AF516253

REFORM AND EMPLOYMENT

REFORM
AND
EMPLOYMENT

Institute of Applied Manpower Research

CONCEPT PUBLISHING COMPANY, NEW DELHI-110059

ISBN 81-8069-000-8

First Published 2002

Published and Printed by
Ashok Kumar Mittal
Concept Publishing Company
A/15-16, Commercial Block, Mohan Garden
New Delhi-110059 (India)
Phones : 5351460, 5351794
Fax : 091-11-5357103
E-mail : publishing@conceptpub.com

CONTENTS

SECTION III: Economic Integration and Employment

SECTION IV : State Experiences

PREFACE

The reform measures initiated in the early 1990s generated intense debate, in particular on its likely impact on employment and poverty. There has so far been no consensus among the scholars about the outcome of these reforms. Some believe that reforms would have positive impact on the poor in the medium and long run through acceleration of investment, output and employment. However, in the short run it might have adverse impact on the poor due to the adoption of stabilisation measures. But there are others who contest this view and argue that economic reforms would have adverse impact on the poor in the short as well as in the long run. Some of the early studies had in fact predicted a decline in the employment opportunities as a significant outcome of the reforms. But then others refuted this hypothesis. Yet some others argue that a market-based economy weakens the links between economic growth and poverty reduction and economic growth and employment growth. The debate continues. However, a decade has elapsed since the reform process was initiated, and the time period is adequate to make an assessment of the situation through empirical investigations.

It is in this context, that the Institute took a lead in organising a National Seminar on Economic Reforms and Employment in the Indian Economy during March 22-23, 2001 to provide a forum for debate on several issues confronting the economy.

A number of scholars were invited to present papers and deliberate upon these issues. This volume is based on the deliberations of the seminar and it consists of 15 papers, which were presented by eminent scholars noted for their contributions in related areas. The papers have since been revised by the authors on the lines of the discussions and suggestions put forward during the seminar. The volume covers a wide spectrum of issues—economic reforms vis-à-vis growth performance, labour market analysis, employment, poverty, social sector development, WTO as well as some state-level experiences. Based on empirical research and presented within theoretical contexts, these papers provide insight and understanding on a range of complex issues in the debate on the impact of economic reforms. It is hoped that the volume will be useful and stimulate further research.

The Institute had constituted a Steering Group under the Chairmanship of Professor G.S.Bhalla, for advice on the design and agenda of the seminar. We appreciate the group's efforts. It is our privilege to thank Professor Bhalla and others who served as members of the Steering Group. We would like to place on record our special thanks to Dr. S.P.Gupta and Dr.M.S.Ahluwalia for their inaugural and valedictory addresses.

The Institute wishes to express its appreciation to the authors, the chairpersons, discussants and the participants who made valuable contributions in making this a rewarding endeavour. The Institute also acknowledges the financial support provided by the Planning Commission in organising the seminar.

At the Institute, Dr. (Mrs.) Mridula Sharma and Shri I.C.Awasthi, faculty members, have been involved in the seminar from the beginning and their efforts have been extremely helpful in organising the seminar and publication of this volume. Dr. Nandita Khadria and Smt. Dipika Sen have helped in editing and production of the book. In addition, other faculty and staff members have contributed in various ways in the organisation of the seminar. Smt. Suhasini Ramaswami helped us in the initial editing of the manuscript. Shri Ashok Mittal, Concept Publishing Company took personal interest in bringing out the volume in a very short time. The Institute is thankful to all of them for their all-round support.

March, 2002 **H. Ramachandran**
New Delhi *Director*

THE SEMINAR

Introduction

Being crisis induced, the initial phase of reforms focused on macro-economic stabilisation. Encouraged by the response of the Indian economy, policy planners introduced a variety of measures in the form of reform of industrial, trade and investment regimes which were much wider and deeper than the ones in the initial phase of reforms. The whole package of first generation reforms introduced in the nineties primarily aimed at inducing dynamism into the economy, enhancing efficiency and growth, reducing the role of government, strengthening the economy to be more resilient to internal as well as external competition and modernising the technology to enhance growth and development of the country.

Although the reform process did not address several critical areas, the overall response of the Indian economy to the reform process was very encouraging and it produced satisfactory results both in the areas of macro-economic stabilisation and economic growth. For instance, GDP growth which was 0.8 per cent in 1991/92 rose to 5.3 per cent in the very next year. During the period 1994/95 and 1996/97 the average rate of growth of GDP was estimated to be 7 per cent per annum. It, however, dropped to 5 per cent in 1997/98 and less than 6 per cent in 1999/2000. The annual rate of inflation came down from 17 per cent in 1991 to 5 per cent in 1997/98. Foreign currency reserves rose from US $ 1 billion in 1991 to US $ 27.4 billion in early 1999. The actual FDI inflows increased from US $ 0.135 billion in 1991/92 to US $ 3 billion in 1997/98.

Contrary to the above, there were some disturbing results as well. The export growth performance has been far from satisfactory. Added to this, sustaining a GDP growth of 7 per cent per annum has been an uphill task. Further, it has been very difficult to contain fiscal deficit.

Moreover, there are no concrete evidences of the impact of economic reforms on the crucial indicators of economic development such as price behaviour, wages, income levels, quality of life, agricultural growth, expansion and diversification of the non-farm sector in both formal and informal segments, and infrastructure development.

One, therefore, needs to look at these issues as the country plans to usher in further reforms. It is against this background that the Institute of Applied Manpower Research organised a National Seminar on the Impact of Economic Reforms on Various Sectors of the Economy with particular reference to Employment in India, with the following objectives:

- To identify basic issues confronting the Indian economy and to prioritise these issues;
- To identify shortcomings and drawbacks of the ongoing reform process;
- To evolve a vision and focus for reforming the Indian economic and social system; and
- To suggest an agenda for the second-phase reforms just commenced.

Fifteen papers under four broad themes viz., Economic Policies, Employment and Poverty; Economic Reforms and the Social Sector; Economic Integration and Employment; and State Experiences, were presented and discussed in the seminar held during March 22-23, 2001.

Summary of Proceedings

In his opening remarks, Dr. H. Ramachandran, Director, IAMR gave a brief background of the seminar and flagged the following points: (a) the degree of political consensus on reforms seen during 1993/94 seemed to have disappeared by 2001; (b) reform experiences have been different in different states—some were more proactive than others in attracting the impulses of reform; (c) reforms in the labour sector (which has larger political dimension) are more difficult than in the industry, finance sectors, etc.; and (d) human resource development and the social sector have not received adequate attention in the reforms. He ended his observations by emphasising that a substantive content of the 'second generation reforms' would have to include the issues of labour and employment, particularly, in the context of GDP growth without a commensurate growth in employment.

Dr. S.P. Gupta, Member, Planning Commission in his inaugural address observed that, although the basic objectives of development such as growth, equity, removal of poverty, full employment and social justice have remained unchanged as yet, the backdrop against which these objectives are to be implemented has changed since 1991.

Growth has now become the operative objective, and the implicit assumption with this operative objective is that there is a multi-collinearity between growth, reduction in poverty, and increase in employment. Moreover, it is assumed that the benefits of growth automatically percolate down to all sections of society and to all regions.

The issues of debate therefore are (a) whether the percolation theory is academically acceptable in the present context, (b) whether one can afford to concentrate on growth and leave employment to be taken care of by itself, and (c) whether there should be separate programmes on employment generation, poverty alleviation, etc., or should these programmes be weeded out altogether and funds allocated to other programmes.

He referred to some studies, which indicate that growth in the post-reform period had no impact on the incidence of poverty and generation of employment. The slow percolation that the country was getting before reforms is also dying out. Now employment is also drastically coming down in the organised as well as unorganised sectors.

He, therefore, suggested that if the growth and employment relation is found not to be working positively then alternatives, such as a comprehensive social security system specially in the informal sector, have to be kept in mind despite some reservations on the desirability of adopting such measures. Labour should be considered as an important input in deciding the growth pattern. The thrust of the policy would be to find ways of converting surplus labour into human resource with appropriate education, training, health care schemes, etc., so that it contributes to the process of growth. The issues of reforms and employment have to be discussed in the current scenario of the open market economy created by the WTO.

Prof. G.S. Bhalla summed up the session by highlighting the issues arising out of the inaugural address and remarked that the views expressed by Dr. Gupta raised some uncomfortable questions that need to be addressed. He added that perhaps what was left unsaid was—why growth did not lead to poverty reduction and employment generation. He felt that sectoral distortion in the growth pattern—growth led by the tertiary sector—cannot be employment oriented. It is only agriculture led growth that can generate much employment in a country like India but this sector was grossly neglected.

I. Economic Policy, Employment and Poverty

In this session four papers were presented. Professor B.B. Bhattacharya concentrated on issues pertaining to macro balances. He emphasised that the economic reform process of about the past decade did not adequately focus on maintaining the macro-economic balance. As a result, there has not been a perceptible increase in the growth rate. He warned that the process of recovery must start now to take the economy into a high trajectory of the growth path.

Moving from macro to regional analysis, Professor Ashok Mathur was of the opinion that national level aggregate figures quite often present a distorted or unrealistic picture of the economy. It is therefore necessary that the impact of economic reforms be seen at regional and sectoral levels. He observed that the content of growth was more important than the aggregates. In this context he emphasised that the industry-based secondary sector needs to be given a boost, as it is the 'engine of growth' for the economy. Therefore, increasing the pace of industrial growth is crucial for economic reforms.

Dr. Arup Mitra highlighted some of the major outcomes of deregulation and economic reforms in urban India that are manifested in terms of (i) tertiarisation, casualisation and feminisation of the work-force, (ii) rise in part-time jobs rather than regular jobs, and (iii) increasing the share of the informal sector in total employment. He argued that in spite of rapid industrial growth during the nineteen-eighties, employment growth in the organised industry has not been impressive. Factor market distortion and adoption of capital-intensive technology possibly led to such a sluggish employment growth in the organised industrial sector. Even in the post-reform period, employment elasticity does not seem to have improved to any significant extent. Given the limited labour demand in this sector, the urban informal sector has acted as repository of surplus labour growing primarily owing to natural growth of population and rural-urban migration.

With reference to urban and rural poverty, Dr. Mitra said that meager earnings accruing to workers in the informal sector have resulted in a high head count ratio of urban poverty, although open unemployment rate in the Indian context has not been striking. Both rural poverty and urban poverty show signs of increase in the nineties.

Dr. Pranob Sen, the discussant, agreed with Dr. Bhattacharya that nothing significant has happened to the broad economic parameters during the period of economic reforms. Some changes such as reduction in duty rates, removal of licensing restrictions etc., have been introduced but private sector investment has not significantly picked up and the real reforms seem yet to take off.

With reference to the presentation of Professor Ashok Mathur, the discussant noted that disparities at different levels and across sectors are inevitable. Economic policies therefore need to be sectorally and regionally balanced. He further extended the argument raised by Professor Mathur of considering the industrial sector as 'engine of growth' and suggested that this may be different in different states.

Dr. Pranob Sen observed that the issue of casualisation is more important in the wake of economic reforms but one should also look into the definitional aspects of 'casual' workforce in the organised sector. He also pointed out that sometimes the value of output could give wrong signals in certain areas if sub-contracting is on the higher side. It would, therefore, be better if one also looks at the employment relationship of organised to unorganised sector.

The issues raised by the participants in response to the presentations and the observations of the discussant may be summarised as follows:

- If we accept the arguments that nothing much happened in the reforms period then we may not be able to explain a number of phenomena such as reduction in the volume of the investment in the poverty alleviation programme, changes in the budgetary allocation on goods and wages and their effect on macro-balances.
- Employment opportunities have declined or at least have been sluggish in the public sector and the organised sector in urban India. Casualisation has also shown an ascending trend. The informal/unorganised sector has been able to provide more jobs.
- Industrial growth has taken place but employment growth has not been noticed. Thus, growth does not necessarily lead to providing employment opportunities.
- Pressure of labour has increased in the urban sector. This may be tackled through (a) programmes of rural development, and (b) programmes of urban employment.
- There has been an increase in wages of casual labour but the increase is more deceptive than real. The employer does not have to bear the burden of rational benefits in regard to casual labour. On the whole, labour has not benefited in the long run.

There was a consensus on the trend of decline in investment in the public sector and not so significant an increase of investment in the private sector that has taken place. Consensus also emerged on the view that growth in the economy and production does not necessarily ensure and signify employment growth. The impact of economic reforms needs to be understood and analysed on a regional and sectoral level. Analysis of national aggregates could be misleading. It was agreed upon that India has to pay particular attention to industry-based secondary sector growth without ignoring the agriculture sector.

Professor Lalit Deshpande and Dr. Sudha Deshpande focused on changes in the nature and shape of the labour market vis-à-vis the economic reforms. They initially discussed the World Bank's advice on labour policy and employment, which suggests that growth flows mainly from efficiency of the market and trade. The process may initially accompany macro-economic decline in general and a sharp decline in the demand for labour in particular. They cited the examples of East Asian and Latin American countries which followed the World Bank Model of development. The Deshpandes were however of the opinion that the World Bank Model can not be implemented universally without ascertaining the ground realities. While discussing the economic and labour reform policies of the World Bank in the context of India, they pointed out that (a) globalisation will weaken the role of the state in assuring social justice; (b) market oriented models have also seen declining trends in the primary sector's share in growth and (c) the stages of economic development are noticeably marked by the shift straight from primary to tertiary sector, with the neglect of growth and development of the secondary sector, which forms an essential base of economic development in any country.

They noted that there has been a shift of workers from low to high productive growth sectors. It is estimated that this will result in a considerable decline of poverty. Further, employment elasticity is also expected to decline. Therefore, in a state where the degree of per capita income is higher and poverty lower, the growth and employment rate will rise.

Shri Shailendra Sharma observed that employment elasticity is to be revised by NSSO (1993/94). And, there is a need to show as to how the quality of employment is being shaped under the impact of economic reforms. He also added that despite increase in the GDP (per capita), the wage per capita is not found to be growing and concluded that the workers are not gaining from the reforms. Issues were also raised by him relating to definitional aspects of employment, unemployment, workforce, labour force, etc.

The discussion that followed flagged the following points: (i) while the presentation of the Deshpandes finds elasticity of employment negative in certain jobs, particularly in agriculture, there is hardly any permanent worker in that sector as workers prefer to work on a casual basis; (ii) there is a vast variation in the technological sphere of the three sectors, and therefore, equating the workforce in quantity without any reference to technology may not yield sound conclusions.

There was a general consensus that the World Bank Model needs to be adjusted to the ground realities in India. The dictum that growth flows mainly from efficiency of the market and trade has to be qualified by the level of development, opening of the economy along with removing the curbs on labour movements. The differences in views persisted on issues such as distress sale of labour during the post-reform period, the effect of casualisation and contractualisation on the position of workers.

The arguments in the paper by Dr. Mahendra Dev were presented by Professor P.K. Chaubey, which may be summarised as follows:

(i) The rate of growth in employment decelerated in the 1990's; (ii) poverty among workers also declined during that period but the pace of reduction was slow; (iii) the rate of growth in rural non-farm employment declined in the post-reform period till 1993/94 but increased in 1999/2000; (iv) the quality of employment deteriorated because of casualisation of labour; and (v) real wages for casual labourers increased at a slow pace (1990s). He argued that agricultural growth is one of the important determinants of rural poverty; hence emphasis must be placed on ensuring healthy growth of agriculture in future. Trade and price reforms alone would not be sufficient to improve agricultural growth. Without infrastructure development and institutional changes the price instrument may not increase aggregate supply. Domestic deregulation seems to be more important than trade liberalisation. It was suggested that there is a need to give greater importance to health and education aspects for reducing poverty.

Dr. Abusaleh Shariff, the discussant, while discussing the paper observed that economic reforms have resulted in low growth to some degree, the services sector did grow in the post-reform period, yet a disaggregated analysis for the same was necessary. With reference to Mahendra Dev's observation that there has been more growth in employment as compared to the findings of the NSS, (that suggests a mere .04 per cent growth) the discussant observed that due discount has to be given to irregular and seasonal nature of employment in rural sector. He suggested that the gross growth in real wages in agriculture sector should be measured with reference to the increase in prices of the primary goods that the workers consume.

II. Economic Reforms and the Social Sector

Four papers were presented under this theme. Professor P.R. Panchamukhi focused on the mutuality of economic reforms and social sector development and set a broad framework of the likely impact on the educational sector. He highlighted that a continuous decline in relative allocations to higher education will not be in the interest of the long-term development of the economy. Further, withdrawal of subsidies from higher education (as has been proposed recently) will have negative effects on R&D and thereby on the growth and development of the country. Development of external funding for financing education may have implications for value formation of the economy as the education sector is considered to be an effective agent for value formation and inter-generational value transmission. The paper invited the attention of the policy makers to take wholesome view of distributional effects of reforms on the education sector, i.e., to what extent (a) the first generation learners would be brought under the fold of education, (b) the children of SC, ST and OBC would enter schools, colleges and universities, (c) the other deprived groups like girls would be encouraged to receive adequate levels of education like their male counterparts, and (d) the less developed regions would get educational facilities.

Professor J.B.G. Tilak, as discussant, described the paper as a valuable document, which has presented the issue in a systematic manner describing the reciprocal linkages in economic reforms and educational policies. However, he added, since expenditure at higher levels of education has declined, analysis merely in terms of ratios would not lead to rational conclusions. A parallel exercise undertaking the extrapolation of the trends without implications of economic policies would have helped to understand the phenomenon in a better way. He further added that in the present paper the analysis is attempted only on the basis of input parameter, that is, expenditure; the output indicators such as enrolment ratio, drop out rate, internal efficiency of the system, and so forth need also to be studied in order to establish the indicative impact of economic reforms on education.

The discussion on the paper raised the following points:

(a) the issue of plan investment on education needs to be studied state wise and mere analysis based on non-plan expenditure is not sufficient;
(b) qualitative indicators of education also need to be analysed at more disaggregated levels; and
(c) the question of equity is an important dimension which needs to be studied in view of public vis-à-vis government schools.

There was a general agreement that the current attitude of the state of minimising its responsibility in terms of financial support to higher education would have an adverse effect in the long run on the growth and development of the country.

The paper by Dr. Anil Gumber examined the impact of economic reforms on health indicators. The focus of the paper was on morbidity and disease prevalence and their treatment, on the utilisation of health services, and on the cost of health care. It also examined in detail the equity dimensions. Dr. Gumber raised three critical issues in the light of the on-going economic reforms. These are: (i) how much progress has the country made in various health outcomes? (ii) what is the status of health-provision and financing? and (iii) have the health equity issues in terms of accessibility and use been adequately addressed?

He pointed out that government spends only about 25 per cent of the total health allocations. This is in contrast with the spendings in OECD and East Asian countries where government spending ranges from 70-90 per cent. He noted that as countries get richer, they spend more of their income on health care, and the government share grows larger. Richer states are spending more on health care resulting in raising the health status of people. Conversely, the per capita health care spending is very low in poorer states. Using various surveys from 1973 to 1995/96, Dr. Gumber showed that rural morbidity rates are higher than urban morbidity rates. He also demonstrated substantial inter-state differentials in both urban and rural morbidity rates. For the country as a whole, nearly 18 and 10 percent of illness episodes in rural and urban areas were not treated. Public sector subsidies benefit the better off more than the poor.

Dr. Sonal Desai, the discussant of the paper, observed that more detailed studies need to be carried out on (i) the utilisation of existing public sector health services by the poor and weaker section of society, (ii) scope for further improvement in services, and (iii) generating awareness. She admitted that considering the large number of people still below the poverty line, the public sector must increase its efficiency and reach.

The general consensus was that the issue of public health can not be left to open market forces and the state should come up to meet the requirements increasingly. The attitude of people towards sanitation and hygiene is as important as the state delivery system. There was a general agreement that the state should provide comprehensive preventive facilities such as immunisation, and take steps against water borne, and sanitation and hygiene related diseases. In this, awareness needs to be given appropriate weightage. The health schemes and preventive and curative provisions need to focus on gender-based health requirement and such other means which promote an appropriate attitude towards health.

Dr. Nirmala Banerjee dealt with issues pertaining to the employment of women workers in manufacturing and services sectors in the post-reform period. She observed that the share of women in the manufacturing sector has increased but only in the organised sector. The 'service sector' has good potential for educated women in urban areas. But there is a possibility of this sector being feminised with lowering wages and increasing casualisation.

Dr. Kumud Sharma, the discussant of the paper, suggested that the analysis of increase in the regular service opportunities needed further disaggregation by sector. She said that in a deregulated wage market women might be pushed further to low paid jobs and this will have negative effects on the quality of employment for women. She further added that the present workers unions are hardly women friendly and even current programmes of skill generation, credit funding, employment generation, etc., are inadequate. Impact of ecronomic reforms on women needs an indepth study with a view to analysing the choice of venture, income levels, skill acquisition routes in the perspectives of changing economic environment.

The paper by Dr. Alakh N. Sharma and Dr. Piush Antony examined the trends in the employment scenario in the post-reform period with the provision of social security and safety net measures under focus. They contended that the performance of the economy as measured by GDP has been somewhat better in the post-reform period. In the initial two years of economic reforms, the rate of growth of employment declined, but it picked up when there was a revival in the economy in terms of growth of GDP. They stressed that the overall pace of employment generation has not declined, but the quality of employment has generally deteriorated, because most of the employment is being created in the informal sector where there is practically no provision of insurance and social security. One of the most conspicuous effects of globalisation is that the small proportion of the labour force that enjoyed job security is gradually shrinking and the proportion of those who are devoid of any security is multiplying. While commenting on the proposed changes in the labour laws, authors showed their concern and stated that it would lead to casualisation and contractualisation, leading to general worsening of labour standards in India.

Dr. Prem Vashisht, the discussant of the paper, agreed that the new economic policy has accelerated the trend of casualisation and contractualisation. The proportion of labour in the unorganised sector has increased considerably. Job and income security are on the decline. An increasing number of workers are slipping out of the social security net. Voluntary Retirement Scheme (VRS) is also being misused and its beneficiaries have not been able to transform the funds so received into capital. There is a need to preserve and promote labour standards and extend social safety net to unorganised sector workers.

III. Economic Integration and Employment

Under this theme three presentations were made. The first paper, by Professor G.K. Chadha, discussed impacts of WTO on employment in the rural areas through demand-supply linkages as well as through changes in the domains of the market of the different economic sectors. While the new economic environment had beneficial impacts on the economy in terms of technology upgradation, better opportunities for skilled and trained workforce, access of domestic producers to the international markets, etc., it also had adverse effects on employment in rural areas. It may further accentuate the problem on the following premise:

(i) Free inflow of imports would have labour displacing effects in rural areas.
(ii) The challenges of international standards, price competitiveness, etc., would lead to a dualism in the labour market. As a result, a sizeable chunk of the rural workforce employed in the small and tiny rural industry would lose, whereas the educated, skilled and trained, mostly urban, would have higher prospects.

Dr. Rajesh Mehta looked into the aspect of the access of industrial goods of the developing countries to the world market in the light of multilateral trade agreements such as the Uruguay Round and WTO. He was of the view that there are a number of challenges, barriers and obstacles that restrict the access of developing countries to the world market. While reviewing India's commitments under the Uruguay Round and WTO, he discussed the various discrepancies, which restrict the access of its products to the world market. Dr. Mehta suggested that the discrepancies should be taken care of by India and other developing countries in the following negotiations and agreements, in order to have access to world markets.

Dr. B. Bhattacharya, the discussant, agreed with Dr. Chadha that rural employment is certainly a critical issue in the context of the WTO regime. He also pointed out that the new regime is bound to create imbalances in trade and agriculture. The developed countries provide heavy subsidy to the agriculture sector. Their export of agricultural produces at competitive prices to India would bring a difficult situation to Indian farmers. Under globalisation, free movement of commodities is advocated but free movement of labour is not even talked about. This is meant to exploit the developing countries.

The third paper in this session, by Professor Biplab Dasgupta, dealt with globalisation, labour market and labour standards. The paper argued that advocacy of a flexible labour market leads to an authoritarian state and indeed such regimes are more effective in bringing a flexible wage system and help to clear the market. However, in the democratic governments repressing of labour is not a feasible proposal. The paper also discussed the negative consequences of structural adjustment, of poverty, disparity and unemployment. Professor Dasgupta highlighted that labour standards under the WTO regime have become highly discriminatory for the LDCs. To follow the WTO in toto would be harmful, because WTO provisions are biased in favour of developed countries, which have adopted multiple approaches,the nature of which is discriminatory.

IV. State Experiences

Four case studies of the states of Punjab, Karnataka, Maharashtra and Assam were presented and discussed to get an insight into regional level linkages of economic reforms with employment and poverty in this session.

Presenting the case of Punjab, Dr. S.S. Gill stated that drastic reduction in public investment in Punjab has slowed down the development process of the state giving rise to serious negative implications for employment generation. The incidence of under-employment has particularly risen in rural areas owing to a continuous decline in the per acre absorption of agricultural labour during the nineties. In urban areas, unemployment is increasing owing to an overall decline in employment of the organised (government as well as private) sector.

Dr. Gill suggested that there was a need for expansion in non-farm employment avenues along with an increase in employment with agriculture and allied activities through crop-diversification. To achieve this, decentralised development with major investment in infrastructure and marketing areas were inevitable. Dr. Gill was of the opinion that such a process can also take care of the growing youth unemployment in the state.

Initiating the discussion, Professor Ravi Srivastava, the discussant, observed that some of the points made by Dr. Gill need re-assertion. For instance, the main issues were: (i) why non-agricultural growth did not take off in the state, (ii) what linkages can be cited between the reforms and the observations made in the paper, and (iii) whether the solutions offered about increased government role are feasible under second-generation reforms.

There was a general agreement that withdrawal of subsidies and full application of WTO agreements might bring about discomfort in the agriculture and industry sectors of the economy, as well as for the labour force. The participants felt that there was an urgent need for creating necessary infrastructure by curbing tax evasion and imposing strict fiscal discipline.

Dr. R.S. Deshpande highlighted the case of Karnataka with its characteristic phases of intermittent growth and stagnation which indicate inability of the state to climb up the developmental hierarchy despite being progressive with many first initiatives such as, pragmatic land reforms, democratic decentralization, well-designed anti-poverty programmes, initiatives in rain-fed agriculture, rigorous participation in international trade, and so on.

Dr. Deshpande mentioned that the most important challenges were (i) facilitating private investment in backward areas, (ii) making funds available for initiating agricultural and rural development schemes in fragile regions and (iii) participating in the process of liberalization by a proper approach which can enable most deserving regions and groups of farmers to take advantage of it. He concluded by emphasising the urgent need to integrate the various actions with different stages of reforms so that the stakeholders across sectors are not taken unawares.

Initiating discussion on the paper, Dr. Prem Vashishth raised some specific questions such as: (i) whether the stagnation in public sector employment has anything to do with reforms, (ii) whether the diversification of agriculture, particularly floriculture, has been looked at from the angle of its capital intensity, (iii) what can be the strategy to relocate certain activities in backward regions, and (iv) without reducing subsidies, particularly regarding water/electricity supplied to farmers at cheaper rates, how was the integration of various stages of reforms with actions proposed.

Dr. Ajit Karnik evaluated the progress made by Maharashtra during the nineties in terms of fiscal balancing measures. He studied fiscal stress ratios (FSRs) and fiscal dependency ratios (FDRs) for the state vis-à-vis the rest of India. He found that FSRs for Maharashtra had increased whereas for others (i.e., the rest of the states), they have been decreasing, which indicates that the state has lagged behind in managing its fiscal stress. Further, even in respect of FDRs, the state is noted to be faring poorly in comparison to the rest of India. The paper on the basis of an econometric analysis demonstrate the adverse impact of fiscal imbalances on the real rate of growth of Maharashtra. Observing similar findings, namely, relatively poor achievement with regard to other aspects such as transparency, local finance, political and institutional aspects and so forth, the author present a discouraging picture so far as second generation reforms in the state are concerned.

Prof. Atul Sharma, the discussant of the paper, appreciated the findings of Dr. Karnik. But he questioned the formulation of a relationship between fiscal imbalances and growth and observed that the relationship seems to have been worked out in haste. Some of the suggestions made during discussion were as follows:

Though the paper has distinctly brought out the grave fiscal situation in Maharashtra, yet the analysis did not specify the reasons behind it. It was suggested that the author analyses it at disaggregated levels to have a comparative view of pre- and post-fiscal reforms, as well as, compare it with the rest of the states in terms of divisions and uniformity.

Shri H.S. Das presented the case of Assam. He stated that during the period of first generation reforms the state could not benefit owing to factors particularly unfavourable to the state. These factors included lower than national per capita income, lower GDP growth rate, high growth rate of population, low agricultural productivity, deteriorating power situation, recurring floods/erosion of soil/environmental degradation, inadequate health care facility particularly in rural areas, low rate of capital formation, industrial stagnation, and brain drain from the state. However, some major steps have been initiated recently. These include opening border trade with neighbouring countries and significant improvement on the agricultural front leading to prospects of a 'mini-green revolution'.

Professor Atul Sharma initiated the discussion on Assam by comparing it with Maharashtra. He observed that while in Maharashtra the concern relates to the state of public finance, in Assam it is more related to the difficult conditions prevailing on the ground. These are mainly of socio-political dimensions, which are no doubt required to be congenial in order to yield positive results for any economic policy. In the light of this, Professor Sharma posed mainly two general questions: (i) given that the problem of fiscal management is common to all the states, what are the perceived reasons for the problem to be so deep in an otherwise progressive state like Maharashtra? and (ii) whether the government of Assam has tried to attract investments like other states.

Professor Amitabh Kundu observed that the experience of the states reveals that unless the state governments initiate matching supportive policy measures, the progress of the states will be lagging. What is actually required is a conducive political and peaceful environment. He mentioned that the experience of the last decade of a higher economic growth at the national level (more than 6 per cent for the last three years in succession) on the one hand and higher employment growth in certain individual sectors on the other appears to lend support to the theory that economic growth does result in an overall favourable impact on employment generation.

Summing Up

Professor Ravi Srivastava, while summing up the deliberations of the seminar identified the key issues relating to the linkages between: (i) the structure and pattern of growth in the pre- and post-reform period, (ii) the emerging nature of employment and the workforce, and (iii) the quality of life in general, and that of the workforce in particular—this aspect being dealt with by looking at education, HRD, social security, provision of health and poverty alleviation programmes.

The tone of the seminar was set by the chief guest Dr. S.P. Gupta, Member, Planning Commission who pointed out that the broad development policy objectives had not changed in India, but there was a shift in emphasis over the years which resulted in a certain risk of conflicting growth with the multiple development policy objectives and one has to be conscious about how these policy objectives could be achieved. In other words many of these objectives perhaps needed independent sets of intervention.

A number of very interesting issues came up in each of the themes. So far as the structure and pattern of growth is concerned the issue of convergence or divergence of state income was discussed. It was pointed out that after the mid 1960s, there was divergence of state incomes, and according to various criteria it was the low and high-income states, which showed considerable divergence.

The issues of the emerging nature of workforce and employment generated considerable debate. Although the papers presented conflicting results on the issue of decline in employment elasticities, there was considerable unanimity on the issue of the tertiarisation of the workforce particularly in the more recent period.

Apart from the above, there were considerable differences of opinion on other questions such as, (i) have the workforce participation rates declined in 1999/2000 as compared to 1993/94? (ii) what has happened to growth rates in employment? (iii) what has happened to unemployment rates? and (iv) what has happened to the thesis of casualisation of labour?

Various issues came up with respect to what is happening in the field of education. It was pointed out that there had been declining public expenditure on higher education which will have serious repercussions on the growth and development of the country in the long run.

In respect to what happened in the field of health, the paper presented pointed out that although there has been improvement between 1992/93 and 1998/99, the improvement has been slow. In any case, the cost of health care increased tremendously in the decade 1986/87 to 1995/96. It was also pointed out that public sector expenditure on health was quite regressive with the top strata possibly using up almost 30-40 per cent of public subsidy.

The paper on social security to labour presented a typology of comprehensive social security. It argued that one needs to think of a comprehensive social security plan, particularly when labour market flexibility and efficiency considerations are to be introduced.

A forceful argument that came up during discussions was the quality of labour that would have strong positive implications on India's competitiveness for growth particularly in the WTO regime.

Though at all India level the nature of the reform process was more or less taken for granted, at the state level there were constraints on the growth process and reforms. What was happening on the way of reforms was discussed at considerable length in this session, and two issues stood out from this. One was that even in the developed state of Maharashtra the fiscal situation was quite alarming. The same was revealed by the case study on Punjab. The other was that reform was at least on the agenda of virtually all the states that were discussed in the session and that various steps were taken to improve the quality of growth in these states.

Dr. Montek Singh Ahluwalia in his valedictory address noted that employment is one of the major objectives of development policy and rightly so in the context of economic reforms. He emphasised that from the policy point of view it is not the net increment in jobs that is really very important but the quality of employment. What is important in any development process is the structure of employment and continuous improvement in it, wherein a lot of new jobs are created and simultaneously, a lot of older type jobs are destroyed.

What was more important, according to him, was to have a multi-dimensional look as to whether we are really getting rid of the low-quality, unattractive jobs and creating better-quality jobs in its place? That is not measured by a net increase in employment as it may be found that the most successful employment strategy in fact is one that does not just focus on the net increment but on increasing the extent to which low-quality jobs get replaced by better-quality jobs. This very often means tolerating the disappearance of certain types of jobs in the system. This may be viewed as a very negative phenomenon, but may not actually be so.

He observed that growth was of course important, and there are many macro-policies that focus on growth. One of the issues that comes in is the belief that because employment is important, one should not lightly adopt technologies which minimise the use of labour or which move from more labour-intensive to less labour-intensive technology.

He emphasised that the issue of a choice between labour intensive and capital-intensive technology calls for some serious thinking. There is no doubt that excess capital intensity is wrong by definition, but the notion that one must always use more labour-intensive technology is also not sustainable. There are evidences to suggest that wherever the government could, it opted for the continuation of on-going technological processes and also the institutional arrangements which keep labour in place, but the cost of that in terms of efficiency and the damage it did to other sectors was not kept in mind.

Dr. Ahluwalia's main concern was that from the policy point of view one needs to look at all the policies that would lead to more rapid growth of the economy because they would enable growth in many labour-intensive sectors, which is being held up very often because of the belief that we need to protect employment.

He pointed out that the issue of diversification in agricultural processing as addressed in some of the papers in the seminar was important. But equally important were the new sectors, which we have not looked at adequately. One such sector is tourism and transport. Even for relatively low-income countries, the employment generating possibility from these sectors is very high. Still, they do not figure in our policy thinking. In fact the only new employment generating areas that have received a lot of attention are the IT and the naval services, where, in the last year or two, there has been a general consensus that these are areas where huge employment possibilities exist. Thus, there is a need to identify many different sectors with possibilities and prospects of growth. The policy constraints, which are holding some of these sectors back, have to be also reviewed.

He observed that one important issue that we need to look at is the role of special employment focused policies. It has been taken for granted that there is a great need for employment focused programmes, simply because the system will not automatically generate all the necessary employment. While supporting such a need, however, Dr. Ahluwalia pointed out that certain programmes had become quite ineffective. He suggested that a fresh review of these programmes for selecting the ones which were more productive, is essential. On the whole, he stressed the need for a complete restructuring of the existing programmes.

Dr. Ahluwalia underlined the importance of education and training, because according to him one can't just talk about a labour-using strategy without ensuring that there is a system that generates skills. In this context he also referred to the two prevailing views about the role of vocational education/training. One view on this issue is that, apart from specialized training in professions, such as, medical, engineering and so on, which are high-income professions, what is needed is good quality schooling, which prepares people to pick up the required skills on the job. The second view stresses the need for formal vocational training and points to the various existing models by which an element of vocationalisation can be brought into the educational system.

Stating his concern about the current vocational education system in India he said that the operation of the existing systems suggest that many of the existing vocational training institutes do not seem to be serving much useful purpose. For instance, many of these are still training people on skills that are no longer in demand, some of them are also staffed poorly and lack the equipment needed for imparting the skills. Thus, the whole question of what should be the role of vocational and technical training in building up a technical labour force is an issue that has not been addressed adequately in the system and the government needs to be better informed about this through further research in the area.

Dr. Ahluwalia expressed that Indian labour laws are undoubtedly the most rigid once amongst developing countries. Liberalisation of labour laws should bring in flexibility. But along with flexibility it is also necessary to have some kind of a minimum safety net—sort of an unemployment insurance mechanism, whereby, if a person loses his or her job, at least for a certain period of time, he or she can get an unemployment insurance benefit on a declining basis, till another job is found.

Regarding the downsizing policy of the government, Dr. Ahluwalia stated that the ability to use VRS is directly related to how capital-intensive the technology is. In a high capital-intensive industry, the wage costs are a very small part of the total value added. In such industries it is possible to do downsizing operation by paying off labour because the implicit cost of that is not very high. But in a labour intensive industry this kind of high VRS settlements may not be feasible. So, the present system provides flexibility at the capital-intensive end of the spectrum and does not provide the same at the labour-intensive end of the spectrum.

He pointed out that the danger in a globalised world lies in the fact that if the regimes were not similar in nature, investment, whether foreign or domestic was likely to move abroad. He also suggested that we need a much stronger awareness amongst everyone concerned as to whether this is indeed a problem, and if so, the way to tackle it in a framework in which a comparable degree of unemployment insurance exists with other countries.

Dr. Ahluwalia concluded by saying that, this is not an easy thing to accomplish since the essence of unemployment insurance is that everybody should be contributing so that the occasional job-losers are compensated. Before the whole system starts functioning, with enough contribution coming in, there may in fact be a burden on the fiscal side in the interim period.

SECTION I

ECONOMIC POLICY, EMPLOYMENT AND POVERTY

1

NATIONAL AND REGIONAL GROWTH PERFORMANCE IN THE INDIAN ECONOMY: A Sectoral Analysis

ASHOK MATHUR

Introduction

This paper sets out to examine seven issues related to national and regional growth in the Indian economy. The main focus of attention is on growth performance during the nineteen-eighties and the nineteen-nineties. However, in order to view growth over the last two decades against the background of the pattern of growth in earlier decades, a broad sweeping analysis of the period since 1950/51 is undertaken on a decadal basis. Section two presents the average decadal growth rates at the national level for each of the three main sectors and the gross domestic product. Sections three and four discuss regional growth rates, their ranks and the changes, if any, that have come about in the relative hierarchy of the state level growth rates. Section five analyses the impact of regional growth performance on state level economic development in terms of their per capita incomes. Section six is devoted to an examination of regional disparities in terms of state level per capita incomes. Section seven discusses the impact of growth on the sectoral structure of the economy, both at the national and regional levels. Section eight poses the question as to which sector can be considered to have been the 'engine of growth'. Finally, a brief resume of the paper appears in section nine.

National Level Sectoral Growth Performance

Growth performance in this section is examined in terms of two sets of data, covering the period 1950/51 to 1999/2000. Till recently the long-term data for this period were available only in terms of national income data at 1980/81 prices from 1950/51 up to 1996/97. Data at 1993/94 prices have been available since 1993/94 but in order to draw upon a single base period series for the maximum period possible, in what we have designated as A series, 1980/81 base year data have been used from 1950/51 to 1996/97 and 1993/94 base year data for the period from 1996/97 to 1999/2000. These data have been taken from the Government of India's Economic Survey (2000 and 2001) for the years 1999/2000 and 2000/2001. In the second, namely, Series D, only Economic Survey 2000/2001 data have been used, making use of the recently released data at 1993/94 prices right from 1950/51 onwards. Series D at 1993/94 prices has the advantage over Series A in so far as, for the more recent period, the 1993/94 prices and weight structure would be more appropriate to reflect the changing commodity/services composition of the national product, whereas for the period prior to the nineteen-nineties the 1980/81 prices and weight structure would be more in tune with the earlier structure.

For examining the trend of growth rates over the last half a century or so one can periodise in terms of shorter time spans on the basis of alternative criteria. If the focus is on comparing the growth scenario prior to and after a certain event, the dividing line between periods would have to be determined by dating of the event. Since in the present paper no such event/events have been kept as the primary concern, we have adopted decadal periodisation. A quinquennial periodisation could also be used, but a decadal period has been considered to have the advantage of longer periods. Further, a decadal periodisation fits in automatically and exactly into periodisation based on pre-reform and post-reform periodisation, since the latter period commences from the beginning of the decade of the nineties, i.e., 1991.

The decadal growth rates can be estimated by alternative methods. The simplest is to estimate compound growth rates between decadal terminal points at 1950/51, 1960/61 and 1999/2000, which is the latest year for which quick estimates are available. A more appropriate version of essentially the same method is to use three yearly averages of data at terminal points since it eliminates, or at least reduces, the influence of fluctuations around terminal points on the decadal growth rates. A more accurate method is to fit semi-logarithmic time trends to annual data separately for each decade. The method which has been used here for estimating decadal growth rates at the national level is different from all these three. It involves estimating the averages of annual growth rates for each decade and has the advantage of taking into account actual annual growth rate for each and every year within any decade (see Kakwani, 1997, for theoretical superiority of this method). The first step for this method was to obtain absolute data for each of the three sectors. The Annual Economic Surveys give aggregated data for the primary sector ('agriculture, forestry and logging, fishing, mining and quarrying'), the secondary sector ('manufacturing, construction, electricity, gas and water supply') and gross domestic product at factor cost. Tertiary sector gross domestic product estimates were derived by aggregating contributions of 'transport, communication and trade', 'banking and insurance, real estate and ownership of dwellings and business services' and 'public administration and defence and other services'. At the second stage, annual growth rates for the three sectors and GDP were obtained, from which the five decadal averages were derived. It may be borne in mind that the decadal growth rates for the nineties are derived by averaging nine annual growth rate observations and not 10, since data for the 10th year (2000/2001) were not available at the time of writing the paper.

Based on the above method, Tables 1.1 and 1.2 give decadal growth rates derived on the basis of A Series and D Series data. Graph 1.1 depicts D Series. As may be observed, for GDP growth rates the decadal estimates show very little difference between the two sets of estimates for each of the five decades, the difference being only of the order of 0.08 at the most. But for sectoral estimates, growth rates based on D Series differ from A Series by a slightly greater margin.

TABLE 1.1 : **Decadal Growth Rates (per cent per annum): A Series**

Sl. No.	Decadal Period	Sector: Primary	Secondary	Tertiary	GDP
1.	Fifties	3.17	6.27	4.14	3.94
2.	Sixties	2.56	5.57	4.64	3.75
3.	Seventies	1.93	4.03	4.34	3.16
4.	Eighties	3.84	7.16	6.53	5.68
5.	Nineties (at 80-81 prices up to 1996-97 and 93-94 prices thereafter)	2.60	6.03	8.20	5.82
6.	1951-2000	2.82	5.86	5.47	4.45

Source : Estimated on the basis of the data given in various issues of the *Economic Survey*, Government of India.

TABLE 1.2: **Decadal Growth Rates (per cent per annum): D Series (at 93-94 prices)**

Sl. No.	Decadal Period	Sector: Primary	Secondary	Tertiary	GDP
1.	Fifties	3.10	6.25	4.27	3.91
2.	Sixties	2.37	5.59	4.77	3.70
3.	Seventies	1.64	3.91	4.41	3.08
4.	Eighties	3.73	6.96	6.72	5.62
5.	Nineties (up to 1999-2000)	2.92	5.88	7.77	5.81
6.	1951-2000	2.92	5.77	5.55	4.44

Source : Same as for Table 1.1.

Coming to the trend of decadal growth rates, four points need to be observed:

(i) First, the aggregate growth of the economy decelerated from the fifties till the seventies but thereafter it registered a sharp increase during the eighties from 3.16 per cent to

5.68 per cent. During the nine years of the nineties the average annual growth rate emerges to be slightly higher by 0.19 per cent at 5.82 per cent according to the D Series, but according to the A Series the increase in growth rate during the nineties is only 0.14 per cent per annum.

(ii) When one looks at the sectoral growth rates, both the agriculture based primary sector and the industry based secondary sector exhibit a declining trend from the fifties till the seventies. The tertiary sector exhibits a fluctuating pattern during the decades of the fifties, sixties and seventies. However, during the eighties all three sectors shared in the steep rise in growth rate.

(iii) From the eighties to the nineties, although the GDP growth rate may have registered a marginal increase, the behaviour depicted by sectoral growth rates is rather disquieting. Both primary and secondary sectors reveal a visible decline in their growth rates. The magnitude and pattern of decline differs depending upon whether one uses Series A or Series D. In respect of the primary sector, Series A exhibits a steeper decline in growth rate than Series D but in the secondary sector Series D shows a steeper decline than Series A.

(iv) It is only the tertiary sector which exhibits a visible rise in the growth rate from the eighties to the nineties and has brought about a slight increase in the overall growth rate during the nineties. This is particularly so during the latter half of the nineties. This is also the period during which recommendations of the Fifth Pay Commission were implemented.

But both the real production sectors based on agriculture and industry have registered a decline in their growth rates. Tertiary sector growth is essentially a reflection of rising factor incomes but without the backing of a corresponding rise in productive growth. The rise in tertiary sector incomes which have contributed to its growth has apparently been much more at the upper end of the income distribution ladder than at the lower end since organised activities have fared much better than unorganised ones (Mathur, 2000a). The sectoral growth trends during the nineties thus do not provide a basis for feeling satisfied with the rise in overall growth rate during the nineties. In fact they are quite disturbing.

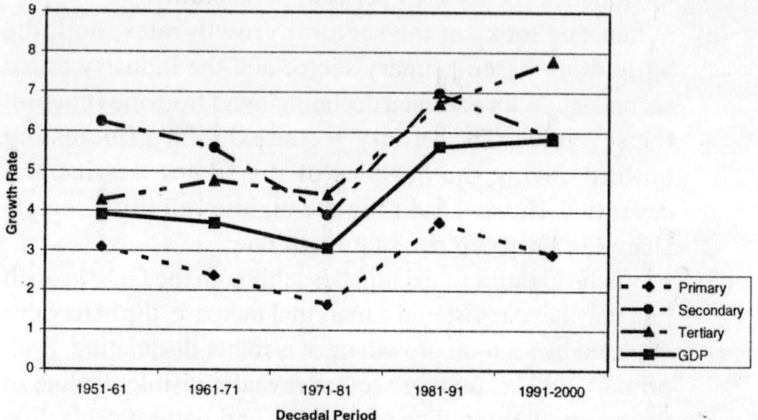

Graph: Decadal Growth Rate (per annum): D Series (at 93-94 prices)

In the light of the picture which emerges from a broad sweeping view of growth during the past five decades, one can discern a distinct break from the end of seventies. Whereas the first three decades display a faltering pace of growth, the next two decades exhibit a visible improvement. But in the light of comparative patterns of growth during the eighties and the nineties, the former depicts a more robust pattern of growth since the latter shows up serious internal weaknesses in the sectoral pattern of growth.

Regional Growth Performance: Level and Ranks

We may now turn to regional growth performance. Estimates of regional growth for the period 1961-89 are based on the author's earlier study (Mathur, 1994). For the period 1980/81 to 1995/96 fresh estimates based on SDP Series at 1980/81 prices, brought together by CSO (Central Statistical Organisations, 2000) from SDP estimates prepared by different State Statistical Bureaus, have been drawn upon.

It may be mentioned here that the entire state level SDP data from 1980/81 to 1993/94 at 1980/81 prices were re-estimated at

1993/94 prices by splicing the series at 1980/81 prices and the state level series at 1993/94 prices, which have now become available for the period 1993-99. However, results based on 1980/81 price data and results based on 1980/81 price data and the estimates based on 1993/94 prices differed considerably for a number of variables. In the light of these two different sets of results, it has been decided to stick to estimates based on 1980/81 price data.

1961-89

We may first present the scenario for the period prior to 1989. Table 1.3 gives the average of annual rates of growth of SDP at constant prices of different States during each decade since 1960, as also during the composite three-decade period of 1961-89. While for the fifties and the sixties the growth rates are based on SDP data at 1960/61 base year prices, for the seventies and the eighties 1970/71 and 1980/81 constant price series of SDP have been used. The ranks of states in terms of their growth rates are given below the growth rates (see also Dholakia, 1985; Singh, 1985).

It may be seen from Table 1.3 that during the three-decade period 1961-89, in terms of the rate of growth of SDP, it is the State of Haryana which tops the list followed by Punjab, Rajasthan, Assam, Karnataka and Maharashtra. At the other end lie Kerala, Himachal Pradesh, Uttar Pradesh and Bihar. When we look at decadal growth rates, a large number of states have not changed their rank ordering substantially. However, some significant changes have occurred in the case of Andhra Pradesh, Madhya Pradesh, Rajasthan, Tamil Nadu and Uttar Pradesh, which have improved growth performance judged in terms of their ranks. On the other hand, Kerala shows a considerable sliding down in terms of growth performance. Punjab has also lost its high rank by four points during the eighties. Orissa's steep descent in rank essentially reflects data inadequacies of the sixties. Maharashtra, in contrast, reveals shifts in rank but in the opposite direction.

1981-96

Table 1.4 gives statewise growth rates of SDP for the period from

1980/81 to 1995/96, which is the latest year for which SDP data were available for all the 16 states considered here. The annual growth rates in this table have been estimated as compound growth rates with three-year averaging of SDP at the terminal points. The table also contains growth rates separately for the decade of the eighties and the first half of the nineties.

For the 15-year period as a whole (1990/91 to 1995/96), the highest growth rate (5.49) emerges in the case of Andhra Pradesh, followed closely by Maharashtra (5.43), Rajasthan (5.08) and Haryana (4.92). At the other end of the spectrum were Bihar (2.72), Assam (2.92), Orissa (2.99) and Kerala (3.29). The other eight states were in the middle category of growth with annual pace of expansion falling between 4.70 (Karnataka) and 3.42 (Madhya Pradesh). The categorisation of states into high, low and middle remains roughly the same if one considers only the eighties. But in the immediate post-reform period there was considerable reordering of the states. The top four category contained Andhra Pradesh and Maharashtra as in the eighties, but Gujarat and Karnataka also moved into this category. On the other hand, Haryana and Rajasthan which were in the top-four category during the eighties slumped to 12th and 11th ranks respectively during 1991-96.

At the other end of the scale, whereas Bihar and Orissa were already in the lowest—four growth rate category, in the nineties Uttar Pradesh and Himachal Pradesh slumped into it from the middle category where they occupied ninth and eighth ranks, respectively.

TABLE 1.3: **Average Annual Growth Rates (g) and Their Variability (C.V.)**

	1961-70		1971-81		1981-89		1961-89	
State	g	c.v.	g	c.v.	g	c.v.	g	c.v.
1	2	3	4	5	6	7	8	9
Andhra Pradesh	2.12	2.85	3.46	2.54	4.72	1.45	3.38	2.12
Rank	14	5	9	7	9	6	11	5
Assam	3.89	1.06	3.70	1.54	5.81	0.57	4.39	0.88
Rank	7	13	7	11	4	16	5	16

(contd.)

TABLE 1.3 *(contd.)*

1	2	3	4	5	6	7	8	9
Bihar	1.55	4.05	3.20	1.29	4.57	1.07	3.05	1.67
Rank	15	3	14	13	12	9	14	9
Gujarat	5.16	1.15	4.38	3.28	5.80	2.33	5.06	2.27
Rank	4	11	4	5	5	2	3	4
Haryana	6.41	1.38	4.80	1.66	6.29	1.29	5.78	1.47
Rank	2	8	1	10	2	7	1	11
Himachal Pradesh	1.08	2.38	3.32	2.37	4.06	1.60	2.79	1.99
Rank	17	6	12	9	16	5	16	7
Jammu & Kashmir	3.72	2.28	4.34	1.08	4.12	0.69	3.68	1.54
Rank	8	7	5	15	15	14	9	10
Karnataka	4.32	1.37	3.38	2.38	5.25	0.79	4.25	1.46
Rank	5	10	11	8	8	13	6	12
Kerala	3.71	0.51	2.30	0.94	1.66	2.23	2.58	1.03
Rank	9	16	6	16	17	3	17	14
Madhya Pradesh	2.56	5.65	3.63	3.41	5.92	1.22	3.95	2.92
Rank	11	2	8	4	3	8	8	1
Maharashtra	2.93	1.05	4.51	1.13	4.57	0.80	4.00	1.00
Rank	10	12	3	14	11	12	7	15
Orissa	10.25	0.60	2.47	5.21	4.40	2.43	3.44	1.87
Rank	1	15	15	1	13	1	10	8
Punjab	5.55	0.46	4.64	0.61	5.64	0.42	5.24	0.51
Rank	3	17	2	17	6	17	2	17
Rajasthan	3.93	3.18	4.10	3.41	7.47	1.82	5.04	2.57
Rank	6	4	6	3	1	4	4	3
Tamil Nadu	2.23	0.99	2.10	4.38	5.64	1.03	3.19	2.40
Rank	13	14	17	2	7	10	13	6
Uttar Pradesh	1.16	8.46	3.39	2.96	4.58	0.61	3.00	2.76
Rank	16	1	10	6	10	15	15	2
West Bengal	2.55	1.38	3.23	1.51	4.31	0.88	3.33	1.22
Rank	12	9	13	12	14	11	12	13
Co-efficient of correlation		0.61		0.23		0.27		0.25

Source: Ashok Mathur (1994), "Regional Economic Development and Policy in India", in G.K. Chadha (ed.), *Policy Perspectives in Indian Economic Development*, Har-Anand Publications, New Delhi.

TABLE 1.4: **Regional Growth Rates of State Incomes**

State	Growth Rate (1981-96)	Rank	Growth Rate (1981-91)	Rank	Growth Rate (1991-96)	Rank
Andhra Pradesh	5.49	1	5.86	4	4.66	1
Assam	2.91	15	3.52	15	1.56	10
Bihar	2.72	16	4.44	12	-1.04	16
Gujarat	4.26	7	4.69	11	3.30	3
Haryana	4.92	4	6.47	2	1.51	12
Himachal Pradesh	3.80	10	4.90	8	1.38	13
Karnataka	4.70	5	5.44	5	3.06	4
Kerala	3.29	13	3.42	16	2.99	5
Madhya Pradesh	3.42	12	4.09	13	1.93	9
Maharashtra	5.43	2	6.20	3	3.72	2
Orissa	2.99	14	4.07	14	0.61	15
Punjab	4.25	8	5.25	7	2.05	8
Rajasthan	5.08	3	6.70	1	1.51	11
Tamil Nadu	4.57	6	5.41	6	2.69	7
Uttar Pradesh	3.63	11	4.86	9	0.93	14
West Bengal	4.20	9	4.83	10	2.78	6

Source : Estimated on the Basis of *Estimates of State Domestic Product*, available on C.S.O. Floppy.

Variations in Sectoral Growth Performance

Sectoral growth rate ranks (Table 1.5) were by and large not widely different from ranks in terms of overall growth rates.

However, in the case of some states the ranks of sectoral growth rates during 1981-96 differed from the rank of overall state growth rate by more than three ranks. The case of such states is discussed below briefly:

1. Whereas Andhra Pradesh ranked first in terms of its overall growth rate, it occupied 11th rank in terms of its primary sector growth rate, reflecting its weak agricultural growth during this period.
2. Whereas Gujarat ranked seventh in terms of overall growth rate, it was way down at 16th rank in terms of primary sector

TABLE 1.5: **Regional Growth Rates of Sectoral Incomes: 1981-1996**

State	Primary Growth Rate	Rank	Secondary Growth Rate	Rank	Tertiary Growth Rate	Rank
Andhra Pradesh	1.93	11	6.76	1	6.26	3
Assam	1.78	12	1.95	16	4.44	13
Bihar	1.19	14	4.11	12	4.02	15
Gujarat	0.40	16	6.66	2	5.74	6
Haryana	3.68	5	6.34	3	5.95	5
Himachal Pradesh	1.66	13	5.15	8	5.70	7
Karnataka	2.92	7	5.70	6	6.16	4
Kerala	2.39	8	3.45	14	4.03	14
Madhya Pradesh	2.20	10	4.17	11	5.11	9
Maharashtra	3.03	6	5.30	7	6.92	1
Orissa	1.14	15	4.60	10	4.93	10
Punjab	4.05	3	5.92	5	3.43	16
Rajasthan	3.78	4	5.97	4	6.56	2
Tamil Nadu	4.07	2	3.76	13	5.46	8
Uttar Pradesh	2.28	9	5.15	9	4.74	11
West Bengal	4.65	1	3.32	15	4.45	12

Source : Same as for Table 1.4.

growth rate. Again, it was near the top occupying rank one terms of its secondary sector growth rate. This essentially shows the wide disparity between agricultural and industrial growth performances in the state.

3. Kerala's overall growth rate rank was 13, but its agricultural growth performance was relatively much better with rank eight in primary sector growth rate.
4. Maharashtra, which occupied second rank in terms of overall growth, was sixth and seventh in terms of its primary and secondary sector growth performance. Since in terms of its tertiary sector growth it ranked first, its growth superiority rested primarily on high growth of service incomes, rather than very high agricultural or industrial growth.

5. Although Orissa occupied 14th and 15th ranks in terms of its overall and primary sector growth, it was relatively better at 10th rank in terms of secondary and tertiary sector growth.
6. In the case of Punjab again there was wide disparity in sectoral growth rates as in the case of Gujarat. Whereas Punjab ranked eighth in terms of its overall growth, it maintained its high relative primary growth position (third), although not the number one position which it had almost invariably occupied since the sixties. Where Punjab lost its rank badly was in terms of tertiary sector growth, with the lowest (16th) rank in this sector.
7. A similar sectoral growth disparity is also evident in the case of Tamil Nadu, whose overall growth rank was sixth. But in primary growth it was second from the top while in secondary sector growth it was 13th.
8. West Bengal depicts a similar position. Its overall growth rank was ninth but in terms of its agricultural growth performance it is known to have shown a very distinct resurgence giving it the first rank in terms of primary sector growth. But in terms of its secondary sector growth it ranked 15th, revealing a continuing weak position in industrial growth.

Thus, distinct sectoral growth disparity appears to have existed in the case of Gujarat, Punjab, Tamil Nadu and West Bengal, all of which have belonged to the category of well developed states. Maharashtra also falls by and large in the same category.

Changes in Growth Rates and their Ranks between 1980s and 1990s

Some idea about reordering in the hierarchy of states in terms of their growth ranks after the reforms was conveyed in Section III (B). Another way of looking at changes in statewise growth performance between the pre- and post-reform periods is to examine statewise change in the growth rates between the eighties (1981-91) and the nineties (1991-96) as well as change in growth ranks. For this purpose, the growth rates and their ranks for 1981-91 given in Table 1.4 have been subtracted from those for 1991-96. These changes are summarised in Table 1.6 for the overall growth rates as well as for each of the three sectors. A negative difference in growth rates obviously indicates a decline in growth rates from the eighties to the nineties and vice-versa. On the other hand, a negative change in ranks depicts improvement in rank position of that state and vice-versa.

The first thing which strikes one by a look at Table 1.6 is that not even a single state exhibited an increase in the aggregate growth rates from the 1980s to the first half of the nineties. The same was by and large true of sectoral growth rates, except in the case of primary sector growth rate which depicted a marginal increase in Karnataka (-0.91) and Gujarat (+0.72). The maximum decline in overall growth rate was in the case of Bihar (-5.47) followed by Rajasthan (-5.19), Haryana (-4.96), Uttar Pradesh (-3.93), Himachal Pradesh (-3.52), Punjab (-3.45) and Orissa (-3.20). It may be observed that a steep decline in growth rates was shared by well developed states like Punjab and Haryana as well as relatively less developed states, but the less developed states were affected much more. The initial impact of the reform process thus affected adversely the less developed states to a greater degree than the more developed states. It may be noted that Ahluwalia's (2000) results differ somewhat from these. This is presumably a consequence of his covering a longer period up to 1997/98, inclusion of 14 states as against 16 covered here and using 1990/91 as the terminal year for the first period but 1991/92 as the base year for the subsequent period.

When we look at change in the ranks in terms of overall growth rates, if we ignore rank changes up to the third, the steepest deterioration took place in the case of Haryana (-10) and Rajasthan (-10), followed by that in the case of Uttar Pradesh (-5), Himachal Pradesh (-5) and Bihar (-4). At the other end of the scale Kerala improved its rank position by 11, followed by Gujarat (8), Assam (5), Madhya Pradesh (4) and West Bengal (4).

The change in the ranks of sectoral growth rates was broadly in conformity with the changes for overall growth. But in a few

TABLE 1.6: **Change in Growth Rates between Eighties and Nineties (90s minus 80s)**

State	Overall	Rank Change	Primary	Rank Change	Secondary	Rank Change	Tertiary	Rank Change
Andhra Pradesh	-1.20	-3	-1.54	-1	-6.20	5	-6.11	8
Assam	-1.97	-5	-1.55	-1	-3.02	-1	-2.38	-6
Bihar	-5.47	4	-5.35	9	-7.94	7	-4.20	4
Gujarat	-1.39	-8	0.72	-6	-1.44	-5	-4.20	-1
Haryana	-4.96	10	-3.35	4	-7.70	11	-5.71	9
Himachal Pradesh	-3.52	5	-3.22	5	-1.28	-9	-5.91	7
Karnataka	-2.38	-1	0.91	-9	-4.98	4	-4.51	-1
Kerala	-0.43	-11	-0.43	-6	-0.08	-11	-0.72	-14
Madhya Pradesh	-2.16	-4	-0.11	-10	-4.25	-1	-4.43	2
Maharashtra	-2.48	-1	-1.69	0	-3.76	-4	-2.21	-3
Orissa	-3.45	1	-2.65	0	-6.42	5	-3.69	-3
Punjab	-3.20	1	-3.26	4	-3.55	-4	-3.00	-1
Rajasthan	-5.19	10	-4.66	11	-4.69	1	-6.53	8
Tamil Nadu	-2.72	1	-1.28	-3	-2.81	-3	-3.57	-3
Uttar Pradesh	-3.93	5	-1.83	1	-7.36	11	-5.08	5
West Bengal	-2.05	-4	-2.93	2	-1.27	-6	-1.92	-11

Source : Same as for Table 1.4.

cases, change in sectoral growth ranking differed visibly from the overall rank change. States where there were marked deviations were:

1. In the case of Gujarat whereas the overall growth rate rank improved by eight, for the tertiary sector it was only one.
2. In Himachal Pradesh, while the overall growth rate rank deteriorated by five positions, in the case of secondary sector growth, there was improvement of nine positions.
3. In Kerala, whereas overall growth rank improved by 11 positions, in the case of the primary sector, although there was improvement in rank, it was only of the order of six positions.
4. In Madhya Pradesh, the overall growth rank improved by four positions, but in the case of primary sector growth it improved by 10 positions while in the case of tertiary sector growth it deteriorated by two positions, thus revealing divergent sectoral trends.
5. Rajasthan's overall growth rank deteriorated by 10 positions, but in the secondary sector growth some cushion seems to have operated since the rank decline was only one.
6. In Uttar Pradesh the overall growth rate decline was five but in the secondary sector the decline was 11.
7. West Bengal depicted a reverse type of situation since its overall growth rank improved by four but in the tertiary sector growth the improvement was by 11. On the other hand, its primary sector growth rank, which was at the top (1) during the eighties declined by two to yield the third rank during 1991-96.

Impact on Regional Development: Levels, Ranks and Relatives

What has been the impact of growth on the levels of regional development? This is the theme to which this section is addressed. The level of economic development of different states is taken to be measured in terms of state domestic product (SDP) per capita, which in brief shall be referred to as income per capita. At first changes in it during the period 1951-1981 are presented (Table 1.7). These results are based on an earlier study by the present writer (1994). The estimates for 1950/51 and 1980/81 are based on data at 1960/61 prices and 1970/71 prices respectively.

As may be observed, the top four states in 1950/51 were West Bengal (1), Punjab (2), Gujarat (3) and Maharashtra (4) while the bottom four were Bihar (16), Orissa (15), Madhya Pradesh (14) and Uttar Pradesh (13). By 1980/81 there were only two visible changes in these ranks and both of these were in the direction of deterioration. There was a downward slide in the position of West Bengal and Uttar Pradesh, both of which lost their position by four ranks. In the case of West Bengal the slide was of course at a much higher level of development than in the case of Uttar Pradesh. The decline in the case of West Bengal was to a considerable extent a consequence of its industrial decline, which started with the 'Gherao' movement of the nineteen sixties.

TABLE 1.7: **State Per Capita Income and Their Ranks**

State	1950-51 at 60-61 Prices NCAER	1960-61 at 60-61 Prices NCAER	1970-71 at 70-71 Prices SSB	1980-81 at 70-71 Prices SSB
1	2	3	4	5
Andhra Pradesh	258	289	585	647
Rank	11	13	10	8
Assam	335	428	535	558
Rank	6	7	13	12
Bihar	181	222	402	441
Rank	17	15	17	17
Gujarat	381	403	829	904
Rank	3	4	3	4
Haryana	364	396	877	1060
Rank	5	5	2	2
Himachal Pradesh	270	295	651	711

(contd.)

TABLE 1.7 *(contd.)*

1	2	3	4	5
Rank	10	10	6	6
Jammu & Kashmir	227	248	548	642
Rank	16	16	12	10
Karnataka	287	313	641	687
Rank	8	9	8	7
Kerala	304	326	594	621
Rank	7	8	9	9
Madhya Pradesh	236	293	484	517
Rank	15	11	16	15
Maharashtra	373	480	783	957
Rank	4	2	4	3
Orissa	252	268	485	477
Rank	13	15	15	16
Punjab	444	485	1070	1354
Rank	2	1	1	1
Rajasthan	256	272	645	537
Rank	12	14	7	13
Tamil Nadu	245	344	581	584
Rank	14	6	11	11
Uttar Pradesh	271	292	486	519
Rank	9	12	14	14
West Bengal	471	462	722	793
Rank	1	3	5	5

Note: Estimates of per capita income of Himachal Pradesh, Jammu & Kashmir, Haryana and Punjab for 1950-51 and 1960-61 have been derived by assuming that the same relative distance existed between them in 1950-51 and 1960-61, as in 1970-71. Admittedly, estimates for these states for the first two periods are less reliable. Assumptions also had to be made for estimating figures for 1989-90 in respect of Madhya Pradesh, for which data are available only at 1970-71 prices, and for four States for which 1989-90 data were not available.

Source: Same as for Table 1.3.

When comparing the levels of development of 1980/81 with 1995/96 on the basis of per capita income at 1980/81 prices (Table 1.8), it may again be observed that there was very little change over the period in terms of ranks of the top four and bottom four states, the top four being Punjab, Maharashtra, Haryana and Gujarat in 1980/81. In 1995/96 the top four were again the same, the only difference being that Punjab and Maharashtra had switched places. Similarly, in the case of the lowest ranking states there was only a slight shift of ranks.

TABLE 1.8: **Per Capita Incomes and Ranks in 1981 and 1996**

State	1980-81	Rank	1995-96	Rank
Andhra Pradesh	1379.87	10	2407.02	9
Assam	1284.47	13	1601.98	15
Bihar	916.96	16	983.40	16
Gujarat	1939.75	4	3516.75	4
Haryana	2370.10	3	3679.06	3
Himachal	1703.56	6	2518.17	8
Karnataka	1520.36	7	2558.37	7
Kerala	1507.56	8	2200.05	10
Madhya Pradesh	1357.55	11	1854.20	12
Maharashtra	2435.25	2	4635.13	1
Orissa	1313.50	12	1633.81	14
Punjab	2674.15	1	4176.13	2
Rajasthan	1221.67	15	1973.76	11
Tamil Nadu	1498.04	9	2819.66	5
Uttar Pradesh	1277.55	14	1654.34	13
West Bengal	1773.38	5	2703.67	6

Source : Same as for Table 1.4.

The absolute magnitude of change in per capita incomes between 1980/81 and 1995/96 and their ranks, have been given in Table 1.9. The change has been measured as 1995/96 minus 1980/81 income per capita. Thus, a positive change indicates an increase in per capita income and vice-versa. As may be observed, the

TABLE 1.9: **Per Capita Overall and Sectoral Income Change (1996-1981)**

State	NSDP	Rank	Primary	Rank	Secondary	Rank	Tertiary	Rank
Andhra Pradesh	1027.15	-7	125.77	-9	340.54	-6	560.83	-6
Assam	317.52	-15	-14.08	-13	40.03	-16	291.57	-11
Bihar	66.44	-16	-121.94	-16	80.08	-15	108.29	-16
Gujarat	1577.00	-2	-110.38	-15	959.84	-1	727.54	-3
Haryana	1308.96	-5	223.38	-4	460.21	-4	625.37	-4
Himachal Pradesh	814.61	-9	58.57	-10	319.36	-7	436.68	-8
Kanataka	1038.01	-6	163.37	-6	288.18	-8	586.46	-5
Kerala	692.48	-11	127.98	-8	156.37	-12	408.13	-9
Madhya Pradesh	496.65	-12	57.87	-11	186.24	-10	252.54	-14
Maharashtra	2199.88	-1	150.02	-7	802.83	-2	1247.03	-1
Orissa	320.31	-14	-41.66	-14	92.90	-14	269.06	-13
Punjab	1501.98	-3	548.79	-1	608.03	-3	345.15	-10
Rajasthan	752.08	-10	243.56	-3	235.59	-9	272.94	-12
Tamil Nadu	1321.62	-4	181.56	-5	405.33	-5	734.73	-2
Uttar Pradesh	376.78	-13	28.84	-12	122.02	-13	225.93	-15
West Bengal	930.29	-8	286.09	-2	178.69	-11	465.51	-7

Source : Same as for Table 1.4.

maximum increase over this period took place in the case of Maharashtra, followed by Gujarat, Punjab, Tamil Nadu and Haryana, all developed states which occupied the top five ranks in 1995/96. In 1980/81 also this ranking was broadly true except that Tamil Nadu occupied the ninth rank. At the other end of the scale are Bihar, Assam, Orissa, Uttar Pradesh and Madhya Pradesh, in whose case income change was the least. All these belong to the less developed category and four of these fall within the 'Bimaru' category. Thus, relative improvement in overall developmental level has been the fate of the better off while decline or meagre improvement has fallen to the share of those lagging behind.

When one looks at the scenario in terms of sectoral per capita income change, one is struck by the fact that whereas the secondary and tertiary sectors, as well as overall per capita incomes recorded an increase in the case of all states over the period 1981-96, per capita primary income declined in the case of four states (Assam, Bihar, Orissa and Gujarat). However, the relative per capita sectoral change has by and large been in conformity with overall per capita income change, as may be observed from Table 1.8. The ranks of sectoral income change are generally two to three or at the most four places away from that of overall per capita income change. But in the case of a few states there has been visible divergence between performance of certain sectors and the overall per capita income change. States where there have been such noticeable deviations are discussed below:

1. In Gujarat, whereas the overall per capita income change is among the highest, per capita primary sector income change is second from the bottom. In fact, in Gujarat there was a decline in per capita primary income, as mentioned earlier. Thus, agricultural performance has been a weak spot amidst commendable overall economic performance in the case of Gujarat.
2. Similarly, in Maharashtra, amidst overall and secondary as well as tertiary sector economic performance of a top level magnitude, primary sector per capita income change falls in the middle category. It has, however, not been as disturbing

a picture as in the case of Gujarat's primary sector.

3. In Punjab whereas the overall as well as primary and secondary sector per capita income changes were among the top three, in tertiary sector incomes the change has been of the 10th rank.
4. The case of Rajasthan was of the reverse type. Its overall, secondary and tertiary per capita income changes were relatively poor, their ranking belonging to the lower middle category. But in terms of its primary sector income change, its position was third from the top, reflecting essentially a resurgence in its agricultural growth.
5. West Bengal presents a picture of sectoral contrasts. Whereas its overall and tertiary income increase belonged to the middle category, in terms of its primary sector income increase it was second from the top, reflecting very commendable agricultural performance during the eighties. On the other hand, per capita secondary income increase was very poor, occupying the 11th rank.

Development ranks in terms of per capita income hide the exact magnitude of difference between incomes of different states. Moreover, they do not allow one to observe a state in relation to overall development of the country. In order to overcome these limitations, we have estimated state income relatives (Nair, 1982) for the four quinquennial points of time during the eighties and nineties (Table 1.10). Here state per capita incomes have been expressed as a percentage of the All-India average, both for overall state income and sectoral per capita incomes. A value of more than 100 indicates states which are more developed than the country as a whole and vice-versa.

It may be observed from the last row of Table 1.10, that whether one considers overall or sectoral development, the number of states above the country average is much less than those below it. In terms of overall per capita income, four to six states belong to the above average group against 10-12 below it. By and large, a similar position exists in respect of the sectors, except that in the case of the tertiary sector the number of above average states has risen

TABLE 1.10: **State Per Capita Income Relatives**

State	Part A : Primary Sector Relatives				Part B : Secondary Sector Relatives			
	1980-81	1985-86	1990-91	1995-96	1980-81	1985-86	1990-91	1995-96
1	2	3	4	5	6	7	8	9
Andhra Pradesh	88.61	88.42	87.22	92.41	59.25	64.89	79.24	79.25
Assam	94.41	94.79	83.93	80.66	38.32	40.95	29.89	26.19
Bihar	69.76	72.69	68.32	46.20	41.10	52.78	47.60	33.25
Gujarat	109.04	91.30	89.26	81.85	136.59	162.20	157.61	207.00
Haryana	178.27	191.15	196.36	182.35	116.26	146.09	141.97	126.57
Himachal	118.16	108.19	112.05	110.11	95.42	84.81	88.33	95.76
Karnataka	96.46	90.02	86.86	103.78	81.60	79.68	83.65	83.99
Kerala	81.47	74.58	79.98	86.45	94.96	79.09	74.86	72.85
Madhya Pradesh	104.03	103.52	100.71	97.70	64.43	51.63	61.02	60.57
Maharashtra	94.28	83.93	96.64	100.27	220.90	212.47	209.79	230.53
Orissa	100.12	106.03	73.35	82.33	52.44	46.05	45.55	41.14
Punjab	182.36	224.06	220.66	225.02	127.70	145.61	144.94	153.28
Rajasthan	87.95	90.73	115.67	105.99	56.94	57.27	61.81	63.40
Tamil Nadu	53.48	61.07	64.13	68.47	129.68	126.48	127.64	126.15
Uttar Pradesh	92.06	88.68	87.54	83.77	50.61	55.20	56.37	44.21
West Bengal	79.64	86.87	82.16	103.85	134.23	114.63	101.01	97.08
No. of states above A-I average	6	5	5	6	6	6	6	5

(contd.)

TABLE 1.10 *(contd.)*

1	2	3	4	5	6	7	8	9
No. of states below A-I average	10	11	11	10	10	10	10	11
Andhra Pradesh	90.39	92.92	103.02	100.08	82.42	84.41	91.20	91.92
Assam	80.32	92.47	79.45	69.56	76.72	81.05	68.34	61.18
Bihar	44.81	44.30	42.08	33.71	54.77	57.63	52.99	37.56
Gujarat	110.41	116.23	115.70	126.22	115.87	117.32	116.90	134.30
Haryana	111.56	121.86	125.39	117.26	141.57	155.24	155.31	140.50
Himachal	84.92	88.85	94.35	85.57	101.76	95.58	99.20	96.17
Karnataka	89.86	91.93	97.88	102.20	90.81	88.24	90.24	97.70
Kerala	97.76	88.98	84.42	89.65	90.05	80.88	80.36	84.02
Madhya Pradesh	62.91	60.84	60.24	56.74	81.09	75.62	75.07	70.81
Maharashtra	159.66	167.96	171.33	200.80	145.46	145.18	154.20	177.01
Orissa	68.38	66.62	60.30	61.17	78.46	77.38	61.23	62.39
Punjab	152.55	138.80	126.00	112.56	159.73	174.36	165.09	159.48
Rajasthan	64.66	60.61	74.10	59.57	72.97	71.80	85.98	75.38
Tamil Nadu	108.34	115.60	112.82	125.81	89.48	96.50	99.02	107.68
Uttar Pradesh	73.66	69.74	70.75	59.90	76.31	73.79	73.13	63.18
West Bengal	120.42	114.47	102.96	106.94	105.93	103.53	94.94	103.25
No. of states above A-I average	6	6	7	8	6	5	4	6
No. of states below A-I average	10	10	9	8	10	11	12	10

Source : Same as for Table 1.4.

progressively from six to eight.

If one tries to categorise states according to whether their index value has risen, fallen or fluctuated, it may be noted that:

(i) Only five states have shown a continuous or almost continuous rise in their index. This group includes Andhra, Gujarat, Karnataka, Maharashtra and Tamil Nadu.
(ii) In contrast, those which have shown by and large a continuous decline in their overall index are Bihar, Madhya Pradesh, Orissa and Uttar Pradesh, which have formed almost a perennial backward group.
(iii) The remaining seven states (Assam, Haryana, Himachal Pradesh, Kerala, Punjab, Rajasthan, West Bengal) have shown fluctuations in the value of their index, which in some cases have been small fluctuations while in others fluctuations have been quite wide as in Haryana, Punjab and Rajasthan.

Impact on Regional Income Disparities

Having examined the level of state per capita incomes in the previous section, this section focusses on inter-temporal behaviour of disparity among the states in terms of their per capita income levels. Theoretical models dealing with this theme have provided divergent conclusions. The neo-classical models developed along the lines of Solow's work postulate a long term trend towards income convergence among spatial units. Neo-classical theoretical expectations lead to this conclusion within the framework of factor mobility among the spatial units as well as without inter-spatial factor mobility. The latter conclusion emerges from the application of the Heckscher-Ohlin theorem to the inter-regional framework. In contrast to the neo-classical formulation, dissident views emerging from the works of Gunnar Myrdal, Raul Prebisch and Andre Gunder Frank postulate primarily divergence among regions during the process of development of the developing regions. The third brand of formulations and their empirical verification lead one to expect a divergence among regions up to some stage of development but an ultimate trend towards convergence, resulting in an inverted U-shaped curve of regional disparities. Albert Hirschman's work and empirical study of J.G. Williamson belong essentially to this category.

There have been a large number of studies of this theme for the Indian economy. An overview of some of the major studies up to the eighties was provided in K.R.G. Nair's *Survey of Regional Economics,* for the ICSSR (1994). Two earlier studies by the author (1983 and1994) on this theme as also some of the other works indicated that in the initial phase of post-independence development, there was some evidence to suggest a tendency towards narrowing down of regional income disparities. But since the mid-sixties, particularly in the wake of the Green Revolution, disparities had started mounting. This trend has continued unabated.

The inter-regional behaviour of regional income disparities can be viewed from two perspectives. One of these is to examine the time trend of some measure of regional income differentials. In this section disparities have been measured in terms of the co-efficient of variation of state level per capita incomes. The second approach is to consider statewise growth over a certain period of time in relation to the initial per capita income of those states at the beginning of that period of time. In case the higher income states systematically reveal a higher pace of growth and vice-versa, it obviously implies an income widening tendency among the states. A negative correlation between these two variables, on the other hand, indicates income convergence tendency. These are essentially parallel to what has been called by Barro, Xavier Salai-Martin (1995) and Quah (1996) as â and ó convergence.

Co-efficient of Variation Test

We may first turn to the inter-temporal behaviour of the co-efficient of variation (CV) of state level per capita incomes or to be more precise per capita SDP. Table 1.11, which is taken from the author's earlier paper (1994), presents weighted CV from 1950/51 to 1980/81. Estimates of CV (unweighted) for the period 1981-96, based on state level SDP data at 1980/81 prices, brought together by C.S.O.

from various State Statistical Bureau estimates, are given in Table 1.11. As may be seen, the CV showed a tendency towards decline till the mid-sixties but thereafter there has been an almost continuous increase. It is this type of behaviour which had prompted the writer to conjecture in his earlier article (1983) that the Indian experience appeared to suggest movement along a U-shaped curve of regional disparities rather than an inverted U-shaped one.

TABLE 1.11: **Spatial Variability of Inter-State Per Capita Incomes (SDP): Estimates of Weighted Co-efficient of Variation (C.V.)**

Year	C.V. at 1960-61 Prices	Based on
1950-51	26.7	NCAER data
1955-56	23.5	NCAER data
1960-61	24.2	NCAER data
1964-65	19.6	CSO data
1965-66	24.6	SSB data
1970-71	24.7	SSB data
1975-76	27.2	SSB data
1980-81	30.2	SSB data

Source: Same as for Table 1.3.

In order to delve into factors operating behind this contrary path of movement, movements in sectoral per capita income disparities for the period 1951-76 had been examined in the earlier study by the author (1983). The analysis suggested an inverted U-shaped curve in the case of the primary sector, the rising part primarily coinciding with the inequitable consequences emerging from the new agricultural strategy associated with the onset of the Green Revolution. In contrast, the secondary sector regional disparities revealed some tendency towards a decline of per capita income disparities. Tertiary sector per capita income disparities, on the other hand followed a path somewhat similar to that of the primary sector regional disparities.

TABLE 1.12: **Co-efficients of Variation of Overall and Sector Income Per Capita (1980-81 to 1995-96)**

Period	Overall	Primary	Secondary	Tertiary
1980-81	29.98	33.55	51.92	33.09
1985-86	33.54	41.37	53.23	33.75
1990-91	34.74	42.55	52.15	33.47
1995-96	39.43	41.74	61.90	42.22

Source : Same as for Table 1.4.

For extending the sectoral analysis of regional disparities into the more recent period, Table 1.12 gives quinquennial estimates of sectoral co-efficients of variation from 1980/81 to 1995/96, all based on SDP data at 1980/81 prices. What emerges from this Table is a perceptible deviation from the earlier trend of sectoral regional disparities. The rising primary sector regional disparities show some tendency to get arrested, to a considerable extent a consequence of the much improved agricultural performance of the agriculturally lagging Rajasthan and West Bengal. But the secondary and tertiary sector disparities show a disturbing trend after the eighties. Between 1990/91 and 1995/96 there was a substantial rise in the co-efficient of variation of the secondary and tertiary sectors from 52.15 per cent to 61.90 per cent and from 33.47 per cent to 42.22 per cent. There is therefore indication that in the post-reform period industrial investments have tended to move in the direction of the better developed regions, shying away from the less developed ones. The service sector incomes have followed the direction of secondary sector growth, as one would normally expect.

Correlation Test

In order to examine to what degree the above tendency is borne out in terms of the second mode of assessing the pattern of movement of regional disparities, we may now turn to the correlation of overall and sectoral rates of growth with the initial levels of state per capita income. For this purpose, statewise compound rates of growth of SDP and sectoral incomes which were discussed for the 15-year period of the eighties and first half of the nineties in Section II (b), have been correlated with the initial per capita income existing in 1980/81 (see Section IV). In addition, in order to view the scenario separately for the eighties and the nineties, statewise compound growth rates were estimated separately for the periods 1980/81-82/83 to 1989/90-91/92 and 1989/90-91/92 to 1993/94-95/96. These growth rates were correlated with respective statewise per capita incomes of 1980/81 and 1990/91. The resulting correlations for the overall economy and each of the three sectors for 1981-96, 1081-91 and 1991-96 are presented in Table 1.13.

TABLE 1.13: **Co-efficients of Correlation of Growth with Initial Per Capita Income**

Period	Overall	Primary	Secondary	Tertiary
1981-96	0.49	0.16	0.20	0.10
1981-91	0.40	0.19	-0.03	-0.10
1991-96	0.41	0.10	0.57	0.61

Source : Same as for Table 1.4.

As may be observed from Table 1.13, for the composite period 1981-96 the correlation for the overall economy is +0.49, which indicates an income widening tendency. The value of the correlation co-efficient, though positive and fairly high, is a little below the 10 per cent significance level since the number of observations in terms of the states included for analysis (16) is not very large. But it does broadly corroborate the finding of an increase in overall regional income disparity in terms of the co-efficient of variation criterion. However, when one looks at the sectoral correlations, though all the three correlations are positive, they are very poor and too low either to confirm or contradict the conclusions based on co-efficient of variation.

By and large similar conclusions emerge in respect of correlations for the eighties (1980/81 to 1990/91). However, when one comes to the post-reform period of 1991-96, the results are rather revealing. Although the overall economy correlation is +0.41, those for the secondary and tertiary sectors reveal significant positive correlation values. In the case of these two sectors during 1991-96 both the co-efficient of variation test and the correlation co-efficient tests lead to an identical conclusion of a rise in regional disparities in the industrial and tertiary activities. Thus, some of the misgivings concerning the likely adverse impact of reforms on regional disparities in industry appear to have been borne out during the first half of the nineties. One would have to wait for fuller results to become available at the regional level before definitive conclusions can be drawn up regarding the whole decade of the nineties.

Disparities within State Sub-categories

It would be useful to refer to some interesting results of a 'convergence' hypothesis study by Das (1998). In the light of the 10th Finance Commission's suggestion that states should be categorised into the High Income, Middle Income and Low Income states, groups the convergence hypothesis has been tested separately for the three groups of states in terms of the σ and β convergence tests. These tests have been applied separately for the period 1960-94 as well as for the sub-periods 1960-65, 1966-82 and 1983-94. A negative β co-efficient indicates a negative relationship between regional growth over a period of time and the initial levels of per capita income thus pointing to convergence, while a positive β co-efficient shows divergence among the states. Similarly, a decline in σ co-efficient indicates convergence tendency and vice-versa. If both σ and β tests indicate convergence, the situation is referred to as that of Absolute Convergence; if both indicate divergence, it is called Absolute Divergence. If σ test reveals divergence but β test indicates convergence, it is referred to as Partial Divergence, while convergence in terms of σ test and divergence in terms of β test is called Partial Convergence in this paper.

The high income states in Das's study include Punjab, Maharashtra, Haryana and Gujarat; the middle category includes Tamil Nadu, Karnataka, West Bengal, Kerala and Andhra Pradesh; while the low income group covers Madhya Pradesh, Rajasthan, Orissa, Uttar Pradesh and Bihar, making up 14 major states. The results for the overall period and three sub-periods for all the states

TABLE 1.14: **Divergence-Convergence Among the States**

	1960-94	1960-65	1966-82	1983-94
		14 Major States		
β Co-efficient	Positive	Negative	Positive	Positive
σ Co-efficient	Increase	Decrease	Increase	Increase
Overall Trend	Absolute Divergence	Absolute Convergence	Absolute Divergence	Absolute Divergence
		High Income States		
β Co-efficient	Negative	Negative	Positive	Positive
σ Co-efficient	Increase	Decrease	Increase	Increase
Overall Trend	Partial Divergence	Absolute Convergence	Absolute Divergence	Absolute Divergence
		Middle Income States		
β Co-efficients	Negative	Negative	Negative	Negative
σ Co-efficients	Decrease	Decrease	Decrease	Decrease
Overall Trend	Absolute Convergence	Absolute Convergence	Absolute Convergence	Absolute Convergence
		Low Income States		
β Co-efficients	Positive	Negative	Negative	Negative
σ Co-efficients	Increase	Decrease	Increase	Increase
Overall Trend	Absolute Divergence	Absolute Convergence	Partial Divergence	Partial Divergence

Source : Tushar Kanti Das (1998), " 'Convergence' and 'Catch-Up' : An Empirical Analysis with Fourteen Major Sates of India", mimeographed, Department of Economics, Utkal University, Bhubaneswar.

as well as the three sub-categories have been summarised in Table 1.14. For the 14 states considered together, there is Absolute Divergence for the period as a whole, as well as for the two major sub-periods, viz. 1966-82 and 1983-94. There was Absolute Convergence only during 1960-65 and that was true of each sub-category of states. This is broadly in conformity with the main conclusions of the two earlier studies of the author referred to earlier in this paper (1983 and 1994).

What is of interest to note is that for the middle income states there was Absolute Convergence for the period as a whole as well as for each sub-period. It is the high income states as well as low income states which displayed either Absolute or Partial Divergence during the overall periods and sub-periods except 1960-65. This does underscore the need for policy to incorporate special measures to uplift the sagging pace of development in the lagging regions.

National and Regional Economic Structure

State per capita income provides only one indicator of State level development, although it can be designated as the most important single indicator of development. Sectoral structure of income can be considered as the second most important indicator of development. In line with the Colin Clark-Kuznets Fisher hypothesis, with a rise in the level of development the share of non-primary activities generally increases at the cost of primary sector. A decline in the share of the primary sector is counterbalanced by a rise in the share of secondary and tertiary activities. As to which of these two sectors is more positively related to development, needs to be assessed.

All-India Sectoral Change

We may first look at the national level sectoral structure and the change in it over the five decades from 1950/51 to 1999/2000, the latest year for which sectoral data are available at present. For this purpose the All India sectoral structure has been estimated from national income data at 1993/94 prices as given in the Economic Survey, 2001 (Appendix Table 1.3, page 5-5). Estimates of the share of primary, secondary and tertiary sections as given in Table 1.15 (A and B) show a substantial decline in the share of primary sector over the five-decade period (-31.96), which is counterbalanced by maximum rise in the share of the tertiary sector (+19.83) followed by that of the secondary sector (+11.34), as may be seen from the last row of Table 1.15(B). The share of the primary sector has declined to 27.23 per cent, which is less than half of what it was in 1950/51 (59.19 per cent).

TABLE 1.15: **All-India Sectoral Structure and Structural Changes : (1951-2000)**

(A) Sectoral Percentages

Year	Primary	Secondary	Tertiary
1950-51	59.19	13.29	28.04
1960-61	54.75	16.61	29.02
1970-71	48.12	19.91	32.18
1980-81	41.82	21.59	36.59
1990-91	34.92	24.49	40.59
1999-2000	27.23	24.63	47.87

(B) Change in Sectoral Percentage: S(t) - S(t-1)

Period	Primary	Secondary	Tertiary
1950/51 - 1960/61	-4.45	3.32	0.98
1960/61 - 1970/71	-6.63	3.30	3.16
1970/71 - 1980/81	-6.30	1.68	4.41
1980/81 - 1990/91	-6.90	2.90	4.00
1990/91 – 2000	-7.69	0.14	7.28
1950/51 – 2000	-31.96	11.34	19.83

Source : Same as for Table 1.4.

The total magnitude of sectoral structural change over the five-decade period, however, hides considerable decadal variations in the magnitude of sectoral shifts in some of the sectors. The magnitude of the primary sector decline has risen every decade except for a slight dip from -6.63 in the sixties to -6.30 in the seventies. In the reverse direction, the magnitude of increase in the share of the tertiary sector has gone up in every decade except for a slight decrease in the magnitude of increase from +4.41 in the seventies to +4.00 in the eighties. In contrast, structural enhancement in the direction of the secondary sector has been much less than in the direction of the tertiary sector. But in addition, there have been considerable variations in the decadal magnitude of secondary sector shift. There was a major decline in the magnitude of shift from +3.30

in the sixties to +1.68 during the seventies; but the decline in the nineties to +0.14 from +2.90 in the eighties has been very phenomenal and disturbing. It is again indicative of the weak health of the industrial sector during the nineties to which attention was drawn in the opening section of this paper.

State Level Sectoral Structure

We may now look at the state level picture. Table 1.16 gives the percentage share of primary, secondary and tertiary sectors in NSDP as well as the ranks of states in terms of these three shares for 1980/81 and 1995/96. For the purpose of comparison, the ranks of the states in terms of per capita NSDP is also given for 1980/81. As may be observed, there does not exist a very close inverse relationship between the level of development as reflected in per capita NSDP and the ranks of primary sector share. Similarly, although there appears to be a broad positive relationship between ranking of per capita incomes and that of the share of other two sectors, it is not a very perfect positive one. In order to examine whether a rise in the level of development as reflected in per capita income is more closely related to the share of the secondary or tertiary sector or decline in the share of the primary sector, these three shares have been correlated with the level of per capita income for three points of time (1981, 1991 and 1996). The value of correlation co-efficients is summarised in Table 1.17.

A look at correlation co-efficients shows that it is the industry based secondary sector which is much more closely related in a positive direction to per capita income than the tertiary sector. Similarly, the positive correlation of the secondary sector is stronger than the negative correlation of the primary sector activities. In fact the relationship with the tertiary sector is not only much more feeble but erratic as well as being mildly negative in 1991 and 1996. On the other hand, the positive relationship with the secondary sector has been gaining in strength over the years, the correlation co-efficient values having risen from +0.42 in 1981 to + 0.67 in 1996. The latter value is significant at 0.01 level. It appears therefore that despite the

TABLE 1.16: **Sectoral Income Structure (State Level)**

(A) 1980-81 Percentages

State	Primary	Rank	Secondary	Rank	Tertiary	Rank	Per Capita Income Ranks (1990-91)
Andhra Pradesh	46.62	10	16.61	13	36.77	4	11
Assam	53.36	5	11.54	16	35.10	6	8
Bihar	55.23	3	17.34	12	27.43	14	16
Gujarat	40.81	12	27.24	4	31.95	10	4
Haryana	54.60	4	18.98	8	26.42	15	2
Himachal	50.35	8	21.67	6	27.98	13	3
Karnataka	46.06	11	20.76	7	33.18	7	7
Kerala	39.23	13	24.37	5	36.40	5	13
Madhya Pradesh	55.63	1	18.36	10	26.01	16	5
Maharashtra	28.10	15	35.09	1	36.80	3	9
Orissa	55.33	2	15.45	14	29.22	12	6
Punjab	49.50	9	18.47	9	32.02	9	1
Rajasthan	52.26	7	18.03	11	29.71	11	12
Tamil Nadu	25.92	16	33.49	2	40.60	1	15
Uttar Pradesh	52.31	6	15.33	15	32.36	8	10
West Bengal	32.60	14	29.28	3	38.12	2	14

(contd.)

TABLE 1.16 *(contd.)*

(B) 1995-96 Percentages

State	Primary	Rank	Secondary	Rank	Tertiary	Rank
Andhra Pradesh	31.95	13	23.67	10	44.38	4
Assam	41.90	6	11.75	16	46.35	2
Bihar	39.10	8	24.31	8	36.59	11
Gujarat	19.37	15	42.32	1	38.31	10
Haryana	41.25	7	24.73	7	34.02	13
Himachal	36.39	9	27.34	4	36.27	12
Karnataka	33.76	10	23.60	11	42.64	6
Kerala	32.70	11	23.81	9	43.49	5
Madhya Pradesh	43.85	3	23.49	12	32.66	14
Maharashtra	18.00	16	35.76	2	46.24	3
Orissa	41.93	5	18.10	15	39.96	8
Punjab	44.84	1	26.39	5	28.77	16
Rajasthan	44.69	2	23.10	13	32.22	15
Tamil Nadu	20.21	14	32.17	3	47.63	1
Uttar Pradesh	42.14	4	19.21	14	38.65	9
West Bengal	31.96	12	25.82	6	42.22	7

Source : Same as for Table 1.4.

TABLE 1.17: **Correlation of State Sectoral Structure and Per Capita Income Value of Correlation Co-efficients**

Sector	1980-81	1990-91	1995-96
Primary	-0.33	-0.24	-0.49
Secondary	0.42	0.49	0.67
Tertiary	0.09	-0.17	-0.03

Source : Same as for Table 1.4.

fact that improvements in overall growth of the economy have come about mainly as a consequence of growth in the tertiary sector incomes, the kingpin of development continues to be the industry based secondary sector activities.

State Level Sectoral Structural Change

The share of the different sectors in SDP conveys only a static picture of the sectoral structure of the regional economies. An equally important facet is to obtain the dynamic picture by examining the magnitude of structural change in different economies and to see whether structural change bears any systematic relationship to either the pace of growth or the level of development of different regional economies.

For this purpose, Table 1.18 gives the magnitude of structural change from 1980/81 to 1995/96 in terms of the share of each of the three sectors in 1996 minus the share in 1981, that is,

R (i) = R (i) 96 - R (i) 81

where i = Primary, Secondary and Tertiary sectors.
R indicates a sector's percentage share in NSDP

As may be observed from Table 1.18, the share of the primary sector decline during 1981 and 1996 was the maximum in Gujarat, followed by Bihar, Andhra Pradesh, Himachal Pradesh, Orissa, Haryana and Karnataka. The counterbalancing rise in the share of the secondary sector was the maximum in Gujarat, followed by that in Punjab, Andhra Pradesh, Bihar, Haryana, Madhya Pradesh and Rajasthan.

TABLE 1.18: **Statewise Change in Sectoral Percentages: (1996-1981)**

State	Primary	Rank	Secondary	Rank	Tertiary	Rank
Andhra Pradesh	-14.67	14	7.06	3	7.61	7
Assam	-11.45	8	0.21	13	11.24	1
Bihar	-16.13	15	6.97	4	9.16	5
Gujarat	-21.44	16	15.08	1	6.36	12
Haryana	-13.35	11	5.76	5	7.60	8
Himachal	-13.96	13	5.67	6	8.29	6
Karnataka	-12.30	10	2.84	10	9.46	3
Kerala	-6.53	4	-0.56	14	7.09	9
Madhya Pradesh	-11.78	9	5.13	7	6.65	11
Maharashtra	-10.10	6	0.67	12	9.44	4
Orissa	-13.40	12	2.66	11	10.74	2
Punjab	-4.66	2	7.92	2	-3.25	16
Rajasthan	-7.57	5	5.07	8	2.51	15
Tamil Nadu	-5.71	3	-1.32	15	7.03	10
Uttar Pradesh	-10.17	7	3.88	9	6.29	13
West Bengal	-0.64	1	-3.47	16	4.10	14

Source : Same as for Table 1.4.

When one comes to the tertiary sector, the maximum shift towards this sector occurred in Assam, whose secondary sector change rank was among the lowest at 13. The second largest change in the tertiary sector was that in the case of Orissa, followed by Karnataka, Maharashtra and Bihar. When we look at the other end of the scale, the slowest pace of shift towards the secondary sector was in West Bengal followed by Tamil Nadu, Kerala, Assam and Maharashtra. It may thus be seen that it is not always in the more developed states that the shift towards secondary or tertiary sector has been substantial. For example, it was found to be high in Bihar, in Assam and Orissa in respect of the tertiary sector and in the medium high range in respect of the secondary sector in the case of

Madhya Pradesh and Rajasthan. On the other hand, in some of the advanced states like West Bengal and Tamil Nadu, secondary sector structural change has in fact been negative. It was very low even in Maharashtra. Similarly, in Gujarat and Tamil Nadu, tertiary sector change was very low. Thus the relationship between the extent of structural change does not appear to be very systematically related to the level of development.

TABLE 1.19: **Correlation of Statewise Structural Change with Initial Per Capita Income**

Period	Primary	Secondary	Tertiary
1981-96	0.18	0.14	0.44
1981-91	0.28	0.01	0.38
1991-96	-0.18	0.31	-0.2

Source : Same as for Table 1.4.

In order to assess the strength of the relationship between structural change and the level of development, Table 1.19 gives values of correlation between per capita Income in 1980/81 and structural change during 1981-91 and during the post-reform period 1991-96. As conjectured in the previous paragraph, the correlation values are rather poor. In the eighties the maximum strength of relationship existed in the tertiary sector (r= -0.38) and that was also the reverse of the expected direction. During 1991-96 the relationship in the tertiary sector was again negative, but in the secondary sector it was in the expected positive direction and also of the highest magnitude. However, the positive value was only +0.31, which is significant only at about 25 per cent.

TABLE 1.20: **Correlation between Statewise Growth Rates and Initial Per Capita Income**

Period	Primary	Secondary	Tertiary
1981-91	0.10	0.08	-0.22

Source : Same as for Table 1.4.

Similarly, the correlation between initial per capita income in

1980/81 and state level growth rates during the decade 1981-91 was studied. The results are reported in Table 1.20. As in the case of the relationship of structural change to the level of development, these relationships are even more feeble and not always in the expected direction.

Which Sector has been the 'Engine of Growth'?

Having examined sectoral levels of development and pace of growth, both in the national and regional contexts, can some sector be considered to have been the kingpin in the process of growth in the Indian economy? This was among the main issues examined as a part of the Kaldorian Growth Laws (Kaldor, 1966 and 1967; Thirlwall, 1983). Kaldor considered this issue in the context of growth in mature capitalist economies and came to the conclusion that the growth of the industrial sector acted as the 'engine of growth'. Could the same be true for a developing economy, which in the present context is the Indian economy?

The Kaldorian postulate can be considered as resting upon a few propositions. Among these, one is the high correlation between the rates of growth of the industrial sector and of overall economic growth observed in the case of the industrially advanced countries considered by Kaldor, as also by other scholars. Since in advanced capitalist economies industrial output forms a major component of domestic output, correlation between growth of the secondary sector and overall output growth is bound to be high. Caution about this correlation has also been expressed by Gomulka (1983) and McCombie et al. (1983). For that very reason, in the developing countries, since it is the primary sector which forms the dominant component of national output, one would expect a high correlation to exist between the growth of the primary sector and the overall rate of economic growth. But it raises the question that in case this expectation is empirically borne out, could we assign the role of 'engine of growth' to the primary sector in the case of developing countries?

In the light of the abovementioned limitation, there is another channel through which industrial growth could be viewed as being related to overall growth. The channel we have in mind here is the input-output linkages of the secondary sector—both of the forward and backward types (Hirschman, 1958)—with the primary and tertiary sectors and through these the influence of secondary sector growth on the overall growth rate. A good bit of the tertiary sector income is generated through the input of its services in the industrial sector though a part of the services also gets utilised in primary sector production and within the tertiary sector itself. On the other side, with the process of development, a rising volume of secondary sector output finds its outlet in the primary sector in the form of inputs like fertilisers, electricity, improved agricultural implements, other capital goods like tractors and manufactured consumer goods. As to how important this third channel is in explaining the relationship of overall economic growth and secondary sector growth, can be revealed only by empirical analysis of the relationship of secondary sector growth rate with rates of growth of the primary and tertiary sector incomes.

It is with this perspective that we now turn to empirical analysis of the Kaldorian postulate in the context of the Indian economy. Inter-sectoral growth relationships have been analysed from two angles—first with the help of the time series analysis at the all-India level covering a span of nearly five decades (1950/51 to 1998/99), and then through a cross-sectional growth analysis using regional data of major Indian states. Empirical estimates have been derived separately for the period up to and beyond 1980/81, using C.S.O. (1979 and 1984) and Economic Survey (1998 and 2000) data. Results up to 1980/81 along these lines have been obtained by the writer in another paper (Mathur, 2001), whereas for the period 1981-96 they have been estimated here.

National Level Inter-Temporal Analysis

First let us look at the national level correlations between annual growth rates of income generated in each of the three sectors with annual growth rates of aggregate domestic product (Table 1.21). The correlation of growth of the secondary sector with that of aggregate domestic output is positive, statistically significant, and free of auto-correlation at 1 per cent level significance for the period 1951-81, thus

TABLE 1.21: **Regression of Aggregate Growth on Sectoral Growth**

(A): 1950-51 to 1980-81		
Primary Sector	$g_y = 2.20 + 0.54^{***}\ g_p$	r = 0.97***
	(20.70)	DW= 1.53
Secondary Sector	$g_y = 1.33 + 0.43^{***}\ g_s$	r = 0.42***
	(2.44)	DW= 2.66
Tertiary Sector	$g_y = -2.34 + 1.19^{***}\ g_t$	r = 0.50***
	(3.06)	DW= 2.50
(B) : 1980-81 to 1998-99		
Primary Sector	$g_y = 4.51 + 0.36^{***}\ g_p$	r = +0.79***
	(5.17)	DW= 1.19
Secondary Sector	$g_y = 2.22 + 0.52^{***} g_s$	r = 0.74***
	(4.39)	DW= 2.43
Tertiary Sector	$g_y = 2.32 + 0.49\ g_t$	r = +0.34
	(1.47)	DW= 2.46
(C): 1950-51 to 1998-99		
Primary Sector	$g_y = 3.03 + 0.48^{***}\ g_p$	r = 0.89***
	(13.37)	DW= 1.09
Secondary Sector	$g_y = 1.16 + 0.56^{***}\ g_s$	r = +0.58***
	(4.88)	DW= 2.55
Tertiary Sector	$g_y = -0.67 + 0.95^{***}\ g_t$	r = +0.56***
	(4.54)	DW= 2.79

Notes: g_y is annual rate of growth of net national income.
g_p is annual rate of growth of primary sector income.
g_s is annual rate of growth of secondary sector income.
g_t is annual rate of growth of tertiary sector income.
t values are given within parenthesis.

Source : Ashok Mathur (2001), "Kaldor's Laws and Economic Growth in India: Some Conceptual Issues and Empirical Evidence" in Raj Kumar Sen and Biswajit Chatterjee (eds.), *Indian Economy : Agènda for the 21st Century*, Essays in Honour of Professor P.R. Brahmananda, Deep & Deep Publications, New Delhi.

reaffirming Kaldor's results obtained for advanced industrial countries. But what is important to note is that the correlation co-efficients of both the other sectors are higher than that of the secondary sector, confirming the doubt that these correlations may essentially be a reflection of the weight occupied by each of the three sectors in national output. The highest correlation during 1951-81 emerges in the case of the primary sector, which accounted for about 50 per cent of the national output. The proportional output contributed by the secondary sector during much of this period had been the least at about 20 per cent, and so also is its correlation co-efficient (+0.42), though it is statistically significant.

Results for the period subsequent to 1980, that is 1980/81 to 1998/99, as may be observed from Table 1.21-B, differ from that for the earlier period in two respects. First, for this period the relationship of secondary sector growth to aggregate growth emerges to be much stronger than what it was during 1951-81. Moreover, the correlation co-efficient of secondary sector growth emerges to be higher than that of the tertiary sector. These changes are a reflection of the growing prominence of the industrial sector in India compared to the initial position in which India had a small industrial base. Simultaneously, the correlation of primary sector growth to aggregate growth declined from 0.97 during 1951-81 to 0.79. It may, however, be noted that the DW value (1.19) for correlation of primary sector growth does not confirm the absence of auto-correlation, although it does not fall within the critical range.

The statistical tests reveal that the correlation co-efficient of each sector is significant and that of the primary sector had an edge over that of the secondary sector during the period 1951-81. But in view of the fact that their hierarchy is basically dependent upon the existing sectoral structure of the economy, particularly for the period 1951-81, on the basis of direct correlations between sectoral growth rates and the overall growth rate it is difficult to designate any one of the three sectors as having been the 'engine of growth' or to attribute a higher causal role to either sector in the growth process.

This brings us to the channel of input-output relations among the three sectors, which has been referred to earlier. Here, instead of basing one's conclusions on direct correlations between growth of individual sectors and overall growth, inter-sectoral growth correlations are studied. Two sets of relationships are examined, the first one of which considers the secondary sector to be at the apex of the growth process and the second visualises the primary sector to be in the key role. These correlations are between:

(i) Growth of the secondary and of the primary sector on the one hand, and growth of the secondary and of the tertiary sector, on the other. Since overall growth is nothing but that derived through aggregation of sectoral data, if these two correlations are positive and significant, the role of the secondary sector as the 'engine of growth' would stand vindicated.

(ii) Growth of the primary sector and of the secondary sector on the one hand, and growth of the primary sector and of the tertiary sector on the other. If both these correlations are positive and significant, the primary sector could be viewed as playing the key role. It is possible for (a) and (b) to be simultaneously valid, which would show strong interdependence between all three sectors in the growth process without signifying greater relative importance of one sector over the other in generating growth.

These two sets of relationships based on annual growth rate series are portrayed in diagrams 1(a)-1(b) for 1951-99, 1(c)-1(d) for 1951-1981 and 1(e)-1(f) for 1981-1999. The corresponding regression equations are given in Table 1.22.

Some important points emerge from these correlations. First, the correlation between growth of the primary and the secondary sector, though positive, is feeble. This is contrary to what may be envisaged, the possible reasons for which formed one of the themes of an earlier article of the author (1990). Secondly, growth of the services sector is closely interlinked to the pace of expansion of the industrial sector. This is true for the period 1951-99 as a whole as also separately for its two sub-sets. It should, however, be noted from regression equations given in Table 1.22 that DW values indicate the presence of auto-correlation for some of the regressions during 1951-99. It is absent for the sub-period 1951-81 and is within the indeterminate range for 1981-99.

TABLE 1.22: **Inter-Sectoral Growth Relationships**

(A): 1951 – 1981		
	$g_p = -0.11 + 0.50\ g_s$	r = 0.26
	(1.44)	DW = 2.75
	$g_t = 3.02 + 0.26^{***}\ g_s$	r = 0.70***
	(5.23)	DW = 1.86
	$g_s = 4.94 + 0.14\ g_p$	r = 0.26
	(1.44)	DW = 1.43
	$g_t = 4.18 + 0.08^{**}\ g_p$	r = 0.40**
	(2.32)	DW = 1.19
(B): 1981 – 1999		
	$g_p = 0.68 + 0.40\ g_s$	r = 0.26
	(1.08)	DW = 2.80
	$g_t = 0.54 + 0.24^{**}\ g_s$	r = 0.48**
	(2.17)	DW = 1.35
	$g_s = 6.18 + 0.16\ g_p$	r = 0.26
	(1.08)	DW = 1.47
	$g_t = 7.28 - 0.07\ g_p$	r = 0.21
	(0.84)	DWG = 0.89
(C): 1951 – 1999		
	$G_P = 0.10 + 0.48^{*}\ g_s$	r = 0.27
	(1.89)	DW = 2.82
	$g_t = 3.50 + 0.32^{***}\ g_s$	r = 0.57***
	(4.75)	DW = 0.88
	$g_s = 5.40 + 0.15^{*}\ g_p$	r = 0.27*
	(1.89)	DW = 1.44
	$g_t = 5.22 + 0.06\ g_p$	r = 0.18
	(1.23)	DW = 0.67

Source : Same as for Table 1.21.

In contrast, growth of the primary sector does not appear to be

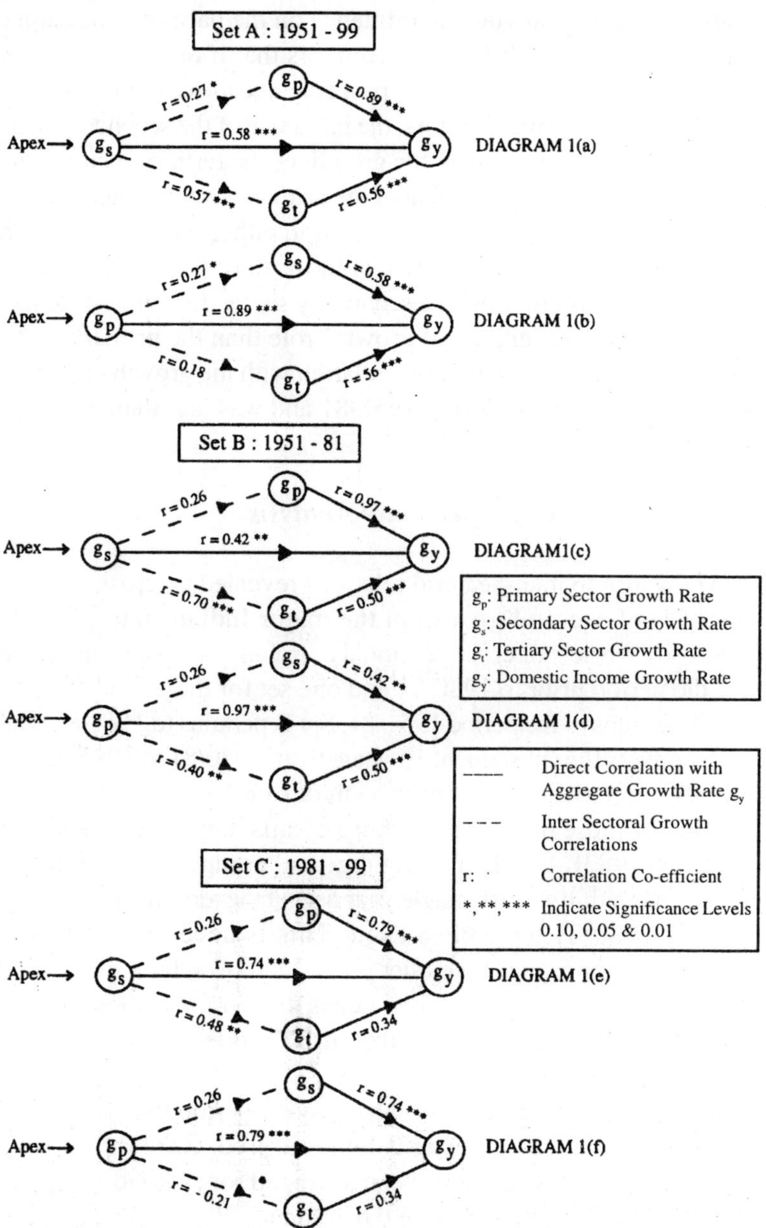

Diagram 1.1: National Level Sectoral Growth Relationships

exercising that important an influence on the pace of expansion of the services sector. It follows from this that if one is viewing the national growth process of the past five decades in terms of interaction of the three main sectors, the influence of the secondary sector through its repercussion on the growth of the tertiary sector stands out more prominently than that of the primary sector, which does not reveal its role in terms of its correlation either with growth of the secondary sector or with growth of the tertiary sector. Therefore, if one goes by this criterion, the secondary sector does emerge to have played a stronger 'engine of growth' role than the primary sector, despite the fact that its direct correlation with the growth of national income was the least during 1951-81 and was less than that of the primary sector during 1981-99.

Regional Level Cross-Sectional Analysis

We now turn to inter-sectoral relations revealed by cross-sectional analysis of sectoral growth in the major Indian states. For this purpose, two sets of cross-sectional correlations have been derived for the period prior to 1980/81 and one set for the period 1981-96. Set A pertains to the period 1951-81, Set B pertains to 1961-81 while Set C covers the subsequent 15 years from 1980/81 to 1995/96. The data for regional analysis of growth during 1951-81 are based on linking of these three series whose details have been spelt out in Mathur (1983). For estimating regional compound growth rates during these thirty years, single year data at the terminal points 1950/51 and 1980/81 have been used. This is necessitated by data availability constraints for earlier years. Moreover, for a span as wide as this three-decade period, one hopes that erratic nature, if any, of a terminal year would get substantially overshadowed by the quantum of growth.

In the case of Set B, only the 20-year period from 1960/61 to 1980/81 is covered but sectoral domestic products of the first three and the last three years have been averaged for estimating regional growth rates in order to reduce the influence of erratic behaviour of annual data on growth rates. This methodology could not be applied to the 30-year period 1951-81, since in the case of the nineteen-fifties initial regional data are available only for one year (1950/51). Thus, while Set B has the advantage of terminal averaging procedure, Set A has the advantage of covering a longer span of time. Set C which covers the period from 1980/81 to 1995/96, is based on the State Statistical Bureaus' data at 1980/81 prices. Compound Growth Rates have been estimated using the same methodology as for Set B.

Table 1.23 and diagrams 2(a)-2(f) give estimates of regressions and correlation co-efficients across states for the three periods. As may be observed from Table 1.23, the direct correlations of sectoral growth with overall growth for the pre-1980 period broadly follow

TABLE 1.23: **Regional Regression Results**

Set A (1951 - 1981)		
Primary Sector	$g_y = 1.11 + 0.94^{***} g_p$	$r = 0.84^{***}$
	(1.85)	
Secondary Sector	$g_y = 0.69 + 0.59^{***} g_s$	$r = 0.80^{***}$
	(4.57)	
Tertiary Sector	$g_y = 1.08 + 0.52^{***} g_t$	$r = 0.70^{***}$
	(3.35)	
Set B (1961-81)		
Primary Sector	$g_y = 1.41 + 0.86^{***} g_p$	$r = 0.79^{***}$
	(4.40)	
Secondary Sector	$g_y = 1.79 + 0.34^{**} g_s$	$r = 0.58^{**}$
	(2.46)	
Tertiary Sector	$g_y = 0.34 + 0.68^{***} g_t$	$r = 0.92^{***}$
	(8.22)	
Set C (1981 - 1996)		
Primary Sector	$g_y = 3.19 + 0.36^{**} g_p$	$r = 0.49^{**}$
	(2.10)	
Secondary Sector	$g_y = 1.98 + 0.66^{**} g_s$	$r = 0.66^{***}$
	(3.29)	
Tertiary Sector	$g_y = 0.67 + 0.66^{***} g_t$	$r = 0.74^{***}$
	(4.15)	

Source : Same as for Table 1.21.

the same pattern as in the case of time series analysis at the national level. The slopes of all three regression lines are also less than unity.

When one shifts attention to regressions based on regional growth rates during the post-1980 period covering the phase 1981-96 (Set-C), one can again observe a broad similarity to changes in the post-1980 period indicated on the basis of national level inter-temporal regressions. But it may be noted that the strength of the correlation coefficient of secondary sector growth with aggregate growth as well as its regression co-efficient is higher during 1981-96 compared to that during 1961-81. These characteristics do point to the growing significance of industrialisation in the process of regional economic growth.

Inter-sectoral growth relationships across regions for 1981-96 reveal a somewhat different pattern than that for 1951-81 (Diagram 1.2). Both Set A and Set B results indicate that regional tertiary sector growth is much more closely linked to growth of the primary sector than was revealed by the time series analysis at the national level. However, results for 1981-96 are much more in alignment with the inter-temporal relationships observed at the national level. Among the inter-sectoral growth relationships across regions for 1981-96, the strongest is that of the secondary sector growth with tertiary sector growth. The relationships of secondary sector growth to primary sector growth and that of primary sector growth to tertiary sector growth are both feeble. The growing significance of secondary sector growth in the development process *via* its relationship to tertiary sector growth thus reaffirms the emerging role of industry based secondary sector growth as the 'engine of growth' in the Indian economy. Attention to this facet was also drawn earlier in the paper, both on the basis of national level inter-temporal correlations and direct correlation of secondary sector growth to aggregate growth across regions. However, designating a sector as the 'engine of growth' does not imply that the process of growth can be generated without sustained growth in other sectors of the economy, each of which has a role to play in supporting overall growth of the economy.

An increased role of industrialisation in generating growth, but a sluggish pace of industrial expansion which was observed in section II, represents an incongruent situation. The policy for

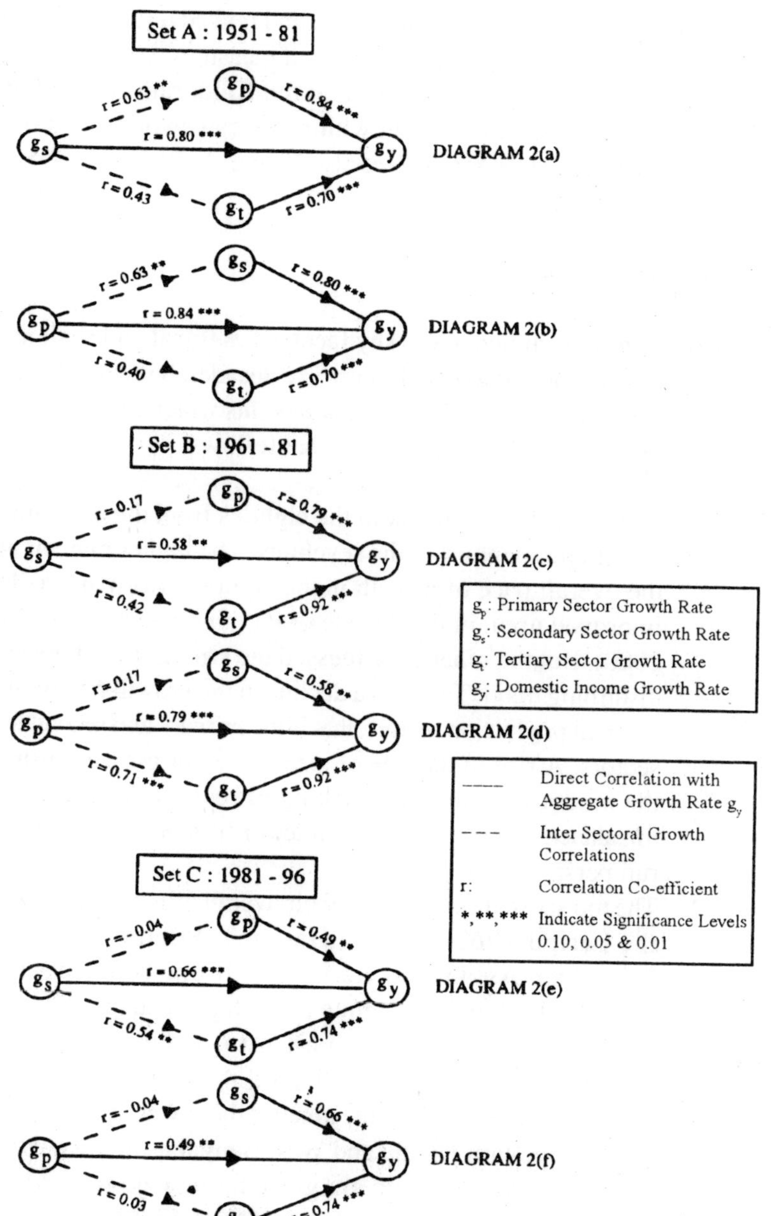

Diagram 1.2: Regional Growth Relationships

sustaining the tempo of industrialisation and related tertiary growth shall have to devise an appropriate blend of measures which provide support to domestic industry based on the Kaldorian concept of 'dynamic increasing returns', but within the framework of a more open and competitive economy (see also Young, 1928; Weiss, 1988; and Mathur, 2000a).

Main Conclusions

This paper has examined a few key facets of national and regional economic growth in India over the past five decades, but with a focus on the eighties and the nineties. The main points which emerge from this analysis are now put together in what follows:

1. There is a distinct break in the eighties from the declining growth momentum of the seventies. The higher plateau of the overall pace of growth in the eighties was marginally improved upon in the decade of the nineties (up to 1999/2000). But the nineties witnessed the emergence of a very disturbing trend. This was a decline in the growth rate of the two real production sectors, that is the primary and secondary sectors. A rise in the rate of tertiary sector growth during the nineties without the backing of real production is an imbalance which cannot be justified or sustained in the longer run perspective.
2. The top six states in terms of their overall growth rate during the period 1961-89 were Haryana, Punjab, Gujarat, Rajasthan, Assam and Karnataka. If one considers the eighties alone, the new group of the top six states contains Rajasthan, Haryana, Maharashtra, Andhra Pradesh, Karnataka and Tamil Nadu (Table 1.4). In the post-reform period of the first half of the nineties there was considerable reordering, with Kerala and West Bengal as the two main new entrants in the top six growth rate category while Haryana and Rajasthan slumped to the lowest growth category states. Andhra Pradesh, Maharashtra and Gujarat emerged as the three fastest growing states.

3. Considerable sectoral growth rate disparity could be witnessed in the case of some of the well developed states during the eighties and nineties. Notable among these were Andhra Pradesh and Gujarat, both of which displayed very poor primary growth performance as against their high growth rank in the other two sectors. On the other hand, a well-placed Punjab displayed the lowest tertiary sector growth in contrast to its high growth rank in the case of primary and secondary sector growth. Similarly, whereas West Bengal had bounced up to the top in terms of primary sector growth, in the secondary and tertiary sector growth it had the lowest ranks.
4. As regards the impact of growth on change in state per capita incomes between 1981 and 1996, it may be observed that the five maximum levels of increase took place in the case of Maharashtra, Gujarat, Punjab, Tamil Nadu and Haryana, all of which are well-developed states. The lowest level of change on the other hand occurred in Bihar, Assam, Orissa, Uttar Pradesh and Madhya Pradesh, all of which belong to the relatively backward category.
5. State Income Relatives, (i.e., index of state-wise regional development) reveal that over the period 1981-96 only four to six states fall in the above All-India average category as against 10-12 below it, showing concentration of high development only within a few states. Moreover, over the period 1981-96 continuous rise in the index occurred in the case of the five developed states (Gujarat, Maharashtra, Karnataka, Tamil Nadu and Andhra Pradesh) while continuous decline occurred in the case of the least developed states (Bihar, Madhya Pradesh, Orissa and Uttar Pradesh).
6. The above tendencies have inevitably brought about a rise in overall regional income disparities as reflected in steep acceleration in the rise of co-efficient of variation of per capita incomes during 1991-96 (Table 1.10). Sectoral trends reveal that whereas rising primary sector disparities have tended to get arrested during the nineties, it is basically

secondary and tertiary sector disparities which have tended to widen sharply during this period.

7. Whereas within the middle income states there has been a tendency towards convergence, it is the high and low income states that have been characterised by income divergence and have primarily been responsible for overall regional income divergence in the country.
8. Structural Income Change at the All-India level during the five-decade period 1951-2000 shows the shift towards the secondary sector to have been the least (+11.34). Moreover, unlike almost a unidirectional change in the case of the primary and tertiary sector shifts (Table 1.14), there have been substantial decadal fluctuations in the case of the secondary sector shift. There was a major dip from +3.30 in the sixties to +1.68 in the seventies. But the decline in the shift from +2.90 in the eighties to a meagre +0.14 during the first half of the nineties has been much more substantial, pointing to the shaky health of the industrial sector during the latter period.
9. The correlation of statewise sectoral percentages with the level of development as reflected in per capita incomes shows the secondary sector to be the most strongly correlated to the level of development in a positive direction. Moreover, this relationship has been gaining in strength from 1981 to 1996 (Table 1.17), indicating that development of the secondary sector continues to occupy a strategic position despite the phenomenal rise of the tertiary sector during the nineties.
10. Rise in the share of secondary sector during 1981-96 was the maximum in Gujarat, followed by that in Punjab, Andhra Pradesh, Bihar, Haryana, Madhya Pradesh and Rajasthan. But the magnitude of this shift bore a very feeble relationship (r = +0.14) to the level of development of the states (Table 1.19).
11. The issue as to which sector has been the 'engine of growth', was examined within a modified Kaldorian framework. The main criticism of the Kaldorian

methodology of directly correlating a sector's growth with aggregate growth of the economy has been that the value of the correlation co-efficient would be closely dependent upon the weight of that sector in the GDP. In order to overcome this criticism, the methodology adopted here considers two hypotheses. The first one is that, in a developing country primary sector growth is the kingpin of the process of growth, and the second one is that the secondary sector is the kingpin. For this purpose, instead of directly correlating sectoral growth with GDP growth, for the first hypothesis the relationship of primary sector growth and GDP growth is inferred by looking at the relationship of primary sector growth with growth of the other two sectors. Similarly, for the second hypothesis secondary sector growth is correlated with primary and tertiary sector growth.
The above mentioned relationships were examined with the help of inter-temporal data at the all-India level and cross-sectional data at the regional level. The inter-temporal relationships at the national level and inter-regional relationships for 1981-96 both reveal that the influence of secondary sector growth through its repercussion on growth of the tertiary sector stands out more prominently than that of the primary sector, which does not exhibit its role that strongly in terms of its correlation either with growth of secondary sector or with growth of the tertiary sector. Therefore, the secondary sector, in conjunction with tertiary sector growth, does emerge to have played a stronger 'engine of growth' role than the primary sector.

12. In order to overcome the weak position of industrial growth during the nineties, and keeping in mind the pivotal position of its role as the 'engine of growth' despite the growing significance of tertiarisation, the reform measures through which industrial growth has been addressed during the nineties need to be examined afresh.

Keeping in mind the points which have emerged from preceding view of the national as well as regional scenarios from different angles, it is doubtful whether a high pace of overall growth can be sustained in the long run on the basis of a high pace of tertiarisation without the backing of equally vibrant industrial and agricultural expansion and policies to support these.

REFERENCES

Ahluwalia, Montek S. (2000), "Economic Performance of States in Post-Reforms Period", *Economic and Political Weekly*, Vol. XXXV, No. 19.

Barro, Robert J. and Xavier Sala-i-Martin (1995), *Economic Growth*, Mc-Graw Hill, New York.

Das, Tushar Kanti (1998), " 'Convergence' and 'Catch-Up' : An Empirical Analysis with Fourteen Major Sates of India", mimeographed, Department of Economics, Utkal University, Utkal University, Bhubaneswar, mimeo.

Dholakia, Ravinder (1985), "Interstate Variation in Economic Growth and State Income Inequality in India", in G.P. Mishra and A. Joshi (eds.), *Regional Structure of Development and Growth in India*, Ashish Publishing House, New Delhi.

Frank, Andre, Gunder (1967), "Capitalism and Underdevelopment in Latin America", *Monthly Review Press*, New York.

Gomulka, S. (1971), *Inventive Activity and Stages of Economic Growth*, Institute of Economics, Aarhus.

Government of India (2000 and 2001), *Economic Survey*, Ministry of Finance, New Delhi.

Hirschman, Albert O. (1958), *The Strategy of Economic Development*, Yale University Press, New Haven.

Kakwani, Nanak (1997), "Growth Rate of Per capita Income and Aggregate Welfare : An International Comparison", *Review of Economics & Statistics*, June.

Kaldor, Nicholas (1966), *Causes of the Slow Rate of Economic Growth of the United Kingdom, An Inaugural Lecture*, Cambridge University Press, Cambridge.

____ (1967), "Problems of Industrialisation in Underdeveloped Countries", in his *Strategic Factors in Economic Development*, Cornell University Press, Ithaca.

Mathur, Ashok (1983), "Regional Development and Economic Disparities in India : A Sectoral Analysis", *Economic Development and Cultural Change*, April.

____ (1994), "Regional Economic Development and Policy in India", in G.K. Chadha (ed.), *Policy Perspectives in Indian Economic Development*, Har-Anand Publications, New Delhi.

____ (1990), "The Interface of Agricultural and Industrial Growth in the

Development Process: Some Facets of the Indian Experience", *Development and Change*, Vol. 22.

____ (2000a), "Industry" Chapter in *Alternative Economic Survey : 1998-2000*, Rainbow Publishers, Delhi.

____ (2000b), "Reformed Swadeshism, Liberalisation and Economic Theory : A Developmental Perspective", *Social Sciences Research Journal*, Vol. 7, No. 2 (Punjab University).

____ (2001), "Kaldor's Laws and Economic Growth in India : Some Conceptual Issues and Empirical Evidence" in Raj Kumar Sen and Biswajit Chatterjee (eds.), *Indian Economy : Agenda for the 21st Century*, Essays in Honour of Professor P.R. Brahmananda, Deep & Deep Publications, New Delhi.

McCombie, John S.L. and John R. de Ridder (1983), "Increasing Returns, Productivity and Output Growth : The Case of the United States", *Journal of Post-Keynesian Economics*, Spring Issue.

Nair, K.R.G. (1982), *Regional Experience in a Developing Economy*, Wiley Eastern, New Delhi.

____ (1994), *Regional Economics: A Survey*, an ICSSR Research in Economics Monograph No. 7, New Delhi.

Prebisch, R. (1984), "Five Stages in My Thinking on Development", in G.M. Meier and D. Seers (eds.), *Pioneers in Development*, Oxford University Press, New York.

Singh, Ajit Kumar (1985), "Inter-State Differences in Levels and Rates of Growth of Income in India : 1951-81", in G.P. Mishra and A. Joshi (eds.), *Regional Structure of Development and Growth in India*, Ashish Publishing House, New Delhi.

____ (1999), "Inter-State Disparities in Per capita SDP: Trends and Causes", *Arth Vijnana*", Vol. XLI, No. 2.

Thirlwall, A.P. (1983), "A Plain Man's Guide to Kaldor's Growth Laws", *Journal of Post-Keynesian Economics*", Spring Issue.

Weiss, John (1988), *Industry in Developing Countries: Theory, Policy and Evidence*, Croom Helm, London.

Williamson, J.G. (1965), "Regional Inequality and the Process of National Development: A Description of the Patterns", *Economic Development and Cultural Change*, Vol. 13, No. 4, Pt. 2.

Young, Allyn (1928), "Increasing Returns and Economic Progress", *Economic Journal*, Vol. XXXVIII, No. 152.

2

GROWTH AND EMPLOYMENT WITH SPECIAL REFERENCE TO ORGANISED INDUSTRY

ARUP MITRA

Introduction

An important aspect of the positive effects of economic growth is its ability to improve the standard of living of the population. In line with this, one of the basic objectives of industrial policy in India since Independence has been to create employment opportunities on a large scale in the industrial sector. The deregulation process initiated in 1984/85, and structural adjustment programmes implemented in July 1991 aimed at increasing the long-run growth rate of GDP through deregulation in both commodity and factor markets. By removing the rigidities in the factor market, that is, removing subsidies in the capital market and discouraging unionisation in the labour market, employment levels in the industrial sector were expected to grow fast. Keeping in view some of these major policy changes, this paper intends to analyse the urban labour market over the last two decades or so. Before turning to the empirical analysis it may, however, be interesting to refer to some of the propositions usually drawn to explain the urban labour market behaviour in developing countries.

An important feature of economic growth, as viewed by Kuznets (1966) is the upward income mobility involving locational (rural-urban), occupational and industrial shifts of individuals and their incomes. In the process of growth, rise in agricultural productivity releases the surplus rural labour to be used in urban based non-agricultural activities (Lewis, 1954). Also, in the absence of agricultural growth, landlessness and rural poverty compel the unemployed and underemployed to migrate and explore opportunities in the urban job market (Hoselitz, 1957; Harris and Todaro, 1970). Even without inter-spatial population mobility a high natural growth of population can explain large supplies of labour in the urban areas (Mitra, 1994).

Large supplies of labour, available at a moderate wage rate, are expected to facilitate the expansion of non-agricultural activities, in particular industry. High productivity activities in the tertiary sector cannot employ them on a large scale as skill requirements are usually much higher than what is available. However, owing to limited spread of the industrial sector (resulting from inadequate infrastructural facilities) and/or sluggish employment growth therein (resulting from the adoption of capital intensive technology), the mismatch between demand and supply in the urban labour market tends to get aggravated. An immediate consequence of this may not be a rising unemployment rate, as not many of them can afford to remain unemployed for long. On the other hand, it may result in a residual absorption of labour in low productivity 'urban informal sector' jobs. This, however, means a sizeable number of urban households being pushed into vulnerability and poverty, and city growth being accompanied by the mushrooming growth of slums and squatter settlements. In turn, all this has serious implications in terms of environmental and health hazards.

In the backdrop of this framework and the major policy changes (mentioned above) that took place in India, this paper is organised as follows. The next section focuses on the changing composition of the workforce in terms of activities, category of employment and gender. The third section evaluates the performance of the organised sector, in particular, the organised industrial sector, as far as the issue of employment generation is concerned. The fourth section examines the magnitude of unemployment rates and the relative size of the informal sector in total employment in the urban areas. The next section comments on urban poverty, and the final, section summarises the major findings.

The data base of the study is mainly drawn from the decennial population censuses and the quinquennial surveys of the National Sample Survey Organisation (NSSO) on employment-unemployment and consumption expenditure. The information based on large sample surveys is not available after the 50th round (1993/94) of NSSO; however, certain aspects of employment and poverty could be covered for the recent years, that is, till 1997/98, on the basis of the thin sample surveys of the NSSO. Employment growth in the organised private and public sectors has been estimated till 1998 from the data provided by the Ministry of Labour.

Structural Shift

It is not just growth but the composition of growth that matters in tackling the 'employment problem'[2] and poverty. In the Indian context, the composition of value added has undergone a change away from agriculture more towards tertiary activities than industry, over the period 1960/61 to 1997/98 (Table 2.1). A large share of the tertiary sector, as the historical experience of the present day developed countries shows, is commensurate only with a very high level of per capita income. In fact, value added from the tertiary sector cannot be treated as similar to that from the commodity producing sector. Rapid growth of the tertiary sector or a predominantly large share of the tertiary sector in low income countries generates a heavy burden on the commodity producing sector, resulting in an adverse balance of payment situation and/or inflation which tends to wipe out the positive effects of growth, if any, on the levels of living (Bhattacharya and Mitra, 1990).

Secondly, compared to the experience of the present day developed countries a major deviation noted in the Indian context is the less than proportionate shift in the workforce structure vis-à-vis the shift in the composition of value added away from agriculture towards the industry and tertiary sectors. While the share of agriculture in total value added has declined over the years (Table 2.1), its share in total employment still persists at a high level (Table 2.2). On the other hand, the employment share of the industrial sector continues to dwindle at an unreasonably low level: both household and

TABLE 2.1: **Gross Domestic Product at Factor Cost by Industry of Origin (%)**

Industry	1960-61	1970-71	1980-81	1990-91	1992-92	1993-94	1997-98	1998-99
Agriculture etc. and mining etc.	52.1	45.8	39.6	32.9	32.2	33.5	29.2	29.2
Manufacturing, construction, electricity, etc.	18.7	22.4	24.4	28.0	27.1	23.7	25.3	24.7
Transport, communication and trade	12.6	14.3	16.7	17.8	18.2	19.3	21.1	21.3
Banking etc., real estate and business services	8.2	8.0	8.8	10.2	11.1	11.5	12.2	12.1
Public adminis-tration, defence and other services	8.2	9.6	10.5	11.1	11.4	12.0	12.3	12.7

Notes: 1. Percentages for the period 1960-61 to 1992-93 are based on figures at 1980-81 prices, and thereafter at 1993-94 prices.

2. Figures for 1997-98 and 1998-99 are based on provisional and quick estimates, respectively.

Source: Economic Survey, 1999-2000, Government of India.

non-household manufacturing accounted for only 10 per cent of the total workforce in 1993/94 (Table 2.2). All this means increasing productivity differentials across sectors and insignificant benefits accruing to individuals through employment generation in the high productivity organised industry. We turn to this point later in section three.

In urban India, the employment structure of both males and females has been dominated by tertiary activities. The share of manufacturing in total male employment rather declined between 1983 and 1997 by almost three percentage points (Table 2.3(a)). A similar pattern is evident among urban females also: the share of manufacturing fell from 29.6 per cent in 1977/78 to 25.1 per cent in 1997. The declining share of manufacturing in total employment of females has been compensated by a rising share of services. (Table 2.3(b)).

TABLE 2.2: **Workforce Structure in India (%)**

Activities	1972-73	1977-78	1983	1987-88	1993-94	1997
Agriculture	73.9	71	68.6	65	64	65.1
Mining & quarrying	0.4	0.4	0.6	0.7	0.7	0.6
Manufacturing	8.8	10.2	10.7	11.1	10.5	10.1
Electricity etc.	0.2	0.3	0.3	0.3	0.4	0.4
Construction	1.9	1.7	2.2	3.8	3.2	3.5
Trade and commerce	5.1	6.1	6.2	7.2	7.4	7.7
Transport etc.	1.8	2.1	2.5	2.6	2.8	2.8
Services	7.9	8.1	8.9	9.3	10.3	9.8
All	100	100	100	100	100	100

Note: Both usual primary and subsidiary status workers have been included.
Source: Quinquennium surveys carried out by National Sample Survey Organisation, Government of India. Key Results on Employment and Unemployment, NSS 50th Round (July 1993-June 1994). "Household Consumer Expenditure and Employment Situation in India, 1997", NSS 53rd Round, January-December, 1997.

Distribution of workers by category of employment shows that among both urban males and females the percentage of casual employment increased over time. Deregulation seems to have ushered in casualisation of the workforce (Table 2.4). On the other hand, regular wage/salaried employment among females rose significantly from 24.9 per cent in 1977/78 to 31.3 per cent in 1997, and this has been matched by a declining share of self-employment among them. A shift in women's employment from home-based activities to more commercial or market based activities is indicative of such a pattern of change. Rising literacy and improvement in levels of education acquired would possibly explain the increasing absorption of women in market-based service activities.

The female-male worker ratio (i.e., the number of female workers per thousand male workers) computed for different activities is reported in Table 2.5. Despite the fact that the female-male population ratio dropped between 1981 and 1991 census years (Mitra, 1993), the number of female workers per thousand male

TABLE 2.3(a): **Employment Pattern in Urban India (%) : Males**

Activities	1972-73	1977-78	1983	1987-88	1993-94	1997
Agriculture	10.7	10.6	10.3	9.1	9.0	7.6
Mining & quarrying	1.0	0.9	1.3	1.3	1.3	1.2
Manufacturing	26.8	27.5	27	25.9	23.6	23.6
Electricity etc.	0.9	1.1	1.1	1.2	1.2	1.5
Consumption	4.4	4.2	5.2	5.9	7.0	7.9
Trade and commerce	20.1	21.6	20.2	21.7	22	20.6
Transport etc.	9.1	9.8	9.9	9.6	9.8	9.3
Services	27.0	24.3	25.0	25.3	26.1	28.2
All	100	100	100	100	100	100

TABLE 2.3(b): **Employment Pattern in Urban India (%) : Females**

Activities	1972-73	1977-78	1983	1987-88	1993-94	1997
Agriculture	32.9	31.9	32	30.5	24.8	16.5
Mining & quarrying	1.4	0.5	0.8	0.7	0.6	0.3
Manufacturing	24.6	29.6	27.1	26.9	24.3	25.1
Electricity etc.	0.1	0.1	-	0.2	0.3	0.5
Consumption	2.7	2.2	3.3	3.5	4.1	6.9
Trade and commerce	9.6	8.7	9	9.9	10.1	9.1
Transport etc.	1.4	1	1.6	0.7	1.3	1.5
Services	27.4	26	26.2	27.6	34.5	40.1
All	100	100	100	100	100	100

Note: See Table 2.2. Results for 1997 are based on thin sample.
Source: Table 2.2.

workers (for all activities combined) rose between 1983 and 1987/88 or 1993/94 in urban India. Rising work participation rate among women is a major component which caused an improvement in female-male worker ratio (Mitra, 1993). An interesting point emerging from the figures in Table 2.5 suggests that between 1987/88 and 1993/94 the number of female workers per 1000 male

TABLE 2.4: **Classification of Urban Workers (Usual Principal-cum-Subsidiary) by Category of Employment (%)**

Year	Male			Female		
	Self-emp.	Regular wage salaried	Casual wage	Self-emp.	Regular wage salaried	Casual wage
1997	40.0	41.5	18.5	39.7	31.3	29.0
1993-94	41.7	42.1	16.2	45.4	28.6	26.0
1987-88	41.7	43.7	14.6	47.1	27.5	25.4
1983	40.9	43.7	15.4	45.8	25.8	28.6
1977-78	40.4	46.4	13.2	49.5	24.9	25.6

Note: See Table 2.3.
Source: Table 2.3.

TABLE 2.5: **Female-Male Ratio of Usual Principal-cum-Subsidiary Status Workers in Urban India**

Activities	1972-73	1977-78	1983	1987-88	1993-94
Agriculture	708	806	783	894	734
Mining & quarrying	319	145	155	144	123
Manufacturing	212	288	253	278	274
Electricity etc.	25	24	-	44	64
Construction	143	143	160	158	156
Trade and commerce	110	108	112	122	114
Transport etc.	35	27	41	19	33
Services	234	286	264	291	329
All	231	268	252	267	266

Note: Figures give the number of female workers per 1000 male workers.
Source: Based on Pravin Visaria (1997), "Youth Unemployment in India: Its Level, Nature and Policy Implications", Institute of Economic Growth, Delhi, mimeo., Alakh, N. Sharma (1997), "Trends in the Structure and Pattern of Employment and Unemployment in India", Institute of Economic Growth, Working Paper Series, No. E/188/97 and NSSO Surveys.

workers remained more or less unchanged in spite of the deceleration which the structural adjustment programmes of 1991 supposedly resulted in. In other words, reforms seem to have brought in feminisation, as female-male wage differentials are substantial even in the urban labour market, and secondly, female labour being more amicable, employers' preference seems to have shifted in their favour. Activity-wise, both in manufacturing and services the female-male employment ratio improved between 1983 and 1987/88, and continued to rise in services in 1993/94. In manufacturing, however, the ratio dropped marginally between 1987/88 and 1993/94.

In 1997, the female-male ratio of workers (all activities combined) fell drastically to 230 in urban India. But this was primarily because of the drop in the number of female workers per thousand male workers in urban agriculture. A significant decline in the relative size of agriculture in total female employment during 1993/94 to 1997 provides support to this point (see Table 2.3(b)). But within non-agricultural activities, manufacturing also registered a fall in the female-male ratio of workers from 274 in 1993/94 to 252 in 1997. However, in services the ratio did not show any tendency of decline during the same period. It would not, therefore, be appropriate to suggest that the feminisation trend in urban non-agricultural acivities, which continued during the eighties was arrested in the mid-nineties.

On the whole, in this section we observe patterns of change favouring tertiarisation, casualisation and feminisation of the urban workforce following the deregulation and economic reforms in the eighties and early nineties respectively.

Organised Sector

Downsizing of the public sector employment is an issue which has been faced by many industrial, developing and transition economies in recent years. The reasons underlying the downsizing vary considerably across countries. It is either due to a move towards a more market oriented economy, or a reduction in the role of the military, or an attempt to reduce a bloated bureaucracy, or it has been necessitated by a fiscal crisis requiring a severe cut-back in government spending (Haltiwanger and Singh, 1999). In the Indian context also, a huge fiscal deficit carried over the years necessitated privatisation and a considerable decline in public spending.

Comparing quite well with this change in policy environment, employment growth in the public sector decelerated over the years. During the seventies the public sector recorded a growth rate of 3.4 per cent per annum which dropped to 1.88 per cent per annum in the eighties and to 0.38 per cent during 1990/91 through 1996-97. Further, between March 1997 and December 1998 the growth rate became negative, namely, - 0.62 per cent (Table 2.6). In the organised private sector, on the other hand, employment growth rate was sluggish both during the seventies and the eighties. Although it picked up to 1.99 per cent per annum in the period 1990/91 to 1996/97, the share of the organised private sector remained at a moderate level of around 30 per cent in 1980/81, 1991 and 1998, which implies that its overall impact on total organised sector employment could not have been significant.

TABLE 2.6: **Employment Growth in Organised Sector**

Period	Growth Rates (% p.a.)	
	Public	Organised Private
1970-71 to 1980-81	3.44	0.89
1980-81 to 1990-91	1.88	0.22
1990-91 to 1996-97	0.38	1.99
1970-71 to 1996-97	2.12	0.8
1996-97 to 1998 Dec.	-0.62	0.96

Note: The year refers to April-March.

Source: Based on data provided by Directorate General of Employment and Training (DGE&T) Ministry of Labour, Government of India.

As mentioned earlier, the industrial sector is expected to play a major role in the process of economic development. We have, therefore, analysed employment in the organised industrial sector in detail using the two-digit level classification. Keeping in view the policy changes, as mentioned earlier, we have considered three sub-periods: (a) the regulated regime, from 1976/77 to 1984/85; (b) the period of deregulation, from 1985/86 to 1990/91; and (c) the post-reform period, from 1990/91 to 1993/94.

Relative to the first sub-period, from 1976/77 to 1984/85, the industrial growth rate both in terms of output and value added accelerated during the latter half of the eighties (Table 2.7). However, as evident from Table 2.7, output growth fell at least in seven industries during the post-reform period, particularly in comparison with the period of deregulation (1985/86 to 1990/91). Food products, jute textiles, wood and wood products, paper and paper products, chemical and chemical products, non-metallic mineral products, basic metal and alloys, and machinery and equipment, registered a decline in the growth rates, which, in fact, brought the overall industrial growth rate down to 8.75 per cent per annum during the post-reform period as compared to 9.24 per cent during the previous sub-period. Even in terms of gross value added originating from jute textiles, chemical and chemical products, non-metallic mineral products, and machinery and equipment, the growth rate decelerated during the early nineties. However, as mentioned above, the third sub-period in our study is too short and, therefore, the analysis based on growth patterns can at best be suggestive. Nevertheless the revival from the initial deceleration of the reforms seems to have been quicker in the Indian context as compared with many other countries, which have also undergone structural reforms. This could be one of the reasons why the industrial output growth rate corresponding to the third period was only marginally lower than that of the second period.

The industrial growth rate subsequent to the reforms is said to be constrained by (a) the balance of payment crisis of 1991 which necessitated an import squeeze affecting availability of inputs and their costs, (b) the tight monetary policy pursued to contain inflation which affected demand and raised the cost of borrowing for industries, and (c) a fall in investment demand owing to reduction in public expenditure and investment. The slow industrial growth in the early nineties is also attributable to inherent adjustment lags in the process of industrial restructuring, early uncertainties about the commitment to the reform policies and the lack of supplementary reforms at the sectoral and local levels (Ministry of Industry, 1996).

TABLE 2.7: Growth Rates of Some Variables (Per cent per annum)

Industry Code	Output			Gross Value Added			Employment		
	1976-7 to 1984-5	1985-6 to 1990-1	1991-2 to 1993-4	1976-7 to 1984-5	1985-6 to 1990-1	1991-2 to 1993-4	1976-7 to 1984-5	1985-6 to 1990-1	1991-2 to 1993-4
1	2	3	4	5	6	7	8	9	10
20-21: Food products	3.97	10.33	2.86	19.73	3.54	7.79	-1.2	3.21	4.08
22: Beverages, tobacco and tobacco products	1.11	4.13	7.29	-1.37	2.36	6.97	2.08	7.16	-0.3
23: Cotton textiles	-2.32	5.87	5.89	-6.8	6.27	8.29	-1.23	-0.99	1.84
24: Wool, silk and synthetic fibers textiles	5.52	9.43	15.08	-1.95	6.87	28.66	5.05	1.94	6.46
25: Jute, hemp and mesta textiles	-0.6	0.47	-0.35	1.98	1.92	-2.29	0	-0.01	-7.11
26: Textile products	2.43	14.31	21.51	1.83	17.59	27.2	1.69	9.76	21.89
27: Wood and wood prod., furniture and fixtures	1.17	11.81	-22.97	-5.41	2.6	15.95	-0.11	-1.29	4.58
28: Paper and paper products and printing and allied industries	5.44	7.66	3.46	2.61	6.67	10.93	2.48	0.23	2.11
29: Leather and leather and fur products	7.11	11.22	18.1	6.8	13.39	26	3.37	8.94	3.63

(contd.)

(Table 2.7 contd.)

1	2	3	4	5	6	7	8	9	10
30: Chemical and chemical products	13.68	10.65	7.15	22.51	15.78	9.77	20.66	1.08	5.2
31: Rubber, plastic, petroleum and coal prod.	1.47	7.87	19.36	-21.75	16.96	20.21	-13.03	5.88	7.07
32: Non-metallic mineral products	8.22	9.59	-1.14	5.52	9.55	-3.68	4.72	0.56	-1.48
33: Basic metal and alloys	9.28	7.95	5.47	6.81	-0.86	20.42	3.64	0.27	2.42
34: Metal products and parts	4.36	10.02	10.11	4.12	-1.05	6.66	0.43	4.83	1.8
35-36: Non-metallic machinery and equipment	5.38	10.13	3.96	2.06	9.7	7.54	2.93	1.87	0.85
37: Transport equipment and parts	8.45	10.68	13.82	5.05	7.98	14.64	5.45	0.01	1.38
38: Other mfg. industries	5.89	14.41	27.5	6.73	13.65	31.46	1.17	5.16	10.33
All industries	5.36	9.24	8.75	2.58	9.39	12.02	1.72	1.89	2.98

Notes: 1. Growth rates of Output, Employment, and Wages corresponding to different periods have been calculated by taking the variables as a function of time and time dummies as explained in the text.

2. Since gross value added figures for industries 20-21 and 27 turned out to be negative for some of the years, the growth rates have been calculated by taking the yearly average.

Source : Based on ASI data.

As mentioned, the process of adjustment, however, seems to have had a much shorter time span compared to the international experience. From April, 1994 industrial recovery seems to have taken place, and this broad based industrial recovery is attributed to a number of factors such as cumulative success of industrial restructuring, resurgence of exports in response to trade and payment policies, declining nominal and real interest rates, cumulative efforts of tax reforms, growing public expenditure on poverty alleviation and employment generation programmes, another agricultural bumper crop, a buoyant infrastructural sector and growth confidence, and improvement in investment climate due to the cumulative success of industrial trade, financial and capital market reforms (Ministry of Industry, 1996).

Despite an appreciable growth of output in the industrial sector during the eighties employment growth was quite sluggish in a large number of industries (see Table 2.7). The overall employment growth in organised industry was only 1.89 per cent per annum between 1985/86 and 1990/91. However, employment growth over the three-year period following the structural adjustment turned out to be highest (2.98 per cent per annum). Nevertheless, some of the industries recorded either a negative or a sluggish, though positive, growth rate of employment even during the early nineties. They are beverages, tobacco and tobacco products, cotton textiles, jute textiles, non-metallic mineral products, metal products and parts, machinery and equipment, and transport equipment and parts.

In order to assess the impact of growth on employment it would be desirable to estimate the employment elasticity. The following equation is estimated to compute the employment elasticity of growth: The logarithmic transform of employment, E, in a particular industry is taken to be a function of gross output of that industry, O, and the wage rate, i.e., wages and salaries per employee, W.

$$\ln E = ?_0 + ?_1 \ln O + ?_2 \ln W \text{ ....(2)}$$

The signs of $?_1$ and $?_2$ are expected to be positive and negative, respectively. Our major objective is to estimate the parameters and examine if $?_1$ has undergone changes over time. The CUSUM and

CUSUM square tests have been carried out to assess if such changes have occurred on a year to year basis. Empirical results (not reported here) are not supportive of any change. Chow-test could not be carried out since the number of observations corresponding to the third sub-period is only three. We have, therefore, tried to capture the possible changes in the parameters in terms of dummy variables. The equation with dummy is as follows:

$$\ln E_i = ?_0 + ?_1 \ln O + ?_2 (\ln O) D_1 + ?_3 (\ln O) D_2 + ?_4 \ln W \quad ..(3)$$

The partial elasticity of employment with respect to output in industry i is $?_1$ for sub period 1, $(?_1 + ?_2)$ for the sub-period 2, and $(?_1 + ?_3)$ for the sub-period 3. Corresponding to each of the industries equations (2) and (3) have been estimated by applying OLS. Wherever DW turned out to be low, Cochrane-Orcutt estimation method has been applied presuming a first order scheme for the error term, i.e.,

$$(?_t = P?_{t-1} + u_t).$$

The regression results reported in Table 2.8 indicate that for some of the equations, particularly in relation to industries 22,27,28,30,32,33 and 34, multicollinearity possibly exists. The results therefore need to be interpreted cautiously. Corresponding to the category of all-industries the average employment elasticity for the period 1976/77 through 1993/94 turned out to be only 0.17. With dummies, the employment elasticity for the sub-periods l and 2 is 0.22 and 0.215, respectively. In the sub-period 3 it is the same as that in sub-period 1 since the t-ratio corresponding to $?_3$, is not significant. With the addition of man-days per labour as an explanatory variable, the partial elasticity of employment with respect to value added goes up to 0.51 and 0.67 for the eighties and nineties respectively, as shown by Goldar (2000). From the econometric point of view it may be noted, therefore, that the estimate of the employment elasticity parameter is highly volatile, and the volatility can be attributed to addition and deletion of other variables in the employment function. Hence, it implies that the employment function needs to be specified

TABLE 2.8: **Elasticity of Employment with Respect to Output and Wages**

Industry	Equ.	Intercept	LnO	LnO(D1)	LnO(D2)	LnW	Adj.R2	DW
1	2	3	4	5	6	7	8	9
20-21	1	18.38	0.12			-0.66	0.71	2.63
		(8.90)*	-1.07			(-3.27)*		
	2	19.05	0.12	-0.004	-0.006	-0.69	0.69	2.85
		(6.29)*	-1.07	1.02	0.88	(-3.31)*		
22	1	9.81	0.34			-0.11	0.54	1.79
		(2.60)*	-1.29			0.51		
	2	11.88	0.19	0.003	0.01	-0.15	0.49	1.72
		(2.27)*	-0.55	-0.35	-0.88	0.57		
23	1	27.89	-0.11			-1.38	0.67	1.32
		(11.88)*	0.8			(-4.33)*		
	2	15.02	0.18	-0.01	-0.02	-0.39	0.9	1.67
		(5.81)*	-1.69	(-5.07)*	(-5.55)*	1.45		
24	1	9.99	0.3			-0.15	0.78	2.42
		(2.79)*	(2.55)*			0.29		
	2	9.51	0.51	-0.007	-0.01	-0.37	0.78	2.4
		(2.62)*	(2.71)*	1.04	1.42	0.71		
25	1	16.24	0.49			-1.04	0.82	2.55
		(11.76)*	(5.38)*			(-8.21)*		
	2	10.24	0.34	-0.02	-0.02	-0.19	0.88	2.64
		(4.27)*	(3.68)*	(-2.69)*	(-2.87)*	0.59		
26	1	15.25	0.75			-1.4	0.97	1.54
		(4.67)*	(14.0)*			(-3.26)*		
	2	12.64	0.86	-0.01	-0.01	-1.25	0.97	2.07
		(3.59)*	(8.96)*	(-2.20)*	-1.72	(-2.68)*		
27	1	15.04	-0.12			-0.3	0.53	1.64
		(10.02)*	1.35			1.63		
	2	12.91	-0.09	-0.007	-0.01	-0.08	0.68	1.95
		(8.61)*	1.27	(-1.94)*	(-2.85)*	0.5		
28	1	13.94	0.45			-0.75	0.4	1.42
		(7.56)*	(2.36)*			1.71		

(contd.)

TABLE 2.8 *(contd.)*

1	2	3	4	5	6	7	8	9
	2	10.48	0.04	-0.005	-0.002	0.18	0.48	2.35
		(5.84)*	-0.22	1.5	0.51	-0.56		
29	1	7.95	0.55			-0.33	0.93	1.31
		(2.61)*	(15.18)*			0.99		
	2	13.1	0.2	-0.001	0.002	-0.41	0.94	1.65
		(4.37)*	-1.64	-0.1	-0.2	(-1.91)*		
30	1	-31.31	2.61			0.22	0.94	1.31
		(-3.93)*	(5.67)*			-0.6		
	2	-5.21	0.81	-0.01	-0.02	0.71	0.86	1.66
		0.91	-1.69	0.78	0.74	-1		
31	1	-2.61	0.95			0.16	0.54	2.4
		0.37	(2.26)*			-0.28		
	2	-13.5	1.55	-0.01	0.02	0.17	0.58	2.14
		0.88	(2.97)*	0.89	-0.7	-0.33		
32	1	11.43	0.16			-0.06	0.92	2.25
		(6.65)*	(1.79)*			0.32		
	2	12.07	0.11	-0.001	0.002	-0.06	0.9	2.13
		(5.31)*	-0.81	-0.22	-0.56	0.31		
33	1	9.97	0.08			0.23	0.68	2.26
		(8.51)*	-1.38			-1.7		
	2	8.96	0.21	-0.006	-0.008	0.15	0.78	1.81
		(8.29)*	(2.47)*	(-2.45)*	(-2.11)*	-1.19		
34	1	11.15	0.37			-0.37	0.81	2.06
		(11.53)*	(6.75)*			(-2.41)*		
	2	9.98	0.41	-0.003	-0.004	-0.3	0.8	1.94
		(6.95)*	(4.98)*	1.12	0.9	1.61		
35-36	1	12.92	0.36			-0.46	0.89	2.32
		(7.54)*	(3.69)*			-1.58		
	2	12.51	0.38	-0.001	-0.001	-0.43	0.88	2.44
		(6.47)*	(3.12)*	0.45	0.34	1.38		

(contd.)

TABLE 2.8 *(contd.)*

1	2	3	4	5	6	7	8	9
37	1	19.17	0.21			-0.91	0.81	2.31
		(5.63)*	-1.67			(-2.66)*		
	2	17.94	0.19	-0.005	-0.003	-0.75	0.81	1.94
		(4.88)*	-1.42	1.42	0.64	(-2.15)*		
38	1	11.39	0.31			-0.39	0.96	1.69
		(10.04)*	(13.32)*			(-2.72)*		
	2	10.57	0.33	-0.004	-0.004	-0.33	0.95	1.75
		(7.22)*	(6.35)*	0.93	0.6	(-1.83)*		
All India	1	15.07	0.17			-0.21	0.7	2
		(12.53)*	(2.03)*			0.94		
	2	13.31	0.22	-0.005	-0.004	-0.12	0.79	2.37
		(11.32)*	(2.47)*	(-2.65)*	1.43	0.58		

Notes: 1. Figures in parentheses are t-ratios. * represents significance at 10 per cent level.
2. Cochrane-Orcutt procedure has been applied to overcome the problem of auto-correlation.

carefully, that is, the time series tests like unit root and co-integration tests have to be carried out on the variables that one intends to add to the employment function. If they do not satisfy these tests, the results could be highly misleading, and the policy conclusions would be fallacious.

Surprisingly, employment elasticity in the case of food products is not only low in magnitude but statistically insignificant also, though one would expect the technology in this sector to have been highly labour intensive. Similar is the case with beverages where all the coefficients are statistically insignificant. But this could have been due to multicollinearity. However, the estimates of $?_1$, $?_2$, and $?_3$ are all low in terms of magnitude also. Within the category of textile and textile products (23,24,25,26), employment elasticity in cotton textile again has been perceptibly low, namely, 0.18, 0,17 and 0.16 for the three sub-periods, respectively. Among the other groups of light industries (wood, paper and leather) employment elasticity in wood turned out to be negative although statistically insignificant. The only two industries which registered a very high employment elasticity are chemical and chemical products and rubber, plastic, petroleum and coal products although there is no sign of change in the elasticity coefficient over time.

Non-metallic mineral products, basic metal and alloys and transport equipments and parts again recorded an unreasonably low elasticity of employment with respect to growth, and in the rest of the industries it has been only moderate. On the whole, two important observations follow: the impact of growth on employment in a large majority of the industries has been either marginal or moderate, and second, there is no evidence of any rise in the employment elasticity over time. In other words, employment generation capabilities of the organised industrial sector in India seem to have remained modest over the years.

Unemployment and Informal Sector Employment

In the preceding section we noted the limited role that the organised industrial sector has played in the context of employment generation. Structural adjustment programmes and exit policy leading to closure of inefficient units and labour retrenchment are supposed to have aggravated the 'employment problem'. Rise in informal sector employment, casualisation and contractual employment even in the organised sector are some of the outcomes that several studies predicted at the time of initiating the reforms (Mundle 1992, Bhattacharya and Mitra, 1993).

Table 2.9 provides no major evidence in support of rising unemployment in the urban areas. Estimates of unemployment rates are presented both in terms of usual status and current status approaches. While the former refers to pure open unemployment rate, the latter in addition captures the extent of underutilisation of labour also. Unemployment rates in the Indian context turn out to be quite modest primarily because open unemployment over a long period of time is mostly unaffordable. Only among females the usual principal status unemployment rate seems to have gone up in 1993/94 compared with 1983, whereas among males it virtually remained unchanged during the same period. As per the current weekly and current daily status estimates, the unemployment rate fell both among females and males between 1977/78 and 1993/94.

TABLE 2.9: **Unemployment Rates (%) by Sex, Residence and Status**

	Male			Female		
Residence	UPS	CWS	CDS	UPS	CWS	CDS
Rural						
1993-94	2.0	3.1	5.6	1.3	2.9	5.6
1987-88	2.8	4.2	4.6	3.5	4.4	6.7
1983	3.1	3.7	7.5	1.4	4.3	9.0
1977-78	2.2	3.6	7.1	5.5	4.1	9.2
1972-73	--	3.0	6.8	--	5.5	11.2
Urban						
1993-94	5.4	5.2	6.7	8.3	7.9	10.4
1987-88	6.1	6.6	8.8	8.5	9.2	12.0
1983	5.9	6.7	9.2	6.9	7.5	11.0
1977-78	6.5	7.1	9.4	17.8	10.9	14.5
1972-73	--	6.0	8.0	--	9.2	13.7

Note: UPS stands for usual principal status and CWS and CDS are current weekly status and current daily status respectively.

Source: Revised Report No. 406, Key Results of 50th Round of NSSO.

A decline in terms of current status unemployment rate is indicative of an increase in demand for part-time, sub-contracted jobs. Casualisation has been quite evident in the case of both urban males and females. Among females the decline in unemployment rate (and by implication a rising work participation rate) as per the current status, and the increase in the share of regular/salaried women workers in the urban areas, need to be interpreted carefully. They are more of a reflection of growth of employment in sectors with low productivity and wages than anything else (Kundu, 1997).

In non-agricultural activities (both rural and urban combined), the relative size of the informal sector, estimated on the basis of the assumption that small establishments and own account enterprises fall into the so-called informal sector, turned out to be around 61 per cent and 72 per cent in 1990 as per the Economic Census data and the data provided by the Ministry of Labour, respectively (Mitra, 1998). Presuming that all organised sector activities are conducted in the urban areas the estimate of urban unorganised/informal sector employment has been derived for several time points, starting from 1983 to 1997. Figures in Table 2.10 are indicative of a rise in the share of urban unorganised sector employment from 59 per cent in 1983 to around 68 per cent in 1997. All this suggests a rise in low productivity and low income jobs in the urban economy during the nineties. Besides, contractual employment and piece rate jobs within the organised sector, which do not necessarily get reflected in the figures on organised sector employment, are also on the rise (Mitra, 1999). Further, the critics of the new development strategy hold that the organised industrial growth rate may not be high in the long run

TABLE 2.10: **Percentage Share of Informal/Unorganised Sector Employment**

Year	Non-Agriculture Activities (All areas)	All Activities* (Urban)
1983		59.2
1987-88		61.8
1989-90	72.36**	63.4
1990-91	61.03**	63.9
1992		64.5
1993-94		67.1
1994-95		67.0
1995-96		67.5
1997		68.1

Notes: 1. *Presuming all organised sector activities are held in urban areas, estimates of unorganised sector have been derived.

2. **Estimates are based on data from DGE&T (1989-90) and Economic Census (1990); Arup Mitra (1998), "Employment in the Informal Sector", *The Indian Journal of Labour Economics*, Vol. 41, No. 3.

and the present low rate of infrastructural investment would slow down even agricultural growth, leading to larger inflows of migrant labour to urban areas from the rural areas, and subsequent expansion of the urban informal sector (Kundu, 1997).

A detailed classification of the informal sector activities suggests that the sector is highly heterogeneous in nature. However, a large majority of the activities correspond to petty trade, transport and services (Mitra, 1994). Only around 20 per cent of the workers are engaged in the commodity producing sector. Further, the linkage between the formal and the informal sectors is found to be weak; the partial elasticities of informal sector employment with respect to employment in various components of the organised sector range between 0.15 and 0.18. In particular, the linkage between organised manufacturing and informal manufacturing is not of a generative sort (Shaw, 1990), which means that workers in the informal sector are not in a position to benefit from inter-sectoral ties.

Urban Poverty

As a consequence of the rise in low productivity activities the head count ratio of urban poverty continues to persist still at a high level. The estimate of urban poverty as presented in Table 2.11 shows that even in 1993/94, around 32 per cent of the urban population belonged to poor households. The observed decline in the urban poverty ratio between 1987/88 and 1993/94 needs to be interpreted cautiously. The decline may be perceived in terms of shrinking employment opportunities in the urban areas and their dampening effect on rural poor who migrate to the urban areas in search of jobs, and in the process who usually transfer rural poverty to the urban areas. Only a marginal fall in the rural poverty ratio during this period (1987/88 through 1993/94) would substantiate this view further.

After 1993/94, poverty in both rural and urban areas increased, crossing 42 per cent and 34.5 per cent in 1998 in rural and urban India respectively. In fact, over the period 1994/95 through 1998 urban poverty appears to have remained around 34 per cent (with the exception in 1994/95). The rise in rural poverty between 1993/94 and

TABLE 2.11: **Head Count Ratio of Urban Poverty (%)**

Year	Rural	Urban
1973-74	56.44	49.01
1977-78	53.07	45.24
1983	45.65	40.79
1987-88	39.09	38.20
1993-94	37.27	32.36
1994-95	38.03	34.24
1995-96	38.29	30.05
1997	38.46	33.97
1998 (Jan.-June)	42.25	34.58

Sources: 1. Estimates for the years 1973-74 through 1993-94 are based on NSSO's large sample data (Modified Expert Group Methodology). Malhotra (1997), "Incidence of Poverty in India: Towards a Consensus on Estimating the Poor", *Indian Journal of Labour Economics*, Vol.40, No.1.

2. Estimates for the years, 1994-95, 1995-96, 1997 and 1998 (Jan. to June) are based on NSSO's thin sample data; taken from S.P. Gupta (1999), "Trickle Down Theory Revisited: The Role of Employment and Poverty", V.B. Singh Memorial Lecture, 41st Annual Conference, Indian Society of Labour Economics. .

1998 is indicative of both a fall in employment opportunities in the rural non-farm sector and the declining role of the urban economy in benefitting the rural migrants. Structural adjustment and fiscal stabilisation affecting the urban organised sector through import compression and fiscal contraction (Tendulkar and Jain, 1995), possibly deteriorated the poverty situation.

The impact of growth on poverty has been a matter of major concern for both policy makers and researchers. Studies suggest that in the process of economic growth, relative inequality might increase but poverty tends to decline (World Bank, 1998). Empirical evidence in the urban context has not been quite supportive of this view though. Even in the highly industrialised states growth seems to have made no dent on poverty as the percolation effect, which is expected to work mainly through the output-employment linkages has not been significant (Mitra, 1992b). Ravallion and Datt (1996) also point out that secondary sector growth did not reduce poverty either in urban or rural areas.

Conclusion

Employment growth in the organised sector, particularly the public sector, has been sluggish during the eighties and nineties. In spite of rapid industrial growth during the eighties employment growth in organised industry has not been impressive. Factor market distortion and adoption of capital intensive technology possibly led to such a sluggish employment growth in the organised industrial sector. Even in the post-reform period employment elasticity does not seem to have improved to any significant extent. The share of industry in total workforce persists at a considerably low level. Given the limited labour demand in this sector, the urban informal sector has acted as a repository of surplus labour, which has been growing owing to the natural growth of population and rural-urban migration. On the whole, some of the major outcomes of deregulation and economic reforms in urban India are manifested in terms of tertiarisation, casualisation and feminisation of the work force, a rise in part time jobs rather than regular jobs, and an increasing share of the informal sector in total employment.

Meagre earnings accruing to workers in the informal sector have resulted in a high head count ratio of urban poverty, although the open unemployment rate in the Indian context has not been striking. Both rural poverty and urban poverty show signs of increase in the nineties. Implementation of rural development programmes possibly can reduce the supply pressure in the urban labour market but profound exercises involving formulation of urban employment programmes need to be attempted by the policy planners to tackle the urban 'employment problem' more effectively.

NOTES

1. Informal sector has been defined in the literature on the subject (ILO, 1970 and 1972) primarily in terms of small size, perfect competition in the product and factor (labour) market, absence of government protection, inadequate physical and financial capital reflected in a low capital-labour ratio and absence of unionisation.
   The informal sector is associated with certain characteristics, which keep the earnings of the workers low. Clearly, it is not defined as a low-income sector but the characteristics associated with this sector lower the level of income accruing to the workers. For example, low capital-intensity, high degree of competition in the product market, free entry, small operational units, and the unskilled nature of labour generate meagre earnings.
   It would be realistic to acknowledge wide diversity even within the informal sector, with many activities serving on the margin as repositories of surplus labour (i.e., segmented market for both labour and output), others selling in a market that represent product differentiation (i.e., segmented market for labour but not for output) and many others performing specific functions in an inter-related production system (i.e., segmented for labour but linked in terms of output). In an empirical enquiry it is worth examining whether some of the segments within the informal sector are predominant so that on the whole the informal sector stands in sharp contrast to the formal sector, that is, a substantial proportion of informal sector participants have a very low level of income as Sethuraman (1985) notes in the case of Indonesia.

2. The term 'employment problem' refers to not only those who are purely unemployed but also those who are engaged in low productivity activities, i.e., the working poor (Joshi and Joshi, 1976).

3. The National Sample Survey Organisation in India defines unemployment as per usual status and current status approaches. The former defines unemployment on the basis of a longer reference period. The current status is expressed in terms of current weekly and current daily status rates. While the usual status approach estimates purely the open unemployment, the current status approach, particularly the current daily status estimate, captures the phenomenon of underemployment as well.

REFERENCES

Bhattacharya, B.B. and Arup Mitra (1993), "Employment and Structural Adjustment : A Look at 1991 Census Data", *Economic and Political Weekly*, September 18.

—— (1990), "Excess Growth of Tertiary Sector in Indian Economy: Issues and Implications", *Economic and Political Weekly*, Vol. 25, No. 44.

Bourguignon, F. and C. Morrisson (1992), "Adjustment and Equity in Developing Countries: A New Approach", Development Centre Studies, OECD, Paris.

Corbo, V., S. Fisher and S.B. Webb (eds) (1992), "Adjustment Lending Revisited: Policies to Restore Growth", World Bank, Washington, DC.

Dupont, V. and Arup Mitra (1995), "Population Distribution, Growth and Socio-Economic Spatial Patterns in Delhi: Findings from the 1991 Census Data", *Demography India,* Vol. 24, Nos. 1 and 2.

Goldar, B. (2000), "Employment Growth in Organised Manufacturing in India", *Economic and Political Weekly*, April 1.

Gupta, Indrani and Arup Mitra (1997), "Migrants in Urban Labour Market: Micro Level Evidence from Delhi Slums", mimeo, Institute of Economic Growth, Delhi.

Gupta, S.P. (1999), "Trickle Down Theory Revisited: The Role of Employment and Poverty", V.B. Singh Memorial Lecture, 41st Annual Conference, Indian Society of Labour Economics.

Harris, J.R. and M.P. Todaro (1970), "Migration Unemployment and Development: A Two Sector Analysis", *The American Economic Review*, Vol. LX, No. 1.

Haltiwanger, John and Manisha Singh (1999), "Cross-Country Evidence on Public Sector Retrenchment", *The World Bank Economic Review*, January, Vol. 13, No. 1

Hoselitz, B.F. (1957), "Urbanisation and Economic Growth in Asia", *Economic Development and Cultural Change*, Vol. VI, No. 1.

International Labour Office (1972), *Employment, Incomes and Equality: A Strategy for Increasing Productive Employment in Kenya*, Geneva, ILO.

—— (1970), *Towards Full Employment: A Programme for Colombia,* Geneva, ILO.

Joshi, H. and V. Joshi (1976) *Surplus Labour and the City : A Study of Bombay*, Oxford University Press.

Kundu, A. (1997), "Trends and Structure of Employment in the 1990s: Implications for Urban Growth", *Economic and Political Weekly*, June 14.

Kuznets, S. (1966), *Modern Economic Growth: Rate Structure and Spread*, New Haven, Yale University Press.

Lewis, A. (1954), "Economic Development with Unlimited Supplies of Labour", *The Manchester School of Economic and Social Studies.*

Malhotra, Rajeev (1997), "Incidence of Poverty in India: Towards a Consensus on Estimating the Poor", *Indian Journal of Labour Economics*, Vol. 40, No. 1.

Mills, E.S. and Arup Mitra (1997), *Urban Development and Urban Ills*, Commonwealth Pub., New Delhi.

Ministry of Industry (1996), *Handbook of Industrial Policy and Statistics*, Office of the Economic Advisor, Government of India, New Delhi.

—— (1997), *Handbook of Industrial Policy and Statistics*, Office of the Economic Advisor, Government of India, New Delhi.

Mitra, Arup, (1998), "Employment in the Informal Sector", The *Indian Journal of Labour Economics*, Vol. 41, No. 3.

—— (1999), "Survey on Changing Labour Market Structure and Its Effects on Women Employment in India", Asian Productivity Organisation, Tokyo.

—— (1994), *Urbanisation, Slums, Informal Sector Employment and Poverty: An Exploratory Study*, B.R. Publishing Corp., Delhi.

—— (1993), "Rural Non-Farm Employment, Poverty and Women", *The Indian Journal of Labour Economics*, Vol. 36, No. 3.

—— (1992a), "Urban Poverty: A Rural Spill-over?" in V. Pandit and S.D. Tendulkar (eds.) *Indian Economic Review*, Special Number.

—— (1992b), "Growth and Poverty: The Urban Legend", *Economic and Political Weekly*, Vol. 27, No. 13.

—— (1990), "Duality, Employment Structure and Poverty Incidence: The Slum Perspective", *Indian Economic Review*, Vol. 25, No. 1.

Mundle, S.(1992), "Unemployment and Financing of Relief Employment in Period of Stabilisation in India", *Economic and Political Weekly*, January 30.

Ravallion, Martin and Gaurav Datt (1996), "How Important to India's Poor is the Sectoral Composition of Economic Growth", *The World Bank Economic Review*, Vol.10, No.1

Sethuraman, S.V. (1985), "The Informal Sector in Indonesia: Policies and Prospects", *International Labour Review*, Vol. 124, No. 6.

Sharma, A.N.(1997), "Trends in the Structure and Pattern of Employment and Unemployment in India", Institute of Economic Growth, Working Paper Series, No. E/188/97.

Shaw, A. (1990), "Linkages of Large Scale, Small-Scale and Informal Sector Industries: A Study of Thana Belapur", *Economic and Political Weekly*, Vol. 25, Nos. 7/8.

Tendulkar, S.D. and L.R. Jain (1995), "Economic Reforms and Poverty", *Economic and Political Weekly*, June 10.

Visaria, Pravin (1997), "Youth Unemployment in India: Its Level, Nature and Policy Implications", Institute of Economic Growth, Delhi, mimeo.

World Bank (1998), *Reducing Poverty in India: Options for More Effective Public Services,* Poverty Reduction and Economic Management Division, South Asia Region, Report No. 17881-IN.

3

REFORMS AND LABOUR MARKET IN INDIA

SUDHA DESHPANDE and LALIT DESHPANDE

Introduction

The Indian economy grew faster in the 1980s than ever before and growth continued to accelerate in the 1990s despite the shocks of deflation, disintegration of the communist block and the Asian meltdown. The adoption, in 1991, of the strategy of market-based growth with greater integration in the world economy did not bring about the doom the policy's critics predicted was round the corner. Not only is the Hindu rate of growth left behind but the poverty ratio and rate of measured unemployment have declined, the former faster in the 1990s than before. Our foreign exchange reserves are comfortable and our buffer stocks of foodgrains are a matter of concern not because they are too low relative to the demand but because, being too high relative to it, they are too costly to hold. Despite these successes, the reforms have not delivered many promises its advocates had made a decade ago. Fiscal stability continues to elude us; the economy is precariously perched on the threshold of a debt trap; our savings rate has declined and we are still a low income poor performer compared with the Chinese dragon fattening itself on the BigMac and the native chop suey and the tigers and the cubs before they were hit by the Asian flu.

This is not the place to review the market-based development strategy *per se*. However, its labour market implications are directly relevant to the theme of this paper. Although Deshpande has recently considered them elsewhere (Deshpande, 2001) we have reproduced much of it here with minor modifications in sections one, two and four. Section one states the labour policy the World Bank advises countries adopting structural adjustment to follow. Section two presents a brief critique of the Bank's policy mostly from the viewpoints of economics and political philosophy. Evaluation of the impact of Reforms needs facts. They are presented in section three which is the most important section of our paper. It is based on the surveys of employment and unemployment undertaken by the National Sample Survey Organisation (NSSO) following the recommendations of the Dantwala Committee (1970). Section four presents briefly the findings of a study of labour flexibility in India done by Deshpande et al. (2001), at the Institute for Human Development, and the implications of the study for the much debated exit policy for the country. Section five sums up the conclusions.

Market-based Development and Labour

It is difficult to find a better advocate of the market-based development strategy than the World Bank and equally so to find a better document than the World Development Report, 1995(World Bank, 1995) to expound it. The Report predates the Asian Crisis but were it to be written now it is doubtful if its recommendation would have been any different. The Report's main conclusion is that the problems of low incomes, poor working conditions, and insecurity affecting many of the world's workers can be effectively tackled in ways that reduce poverty and regional inequality but to do so will require sound domestic policy and supportive international environment. The first implies that the government must:

1. pursue market-based growth paths that generate rapid growth in demand for labour, expansion in the skills of the workforce, and rising productivity;
2. take advantage of new opportunities at the international level by opening up to trade and attracting capital – but manage

the dislocations that international changes sometimes bring; and

3. construct a framework for a labour policy that complements informal and rural labour markets, supports collective bargaining in the formal sector, provides safeguards for the vulnerable, and avoids biases that favour relatively well-off workers.

Development Strategy and Workers

The Bank's advocacy of the market based development strategy is based on three assumptions. First, growth trickles down and a high rate of growth translates itself, sooner or later, into a high demand for labour. Secondly, labour markets are more competitive than capital markets. The Bank claims that the two assumptions are borne out by the contrast in the developmental experience in East and South East Asian economies on the one hand and that in the Latin American economies on the other. Market based development, which encourages firms and workers to invest in physical capital, new technologies and skills is, to the Bank, the best way to deliver growth, raise living standards for workers and to end discrimination in the labour market. The Bank buttresses its argument by referring to the failure of the countries that have attempted to help workers by biasing investment against agriculture and towards industry, protecting the jobs of a favoured few industrial workers against international competition, dictating wage increases, or creating unneeded jobs in the public sector.

Employment in an Integrating World

The third assumption of the Bank is that International flows of goods, services, capital, and people bring new opportunities for most workers. This view is widely shared. The World Employment Report 1998/99 (ILO, 1998) voices it. The WDR 1995 points out that real wages have risen fast where exports have grown fast. Foreign direct investment, which accounted for 30 to 40 per cent of capital flows to low and middle-income countries, is creating many new jobs; 60 per cent of worldwide growth in the pay-roll of multinational corporations occurred in these countries. International migration, though restricted, has usually brought income gains to those who move, higher remittances for those who stay and increased production of goods and services in the host countries. But there are great fears, mostly baseless, in both developed and developing economies that the integration is harmful to them (Lee, 1996). Some workers will indeed be hurt if they are stuck in declining activities and lack the flexibility to change. Restraining trade or capital is not an effective way of dealing with this problem. A better strategy, according to the Bank, is to improve the skills or to ease their transition to new jobs.

Capital has become more mobile. But far from rendering national governments impotent, international capital movements intensify the impact of domestic policy on labour outcomes, a richly rewarding policy when it is sound but punishing it hard when it is unsound. Faster and broader capital flows and greater openness in trade are making domestic policy more important for workers.

The Bank's Advice on Labour Policy

Labour policies in low and middle-income countries do not affect the majority of workers who work in the informal sector. They are not enforced in many firms in the formal sector. This does not mean that governments should not intervene. Public action can complement community arrangements and enhance the welfare of informal workers by improving the environment in which they operate. In the formal sector, public action is sometimes needed to improve market economies, enhance equity and protect vulnerable workers. Provision of water and sanitation, roads and drainage and environmental health are some of the measures to improve working conditions in the informal sector. Informal income security arrangements can be complemented by public transfer programmes: public works are usually the best transfer method for able-bodied men and women. Thus the Bank is not, as popularly thought, against all kinds of interventions and much less against all kinds of security.

Labour Policy for the Formal Sector

For the formal sector collective bargaining between firms and independent unions is an effective way to determine wages and working conditions. Governments do need to establish the rules for labour management negotiations, spelling out the rights of workers and firms, establishing dispute resolution mechanisms, and promulgating basic health and safety regulations, which unions can monitor. Where unions cover only a small proportion of the workforce decentralised bargaining under conditions of competitive markets produces the best results.

Governments also have to set policy for public employment. In some countries the quality of public service has suffered as its ethos has been destroyed by a combination of over-staffing, inadequate pay and weak governance. Restoring levels of pay and reducing the number of public workers are often essential reforms, to be combined with improvements in the recruitment, promotion, and accountability of civil servants, teachers, nurses and policy makers. The redefinition of the role of the state makes it all the more important that governments be effective in those areas where they continue to be involved.

Abolition of Child Labour

The Bank supports direct government intervention in dealing with child labour and in other cases where the market may produce adverse outcomes, such as discrimination against minorities. But legislation alone has been ineffective.

Labour Standards and Trade Sanctions

Though the Bank supports direct action to eliminate child labour, it does not support trade sanctions against countries which violate this or any other labour standard. The Bank opines that it is best to keep international trade agreements confined to directly trade related issues, to prevent protectionist interests from misusing such links to reduce the trade that workers in low and middle income countries need if their incomes are to rise. This is precisely the stand that the Government of India has taken on the issue.

The Bank's Advice on Managing Major Changes

Many countries are trying to integrate themselves in the global economy and to shift from state-driven to market-driven development. These changes can have a powerful labour market dimension. Their key characteristic is an acceleration in the destruction of non-viable jobs and creation of new ones. The process is often accompanied by macroeconomic decline and by a sharp drop in the demand for labour. In the short run, real wages fall, unemployment rises and employment shifts into informal activities. Moving the economy as quickly as possible to a new growth path is the key to minimising the pain and social costs of adjustment; macroeconomic stability and credibility of the overall reform package are therefore critical. Is a strategy of gradual transition better for workers? Where initial conditions allow gradual job destruction without jeopardising the reform that is needed to generate new jobs, gradualism makes sense, as in China. In other countries either macroeconomic imbalance or the costs of inefficient sectors make gradualism a non-starter.

Microeconomic policies that affect the mobility and incomes of workers can play a major role both in influencing the pace of change and safeguarding the welfare of workers. Good policy would involve action in three areas: enhancing mobility, reducing income insecurity and equipping workers for change. These are highly complementary. However, it is also important to consider the needs of those at risk of steep income decline. Income transfers can play an important role here. Retraining can help certain groups of workers but is unlikely to provide a panacea.

Divergence or Inclusion

The Report saw no worldwide trend toward convergence between rich and poor workers. There is substantial risk that inequality between the rich and the poor would grow over the coming decades, while poverty deepens. But it need not be so if countries choose the right international and domestic policies. Preserving open trading relations, preventing rich country fiscal deficits from crowding out investments elsewhere, and delivering high and stable growth in the high income countries will maintain global demand and help head off any protectionist pressures in rich countries that might result from persistently high unemployment.

Review of the World Bank's Policies from Liberal Viewpoints

Most of the economic policies advocated by the World Development Report are in keeping with one or the other school of liberal political philosophy. Liberals have tended to praise the market to the extent that it acts as a stimulus to the individual initiative and discovery that brings about the progress of society. In this respect, the virtues of free market in labour and commodities parallel those of the free market in ideas – they promote the good and weed out the bad (Bellamy, 1993). When these advantages are missing, liberals have often proved less enthusiastic about laissez faire. Even the Classical liberals accepted the need for state intervention in cases of imperfect markets, missing markets and market failures. In some forms of social liberalism the state's tasks are held to involve considerable economic intervention and social provision of an enabling nature. Such activities might range from a publicly funded transport system to state schools and welfare schemes. To the extent that the Bank's labour policy advocates some of them and is not opposed to others subject to the condition of capacity to manage them efficiently, there is not much one can fault it for on this score.

The major exponent of contemporary social democratic liberalism is John Rawls. For him fairness rather than truth or goodness is the only acceptable criterion of modern justice. According to him, there are two principles for fairness. According to the first principle, the state must provide the most extensive system of equal liberties possible. And according to the second principle, there must be equal opportunities to obtain positions and status in society regardless of colour, gender, creed etc. To help achieve this each person is to have an equal share of wealth except when an unequal distribution would improve the welfare of the least well-off in society, by providing incentives that encourage people to work harder and produce more in ways that raised the living standards of every one. Progressive taxation would be necessary if the trickle down effect failed to produce any benefits from this greater affluence for those at the bottom of society (Bellamy, 1993).

Standing (1999) bases his concept of a good labour market on Rawls' utopia of good society as extended by Sen. As Bellamy points out, the thought experiment which forms the basis of Rawlsian social liberalism is questioned by socialists. But in times when the models of state socialism and welfare state capitalism have failed, the search for a good society and by implication for a good labour market assumes urgency. The World Bank's liberalism holds little promise for progress in this search.

In the last century, it was fashionable to argue that the trust in the market mechanism was an anachronism in the twentieth century in the context of Fordism and large government bureaucracies. Both of these, it was claimed, had long dethroned Consumer, the King for whom tolled the bells of the eighteenth century capitalists. This criticism has been blunted a bit by the spread of decentralised production, flexible specialisation, batch production, lean bureaucracies, all oriented to cater to the idiosyncrasies and convenience of the consumer. Advances in information technology have helped in the coronation of the consumer and so has the growth of competition among producers consequent on globalisation.

Microeconomic and Macroeconomic Criticisms

The second of the two fundamental theorems of welfare economics states that under some stricter conditions including non-increasing returns to scale, Pareto-optimum allocation can be attained through the price system if the initial distribution were fixed appropriately. The trouble is that it cannot be. Primarily because the state would lack information regarding incomes of individuals who would not divulge their true income to the tax authorities. In general there are enormous problems in attaining the general equilibrium defined by Walras. Following Stiglitz (1991), they could be classified under two heads:

(i) Those that arise because information is imperfect.
(ii) Those that arise from the view that human behaviour is based on strategic consideration rather than on exclusive pursuit of self interest.

The information required by an economic agent to make rational choices today is so vast that it is impossible for any individual to posses it. The fundamental theorems of welfare economics require markets to exist in all commodities contingent on all possible outcomes in the world. This is impossible. Human beings are fallible. They may make mistakes in processing such vast information. The competitive theory assumes away transaction costs. In practice, every transaction involves costs. Like information costs they too are asymmetric and distort the prices from the equilibrium prices. The theory assumes that the cost of enforcing contracts and property rights is zero, which is patently unrealistic. Uncertainty creates information problems. They give rise to demand for insurance. Insurance markets are notoriously inefficient. They create a moral hazard.

Human Behaviour, Strategy and Self Interest

The competitive theory assumes that human behaviour is motivated by self-interest and everyone pursues self-interest independently of others. Critics challenge this assumption. They point out that many situations in life resemble prisoners' dilemma where actions of one individual influence the outcomes for others. The morale of the dilemma is that society would be better off if its members co-operated with one another than when each member pursued his interest independently of others. This defect arising from methodological individualism has been highlighted among others by Fine (1998). A sympathetic critic of the neo-classical theory comments that economists have neither theory nor evidence to suggest that the invisible hand will always bring about an equilibrium (Hahn, 1991).

GEA and the Labour Market

In the GEA, labour services are not treated any differently from commodities and all assumptions of goods market are applied to the labour market. Assuming rationality, homogeneity, perfect knowledge, large number of buyers and sellers, absence of collusion, free mobility and substitutability of resources, it can be proved that the labour market would be cleared at a wage that would be consistent with the equilibrium price set. However, existence of unemployment shows that, at least one of the markets is imperfect and the economy is out of equilibrium most of the time in most countries.

The principal-agent problem also belongs to the set of problems caused by incomplete knowledge. When an employer hires a worker he does not know how productive he would be in his job. In many cases, the principal finds it difficult to monitor an employee's performance. Under the circumstance, wage would not equal marginal product and thereby violate the condition of competitive equilibrium. Difficulties of monitoring worker performance often lead to devising interventions, which aim at evoking proper behaviour from workers. The real difficulty, according to Standing(1999), is that no one can write a complete contract and all explicit contracts have an implicit complement. He rejects the solution offered by the theory of optimal contracts. He argues that the basic flaw in this argument is that the labour market is not all about outcomes but largely about processes and interactions of institutional arrangements. Human beings are not motivated by gains alone and certainly not by financial gains alone. Nor are motivations fixed at the beginning of the contract and invariant later. They respond to institutional and power arrangements. The principal-agent model focuses on formal relations whereas informal relations and trust play an important role in labour relationships. The labour market is, as Solow (1990) argues, more a social than an economic institution. Social and cultural norms play a crucial role (Standing,1999).

The criticisms are formidable. They show that the claims made on behalf of the invisible hand and Pareto-optimality are too tall to be defended. What can be defended is the milder version of the

Hayekian view of markets. According to Hayek, no one knows the feasibility set or the possibility set. The market is the mechanism by which progressive uncovering of these sets takes place. Market prices convert an economy with dispersed information into a full information economy. The latter is a fiction but over time markets tend towards it. Competition creates a market for information. It sets in motion a learning process with incentives to move to the ideal (Hahn, 1991). Those who learn from their mistakes earn profits and those who do not learn incur losses. So long as we do not claim that the market is the best way to allocate resources we keep clear of dogma. We can then consider the functional merits of a competitive system in a given cultural and institutional set-up. This interpretation of competitive markets, including labour markets, would be the first step towards embedding the market into society, as Polanyi (1944) would have wished, rather than society into the market.

Strategy not Based Wholly on Supply-side Economics

For Keynes the worst effects of a free market arose from leaving savings and investments to chance of private judgement and profit, particularly when there existed gross inequalities in the distribution of wealth. Hence the policy to manage the aggregate demand at full employment level and progressive taxation to regulate consumption and fund investment and welfare. But Keynesianism could not explain the coexistence of inflation and unemployment in most industrialised countries. The Bank's development strategy advocates high and rising demand for labour and income security through public works programmes and to that extent differs from pure supply-side economics, a point often missed by the critics of the Bank in the LDCs.

Relevance of East Asia and its Labour Markets Overdone by the Bank

Usually, public policy is used to make up for coordination failures in most markets. According to the Bank, in case of labour markets coordination failures are limited, and information, although not perfectly symmetric between workers and employers, is better than in capital markets. Externalities primarily affect investment decisions in human capital, not interactions in the labour market. Thus there is a presumption that, if left to themselves, labour markets would perform their coordinating role quite well. This generalisation is often questioned by referring to the low rates of growth of many African, South Asian and Latin American economies despite very large investments in human capital. These economies are plagued by high and growing educated unemployment. While human capital accumulation may be a necessary condition for sustained rapid growth, it certainly is not a sufficient condition. Using human capital in activities that yield higher returns on the prior investment in education, training is as important to growth as the accumulation of human capital. The argument has great relevance to India in the context of massive waste of national resource in the form of educated unemployment.

Two conditions must be fulfilled, according to the Bank, for a growing supply of educated labour to be utilised in high return activities. First, there must be rapid growth of labour demand relative to supply and, in particular, of demand for skilled labour. Second, the labour market must perform well. It must be efficient, flexible, and responsive to changing conditions so as to ensure that workers are employed in jobs in which their skills are most productively utilised. This is a reiteration of the view expressed earlier in the World Bank Policy Research Report, *The East Asian Miracle* (1993).

The Bank cites the example of East Asia where, according to it, governments resisted the temptation to intervene in the labour market to counter outcomes unpalatable in the short run or to particular groups. A relatively high level of efficiency in the allocation of labour was achieved by allowing wages and employment to be determined largely by interaction between those supplying and those demanding labour services, rather than by government legislation, public sector leadership or union pressure.

East Asia's Flexible Labour Markets

By not allowing the price of labour in some sectors to rise well above what workers would earn elsewhere in the economy, the High Performing Asian Economies (HPAEs) avoided creation of a high wage labour elite. For example, there is evidence from Taiwan of a remarkably integrated labour market; there is no significant correlation between the growth rate of earnings and growth of output within sectors. Manufacturing wages for unskilled labour are only 20 per cent higher than agricultural wages. Another remarkable feature is the modest size of the gap between skilled and unskilled wages in the non-agricultural sector. The small gap did not result from minimum wage legislation pushing up unskilled wages. Rather the growth of demand for unskilled labour in combination with the marked increase of educated workers compressed the occupational structure of wages. One benefit of the compressed wage structure was that it reduced the incentive for educated workers to conduct a lengthy search for a relatively high wage job, and thereby remain unemployed, rather than fill a job slot at a lower occupational level. Conversely, a segmented labour market may provide an incentive to workers in low-income employment, and to the unemployed, to lobby the government to provide more high-wage jobs than justified by the derived demand for labour.

Rapid growth was a key factor in making wages more flexible in the HPAEs. Workers are generally more willing to accept flexibility of wages around a rapidly rising trend because downward adjustment implies a slower rate of increase rather than an absolute decline in real earnings (Shah and Mathur, 1992). This is manifested in wage setting practices that tie compensation to enterprise performance.

East Asia: Not a Model

Hong Kong, Japan, Korea and Taiwan did not repress wages but Singapore did. Korea, Singapore, Taiwan suppressed independent unions. Malaysia has independent unions but highly restrictive labour laws. Hong Kong and Japan do not intervene in labour relations. In Japan most unions are company based. Hong Kong is the least interventionist state in the world. Unions are weak. In Japan union membership is high yet unions did not exact economic benefits for their members at the expense of economic growth (Freeman, 1993). There was substantial diversity within the group to justify putting them in one basket. Even when they are considered a homogeneous lot, according to Mazumdar (2000), their experience in dealing with labour problems could hardly be emulated, depending as it did on the social and political conditions peculiar to the region. He doubts if ESEA could serve as a model for other countries.

Lessons of Comparative Studies

Recently many researchers have undertaken comparative studies of business groups, industrial orders and social systems of production across countries and have highlighted the close connection between firms' competitive strategies and their internal structures and external relationships. They have also emphasised the strong interdependence between dominant forms of organisation of economic activities in particular regions and the economies, and the institutional context in which these developed. How economic transactions are organised between different kinds of economic actors and related to particular production systems differ significantly between institutional environments so that they constitute qualitatively distinct systems of economic organisations that are unlikely to converge into a single one (Whitley, 1999). In short, capitalist business systems in India are likely to diverge substantially from East Asian or Latin American systems. Similarly, the analysis of conditions encouraging and inhibiting the development and widespread adoption of different kinds of work systems emphasises the "societal effect" in explaining variations in work organisation and control across capitalist economies. The highly society-specific nature of many labour market institutions, education and training systems, and state structure and policies have generated varied forms of interest representation, capital-labour relations and patterns of work organisation and control. It is true that some features of work organisation are being transferred across countries by some multinational firms, but these typically vary between firms and contexts as interest group structures and institutional arrangements differ in nature and strength across contexts. The simple assumption that competition will automatically standardise work systems in India on the pattern of those in East Asian economies is patently inadequate. In a similar vein, Banuri and Amadeo (1991) have extended the argument that institutional arrangements place constraints upon policy making and should be taken into account in policy prescriptions by showing that the feasible range of institutional changes is also circumscribed and constrained by historical and social factors peculiar to each country or region.

Impact of Reforms

Evidence from the NSSO

Starting with 1972/73 the NSSO has carried out six surveys using large samples, each at an interval of roughly five years. We have excluded the first of these because we are not wholly convinced whether its results, even when adjusted, are strictly comparable with those of the five that followed it. Of the last five surveys, three were conducted before and two after the liberalisation of the Indian economy in 1991. The 'before and after' comparison is the crudest method of assessing the impact of any change but we prefer it because it is simpler than the alternatives such as 'planned versus actual' and 'with and without'. We have not given much credence to small changes from one survey to another and when a variable traces a zigzag course, we average it over the three surveys preceding liberalisation on the one hand and over the two surveys following liberalisation on the other. The averages are not given in the tables but can be easily calculated by the reader. They help us in judging if the situation had improved, deteriorated or remained the same.

Impact on Work Participation Rates (WPRs)

The analysis that follows relates to usual status principal workers. In doing so we follow the advice of the NSSO. According to the Organisation, 'usual principal status approach is best suited as a measure of economic activity in an economy with seasonal fluctuations in employment. This is because in this approach the criterion used is the pattern of activities followed by the person for a relatively long period of time'. Inclusion of subsidiary workers, the transient element, increases the participation rate and decreases the unemployment rate over time.

Many economic, demographic and social factors influence WPR. The first influences it in the short as well as the long run whereas the second and the third do so in the long run. Stabilisation is an important condition of success of structural adjusfment (Toye, 1995). The sudden deflation of the economy in crisis increases unemployment as firms retrench or close while population and labour force continue to grow at their trend rates. This would lead one to expect a fall in the WPR, particularly of men. Table 3.1 shows that the work participation of rural men remained much the same in 1993/94 as before liberalisation but that of urban men increased. The participation of rural women declined but that of urban women

*TABLE 3.1: **Work Participation Rates of Principal Status Workers, 1977/78-1999/00**

(Per cent)

	Rural			Urban		
Year	Persons	Males	Females	Persons	Males	Females
1977/78	38.5	53.7	24.8	31.9	49.7	12.3
1983	39.1	52.8	24.8	32.0	50.0	12.0
1987/88	38.5	51.7	24.5	31.5	49.6	11.8
1993/94	39.0	53.8	23.4	32.7	51.3	12.1
1999/00	38.0	52.2	23.1	32.4	51.3	11.7

	Total		
Year	Persons	Males	Females
1977/78	37.0	52.8	22.1
1983	37.4	52.1	21.8
1987/88	36.8	51.2	21.4
1993/94	37.3	53.1	20.4
1999/00	36.4	51.9	19.9

Note : * All the Tables in this chapter are based on different NSS Rounds.

remained unchanged. The changes in either direction were marginal, hardly a percentage point more or less on the average. A decline in the WPR does not imply a fall in the number of workers. The number of rural men at work increased from 158 million in 1987/88 to 181 million in 1993/94 while urban workers increased from 52 million in 1987/88 to 63 million in 1993/94. The increase in women workers was from 71 million to 74 million in rural India and from 11 million to 14 million in urban India.(see note at the end of the text)

The male participation rate in 1999/00 was about one percentage point lower than in 1993/94 in rural India but remained unchanged in urban India. The change in female participation rate was negligible, much to the dismay of the believers in the encouraged worker hypothesis or discouraged worker hypothesis. The absolute increases in employment in this period were lower than in the earlier sub-period, the comparison being marred by the drought of 1987/88. As before, the increase could be attributed to the use of the revised rate of growth of population and a genuine component that shows the net effect of positive and negative economic factors.

The regional structure of WPRs showed considerable stability after liberalisation with the structure prevailing before. The stability was ascertained in terms of correlation coefficients between the participation rates in 17 major states in 1983 with those in 1987/88, 1993/94 and 1999/00 given in Table 3.2. The participation rates of men as well as women in rural India were highly correlated. The correlation coefficients in the successive survey rounds of the NSSO starting with 1983, were positive and significant at 1 per cent. So also were the coefficients of the structure of participation of urban females. The correlation in the structure of activity rates of urban men was significant at more liberal tests of significance of 5 per cent in 1993/94 and of 10 per cent in 1999/00. There is a faint suggestion that liberalisation may be loosening the ties with the past.

The regional structure of participation rates of rural and urban males was quite compressed. The coefficients of variation reported in Table 3.2 ranged between 7 per cent and 8 per cent in case of rural males and 5 per cent and 8 per cent in that of urban males. The structure for women was relatively much dispersed with coefficients of variation varying between 55 and 63 per cent in the case of rural

TABLE 3.2: **Correlation Coefficients between Work Participation Rates in 17 States in 1983 with those in 1987/88, 1993/94 & 1999/00**

	1987/88	1993/94	1999/00
Rural males	0.938***	0.861***	0.711***
Rural females	0.976***	0.958***	0.945***
Urban males	0.717***	0.434**	0.356*
Urban females	0.744***	0.614***	0.561***

Coefficients of Variation between Work Participation Rates for 17 States

(Per cent)

	1977/78	1983	1987/88	1993/94	1999/00
Rural males	8.13	8.19	7.02	7.89	7.66
Rural females	58.33	58.02	55.05	61.8	63.02
Urban males	7.19	4.87	6.14	6.97	7.99
Urban females	37.99	33.66	41.54	36.91	39.48

Notes: 1. *** denotes that the coefficient was significant at 1 per cent.
2. ** denotes that it was significant at 5 per cent and
3. * denotes that it was significant at 10 per cent.

women and between 34 and 42 per cent for urban women. The difference in the dispersal of the structures for men and women is consistent with the finding that proportionately more men than women move from one state to another, unifying the labour market for men more than for women. As to the impact of liberalisation, we observe that regional inequalities in the structure of participation that declined on the immediate impact may widen in the future.

Age-Specific Participation Rates

The abolition of child labour is an important part of the social policy in India. The critics of the reforms predicted an increase in the participation of children as a consequence of impoverishment of population that they felt would follow reforms as surely as day follows night. Contrary to the expectation, the data for 1983, 1987/88,

TABLE 3.3: **Child Labour in Ages 0-14 Years, 1983, 1987/88, 1993/94 and 1999/00**

	Volume of Child Labour (in millions)					
	Rural			Urban		
Year	Persons	Males	Females	Persons	Males	Females
1983	19.36	10.69	8.67	2.09	1.37	0.72
1987/88	14.75	8.56	6.98	1.86	1.11	0.75
1993/94	11.51	6.19	5.32	1.67	1.04	0.62
1999/00	7.95	4.39	3.55	1.21	0.78	0.43
	Growth Rates Per Annum (Per cent)					
1983-87	-6.8	-5.6	-5.4	-2.9	-5.3	1.0
1987-93	-4.1	-5.4	-4.5	-1.8	-1.1	-3.2
1993-99	-6.2	-5.7	-6.7	-5.3	-4.7	-6.2
	Work Participation Rates 0-14 Years (Per cent)					
1983	13.0	13.5	12.5	4.9	6.1	3.6
1987/88	9.5	10.2	9.7	3.9	4.5	3.4
1993/94	7.2	7.2	7.1	3.5	3.7	2.5
1999/00	4.4	4.5	4.2	1.9	2.4	1.4
	Work Participation Rates 15 Years and Over (Per cent)					
1983	56.4	70.9	41.6	43.5	65.9	18.1
1987/88	55.5	70.4	39.9	43.3	65.1	18.9
1993/94	56.3	71.5	46.7	43.5	66.2	19.1
1999/00	59.1	82.9	35	46.8	74.5	16.6

	Total		
Year	Persons	Males	Females
1983	21.45	12.06	9.49
1987/88	16.94	9.51	7.43
1993/94	13.18	7.24	5.94
1999/00	9.16	5.18	3.98

(contd.)

TABLE 3.3 *(contd.)*

Year	Persons	Males	Females
	Growth Rates Per Annum (Per cent)		
1983-87	-5.9	-5.9	-6.1
1987-93	-4.2	-4.5	-3.7
1993-99	-6.1	-5.6	-6.7
	Work Participation Rates 0-14 Years (Per cent)		
1983	11.2	11.9	10.6
1987/88	8.3	8.8	7.9
1993/94	6.2	6.4	6.0
1999/00	3.8	4.0	3.6
	Work Participation Rates 15 Years and Over (Per cent)		
1983	47.6	69.6	36.1
1987/88	52.4	69.0	32.3
1993/94	53.0	70.0	34.9
1999/00	55.8	80.6	30.1

1993/94 and 1999/00 reported in Table 3.3 show substantial decline in the participation of children aged 5-9 and 10-14. The decline is steeper in rural than in urban India. Applying the NSSO participation rates to the estimated population aged 5-14, we derived the absolute number of children at work in the four survey rounds of the NSSO. There were, in rural India, 11 million boys and nine million girls at work in 1983, nine million boys and seven million girls in 1987/88, six million boys and five million girls in 1993/94 and four million boys and four million girls in 1999/00. In urban India the number of boys at work declined from one million in the first three rounds to 0.8 million in the last; the number of girls at work declined from 0.7 million in 1983 to 0.4 million in 1999/00.

To many, the data lack credibility. The attendance ratios in the school-going ages reported by the NSSO are often criticised as too high to be true. According to the National Fertility Health Survey, 19 per cent of the boys and 30 per cent of the girls, both 5-14 years of age, did not attend school in 1998/99 (IIPS, 2000). Assuming that all of them were at work, we estimate that there were 24 million boys and 35 million girls or 59 million children at work in the country. The truth is likely to lie somewhere in-between. There is much scope for improving the methodology of the surveys the NSSO conducts and for involving NGOs in them to capture the true extent of child labour in the country (Government of India, Ministry of Labour, 2000). Though the absolute number of children at work may be questioned there may be much less reason to doubt the trend revealed by the NSSO. The bits and pieces of circumstantial evidence in support of this presumption are the substantial increase in school attendance, an increase in per capita income and reduction in poverty.

The participation of men of prime ages in Table 3.4 shows little variation and little or no scope for improvement as around 97 per cent of the men aged 25-49 were at work. In the male dominated Indian society men have to earn to keep the pot boiling and women toil unsung, unheard and unseen. Women aged 25-49 were economically more active in the villages and less active in the cities after liberalisation than before though only marginally so. Consistent with the improvements in incomes of the poor is the decline in the participation of the population 60 years and over.

TABLE 3.4: **Age-Specific Work Participation Rates, 1983,1987/88, 1993/94 and 1999/00**

(Per cent)

	1983			
	Rural		Urban	
Age Group	Males	Females	Males	Females
5-9	2.0	1.8	0.5	0.5
10-14	21.3	17.0	9.3	5.4
15-29	78.9	36.1	64.0	14.5
30-44	98.1	45.8	97.2	23.4
45-59	95.0	40.7	92.1	22.8
60+	64.1	15.5	48.6	11.6
All ages	61.3	28.7	56.8	13.6

(contd.)

TABLE 3.4 *(contd.)*

Age Group	Rural Males 1987/88	1993/94	1999/00	Rural Females 1987/88	1993/94	1999/00
5-9	0.7	0.9	0.5	0.6	1.1	0.6
10-14	14.5	11.2	8.2	12.6	10.4	7.4
15-19	53.0	52.3	47.5	30.1	26.4	23.4
20-24	83.1	82.4	82.3	35.3	31.8	31.0
25-29	94.4	94.7	94.2	39.9	35.4	37.3
30-34	97.7	98.0	97.4	44.2	40.7	42.2
35-39	98.3	98.8	98.1	47.0	43.5	45.3
40-44	97.4	98.5	98.1	48.4	44.0	46.2
45-49	97.5	98.0	97.7	45.7	43.8	45.0
50-54	95.2	96.5	94.9	41.5	40.7	39.9
55-59	91.7	93.6	91.9	34.5	33.7	35.1
60+	64.6	84.8	62.2	16.0	25.6	17.4
65+		56.5			11.7	
All ages	51.7	53.8	52.2	24.5	23.4	23.1
	Urban Males			Urban Females		
5-9	0.5	0.4	0.3	0.3	0.3	0.1
10-14	7.3	5.9	4.6	4.5	3.5	2.8
15-19	32.3	33.7	30.3	11.0	9.4	8.7
20-24	64.5	65.4	64.4	13.9	13.6	13.0
25-29	90.3	89.2	87.8	17.5	17.5	16.1
30-34	96.6	96.1	95.8	20.9	20.8	19.8
35-39	97.8	98.2	97.3	23.8	23.3	23.5
40-44	98.0	98.0	97.3	25.2	25.7	24.2
45-49	97.0	97.1	96.8	24.1	25.3	23.4
50-54	93.2	94.1	93.3	22.6	24.0	22.5
55-59	83.5	84.5	80.3	18.8	18.5	18.1
60+	46.1	55.6	38.6	9.3	13.5	8.2
65+		34.7			6.6	
All ages	49.6	51.3	51.3	11.8	12.1	11.7

Education-Specific Participation Rates

Since liberalisation and globalisation have gone hand in hand with spread of information technology, it is expected that the participation rates of the more educated would improve and those of the less educated would deteriorate over the medium to long term. Unfortunately absence of data prevents verification for the medium term. In the short run, the education specific participation rates of rural and urban males, 15 years and over, reported in Table 3.5 shows no variation over the three survey rounds of 1983, 1987/88 and 1993/94. Comparable data for the latest round are yet to be published. The rates for women show substantial variation for some levels of

TABLE 3.5: **Education-Specific Participation Rates for Workers Aged 15 Years and Over**

	Rural Males				Rural Females			
Education Level	1983	1987/88	1993/94	1999/00	1983	1987/88	1993/94	1999/00
Illiterate	91.0	90.2	91.3	N.A.	70.7	41.4	39.1	N.A.
Upto Primary	88.5	87.0	88.9	N.A.	27.7	27.4	28.6	N.A.
Middle	70.2	68.8	73.5	N.A.	15.8	17.6	17.7	N.A.
Secondary	66.5	66.4	68.3	N.A.	15.8	17.5	15.3	N.A.
HSC	N.A.	N.A.	62.9	N.A.	N.A.	N.A.	16.1	N.A.
Graduate+	77.4	76.6	79.2	N.A.	22.0	25.0	29.3	N.A.
Total 15+	85.6	93.9	84.6	82.9	37.3	37.3	34.6	35.0
	Urban Males				Urban Females			
Illiterate	86.3	85.5	86.6	N.A.	24.1	23.0	23.3	N.A.
Upto Primary	84.1	82.7	84.4	N.A.	13.4	13.2	15.1	N.A.
Middle	68.8	66.2	71.3	N.A.	7.1	8.1	9.1	N.A.
Secondary	65.2	64.5	66.3	N.A.	17.4	12.5	10.8	N.A.
HSC	N.A.	N.A.	58.9	N.A.	N.A.	N.A.	12.6	N.A.
Graduate+	81.0	79.9	80.7	N.A.	27.9	29.7	28.2	N.A.
Total 15+	76.9	75.4	75.8	74.5	18.1	14.5	17.5	16.6

Note : NA: Data is not available.

education. For example, participation of illiterate rural women declined from 71 per cent in 1983 to 41 per cent in 1987/88 and further to 39 per cent in 1993/94. The decline owes not so much to reforms as to spread of women's education in the 1980s. The participation of graduate women in rural areas improved from 22 per cent to 29 per cent between 1983 and 1993/94; that of urban women did not show much perceptible change.

Unemployment Rates

We expect unemployment to increase in the short to medium term following reforms particularly if the economy lacks price flexibility and factors of production do not quickly move out of non-traded to traded sectors. Usual status unemployment expressed as a rate increased marginally for both men and women in rural India but declined in urban India (Table 3.6). The average of the three pre-liberalisation rates for men in rural areas was 2.4 per cent and that of the two post-liberalisation survey rounds was 2.1 per cent; for women the average declined from 3.5 per cent before liberalisation to 1.4 per cent after liberalisation. In urban India, the corresponding average of the unemployment rates declined from 6 per cent to 5 per cent for men and from 11 per cent to 8 per cent for women.

The current weekly status (CWS) unemployment rate for men, given in Table 3.7, remained much the same before and after liberalisation and for women it declined by one percentage point in rural India. In urban India the male unemployment rate declined by two percentage points and that of females by one percentage point. The urban CWS unemployment rate was higher than the rural both for men and women and was higher for women than for men within each type of residence. The difference was marginal in rural areas but marked in urban India. Unemployment rate by current daily status, reported in the same table, did not change for rural males but declined from an average of 8.3 per cent before liberalisation to 6.3 per cent after it for rural females. In urban India the average rate declined from 9 per cent to 7 per cent for males and from 13 per cent to 5 per cent for females. Taking all the three indicators of unemployment there is no evidence to suggest that liberalisation led to an increase in unemployment.

TABLE 3.6: **Unemployment Rates by Usual Status Principal**

(Per cent)

	Rural			Urban		
Year	Persons	Males	Females	Persons	Males	Females
1977/78	3.2	2.2	5.5	8.7	6.5	17.8
1983	1.9	2.1	1.4	6.1	5.9	6.9
1987/88	3	.8	3.5	6.5	6.1	8.5
1993/94	1.8	2	1.3	5.9	5.4	8.3
1999/00	1.9	2.1	1.5	5.2	4.8	7.1

	Total		
Year	Persons	Males	Females
1977/78	6.7	3.2	7.2
1983	3	3	2.1
1987/88	4	3.6	4.2
1993/94	3	2.9	2.5
1999/00	3	2.9	2.5

TABLE 3.7: **Unemployment Rates by Current Weekly Status and Current Daily Status**

(Per cent)

	Current Weekly Status				Current Daily Status			
	Rural		Urban		Rural		Urban	
Year	Males	Females	Males	Females	Males	Females	Males	Females
1977/78	3.6	4.1	7.1	10.9	7.1	9.2	9.4	14.5
1983	3.7	4.3	6.7	7.5	7.5	9.0	9.2	11.0
1987/88	4.2	4.4	6.6	9.2	4.6	6.7	8.8	12.0
1993/94	3.1	2.9	5.2	7.9	5.6	5.6	6.7	10.4
1999/00	3.9	3.7	5.6	7.3	7.2	7.0	7.3	9.4

The regional structure of unemployment rates was very stable with all except one of the 12 values of correlation coefficients, being significant at 1 per cent (Table 3.8). The structure, though stable, was dispersed with coefficients of variation ranging between 72 per cent and 113 per cent in the case of rural males and between 39 per cent and 53 per cent for urban males. The regional structure of unemployment rates for rural women was more unequal with the coefficients varying between 115 and 174 per cent. It was less dispersed for urban than rural women. The coefficients of variation ranged between 83 per cent and 117 per cent. The labour market is more integrated nationally for men than for women. It appears that liberalisation affected the regional unemployment structures of males and females differently. It compressed the regional structure in the case of men but opened it up in the case of women, a result quite consistent with the tradition that grants freedom of movement to men but confines women to the kitchen of either the father or the husband.

TABLE 3.8: **Correlation Coefficients between Unemployment Rates in 17 States in 1983 with those in 1987/88, 1993/94 & 1999/00**

	1987/88	1993/94	1999/00
Rural males	0.934***	0.811***	0.847***
Rural females	0.829***	0.787***	0.814***
Urban males	0.919***	0.471**	0.539***
Urban females	0.898***	0.747***	0.796***

Notes: 1. *** denotes that the coefficient was significant at 1 per cent.
2. ** denotes that the coefficient was significant at 5 per cent.

Coefficients of Variation between Unemployment Rates for 17 States

(Per cent)

	1977/78	1983	1987/88	1993/94	1999/00
Rural males	112.66	95.53	75.11	78.61	72.28
Rural females	114.83	167.96	125.09	145.09	173.76
Urban males	53.33	39.28	39.52	38.00	42.6
Urban females	92.59	79.33	83.18	84.06	117.18

Age-Specific Unemployment and Distribution of Unemployment by Age

Comparable age-specific unemployment rates are available for three years, 1987/88, 1993/94 and 1999/00 and are given in Table 3.9. The rates of unemployment reported for rural men aged 35 and over, and for urban men 40 years and older are negligible. They are high for the young, aged 15-19 and 20-24. In rural India they show a common pattern, starting with high rates in 1987/88, a dip in 1993/94 and a rise in 1999/00. For both rural men and women the rates are lower after liberalisation than before. Urban men and women aged 15-19, 20-24 and 25-29 suffered extremely high rates of unemployment, two and a half to three times the average for all ages. The rate for fresh entrants to the male labour force aged 15-19 was 21 per cent in 1987/88, which declined to 13 per cent in 1993/94 and rose to 15 per cent in 1999-00. The corresponding rates for women were 19 per cent, 17 per cent and 16 per cent respectively. Women aged 20-24 suffered the highest rate of unemployment of 24 per cent in 1987/88, 28 per cent in 1993/94 and 23 per cent in 1999/00. The young

TABLE 3.9: **Age-Specific Unemployment Rates, 1983,1987/88, 1993/94 and 1999/00**

(Per cent)

	1983			
	Rural		Urban	
Age Group	Males	Females	Males	Females
5-9	0.0	0.0	0.0	0.0
10-14	0.7	0.2	1.2	0.1
15-29	3.9	1.0	8.9	2.7
30-44	0.5	0.3	1.4	0.5
45-59	0.2	0.2	0.7	0.2
60+	0.2	0.1	0.3	0.0
All ages	1.3	0.4	3.5	1.0

(contd.)

TABLE 3.9 *(contd.)*

Age Group	Rural Males 1987/88	1993/94	1999/00	Rural Females 1987/88	1993/94	1999/00
5-9	0.0	0.0	0.0	0.0	0.0	0.0
10-14	3.3	1.8	2.4	3.1	1.0	0.0
15-19	7.7	4.7	6.3	5.9	2.9	4.1
20-24	7.8	6.6	6.2	5.9	4.8	1.9
25-29	3.6	3.2	3.1	4.1	1.9	2.4
30-34	1.1	0.7	1.0	2.6	0.5	0.7
35-39	0.6	0.2	0.4	2.7	0.5	0.2
40-44	0.6	0.2	0.1	2.4	0.2	0.2
45-49	0.5	0.1	0.1	2.4	0.2	0.2
50-54	0.5	0.0	0.0	1.7	0.2	0.3
55-59	0.3	0.1	0.1	1.4	0.0	0.0
60+	0.5	0.0	0.3	1.8	0.0	0.0
65+		0.0			0.8	
All ages	2.8	2.0	2.1	3.5	1.3	1.7
	Urban Males			Urban Females		
5-9	0.0	0.0	0.0	0.0	0.0	0.0
10-14	9.9	4.8	8.0	2.2	0.0	3.4
15-19	20.6	13.1	15.4	19.1	16.8	15.5
20-24	17.3	13.9	13.9	24.0	27.7	22.6
25-29	6.5	6.7	7.5	12.5	12.9	11.5
30-34	1.9	2.1	2.2	5.0	5.5	4.8
35-39	1.1	0.6	1.2	3.3	1.7	2.1
40-44	0.6	0.3	0.6	1.6	0.4	1.2
45-49	0.6	0.4	0.5	1.6	0.4	0.8
50-54	1.0	0.4	0.5	0.9	0.4	0.9
55-59	0.6	0.2	0.2	0.0	0.5	0.5
60+	1.1	0.5	0.0	0.0	0.0	0.0
65+		0.0			0.0	
All ages	6.1	4.6	4.8	8.5	8.3	7.1

are doubly disadvantaged first because they are young and inexperienced and secondly, because they are likely to be more educated.

As can be expected from the rates, the volume of unemployment is concentrated in the age group 15-29 both for men and women, rural and urban. Table 3.10 shows that at least 82 per cent of the unemployed rural men, 58 per cent of rural women, 85 per cent of the urban men and 81 per cent of such women were concentrated in these ages. The concentration increases in 1993/94 and 1999/00 relative to 1987/88 for unemployed rural men and women. For urban men it decreases and for urban women it does so only after increasing in 1993/94.

Education-Specific Unemployment and Distribution of Unemployment by Education

Unemployment rates for the illiterates and the less educated aged 15 years and over, given in Table 3.11, show that these groups experience very low unemployment irrespective of the place of residence or gender. It is the secondary passed but much more the

TABLE 3.10: **Percentage Distribution of Unemployed by Age**

(Per cent)

	1983			
	Rural		Urban	
Age Group	Males	Females	Males	Females
5-9	0.1	0.7	0.1	0.0
10-14	7.6	7.0	4.6	2.0
15-29	82.1	74.1	84.7	86.8
30-44	7.2	11.7	7.9	9.3
45-59	2.1	4.6	2.2	1.8
60+	0.9	1.9	0.5	0.1
All ages	100.0	100.0	100.0	100.0

(contd.)

TABLE 3.10 *(contd.)*

	Rural Males			Rural Females		
Age Group	1987/ 88	1993/ 94	1999/ 00	1987/ 88	1993/ 94	1999/ 00
5-9	0.0	0.0	0.0	0.0	3.6	0.0
10-14	4.2	2.3	2.3	5.2	3.1	0.0
15-19	28.4	25.0	28.7	19.2	20.8	22.1
20-24	36.2	44.0	37.7	23.2	42.2	34.6
25-29	17.3	21.5	20.4	15.7	17.3	18.8
30-34	4.6	4.5	6.0	9.0	4.3	5.6
35-39	2.2	1.2	2.4	8.7	3.6	1.7
40-44	2.5	0.9	0.5	6.6	1.5	1.3
45-49	1.4	0.4	0.4	5.6	1.4	1.1
50-54	1.2	0.0	0.0	2.9	1.1	0.9
55-59	0.6	0.3	0.3	1.6	0.0	0.0
60-64	1.3	0.0	1.3	2.2	0.0	0.0
65+		0.0			1.2	
All ages	100.0	100.0	100.0	100.0	100.0	100.0
	Urban Males			Urban Females		
5-9	0.0	0.0	0.0	0.0	0.0	0.0
10-14	0.0	1.4	1.8	1.1	0.0	1.3
15-19	29.1	23.5	23.4	23.8	18.2	18.6
20-24	42.6	41.8	38.4	39.8	47.3	40.6
25-29	17.4	22.2	23.2	19.9	21.6	21.6
30-34	4.4	6.6	6.3	6.9	8.7	9.2
35-39	2.3	1.7	3.4	4.7	2.7	4.4
40-44	1.0	0.7	1.5	1.8	0.5	2.0
45-49	0.9	0.8	1.0	1.5	0.4	1.1
50-54	1.0	0.6	0.7	0.6	0.3	0.8
55-59	0.4	0.2	0.2	0.0	0.3	0.3
60-64	0.9	0.3	0.0	0.0	0.0	0.0
65+		0.0			0.0	
All ages	100.0	100.0	100.0	100.0	100.0	100.0

TABLE 3.11: **Education-Specific Rates of Unemployment, 15 years and Over**

(Per cent)

Educational Level	Rural Males				Rural Females			
	1983	1987/88	1993/94	1999/00	1983	1987/88	1993/94	1999/00*
Illiterate	0.4	0.9	0.3	0.4	0.2	2.4	0.2	0.3
Upto primary	1.3	2.1	0.8	1.4	0.6	3.5	1.0	1.3
Middle	3.9	5.4	3.0	3.2	2.5	13.7	5.3	5.9
Secondary	7.8	10.5	6.7	5.9	8.0	33.5	19.9	19.2
HSC			9.8	8.2			29.1	28.8
Graduate+	11.4	15.0	13.2	12.0	15.6	37.3	34.6	46.2
	Urban Males				Urban Females			
Illiterate	1.7	1.8	1.1	1.3	0.2	2.1	0.4	0.8
Upto primary	3.6	4.6	2.5	3.2	0.7	6.4	4.5	2.8
Middle	6.4	8.8	5.7	5.6	2.1	21.6	15.7	12.9
Secondary	6.5	8.8	6.3	5.5	4.0	22.8	20.0	16.5
HSC			8.5	8.4			22.0	21.7
Graduate+	6.4	7.4	6.4	6.7	7.4	21.0	20.6	18.7

Note: * Data for 1999/00 relate to unemployed 5 years and older.

graduates among men who suffer very high rates of unemployment in rural India. In urban India the rates of unemployment among graduates do not differ much from those among secondary and HSC passed. Women who have completed middle school and all higher levels of education suffer from rates of unemployment ranging between 2.5 per cent to 46 per cent in rural India and from 16 per cent to 23 per cent in urban India.

The waste and mal-allocation of educational resources is brought out more vividly in the distributions of the unemployed by education reported in Table 3.12. Men who have at least passed the secondary school examination formed upwards of 40 per cent of the unemployed in rural India and upwards of 44 per cent in urban India. Women who have passed the secondary level formed between 24 per cent and

63 per cent of the unemployed in rural India and between 61 per cent and 74 per cent in urban India.

TABLE 3.12: **Distribution of Unemployed Aged 15 years and Over by Education**

(Per cent)

	Rural Males				Rural Females			
Education Level	1983	1987/ 88	1993/ 94	1999/ 00	1983	1987/ 88	1993/ 94	1999/ 00*
Illiterate	11.4	14.4	6.4	7.3	29.0	56.3	17.1	9.6
Upto primary	20.5	20.7	11.1	15.8	14.3	9.3	9.3	10.2
Middle	27.1	22.1	21.0	21.6	19.8	10.3	14.4	17.4
Secondary	32.1	31.3	25.8	23.2	28.7	19.4	27.3	26.3
HSC			16.9	14.7			15.3	13.1
Graduate+	8.9	11.5	18.8	17.4	8.2	4.7	16.6	23.4
Total 15+	100.0	100.0	100.0	100.0	100.0	100.0	100.0	100.0
Secondry+	41.0	42.8	61.5	55.3	36.9	24.1	59.2	62.8
	Urban Males				Urban Females			
Illiterate	7.2	5.8	4.3	4.4	7.1	7.8	2.8	4.2
Upto primary	21.6	22.7	14.1	14.7	12.3	12.5	8.8	6.0
Middle	26.8	24.6	22.1	21.8	19.8	16.5	15.2	15.5
Secondary	31.6	31.5	22.1	19.3	37.3	34.0	21.5	18.8
HSC			16.9	16.5			16.3	17.5
Graduate+	12.8	15.4	20.5	23.3	23.5	29.2	35.4	38.0
Total 15+	100.0	100.0	100.0	100.0	100.0	100.0	100.0	100.0
Secondry+	44.4	46.9	59.5	59.1	60.8	63.2	73.2	74.3

Note: * Data for 1999/2000 relate to unemployed 5 years and older.

Educated Unemployment Aged 15 years and Over

Rates of unemployment for rural males, rural females and urban females who have passed the secondary and higher levels and graduation are very high, running into double digits, in most survey rounds (Table 3.13). Irrespective of residence and level of education, unemployment was higher for women than for men. For the secondary passed, the rates are lower in the post-liberalisation than in the pre-liberalisation years but opposite is the case of graduates. The concentration of the unemployed who have passed secondary school and graduation increased after liberalisation. India shares the high wastage of educated manpower with many neighbouring, African and Latin American countries. The educated in East and South East Asia do not experience such high unemployment. The World Bank attributes the difference to the fact that the relative wages of the educated in the former set of countries are determined more by non-market than market forces whereas in the East and South East Asia they are determined more by the market than non-market forces.

TABLE 3.13: **Unemployment Rates among Educated Unemployed 15+, 1983-1999/00**

(Per cent)

	1983	1987/88	1993/94	1999/00
Rural Males				
Secondary and above	10.9	11.4	8.9	6.9
Graduate and above	11.4	13.5	13.4	10.7
Rural Females				
Secondary and above	35.0	34.1	24.3	20.4
Graduate and above	15.6	14.9	32.3	35.1
Urban Males				
Secondary and above	8.4	8.3	6.9	6.6
Graduate and above	6.4	6.4	6.4	6.6
Urban Females				
Secondary and above	22.2	22.0	20.7	16.3
Graduate and above	7.4	7.9	20.5	16.3

Underemployment

The NSSO estimates the extent of visible underemployment by cross-tabulating principal status workers by their current daily activity status. The cross tabulation in Table 3.14 shows that the extent of visible underemployment was higher among women than men irrespective of their rural-urban residence. The usually employed who do not find work by CDS may either seek work or withdraw from the labour force. Proportionately more women than men chose to withdraw. Liberalisation has reduced visible underemployment quite perceptibly among women and to a small extent among urban males. The extent of visible underemployment remained more or less the same among rural men.

TABLE 3.14: **Distribution of Usual Status Workers by their Current Daily Status: Visible Underemployment**

(Per cent)

Current Daily Status	1983	1987/88	1993/94	1999/00
Rural				
		Males		
Employed	87.6	92.6	90.9	89.7
Unemployed	5.7	2.7	4.0	5.3
Not in Labour force	6.7	4.7	5.1	5.1
Total	100.0	100.0	100.0	100.0
		Females		
Employed	58.1	63.8	66.3	67.6
Unemployed	5.0	2.6	3.0	4.1
Not in Labour force	36.9	33.6	30.6	28.3
Total	100.0	100.0	100.0	100.0
Urban				
		Males		
Employed	92.1	93.8	94.9	94.2
Unemployed	4.1	3.7	2.7	2.7
Not in Labour force	3.8	2.5	2.5	3.1
Total	100.0	100.0	100.0	100.0
		Females		
Employed	70.1	71.6	76.6	79.1
Unemployed	3.8	3.7	2.4	2.2
Not in Labour force	26.1	24.7	21.0	18.7
Total	100.0	100.0	100.0	100.0

The extent of invisible unemployment is derived by asking usually employed principal workers, if they were seeking or available for additional work. As Table 3.15 shows, invisible underemployment, averaged over the two pre-and two post-liberalisation rounds, is lower after than before liberalisation. It is higher for rural men than for rural women and higher for urban women than for urban men. Male workers were casualised to a greater extent than female workers in rural areas, but the opposite was the case in urban India. We think that casual workers are more likely than the regular wage/salaried to report available for work.

TABLE 3.15: **Percentage of Usual Status Principal Workers who Sought or were Available for Additional Work: Invisible Underemployment**

	Rural		Urban	
Year	Males	Females	Males	Females
1983	20.3	18.1	13.1	14.6
1987/88	12.6	8.2	9.1	12.2
1993/94	6.9	6	4.4	5.1
1999/00	10.5	8.3	6.1	5.8

Structure of Employment by Sectors

Students of development economics have always watched closely the changes in the structure of income and employment in the process of development. Since liberalisation apprehensions have been expressed regarding the pace of change away from the primary sector. While the primary sector's share in total employment has been declining, many critics feared that the pace of decline had slowed down considerably in the 1990s. The fears were based on the data from the thin rounds of the NSSO, available in the early 1990s. The data from the large sample of the 50th Round of the NSSO confirmed the fears. The share of the primary sector declined by 1.1 per cent compound per annum between 1983 and 1987/88 and by 0.4 per cent per annum between 1987/88 and 1993/94. The key results of the 55th round given in Table 3.16, show an annual decline of 1.3 per cent compound, the fastest since 1977/78. The changes between 1983 and 1987/88, and 1987/88 and 1993/94 are distorted by the drought in 1987/88 and once the weather gods became kinder the pace of shift away from the primary sector quickened as never before. Liberalisation benefited the tertiary sector the most. Its share in 1999/00 shows an increase of 3.3 percentage points over 1993/94. Of the 4.7 percentage points lost by the primary sector, the tertiary sector picked up 3.3 while the secondary sector picked up 1.6.

TABLE 3.16: **Distribution of Workforce by Sectors, 1977/78-1999/2000**

(Per cent)

Sector	1977/78	1983	1987/88	1993/94	1999/00
1	2	3	4	5	6
		All-India Persons			
Primary	70.5	67.8	64.4	63.0	58.3
Secondary	12.7	14.1	16.1	15.3	16.8
Tertiary	16.8	18.1	19.5	21.7	24.9
Total	100	100	100	100	100
		Rural			
Primary	83.4	81.5	78.3	78.2	75.1
Secondary	8.0	9.0	11.3	10.2	11.6
Tertiary	8.6	9.5	10.4	11.5	13.3
Total	100.0	100.0	100.0	100.0	100.0
		Urban			
Primary	15.2	14.8	13.6	12.3	7.9
Secondary	33.2	33.9	33.6	32.2	32.3
Tertiary	51.6	51.3	52.8	55.5	59.8
Total	100.0	100.0	100.0	100.0	100.0
		All-India Males			
Primary	65.6	61.9	58.4	57.2	53.1
Secondary	14.2	15.8	17.6	16.8	18.3

(contd.)

TABLE 3.16 *(contd.)*

1	2	3	4	5	6
Tertiary	20.2	22.3	24.0	26.0	28.6
Total	100.0	100.0	100.0	100.0	100.0
		Rural			
Primary	80.7	77.8	74.6	74.0	71.3
Secondary	8.8	10.0	12.1	11.2	12.6
Tertiary	10.5	12.2	13.3	14.8	16.1
Total	100.0	100.0	100.0	100.0	100.0
		Urban			
Primary	10.6	10.3	9.1	9.0	6.5
Secondary	33.7	34.6	34.3	33.1	33.0
Tertiary	55.7	55.1	56.6	57.9	60.5
Total	100.0	100.0	100.0	100.0	100.0
		All-India			
		Females			
Primary	81.8	81.2	77.7	78.0	70.0
Secondary	9.5	10.3	12.8	10.9	13.5
Tertiary	8.7	8.5	9.5	11.1	16.5
Total	100	100	100	100	100
		Rural			
Primary	88.2	87.8	84.8	86.1	84.0
Secondary	6.7	7.4	10.0	8.3	9.3
Tertiary	5.1	4.8	5.2	5.6	6.7
Total	100.0	100.0	100.0	100.0	100.0
		Urban			
Primary	31.9	32.0	30.5	24.8	14.6
Secondary	32.4	31.2	31.3	29.3	29.3
Tertiary	35.7	36.8	38.2	45.9	56.2
Total	100.0	100.0	100.0	100.0	100.0

The fears relating to stagnation of the development process are better examined in the rural sector. The share of the primary sector in total employment shows a decline of 0.4 per cent per annum between 1977/78, and 1983, 0.9 per cent per annum between 1983 and 1987/88, and hardly at all immediately after liberalisation. However, the share declined at 0.7 per cent per annum compound in the six years following 1993/94. The share of the secondary sector increased from 8.0 per cent in 1977/78 to 10.2 per cent in 1993/94 and further to 11.6 per cent in 1999/00. The share of the tertiary sector increased from 8.6 per cent to 13.3 per cent between 1977/78 and 1999/00. In urban India the share of the primary sector declined from 15.2 per cent in 1977/78 to 7.9 per cent in 1999/00, the decline being the fastest, 7.4 per cent per annum compound, between 1993/94 and 1999/00. The share of the secondary sector shows stagnation throughout the two decades. The tertiary sector was the beneficiary of this structural change.

The analysis of the change in the structure of employment of main male workers of the Census of 1971 and 1981 had shown that the decline in the share of agriculture had improved the share of industry more than it did the share of tertiary sector (Deshpande and Deshpande, 1985). This was the classical pattern followed by industrialised countries in their early stages of development. The analysis of change in the 1980s based on the Census of 1991 showed that the boot was on the other leg in the sense that the tertiary sector became the major beneficiary of the decline of agriculture (Deshpande, 1996). The data from the NSSO for the two decades covering the 1980s and the 1990s shows that India has departed from the classical pattern to follow the East Asian path of development, giving precedence to the tertiary over the secondary sector.

Structure of Employment by Industry

Changes in the structure of employment by industry given in Table 3.17 show that in the long haul from 1977/78 to 1999/00 agriculture dropped 12.2 percentage points, manufacturing picked up by barely 0.9 percentage points and trade by 4.6, construction gained by 2.9 and services by 1.8 percentage points, the gain being bigger than that

TABLE 3.17: **Distribution of Workers by Industry Division, 1977/78-1999/00**

(Per cent)

Sector	1977/78	1983	1987/88	1993/94	1999/00
1	2	3	4	5	6
		All-India			
		Persons			
Agriculture	70.5	67.8	64.4	63	58.3
Mining & quarrying	0.5	0.6	0.7	0.7	0.6
Manufacturing	10.3	10.9	11.3	10.9	11.2
Electricity, gas etc.	0.2	0.3	0.4	0.4	0.3
Construction	1.8	2.3	3.8	3.2	4.7
Trade	6.2	6.4	7.3	7.8	10.8
Transport & storage	2.2	2.6	2.7	2.9	4.0
Services	8.3	9.1	9.6	10.9	10.1
Total	100.0	100.0	100.0	100.0	100.0
Workers in '000s	242230	269340	291220	331980	363400
		Rural India			
		Persons			
Agriculture	83.4	81.5	78.3	78.2	75.1
Mining & quarrying	0.4	0.5	0.6	0.6	0.5
Manufacturing	6.2	6.8	7.2	7.1	7.4
Electricity, gas etc.	0.1	0.1	0.2	0.2	0.2
Construction	1.3	1.6	3.3	2.3	3.5
Trade	3.3	3.4	4.0	4.3	5.4
Transport & storage	0.8	1.1	1.3	1.4	2.3
Services	4.5	4.9	5.1	5.8	5.6
Total	100.0	100.0	100.0	100.0	100.0
Workers in '000s	196580	214140	228490	255260	272730
		Urban India			
		Persons			
Agriculture	15.2	14.8	13.6	12.3	7.9
Mining & quarrying	0.8	1.2	1.2	1.2	0.8
Manufacturing	27.9	27.0	26.1	23.7	22.6

(contd.)

TABLE 3.17 *(contd.)*

1	2	3	4	5	6
Electricity, gas etc.	0.8	0.9	0.9	1.0	0.7
Construction	3.7	4.8	5.4	6.3	8.2
Trade	18.8	17.8	19.2	19.5	27.0
Transport & storage	8.0	8.2	7.8	8.0	9.0
Services	24.8	25.3	25.8	28.0	23.8
Total	100.0	100.0	100.0	100.0	100.0
Workers in '000s	45650	55200	62730	76720	90670

of manufacturing. In rural India, the share of agriculture declined from 83.4 per cent in 1977/78 to 75.1 per cent in 1999/00. Construction gained 2.2 percentage points of the 8.3 points lost by agriculture. The rest were picked up by trade, transport, services and manufacturing. In urban India agriculture lost 7.3 percentage points, manufacturing 5.2 and services one percentage point. Trade gained most, 8.2 percentage points followed by construction, 4.5 percentage points. Of the 5.2 percentage points lost by manufacturing, nearly 1.8 were lost before liberalisation and 3.5 after. In other words, it was urban and not rural India that was de-industrialised by liberalisation. As we shall see later these changes have not reduced the productivity of labour in the growing sectors.

Gender Composition of the Workforce

Given the alleged preference of women to work from home we expected that the share of women would be higher among the self-employed than among wage paid labour, regular and casual. NSSO data given in Table 3.18 show that women form a higher proportion of the casual than of the self-employed. Their share was the lowest among regular wage/salaried workers. These conclusions hold good irrespective of rural-urban residence. Excluding the abnormal drought year, the data suggest that, women's share in casual and the self-employed marginally declined and that among the regular wage/salaried marginally increased after liberalisation than before it.

Table 3.19 shows that women formed about a third of the workers in agriculture both in urban and rural India in 1999/00. They

TABLE 3.18: **Gender Composition of the Workforce by Employment Status**

(Per cent)

Employment Status	1977/78	1983	1987/88	1993/94	1999/00
		All India			
Self-employed	27.1	27.0	27.7	24.9	25.3
Regular/Salaried	12.7	13.3	15.4	14.6	15.8
Casual	38.5	37.5	34.9	33.8	32.7
Total	28.1	28.1	28.0	26.3	26.3
		Rural India			
Self-employed	28.4	26.8	29.9	26.9	27.6
Regular/Salaried	13.1	13.5	17.4	14.0	15.3
Casual	39.4	38.6	35.9	34.8	34.3
Total	30.5	30.8	30.9	29.0	29.3
		Urban India			
Self-employed	18.6	16.4	16.9	15.8	16.3
Regular/Salaried	12.3	13.1	14.0	15.0	16.1
Casual	31.1	30.0	27.7	26.9	22.2
Total	17.7	17.5	17.5	17.5	17.3

formed 31 per cent and 18 per cent respectively of rural and urban manufacturing; and 22.5 per cent and 27.4 per cent respectively of rural urban services. Trade and construction employed a little more than a tenth. Surprisingly, no woman was employed in electricity and gas, and transport and storage, the two sectors dominated by public ownership. Liberalisation is expected to lead to feminisation of the workforce. However, the gender composition by industry, all India, rural and urban has remained stable, as shown by the correlation coefficients, over the last five survey rounds spanning two decades.

Distribution of Workers by Level of Education

The spread of education in the population improves with time as the access to education and demand for education increases. The distribution of workers aged 15 years and older by education given

TABLE 3.19: **Gender Composition of Workforce by Industry Division, 1977/78 -1999/00 (Per cent Share of Women in Total Employment)**

Sector	1977/78	1983	1987/88	1993/94	1999/00
		All-India			
Agriculture	32.5	33.4	33.7	32.1	32.8
Mining & quarrying	13.9	15.9	16.9	15.4	18.3
Manufacturing	23.8	23.2	23.8	23.5	24.1
Electricity, gas etc.	1.4	0.0	2.1	3.2	2.7
Construction	12.7	12.8	20.9	10.7	10.7
Trade	12.6	12.4	12.1	11.2	11.2
Transport & storage	2.7	3.2	1.9	2.6	2.7
Services	19.4	17.9	18.5	19.7	25.4
Total	28.1	28.1	28.0	26.3	26.3
		Rural India			
Agriculture	32.3	33.2	33.4	31.9	32.8
Mining & quarrying	15.2	18.5	20.6	19.3	23.5
Manufacturing	29.0	29.0	29.6	29.0	30.5
Electricity, gas etc.	0.0	0.0	0.0	0.0	0.0
Construction	14.1	13.5	25.3	10.1	10.1
Trade	18.5	17.2	16.2	14.2	12.5
Transport & storage	3.8	2.8	2.4	2.1	1.3
Services	20.3	17.6	18.2	17.0	22.5
Total	30.5	30.8	30.9	29.0	29.4
		Urban India			
Agriculture	37.2	37.8	39.1	35.3	31.9
Mining & quarrying	11.1	11.7	10.2	8.8	8.6
Manufacturing	18.8	17.5	18.0	17.9	17.7
Electricity, gas etc.	2.2	0.0	3.9	5.3	4.9
Construction	10.6	12.0	11.3	11.4	11.6
Trade	8.2	8.8	9.0	9.1	10.5
Transport & storage	2.2	3.4	1.6	2.8	3.8
Services	18.6	18.1	18.7	21.6	27.4
Total	17.7	17.5	17.5	17.5	17.2

TABLE 3.20: **Distribution of Workforce Aged 15 years and Over by Education, 1983-1999/00**

(Per cent)

	Rural Males				Rural Females			
Educational Level	1983	1987/88	1993/94	1999/00	1983	1987/88	1993/94	1999/00*
Illiterate	52.9	49.9	44.4	40.3	87.1	84.9	79.8	74.9
Literate upto	29.4	29.9	29.4	27.7	10.1	11.0	13.8	15.7
Primary	0.0	0.0	0.0	0.0	0.0	0.0	0.0	0.0
Middle	10.5	10.9	13.4	15.9	1.8	2.4	3.7	5.6
Secondary	5.9	7.5	7.2	9.0	0.8	1.4	1.6	2.3
HSC	0.0	0.0	3.1	4.0	0.0	0.0	0.6	0.7
Graduate+	1.3	1.8	2.5	3.1	0.2	0.3	0.5	0.8
Total 15+	100.0	100.0	100.0	100.0	100.0	100.0	100.0	100.0
	Urban Males				Urban Females			
	1983	1987/88	1993/94	1999/00	1983	1987/88	1993/94	1999/00*
Illiterate	22.6	20.6	18.5	16.4	60.4	54.6	48.4	44.1
Literate upto	30.7	31.0	26.0	22.3	17.9	18.5	18.6	17.8
Primary	0.0	0.0	0.0	0.0	0.0	0.0	0.0	0.0
Middle	17.6	15.8	17.3	18.8	5.2	5.7	7.4	9.2
Secondary	19.2	21.1	15.3	16.7	9.7	11.2	7.8	8.5
HSC	0.0	0.0	8.6	9.2	0.0	0.0	5.2	5.7
Graduate+	9.9	11.5	14.3	16.6	6.8	10.0	12.6	14.7
Total 15+	100.0	100.0	100.0	100.0	100.0	100.0	100.0	100.0

Note: * Data for 1999/00 relate to workers 5 years and older.

in Table 3.20 shows a qualitative improvement indicated by a rise in the shares of higher levels of education and a decline in those of the lower levels. The share of secondary plus among rural male workers increased from 7.2 per cent in 1983 to 16.1 per cent in 1999/00 and from 29 per cent to almost 43 per cent in urban India: that of women who have passed at least the secondary stage increased from one per cent in 1983 to 3.8 per cent in 1999/00 in rural India and from 16.5 per cent to 28.9 per cent in urban India.

Structure of Employment by Employment Status

Liberalisation is expected to increase the share of casual and the self-employed and reduce that of the regularly employed. We find in Table 3.21 that the share of casual workers among rural men increased from 27 per cent in 1977/78 to 37 per cent in 1999/00. In urban India, it increased from 13 per cent to 17 per cent. The share of regular wage/salaried men declined in both places of residence. Share of self-employed decreased from 62 per cent in 1977/78 to 54 per cent in 1999/00 in rural and, contrary to expectation, increased marginally in urban India. There was casualisation of rural women

TABLE 3.21: **Distribution of Workers by Employment Status, 1977/78-1999/00**

(Per cent)

	Males			Females		
Year	Self-employed	Regular/ Salaried	Casual	Self-employed	Regular/ Salaried	Casual
			Rural			
1977/78	62.2	10.8	27.0	56.3	3.7	40.0
1983	59.5	10.6	29.9	54.1	3.7	42.2
1987/88	57.5	10.4	32.1	54.9	4.9	40.2
1993/94	56.9	8.5	34.6	51.3	3.4	45.3
1999/00	54.4	9.0	36.6	50.0	3.9	46.1
			Urban			
1977/78	39.9	47.2	12.9	42.2	30.8	27.0
1983	40.2	44.5	15.3	37.3	31.8	30.9
1987/88	41.0	44.4	14.6	39.3	34.2	26.5
1993/94	41.1	42.7	16.2	36.4	35.5	28.1
1999/00	41.2	41.9	16.9	38.4	38.5	23.1

who captured the points lost by the self-employed. In urban India, the share of regular wage/salaried among females increased by eight percentage points at the cost of the self-employed and casual workers. Both lost 4 percentage points each.

Labour Absorption by Industry

The percentage distribution of workers by industry in a given year gives us a snapshot of the industrial structure in that year. The percentage distribution of the absolute change in workers by industry given in Table 3.22 tells us the extent of flows into and out of each industry. For example, between 1977/78 and 1983, employment in India increased by about 27.1 million of which 11.8 million (43.6 per cent) had entered agriculture. In contrast, between 1993/94 and 1999/00, employment increased by 31.4 million but the share of agriculture had declined from 63.0 per cent to 58.3 per cent. This means that 2.9 million or 9.3 per cent of the 31.4 million additional workers had entered agriculture. We note first the percentage distribution of the change for the country as a whole irrespective of place of residence and sex. Our interest lies in the comparison of the distributions before and after liberalisation. Although the table gives the distributions between 1983 and 1987/88 and 1987/88 and 1993/94, we know that the drought of 1987/88 affected the industrial distribution substantially. Hence our comparison is restricted to changes between sub-periods 1977/78-1983 (before liberalisation) and 1993/94-1999/00 (after liberalisation).

TABLE 3.22: **Distribution of Net Additions to Workforce**

(Per cent)

Sector	1977-78 to 1983	1983 to 1987-88	1987-88 to 1993-94	1993-94 to 1999-00
1	2	3	4	5
		All-India		
Agriculture	43.6	21.7	53.0	9.3
Mining & quarrying	2.1	1.8	0.8	-1.2
Manufacturing	16.8	15.3	8.5	13.9

(contd.)

TABLE 3.22 *(contd.)*

1	2	3	4	5
Electricity, gas etc.	0.6	1.4	0.6	-0.3
Construction	6.8	22.2	-0.5	20.0
Trade	7.5	18.6	11.7	42.2
Transport & storage	6.1	4.5	4.5	15.0
Services	15.8	15.4	20.7	1.8
Total	100.0	100.0	100.0	100.0
		Rural India		
Agriculture	60.2	30.5	77.3	29.8
Mining & quarrying	1.6	2.1	0.6	-1.0
Manufacturing	13.5	13.2	6.2	11.8
Electricity, gas etc.	0.1	1.7	0.2	0.2
Construction	5.0	28.7	-6.2	21.0
Trade	4.5	13.0	6.9	21.5
Transport & storage	4.5	4.3	2.3	15.5
Services	9.4	8.1	11.8	2.7
Total	100.0	100.0	100.0	100.0
		Urban India		
Agriculture	12.9	4.8	6.5	-16.3
Mining & quarrying	3.1	1.2	1.2	-1.4
Manufacturing	22.7	19.5	12.9	16.6
Electricity, gas etc.	1.4	0.9	1.4	-0.9
Construction	10.1	9.8	10.3	18.6
Trade	13.0	29.5	20.8	68.2
Transport & storage	9.2	4.9	8.9	14.5
Services	27.7	29.5	37.9	0.7
Total	100.0	100.0	100.0	100.0

We find that in the sub-period after liberalisation, as noted above, agriculture absorbed less than a 10th, trade absorbed 42 per cent, construction 20 per cent, transport 15 per cent and manufacturing 14 per cent of the net addition to the workforce. Services absorbed less than 2 per cent. Before liberalisation, agriculture absorbed 43.6 per cent of the total increase, manufacturing 16.8 per cent, services 15.8 per cent, trade barely 8 per cent and construction, about 7 per cent. Table 3.23 shows that, except construction, nowhere did the additions to the workforce reduce labour productivity. Agriculture has the lowest

TABLE 3.23: **GDP Per Worker (in Rs.) at 1980/81 Prices by Sector of Origin**

Sector	1977/78	1983	1987/88	1993/94	1999/00
Agriculture	2710	2888	2853	3373	3968
Mining & quarrying	13643	14050	14503	18302	23968
Manufacturing	7971	9082	10608	13433	19346
Electricity, gas etc.	30920	35795	36141	47428	78549
Construction	13742	10647	7117	9794	9251
Trade & transport	11974	13906	14647	16960	18519
Services	8195	8733	10209	11923	17379
GDP per worker	4713	5277	5849	7204	9756
GDP per capita	1791	1979	2154	2693	3559

Compound Rates of Growth Per Annum (Per cent)

Sector	1977/78 to 1983	1983 to 1987/88	1987/88 to 1993/94	1993/94 to 1990/00
Agriculture	1.1	-0.3	2.8	2.7
Mining & quarrying	0.5	0.7	3.9	4.5
Manufacturing	2.2	3.5	3.9	6.1
Electricity, gas etc.	2.4	0.2	4.5	8.4
Construction	-4.3	-9.0	5.3	-1.0
Trade & transport	2.5	1.2	2.4	1.5
Services	1.1	3.5	2.6	6.3
GDP per worker	1.9	2.3	3.5	5.1
GDP per capita	1.7	1.9	3.7	4.6

labour productivity, Rs.3968, trade and transport, which together attracted the biggest flow, records output per worker of Rs.18519, manufacturing had a GDP per worker of Rs.19346. Despite the fall in productivity in construction after liberalisation, labour productivity in it remained higher than in agriculture. Workers may not be able to maximise incomes but the process is rational enough to support some faith in the market mechanism.

It would be more instructive to observe from Table 3.22 the changes in rural and urban residence separately. During 1977/78-1983 agriculture absorbed almost 60 per cent and manufacturing 13.5 per cent of the net additions to the rural workforce. After liberalisation agriculture absorbed 30 per cent and manufacturing 11.8 per cent, two percentage points less than in 1977/78-1983. Construction and trade absorbed about five per cent each of the net addition to the rural workforce between 1977/78-1983. They absorbed four times as many after liberalisation. The other changes are consistent with the effects of the drought in 1987-88 and the tendency of workers to take up their normal industrial affiliation later.

In urban India, after liberalisation, there was a net flow out of agriculture. Trade absorbed 68.2 per cent of the additional workers, manufacturing 16.6 per cent and construction 18.6 per cent. During 1977/78-1983 agriculture absorbed 13 per cent, manufacturing 23 per cent, construction 10 per cent, trade 13 per cent and services 28 per cent of the net addition.

Earlier, while discussing changes in the gender composition of the workforce, we stated that it had remained stable over time. We try to find out if liberalisation is causing a change at the margin, which would lead to feminisation of the workforce in the future. We do this by noting the shares of women in the incremental workforce in each industry. In Table 3.24 we find that, for the country as a whole, the share of women, 28 per cent in the incremental workforce in 1977/78-1983, decreased to 27 per cent in the inter-round period 1983-1987/88, dropped further to 15 per cent in the next but increased to 26 per cent in 1993/94-1999/00. The sectors that are likely to be feminised most in the future are agriculture, services and manufacturing in rural India and services and agriculture in urban India.

TABLE 3.24: **Share of Female Entrants in Net Addition to Workforce**

(Per cent)

Sector	1977-78 to 1983	1983 to 1987-88	1987-88 to 1993-94	1993-94 to 1999-00
1	2	3	4	5
		All-India		
Agriculture	47.1	45.1	18.0	84.6
Mining & quarrying	19.7	21.4	5.4	-1.7
Manufacturing	19.9	29.0	20.2	29.2
Electricity, gas etc.	-5.4	7.1	7.2	9.2
Construction	13.2	31.1	513.0	10.8
Trade	10.7	10.9	7.3	11.3
Transport & storage	4.8	-7.5	5.5	3.1
Services	11.0	22.6	23.8	389.8
Total	28.0	26.8	14.6	26.3
		Rural India		
Agriculture	47.8	43.1	18.8	67.8
Mining & quarrying	27.4	28.1	8.6	-14.4
Manufacturing	28.9	34.1	23.1	44.2
Electricity, gas etc.	0.0	0.0	0.0	0.0
Construction	11.7	35.1	78.6	10.0
Trade	6.9	12.3	4.0	7.7
Transport & storage	0.8	0.7	0.6	0.2
Services	3.0	23.2	12.7	198.0
Total	34.3	31.8	12.9	34.6
		Urban India		
Agriculture	41.0	69.6	-1.0	46.1
Mining & quarrying	12.3	-0.6	2.3	9.2
Manufacturing	10.0	22.5	17.6	15.8
Electricity, gas etc.	-6.2	32.3	9.1	6.8
Construction	14.6	8.8	11.6	11.9

(contd.)

TABLE 3.24 *(contd.)*

1	2	3	4	5
		Urban India		
Trade	13.2	9.7	9.3	12.7
Transport & storage	8.4	-21.2	7.9	6.8
Services	16.0	22.3	30.4	1306.5
Total	16.2	17.3	17.7	15.8

Income Elasticity of Employment

Table 3.25 shows that elasticity of employment with respect to income has declined over successive survey rounds from 0.46 in 1977/78-1983 to 0.20 in 1993/94-1999/00. The sad point is that this decline refers to total employment, not merely to that in the organised sector. When the organised sector forms barely eight per cent of the total employment it is difficult to argue that the decline in it would cause elasticity of total employment to decline so steeply. That it should decline in the medium term after liberalisation is no less

TABLE 3.25: **Elasticity of Employment by Sectors***

All India	1977-78 to 1983	1983 to 1987-88	1987-88 to 1993-94	1993-94 to 1999-00
Agriculture	0.50	1.91	0.36	0.07
Mining & quarrying	0.92	0.85	0.34	-1.28
Manufacturing	0.53	0.38	0.26	0.20
Electricity, gas etc.	0.57	0.97	0.39	-0.14
Construction	3.96	3.95	-0.06	1.18
Trade & transport	0.42	0.78	0.54	0.79
Services	0.74	0.42	0.57	0.18
Total	0.46	0.41	0.35	0.20

Note: * Elasticity of employment is derived by dividing percentage change in employment by percentage change in GDP at 1980/81 prices for each inter-round period.

shocking because one of the major justifications for liberalisation was that it would alter the structure of production in favour of labour intensive industries and help increase employment intensity. This may be the reason why the finance minister was persuaded to deregulate the labour market. As the elasticities stand today, it is construction and trade and transport in which employment responds the most to income.

Trickle Down

In India there has been heated debate on the relevance of the trickle down theory. If one goes by the estimates of poverty for the year 1999/00 released recently by the Planning Commission there is some evidence to suggest from the cross-section data that the trickle down may be valid. In the absence of the latest figures of per capita NDP for states for the year 1999/00, we related the per capita state NDP of 17 states for the year 1998/99 to the estimated share of population below poverty line in 1999/00. The correlation coefficient of 0.412 was significant at 5 per cent and carried a negative sign as could be expected from the trickle down hypothesis. We also related changes in the number of unemployed males, to changes in per capita state NDP. The results are reported in Table 3.26. The correlation coefficient was -0.633 for the period 1983-1987/88, -0.416 for 1987/88-1993/94 and -0.207 for 1993/94-1999/00. The first was significant at 1 per cent, the second at 5 per cent and the third was not significant even at 10 per cent, though all the three carried the expected negative sign.

TABLE 3.26: **Correlation Coefficients between Per cent Change in Per Capita State NDP and Number of Unemployed Males by Usual Status**

Period	Correlation Coefficient
1983-1987/88	-0.633***
1987/88-1993/94	-0.416***
1993/94-1999/00	-0.207

Note: *** shows that the coefficient was significant at 1 per cent.

Labour Flexibility and Exit Policy

Since the case for deregulation of the labour market is based on organised sector employment growing slower than GDP, population, workforce and labour force, especially in the 1980s and the 1990s, we have given their rates of growth in four sub-periods spanning 1977/78 to 1999/2000 (in Table 3.27). The table shows that total employment in the organised sector grew slower than output in each sub-period and the gap widened in the 1990s. Both public and private organised sector grew slower than output. While the public sector decelerated continuously, the private sector accelerated in the last two sub-periods. Organised sector employment grew slower than population, workforce (usual status principal and subsidiary workers taken together) and labour force. This shows that either unorganised sector or unemployment, probably both may have increased. Data

TABLE 3.27: **Rates of Growth in Output (GDP), Organised Sector Employment,Workforce, Labour Force and Unemployment, 1977/78 - 1999/00**

Year	GDP at 1993/94 Prices	Population	Organised Sector Employment		
			Total	Public	Private
1977/78-1983	3.8	2.0	2.0	2.6	0.6
1983-1987/88	4.1	2.1	1.1	1.5	0.1
1987/88-1993/94	5.6	2.0	1.0	1.0	1.2
1993/94-1999/00	6.5	1.9	0.7	0.1	2.2

Year	Workforce P+S	Labour Force P+S	Workforce P	Labour Force P	Unemloyment	
					Live Register	Estimated from NSSO Data
1977/78-1983	2.1	2.0	1.8	1.8	10.3	-11.8
1983-1987/88	1.8	2.0	1.7	2.2	6.1	9.1
1987/88-1993/94	2.1	2.2	2.2	2.2	3.3	-2.7
1993/94-1999/00	0.8	0.9	1.5	1.3	1.9	1.2

from employment exchanges shows unemployment growing faster than total organised sector labour force and workforce, calculated with and without subsidiary workers. The growth of unemployment derived from the NSSO shows wide fluctuations. However, so far as deregulation is concerned the evidence of the late 1980s and the 1990s shows private sector organised employment picking up and running ahead of workforce and labour force defined broadly.

The income elasticity of employment with respect to output in manufacturing declined from 1.14 in 1973-78 to 0.53 in 1978-83, 0.42 in 1983-88 and 0.33 in 1988-94. The organised manufacturing sector reported by the Annual Survey of Industries (ASI) increased slower than output but faster than the demographic variables in the 1990s. Manufacturing employment grew at 3.2 per cent per annum compound between 1991/92 and 1997/98 compared to 1.5 per cent per annum between 1985/86 and 1991/92(Sharma, 2000). Though the comparison raises some doubts regarding the role of rigidities the study of Fallon and Lucas (1991) has provided the strongest justification for deregulation. It estimates that the amendment in 1976 of the exit clause of the Industrial Disputes Act of 1947, which prohibited the employers of 300 or more workers instead of 500 and more earlier, to retrench or close down without permission three months in advance of the closure or retrenchment reduced the demand for labour by 17.5 per cent. Lowering of the employment limit from 300 to 100 workers by the amendment of 1984 is likely to have reduced the potential employment more drastically. The wage increases and the amendments have allegedly increased the real cost of employing workers to employers. The real costs consist of pecuniary costs and psychological costs. The former would include the cost of excessive wage increases, strikes and deterioration of work ethic engendered by excessive employment. Should this happen unit labour costs would increase. There is no evidence to show that they have. On the contrary, there is plenty to show that they might have declined. Labour productivity in the manufacturing sector of the ASI has increased ahead of real wages. Papola (1994) reports high correlation between productivity and real wages at two-digit industry level during 1970/71-1987/88. This implies a decline in unit labour cost. But the capital intensity with respect to labour did increase. It would be wrong to argue that an employer would increase capital per worker only if unit wage cost increased. The fear that he would not be allowed to retrench the worker in the future could drive him to substitute capital for labour and justify deregulation. Besides, the high correlation between productivity and wages suggests that productivity gains were appropriated by the workers at the source. This would go against competitive hypothesis and thereby support the demand for deregulation.

The studies based on industry data show the net change which is a consequence of increase and decrease in employment by a large number of employers, each one of whom may be reacting not only to the changes in law or union behaviour. Hence, the proper unit of study should be individual employers. Many factors affect employment. They could be broadly classified as those relating to product market, factor market, the nature of industry, the size of employment, the state where the unit is located, presence of unions, and choice of technology, to mention a few. In a recent study, based on 1300 firms belonging to nine industries in 10 states and eight size groups of employment, Deshpande and Sharma tried to identify the determinants of levels and change in employment between 1991 and 1998, extent of labour flexibility, impact of unions and legislation and regional location (Deshpande et al., 2001).

Impact of Unions and Collective Bargaining

A union is both an economic and a political institution. Its impact depends on many things such as its quantitative and qualitative strength and its leadership. Our survey revealed that only 28 per cent of the firms reported presence of unions and of them 30 per cent had more than one union. Larger firms are more unionised than smaller ones; one in every 10 of the small firms employing 10-19 workers, but nine of every 10 firms employing 1000 or more workers were unionised. Hence, though unions may not be plentiful enough to influence the manufacturing sector as a whole, they may have a substantial impact on large firms..

Our sample showed that both unionised and non-unionised

firms increased capital per worker. Hence, unions could not be blamed for forcing employers to adopt capital intensive technology. Union absence appears to be slightly more conducive to growth of employment than union presence. Union presence is likely to be a deterrent to the growth of employment in so far as proportionately more unionised than non-unionised firms have reduced their employment. Firms located in Delhi and Uttar Pradesh(11 per cent) were less likely to be unionised whereas those located in West Bengal(59 per cent) and Kerala(56 per cent) were more likely to report a union.

Holding other factors constant, firms with unions paid the unskilled and skilled workers about 17 per cent more than those without unions. Older firms paid higher wage than the new firms. The greater the share of women in employment, the lower was the wage paid both to the unskilled and skilled male worker but higher the share of contract workers, higher was the wage paid to the skilled worker. Controlling for other factors, size did not affect the wage levels significantly. Firms situated in Maharashtra paid 20 per cent higher wages to the unskilled and those situated in West Bengal paid 28 per cent less to the unskilled and 39 per cent less to the skilled male worker than those situated in Andhra Pradesh. Generally unions raised the wages of the unskilled more than those of the skilled and thereby narrowed wage differentials based on skill. The differentials were narrower in Kerala and West Bengal, the two states ruled by communists and also in Gujarat where the wages of the unskilled may have been pulled up by the growing demand for labour. Taking all the evidence of what unions do and their limited presence in manufacturing it seems unlikely that they are capable of influencing allocation of resources effectively.

Impact of State Regulation

The state in India has a pervasive influence on employment, wages and conditions of work in the organised manufacturing sector. Close to half of the firms reported that their basic wage was determined by minimum wage law. The importance of minimum wage law declines as union presence increases by industry and size of employment. Minimum wage law is the most important determinant of wages in the beverages and tobacco industry (NIC 22) which is least unionised. Nearly two-thirds of the firms employing less than 10 workers relied on minimum wage law for determining their basic wage, while of the firms employing 1000 or more workers only 17 per cent did so. Payment of bonus is determined entirely by the Payment of Bonus Act.

We treated size of employment as a proxy for the role of the state. All labour laws apply to firms which employ 100 workers or more. This is particularly true of the provisions relating to retrenchment and closure. We found that firms employing less than 100 workers increased their employment faster than those employing 100 workers or more. Holding all other factors constant, the advantage of the small firms appears to be marginal as far as total employment is concerned and disappears altogether in the case of manual employment.

Labour Process Flexibility

In the developed countries industrialisation was associated with greater security of employment and income. Critics of liberalisation and globalisation forecast dualistic labour markets coming into existence everywhere. Indian labour markets have been dualistic and the new economic policy, according to the critics, is likely to widen this dualism. We found that over the seven years of liberalisation dualism did increase. The share of permanent manual workers declined from close to 68 per cent in 1991 to 64 per cent in 1998. It increased sharply in non-metallic minerals (NIC 32) and beverages and tobacco (NIC 22) categories. Not only did the share of non-permanent workers increase but the share of the casual in non-permanent increased even faster. It is the big firms that resorted to the greater use of non-permanent workers. Holding all other factors constant, firms employing 50-99 workers and those employing 500 or more workers increased the share of non-permanent workers significantly between 1991 and 1998. Also, firms employing 500 workers or more increased the share of temporary workers. Casual employment did not show an association with size of employment, nor did bigger firms take to casualisation of their workforce between 1991 and 1998. A large share of the firm's employment was non-regular, comprising 33 per cent non-permanent and eight per cent contract. All larger employers used significantly smaller shares of contract labour. Women workers were mostly employed in large firms. Firms employing 1000 workers or more accounted for more than 75 per cent of all women workers. Firms, which employ a higher share of non-permanent, also employ a higher share of women. Firms employing 50-99 workers and 500 and over reported an increase in the share of female workers.

Impact of Ideology and Administrative Efficiency

We expected firms located in Kerala and West Bengal to grow slower between 1991 and 1998. Left ideology of the governments and their support to unions would raise the real cost of employment to the employers situated in these states higher than to those located in other states. We found that total employment increased faster in Kerala but much slower in West Bengal; the finding with regard to Kerala was statistically significant whereas that with respect to West Bengal was not. Changes in production process workers did not show statistically significant relationship with location.

In relation to Andhra Pradesh, the excluded dummy in our regression analysis, employers in most other states employed a lower share of non-permanent in total employment and also in manual employment. However, the relationship between location and share of non-permanent was not significant in the case of manual workers. It was significant in the case of total employment in Kerala, Madhya Pradesh, Maharashtra and West Bengal. Firms located in Madhya Pradesh, Maharashtra, Tamil Nadu, Uttar Pradesh and West Bengal employed a smaller share of casual workers in total and manual employment. Again, the relationship was significant only in case of total employment. Of these only West Bengal was ruled by the Left. Contract labour was negatively associated with five of the eight states, as expected. These five include Kerala and West Bengal, but the presence of others, viz., Uttar Pradesh, Tamil Nadu and Maharashtra suggests that ideology may not be the only discouragement for the use of contract labour. The share of female labour in 1998 was significantly higher only in Kerala. Even West Bengal showed a lower share of women than Andhra Pradesh. Again, Madhya Pradesh, Maharashtra and West Bengal reduced the share of women in manual employment significantly. Thus on the evidence given by the employers themselves, the state regulation, be it the MWL or the Bonus Act, the employment of flexible categories such as contract labour does not appear to have failed as widely as it is claimed to have done by its critics.

Implications for Policy

Since the jobless growth of the 1980s, and particularly since the change in the economic policy in 1991, the lack of deregulation of the labour market has come in for much criticism. It relates primarily to the restrictions on exit, which allegedly have reduced the freedom of the employers to close down or retrench workers. Our survey shows that:

1. Employment in the factory sector of manufacturing has increased ahead of population.
2. The share of employers covered by the exit ban reporting decrease in employment is not only higher than that of the employers not restrained by the 1984 amendment but it increases with the size of the firm. In other words, a larger proportion of bigger rather than smaller firms have been able to reduce employment. The number of firms that have closed down is not known but the general impression is that it has increased.

The two facts show that employers can and do increase or decrease employment though perhaps not as much as they want. These two considerations weaken the case for total removal of the exit clause. Some participants in the debate have suggested that firms employing less than 300 or 500 workers should be allowed to exit without having to obtain prior permission. Thirty per cent of the workers in manufacturing are employed in firms employing less than

100 workers and 62 per cent are employed in firms employing less than 500 workers apiece. This could be a better alternative to scrapping the provision totally in one sweep, particularly when growth of manufacturing has decelerated sharply.

We found that employers who increased employment resorted to employing flexible categories of workers such as temporary, casual, contract and women. Even if the exit clause were rolled back employment of non-regular categories is likely to increase, thereby increasing the dualism in the labour market. One has then to increase employment fast enough to reduce unemployment close to its natural rate so as to put pressure on the unskilled wage to increase and narrow the wage differentials based on skill, gender and region. Since the market based development strategy precludes the state from adopting the Keynesian strategy to increase employment, the burden of producing full employment would devolve entirely on the private sector. The flows of FDI would have to increase manifold. It is doubtful if private investors, native as well as foreign, were deterred exclusively by the exit clause. Hence the resolve to raise the limit inviting its application from 100 to 1000 announced by the Finance Minister in his recent budget runs the risk of backlash on the reform process itself.

Summary and Conclusions

The World Bank's market based development strategy aims at maximising growth by achieving macro-economic stability, integration with the world economy and by helping the markets to work more efficiently. It argues that such a policy would raise the demand for labour to near-full employment levels without producing inflation. If workers caught in the declining industries and depressed regions were hit by globalisation the Bank recommends that the state should provide security of income through public works.

The Bank points out in justification of this policy that the informal sector would gain by growth of employment and improvement in the infrastructure of transport, public health, drinking water, sanitation and education. For the formal sector, the Bank advises encouragement of unions and collective bargaining at the plant level, and establishment of norms and rules for conducting labour management relations, basic health and safety regulations, and abolition of child labour and discrimination. In short, the policy should enhance mobility, reduce income insecurity and equip workers for change.

One should not equate the Bank's market-based development strategy with Walras' general equilibrium approach. It is close to the hypothesis of "workable competition". The Bank seeks empirical justification for its policy in the experience of South and East Asia. This justification is unwarranted and irrelevant.

The market based strategy is consistent with most schools of liberal political philosophy except that of social democrats led by Rawls. Whereas Rawls would minimise the difference in the freedoms available to the least advantaged citizen and the others on the average, Sen would widen the scope of freedoms to include capabilities and functionings. Standing has applied the Rawls-Sen definition of good society to the labour market. According to him, a good society and a good labour market are those that reduce the insecurity faced by the least insecure individual and the society on the average. Standing (1999) regards his strategy to be one which would meet with approval from egalitarians as well as libertarians. This is unlikely. The Bank would go along with the proposal in so far as assuring income security through public works programme to the able-bodied willing to work was concerned. It would accept the need to levy progressive income tax to redistribute income but we are not sure the Bank would support Standing completely on the citizenship income. The income transfers required to implement his proposal may turn out to be too high to be compatible with the enhanced mobility of capital. Compared to Standing's proposal the policies recommended by the Bank are moderate and, if implemented, would not have strained the state's capacity and willingness to tax too much. Nor would they have scared away foreign investors. The labour market could have been deregulated when the going was good. Instead, deregulation is being proposed at a time when industry is in recession and the prospects for exports are not bright.

India's "entigerment" has occurred at a snail's pace in a decade marred by much national and international political and economic turmoil. This does not mean that liberalisation has been all in vain. If the Indian statistical systems could be trusted for the direction rather than the magnitudes of change they reveal, one could conclude that the improvement in growth has been accompanied by a decrease in poverty ratio, numbers unemployed and child labour. The slow pace has not affected the labour market outcomes and processes much. The structure of work participation and unemployment rates has remained impervious to liberalisation and globalisation in the past decade.

Students of development economics have always followed closely the changes in the structure of income and employment in the process of development. Since liberalisation apprehensions have been expressed regarding the pace of change away from the primary sector (Bhalla, 1996). The fears were based on the data from the thin rounds of the NSSO, available in the early 1990s. The data from the large sample of the 50th Round of the NSSO (1993/94) confirmed them. The movement away from primary quickened as never before since 1993/94. Unlike in the 1980s, it is the tertiary sector, not the secondary sector, that has gained from the decline of the primary sector. This is true much more in urban than rural India. The analysis of labour absorption by industry show that labour has moved out of low productive agriculture to high productive services and manufacturing, raising the incomes in the former and reducing them in the latter. India has moved away from the classical model of structural change and appears to be following the East Asian model.

Note on Estimation of Population and Workforce in 1993/94 and 1999/00

To study the process of labour absorption by sector and industry in absolute terms in the four inter-round periods: 1977/78-1983, 1983-1987/88, 1987/88-1993/94 and 1993/94-1999/00, we needed estimates of population and workforce in the respective year of the survey rounds. Visaria (1996) had estimated population and workforce by sex and their rural-urban residence for all NSSO Survey rounds starting from 1972/73 up to 1993/94. However, the population for 1993/94 was estimated by extrapolating the rate of growth of population that prevailed in the 1980s. The rate of growth of population used for this estimation of 2.1 per cent per annum compound, was higher than 1.9 per cent per annum compound, used by the Registrar General (1996) for population projections 1996-2016. The census count of 1027million for 2001, released recently by the Registrar General Office was higher than the projected population by barely 1.45 per cent. India's population grew at 1.9 per cent per annum compound over the 1990s, and not at 2.1 per cent assumed by Visaria in his estimates. We have therefore accepted Visaria's estimates of population and workforce for the three years namely 1977/78, 1983 and 1987/88 but rejected those made by him for the year 1993/94.

We estimated the population and workforce, by sex and rural-urban residence, in 1993/94 and 1999/00 in the light of the 2001 Census data by sex as follows:

1. We first derived the compound rates of growth of population for males and females separately and estimated population by sex in each inter-censal year.
2. The estimates of population by sex for 1993/94 and 1999/00 for the country as a whole were arrived at by averaging the respective population in the years 1993 and 1994 and 1999 and 2000.
3. We needed to distribute this total population by sex by their rural urban residence. Census data on distribution of population by their rural-urban residence are yet to be published. But in addition to total population, the Registrar General provides projections of urban population. By using the shares of urban population given by the Registrar General's projections of urban population, we first estimated the urban population by sex in the two survey years. The difference between the total and the urban population by sex gave us the estimates of rural population for each sex.
   By applying the WPRs reported by the NSSO for their 50th Survey Round (1993/94) and 55th Survey Round (1999/00) separately to the estimated population of rural males, rural females, urban males and urban females, we estimated the

workforce by sex and rural-urban residence in 1993/94 and 1999/00 . The workforce by sex so estimated was added to get estimates of total rural and urban workforce and the two together gave us the workforce for the country in the two years.

REFERENCES

Banuri, Tariq and Edward J. Amdeo (1991), "Worlds within the Third World: Labour Market Institutions in Asia and Latin America" in Tariq Banuri (ed.) *Economic Liberalization: No Panacea,* WIDER Studies in Development Economics, Clarendon Press, Oxford.

Bellamy, Richard (1993), "Liberalism" in Roger Eatwell and Antony Wright (eds.) *Contemporary Political Ideologies,* Pinter Publishers, London.

Bhalla, Sheila (1996), 'Workforce Restructuring, Wages and Want: Recent Events, Interpretations and Analysis" in *The Indian Journal of Labour Economics,* Volume 39, Number 1, January-March.

Deshpande, L. K. (2001), *Labour Flexibility in India,* Fourth V. V. Giri Memorial Lecture, V.V. Giri Institute of Development Studies, Lucknow, February 26.

Deshpande, Sudha (1996), "Changing Structure of Employment in India, 1981-1991" in *The Indian Journal of Labour Economics,* Volume 39, Number 4, October-December.

—— and L.K. Deshpande (1985), "Census of India 1981 and The Structure of Employment" in *Economic and Political Weekly,* Vol. XX, No. 2, June 1.

Deshpande L. K.; Alakh N. Sharma; Anup Karan and Sandip Sarkar (2001), *Economic Liberalisation and Labour Market Flexibility in India.*

Fallon. P. and R. Lucas (1991), "Impact of Changes in Job Security Regulations in India and Zimbabwe" in *World Bank Economic Review,* Vol. 5, No. 3.

Fine, Ben (1998), *Labour Market Theory: A Constructive Reassessment,* Routledge, London.

Freeman, Richard (1993), "Labour Market Institutions and Policies: Help or Hindrance to Economic Development?" *Proceedings of the World Bank Annual Conference on Development Economics, 1992.* Washington DC.

Government of India (1970), *Report of the Expert Committee on Unemployment Estimates (Chairman: Prof. M. L. Dantwala),* Planning Commission, New Delhi.

—— (2000), *Report of The Study Group on Labour Statistics* (Chairman: Prof. L.K. Deshpande), Ministry of Labour, New Delhi.

Hahn, Frank (1991), "The Welfare Economics of Market Economies" in David Vines and Andrew A. Stevenson (eds.) *Information, Strategy and Public Policy,* Basil Blackwell Inc., Oxford.

International Institute for Population Sciences (IIPS) (2000), *India: National Family Health Survey (NFHS-2) 1998-99,* Mumbai.

International Labour Office (1998), *World Employment Report,* ILO, Geneva. Lee, Eddy (1996), "Globalisation and Employment: Is Anxiety Justified?" in *International Labour Review,* Volume 135, Number 5.

Mazumdar, Dipak (2000), "Introduction" in the Special Issue on East Asian Labour Markets: Long-term Trends and Impact of the Crisis, in *The Indian Journal of Labour Economics,* Volume 43, Number 3, July-September.

NSSO, Key Results of the Quinqunnial Employment Unemployment Survey Rounds: the 32nd Round (1977-78), the 38th Round (1983), the 43rd Round (1987-88), the 50th (1993-94) and the 55th Round (1999-2000).

Papola, T. S. (1994), "Structural Adjustment, Labour Market Flexibility and Employment" in *The Indian Journal of Labour Economics,* Volume 37, Number 1, January-March.

Polanyi, Karl (1944), *The Great Transformation,* Beacon Press, Beacon Hill, Boston, USA.

Registrar General and Census Commissioner (1996), *Population Projections For India and States 1996-2016,* Government of India, Ministry of Home Affairs, New Delhi.

Shah, Shekhar and Subodh C. Mathur (1992), "Sources of Labour Market Flexibility in East Asia: A Review of Selected Issues", Background Paper for World Bank cited in *The East Asian Miracle,* Washington, D.C.

Sharma, Alakh N. (2000), "Employment Generation Policy in India and Social Safety Needs", Working Paper, Institute for Human Development, New Delhi.

Solow, Robert (1990), *Labour Market as a Social Institution,* Basil Blackwell Ltd. London.

Standing, Guy (1999), *Global Labour Flexibility Seeking Distributive Justice,* MacMillan Press Ltd., London.

Stiglitz, Joseph E. (1991), "The Invisible Hand and Modern Welfare Economics" in David Vines and Andrew A. Stevenson (eds.)

Toye, John. (1995), *Information, Strategy and Public Policy,* Basil Blackwell Inc., Oxford, *Structural Adjustment and Employment Policy: Issues and Experience,* ILO, Geneva.

Visaria, Praveen (1996), "Structure of Indian Workforce, 1961-1994" in *The Indian Journal of Labour Economics,* Volume 39, Number 4, October-December.

Whitely, Richard (1999), *Divergent Capitalisms: The Social Structuring and Change of Business Systems,* Oxford University Press, New York.

World Bank (1993), *The East Asian Miracle Economic Growth and Public Policy,* A World Bank Policy Research Report, Published for the World Bank, Oxford University Press, New York.

—— (1995), *Workers in an Integrating World Development Report,* Published for the World Bank, Oxford University Press, New York.

4

ECONOMIC REFORMS, EMPLOYMENT AND POVERTY

S. MAHENDRA DEV

Introduction

The economic reforms in India were initiated in mid-1991 in response to the economic crisis and to improve the economic situation. There has been a debate whether the reform measures have adverse effects on poverty and employment. According to some researchers, reforms would benefit the poor in the medium and long run, although they may have adverse effect in the short run (Bhagwati and Srinivasan 1993; Tendulkar 1998; Joshi and Little1997). Some others argue that the reform package has internal contradictions and it might have an adverse effect on the poor in both the short and long runs (Nayyar 1993; Ghosh 1995; Bhaduri 1996).

The pro-reformers argue that reforms would increase efficiency and lead to higher growth and in turn reduce poverty. It is also argued that one has to look at the counterfactual situation while analysing the impact of reforms. According to them, the strategy of the 1980s (public expenditure led growth) is not sustainable and there is no alternative to reforms. They also argue that intensification of reforms (second generation) is needed to have a significant impact on growth and on the poor. On the other hand, anti-reformers argue that economic reforms would adversely affect the poor and one can have an alternative strategy to the economic policies which are being followed in the country.

The objective of the present paper is to put together the evidence on employment and poverty in the pre-reform and post-reform periods. Generally, 'before and after' approaches are used for analysing the impact of economic reforms. The limitations of this approach are well known. One has to keep in mind that the observed employment/unemployment and poverty situation is caused by reform related policies as well as long term structural factors. They are also influenced by exogenous factors like the weather and other external factors.

The paper is organised as follows: Section two provides trends in employment while section three deals with trends in poverty. Section four examines policy issues. The last section provides the conclusions.

Trends in Employment, Unemployment and Wages

Here, we examine trends in employment, unemployment and wages in the pre- and post-reform periods. These are mostly based on National Sample Survey data on Employment and Unemployment for various surveys. Some aggregate results for the year 1999/2000 (55th round) were released recently which have been used in this study.

There has been a debate on the employment trends in the country in the post-reform period. Using the data from the earlier NSS rounds, Gupta (1999) says that there has been jobless growth in the 1990s. The National Sample Survey Organisation (NSSO) has recently released the findings of its 55th survey round on employment trends in the country. The survey pertains to the period July 1999 to June 2000 and since it is based on a large sample, the results can be compared with the earlier large sample round, namely, the 50th round, which pertained to the July 1993 to June 1994 period. In this section, we examine the trends in employment up to 1999/2000.

Decline in Labour Force Participation Rates

It is seen from Table 4.1 that compared to the rates in 1993/94, among rural males, the labour force participation rates (LFPR) declined in 1999/2000 for all categories except urban males. However, one has to see LFPR by age groups. Table 4.2 shows that LFPR declined in the younger age groups as well as for those aged 50 years and above during 1999/2000. It has remained the same for age groups 25 to 49 years. In the case of rural females, however, the LFPR declined for all age groups. The patterns in urban areas are similar to those for rural areas. Thus, the labour force population proportion seems to have declined in the 1990s.

TABLE 4.1: **Labour Force (per 1000 persons)**

	Usual Status – All		Usual Status—Principal	
	1993-94	1999-00	1993-94	1999-00
Rural male	561	540	549	533
Rural female	331	302	237	235
Urban male	542	542	537	539
Urban female	164	147	132	126
Overall	428	406	384	376

Source: NSSO (2000), *Employment and Unemployment in India: 1999-2000: Key Results*, NSS 55th Round, December, 2000.

TABLE 4.2: **Age-specific Usual Status Labour Force Paricipation Rates in NSS 50th and 55th Rounds (All India)**

Age Group	Rural Male		Rural Female		Urban Male		Urban Female	
	50th	55th	50th	55th	50th	55th	50th	55th
1	2	3	4	5	6	7	8	9
5-9	11	7	14	7	4	3	4	2
10-14	139	93	142	96	71	52	47	37
15-19	598	532	371	314	404	366	142	121
20-24	902	889	470	524	772	755	230	191
25-29	980	975	528	498	958	951	248	214
30-34	988	987	587	557	983	980	283	245

(contd.)

TABLE 4.2 *(contd.)*

1	2	3	4	5	6	7	8	9
35-39	992	986	610	579	990	986	304	289
40-44	989	984	607	586	984	980	320	285
45-49	984	980	594	566	976	974	317	269
50-54	970	953	543	515	945	939	287	264
55-59	941	930	468	450	856	811	225	208
60+	699	640	241	218	443	402	114	94
All	561	540	331	302	542	542	164	147

Note: 'all' includes n.r. cases of age.

Source: Same as for Table 4.1.

Subsidiary status labour reflects the category of those persons, who are not available for work for most period of the year, but make themselves available for some period – in non-technical terms, it is the category of occasionally working people. The Table 4.2 shows that it is this particular category, which has actually shrunk in size between 1993/1999.

The fall in subsidiary status labour is particularly marked among rural females. Such an outcome is possible in two scenarios. First, if the male members are earning well, then females may be less inclined to work. The second possibility is that if the male members are not finding higher remunerative non-farm employment opportunities, then they remain on the farm, making it less necessary for the females to turn up for work. But as we see later, rural non-farm jobs have risen at a much higher rate than farm jobs. So, the first explanation is more possible.

Work Participation Rates

The work participation rates given in Table 4.3 show that the employed per 1000 persons declined for all categories in 1999/2000 as compared to 1993/94. This is true for current weekly status (CWS) as well as current daily status (CDS) (Table 4.4).

TABLE 4.3: **Number of Persons Employed per 1000 Persons according to Usual Status (ps+ss) During 1972-73 to 1999-2000 in Different NSS Rounds (All-India)**

	Employed (all workers)					
Round (year)	Male	Female	Person	Male	Female	Person
55 (1999-00)	531	299	417	518	139	337
50 (1993-94)	553	328	444	520	154	347
43 (1987-88)	539	323	434	506	152	337
38 (1983)	547	340	445	512	151	340
32 (1977-78)	552	331	444	508	156	341
27 (1972-73)	545	318	*	501	134	*

Note : * denotes proportions not derived in NSS 27th round.
Source: Same as for Table 4.1.

TABLE 4.4: **Number of Persons Employed per 1000 Persons according to Current Weekly Status and Current Daily Status during 1972-73 to 1999-2000 in Different NSS Rounds (All-India)**

	CWS Employed				CDS Employed			
	Rural		Urban		Rural		Urban	
Round (year)	Male	Female	Male	Female	Male	Female	Male	Female
55 (1999-00)	510	253	509	128	478	204	490	111
50 (1993-94)	530	267	511	139	504	220	498	120
43 (1987-88)	504	220	492	119	501	207	477	110
38 (1983)	511	227	492	118	482	198	473	106
32 (1977-78)	519	232	490	125	488	194	472	109
27 (1972-73)	530	277	491	123	503	231	477	108

Source: Same as for Table 4.1.

Employment Growth

According to some estimates, rural employment growth declined from 2.03 per cent in 1987/88 to 1993/94 to 0.67 per cent per annum during 1993/94 to 1999/2000 (Table 4.5). Similarly, growth of urban employment declined from 3.39 per cent to 1.34 per cent during the same period.

TABLE 4.5: **Employment Growth in the Last Two Decades**

Period	Rural	Urban
1983 to 1987-88	1.36	2.77
1987-88 to 1993-94	2.03	3.39
1993-94 to 1999-2000	0.67	1.34

Source: C.P. Chandrasekhar and Jayati Ghosh (2001), "Disturbing Employment Trends", *Business Line*, January 23, 2001.

Organised Employment and Its Growth

It is important to distinguish between organised sector employment and other employment. The preference for organised sector employment reflects the fact that these jobs typically provide much higher incomes to wage earners than the unorganised or informal sector and also provide much greater job security and other benefits. Organised sector employment, however, is small and job potential is limited.

The available information on the share of the organised sector in the total employment generated in each sector of the economy is summarised in Table 4.6. It shows that organised sector employment is only 28.25 million, or about seven per cent of the total employment of over 374 million in the economy. Furthermore, as much as 19.56 million, or almost 70 per cent of total organised sector employment is in the public sector.

The share of organised sector employment in total employment varies from sector to sector. It is almost miniscule in agriculture and as much as 65 per cent in a highly capital intensive sector such as electricity. However, it is interesting to note that the share of the organised sector in the total employment generated is quite low in most sectors indicating the preponderance of the unorganised sector.

For example, in the manufacturing sector it is as low as 16 per cent. In other words, as much as 84 per cent of the employment generated is in the unorganised sector, which consists of the tiny sector, handlooms and power looms and other village industries and the smaller SSI units.

TABLE 4.6: **Organised Sector Jobs in Employment by Industry: 1997**

Industry	Employment (million)	% in Organised Sector	Total Organised Sector
Agriculture	240.17	1.44	0.6
Mining & quarrying	2.89	1.07	37.3
Manufacturing	43.9	6.90	15.8
Electricity	1.55	1.00	64.9
Construction	14.85	1.18	8.0
Wholesale & retail trade	35.05	0.48	1.4
Transport, storage & communication	12.05	3.15	26.3
Financial services	4.59	1.61	35.4
Community, social & personal services	39.28	11.42	29.3
All sectors	394.33	28.25	7.2

Sources: 1. DGE&T for employment in organised sector.
2. Total employment as projected on the basis of trends.

Not only is organised sector employment a relatively small percentage of the total, the growth of this type of employment has also decelerated in the 1990s (Table 4.7). Organised sector employment had grown at 1.59 per cent per annum during 1980 to 1990, but it decelerated to 0.86 per cent between 1991 and 1997. It is interesting to note that the reason for this deceleration was the slowing down in employment creation by the public sector. Between 1980 and 1990 the growth of organised sector employment in the public sector was 2.22 per cent but it plummeted to 0.38 per cent in 1990-97. In contrast, the growth in the private sector in the 1980s was only 0.16 per cent per annum but it accelerated sharply to 2.0

per cent in the 1990s. The faster growth in private sector employment did not offset the effect of the slow down in public sector employment in the organised sector because the private sector share of the employment in the organised sector was only one-third.

TABLE 4.7: **Total Employment and Organised Sector Employment**

	Employment (million)			Growth Rate (% per annum)	
Sector	1980	1990	1997	1980-90	1991-97
Total employment [a]	269.19	324.29	374.4	1.88	2.43
Organised sector employment [b]	22.31	26.34	28.25	1.59	0.86
Public sector [b]	15.08	18.76	19.56	2.22	0.38
Private sector [b]	7.23	7.58	8.69	0.16	2.00

Notes : 1.[a] UPSS basis as reported by NSSO surveys. The absolute figures are for the years 1978, 1988, and 1993-94.

2.[b] Number of employees reported by Employment Market Information System of Ministry of Labour.

3. The rate of growth of total employment are compound rates of growth of employment as revealed by NSSO surveys.

4. The organised sector employment growth rates are trend growth rates.

Some of these trends in employment in the organised sector are likely to continue at least over the next decade. It is well known that employment in the government sector is bloated and the severe financial constraints that both central and state governments are facing make it very difficult to envisage rapid growth of employment in these sectors. There is certainly need to expand employment in some areas within the state government sector, especially in education and health, but in order to finance expansion in these critical areas it will be necessary to make economies in other areas. The total volume of employment in the government sector is therefore not likely to increase rapidly in future.

Rapid growth in organised sector employment in future must therefore depend upon faster growth in organised sector employment provided by the private sector. In this context, the experience of the 1990s is reassuring because it does show faster growth in organised sector employment in the private sector. If this growth can be sustained, and hopefully accelerated in future, it will in due course lead to an increase in the relative size of the private sector which in turn will pull up the growth in total organised sector employment over a period of time.

In the next decade, therefore, we must recognise that the bulk of the growth in employment will have to come from the unorganised sector as defined and identified under present conditions. This points to the special importance of promoting self-employment in areas which can yield reasonable levels of income. It also points to the need to encourage the process of modernisation and structural change which can accelerate the transformation of presently unorganised sector activity into organised sector activity, providing better quality employment opportunities as fast as possible.

Casualisation of Labour

Even in the past rounds of the NSSO, a shift was seen in the type of employment towards casualisation. It has continued in the latest round also. Out of every 1000 persons employed in 1993/94, 316 were casual labourers (Table 4.8). This proportion has now gone up to 331. Interestingly, contrary to what we normally believe, the share of regular employees has also gone up from 131 to 140 per 1000. The fall is in the 'self employed' category. This category could include owner farmers and their family members and owners of small businesses. In 1999/2000, nearly 53 per cent of the workforce was self employed, compared to 55 per cent in 1993/94. The detailed break-up shows that this dip is mainly in the case of the rural workforce. It could be because of the shift of smaller farmers to other professions and/or some consolidation of farms.

Employment by Sector: Increase in the Share of Rural Non-Farm Employment

In rural areas, about 71 per cent of male workers and 65 per cent of

TABLE 4.8: **Type of Employment (per 1000 working persons)**

	1993-94			1999-00		
	Self-employed	Regular Employees	Casual Labour	Self-employed	Regular Employees	Casual Labour
Rural male	579	83	338	550	88	362
Rural female	585	28	387	573	31	396
Rural	581	63	356	558	68	374
Urban male	417	421	162	415	417	168
Urban female	454	286	162	453	333	214
Urban	425	392	162	422	400	177
Overall	549	131	316	529	140	331

female workers were employed in the primary sector (Table 4.9). The tertiary sector was a more important source of employment for rural males than for rural females. The secondary sector accounted for about 13 per cent of male employment and about 9 per cent of female employment in rural areas. Although the broad pattern in the structure of employment remained the same during the period 1983 to 1999/2000, it shows a decreasing trend in the share of employed in the primary sector. While the share of female workers employed in the tertiary sector remained virtually stagnant in the range of five per cent to six per cent during this entire period , the corresponding share for male workers increased from 12 per cent to 16 per cent. In the case of urban areas, the pattern of changes in the distribution remained broadly the same. However, the share of employment in the tertiary sector rose steadily during the period 1983 to 1999/2000 for both males and females. This rise was much higher for females.

Unemployment Rates

The unemployment rates (Table 4.10) show that compared to 1993/94, the unemployment rate for usual status has not shown significant changes in 1999/2000. In the case of current daily status (CDS), the unemployment rates increased in (except for urban females) 1999/2000 as compared to those for 1993/94.

TABLE 4.9: **Distribution of Usually Working by Broad Groups of Industry in Different NSS Rounds (per 1000) All India**

	Male						Female					
	Primary		Secondary		Secondary		Primary		Secondary		Secondary	
Round	PS	All	PS	All	PS	All	PS	All	PS	All	PS	All
						Rural						
55	712	714	127	126	161	160	841	854	93	89	66	57
50	737	741	113	112	149	147	847	862	91	83	63	56
43	739	745	123	121	138	134	825	847	112	100	63	53
38	772	775	102	100	123	122	862	875	78	74	57	48
						Urban						
55	65	66	329	328	606	606	146	177	293	293	561	529
50	87	90	331	330	581	579	193	247	295	291	510	463
43	85	91	343	340	572	569	218	294	324	317	458	389
38	97	103	344	342	551	550	255	310	307	306	430	376

TABLE 4.10: **Unemployment Rates from 1972-73 to 1999-2000 in Different NSS Rounds**

All India

	Unemployment Rate							
	Male				Female			
Round (year)	US	US (adj.)	CWS	CDS	US	US (adj.)	CWS	CDS
				Rural				
55 (1999-2000)	21	17	39	72	15	10	37	70
50 (1993-94)	20	14	31	56	13	9	29	56
43 (1987-88)	28	18	42	46	35	24	44	67
38 (1983)	21	14	37	75	14	7	43	90
32 (1977-78)	22	13	36	71	55	20	41	92
27 (1972-73)	-	12	30	68	-	5	55	112
				Urban				
55 (1999-2000)	48	45	56	73	71	57	73	94
50 (1993-94)	54	41	52	67	83	61	79	104
43 (1987-88)	61	52	66	88	85	62	92	120
38 (1983)	59	51	67	92	69	49	75	110
32 (1977-78)	65	54	71	94	178	124	109	145
27 (1972-73)	-	48	60	80	-	60	92	137

The problem with these estimates is that we do not know how well employed are the persons who are seen as employed. In other words, we do not know about the productivity and incomes of the employed.

Unemployment by Income or Expenditure Criterion (Poverty among Workers)

One way of looking at unemployment by income or expenditure criterion is to look at the poverty ratios among the employed. The large gap between unemployment rates by time criterion shows low earnings for many of the workers. Distribution of employed across expenditure classes shows (Table 4.11) that poverty among rural and urban workers has declined over time but it is still substantial. The proportion of poor among rural workers declined from 38 per cent in 1987/88 to 35 per cent in 1993/94. The rate of decline in the post-reform period was slower than that for earlier periods. Poverty among urban workers, however, declined faster than for rural workers in the post-reform period.

TABLE 4.11: **Poor among Employed**

Year	Percentage of Poor among Employed	
	Rural	Urban
1977-78	51.81	37.99
1983	45.25	39.69
1987-88	38.02	36.94
1993-94	35.25	30.61

Source: Planning Commission.

Quality of Employment

Security of employment can be used as a proxy for quality of employment. NSS provide employment data for three categories, as for example, self-employed, regular and casual. The NSS data show that the share of self-employed and regular wage workers has been declining and casualisation of labour has been increasing over time. The casualisation phenomenon got accentuated with economic liberalisation. Ghose (1999) has estimated the employment quality index (EQI) using NSS data for the period 1977/78 to 1993/94. The EQI given in Table 4.12 reveals that (a) quality of employment has been the highest in services and it has been lowest in agriculture; (b) the quality of employment deteriorated in the aggregate economy and in all the three sectors; (c) the deterioration has been slower in services; and (d) the deterioration has been higher for males as compared to females for the aggregate economy.

Another notable feature of the 1990s has been the decline in the rate of growth of rural non-farm employment. It is known that there was significant growth in rural non-farm employment in the late 1970s and 1980s (for more details see Mahendra Dev, 1999).

TABLE 4.12: **Employment Quality Index: 1977-78 to 1993-94**

	1977-78	1983	1987-88	1993-94
Males	0.737	0.731	0.725	0.717
Females	0.687	0.680	0.686	0.675
Aggregate economy	0.723	0.717	0.715	0.706
Agriculture	0.694	0.688	0.687	0.675
Industry	-	0.749	-	0.715
Services	-	0.791	-	0.782

Note: Employment Quality Index is constructed by applying weights to the types of employment (regular, self-employed, casual labour).

Source: Based on Ajit K. Ghose (1999), "The Question of Employment Security in India: A Note", Paper presented at the Conference on Social Security in India, New Delhi, April 15-17.

Changes in Real Wages, NSS Data: Real wages for casual workers over the period 1983 to 1993-94 are given in Table 4.13. Real wages have increased in the 1990s but the rate of growth during 1988-94 has been lower than that for earlier periods. The growth rate of real wages for the tertiary sector during 1987/88 to 1993/94 was the lowest among all the sectors.

The data on real wages for agricultural labourers also show that the growth rate was lower in the 1990s as compared to the 1980s (Economic Survey, 2000-2001).

To sum up, the trends in employment show: (a) employment growth declined in 1990s; (b) poverty among workers declined but the pace of reduction was slow in the 1990s; (c) rate of growth in rural non-farm employment declined in the post-reform period till 1993-94 but increased in 1999-200; (d) quality of employment deteriorated because of casualisation of labour; (e) real wages for casual labourers increased but there was slow growth in the 1990s.

TABLE 4.13: **Trends in Average Real Earnings Per Day of Rural Casual Labour (1983 to 1993-94) at 1993-94 Prices**

	Real Wages (in Rs.)			Compound Growth per Annum	
	1983	1987-88	1993-94	1983 to 1987-88	1987-88 to 1993-94
Casual labour in public works	16.62	20.17	22.38	4.40	1.75
Other casual labour					
(a) Primary sector	13.95	17.29	18.98	4.89	1.57
(b) Secondary sector	20.43	24.05	27.08	3.69	2.00
(3) Tertiary sector	14.82	19.07	20.21	5.76	0.97

Source: S. Mahendra Dev and Alakh N. Sharma (forthcoming), *Economic Reforms, Employment and Poverty*, Institute for Human Development, Delhi.

Trends in Poverty

The concept of poverty is two-dimensional (viz., income poverty and non-income poverty). It covers not only levels of income and consumption, but also health and education, vulnerability and risk; and marginalisation and exclusion of the poor from the mainstream of society.[1] The performance of India in terms of income and non-income indicators has not been satisfactory. This is not to to deny that progress has certainly been made in reduction in both income and non-income poverty.

Apart from official estimates, some researchers have estimated using different price indices. The studies by Datt (1999), Gupta (1999) and Sundaram and Tendulkar (2000) showed that rural poverty declined in the seventies and eighties. But, it has not shown a decline in the 1990s (Table 4.14). On the other hand urban poverty showed a decline in the 1990s.

Recent Trends up to 1999-2000: The estimates in Table 4.14 are only up to 1998. Based on consumer expenditure data from the NSS

TABLE 4.14: **Estimates of Poverty in India (Head Count Ratios)**

		Rural			Urban		
NSS Round	Year	Datt	Gupta	Tendul-kar Sunda-ram	Datt	Gupta	Tend-ulkar Sunda-ram
27	October 72-September 73	55.4	NA	57.2	45.7	NA	47.0
28	October 73-June 74	55.7	NA	56.2	48.0	NA	49.2
32	July 77-June 78	50.6	NA	54.5	40.5	NA	42.9
38	January-December 83	45.3	45.6	49.0	35.7	40.8	38.3
42	July 86-June 87	38.8	NA	45.2	34.3	NA	35.4
43	July 87-June 88	39.2	39.1	44.9	36.2	38.2	36.5
44	July 88-June 89	39.1	NA	42.2	36.6	NA	35.1
45	July 89-June90	34.3	33.7	36.7	33.4	36.0	34.8
46	July 90-June 91	36.4	35.0	37.5	32.8	35.3	35.0
47	July-December 91	37.4	NA	40.1	33.2	NA	34.8
48	January-December 92	43.5	41.7	46.1	33.7	37.8	36.4
49	January-June 93	NA	NA	44.2	NA	NA	38.9
50	July 93-June 94	36.7	37.3	39.7	30.5	32.4	30.9
51	July 94-June 95	41.0	38.0	43.6	33.5	34.2	34.1
52	July 95-June 96	37.2	38.3	40.1	28.0	30.0	28.7
53	January-December 97	35.8	38.5	38.3	30.0	33.9	31.0
54	January-June 98	NA	45.3	44.9	NA	34.6	NA

Source: Abhijit Sen (2000), "Estimates of Consumer Expenditure and Its Distribution: Statistical Priorities after NSS 55th Round", *Economic and Political Weekly*, Vol. 35, No. 51.

55th Round, the Planning Commission has recently released poverty ratios for the year 1999/2000. Table 4.15 provides official estimates from 1973/74 to 1999/2000. Based on the 30-day recall methodology, the NSSO data reveals that the poverty at the all India level was 26.1 per cent (over 26 crores of population) as against 36 per cent, as recorded by the 1993/94 NSS data. However, the poverty ratio in 1999/2000 was much higher than the target of 16 per cent set for the end of the Ninth Plan period. Rural poverty declined from 37.3 per cent to 27.1 per cent during this period while urban poverty declined from 32.4 per cent to 23.6 per cent.

TABLE 4.15: **Official Estimates of Poverty: 1973-74 to 1999-2000: All-India**

Year	Total	Rural	Urban
1973-74	54.9	56.4	49.0
1977-78	51.3	53.1	45.2
1983	44.5	45.7	40.8
1987-88	38.9	39.1	38.2
1993-94	36.0	37.3	32.4
1999-2000			
30-day recall	26.1	27.1	23.6
7-day recall	23.3	24.0	21.6

Source: Planning Commission.

Controversy on Recall Period for 55th Round: There is, however, controversy regarding the NSS 55th Round estimates. In all the earlier NSS rounds, the reference period has been uniform with respondents asked about their consumption during the 'past 30 days'. Since 1994/95 NSS has also been collecting data on food and some other items using reference period of a week. Visaria (2000) has given some alternative estimates for the period 1994/95 to 1998 based on the reference period of a week. The estimates show that poverty was 23.6 per cent and 20 per cent in rural and urban areas respectively. In the 55th round, however, it collected expenditure data on food, *paan*, tobacco and intoxicants for two different reference periods of one week and one month for the same households. For the remaining items, the data was collected only with a 365-day reference period. In the thin sample surveys of the 51st to 54th rounds, the NSSO had experimented with the recall period by dividing the entire sample into two halves and using a 30-day recall for one half. For the other half, it used a one-week recall period for food, *paan*, tobacco and intoxicants. In the earlier experimental rounds, the one-week recall had consistently shown about 30 per cent higher consumption of food, beverages, *paan*, tobacco and intoxicants than by the 30-day recall (see the poverty ratios in Table 4.16).

TABLE 4.16: **Poverty Estimates**

	Rural		Urban	
Round Year	Type 1	Type 2	Type 1	Type 2
51 Jul 94-Jun 95	41.2	22.8	35.5	18.3
52 Jul 95-Jun 96	37.6	19.1	29.9	15.2
53 Jan 97-Dec98	35.9	20.7	32.3	17.8
54 Jan 98-Jun 98	42.6	23.6	32.9	20.0

Note : Poverty Estimates are made from Type 1 and Type 2 Schedules of Rounds 51 to 54, and by the 30-day and 7-day Recalls in Sub-rounds 1 and 2 of the 55th Round.

Source: Pravin Visaria (2000b), "Polemics on Poverty", *Business Standard*, October 30, 2000. Quoted in A. Sen (2000) For the 55th round, the result from the 30 day recall for food is shown under Type 1, although this schedule in Rounds 51 to 54 did not use the 365 day recall, and is not strictly comparable. The results from the 7 day recall is under Type 2.

However, the 55th Round shows a difference of only about 5 to 6 per cent. Thus, either the presence of the one-week question has biased upward the one month estimates, or the presence of the one-month question has biased down the one-week replies or answers to both sets of questions have been influenced by the presence of each other. Thus, the 1999/2000 estimates of poverty are not fully comparable with the earlier estimates.

Differences between NSS (National Sample Survey) and NAS (National Accounts Statistics)

The poverty estimates based on NSS (official or independent) generally show that poverty has declined significantly in the 1980s but it has not declined (or the rate of decline is low) in the post-reform period. Some analysts argue that these trends based on NSS data are not correct because consumption, based on National Accounts Statistics (NAS), is showing different trends. There has been considerable discrepancy in the consumer expenditure data between these two estimates and the discrepancy has been growing. Owing to this, questions have been raised about the validity of the finding that poverty has not declined in the 1990s. NSS data has been blamed for this finding[2]. Using the National Accounts data with NSS distribution, Bhalla (2000) concludes that poverty in India in 1998 was around 12 per cent. Similarly, Lal et al. (2000) using the NCAER data show that poverty was less than estimates based on NSS.

It is true that NSS estimates are subject to sampling and non-sampling errors. The sample sizes and duration of rounds varied significantly over time. Another criticism of NSS data has been that it does not fully capture the consumption of the rich deciles. Though, absolute poverty estimates may not be affected by this limitation, inequalities in consumption distribution (gini coefficient) can be underestimates. Visaria indicates that with a reference period of a week, the rural households reported spending about 27 to 32 per cent on food items. These estimates seem to be closer to NAS based estimates. However, these estimates are based on thin samples and one has to wait for the quinquennial survey of 1999/2000 to confirm the closeness between NAS and NSS estimates based on reference of a week. Moreover, we do not have these estimates for the pre-reform period.

One can argue that in order to find out the discrepancy between NSS and NAS, one has to check the validity of both these sources instead of blaming only NSS. In fact, the Lakdawala Committee looked at this problem.[3] As the Committee report says, "the National Accounts Estimate of private consumption is derived as a residual by deducting from estimated production of the various goods and services (adjusted for foreign trade), the estimated use for capital formation and public consumption. Apart from the lack of reliable data on production for a sizeable segment of the economy, the adjustments for uses other than private consumption are based on scanty data, often of the distant past, and subjective judgements" (p.13). According to the sources and methods of National Accounts(1980) the consumption expenditure is derived "by commodity flow method from the total value of output, the expenditure incurred by industries as intermediate consumption and all final consumption (including exports & imports) other than those by households and non-profit institutions are deducted to obtain the estimates of private final consumption expenditure" (p.79).

In a recent paper, Ravallion (2000) of the World Bank says that given the way the private consumption component of the National Accounts is calculated in India (as elsewhere), one can not be confident in any claim that the data problem lies entirely with the NSS. Ravallion also indicates that the discrepancy between the private consumption component of the National Accounts and the survey-based mean consumption is found in other countries also. In the United States, for example, survey based consumption grew at the rate of 0.7 per cent per year over 1961-95, as compared to a 2.2 per cemt average growth rate for the National Accounts based private consumption over the same time.

Srinivasan (2000) also discusses the problems of National Accounts data on private consumption. First, the NAS based estimates refer to the private non-corporate sector that covers the current account of resident and non-resident households in the domestic market and non-profit making bodies serving households. Therefore, NAS consumption estimates would be higher than those of NSS. Secondly, serious measurement errors may arise in the application of the commodity flow method while deriving private consumption. According to Srinivasan, 'A fresh look at the issue is needed. But without such a reexamination, it will be hazardous to accept the recent trends in one or the other estimate as firmly established. However, one can not deny that using NSS data both for the distribution and its mean for all periods has the virtue of consistency' (p.8). Also, the differences in NAS and NSS are not increasing in the case of nominal consumption as shown in Table 4.17.[4]

Owing to the above reasons, one should not blame only the NSS for the reliability of data. Perhaps the National Statistical Commission headed by the Governor of Andhra Pradesh, Dr. Rangarajan should take a fresh look at the discrepancy in the consumption data between NSS and National Accounts.

Non-Income Indicators: Trends in Human Development

The performance of India in terms of human development has not

TABLE 4.17: **Ratio of NSS Nominal Consumption by Item to Corresponding Estimates from the NAS (1980-81 Base)**

Item	1977-78	1983	1987-88	1988-89	1989-90	1990-91	1992	1993-94	1994-95	1995-96	1997
Cereals	1.09	1.08	1.02	1.02	1.02	0.96	1.03	0.95	0.99	0.95	0.98
Pulses	1.09	1.12	1.29	1.17	1.24	1.23	1.30	1.17	1.27	1.41	1.50
Sugar	0.60	0.49	0.50	0.60	0.52	0.51	0.46	0.45	0.45	0.49	0.48
Edible oils	0.73	0.65	0.67	0.64	0.73	0.81	0.72	0.68	0.71	0.71	0.66
Fruits and vegetables	0.58	0.70	0.75	0.74	0.71	0.75	0.68	0.71	0.62	0.69	0.65
Milk and products	0.86	0.74	0.73	0.74	0.75	0.72	0.73	0.72	0.68	0.73	0.79
Meat, fish and eggs	0.96	0.77	0.68	0.71	0.67	0.64	0.60	0.51	0.48	0.49	0.48
Other food and beverages	1.22	1.34	1.59	1.56	1.54	1.49	1.57	1.46	1.28	1.16	1.03
Pan, tobacco etc.	0.51	0.52	0.62	0.63	0.60	0.58	0.52	0.51	0.45	0.38	0.35
Fuel and light	1.20	1.08	1.07	1.06	1.10	1.13	1.16	1.17	1.17	1.30	1.42
Clothing	0.61	0.63	0.46	0.50	0.44	0.34	0.43	0.36	0.43	0.49	0.47
Footwear	1.03	1.00	0.83	0.73	0.76	0.52	0.74	0.75	0.86	1.14	1.24
Other goods and services	0.62	0.52	0.53	0.49	0.49	0.47	0.50	0.53	0.52	0.56	0.56

Source: Same as for Table 4.14.

been satisfactory as compared to many of the developing countries. According to the UNDP's *Human Development Report 1994*, between 1960 and 1992, the Human Development Index (HDI) for India increased from 0.206 to 0.382 but, in 1999, the country ranked 132nd among 174 countries in the world. As shown in Table 4.18, the human development indicators for India are much lower than in East and South East Asian countries like China, Indonesia, Republic of Korea, Malaysia, Philippines and Thailand. The changes in human development indicators since Independence at the all India level have been as follows.

(a) Life expectancy at birth increased from 32 years in 1951 to 62 years in 1996 (Table 19). Control of famines and epidemics has had an important role in improving the longevity of Indians. But, this level is not very high compared to other countries. In 1951, the female life expectancy (31.7) was lower than that of males (32.4) but the gap has narrowed slowly and only recently has life expectancy for women (61.4) become higher than that for men (60.4).

(b) Literacy rate increased from 18.3 per cent in 1951 to 62 per cent in 1997. In other words, around 40 per cent of the Indian population are illiterate even after 50 years of independence (Table 4.7). Female literacy at 50 per cent in 1997 is much lower than that for men (73 per cent).

(c) Between 1951 and 1998, infant mortality declined from 146 per thousand to 72 per thousand. Infant mortality, though reduced to half during the last four and a half decades, is still higher than that of many a developing countries. During the same period the death rate declined from 27.4 to 9.0. The performance in terms of decline in birth rate has not been satisfactory. The birth rate has declined from 39.9 per cent in 1951 to only 26.4 in 1998.

Also, food and nutrition deficiencies in households are much larger than what one would conclude by looking at the income poverty estimates. A study concludes that energy, protein and micronutrient deficiencies continue upto and including the seventh decile.[5] It is, therefore, not surprising that more than half of India's children are moderately or severely undernourished, and 30 per cent of newborns are significantly underweight.

TABLE 4.18: **Indicators of Human Development for India and Some Asian Countries**

Country	Life Expectancy at Birth (years)	Infant Mortality Rate (per thousand births)	Adult Literacy Rate (per cent)
India	62.4	71	62
Kerala State (India)	72.0	12	93
Bangladesh	58.1	81	39
China	69.8	38	83
Indonesia	65.1	45	85
Korea, Republic	72.4	6	97
Malaysia	72.0	10	86
Pakistan	64.0	95	41
Philippines	68.3	32	95
Thailand	68.8	31	95

Source: Economic Survey, 1999-2000, Government of India.

TABLE 4.19: **Trends in Human Development Indicators**

Year	Life Expectancy at Birth (years)	Literacy Rate (per cent)	Birth Rate	Death Rate	Infant Mortality Rate
			Per Thousand		
1951	32.1	18.3	39.9	27.4	146
1961	41.3	28.3	41.7	22.8	146
1971	45.6	34.5	36.9	14.9	129
1981	50.4	43.6	33.9	12.5	110
1991	59.4	52.2	29.5	9.8	80
1996	62.4	NA	27.5	9.0	72
1997	NA	62	27.2	8.9	71
1998	NA	NA	26.4	9.0	72

Source: Same as for Table 4.18.

Regional Disparities in Poverty Trends

In a continental economy like India, it is more important to look at trends in poverty at a disaggregate level. Table 4.20 provides state level poverty estimates which are computed by broadly following the Expert Group Method (Datt, 1998). While estimating poverty ratios, adjustments were carried out to the Consumer Price Index Numbers for Agricultural Labourers by updating the nominal price of firewood. The estimates for 1987/88 and 1993/94 are based on 'large samples' while those for 1990/91 and 1992 are based on 'thin samples'. The poverty ratios show that as compared to 1990/91, rural poverty increased significantly in 1992 in all the states except West Bengal. On the other hand, urban poverty recorded increase in only seven states (Andhra Pradesh, Bihar, Karnataka, Orissa, Uttar Pradesh and West Bengal). Four states (Assam, Gujarat, Madhya Pradesh, Tamil Nadu) showed a decline in urban poverty during the same period.

TABLE 4.20: **Poverty Across States: Head Count Ratio 1987-88 to 1993-94**

States	1987/88 Jul-Jun	1990/91 Jul-June	1992 Jan-Dec	1993/94 Jul-Jun
1	2	3	4	5
		Rural		
Andhra Pradesh	34.02	36.90	41.85	28.93
Assam	43.01	42.40	56.61	48.99
Bihar	58.57	58.29	67.81	63.51
Gujarat	42.93	43.13	46.78	35.35
Karnataka	43.49	42.73	56.94	40.97
Kerala	34.67	33.80	34.15	31.07
Madhya Pradesh	47.80	47.93	56.09	45.36
Maharashtra	52.32	43.05	60.63	47.81
Orissa	47.86	27.14	36.57	40.28
Punjab & Haryana	20.00	18.55	18.14	25.23
Rajasthan	50.35	38.96	50.90	47.52

(contd.)

TABLE 4.20 (*contd.*)

1	2	3	4	5
Tamil Nadu	48.35	42.02	46.65	36.74
Uttar Pradesh	41.36	36.88	46.67	41.60
West Bengal	34.87	39.11	28.15	27.27
All-India	39.23	36.43	43.47	36.66
		Urban		
Andhra Pradesh	39.98	31.96	33.05	30.82
Assam	12.26	19.34	6.55	9.95
Bihar	52.94	41.13	46.32	39.72
Gujarat	38.51	44.19	37.14	30.46
Karnataka	42.04	34.80	37.76	29.71
Kerala	38.02	34.77	34.01	23.07
Madhya Pradesh	43.45	40.22	34.45	39.83
Maharashtra	38.79	38.03	38.15	36.23
Orissa	47.53	40.42	48.74	40.76
Punjab & Haryana	19.25	13.44	16.02	11.42
Rajasthan	37.68	29.98	29.13	29.38
Tamil Nadu	39.74	33.80	30.50	31.32
Uttar Pradesh	41.36	36.88	46.67	41.60
West Bengal	32.19	23.27	25.66	22.45
All-India	36.20	32.76	33.73	30.51

Source: G. Datt (1998), "Poverty in India and Indian States: An Update", *The Indian Journal of Labour Economics*, Vol. 41, No. 2.

As compared to the year 1992, however, rural poverty declined significantly in all the states in 1993/94 except in Punjab, Haryana and Orissa. If we concentrate only on quinquennial surveys because of large samples, rural poverty declined in most of the states except in four states (Assam, Bihar, Haryana and Uttar Pradesh) in 1993/94 as compared to those for 1987/88. The rate of decline in rural poverty during the period 1987/88 to 1993/94 was lower in most of the states as compared to the periods 1983 to 1987/88 and 1977/78 to 1983.

Urban poverty showed a higher rate of decline in nine out of 17 states during 1987/88 to 93/94 as compared to previous periods. The state level analysis also shows similar trends in both rural and urban poverty regarding the impact of reforms on the poor. The poverty increased in the first two years of the reform period and showed a decline in 1993/94 but the rate of decline was lower than that for 1980s.

If we look at long term changes, the ranks of states in terms of head count ratio are quite different in average over 1990-94 as compared to those in average over 1957-60. For example, Kerala which had the second highest incidence of rural poverty around 1960 moved to the rank of the fifth lowest in the 1990s. States like Andhra Pradesh, Orissa and Tamil Nadu have also moved up significantly in their ranking. Similar changes in rankings were noticed in urban areas.

However, some of the differences in poverty at state level persisted over time. Punjab and Haryana had the lowest incidence of poverty in both the 1960s and 1990s while Bihar had a much higher incidence of poverty for the last three decades. The disparity in the incidence of poverty is much higher if we look at the level of NSS regions (below state level). Dubey and Gangopadhyay (1998) estimated head count ratios at the level of NSS regions for the years 1987/88 and 1993/94. The estimates based on expert group methodology for 58 major regions show that rural poverty varies from around 5 per cent in Punjab Northern to 69 per cent in Orissa Southern in 1993/94. Similarly, in urban areas it varies from 5 per cent in Assam Hills to 67 per cent in Uttar Pradesh Southern. Changes in incidence of rural poverty by quartiles reveal that 19 regions got poorer while 18 regions have improved their position in 1993/94 as compared to those for 1987/88. In the case of urban areas, 14 regions got poorer while 15 improved in terms of moving to a lower quartile during the same period. There are also significant intra-state variations in some of the states.

Increase in Overall Rural Poverty in the 1990s: Divergence of States

There seems to be some divergence in the trends of rural poverty between two groups of states in the post-reform period. For the period 1950/51 to 1997, Srinivasan (1999) indicates that the trends in rural poverty in one group of states (Andhra Pradesh, Gujarat, Karnataka, Kerala, Maharashtra, West Bengal and Punjab) began to diverge from that in another group of states (Bihar, Madhya Pradesh, Orissa, Rajasthan and Uttar Pradesh) since 1977/78. In the first group poverty decline seems to have continued in the post-reform period at a slow pace while the second group has not shown any such decline.

Recent Trends in Poverty at State Level

Table 4.21 provides the recent official estimates of poverty for the period 1999/2000. It shows that Orissa had the highest poverty (47 per cent), followed by Bihar (42.6 per cent). It is true that one can not compare with earlier periods. However, if we accept the numbers based on the changed methodology, some of the states showed very low incidence of poverty. The poverty in seven states was less than 16 per cent (Andhra Pradesh, Gujarat, Haryana, Himachal Pradesh, Jammu & Kashmir, Punjab and Rajasthan).

Human Development at State Level

Although the human development indicators improved and poverty declined in all the states, progress was generally higher in fast growing states which are mostly high income states (Table 4.22). The standard deviation of poverty incidence worsened slightly and the disparity in health indicators widened significantly although disparities in literacy declined.

Lack of Correlation between Income and Human Development: Income is not correlated with some of the human development indicators. For example, infant mortality in Uttar Pradesh was five times higher than that of Kerala, with both having similar levels of poverty in the 1970s and 1980s. Kerala has higher human development but the economy (both agriculture and industry) has

TABLE 4.21: **Poverty Ratios: 1999-2000 (30-day recall period)**

State	Rural	Urban	Total
Andhra Pradesh	11.05	26.63	15.77
Assam	44.04	7.47	36.09
Bihar	44.30	32.91	42.60
Gujarat	13.17	15.59	14.07
Haryana	8.27	9.99	8.74
Himachal Pradesh	7.94	4.63	7.63
Jammu & Kashmir	3.97	1.98	3.48
Karnataka	17.38	25.25	20.04
Kerala	9.38	20.27	12.72
Madhya Pradesh	37.06	38.44	37.43
Maharashtra	23.72	26.81	25.02
Orissa	48.01	42.83	47.15
Punjab	6.35	5.75	6.16
Rajasthan	13.74	19.85	15.28
Tamil Nadu	20.55	22.11	21.12
Uttar Pradesh	31.22	30.89	31.15
West Bengal	31.85	14.86	27.02
All India	27.09	23.62	26.10

Source: Planning Commission.

been stagnant and unemployment rates are high. Punjab and Haryana have very high per capita incomes but gender inequalities are much higher than in the Southern states. The association between poverty and child mortality is also weak. The basic point is that there is no 'the problem' region in India. Each state has its own problems. In general, the Northern (except Punjab and Haryana where gender bias is evident) and Eastern states like Bihar and Orissa have a lower level of social development as compared to the southern states.

TABLE 4.22: **Poverty and Human Development Indicators at State Level**

	Poverty Ratio		Literacy		Female Literacy		Birth Rate		Infant Mortality	
States	1978	1994	1981	1997	1981	1997	1981	1997	1981	1997
Maharashtra	67.8	43.5	53.5	74.0	39.6	63.0	29.8	23.2	79	47
Punjab	26.9	21.6	46.4	67.0	38.4	62.0	30.2	23.5	81	51
Haryana	—	—	41.7	65.0	25.8	52.0	35.9	28.8	101	68
Gujarat	39.9	33.8	49.9	68.0	36.9	57.0	34.2	25.5	116	62
Tamil Nadu	54.9	34.9	52.6	70.0	39.4	60.0	27.9	19.2	91	53
West Bengal	51.8	26.0	46.3	72.0	34.4	63.0	32.0	22.8	91	55
Karnataka	52.9	37.6	43.9	58.0	31.7	50.0	29.1	23.0	69	53
Kerala	53.2	29.2	78.9	93.0	73.4	90.0	24.9	17.8	37	12
Rajasthan	51.6	43.5	28.4	55.0	13.4	35.0	40.1	32.3	108	85
Andhra Pradesh	47.0	29.4	34.1	54.0	23.3	43.0	30.8	22.7	86	63
Madhya Pradesh	63.9	44.1	32.3	56.0	18.0	41.0	38.5	32.4	142	94
Uttar Pradesh	46.7	40.2	31.4	56.0	16.3	41.0	38.4	34.0	150	85
Orissa	62.1	40.3	38.8	51.0	24.0	38.0	34.0	26.8	135	96
Bihar	64.8	60.4	30.3	49.0	15.8	34.0	37.2	32.1	118	71
Standard Dev.	0.24	0.26	0.27	0.17	0.45	0.27	0.13	0.19	0.34	0.49

Source: *Economic Survey, 1999-2000*; World Bank (2000), *India: Policies to Reduce Poverty and Accelerate Sustainable Development*, Washington DC, World Bank..

Policies

For examining policies, it would be useful to look first at determinants of poverty.

Determinants of Poverty

What are the factors responsible for temporal and spatial variations in poverty? Regarding rural poverty, since agriculture is the most important source of employment and income generation in rural areas, it is natural to expect that performance of agriculture will have an impact on poverty.

However, if the distribution of land and other assets are highly skewed, the benefits of agricultural growth may not be shared by the rural poor. In other words, the incidence of poverty is determined by two major factors, namely, the average level of living in a region and the distribution parameters. In literature, several variables were used to explain the variation in poverty.

Ahluwalia (1978) was perhaps the first to examine the Indian evidence in a fairly comprehensive manner both at the all India level and at the level of major states. This study showed a strong inverse relationship between per capita agricultural value added and incidence of poverty during the period 1956/57 to 1973/74 at the all India level. The results at the state level are somewhat mixed. On the basis of this analysis, Ahluwalia indicates that a 'trickle down mechanism' operated in rural India over the period analysed. Dev (1988) showed that labour productivity in agriculture accounted for a large part of the variations in poverty. Mellor and Desai (1985) state that Dharm Narain had used nominal prices in addition to time and agriculture income per head in explaining time series variation in rural poverty. In the 1980s, poverty alleviation programmes also had an impact on the reduction of poverty.

Tendulkar et al. (1996) examined the impact of macro policies on temporal variations in poverty. Their study shows that both rural and urban poverty showed a significant (statistically) decline over the period 1966/67 to 1993/94. Income per head of the population (agricultural income for rural and non-agricultural income for urban areas) and relative prices of food explain the temporal variations during the above mentioned period. The impact of income per head on rural poverty was higher as compared to urban poverty while the impact of relative prices of food has been more on urban than on rural poverty . Their study (Tendulkar et al., 1996) shows that temporal variations in rural and urban prices were explained by food stocks and central government's gross fiscal deficit. Thus, macro policies relating to agricultural and non-agricultural growth, fiscal deficit, food stocks, and relative food prices are important for reducing poverty in both rural and urban areas. A study on rural poverty by Sen (1996) suggests that agricultural growth, relative prices of food, developmental public expenditure and non-agricultural employment are the crucial variables influencing temporal variations in rural poverty.

Some studies have also examined the factors responsible for inter-state variations in poverty by using pooled time series and cross-section regressions. The analysis of Tendulkar et al. (1996) broadly shows that income per head and relative prices matter for inter-temporal and inter-regional variations in both urban and rural poverty. Sen (1996) also uses pooled time series and cross-section regressions for explaining inter-state variations in rural poverty. In his study, poverty was regressed against agricultural output per rural person, state per capita SDP, a relative food price index calculated by dividing the index of the food price in the CPIAL by the SDP deflator, an inflation index based on SDP deflator and per capita real state development expenditure. The results show that all variables except per capita SDP were significant. The relative food price variable was the most important in terms of its impact on poverty. State development expenditure was the next important variable, followed by agricultural output per capita.

Datt and Ravallion (1997) examined the question of why some Indian states have done better than others in reducing poverty. They also use pooled time series and cross section data at the state level. Two dependent variables are used in the study: deviation from trend in poverty and trend in poverty. For explaining the deviations from the trend rates of rural poverty, variables such as current plus lagged real agricultural output per hectare, current plus lagged real non-agricultural output per capita, rate of inflation and lagged real state development spending per capita were used. All independent variables have the expected signs and are statistically significant. Only the variable relating to state development expenditure is not significant. Other variables in the model may themselves be affected by development spending. In the case of determinants of trends in rural poverty, real agricultural output per hectare and differing initial conditions such as irrigation ratio, female literacy, infant mortality have expected signs and are statistically significant. In other words, states which have started with better infrastructure and human resources recorded significantly higher long term rates of poverty reduction.

Fan et al. (1999) examine the causes of decline in rural poverty in India and the study particularly concentrates on the impact of government spending on productivity and poverty. The study finds that investment in rural roads and agricultural research and development have the greatest impact, while government spending specifically targeted to poverty reduction such as rural development and employment programmes have only modest effects.

Thus variables such as agricultural output, inflation rate/relative food prices, non-agricultural employment, government's development expenditure, infrastructure and human development are important determinants of rural poverty. Most of these variables (with replacement of agricultural output with non-agricultural output) particularly inflation rate/relative food prices are important for explaining variations in urban poverty also. The importance of these factors , however, differed from period to period. For example, green revolution led agricultural growth was responsible for the decline of poverty in the 1970s. In the 1980s, rural non-farm employment and public expenditure were more responsible for reduction in rural poverty.

Regarding recent trends of rural poverty, we have already mentioned about the divergent trends in per capita income of two group of states. There was reduction in the per capita development expenditure, particularly in the early 1990s. There was a decline in the rate of growth of real wages and rural non-farm employment in many states. Relative food prices increased faster in the 1990s as compared to the 1980s. Also, agricultural growth in the 1990s was lower than that in the 1980s. All these factors might have contributed to the lack of decline in rural poverty in the 1990s.

Macro Policies: Agriculture and Industry

Agricultural Growth: Food and Agricultural Policies

For reducing rural poverty, agricultural growth is important. The Indian evidence clearly shows that the growth of foodgrains production in the post-reform period has been lower than that in the earlier periods despite successive good monsoons for the last ten years. Even the growth rate of non-foodgrains has been lower in the post-reform period. This is inspite of increase in terms of trade and private investment.

Terms of Trade and Private Investment: The pre-reform regime has been characterised as biased against agriculture, owing to heavy protection to industrial goods, an over valued exchange rate and rigid controls on export and movement and price (through levies) of agricultural goods. Hence, even though the structural adjustment that followed in the wake of economic reforms concentrated on industrial delicencing and liberalising the foreign exchange regime, it did improve the terms of trade in favour of agriculture from 81 per cent to almost 99 per cent in terms of the 1970/71 levels.

These increasingly favourable terms of trade for agriculture are supposed to attract private investment into agriculture, thereby leading to growth in output and demand for rural labour in a simple neoclassical framework. Since agriculture is more labour intensive, a rise in the relative price of its output (i.e., food) leads to an increase in real wages and investment in agriculture. There is strong evidence of growth in private sector investment in agriculture especially since the late 1980s. Whether this increase in private investment alone can lead to sustained growth in agriculture remains to be seen. This is especially so in the light of the complementarity between public and private investment, as manifested by the state of rural infrastructure, public irrigation, roads and power. Thus even though the terms of trade are becoming favourable, unless non-price factors also become favourable, it may be too early to see the impact on growth.

Subsidies and Investments in Agriculture : Unsustainability of farm subsidies has emerged as an important issue in recent policy debates. Since the mid-70s, the central and state governments have followed a policy of supplying inputs at prices which do not fully cover costs. There has been an enormous increase in the amount of agricultural subsidies over the last two decades. There seems to be a trade-off between subsidies and investments in agriculture. Higher investment in agriculture and rural infrastructure is a necessary condition for increasing agricultural growth. Government's role seems to be much more important for not only raising public investment but also for inducing private investment. The worrying aspect is that the growth rate in agricultural investment rose only for a decade following the Green Revolution and later it declined significantly for both the public and private sectors. As mentioned above, private investment in agriculture has been steadily increasing .The rising trend in private investment partly reflects the improved trade policy regime for agriculture vis-à-vis the reform period. Public investment in agriculture which had been generally rising till the 1970s, decelerated during the 1980s and 1990s. The decline in public investment is attributed to diversion of resources from investment to current expenditure. A large portion of public expenditure on agriculture in recent years went into current expenditure in the form of increased output and input subsidies.

How do we increase investments in agriculture? As noted earlier, input subsidies are a major strain on the government's resources. Reducing these subsidies suggests itself as a source of finance for public investments in agricultuie. However, in the short run, it may be difficult to remove all the subsidies. The process of reduction of subsidy will have to be gradual. In the short run, therefore, public investment for agriculture has to come from other sources in the central and state budgets. Much of the agricultural investments particularly on irrigation is in the areas which are the responsibility of the states. They have to increase investments for creating productive assets by reducing funds for populist and unproductive activities. One of the factors determining private investment is public investment because of the complementarity between the two. Institutional credit seems to be another crucial variable in determining private investment. In a credit constrained economy, credit policy should play a vital role in determining private investment and agricultural performance.

Agriculture Research and Technology: The future of economic and social development is largely dependent upon the technological improvements in agriculture. A massive application of science and technology can enable Indian agriculture to face the serious challenges of food security, and ensure a place for Indian agricultural products globally by the enhancement of value addition process. For agricultural research and education, the country has one of the strongest National Agricultural Research Systems (NARS) in the world. The objective here is to harvest the power of science and technology to improve the living conditions of the poor. It is rather difficult to obtain incremental production from the conventional Green Revolution areas. For the second Green Revolution it is necessary for making the grey areas green. Hence, major support for rainfed areas, especially in Eastern and arid peninsular India would be necessary. Public sector research and technology missions on various crops would play a crucial role in improving crop productivity. For example, the technology mission on oilseeds has already paid rich dividends. Much scope exists for reducing the yield gap between the laboratory and the field particularly for dry land crops. Agricultural research and extension programmes, complemented by the schooling of farmers and farm workers are now recognised as important determinants of farmer's efficiency and productivity. There is considerable scope for bridging the gap between potential and actual yields in many regions of India.

Trade Liberalisation: What is the impact of trade liberalisation on agricultural growth and the poor? Some studies show that India will improve agricultural growth and conditions of the poor with trade liberalisation (Gulati and Kelly, 1999). Using a dynamic nine-sector, seven-income classes computable general equilibrium (CGE) model, Storm (1997) analyses the medium run effects of agricultural trade liberalisation. The simulation results show that, given empirically plausible price response elasticities, the improvement in the incentive structure for farmers consequent upon trade liberalisation in itself is likely to increase substantially agricultural productivity and real incomes in a broad based and sustained manner. The analysis shows that wholesale liberalisation of India's agricultural trade may not be a wise course, if the trade reforms are not supplemented by adequate policy measures like improving rural infrastructure and institutions.

One issue which has been debated in recent years relates to liberalisation of trade in foodgrains. From the point of view of food security, a majority of researchers and policy makers feel that India should not depend on trade for foodgrains. One of the arguments against trade liberalisation in the case of foodgrains is the following. As mentioned above, although India has been a 'small' country in terms of its share in world trade in agriculture, in terms of output shares in the world India is really a 'large' country. The implication of this is that unilateral trade liberalisation by India will substantially alter the nature of world equilibrium in terms of prices, and subsequently, outputs. This is likely to be true especially in the case of rice and edible oils where the world trade in these items itself is very small. This is in fact borne out by the simulations done by Parikh et al. (1995) in the case of rice. Their results show that if India were to export rice freely, the world market price of rice is likely to fall, given the thinness of the world market for rice. International prices for agricultural produce fluctuate considerably and these fluctuations may lead to destabilising movements in domestic prices with an adverse impact on food security.

Domestic Deregulation: There are still some restrictions on storage, marketing and movement of agricultural products particularly at the state level. Most of the government orders are in the form of controls on inputs and output. For example, the Fertiliser Order, 1985 puts controls on price, distribution, sales etc. Regarding cotton, Maharashtra's Monopoly Cotton Procurement Scheme puts a lot of restrictions. There is a need to review these restrictions so that farmers can avail themselves of better opportunities. This is also important for attracting investment to these activities. For example, a modification of the Milk and Milk Product's Order may attract greater investments in the milk industry.

Similarly, a large part of the food processing industry is currently reserved for the small scale sector, for example, milk, oil processing, rice, ice-cream, bread. An expert Group on "Small Enterprise" (1997) has recommended that reservations for the small scale sector should be abolished completely. According to the Committee, the opportunity cost of the reservation policy is extremely high since important sectors like light engineering and food processing have not been able to grow owing to these limitations. If these recommendations are accepted, it would be easier for the food processing industries to upgrade their technology.

Infrastructure and Institutions: One major issue regarding agricultural growth is whether trade reforms or mere withdrawal of the protectionist policy towards industry are sufficient to increase productivity in agriculture. Without infrastructure development and institutional changes, the price instrument may not improve agricultural performance. Not only has infrastructure development in the Eighth Plan fallen short of targets, even its achievements have been lower than those of the Seventh Plan. This is partly due to the reliance that was placed on private sector investment, which did not materialise in adequate measure. Investment in rural infrastructure is more important for agricultural growth than trade liberalisation per se. The role of public and private investment in infrastructure becomes crucial in this context. Infrastructure includes irrigation, electricity, agricultural research, roads and communications and new technology. It plays an important role from the point of view of both input and output. It helps to ensure timely and adequate delivery of inputs to the farmers, and on the output front, it helps integrate local markets with national and international markets. The major responsibility lies with the public sector for making improvements in general infrastructure like roads, power supply and communications. Private domestic and foreign direct investment also should be encouraged to invest in infrastructure.

Institutional reforms are important, particularly in the domain of public systems for sustained technical progress and output growth in agriculture. Land reforms and reforms in the irrigation and credit sectors are needed. Andhra Pradesh has gone a big way in implementing participatory irrigation management through water users' associations.

Industrial Policies and Employment

There is a debate relating to the organised manufacturing sector in India. The World Bank (1989) says that in the 1980s, there was a significant trade off between the higher cost of labour and employment. The wage rate increased by 7.2 per cent per year in the first half of the 1980s. According to the World Bank, employers responded by virtually stopping new hiring and retrenching existing workers to the extent possible. In other words, wage rigidities were responsible for the slow growth of employment. Ahluwalia (1992) also views policy-induced rigidities in the labour market as the principal reason for the decline in employment. On the other hand, Nagaraj (1994) showed that labour market rigidities might not have been responsible for the slow down in employment in the 1980s. The conclusions of his study are: (a) while real earnings per worker had grown annually at 3.2 per cent during the decade since 1979/80, real wages per man day had grown only half as much (1.6 per cent per year) which implies that workers had worked more hours (and shifts) that boosted their earnings; (b) a distinct decline occurred in the power of organised labour, used as a proxy for the reported rigidities in the labour market; (c) structural changes can be seen in employment in manufacturing industries in favour of the unregistered sector and within registered manufacturing towards smaller sized factories. These long term tendencies would have further undermined the power of the organised working class to induce flexible use of labour; (d) there was no systematic correlation in the postulated relationship between earnings per worker, the capital-labour ratio and employment at a disaggregated level. ILO (1996) has shown that while the real wage growth was much faster than the product-wage growth in the 1970s, the reverse was the case in the

1980s. The reason seems to be that the terms of trade were shifting in favour of industry in the 1970s and in favour of agriculture in the 1980s. The important thing to note is that intersectoral terms of trade and hence macroeconomic factors play a role in determining labour costs in Indian industry rather than growing rigidities in the labour market.

Recent data for India shows that there has been a significant growth in employment in the organised (formal) manufacturing sector .The following conclusions can be drawn from Table 4.23.[6]

TABLE 4.23: **Growth Rates of Registered Manufacturing Sector in India: 1973-74 to 1995-96**

Years	Growth Rate (per cent)
1973-74 to 1979-80	1.4
1980-81 to 1988-89	-0.6
1973-74 to 1982-83	3.4
1986-87 to 1994-95	2.1
1986-87 to 1995-96	4.0

Source: R. Nagaraj (1994), "Employment and Wages in Manufacturing Industries: Trends, Hypothesis and Evidence", *Economic and Political Weekly*, Vol. 29, No. 4, pp.177-186, and "Wages and Employment in Indian Manufacturing", in *Growth and Reforms in India: A Study of Selected Aspects*, Oxford University Press, New Delhi (forthcoming).

(a) The growth rate declined from 1.4 per cent during 1973-80 to –0.6 during 1980-89.

(b) The negative growth rate in the 1980s is misleading as the figures show that there were only four years during 1983/84 and 1987/88 when employment fell in absolute figures. After negative growth in the mid-80s, employment showed a steady increase and the absolute levels are higher in the 1990s.

(c) Employment growth was quite high in the post-liberalisation period reaching around four per cent if we consider the period 1986/87 to 1995/96. The growth in 1995/96 was quite high and was associated with high industrial growth of 13 per cent in that year.

(d) Growth in employment was not affected by negative growth in output during 1992-94. Employment growth reflects the rise in fixed capital formation after the reforms.

(e) Contrary to much apprehension, liberalisation programmes introduced in 1991 have not affected adversely if we look at the aggregate level.

High Employment Growth in Spite of Rigidities in the 1990s: There were no significant changes in the labour market policies regarding rigidities. In spite of that, as discussed above, employment grew at the rate of four per cent during the period 1986/87 to 1995/96. It shows that the argument of labour market rigidities was perhaps overdone. As Nagaraj (forthcoming) indicates, (a) unit labor cost has steadily declined right through the 1980s and 1990s; (b) Wage-rental ratio did not increase in the 1980s and 1990s. Further research is, therefore, needed on the issue of labour rigidities (and consequent higher wages) and capital labour substitution .

Education

In order to reduce poverty and increase productive employment basic education and skill improvements are important. The majority of the workers in India are either illiterate or have studied only up to the primary level. Unless there is improvement in skills, we can not shift labour force from agriculture to non-agricultural activities.

Summary and Conclusions

This paper analyses the trends in employment and poverty and policies which have affected them. Major conclusions are summarised as follows.

1. The trends in employment show: (a) employment growth declined in the 1990s; (b) poverty among workers declined but the pace of reduction was slow in the 1990s; (c) the rate of growth in rural non-farm employment declined in the

post-reform period till 1993/94 but increased in 1999/2000; (d) quality of employment deteriorated because of casualisation of labour; (e) real wages for casual labourers increased but there was slow growth in the 1990s.

2. The poverty ratios have not shown any trend during 1950/51 to 1973/74 and declined significantly in the late 1970s and in the 1980s. In the post-reform period rural poverty reduction has been arrested till 1993/94. On the other hand, urban poverty recorded a significant decline in the 1990s. Rural poverty also declined significantly between 1993/94 and 1999/2000. However, there are problems of comparability between 1993/94 and 1999/2000 NSS data. The trends in human development indicators show that India has a long way to go to attain the average level of even the 'medium' human development category of countries.
3. Inter-state inequalities have been increasing in the 1990s and there is a sign of divergence rather than convergence. In the 1990s, poorer states like Bihar, Madhya Pradesh, Rajasthan, Uttar Pradesh and Orissa have not shown reduction in poverty while richer states such as Andhra Pradesh, Gujarat, Karnataka, Kerala, Maharashtra, Tamil Nadu, West Bengal and Punjab recorded a decline in poverty. Divergence in these two groups of states could be one of the reasons for the lack of decline in poverty at the aggregate level in the 1990s. Inequalities in infant mortality are increasing although they fell in the case of literacy.
4. Regarding determinants, agricultural growth is one of the main determinants of rural poverty . Another important determinant of rural and urban poverty is relative food prices. Rural non-farm employment, wages and development public expenditure were also important determinants in the 1980s. An analysis of the impact of public expenditure on poverty revealed that expenditure on roads and agricultural research had a greater impact than the expenditure on direct poverty alleviation programmes.
5. On macro policies we discussed more about agricultural policies as agriculture growth is important for reduction in

rural poverty. One paradox in the agriculture sector in the 1990s is that agricultural growth was lower in the 1990s inspite of increase in the terms of trade and increase in private investment.

6. Since a large number of poor are in the agriculture sector, greater emphasis must be placed on ensuring healthy growth in agriculture. However, as we argued earlier, the incentives for growth can not be solely 'price' driven but must involve non-price factors such as infrastructure, institutions and technology. Trade and price reforms alone would not be sufficient to improve agricultural growth. Without infrastructural development and institutional changes, the price instrument may not increase the aggregate supply response. Domestic deregulation seems to be more important than trade liberalisation.
7. Regarding industrial employment, contrary to apprehensions, liberalisation programmes introduced in 1991 have not affected adversely if we look at the aggregate level. Employment growth was quite high in the post-liberalisation period reaching around four per cent if we consider the period 1986/87 to 1995/96. the analysis also raises doubts regarding the hypothesis that labour market rigidities are responsible for low employment growth in the 1980s. There were no significant changes in the labour market policies regarding rigidities in the 1990s. Inspite of that employment showed significant growth.
8. In the medium and long run, India needs to improve education and skills of the workers in order to improve productivity and reduce poverty. Particular emphasis has to be given to women's education to improve productivity and human development.

Our analysis in the paper shows that macro policies[7] seem to be important for reduction in poverty. The second generation of reforms should concentrate more on agricultural growth and rural infrastructure. Food prices have to be lower as a majority of the poor are net purchasers of food. The impact of direct anti-poverty programmes seem to be modest in a normal year as compared to that in a drought year. However, these programmes have relevance even now. There has been a debate about the efficacy of growth-led poverty reduction *versus* a strategy based on improved social services and programmes targeted at the poor. They are all required under different circumstances if broad-based poverty reduction is to be achieved. There is also need for developing local level institutions[8] for helping the small and marginal farmers and landless labourers as the growth process has marginalized some of these sections of the society. Also, there is a need to give more emphasis to health and education for reducing poverty.

NOTES

1. "There has been much debate about how exactly poverty should be defined. In popular understanding, poverty is identified with lowness of income which prevents a family from obtaining and enjoying the basic necessities of life, including a minimum of food, clothing, shelter and water. This concept is defined as income poverty. For comprehensive picture of poverty those other deprivations, such as in relation to health, education, sanittion and insurance against mishaps, must be taken into account" (Chellaiah and Sudarshan, 1999), p. xiii.
2. See Bhalla (2000), Aiyer (2000), Lal et al. (2000). Tendulkar and Sundaram (2000) on the other hand show that poverty increased in the 1990s.
3. For more on this see Mahendra Dev (2000).
4. Tendulkar and Sundaram (2001) have shown that in the case of cereals the differences are not high. It is known that cereals form considerable proportion in the consumption basket of the poor.
5. Shariff and Mallick (1999).
6. The discussion on employment growth in manufacturing sector is based on Nagaraj (forthcoming) and personal communications with him.
7. On economic reforms for the next decade, see Chelliah (1999).
8. On the marginalisation process in agriculture, see Rao and Hanumappa (1999).

REFERENCES

Ahluwalia, M.S. (1978), *Rural Poverty in India: 1956-57 to 1973-74 in India,* Washington DC, World Bank.

Ahluwalia, Isher J. (1992) *Productivity and Growth in Indian Manufacturing*, Delhi, Oxford University Press.

Aiyer, S. (2000), "Has Economic Reforms Bypassed the Poor?", *The Times of India*, April 23.

Bhaduri, Amit (1996), "Employment, Labour Market Flexibility and Economic Liberalisation in India", *The Indian Journal of Labour Economics*, Vol. 39, No. 1.

Bhagwati, J. and T.N. Srinivasan (1993), "India's Economic Reforms", Ministry of Finance, Government of India, New Delhi.

Bhalla, S. (2000), "Growth and Poverty in India—Myth and Reality", mimeo.

Chandrasekhar, C.P. and Jayati Ghosh (2000), "NSS 55th Round: A Failed Experiment?" *Business Line,* November 14, 2000.

—— (2001), "Disturbing Employment Trends", *Business Line*, January 23, 2001.

Chelliah, R.J. (1999), "Economic Reform Strategy for the Next Decade", Dr. Waheeduddin Khan Memorial Lecture delivered at Centre for Economic and Social Studies, Hyderabad, August 9.

—— and R. Sudarshan (1998), *Income Poverty and Beyond: Human Development in India,* Social Science Press, New Delhi.

Datt, G. (1998) "Poverty in India and Indian States: An Update", *The Indian Journal of Labour Economics*, Vol. 41, No. 2.

—— (1999), "Has Poverty Declined Since Economic Reforms?", *Economic and Political Weekly,* Vol. 34, No. 50.

—— and M. Ravallion (1997), "Why Have Some States Performed Better than Others at Reducing Poverty?", Discussion Paper No.26, Washington D.C., International Food Policy Research Institute.

Dev., S. Mahendra (1988) "Regional Disparities in Agricultural Labour Productivity and Rural Poverty in India", *Indian Journal of Agricultural Economics,* Vol. 23, No. 2.

—— (1996),"Experience of India's (Maharashtra) Employment Guarantee Scheme: Lessons for Development Policy", *Development Policy Review,* 14.(3).

—— (1999), "An Overview of Social Security in India", *The Indian Journal of Labour Economics,* Vol. 42, No. 3, pp. 361-392.

—— (2000), " Poverty Debate, NSS *vs.* National Accounts", *Economic Times*, September 15.

—— and Alakh N. Sharma (forthcoming), *Economic Reforms, Employment and Poverty*, Institute for Human Development, New Delhi.

Dubey, A. and S. Gangopadhyay (1998) "Counting the Poor: Where are the Poor in India?", *Sarvekshana,* Analytical Report No. 1, New Delhi, Department of Statistics, Government of India.

Fan, S., P. Hazell and S. Thorat (1999) *Linkages between Government Spending, Growth, and Poverty in Rural India,* Research Report No. 110, Washington DC, International Food Policy Research Institute.

Ghose, Ajit, K. (1994) "Employment in Organised Manufacturing in India", *The Indian Journal of Labour Economics,* Vol. 37, No. 2, pp. 143-62.

—— (1999), "The Question of Employment Security in India: A Note", Paper presented at the Conference on Social Security in India, New Delhi, April 15-17, 1999.

Ghosh, Jayati (1995), "Employment and Labour under Structural Adjustment: India Since 1991", *The Indian Journal of Labour Economics*, Vol. 38, No. 4.

Gulati, A. and T. Kelly (1999) *Trade Liberalisation and Indian Agriculture*, Oxford University Press, New Delhi.

Gupta, S.P. (1999) "Trickle Down Theory Revisited: The Role of Employment and Poverty", V.B. Singh Memorial Lecture, 41st Annual Conference of the Indian Society of Labour Economics, IGIDR, Mumbai, November 18-20, 1999.

ILO-SAAT (1996) *India: Economic Reforms and Labour Policies*, ILO, New Delhi.

Joshi, V. and I.M.D. Little (1997), *India's Economic Reforms*, Oxford Unviersity Press.

Lal, Deepak, I.Natarajan and Rakesh Mohan (2000), "Economic Reforms and Poverty Alleviation: A Tale of Two Surveys", NCAER and UCLA, mimeo.

Mellor, J.W. and G. Desai (eds.)(1985), *Agricultural Change and Rural Poverty*, Oxford University Press, New Delhi.

Nagaraj, R. (1994), "Employment and Wages in Manufacturing Industries: Trends, Hypothesis and Evidence", *Economic and Political Weekly*, Vol. 29, No. 4, pp.177-186.

—— (forthcoming), "Wages and Employment in Indian Manufacturing", *Growth and Reforms in India: A Study of Selected Aspects*, Oxford University Press, New Delhi.

Nayyar, Deepak (1993), "Economic Reforms in India: A Critical Assessment, ILO-ARTEP, New Delhi.

NSSO (2000), *Employment and Unemployment in India: 1999-2000: Key Results*, NSS 55th Round, December, 2000.

Nurkse, Ragnar (1957), *Problems of Capital Formation in Underdeveloped Countries*, Oxford: Basil Blackwell.

Parikh, K.S. (1994) "Who Gets How Much from PDS? How Effectively Does it Reach the Poor?", *Sarvekshana*, Vol. 17, No. 3.

——, N.S.S.Narayana, Manoj Panda and A.Ganesh Kumar (1998), "Agricultural Trade Liberalisation, Growth, Welfare and Large Country Effects", *Agricultural Economics* , Vol. 17, No. 2, pp. 1-20.

Rao, V.M and H.G. Hanumappa (1999), "The Marginalisation Process in Agriculture: Indicators, Outlook and Policy Implications", Bangalore: Institute for Social and Economic Change, mimeo.

Ravallion (2000), "Should poverty measures be anchored to the National Accounts", *Economic and Political Weekly*, August 26.

Sen, Abhijit, (2000), "Estimates of Consumer Expenditure and its Distribution: Statistical Priorities after NSS 55th Round", *Economic and Political Weekly*, Vol. 35, No. 51.

Sen, Abhijit (1996) "Economic Reforms, Employment and Poverty: Trends and

Options", *Economic and Political Weekly,* Vol. 31, No. 35.

Shariff, A. and A.C. Mallick (1998), "Dynamics of Food Intake and Nutrition according to Expenditure Class", mimeo, National Council for Applied Economic Research, New Delhi.

Srinivasan, T.N. (2000), "Growth, Poverty Reduction and Inequality", mimeo, Yale University.

—— (1999), "Poverty and Reforms in India", Paper presented in the Conference on Reforms, organised by NBER and NCAER, December 14-15, 1999, Neemrana Fort Resort, Rajasthan.

Storm, Servaas, (1997), "The Unfinished Agenda: Indian Agriculture under the Structural Reforms", The *Journal of International Trade & Economic Development,* 6(2).

Sundaram, K. and S.D. Tendulkar (2000) "Poverty in India: An Assessment and Analysis", mimeo, Delhi School of Economics.

—— (2001), "Estimates of Private Consumption: Disaggregated NAS-NSS comparison", *Economic and Political Weekly,* Vol.36, No.2.

Tendulkar, S.D., K.Sundaram and L.R.Jain (1996), "Macroeconomic Policies and Poverty in India: 1966-67 to 1993-94", Paper Prepared for ILO, New Delhi

—— (1998), "Indian Economic Policy Reforms and Poverty: An Assessment", Ch. 12 in the volume in honour of Manmohan Singh edited by I.J. Ahluwalia and I.M.D. Little, New Delhi, Oxford University Press.

Visaria, Pravin (2000), "Alternative Estimates of Poverty in India" *The Economic Times,* June 27, 2000.

Visaria (2000b), "Polemics on Poverty" *Business Standard,* October 30, 2000.

World Bank (1997), *India: Achievements and Challenges in Reducing Poverty,* Washington DC, World Bank .

World Bank (2000), *India: Policies to Reduce Poverty and Accelerate Sustainable Development,* Washington DC, World Bank.

SECTION II

ECONOMIC REFORMS AND SOCIAL SECTOR

5

SOCIAL SECTOR DEVELOPMENTS AND ECONOMIC REFORMS:
A Focus on The Education Sector

P.R. PANCHAMUKHI

That economic reforms, cryptically described by the term LPG, (Liberalisation, Privatisation and Globalisation), have far reaching effects not only on the economy but also on the society of a country, has now been amply appreciated. A close examination of the nature and the extent of such effects would greatly help the policy maker to suggest suitable steps to be taken in different sectors both to strengthen or at least to sustain the positive effects of the reforms on these sectors and also to control the negative effects of the reforms, if any. It should be emphasised that just as economic reforms might have effects on the components of the social sector, similarly social sector developments would have implications for economic reforms. It is desirable to have a clear idea about these direct and reciprocal linkages between the reforms and the components of the social sector for the purpose of meaningful policy interventions. In the present paper an attempt has been made to examine the effects of the reforms on the social sector in general and the educational sector in particular, with a view to suggesting measures to tackle the likely adverse effects of the reforms. The paper also touches upon the implications that educational development is likely to have on reforms.

Discussion in the paper is divided into the following sections : Section one presents a framework for analysing the effects of various economic reforms on various aspects of the educational sector. Here, we present a brief account of economic reforms as introduced in India during the past decade or so. Section two briefly presents the facts and figures relating to some of the effects of economic reforms on the educational sector. It should be mentioned that since relevant data for all the aspects of these linkages between education and economic reforms are not available in required details the empirical analysis contained in this section is not to be considered as comprehensive and complete. Section three briefly presents an outline of measures for safeguarding the interest of the educational sector during economic reforms. Section four briefly considers the reciprocal linkages from educational development to the reform formulation indicating the scope of the subsequent generations of reforms. Section five summarises the main policy conclusions of the study.

A Framework for Analysing the Effects of Economic Reforms on Education

During the past decade or so India has introduced a number of economic reforms, touching different sectors ranging from international trade to agriculture. In the present inter-sectorally interdependent framework any type of change introduced in these sectors is bound to have a direct or indirect implication for the educational sector. We outline below major economic reforms introduced in India and then present a framework for analysing their effects so far as education is concerned. This is presented primarily as an outline of issues for empirical testing.

Economic Reform Measures in India

The following paragraphs indicate the scope of the economic reforms introduced during 1991 to 1998/99 relating to the different sectors.

Trade Related Reforms

1. Tariff reductions from 300 per cent to 40 per cent (1997/98) Reduction in import tariff from 87 per cent to 20 per cent
2. Import licensing system abolished.
3. CSS – Cash Compensatory Scheme withdrawn for exports
4. Devaluation of rupee (twice)
5. Real exchange rate system abolished
6. Liberalisation of foreign exchange
7. Licensing regime diluted

— Shifting of large number of items from restricted list to open general licence.

Industrial Sector Reforms

1. Drastic sealing back of industrial licensing system for all but 18 core sectors
2. Policies promoting capital mobility
3. Relaxation of MRTP Act
4. Opening up of industries to the private sector – privatisation
5. Liberalisation of FDI and foreign portfolio investment
6. Relaxation of FERA
7. Foreign investment up to 51 per cent of equity holdings permitted in 34 industries

Financial Sector Reforms

1. CRR and SLR lowered, implying less access of the government to the resources of commercial banks
2. Interest rates deregulated
3. Post of controller of capital issues was abolished but Security Exchange Board of India (SEBI) was established
4. Increased level of foreign portfolio investment

Fiscal Policy Reforms

1. Reduce fiscal deficit

— Non-plan expenditure to be reduced

2. Tax rate reduction (all taxes)
3. Relative importance of direct taxes vs. indirect taxes raised (1.3 per cent to 3 per cent)
4. Widening of tax base
5. Introduction of presumptive taxation
6. Bank credit to the government reduced by 44 per cent
7. General government debt held by RBI reduced from 15 per cent to 10 per cent
8. Central government budget deficit financed by RBI reduced by 33 per cent to less than 25 per cent
9. Net general government debt held by RBI reduced by 15.6 percent of GDP to 9 per cent of GDP
10. Net external borrowing declined significantly (?) (share declined)
11. Corporation and income tax together increased from 2 per cent to 3 per cent of the GDP
12. Excise and custom duties share declined 9 per cent to 7 per cent of GDP
13. Non-interest expenditure reduced from 16 per cent to 13 per cent of GDP
14. Reduction of subsidies

— Food and fertiliser subsidies not significantly reduced
— Total subsidy share in GDP declined from 3.5 per cent to 2.3 per cent and recently to 1.3 per cent
— Debt relief for farmers reduced

Agriculture Sector Related Reforms (no significant reforms)

1. Abolition of GOI restriction on the movement of agricultural commodities between zones
2. Freeing of prices on some fertilisers
3. Quantitative restrictions on agricultural trade dismantled

As can be noticed from the above listing, a large number of reform measures have been introduced covering largely the economic sectors. There have, of course, been some initiatives impinging upon the major components of the social sector such as primary education, higher education, water supply, electricity tariffs, etc. However, the main thrust of major reform measures seems to be economic sectors rather than the social sector, as the term economic reform itself connotes.

What are the Main Objectives of These Economic Reform Measures?

Against the background of a slow rate of economic growth witnessed by the country during the four decades of planning after Independence there was a felt need to introduce some measures in order to raise the tempo of overall development of the economy. It is not that there were no serious efforts introduced in the country during the long period of four decades. In fact, some observers have commented that India has been a laboratory of a number of experiments in the field of economic and social sectors. However, despite all these initiatives, the potentials of development of the economy were reportedly not fully exploited. It is in this background that the new measures were visualised and introduced, perhaps coincidentally, at the instance of the IMF and the World Bank. It was also a coincidence that such measures were being tried out in other countries as well. Hence, the main objective of these measures was to improve the tempo of economic development, which is sustainable over a long period of time. Too much of soft state ethos, less scope for the play of competitive forces and too much of protectionism have been diagnosed to be the factors for the relatively unsatisfactory performance of the Indian economy during the long plan period. The new philosophy of economic reforms emphasised the role of competitive forces at the national as well as the international levels by the forces of liberalisation, privatisation and globalisation (LPG measures). The reforms listed above aim at introducing and strengthening these forces.

How Would These Reform Measures Influence the Educational Sector?

The economic reform measures seem to influence the educational sector from the following points of view :

(a) influence on the availability of resources for the educational sector
(b) influence on the decision making-process for different sub sectors of the educational sector
(c) implications for funding composition
(d) implications for value formation in society

We may try to outline the likely implications of each of the economic reforms listed for some of the above four aspects relating to education.

Trade Sector Reforms and Educational Sector

Steep reduction in tariffs particularly import tariff would help the educational sector by lowering the purchase price of goods and services relevant to the educational sector and those which enter into the international trade. For example, if the educational sector requires certain equipment used abroad, it can be imported at relatively lower prices because of the tariff reductions. Computer education and education through computers can be cited as examples which might be favourably influenced by these measures. In most schools, particularly in the urban areas of the country, computer education is becoming increasingly popular. The governments of some states have initiated a policy of assisting selected schools by providing computers for the purpose of starting computer education programmes. In some educational institutions education is imparted through computers. For example, at the higher educational level, facilitating conferences among more than three participants. At the higher educational level, the opening up of the floodgates of information through the Internet has provided tremendous opportunities for learners. Even at the school level, children are now accessing vast information (good, bad or indifferent) through the Internet. It is worth exploring to what extent the educational objectives of curriculum coverage are achieved through the import price reduction in the case of computers. In the same way, other equipments used in science laboratories in schools and higher educational institutions are likely to be available at lower costs on account of tariff reductions. To what extent this has happened is a matter for empirical investigation.

Abolition of import license system has also facilitated the flow of imports. If imports are useful for the educational sector, then the unnecessary irritants for the educational sector in respect of procurement of necessary goods and services from abroad would be removed. How far has this actually happened in the case of different levels of education and different states of the country? This needs to be empirically tested.

As against the above measures, devaluation of the Indian rupee might make India's exports cheaper and imports costlier suggesting that the general measures of devaluation may act counter to the specific measures of tariff reduction. However, the likely promotion of exports through devaluation and dilution of the licensing regime might contribute to education indirectly by improving the capacity to fund education by exporters and industrial entrepreneurs. It may be useful to examine how far exporters and industrialists have been favourably influenced by these trade related measures and how far they have increased their contribution to different levels of education.

If the fiscal measures of tax exemptions of donations to educational institutions are considered together with these measures, then, one should expect a better account of donations and charitable contributions to education, induced by the economic reform measures. How many industrialists and exporters have contributed, and to what extent, to the starting of schools and colleges and to creating chairs in universities in different parts of the country? In fact, even the aggregative picture about the quantum of donations and the contributions to the educational sector cannot be developed because of non-availability of such data for different regions and the country as a whole. It would be desirable to pursue this question with the help of ad hoc empirical studies in different regions of the country.

Industrial and Financial Sector Reform Measures

Industrial policy reforms have largely aimed at removing the irritants and restrictions in the functioning of existing industries and in the process of starting of new ones. In the previous regime of the License Raj, the costs in terms of delays and also in terms of financial outgoes were significantly large. Policies promoting capital mobility, relaxation of MRTP Act, opening up of industries to the private sector, etc., are expected to reduce such costs. If the prices of the products of these industrial units are a function of the costs, then, there is no reason why prices should continue to rise on account of cost factors. This should help all the sectors including education which use these products.

The relaxation in FERA and permission for foreign investment up to 51 per cent of equity capital should also help the educational sector if the foreign investors are interested in investing in the industries whose products are used by the educational sector. Incidentally, flows of NRI funds and the funds of foreign investors may be channelised even into education. Education such as management education, engineering education and higher education in specialised scientific disciplines may be the areas where foreign capital is likely to flow in. It is worth examining to what extent this has actually happened in the case of India.

Financial sector reforms are expected to release large amounts of funds for private sector initiatives. Banks and financial institutions do not have to keep their funds captive for being accessed only by the government. In case private entrepreneurs find investment in educational enterprise more rewarding, then, the liquidity advantages arising out of the financial sector reforms should promote the educational sector. Which level of education and which type of education would find itself encouraged by these liquidity advantages is also an important point to be borne in mind while evaluating the implications of these reforms for the educational sector. Interestingly, the reduced interest rate regime, which is part of financial sector reform, is also expected to help the educational-entrepreneur-borrower causing loan-financed educational activity less costly for him. These aspects need to be examined considering the data of the end use of credit focusing particularly on credit for educational purposes, both for supplying educational facilities and for using educational opportunities.

Some measures promoting foreign portfolio investment might also help the educational sector. We do not have data about individual investors from abroad investing in school level education. At the school level, particularly elementary school level, foreign institutional investors and government have been taking interest in promoting certain activities. For example, the investments for District Primary Education (DPEP) have largely come from external sources to start with. Such foreign initiatives need to be evaluated in the background of the functioning of non-DPEP regions and also the sustainability of such programmes in the DPEP regions after the foreign funding ceases.

In the same way, if the sectors supplying their products to the educational sector receive increased portfolio investments from abroad, then, this might indirectly promote the educational sector. One has to see whether and in respect of which goods and services the prices would be higher than what they used to be before the foreign portfolio investment and in respect of which they would be lower during the reform process. The net advantages for the educational sector would depend upon which effect would be stronger.

Thus, there are likely to be liquidity effects and also cost effects for the education sector on account of financial sector reforms. A detailed empirical study according to the type and level of education, presenting a clear balance sheet of gains and losses would be extremely helpful.

Fiscal Policy Reforms

Fiscal policy reforms are likely to have significantly long range effects on the educational sector. Governmental decision making with regard to education has been swinging as a pendulum of favoured treatment of education and less favoured treatment, mostly the latter. Even during the period of the 20-Point Programme, the items of the social sector like education, health, etc., used to be quite low in the serial order, suggesting that the actual decision making with regard to these sectors would not have received very significantly serious attention in the crucial meetings. By the time the points relating to education were to be taken up for discussion after the priority items such as irrigation, power, industry, etc., the patience of the participants would have been exhausted and the time of the meeting would have almost expired. It is in this context that ad hoc decisions in terms of not allocating significant public funds to education or residual treatment for the components of the social sector, used to be taken. Normally, soft sectors such as education and health would receive this indifferent treatment at the hands of the decision makers. It is natural that if a dam remains half built, people raise a hue and cry. But, when a school building remains half completed or the vacancies of teachers are not filled, then, it hardly receives any public attention. It is on account of this reason that when a decision is taken to cut the outlays, then, the first target are sectors like education. However, when a decision is taken for allocating additional funds, then such sectors are likely to be lowest in the priority ranking.

This lukewarm treatment of the educational sector is strengthened by the policy of reduction of fiscal deficit and also the policy of economy in non-plan expenditures. Generally, when there are large fiscal deficits, there is a chance of sectors like education getting some share in public funding. But, when deficits are cut, then, these sectors also suffer the resource crunch. Preliminary calculations show that the rank correlation coefficients between public sector outlay on education and the quantum of fiscal deficit are positive and fairly high. This is observed not only when the fiscal deficits are considered at the central government level but also at the level of the state governments.

The policy of economising on non-plan expenditures would directly affect the public funding of education, for, nearly 85 to 90 percent of expenditures of the educational institutions is on non-plan account. In case economies are introduced in non-plan expenditures, then it is but natural that the maintenance of the educational institutions, which is already deplorable, would suffer further. Since the salaries of the non-plan staff cannot be cut, the major brunt falls on the maintenance and upkeep of the buildings of the educational institutions, laboratories, equipments, approach roads, water supply and sanitation, etc., which are so crucial for proper functioning of the educational institutions. It would be useful to examine to what extent the reduction in non-plan expenditures at the central government level and also at the level of individual state governments has actually affected the maintenance and upkeep of the basic infrastructure of the educational institutions in different states during the period of the 90s. This is essentially a subject matter for micro level empirical investigation.

One may argue that reduction of the fiscal deficits and control on non-plan expenditures would improve the fund availability for private sector initiatives. This might be true. It is also likely that the bureaucratic hurdles in getting government grants may become irrelevant in this new regime of better liquidity in the entire economy in which the educational sector may also have a share. One should also note that this share is available strictly at the conditionality of the banks and the financial institutions. To what extent the educational entrepreneurship can meet these conditions is also a subject matter for empirical investigation. Thus, to what extent all this would favourably influence the educational sector is a matter for a detailed empirical study. A study of how many private sector initiatives have been taken during the period of the 90s for the purpose of development of schools, colleges and universities and to what extent this tempo is better than that during the period before 90s may, to some extent help resolve this issue. One should also note that by and large, conventional investors shy away from the educational sector. But in recent years investment in education by educational entrepreneurs is found to be much more rewarding than investment in non-educational or non-social-sector activities. The rates of return from education for the suppliers of education at all levels are found to be high, even higher than for other activities. Also, the returns are surer and are likely to be realised within a period of a few years of the course of education itself. From the point of view of the economy as a whole also, the rates of return from different levels and types of education are likely to be quite attractive. If these considerations work in the minds of entrepreneurs, then, they might take interest in funding education from borrowed funds. Even private beneficiaries from education like students and parents might think of funding education through borrowed funds in view of the high private rates of return, which are normally higher than those for other investments. As stated earlier, the effects of fiscal reforms in terms of improving liquidity and reducing the cost of borrowings have to be studied with detailed micro level data from the point of view of the suppliers of and individual beneficiaries from education. In case the contents of education are useful for the employers, then, they may also take the initiative of recruiting educated individuals and meeting their costs with the help of low cost borrowed funds, which are available on account of the positive liquidity effects of reduction of fiscal deficits and cuts on non-plan expenditures of the government.

The other important fiscal reform measures introduced in recent years relate to taxation. Reduction of the rates of all taxes might lead to favourable income effects and substitution effects, other things remaining the same. It is also argued on the basis of the Laffer Hypothesis that reduced tax rates might improve revenue collections for the government. In that case, the capacity of the government to fund its activities including education might increase. Whether or not this has actually happened may require statistical testing with empirical data. Similarly, with reduced tax rates the overall economic activity is likely to be favourably affected, according to the Laffer Hypothesis and perceptions of the supply-siders. Once again, whether or not this favourable effect for the economy as a whole would actually filter down to the educational sector is also an empirical question worth probing.

One of the tax reform measures consists of reduced share of indirect taxes as compared to the direct taxes. The conventional public finance theory suggests that the fiscal illusion operates more strongly in the case of indirect taxes than in the case of direct taxes indicating that the revenue effects and the 'spite effects' from a relatively larger direct tax burden are not likely to be favourable. From this point of view, one has to quantify the net effects of rate reduction, larger direct tax share and also greater rigour in tax administration (which also is a component of the fiscal reform measures), and weigh their relative importance, as some of them might work favouring the educational sector and some not so favourable to it.

Widening of the tax base particularly with regard to direct taxes (with the introduction of presumptive taxation, rigorous tax administration, etc.,) might also have similar positive and negative effects so far as the educational sector is concerned. Those who would have remained outside the tax net before these measures might find their ability to pay for education (which, incidentally, is likely to be costlier in the new situation) reduced. Thus, from the demand side the effect of this measure may be unfavourable for the educational sector.

The economic reforms have emphasised the policy of total withdrawals of subsidies or reduction of subsidies. Since education is one of the sectors where payments by beneficiaries are at much lower levels than the costs of their provision, implying high subsidy levels, the ethos of subsidy reduction has certainly affected the educational sector. There is also a move to raise the fees in the educational sector, particularly at higher educational levels, which has significant implications for the aspirants of education. Since the government grants are now shying away from education particularly at the higher levels, educational entrepreneurs particularly from the private sector are required to mobilise their own resources from the individual beneficiaries and also the employers. There is a limit on capacity to pay for education so far as the individual beneficiaries from education are concerned. Since there are also limits of the educational institutions to mobilise funds from the institutional beneficiaries in view of their niggardliness and absence of any statutory binding on them for such cost sharing of education, the educational sector is likely to be adversely affected on the whole on account of such a policy.

Agriculture Related Reforms

Reduction of debt relief for farmers: also an integral part of the new economic reforms, might force the farmers to set a new tradition of 'paying off their debts'. For a number of years, the ethos of debt relief for farmers had created high expectations about the government's role as a welfare agent. This sudden shift in the ethos has shaken the farmers' very approach towards their economic activity. In fact, a number of suicide deaths of the farmers reported in different states might be attributed to this sudden shift. Obviously, the farmers' ability to pay for the education of their wards has been very greatly affected during the period of the reform. It is a matter of empirical investigation to test to what extent the measure of debt relief withdrawal has affected the educational expenditures of farmers. Such developments in different states may have different types of effects on the period of reaching the target of UEE by the states. This question also deserves special attention by researchers.

The removal of quantitative restrictions on agricultural trade: together with freeing of prices of fertilisers and abolition of restrictions on the movement of agricultural commodities between the zones, etc., may have mixed effects on the educational sector. Free mobility might reduce the scarcity advantages for the farmers in some regions of the country. Also, mobility might lead to lower prices and larger availability of agricultural commodities. This might favourably influence the economic condition of the people in different parts of the country leading to greater ability to pay for education. Availability of foodgrains in different parts of the country might also improve the nutritional status of children encouraging them to attend schools without interruptions on account of nutritional deficiency related illness episodes. These are all conjectures about the likely effects. Obviously, these need to be empirically verified in different parts of the country.

Economic reforms, would thus, have mixed effects on the liquidity position relevant for the educational sector and positive substitution effects relating to the educational sector, though their precise quantitative magnitudes are a subject matter for empirical study.

The other aspects which should receive the attention of policy makers are the distributional effects of reforms on the educational sector. To what extent the first generation learners would be brought under the fold of education, the children of SC, ST and OBC would enter schools, colleges and universities, the other deprived groups like girls would be encouraged to receive adequate levels of education like their male counterparts, the less developed regions would get educational facilities, etc., are equally if not more important, considerations for an educational policy maker. It would be highly useful to study if the changes with regard to these aspects during the period of economic reforms, are brought out clearly. The first impressions suggest that economic reforms would have adverse distributional effects in general, and with regard to education in particular. Studies have shown that relative poverty has become more pronounced during the period of reforms. Since the relative income elasticity of household expenditures on education is likely to be fairly high, increases in the relative poverty measures in different states might adversely affect the efforts for promotion of education, particularly UEE. This also needs to be verified with facts and figures during the reform period.

Societal Value Related Effects of Economic Reforms

The more disturbing development worth the serious attention of educational policy makers during the reform period is the erosion of values and the shaking of the country's cultural identity. Globalisation and the information revolution through Internet access has in a sense led to the emergence of a global village wherein individual countries' identities are lost. Further, the cheap values that are being floated through the internet or TV (such as advertisements of a number of luxury items of consumption inducing consumerism, different lifestyles unknown to the Indian cultural ethos, such as observing Valentine's Day, etc.,) have totally debased the life style and thought process of children and the young and hence of future generations as a whole. Closer observers of developments in society have been feeling terribly concerned about such cultural imperialism from the developed world having a different cultural ethos than that of India. In this background, the educational sector, which is supposed to be the agent for inter-generational transfer of culture and heritage, has a tremendous role to play in protecting, reviving and to some extent strengthening the cultural base of the country. It is a subject matter for a multi-disciplinary investigation to study such developments in different community groups and regions in the country during the reform period.

The above general outline shows that the analysis of economic reforms on the educational sector would obviously require a strong analytical framework and a dependable database. In order to facilitate future quantitative research in this area we present below a chart indicating the likely issues of importance in this field and the needed database for examining various analytical issues involved. This chart is essentially illustrative and may not be considered to have covered all the relevant issues in this connection. The chart essentially aims at summarising the main points of discussion in the above paragraphs.

CHART : **Issues to be Tested for Analysing the Nexus between Economic Reforms and the Education Sector**

Reform Item	Issues for Empirical Testing and Development of Database
I. Trade Sector	
1. Import tariff 2. Export tariff 3. Withdrawal of CCS 4. Dilution of licensing system 5. Devaluation 6. Dual exchange rates	i) Has reduction in tariffs reduced the costs of goods and services for providers of educational opportunities and for students and parents ? ii) What are the indirect effects of these cost reductions on parents' decision making to finance education and supply of educational care services ? iii) What is the import content of different types and levels of education ? iv) Have different doses of devaluation and abolition of dual exchange rate regime led to positive income effects for the exporters of goods and services of the educational sector (like books, laboratory material, computer software, etc.,) produced through the educational sector? v) What is the extent of import content of the educational sector related export activities? vi) Has devaluation and abolition of the dual exchange rate regime caused a rise in the import bill of the exporters of education sector related goods and services?

(contd.)

CHART *(contd.)*

Reform Item	Issues for Empirical Testing and Development of Database
II. Industrial Sector	
1. Drastic scaling back of industrial licensing system (except 18 core sectors) 2. Policies promoting capital mobility 3. Relaxation of MRTP Act 4. Opening up of industries to the private sector-privatisation 5. Liberalisation of FDI and foreign portfolio investment 6. Relaxation of FERA 7. Foreign investment up to 1 per cent of equity holdings permitted in 34 industries	i) What are the direct and indirect effects of the reforms relating to the industrial sector on the industry producing goods and services used in the educational sector? ii) Have the promotional policies relating to the industrial sector resulted in larger investment in the education sector related industrial activity? iii) Have these policies led to cost advantages and positive income effects for the entrepreneurs in the education sector related activities? Have these measures finally led to larger resource availability for the educational sector? iv) Have the measures to relax FERA and permission for foreign investment up to 51per cent of equity capital led to larger investment flow from abroad into the educational core sector? v) What relative advantages are attained by the educational sector as compared to other sectors as a result of NRI funds flow? vii) How many foreign collaborative initiatives have been signed in activities that are of relevance to the educational sector during the period after the introduction of these industrial sector reforms? What are their effects on supplies of education sector related services? viii) Have the income effects arising out of the industrial sector reforms affected the availability of educational opportunities in rural areas in particular?

(contd.)

CHART *(contd.)*

Reform Item	Issues for Empirical Testing and Development of Database
III. Financial Sector Reforms	
1. CPR and SLR lowered, implying less governmental access to the resource of commercial banks. 2. Interest rates deregulated and brought down. 3. Post of Controller of Capital Issues was abolished but Security Exchange Board of India (SEBI) was established. 4. Increased level of foreign portfolios investments.	i) Have measures of financial sector reforms led to larger availability of funds for private initiative in the educational sector? ii) Have the liquidity advantages for the education sector related activities of the private sector caused a corresponding disadvantage for the public sector initiated educational activities? iii) What is the effect of this on the supply of educational opportunities for the less privileged sections of the population and also for the people in the rural areas who normally depend upon the public sector supply of educational opportunities? iv) Have the budgets of the Depts. of Education got compressed during the reform period? v) What is the incidence of this budgetary compression at the micro level ? In other words, which components of the education budget are affected as a result of the liquidity disadvantages for the public sector initiatives? vi) How far are the expenditures/investments in the educational sector interest elastic? vii) Have reductions in interest rates favourably affected investments by private sector borrowers for starting new education related ventures? viii) Have these ventures been initiated in rural areas as well? ix) Have private educational entrepreneurs found the interest rate reduction advantageous to start educational activities with borrowed funds?

(contd.)

CHART *(contd.)*

Reform Item	Issues for Empirical Testing and Development of Database
	x) How many such new initiatives are taken by private entrepreneurs, with borrowed funds during the reforms?
	xi) Have public sector initiatives (for starting educational institutions etc.,) also started depending upon borrowing from the banking system in the open financial markets for the purpose of meeting their budgetary needs in education?
IV. Fiscal Policy Reforms	
1. Reduction of fiscal deficit 2. Economy in non-plan expenditures 3. Tax rate reduction (all taxes) 4. Relative importance of direct taxes vs. indirect taxes raised (from 1:3 to 2:3) 5. Widening of tax base 6. Introduction of presumptive taxation 7. Bank credit to the government reduced by 44 per cent 8. Central government debt held by RBI reduced from 15 per cent to 10 per cent 9. Central government budget deficit financed by RBI reduced by 33 per cent to less than 25 per cent 10. Net central government debt held by RBI reduced	i) Are fiscal deficits and outlay on the education sector related? A study of this behaviour at the union government and the state government levels could be done. ii) How have the economy measures in non-plan expenditures affected education expenditures of government? What effects are seen from these measures on maintenance and up keep of different components of the activities of the education sector? How have these measures affected the quality of educational services? Has there been a differential effect on the educational services supplied in the urban areas and the rural areas, as a result of the measures of the economy in non-plan expenditures? iii) What are the liquidity advantages for private sector initiatives relating to the social sector in general and to education in particular, owing to reduction in fiscal deficit and economy in non-plan expenditures at the union government and the state government levels? iv) Have measures for reduction in rates of income tax caused positive income and

(contd.)

CHART *(contd.)*

Reform Item	Issues for Empirical Testing and Development of Database
by 15.6 per cent of GDP to 9 per cent of GDP	substitution effects for the supply of educational facilities at different levels ?
11. Net external borrowing declined significantly (share declined)	v) How has the reduction in indirect taxes, excise duties and sales taxes (and other types of indirect taxes) affected the costs of supplies of educational services?
12. Corporation and income tax together increased from 2 per cent to 3 per cent of the GDP	vi) Have these cost advantages due to tax rate reduction been transferred to the users of such facilities, such as students or parents?
13. Excise and customs duties' share reduced from 9 per cent to 7 per cent of GDP	vii) What effects have been felt on account of the dilution of fiscal illusion due to dominant direct tax share in the overall tax burden in the economy?
14. Non-interest expenditure reduced from 16 per cent to 13 per cent of GDP	viii) Has widening of the tax base, bringing the hitherto non-taxed persons under the tax net (say, through presumptive taxes) affected the disposable income of such new tax payers and thereby affected their expenditure on education of themselves or of their wards? In other words does a close study show the changes in household expenditures on education and education related activities during the reform period and analysis of the factors responsible for these changes?
15. Reduction of subsidies	ix) What are the effects of reduction in subsidies relating to the goods and services that are relevant to the education sector on the composition and size of the educational budgets of households? Similarly, what are the effects of subsidy reduction on the producers and suppliers of educational facilities, at the state and the sub-regional levels?
	x) Have the proposals relating to the plan and non plan needs of the educational

(contd.)

CHART *(contd.)*

Reform Item		Issues for Empirical Testing and Development of Database
		sector, submitted by the state government been sharply cut in the plan discussions and also in discussions with the Finance Commission during the reform period?
	xi)	What is the extent of the *'coefficient of distrust'* in the course of decision making for plan financing and also the financing of the non-plan expenditures relating to the education sector?
	xii)	Information about subsidiary points needs to be analysed. How far have the fiscal policy reforms introduced at the union and the state government levels affected the process of decentralisation relating to the educational sector? What are the effects on the expenditures of the districts, in selected states?
VI. Overall Effect of Economic Reforms	i)	What are the effects of considering price as a major instrument of planning and resource mobilisation so far as the educational sector is concerned since price is emerging as a major instrument?
	ii)	What are the implications of such a system of funding on the composition of the educational sector? What are the effects of a mixed system of funding consisting of 'price', based upon the *quid-pro-quo* principle with regard to some components of education and another, based upon the general system of non-price linked financing? Has the economic reform process affected the composition of the supply of services within the educational sector ?
	iii)	What are the effects of considering price as a major instrument of exclusion, on distribution and utilisation of educational

(contd.)

CHART *(contd.)*

Reform Item	Issues for Empirical Testing and Development of Database
	services? Have the socio-economically less privileged sections of the population been feeling a greater degree of deprivation in the course of the economic reforms?
	iv) Have multi-nationals taken any initiative in improving the access to and utilisation of educational opportunities in rural areas?
	v) Has there been a differential treatment of the rural areas of the developed and less developed states? Analysis of this issue with a mapping of educational facilities in the states is indicated.
	vi) Classification of educational opportunity indicators which are likely to be affected by the economic reforms in the short run, medium run and long run needs to be done.
	vii) The effects of economic reforms on the educational opportunities of different population groups, male and female child population, SC, ST population, religious groups, educational aspirants from HHs of workers in the organised sector, workers in the unorganised sectors etc., need to be studied.
	viii) Analysis of the effects of reforms on these population groups in different states with varying levels and rates of development. Are the less developed states being treated less favourably by the economic reforms as compared to the developed states?
	What changes are felt during the economic reforms in the access and utilization of educational opportunities by the specific population groups in the states of different level, and rates of development?

It is hoped that studies will be initiated in future with the above perspectives and these will generate a comprehensive database useful for policy making. Countervailing measures can be taken firmly on the basis of such an analysis and data.

Comparative Facts in the Indian Context

A comparative analysis of inter-temporal data relating to education and other relevant variables might help firming up some of the conclusions about the effect of economic reforms on education in the Indian context. It is true that not all changes in education can be attributed to economic reforms. Also, as stated earlier, for all the relevant aspects of educational change that are likely to be affected by the reforms, systematic and comprehensive data are not available. It is with these limitations that the following statistical analysis should be viewed.

Changes in the Governmental Initiatives Towards the Social Sector

Researchers have advanced a hypothesis of compression of public sector outlay on education and health during the reform period. Government expenditures on social services and education have registered an increase in absolute terms over the period of time, illustrating, as it were, Wagner's Law of increasing state activity. Thus, during the six year period before the intensive reform process of 1991, the state government expenditures on social services aggregated to Rs.10491 crores, which increased to Rs.13438 crores during the six year period after 1991/92. Similarly, expenditures on education, Medical & Public Health, Housing, Urban Development, etc. also registered significant increases during the same period. This can be seen from the Appendix Table.

But, what is worth noting is the decline in the share of expenditures of some of the crucial components of the social sector during the reform period. Thus, before the reform period social services constituted about 39.4 per cent of total government expenditures. This percentage declined to 36 during the period 1991/92 to 1996/97. Similar trends are seen in the case of education, sports, art and culture, medical and public health, water supply and sanitation, housing, labour and labour welfare, social security and welfare relief on account of natural calamities, etc. Table 5.1 presents the percentage share of some of these crucial components of the social sector.

TABLE 5.1: **Expenditure of All States on Social Sector (Per cent to Total Government Expenditure)**

Components of Social Sector	Pre-Reform Period (1985-86 to 1990-91)			During Reform Period (1991-92 to 1998-99)		
	Plan	Non-Plan	Total	Plan	Non-Plan	Total
Social services	9.18	30.20	39.39	8.32	27.68	36.00
Education, sports, art and culture	2.11	18.89	21.00	2.28	17.58	19.86
Medical & public health	2.18	4.60	6.78	1.77	4.06	5.83
Water supply and sanitation	1.71	0.84	2.55	1.22	0.89	2.11
Housing	0.17	0.38	0.55	0.19	0.28	0.47
Urban development	0.35	0.45	0.80	0.45	0.41	0.86
Welfare of SC, ST and OBC	1.29	1.25	2.53	1.18	4.85	6.03
Labour and labour welfare	0.18	0.53	0.71	0.14	0.42	0.56
Social security and welfare	0.67	1.36	2.04	0.60	1.16	1.76
Nutrition	0.46	0.29	0.75	0.34	0.57	0.91
Relief on account of natural calamities	0.01	1.35	1.37	0.10	0.92	1.01
Others	0.05	0.27	0.32	0.06	0.22	0.28

Source: RBI Bulletins, 1985-1999.

Thus, in most of the components of the social sector, the percentage share of state government expenditures has declined during the reform period. This is worth noting. The share of plan expenditures has also declined in the case of a number of components of the social sector. From this point of view, it appears that the reforms are not associated with fresh initiatives (i.e., plan programmes) of the government with regard to the social sector.

When the data for state government expenditures on social sector on revenue account were considered according to major states, the picture became more revealing. The data were classified according to whether the states are poor states, medium developed states and developed states. The classification was done according to the per capita income for the year 1991. Table 5.2 brings out this revealing picture.

That the shares of major components of the social sector in the total revenue expenditures of the states have fallen is brought out more clearly from the following graphs which present this picture about expenditures on education.

It can be seen that even in many of the poor states, the expenditure share of education in revenue expenditure has fallen during the reform period. This decline in the relative expenditures on the social sector is quite expected in the course of the reforms, which aim at the goal of efficiency in the allocation of resources. A cautious and responsive policy maker has to immediately attend to these challenges and introduce the necessary correctives.

Plan expenditure on different sectors of education during the period prior to reform and of reform also brings out certain interesting aspects. For example, as the following table shows, the share of elementary education in plan outlay on education has been showing significant declines. While increase in the share of elementary education is desirable the decline in the case of higher education is a cause for concern because of their long-term effects on equal access to educational opportunities and technical competency of the entire economy. Table 5.3 brings out these trends.

Budgetary expenditure on education as percentage of total budget has shown significant declines in the case of some of the states where education needs to receive much encouragement. For example, in the case of the less developed states of Madhya Pradesh,

TABLE 5.2: **Pre- and During Reform Period Statewise Expenditure on Major Components of Social Sector (Revenue Account) (% to Total Expenditure)**

Sl.No.	State	Period	Social Services			Education, Sports Art & Culture			Medical & Public Health			Water Supply & Sanitation		
			Plan	Non-plan	Total	Plan	Non-plan	Total	Plan	Non-plan	Total	Plan	Non-plan	Total
1	2	3	4	5	6	7	8	9	10	11	12	13	14	15
		Poor States												
1.	Assam	Pre-Reform	12.22	28.26	40.48	4.65	33.50	23.51	2.30	22.80	5.74	2.74	21.28	3.91
		Reform period	15.08	25.93	41.01	8.37	18.72	27.11	2.47	3.10	5.57	1.97	0.62	2.59
2.	Bihar	Pre-Reform	6.37	32.89	39.26	2.04	21.54	23.57	2.43	3.83	6.26	0.10	1.30	1.40
		Reform period	6.42	31.38	37.80	1.27	22.41	23.68	2.54	3.85	6.38	0.09	1.18	1.27
3.	J&K	Pre-Reform	7.20	26.44	33.63	3.17	12.62	15.78	1.94	5.46	7.40	0.75	2.33	3.08
		Reform period	6.78	27.30	34.08	3.09	13.36	16.45	1.68	5.21	6.89	0.84	2.65	3.48
4.	Karnataka	Pre-Reform	10.40	31.81	42.21	1.52	19.53	21.05	2.40	4.72	7.13	1.85	0.29	2.14
		Reform period	13.31	24.48	37.78	3.66	16.08	17.74	2.26	3.82	6.08	2.12	0.14	2.26
5.	Kerala	Pre-Reform	6.01	41.18	47.19	1.54	26.72	28.26	2.05	5.83	7.87	0.84	0.93	1.79
		Reform period	6.53	33.35	39.88	1.13	23.19	24.32	1.46	5.07	6.53	1.16	0.61	1.77
6.	Madhya	Pre-Reform	12.48	27.00	39.48	2.86	15.56	18.42	2.82	3.47	6.29	2.84	1.40	4.23
	Pradesh	Reform period	10.76	24.76	35.52	2.63	13.76	16.39	2.14	3.08	5.22	1.53	1.46	2.99

(contd.)

TABLE 5.2 *(contd.)*

1	2	3	4	5	6	7	8	9	10	11	12	13	14	15
7.	Manipur	Pre-Reform	9.16	29.73	38.89	3.93	20.09	24.02	1.99	3.89	5.87	0.00	1.70	1.70
		Reform period	10.46	27.71	38.17	4.43	20.96	25.39	1.64	3.87	5.52	0.53	0.42	0.95
8.	Meghalaya	Pre-Reform	9.92	24.79	34.71	4.43	13.46	17.89	2.02	5.45	7.47	0.59	2.53	3.12
		Reform period	13.35	24.34	37.69	7.37	13.12	20.49	2.19	4.48	6.67	0.42	3.5	3.91
9.	Mizoram	Pre-Reform	10.69	23.43	34.13	3.56	11.46	15.02	1.57	3.27	4.84	1.83	2.5	4.33
		Reform period	11.85	22.68	34.53	3.18	13.24	16.41	2.44	2.96	5.4	1.52	1.75	3.27
10.	Orissa	Pre-Reform	14.76	26.67	41.42	4.27	16.63	20.9	3.26	3.75	7.01	1.88	0.8	2.68
		Reform period	14.21	23.73	37.94	5.12	14.66	19.78	2.11	3.24	5.35	1.63	0.65	2.28
11.	Rajasthan	Pre-Reform	7.6	31.67	39.27	3.01	18.72	21.73	2.4	4.78	7.17	0.38	3.94	4.32
		Reform period	7.86	31.53	39.4	3.71	19.1	22.81	.14	4.54	6.68	0.07	4.12	4.19
12.	Tripura	Pre-Reform	17.24	25.47	42.71	5.14	16.15	21.29	2.09	3.59	5.68	0.81	0.55	1.36
		Reform period	15.23	23.71	38.95	5.14	15.56	20.7	2.19	2.77	4.96	0.52	0.43	0.94
13.	Uttar	Pre-Reform	8.59	27.27	35.82	1.83	19.75	21.58	2.65	4.32	6.97	1.96	0.3	2.26
	Pradesh	Reform period	7.5	24.29	31.79	1.88	17.02	18.9	1.53	4.1	5.63	1.5	0.28	1.78
14.	West Bengal	Pre-Reform	7.64	35.83	43.48	1.78	23.4	25.18	1.66	6.29	7.94	0.87	0.56	1.42
		Reform period	7.01	32.94	39.95	1.21	22.11	23.32	1.47	5.43	6.89	1.19	0.57	1.76

(contd.)

TABLE 5.2 *(contd.)*

1	2	3	4	5	6	7	8	9	10	11	12	13	14	15
					Medium Developed States									
15.	Andhra	Pre-reform	11.33	29.42	40.75	1.8	17.6	19.4	2	4.11	6.11	2.3	0.3	2.59
	Pradesh	Reform period	8.75	29.13	37.87	1.47	14.85	16.32	1.8	3.86	5.66	1.59	0.41	2
16.	Arunachal	Pre-reform	9.15	19.54	28.69	4.59	9.92	14.51	1.37	4.53	5.9	2.35	1.01	3.35
	Pradesh	Reform period	15.17	14.98	31.15	7.37	7.69	15.13	1.77	4.08	5.85	4.17	0.49	4.66
17.	Gujarat	Pre-reform	6.15	33.5	39.66	0.96	20.18	21.15	0.64	5.54	6.17	1.29	0.6	1.89
		Reform period	5.89	29.73	35.62	0.92	17.75	18.67	0.85	4.72	5.58	0.48	0.72	1.2
18.	Himachal	Pre-reform	9.37	29.94	39.31	3.31	17.32	20.63	2.36	5.05	7.41	1.84	2.21	4.05
	Pradesh	Reform period	12.56	22.66	35.23	5.41	13.08	18.49	2.84	4.14	6.98	1.57	2.13	3.7
19.	Nagaland	Pre-reform	5.65	24.79	30.44	1.98	10.2	12.17	1.27	5.42	6.69	0.07	33.17	3.24
		Reform period	5.21	21.79	27	2	11.1	13.1	1.37	3.65	5.02	0.07	3.33	3.4
20.	Sikkim	Pre-reform	14.51	19.28	33.78	7.59	10.49	18.08	1.93	3.47	5.4	2.1	0.9	3
		Reform period	6.11	7.87	13.98	2.36	4.43	6.79	1.04	1.41	2.45	0.44	0.35	0.8

(contd.)

TABLE 5.2 *(contd.)*

1	2	3	4	5	6	7	8	9	10	11	12	13	14	15
21.	Tamil Nadu	Pre-reform	12.46	31.52	43.97	1.96	19.87	21.82	2.25	4.97	7.22	2.58	0.18	2.76
		Reform Period	8.33	31.03	39.37	1.2	18.95	20.16	1.64	4.45	6.09	1.82	0.38	2.21
						Rich States								
22.	Goa	Pre-reform	8.8	32.01	40.81	5.32	18.79	24.11	1.14	7.34	8.49	0.59	3.01	3.6
		Reform period	6.1	21.72	27.71	2.29	13.2	15.39	1.09	4.44	5.43	1.75	2.55	4.19
23.	Haryana	Pre-reform	11.62	22.54	34.16	2.13	14.94	17.06	1.94	2.98	4.92	2.44	0.6	3.03
		Reform period	6.94	18.49	25.43	2.02	10.88	12.9	1.01	2.27	3.28	0.22	2.17	2.39
24.	Maharashtra	Pre-reform	7.18	28.18	35.36	1.2	17.99	19.2	1.91	4.42	6.33	2.33	0.17	2.49
		Reform period	8.21	26.95	35.16	1.66	18.13	19.8	1.46	3.36	4.82	1.96	0.26	2.21
25.	Punjab	Pre-reform	5.65	33.38	39.04	1.56	20	21.56	1.71	5.44	7.15	1.11	1.05	2.16
		Reform period	4.98	21.21	26.18	2.11	13.18	15.29	1.39	3.52	4.91	0.87	0.94	1.81

Notes: 1. Pre-reform Period: 1985 to 1990.
Reform Period: 1991 to 1999.
2. The percentage share of average expenditure in total revenue expenditure for the above two periods have been presented here.
3. States have been classified as Poor, Medium and Rich taking into account the per capita income for the year 1990/91.

Pre-Reform & Reform Period, Share of Expenditure (Revenue Account) on Education (State-wise) % to Total Expensditure
FOR POOR STATES

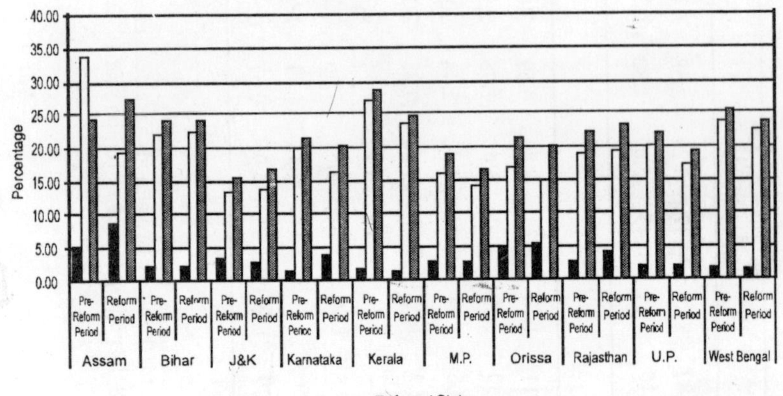

Reform / State

Education Sports Art & Cl. Plan | Education Sports Art & Cl. Non-Plan | Education Sports Art & Cl. Total

Pre-Reform & Reform Period, Share of Expenditure (Revenue Account) on Education (State-wise) % to Total Expenditure
FOR MEDIUM STATES

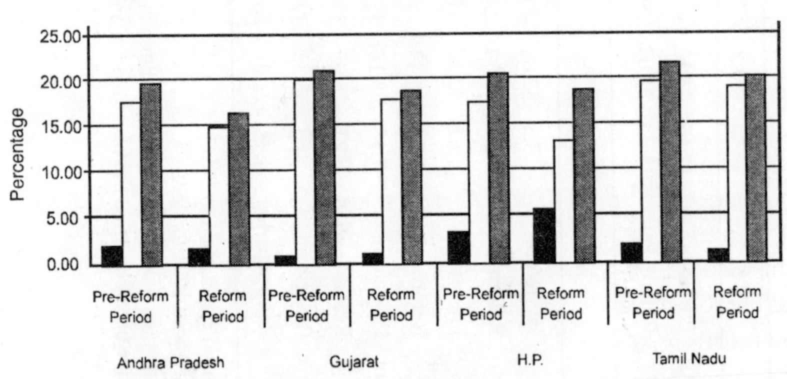

Reform / State

Education Sports Art & Cl. Plan | Education Sports Art & Cl. Non-Plan | Education Sports Art & Cl. Total

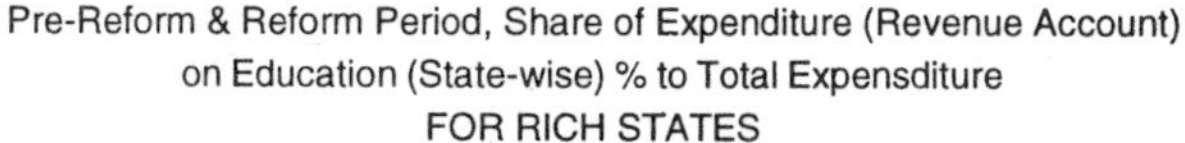

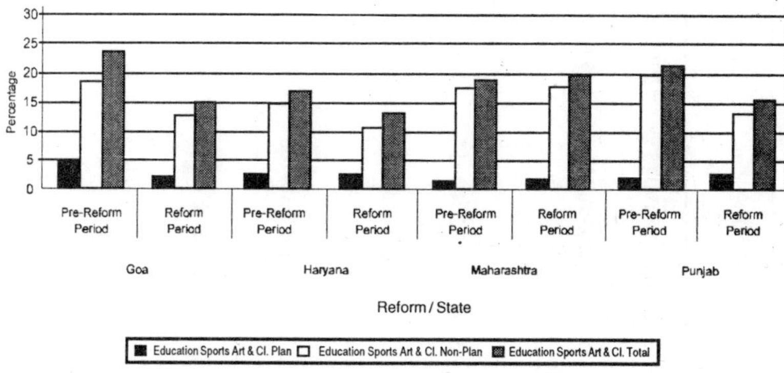

Bihar, Orissa, Uttar Pradesh, etc. the share of budgetary expenditure on education in the total budget has been actually showing a declining trend from 1990/91 to 1996/97. For all the states and UTs also, this share has declined from 28.25 per cent in 1990/91 to 19.6 per cent in 1996/97. Budgetary expenditure on education as percentage of SDP has also shown a decline during the reform period, particularly for the less developed states. Table 5.4 brings out these trends.

States and UTs finance their expenditures through own sources and also through assistance from the Union Government. A close scrutiny of the assistance from the Union Government to the states for education reveals that in recent years during the reform period, the share of central loans to the states for education is showing signs of an increasing trend as compared to the share of central grants. This also shows that the poor states in particular are likely to be under the burden of central loans for financing the educational sector during the reform period.

Thus, the developments during the reform period bring out the following main issues for consideration of the policy makers :

i) The share of plan expenditure is declining;
ii) The share of non-plan expenditure which is so crucial in the

TABLE 5.3: **Plan Expenditure on Different Sectors of Education**

Sector	Ist Plan 51-56	IInd Plan 56-61	IIIrd Plan 61-66	Annual 66-69	IV Plan 69-74	Vth Plan 74-79	VIth Plan 80-85	VIIth Plan 85-90	Annual 90-92	VIIIth Plan 92-97
1. Elementary Education	850 (56)	950 (34)	2010 (34)	750 (24)	2390 (30)	8360 (31)	8360 (31)	28490 (33)	17290 (32)	92010 (42.5)
2. Secondary Education	200 (13)	510 (19)	1030 (18)	530 (18)	1400 (18)	5300 (20)	5300 (20)	18320 (21.5)	10530 (19)	34980 (16)
3. Adult Education	—	—	—	—	—	—	2240 (8)	4700 (5.5)	4160 (8)	18480 (8.5)
4. Higher Education	140 (9)	870 (15)	870 (15)	770 (24)	1950 (25)	2050 (23)	5590 (21)	12010 (14)	5880 (11)	15160 (7)
5. Others	140 (9)	730 (12)	730 (12)	370 (11)	1060 (14)	1070 (12)	2730 (10)	10830 (13)	8230 (15)	27860 (13)
6. Technical Education	200 (13)	1250 (21)	1250 (21)	810 (25)	1060 (13)	1070 (12)	2730 (10)	10830 (13)	8230 (15)	27860 (13)
7. Total	1530(100)	5890(100)	5890(100)	3230(100)	7860(100)	8920(100)	26950(100)	85180(100)	543320(100)	216350(100)

Notes : Figures in brackets denote percentage to total expenditure.

Source: R.V. Vaidyanatha Ayyar, "Educational Planning and Administration in India: Retrospect & Prospect", *Journal of Educational Planning and Administration*, Vol. VII, No. 2, NIEPA. New Delhi.

TABLE 5.4: **Budgetary Expenditure on Education as Percentage of SDP**

States	1985-86	1992-93	1994-95
Andhra Pradesh	5.12	4.47	4.60
Bihar	4.48	5.53	4.75
Karnataka	4.66	3.99	4.09
Madhya Pradesh	3.99	4.91 (1991-92)	4.68
Tamil Nadu	5.11(1991)	4.75	4.35
Uttar Pradesh	4.73(1991)	4.55	4.18
West Bengal	4.73(1991)	3.58	3.74

case of education is also showing a decline, indicating heavy pressures on the educational sector for the purpose of maintenance of existing facilities and infrastructure;

iii) The developments in the case of poor states are particularly intriguing during the reform period since the share of plan and non-plan expenditures in total revenue expenditures of this group of states are not showing a rising trend;

iv) Intra-sectoral shares of expenditures among different levels of education also do not seem to be in the interest of long term development of the economy since relative allocations to higher education are showing a declining trend;

v) Central assistance to the states for development of education appears to be more in the form of loans rather than grants indicating increasing loan burden on the states for the purpose of educational development; and

vi) Increasing interest of the Union Government in the states' responsibility towards education suggests induced abridgement of states' initiative for educational development. Some of the recent initiatives in education with the central support and funding from external sources (such as DPEP) also suggest the dependence of the educational sector of the states on the remoter sources of funding, implying not only dependency but also uncertainty in the pace of development of the educational sector.

Corrective Measures for Safeguarding the Interest of the Educational Sector during the Reform Period

In order to safeguard the interests of the educational sector timely correctives are needed. Some of the correctives may be suggested as follows :

a) Protecting the allocations to the educational sector as a whole,
b) Non-abridgement of the role of the government in education during the reform period, suggesting that the government cannot absolve itself from the responsibility towards provision of educational facilities *at all levels* of education including secondary and higher education in the interest of equality and equity,
c) Trying out less expensive methodology of education particularly at school level. The methodology of an educational guarantee scheme tried out in some states may be effectively implemented in all other states, for which the goal distance from UEE is still long,
d) Discriminatory pricing of education at all levels,
e) Mobilisation of resources from the community for the purpose of meeting increasing costs of education.

Recent initiatives to declare education as a fundamental right in the Indian Constitution and also to introduce Sarva Shikha Abhiyan may be interpreted as the responses to the likely unfavourable effects from the reform processes. This safety net approach needs to be extended further to secondary and higher educational levels also for the reasons explained above.

Reciprocal Linkages

Just as reforms have implications for the educational sector, the developments in the case of the educational sector also have implications for the reform process. Such reciprocal linkages need to be clearly recognised in order to increase the effectiveness of reforms for the educational sector itself. The following reciprocal linkages may be considered.

1. If in the course of economic reforms, subsidies are increasingly withdrawn particularly from the upper stages of education, the contribution of education to the economy and society in the long run is likely to be affected. India, which, at one time, used to boast of being a top ranker as a scientific and technical manpower reservoir, can no longer have this distinction in the future, if its higher education in particular is left to fend for itself. At any point of time, weakening of the higher educational sector, would weaken the forces of competitiveness and efficiency in the functioning of different sectors of the economy. This development would also increase the dependency of the developing countries like India, on technologically better-developed countries of the world. In fact, the strategy of human resource development as advanced by Harbison and Myers during the mid 60s for countries in different stages of development has proved to be counter-productive particularly for the developing and less developed countries.
2. External funding of and special attention to some of the activities in the educational sector seem to have changed the work ethos within some of the wings of the department of education and introduced the elitist trends therein. Such developments might have implications for value formation in the economy. The educational sector is considered to be an effective agent for value formation and inter generational value transmission. The elitist overtones in the educational sector might have implications for this role of the sector.
3. Globalisation within the educational sector might make the educational outputs more outward oriented rather than oriented towards national development itself. While India's education sector is considered to be a major supplier of scientific and technical manpower to developed countries,

in the long run, the national economy is likely to be starved of such competent personnel, weakening the competitive strength of the economy in international competition. Thus, the reform process aiming at efficiency may itself get weakened on account of such changes within the educational sector realised through the reform process itself.

4. In order that the effect of economic reforms on the educational sector is favourable it is necessary to introduce reforms within the education sector itself. Measures for improving internal and external efficiency of the sector need to be introduced in such a way that the equity effects of such efficiency-oriented reforms are not unfavourable.

Concluding Observations

In this paper an attempt is made to present a framework for analysing the effects of economic reforms for the educational sector. This framework also presents the data compilation plan for analysing the effects of reforms.

The data available for analysing the effects of economic reforms on educational sector suggest the need for urgent corrective measures to safeguard the outlays of the educational sector and arrest the process of abridgement of the governmental initiative and responsibility towards all levels of education including upper stages of education. The pattern of funding of education during the reform period calls for an urgent attention to the equity effects of this emerging pattern, effects on the federal working in the field of education and the dangers of elitists developments The paper also urges us to take note of the likely adverse effects of reforms on the values of Indian society and the economy and suggests the immediate attention of policy makers and opinion makers to take suitable measures to strengthen the role of education as an agent for value formation and value transmission. On the whole, while the reforms have some positive implications for education, the overall balance sheet does not seem to be very favourable for the social sector in general and for education in particular.

Appendix Table

Pre- and During Reform, Statewise Total Expenditure on Selected Items of Social Sector (Revenue Account)

(Rs.in crores)

Sl. No.	State	Period	Social Services	Education Sports Art & Culture	Medical & Public Health	Water Supply & Sanitation
1	2	3	4	5	6	7
1.	Assam	Pre-Reform	567.66	329.65	80.44	54.85
		During Reform	1402.16	927.03	190.44	88.59
2.	Bihar	Pre-Reform	1229.59	738.31	195.99	43.83
		During Reform	3187.47	1996.62	538.05	106.99
3.	J&K	Pre-Reform	293.94	137.96	64.69	26.88
		During Reform	862.39	416.28	174.44	88.15
4.	Karnataka	Pre-Reform	1166.43	581.55	196.98	59.15
		During Reform	312.45	1684.82	518.91	192.51
5.	Kerala	Pre-Reform	30.68	563.57	157.02	35.63
		During Reform	67.29	1453.69	390.39	105.71
6.	Madhya Pradesh	Pre-Reform	91.14	600.07	205.01	137.93
		During Reform	3380.2	1559.8	496.79	284.32
7.	Orissa	Pre-Reform	647.15	326.52	29.31	41.84
		During Reform	1754.74	914.96	75.24	105.48
8.	Rajastan	Pre-Reform	943.02	521.82	9.17	103.69
		During Reform	2916.42	1688.85	5.1	309.9
9.	Uttar Pradesh	Pre-Reform	1663.22	1001.91	91	104.82
		During Reform	5563.05	3307.26	262.26	310.87
10.	West Bengal	Pre-Reform	1303.37	754.7	25.99	42.7
		During Reform	3335.32	1947.03	99.36	146.95
11.	Andhra Pradesh	Pre-Reform	1638.39	780.07	245.75	104.29
		During Reform	4098.08	1765.63	612.4	216.95

(contd.)

APPENDIX *(contd.)*

1	2	3	4	5	6	7
12.	Gujarat	Pre-Reform	1220.77	650.95	190.05	58.3
		During Reform	2911.77	1526.04	456.02	97.55
13.	Himachal	Pre-Reform	65.73	33.25	13.51	7.68
	Pradesh	During Reform	149.47	75.01	29.01	23.1
14.	Tamil Nadu	Pre-Reform	1630.86	809.41	267.65	102.37
		During Reform	4362.05	2233.71	674.61	244.44
15.	Goa	Pre-Reform	85.44	50.48	17.77	7.53
		During Reform	160.78	89.27	31.48	24.33
16.	Haryana	Pre-Reform	462.38	230.94	66.58	41.06
		During Reform	1324.78	671.91	171.02	124.54
17.	Maharashtra	Pre-Reform	2229.06	1210.08	398.99	157.17
		During Reform	6057.53	3410.9	829.71	381.54
18.	Punjab	Pre-Reform	677.98	374.44	124.24	37.56
		During Reform	1584.11	925.28	297.26	109.68

Note: Pre-reform Period—1985 to 1990.
During Reform Period —1991 to 1999.

6

ECONOMIC REFORMS AND THE HEALTH SECTOR TOWARDS HEALTH EQUITY IN INDIA[1]

ANIL GUMBER

Background

Since mid-1991 a wide range of economic and policy reforms have been initiated in India with the broad objective of attaining a higher and sustainable growth rate coupled with equity and human development. The economic reforms process comprised two major components: (a) stabilisation of the macro-economy aimed at controlling the fiscal and balance of payment deficits and lowering the rate of inflation, and (b) opening up the economy to international trade and investment through structural adjustments including internal and external deregulations, leading to a shift towards a neutral foreign trade regime. More recently, in the union budget 2001/02, a second degree of economic reforms have been announced by focusing amongst other things on human development specifically on demand creation, investment generation, strengthening rural infrastructure, government downsizing, employment and labour flexibility and social security.

In the light of these reforms the paper attempts to raise some critical issues: (a) How much progress has the country made in various health outcomes? (b) What is the status of health provision and financing? (c) Are the health equity issues in terms of accessibility and use adequately addressed?

During the period of macroeconomic adjustments and structural changes, some of the critical health parameters and their determinants are affecting the people. For instance, the growing incidence of lifestyle diseases owing to changes in the demographic structure, the emerging new public health threats (spreading of HIV infection and injury) and increasing health risks because of the high prevalence of alcohol and tobacco consumption. While these are not directly the result of policy initiatives they are certainly susceptible to policy impact and raise important equity concerns. It is well understood that there are no straightforward impacts of economic reforms on the health status of people; however, certain important parameters which affect the purchasing power of people in turn exhibit a significant impact on health outcomes. In fact there is a strong association between poverty and health, and any policy changes influencing poverty (such as employment generation, income growth, income distribution, prices, income transfers and safety nets) would also impinge on health, of course with a lagged effect.[2] The impact of reform measures initiated in 1991 at the macro level appears to be satisfactory. However, its impact at the micro level has become a subject of debate among scholars and policy makers. Evidence from Latin America and other countries shows that faster growth has brought about a corresponding widening of the set of available economic opportunities and increase in poverty. In India the relative increase in the level of poverty in the initial period of reform appears to be marginal.

The primary focus of this paper is on morbidity and disease prevalence and their treatment, on the utilisation of health services and on the cost and burden of health care. The paper also looks in detail at the socio-economic equity dimensions with respect to area of residence (rural and urban), scheduled and non-scheduled populations, economic status in terms of quintile of monthly per capita expenditure (MPCE) and gender differentials. The paper draws heavily upon data from the two surveys of health care utilisation undertaken by the National Sample Survey Organisation in the mid 1980s and mid 1990s and the National Council of Applied Economic Research (NCAER) survey on a similar subject during 1993.

Health Care System

According to World Bank estimates for 1990, India spent about 6 per cent of GDP on health care, which amounts to Rs. 320 per capita. By 1993 per capita health spending in India had increased further to Rs. 334 (see Appendix). This is a very high proportion when compared to OECD and Asian countries. For instance, OECD countries including Canada are spending between 7 and 8 per cent of GDP and some Asian countries such as China, Sri Lanka, Indonesia, Philippines and Thailand are spending between 2 and 5 per cent of GDP. However, the quality of life (measured in terms of life expectancy, infant and child mortality, maternal mortality, child malnutrition, etc.,) in these countries is much better.

The question therefore arises as to why India's health sector seems to perform relatively poorly? One has to really gauge various health outcomes in relation to the health spending pattern in the Indian economy. Some broad issues emerge when we look closely into the nature and pattern of health spending:

1. Government's share in the total health spending is just 25.1 per cent with wide inter-state differentials (it ranged from 13.6 per cent in Andhra Pradesh to 42.3 per cent in Jammu & Kashmir). This indicates that the household out-of-pocket expenditures on health care are enormous. In contrast, government health spending ranges between 70-90 per cent in OECD countries (including Canada) and between 50-65 per cent in several Southeast Asian countries.
2. A cross-country analysis suggests that as countries get richer, they spend more of their income on health care, and the government's share grows larger (World Bank 1993:110). However, among Indian states this does not seem to hold true. In spite of the fact that Indian economy has grown at around six per cent during the post-reform period, in real terms the per capita government spending on health (as percentage of GDP/NSDP as well as in relation to other sectors) has actually declined in the initial years of reforms.

This clearly reflects that health is yet to be considered as a priority sector.

3. Both health provision and financing are considered to be states' subjects. On an average, out of the total government health spending, the state's share is about 80 per cent. There is a clear demarcation between central and state provision and financing of various health services. The state fully finances hospital services, primary health care facilities and ESIS (Employees' State Insurance Scheme), whereas the family welfare programmes are fully financed by the central government. Most of the national disease control programmes are funded on a 50:50 share arrangement with the states. (However, in terms of total expenditure on these programmes, the state's contribution turns out to be about three-fourths i.e., only basic inputs are shared equally, and the state has to bear all the administrative cost including staff salaries). Centre and states share capital investment equally. Out of the total expenditure on medical education and research, the central government's share is little over 40 per cent. Thus, by and large, the State fully finances all the curative care services. It implies that the state economic conditions and financial and human resources have direct bearing on the health outcomes especially during the post-reform period.
4. The other major difference in the nature of Indian health care spending with respect to Southeast Asian countries is that both central and state governments are spending far less on preventive and promotive care. India spends only one-third on preventive and promotive health care whereas the proportion is as high as two-thirds in China and Sri Lanka. Preventive and promotive health care services include immunisation, antenatal, maternity and postnatal care, contraceptives and other family planning measures, and community based services such as spraying for malaria, and health education. Further, out of the total curative care spending, nearly three-fourths is spent on secondary and

tertiary hospitals (which are primarily located in urban areas). In this country where a majority of the population resides in rural areas, government is spending very little on their day-to-day health care needs. The important issue remains as to how the state can strengthen primary health care services both in terms of resources and accessibility.

5. There are close relationships between per capita state domestic product, per capita state health expenditure and the health status of the population. In other words, richer states are spending higher on health care, resulting in raising of the health status of people. Conversely, the per capita health care spending is very low in poorer states, they are unable to raise matching funds for implementation of several centrally executed public health programmes and thus have not succeeded much in improving the health status of the people. In the light of this argument one has to examine the achievements of various state governments in the post-reform period.

Health Outcomes: Achievements and Pitfalls

Before demonstrating the performance of various states as well as the country as a whole in broad health outcome indicators, it is better to understand the conceptual framework of health care development in India and its linkages to health outcomes.

The conceptual model is designed to offer a better visual representation of the relationships in abstract form that are proposed to exist between concepts. A conceptual framework of Indian health system development and outcomes is depicted in the following Chart. The issues selected for discussion in this paper including the economic reforms process and its impact, are reflected as the concepts of this model. The model presumes that there are essential interrelationships among the political, policy level (including professional associations), social and cultural environments within which the Indian health system operates. These relationships including constitutional commitments of the government to provide

Chart : **Conceptual Framework of Health Care System and Health Outputs**

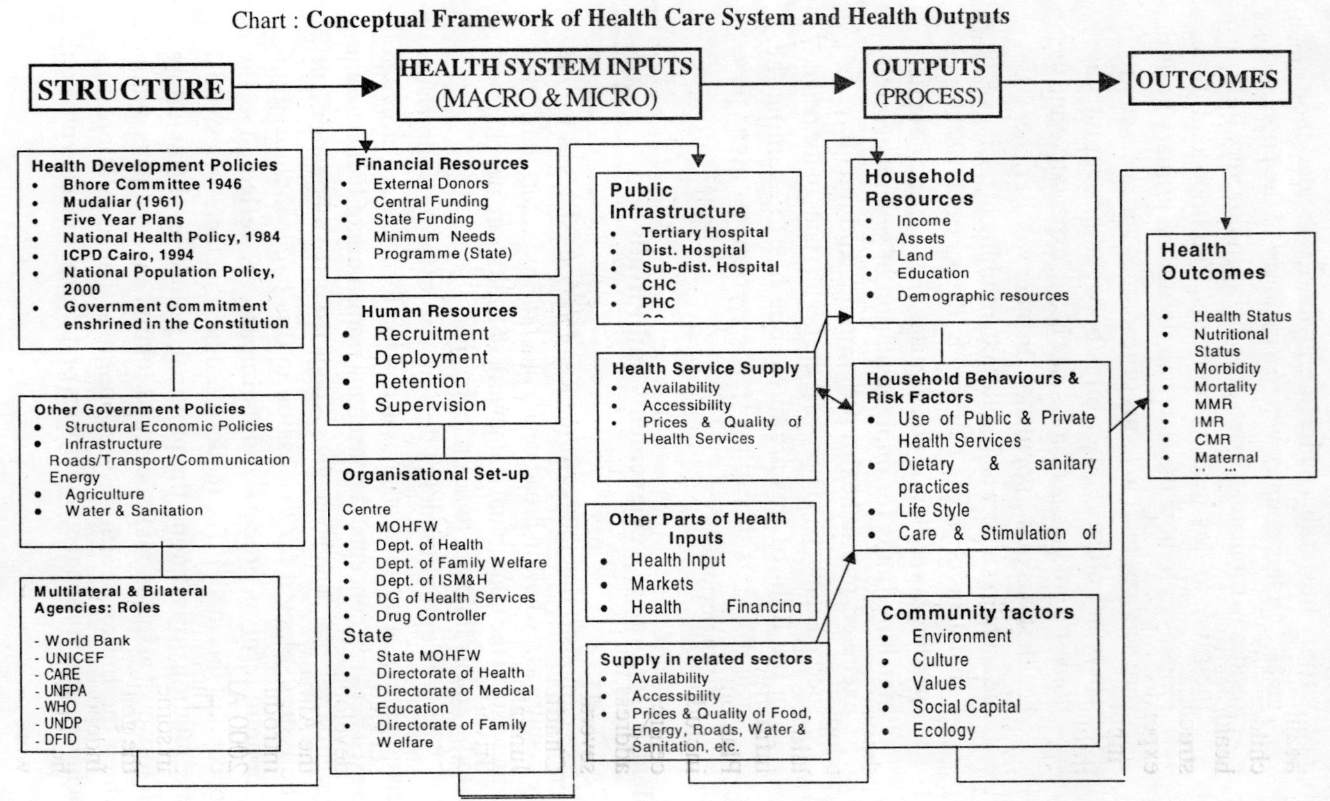

health services, legislation and advocacy for the rights of women, children and vulnerable population, affect the setting of priorities for health care provision, financing and delivery of quality services. This structural framework affects the nature and extent of efforts that are expended to improve health service delivery (both macro and micro 'inputs'). The impact of each of these input factors is mediated through, or buffered by the process through which health services are actually provided ('outputs'). The outcomes of care (measured through several health indicators) are the results of the synergy, or reflect the barriers to effective interaction, between and among all other elements of the framework.

The current state of the Indian health sector is the reflection of the nature of health investments, programmes and policy prescriptions adopted since Independence. In fact the Bhore Committee (1946) laid the foundation and direction for the development of public infrastructure in the health sector. Right from the First Five Year Plan onwards, the emphasis was on creating health infrastructure including a three-tier structure (sub-centres, primary health care centres and community health centres) currently under operation to address the health needs of rural populations. From time to time several Expert Committees such as the Mudaliar Committee (1962), Chadha Committee (1963), Mukherjee Committee (1966), Jungalwala Committee (1967), Katar Singh Committee (1973), Srivastava Committee (1975), Bajaj Committee (1987) and Bajaj Committee (1996) were set up to review and suggest important strategies for improvement in the public health infrastructure and service delivery systems. However, the major shift in health development policies took place when India became the signatory of the Alma-Ata declaration of 1978. The National Health Policy was introduced in 1984 for achieving the goal of "Health for all by 2000 AD" set in the Alma-Ata.

The following Statement presents the achievements and pitfalls in some of the critical health indicators by the end of 2000 vis-à-vis the goal set up in the National Health Policy, 1984. No doubt, since Independence the country has made considerable progress in various health outcomes but once we compare these with the targets which were set 20 years ago, the progress is sluggish.

STATEMENT : **National Health Policy : Goals and Achievements**

Indicators	Past Levels	Goals by 2000 AD	Achievements
Crude birth rate (per 1000 population)	40.8 (1951)	21	26.4 (1998)
Crude death rate (per 1000 population)	25.1 (1951)	9	9 (1998)
Infant mortality rate (per 1000 live births)	146 (1951-61)	Below 60	72 (1998)
Child mortality rate (1 to 4 years)		10	31 (1998)
Maternal mortality rate (per 100,000 live births)	437 (1992-3)	Below 200	407 (1998)
Life expectancy at birth (years)		64+	
Male	37.1 (1951)		62.4
Female	36.1 (1951)		63.4
Universal immunisation	40 (1985-86)	85-100%	92 (GOI)
			42 (NFHS-2)
			86 (Any Dose)
Antenatal care	40 (1985-86)	100%	83 (1998)
Delivery by trained attendant	50 (1985-86)	100%	76 (1998)

Sources: 1. *Annual Report 1999-2000*, Ministry of Health and Family Welfare, Government of India.
2. *National Family Health Survey* (NFHS-2), 1998-99.

An important issue is to examine how various states have performed in health outcomes during the economic reform process. With the availability of results from the National Family Health Survey (NFHS-2) of 1998/99, an interesting comparative analysis with the previous NFHS survey (1992/93) can be attempted. Incidentally, the first NFHS survey coincides with the period when the economic reform process began. We have presented the progress of major states in three critical health outcome and three service delivery indicators during the period 1992/93 to 1998/99 (i.e., over seven years). An effort is also made to relate these indicators with the availability of health infrastructure (measured in terms of population served per hospital bed) in the state. The following are the key findings:

1. Almost all the states have recorded decline in infant mortality rate; however for backward states (Uttar Pradesh, Madhya Pradesh, Orissa and Rajasthan) the rate continued to remain high. In fact, progress is found to be sluggish in Madhya Pradesh, Rajasthan and Punjab. The relationship of IMR with health facility indicates that the better the health facility the lower is the IMR and over time this relationship has become stronger (as revealed by higher value of R^2 during 1998/99).
2. The progress of states on child mortality (${}^{0}q_5$) is better than that shown by IMR (the value of R^2 for the former is higher than the latter one). However, the backward states (Uttar Pradesh, Madhya Pradesh, Orissa and Rajasthan) continue to report a higher child mortality rate. In a few states such as Madhya Pradesh, Rajasthan, Jammu & Kashmir and Punjab the situation worsened over time. The relationship between the child mortality rate and health facility indicates that the better the health facility the lower is the child mortality and over time this relationship has become stronger (as revealed by higher value of R^2 during 1998/99).
3. The third and final health outcome indicator shows the progress of states in terms of total fertility rate (i.e., depicting health status of women in reproductive ages). Almost all the states have recorded decline in fertility rate; however, the backward states of Uttar Pradesh, Rajasthan, Bihar and Madhya Pradesh continue to report a higher fertility rate. Surprisingly, in Rajasthan the situation got further worse. The relationship between fertility rate and health facility indicates that the better the health facility the lower is the fertility rate; however, over time the relationship has become weaker (as revealed by the lower value of R^2 during 1998/99 than that for 1992/93).

4. Three service delivery indicators taken into account are: use of antenatal services, institutional births and child immunization. Although all these service delivery indicators have shown wide inter-state differentials almost all the states have recorded progress over time. In Punjab and Haryana for antenatal care and in Jammu & Kashmir for child immunisation the situation deteriorated during 1998/99. All the three service indicators have shown significant positive relationships with health facilities and over time the relationship has become stronger.

Level and Pattern of Morbidity

There are only two agencies in the country, namely, the National Sample Survey Organisation (NSSO) and the National Council of Applied Economic Research (NCAER) which have disseminated household data on morbidity, health care utilisation and expenditure on treatment. The detailed data made available by the NSS pertains to 1986/87 and more recently for 1995/96 and that by NCAER for 1990 and 1993.

Differentials in Morbidity Levels

Table 6.1 shows the estimated annual morbidity rate for rural and urban population across major states from five surveys pertaining to the period between 1973/74 and 1995/96. The annual morbidity rate ranged between 605 and 2056 per thousand population in rural India and between 612 and 1760 in urban India during 1973/74 to 1995/96. The rural rates were higher than the urban rates in all the five surveys. However, the rural-urban differences have narrowed down during the 1990s. Overall the morbidity rate, both in rural and urban areas, shows a steady increase during the 1980s and 1990s which could also be a reflection of better designing of survey instruments and methodologies for morbidity reporting. The estimated annual level of morbidity in the population has remained below two illnesses per person.

All the five survey reports substantial inter-state differences in

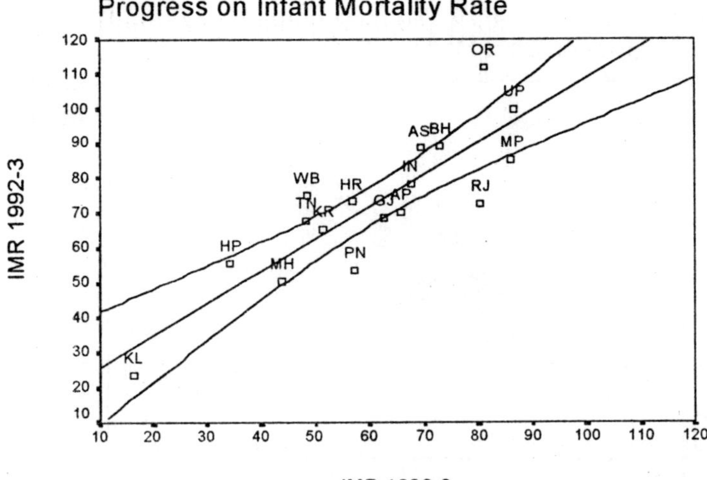

IMR 1998-9

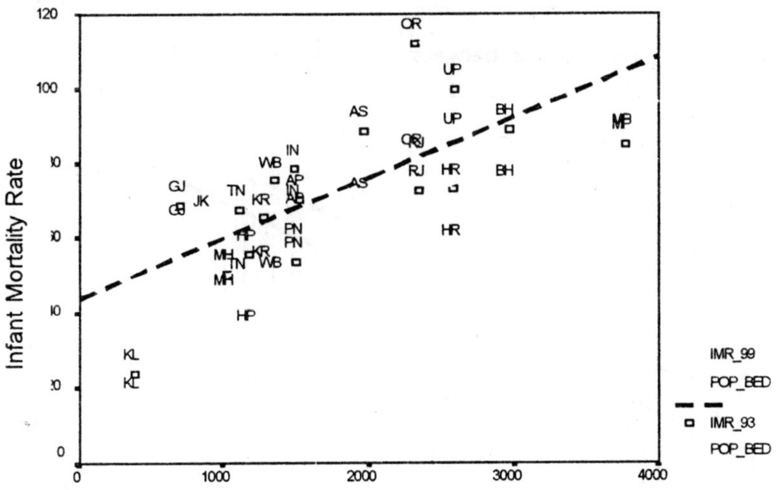

Population served per hospital bed

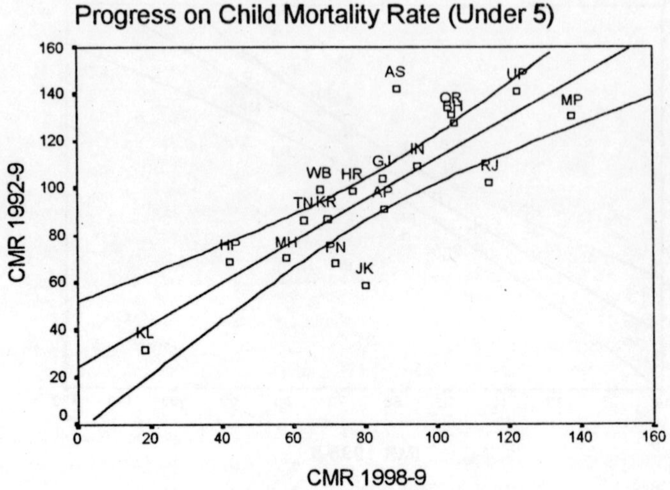
Progress on Child Mortality Rate (Under 5)
CMR 1992-9
CMR 1998-9
AS
UP
OR
BH
MP
IN
RJ
GJ
WB
HR
AP
TN
KR
HP
MH
PN
JK
KL

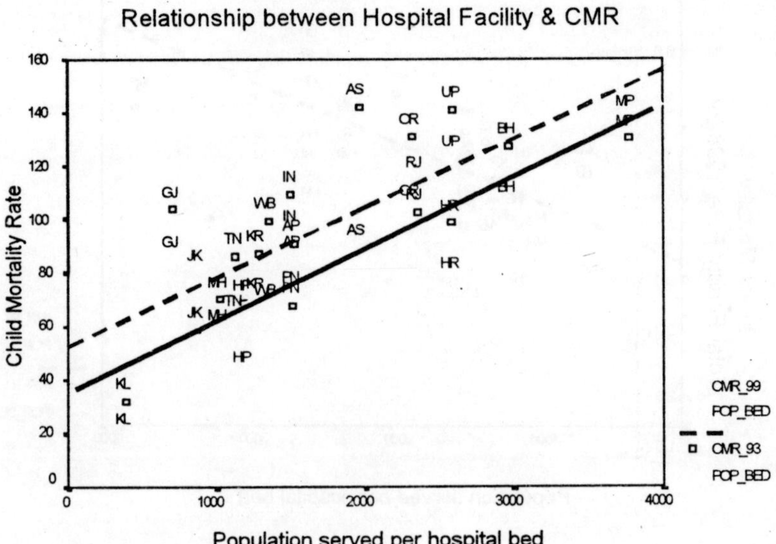
Relationship between Hospital Facility & CMR
Child Mortality Rate
Population served per hospital bed
CMR_99
POP_BED
CMR_93
POP_BED

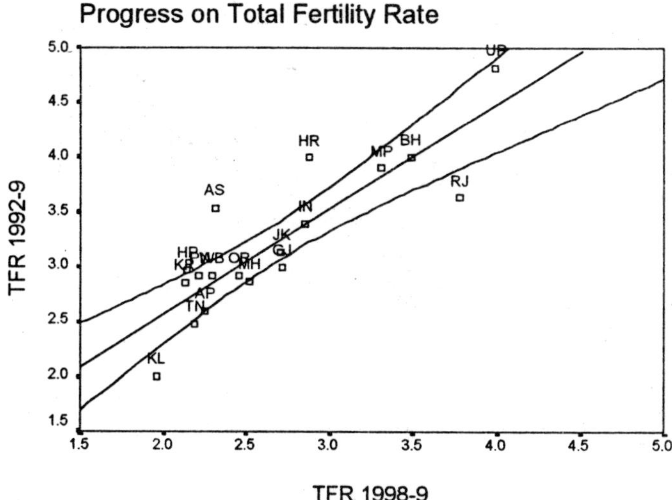
Progress on Total Fertility Rate
TFR 1992-9
TFR 1998-9
UP
HR
MP
BH
RJ
AS
IN
JK
GJ
HP
KR
PN
WB
OR
MH
AP
TN
KL
5.0
4.5
4.0
3.5
3.0
2.5
2.0
1.5

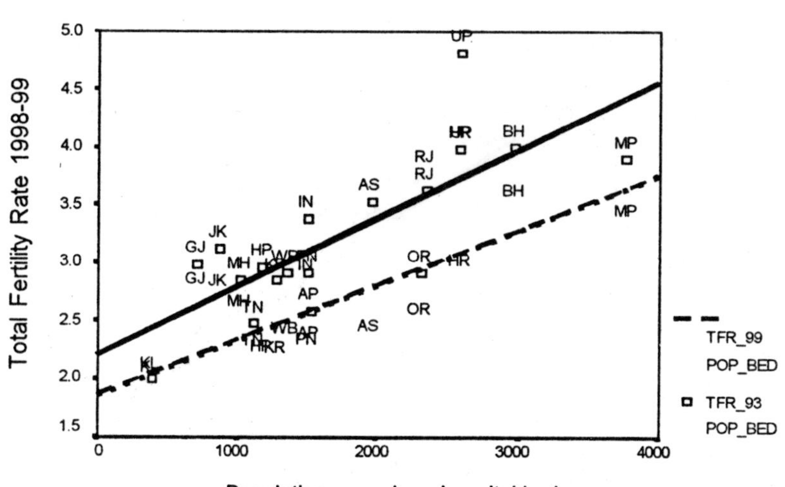
Relationship between Health Facility & Fertility Rate
Total Fertility Rate 1998-99
Population served per hospital bed
TFR_99
POP_BED
TFR_93
POP_BED
0
1000
2000
3000
4000

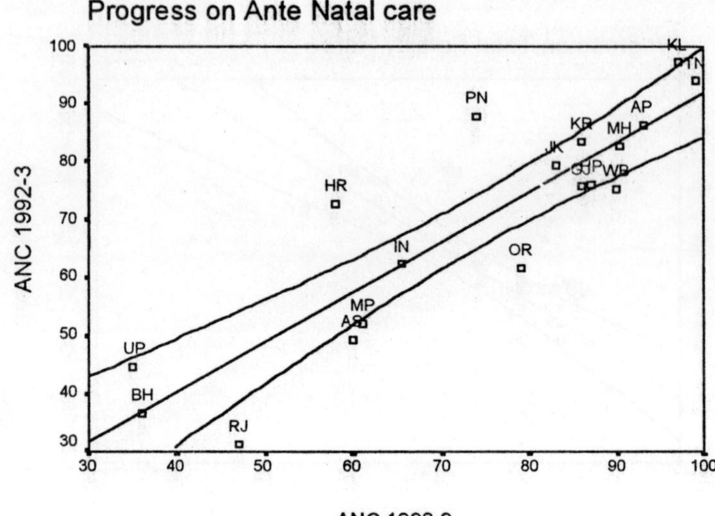
Progress on Ante Natal care
ANC 1992-3
ANC 1998-9
KL
TN
PN
AP
KR
MH
JK
GJ
HP
WB
HR
IN
OR
MP
AS
UP
BH
RJ

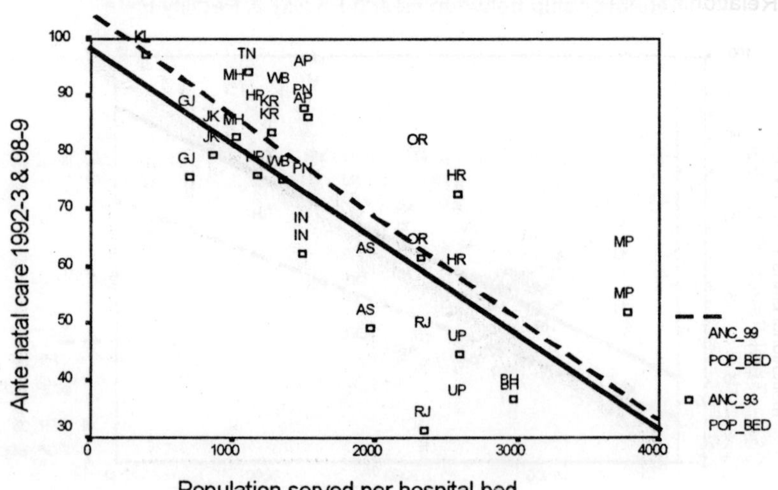
Relationship between Health Facility and Ante Natal Care
Ante natal care 1992-3 & 98-9
Population served per hospital bed
ANC_99
POP_BED
ANC_93
POP_BED

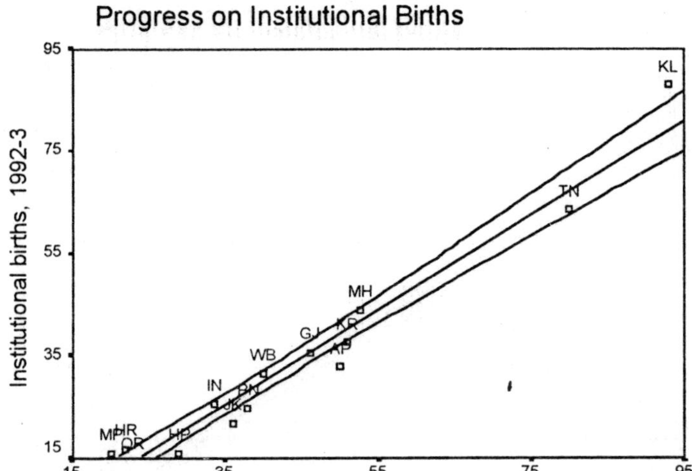
Progress on Institutional Births
Institutional births, 1992-3
Institutional births, 1998-9
95
75
55
35
15
15
35
55
75
95
KL
TN
MH
GJ
KR
AP
WB
IN
PN
JK
MP
HR
OR
HP

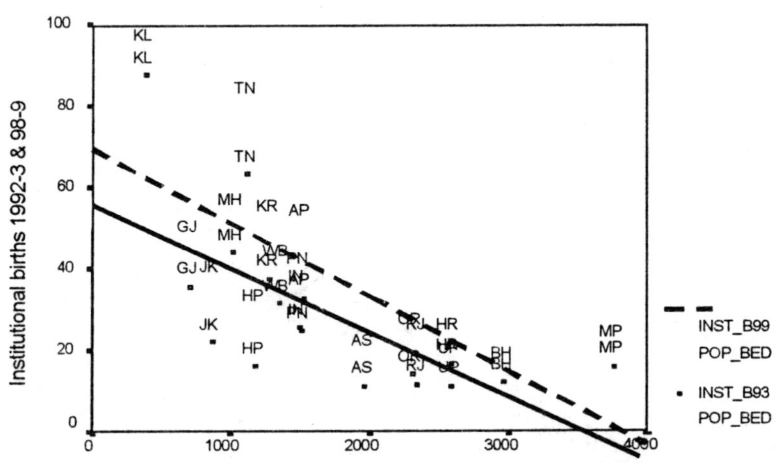
Relationship between Health Facility and Institutional Births
Institutional births 1992-3 & 98-9
Population served per hospital bed
100
80
60
40
20
0
0
1000
2000
3000
4000
INST_B99
POP_BED
INST_B93
POP_BED
KL
TN
MH
KR
AP
GJ
JK
HP
AS
HR
MP
BH
WB
PN
OR
RJ
UP
IN

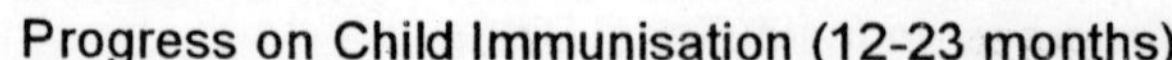
Progress on Child Immunisation (12-23 months)

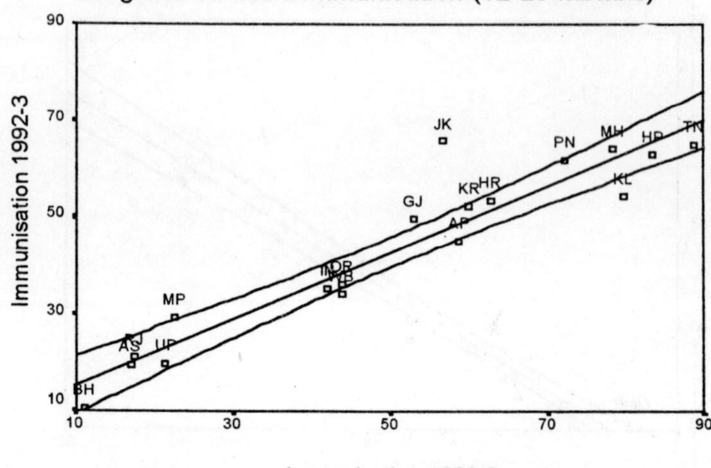
Immunisation 1992-3
Immunisation 1998-9
JK
PN
MH
HP
TN
KL
KR
HR
GJ
AP
IN
OR
WB
MP
RJ
AS
UP
BH

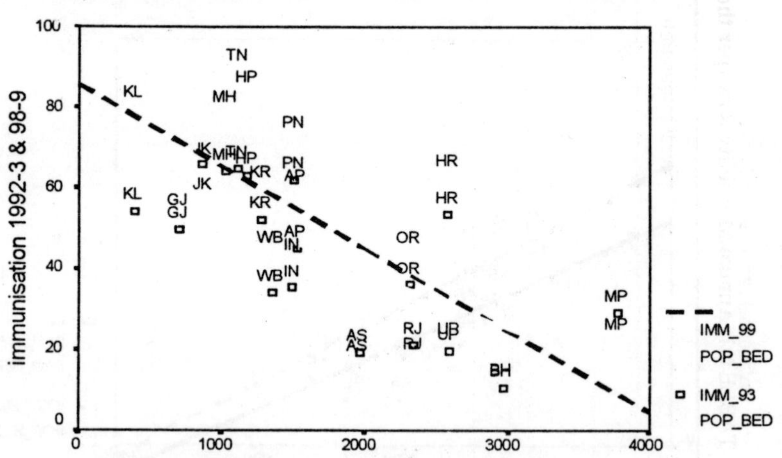
Relationship between Health Facility and Child Immunisation
immunisation 1992-3 & 98-9
Population served per hospital bed
IMM_99
POP_BED
IMM_93
POP_BED

TABLE 6.1: **Annual Morbidity Rate (per thousand population) for Major States, 1973-74 to 1995-96**

	Rural Population					Urban Population				
	NSS			NCAER		NSS			NCAER	
Major States	1973-74	1986-87	1995-96	1990	1993	1973-74	1986-87	1995-96	1990	1993
1	2	3	4	5	6	7	8	9	10	11
Andhra Pradesh	847	1094	1082	1955	1452	735	492	1035	1687	1644
Assam	468	677	1770	395	1020	325	393	1829	4236	780
Bihar	288	428	648	2321	1176	319	203	801	2498	1224
Gujarat	270	425	877	1344	900	170	318	664	1441	1008
Haryana	435	918	1183	660	888	453	605	1161	836	1044
Himachal Pradesh	NE	597	1072	1726	1752	NE	497	837	1653	2139
Jammu & Kashmir	472	781	1066	3359	NE	351	317	1144	3487	NE
Karnataka	399	622	782	1138	1392	359	393	711	1288	1116
Kerala	1935	1925	2054	3479	2196	1157	1024	1576	2677	2100
Madhya Pradesh	555	515	888	2200	1320	578	115	752	2129	1404
Maharashtra	733	534	934	1832	792	853	129	891	1425	936
Orissa	657	838	1381	3115	2124	657	342	1291	2273	1956

(contd.)

TABLE 6.1 *(contd.)*

1	2	3	4	5	6	7	8	9	10	11
Punjab	737	1768	1396	981	1548	658	965	1502	1292	1740
Rajasthan	463	729	549	707	1308	335	228	607	834	1800
Tamil Nadu	906	729	980	2674	936	851	370	1108	1659	900
Uttar Pradesh	359	910	1212	2003	1284	286	359	1416	2029	948
West Bengal	755	1297	1174	1755	960	919	599	1230	1520	972
All-India	605	805	1048	2056	1248	612	434	1032	1760	1212

Note: The estimates for 1973/74 included the prevalence of chronic diseases and the rates for rural and urban India were 21 and 20 per thousand population. The estimates for 1986/87 included annual incidence of hospitalization (26 and 57 per thousand population for rural and urban India respectively). The estimates for 1995/96 included chronic rate (13 for rural and 14 for urban) and hospitalization rate (13 for rural and 20 for urban population). NE—Not Estimated.

Source: NSS (1980); *Sarvekshana*, Vol. 4, Nos. 1 & 2, July-Sept.; (1992) *Sarvekshana*, Vol. 15, No. 4,; Pravin Visaria and Anil Gumber (1994) *Utilization of and Expenditure on Health Care in India, 1986-87 (A Study of Five States)*, Gujarat Institute of Development Research, Ahmedabad; (1997) *Level and Pattern of Morbidity, Health Care Utilization and Expenditure in India, 1986-87*, Gujarat Institute of Development Research, Ahmedabad; Pravin Visaria, Anil Gumber and Paul Jacob (1996) *Morbidity, Health Care Utilization and Expenditure Pattern in Andhra Pradesh, Kerala, Madhya Pradesh and Punjab, 1986-87*, Gujarat Institute of Development Research, Ahmedabad.; Ramamani Sundar (1992), "Household Survey of Medical Care", *Margin*, Vol. 24, No. 2, January-March, pp. 169-175.; Abusaleh Shariff (1995), "Health Transition in India", Working Paper No. 57, National Council of Applied Economic Research, New Delhi. .

both rural and urban morbidity rates. Although there is no clear pattern in the differences in morbidity rates across states, some states have shown a consistently higher rate than the national average. For example, all the five surveys confirm that the reported level of morbidity in rural areas was the highest in Kerala and higher than the national average for Orissa. In four out of five surveys, the rural morbidity rates were higher than the national average for Andhra Pradesh and Punjab whereas they were lower for Bihar, Gujarat, Karnataka, Maharashtra and Rajasthan. A somewhat similar pattern was also observed for the urban morbidity rate. All the five surveys reported a higher urban morbidity rate than the national average for Kerala and Andhra Pradesh and lower rates for Gujarat and Karnataka. In four surveys the rate was higher for Orissa and Punjab and lower for Maharashtra and Rajasthan. In summary Kerala, Andhra Pradesh, Punjab and Orissa fall in the high morbidity zone whereas Gujarat, Maharashtra, Karnataka and Rajasthan are in a low morbidity zone though the inter-state variation in morbidity rates has declined over time particularly for rural areas.

Correlates of Morbidity

The important question is whether the state level morbidity rates exhibit some relationship with select socio-economic indicators. Interestingly, it is observed that there is no clear correspondence between the level of morbidity reported either during 1986/87 and 1995/96 and the life expectancy across 17 states. However, the latter was inversely related with population served per hospital bed and positively with per capita state domestic product as well as per capita state health expenditure.

The incidence of morbidity was marginally higher for females, but the gender differential was larger in urban than in rural India. Both the NSS and NCAER data reveal that the incidence of morbidity for women in the reproductive age group 15-44 is considerably higher than that for men (Gumber, 1997). The NSS data suggest that the illness and hospitalisation rates tend to increase with the economic status of the household measured in terms of monthly per capita expenditure (MPCE). The surveys also confirm that the scheduled caste and tribe population reports lower hospitalisation rate, which is largely due to their lack of access to health care facilities on the one hand and scarcity of resources on the other.

Health Care Use Pattern

Untreated Illnesses and Reasons for Non-Treatment

It is not true that those who have reported illnesses also seek treatment. For the country as a whole, nearly 18 and 10 per cent of illness episodes in rural and urban India were not being treated (Table 6.2). The percentage of non-treatment was marginally higher among females than among males. In few states such as Assam, Andhra Pradesh, Madhya Pradesh and Orissa the level of non-treatment for rural population was quite high. These states also have a higher concentration of tribal population who tend to rely more on traditional healers and/or go for home remedies. However, the degree of non-treatment in most of the states has declined by 1995/96. It is revealing that the probability of not seeking treatment is found to be higher among females, the elderly (aged 60 years and above), and the never married individuals. The probability tends to be higher among the scheduled castes and tribes and those belonging to lower MPCE quintile (Gumber 1997). The belief that the ailments were not considered serious enough for treatment was the most important reason for non-treatment in both rural and urban India during 1986/87 and 1995/96. However, accessibility, physical proximity and financial constraints were extremely important for taking decisions to seek treatment, especially among the poor households. And as compared to 1986/87 their percentage share has risen in 1995/96 (Table 6.3).

Use of Government Facilities

Both the NSS and NCAER data confirm that the rural and urban patients have overwhelmingly chosen public hospitals for inpatient care. The reliance on public facilities for inpatient care was much greater in hilly and backward states, among the scheduled castes and

TABLE 6.2: **Share of Treated Illnesses (as percentage of all illnesses not requiring hospitalisation) by Gender, 1986-87 and 1995-96**

State	Males				Females				Both Sexes			
	Rural		Urban		Rural		Urban		Rural		Urban	
	1986-87	1995-96	1986-87	1995-96	1986-87	1995-96	1986-87	1995-96	1986-87	1995-96	1986-87	1995-96
1	2	3	4	5	6	7	8	9	10	11	12	13
Andhra Pradesh	63.2	76.9	77.3	87.2	56.3	71.9	66.2	82.8	59.7	74.5	71.4	85.0
Assam	77.1	56.2	90.0	68.5	76.3	55.7	84.8	59.6	76.7	56.0	87.3	63.6
Bihar	85.2	78.6	92.7	84.2	84.1	77.6	91.2	84.8	84.7	78.1	91.5	84.5
Gujarat	89.1	94.7	94.3	95.8	87.9	89.4	95.2	97.1	88.5	92.1	94.7	96.5
Haryana	90.3	98.7	91.0	97.8	90.7	95.4	91.0	98.8	90.5	97.0	91.0	98.4
Himachal Pradesh	94.8	89.0	100.0	96.9	98.1	86.2	100.0	97.6	96.5	87.5	100.0	97.2
Jammu & Kashmir	90.5	94.7	98.3	96.8	85.1	92.7	98.1	98.6	87.9	93.7	98.2	97.6
Karnataka	88.5	83.9	93.4	89.6	87.3	72.0	96.7	93.2	87.9	77.5	95.1	91.4
Kerala	93.4	87.9	91.5	89.6	91.2	88.6	89.4	88.8	92.2	88.3	90.4	89.2
Madhya Pradesh	74.5	85.1	88.6	94.8	71.8	82.4	86.3	91.5	80.0	83.7	95.4	93.3
Maharashtra	79.8	90.4	95.2	92.2	80.2	86.8	95.5	92.4	73.3	88.6	87.4	92.3

(contd.)

TABLE 6.2 *(contd.)*

1	2	3	4	5	6	7	8	9	10	11	12	13
Orissa	70.7	69.3	88.4	84.3	68.8	66.1	89.5	88.6	69.7	67.7	88.9	86.6
Punjab	94.6	99.4	97.4	96.5	93.0	98.6	95.3	96.5	93.8	99.0	96.4	96.5
Rajasthan	84.5	86.0	90.0	80.6	81.7	95.1	90.3	88.5	83.2	89.8	90.2	89.6
Tamil Nadu	75.2	75.9	89.2	90.9	75.7	79.2	88.4	92.8	75.3	77.6	88.8	92.0
Uttar Pradesh	89.0	91.3	87.9	94.7	85.5	89.9	87.7	92.6	87.4	90.6	87.8	93.5
West Bengal	84.4	79.4	90.7	91.0	81.5	80.8	85.2	88.8	83.0	80.1	87.9	89.9
All-India	82.8	83.8	90.2	91.0	80.2	81.6	88.1	90.3	81.5	82.7	89.1	90.7

Source: 1986-87: *Sarvekshana*, Vol. 15(4), No. 51, April-June 1992.
1995-96: NSS Report, No. 441, August 1998.

TABLE 6.3: **Percentage Distribution of Untreated Ailments by Reason for Non-Treatment, 1986-87 and 1995-96**

		Reason for Non-treatment (Rural Population)						Reason for Non-treatment (Urban Population)					
State	Survey Year	No Nearby Medical Facility	Lack of Faith	Long Waiting	Financial Reasons	Ailment not Considered Serious	Others	No Nearby Medical Facility	Lack of Faith	Long Waiting	Financial Reasons	Ailment not Considered Serious	Others
1	2	3	4	5	6	7	8	9	10	11	12	13	14
Andhra Pradesh	1986-87	0.9	1.1	0.2	10.1	74.4	7.2	0	1.2	0.8	8.0	84.6	5.5
	1995-96	3.2	4.7	0.3	26.2	56.2	7.9	0	10.7	2.1	20.3	54.8	10.7
Assam	1986-87	0.5	1.1	1.1	5.3	87.7	4.3	0	0.1	5.7	3.7	82.9	7.7
	1995-96	11.5	4.5	0.9	9.2	58	13.0	0.2	8.7	0.3	20.5	58.0	10.9
Bihar	1986-87	1.9	1.3	0.8	18	74.7	3.3	0	0.2	0	9.1	86.1	4.5
	1995-96	5.3	1.5	1.9	40.4	36.8	9.6	0	2.9	0.8	24.9	55.4	13.0
Gujarat	1986-87	0.3	0.6	9.0	17.4	74.7	6.0	0	5.7	0	13.3	77.2	3.8
	1995-96	23.1	2.7	0	2.8	66.4	5.0	0	5.5	19.2	0	52.4	9.7
Haryana	1986-87	0.6	3.6	1.0	14.1	70.6	10.2	0	6.2	0	7.1	75.1	11.6
	1995-96	9.6	16.6	0	12.9	55.9	5.0	0	0	0	12.9	22.8	64.3
Himachal Pradesh	1986-87	14.1	4.1	1.1	4.3	70.9	5.5	0	0	0	0	0	0
	1995-96	2.4	7.4	0.6	0.5	52.9	32.3	0	0	0	0	63.2	35.9
J & K	1986-87	3.9	8.1	0	67.5	15.2	5.3	0	5.3	0	4.5	90.2	0
	1995-96	14.3	0	4.4	0.3	73.3	7.7	0	0	6.4	13.6	57.2	19.9
Karnataka	1986-87	5.3	3.4	0.2	14.6	67.6	8.9	0.7	1.7	0	11.3	81.6	4.7
	1995-96	7.5	4.8	0	22	58.4	5.4	0	1.6	0	11.6	73.7	12.9

(contd.)

TABLE 6.3 *(contd.)*

1	2	3	4	5	6	7	8	9	10	11	12	13	14
Kerala	1986-87	0	1.7	0	14.7	81.0	2.6	0	0.2	0	4.5	88.9	6.4
	1995-96	5.7	1.2	0	12.9	69.8	9.1	1.1	1.3	0	12.4	68.6	14.4
Madhya Pradesh	1986-87	5.4	2.5	Negl	15.8	73.3	3.0	0.3	2.6	0.4	8.6	88.8	4.3
	1995-96	19.8	2.6	0	21.0	45.4	7.5	10.8	15.3	0	10.4	52.4	10.9
Maharashtra	1986-87	1.6	1.4	0.8	7.2	85.5	3.5	0.5	0.4	2.7	8.2	80.4	7.8
	1995-96	8.2	3.4	0	20.1	63.7	4.2	0	0	0.3	25.1	63.3	11.3
Orissa	1986-87	6.6	1.2	0	68.6	17.4	6.2	0.9	0	0	12.1	85.5	1.5
	1995-96	19.5	5.1	0.4	23	38.3	10.8	0	0	4.0	45.4	35.6	10
Punjab	1986-87	1.3	3.1	0	6.2	82.7	6.7	0	2.0	0	2.1	93.2	2.8
	1995-96	21.3	5.5	0	49.0	7.7	16.5	0	4.5	0	47.3	48.2	0
Rajasthan	1986-87	8.6	3.2	0.7	69.5	14.7	3.3	0.1	0.6	0.3	11.2	86.4	1.5
	1995-96	7.1	2.2	0	60.3	25.7	4.7	0	1.3	0	4.9	72.2	21.6
Tamil Nadu	1986-87	1.6	2.5	1.3	15.1	71.6	8	0	0.9	2.5	7.5	79.9	9.2
	1995-96	0.8	4.7	1.1	21.6	66.1	5.6	0	5.1	0	11.7	46.6	36
Uttar Pradesh	1986-87	2.9	2.6	0.1	18.6	73.8	2.0	0.4	0.8	0.9	15.1	75.7	7.2
	1995-96	10.8	4.5	0	22.4	51	9.6	0	11.2	1.0	22.5	64.6	0.7
West Bengal	1986-87	3.9	2.0	0	12.1	78.3	3.7	0.1	1.5	2.1	11.8	78.4	6.0
	1995-96	7.9	0.5	0	43.1	34.6	13.2	0	2.0	0.3	19.7	65.9	10.6
All-India	1986-87	2.9	1.9	0.3	15.3	74.6	5.0	0.1	1.8	1.1	9.6	81.1	6.3
	1995-96	8.8	3.7	0.5	24.2	51.1	9.9	0.8	5.3	1.1	19.8	59.4	12.4

Source : Same as for Table 6.2.

tribes and those belonging to lower MPCE quintile. On the other hand, private facilities are used largely for outpatient care. Unlike public facilities, which are centrally located, the private practitioners are found even in the remote and backward areas. (For instance, 70 per cent of hospitals and 85 per cent of hospital beds in the public sector are located in urban areas.) Private practitioners are usually contacted first for day-to-day health care needs before seeking the distantly located public facility.

It is quite discouraging to note that reliance on public facilities for both inpatient and outpatient care has been declining. The percentage share of public facilities in inpatient care declined from 60 to 44 per cent in rural and from 60 to 42 per cent in urban India during 1986/87 and 1995/96; in the case of outpatient care the respective decline was from 26 to 19 per cent and 27 to 20 per cent (Table 6.4). In certain states it definitely reflects on the efficiency of the public system together with quality of services. Also, from the mid 1990s, a nominal level of user charges at different levels of facilities is being introduced in several states under the World Bank Assisted State Health System Project. For instance, since 1998 user charges have been levied in all the secondary and tertiary level hospitals in Andhra Pradesh and the collection forms as low as two per cent of recurring expenditure in secondary level hospitals to as high as 80 per cent in a super specialist hospital.

In a few states the situation is rather different. The private sector has played a dominant role in handling both inpatient and outpatient loads and that reliance on the government facility has been declining. It is likely that there are large inter-district/regional variations because the for-profit private sector has not made much headway in the backward, remote and hilly areas. A key task would be to map the utilisation statistics at the regional/district level to understand better the reasons for such patterns.

It is also observed that public facilities are used more often in the cases of severe and catastrophic illnesses as well as for certain diseases such as tuberculosis, complications of pregnancy and childbirth, injury and STDs, which the private practitioners are reluctant to deal with. The most common diseases like malaria, typhoid, diarrhoea, acute respiratory infection, pneumonia, etc., are mostly treated by the private health care providers.

TABLE 6.4: **Share of Public Providers in Treated Illnesses, 1986-87 and 1995-96**

State	Inpatient Care				Outpatient Care			
	Rural		Urban		Rural		Urban	
	1986-87	1995-96	1986-87	1995-96	1986-87	1995-96	1986-87	1995-96
Andhra Pradesh	30.8	22.2	41.7	35.4	21.6	22	22.6	19
Assam	89.8	69.2	82.4	63.0	53.0	29	29.6	22
Bihar	50.1	24.1	46.8	31.9	16.9	13	18.0	33
Gujarat	56.0	31.4	61.8	36.3	35.1	25	19.6	22
Haryana	54.1	30.3	56.7	37.0	16.9	13	21.7	11
Himachal Pradesh	88.0	86.5	78.9	91.3	60.7	39	47.7	48
Jammu & Kashmir	96.5	97.7	96.1	95.9	59.8	44	47.4	28
Karnataka	59.8	45.0	50.0	29.3	36.4	26	31.3	17
Kerala	43.6	39.5	56.3	37.3	34.0	28	34.8	28
Madhya Pradesh	80.4	40.4	79.0	54.7	27.1	23	25.9	19
Maharashtra	45.8	30.9	49.4	30.7	36.5	16	35.3	17
Orissa	90.7	84.2	82.2	77.9	52.7	38	47.9	34
Punjab	49.2	37.7	52.0	26.5	13.4	7	15.6	6
Rajasthan	81.0	63.3	86.5	72.1	56.1	36	57.5	41
Tamil Nadu	56.9	40.4	58.2	34.2	38.7	25	35.5	28
Uttar Pradesh	58.3	46.1	61.1	39.0	10.4	8	17.2	9
West Bengal	91.9	79.9	75.9	71.3	19.6	15	25.3	19
All-India	59.7	43.8	60.3	41.9	25.6	19	27.2	20

Note: The percentages for outpatient care (1995-96) are without decimal points.

Source: Same as for Table 6.2.

Provision of Free Health Services by the Public Sector

The share of private sector agencies in the provision of free health services for both inpatient and outpatient care is negligible.

Therefore, those who avail themselves of government facility also receive free treatment. To capture this aspect, Table 6.5 provides information on percentage of patients who received free hospital beds (as a proxy for free inpatient care) and free medicine (as a proxy for free outpatient care). Both rural and urban patients using government facility for inpatient care had also received free care during 1986/87 and 1995/96. However, in the case of outpatient care between 68-72 per cent of patients in 1986/87 and between 41-46 per cent of patients in 1995/96 received free care from the public sector agencies. The decline in the provision of free care reflects not only on the imposition of user charges but also on the non-availability of drugs and medicines in the government hospitals, and as a result the patients are forced to buy these from the market. The situation in regard to the provision of free medicine was found to be much worse in the backward and hilly states (Bihar, Himachal Pradesh, Madhya Pradesh, Orissa and Rajasthan).

A detailed analysis of the 1986/87 data suggests that the receipt of free health services varied inversely with the MPCE quintile for inpatient care but remained more or less stable for outpatient care. Interestingly, a good proportion of inpatients belonging to the top quintile did not pay for any health service (Gumber, 1997:149). Government agencies appear to provide free services without discrimination between various sections of the society, which raises an important issue of wrong targeting of public subsidies.

Cost and Burden of Treatment

Undoubtedly, price is the most important consideration in choosing the public over the private facility especially for the treatment of chronic and catastrophic illnesses. According to the NSS data the average cost of treatment in the private sector for rural inpatients was 1.6 and for urban inpatients 2.4 times higher than in the public sector during 1986/87. The gap got widened further to 2.1 for rural patients in 1995/96 and remained same for the urban patients. The difference in the cost of treatment between private and public sector

TABLE 6.5: **Percentage of Patients Received Free Hospital Bed (Inpatient Care) and Free Medicine (Outpatient Care), 1986-87 and 1995-96**

State	Free Hospital Bed (Inpatient Care)				Free Medicine (Outpatient Care)			
	Rural		Urban		Rural		Urban	
	1986-87	1995-96	1986-87	1995-96	1986-87	1995-96	1986-87	1995-96
Andhra Pradesh	33.3	21.9	41.3	36.8	20.8	20.1	24.2	8.5
Assam	95.5	76.5	76.1	58.0	31.0	12.6	10.5	6.0
Bihar	47.7	20.0	56.5	38.9	5.2	1.5	26.6	10.4
Gujarat	40.0	26.1	39.4	25.4	21.5	9.5	13.9	10.2
Haryana	54.0	29.6	53.3	16.7	8.2	3.7	12.2	1.7
Himachal Pradesh	86.5	79.0	77.3	71.0	24.1	4.5	8.8	6.8
Jammu & Kashmir	93.4	96.8	91.6	88.1	20.3	5.1	12.7	5.2
Karnataka	58.8	37.8	36.6	25.3	26.5	16.3	25.4	8.2
Kerala	45.1	37.5	45.2	31.7	29.8	9.3	25.4	8.7
Madhya Pradesh	77.2	39.2	73.3	49.1	24.5	3.3	17.9	7.8
Maharashtra	42.8	28.7	39.7	28.6	17.0	8.6	21.9	8.8
Orissa	88.7	83.1	88.0	75.2	25.0	8.0	24.6	5.0
Punjab	46.3	26.8	46.1	18.7	6.5	0.6	7.6	2.3
Rajasthan	81.8	65.8	84.9	70.5	15.6	0.1	17.5	9.8
Tamil Nadu	59.5	42.9	57.8	38.9	37.3	27.8	34.3	25.1
Uttar Pradesh	59.1	39.8	56.1	32.6	6.0	1.8	10.5	4.0
West Bengal	90.4	79.6	69.4	64.5	15.4	3.7	18.5	8.2
All-India	60.7	41.6	55.2	38.2	17.5*	7.7	19.7*	9.3

Note: * denotes the All-India average based on the weighted average of 17 major states (states are weighted according to their share in the total estimated hospitalised/ill persons).

Source: Same as for Table 6.2.

was much higher in Tamil Nadu, West Bengal and to some extent in Andhra Pradesh and lower in Bihar, Haryana, Punjab, Rajasthan and Uttar Pradesh (Table 6.6).

TABLE 6.6: **Ratio of Cost of Treatment between Private and Public Provider, 1986-87 and 1995-96**

	Inpatient Care				Outpatient Care			
	Rural		Urban		Rural		Urban	
State	1986-87	1995-96	1986-87	1995-96	1986-87	1995-96	1986-87	1995-96
Andhra Pradesh	2.2	3.8	5.2	5.4	1.8	4.1	4.2	2.3
Assam	0.6	1.0	3.4	3.2	0.8	0.6	0.4	0.9
Bihar	1.3	1.2	1.6	1.6	0.6	1.2	1.7	3.0
Gujarat	2.3	2.2	2.9	2.2	1.6	2.3	1.5	1.7
Haryana	1.5	1.3	1.9	0.6	1.6	0.8	1.9	0.5
Himachal Pradesh	1.8	1.1	3.0	3.2	0.8	NE	1.3	NE
Jammu & Kashmir	2.1	1.0	5.5	2.6	0.8	NE	1.0	NE
Karnataka	2.8	2.3	3.3	2.9	1.8	2.0	1.4	1.4
Kerala	1.6	1.7	2.6	1.5	1.5	1.6	1.6	1.6
Madhya Pradesh	1.7	1.6	2.8	2.3	1.7	1.7	1.9	0.5
Maharashtra	2.9	2.5	5.1	3.7	1.2	2.0	1.3	1.6
Orissa	2.0	1.5	0.9	5.5	0.7	1.2	1.9	0.9
Punjab	1.3	1.7	2.1	1.1	0.8	1.2	1.0	0.8
Rajasthan	1.1	1.5	1.2	1.9	0.9	0.8	1.0	1.3
Tamil Nadu	9.0	5.8	12.4	6.2	5.1	7.5	4.1	5.0
Uttar Pradesh	1.4	1.1	1.5	1.3	0.7	0.6	0.7	0.9
West Bengal	6.0	2.1	5.6	5.8	1.4	0.8	1.9	1.9
All-India	1.6	2.1	2.4	2.4	0.7	1.4	0.9	1.2

Sources: Same as for Table 6.2.

Interestingly, as compared to the public sector the cost of

treatment for outpatient care was lower in the private sector during 1986/87. However, over time the private sector has become costlier by 40 per cent for rural and by 20 per cent for urban patients. The inter-state variations continue to exist and here once again (as observed for inpatient care) the private-public cost ratio was the highest in Tamil Nadu and in Uttar Pradesh the private sector turned out to be cheaper than the public sector. This clearly reflects that the public delivery system in Tamil Nadu is managed better and run efficiently compared to that in several other states including Uttar Pradesh.

The average expenditure on treatment (such as fees, medicines, clinical and diagnostic tests, surgery, and hospital bed charges) per hospitalisation episode in 1995/96 was Rs. 3202 for rural and Rs. 3921 for urban patients for the country as a whole (Table 6.7). As expected, the cost of treatment was higher for urban than rural patients due to cost of living and the nature of care sought. The inpatient care was much cheaper in Orissa, Assam and West Bengal and costlier in Andhra Pradesh, Punjab and Uttar Pradesh for both rural and urban patients and was also costlier in Haryana for urban patients. Although the cost of treatment depends upon the type of disease, insurance coverage and the type of services availed of, the inter-state differentials in costs also reflect the affordability, level of income and the purchasing power of the people.

The cost of outpatient care was much lower than the inpatient care and on the average rural and urban patients were spending between Rs. 176-Rs. 194 for treatment during 1995/96. Care was costlier in those states where the public delivery was also poor (e.g., in Bihar and Uttar Pradesh) and the other way round in the case of Tamil Nadu, West Bengal and Kerala. The cost of care was also found to be higher in urban areas of Haryana and Madhya Pradesh.

The comparison of cost of care with the previous NSS data for 1986-87 shows an alarming increase in health care prices. On an average the cost of health care has grown enormously with an annual arithmetic growth rate of 26-31 per cent for inpatient care and of 15-16 per cent for outpatient care. For inpatient care the increase in cost of care overtime was much faster for rural patients of Andhra Pradesh, Tamil Nadu, Kerala and West Bengal and for urban patients

TABLE 6.7: **Cost of Treatment for Inpatient and Outpatient Care, 1986-87 and 1995-96**

State	Inpatient Care						Outpatient Care					
	Rural			Urban			Rural			Urban		
	1986-87	1995-96	% Annual Change	1986-87	1995-96	% Annual Change	1986-87	1995-96	% Annual Change	1986-87	1995-96	% Annual Change
1	2	3	4	5	6	7	8	9	10	11	12	13
Andhra Pradesh	686	6428	93.0	781	4886	58.4	67	165	16.3	63	172	19.2
Assam	478	1945	34.1	879	3790	36.8	84	151	8.9	12	180	155.6
Bihar	1110	3860	27.5	1054	3724	28.1	158	213	3.9	93	212	14.2
Gujarat	787	2663	26.5	1107	3327	22.3	82	157	10.2	93	218	14.9
Haryana	1295	3224	16.6	739	6537	87.2	72	189	18.1	71	414	53.7
Himachal Pradesh	913	2530	19.7	989	2643	18.6	131	87	-3.7	118	133	1.4
Jammu & Kashmir	618	2548	34.7	610	3612	54.7	102	188	9.4	82	149	9.1
Karnataka	864	2997	27.4	1142	3593	23.8	47	122	17.7	66	172	17.8
Kerala	423	2293	49.1	448	1927	36.7	61	136	13.7	51	120	15.0
Madhya Pradesh	640	2191	26.9	553	2774	44.6	75	155	11.9	117	376	24.6
Maharashtra	865	3089	28.6	1425	3997	20.1	101	165	7.0	102	185	9.0

(contd.)

TABLE 6.7 *(contd.)*

1	2	3	4	5	6	7	8	9	10	11	12	13
Orissa	719	1641	14.2	681	3868	52.0	62	147	15.2	59	136	14.5
Punjab	1341	4988	30.2	1485	5712	31.6	82	175	12.6	80	162	11.4
Rajasthan	986	3038	23.1	706	3149	38.4	100	192	10.2	110	198	8.9
Tamil Nadu	449	2840	59.2	662	3934	54.9	41	102	16.5	46	129	20.0
Uttar Pradesh	1204	4349	29.0	1735	5896	26.6	90	224	16.5	125	227	9.1
West Bengal	402	1957	43.0	1017	3217	24.0	52	131	16.9	87	137	6.4
All-India	853	3202	30.6	1183	3921	25.7	75*	176	15.0	81*	194	15.5

Note: * denotes the All-India average based on the weighted average of 17 major states (states are weighted according to their share in the total estimated hospitalised/ill persons).

Source: Same as for Table 6.2.

of Haryana, Andhra Pradesh, Tamil Nadu, Jammu & Kashmir and Orissa. These states have reported faster growth in the cost of outpatient care as well. Only Himachal Pradesh and Gujarat have reported a slow increase in the costs of both inpatient and outpatient care.

The expenditure on treatment as a percentage of MPCE constitutes the burden of treatment. Overall, the burden for inpatient treatment ranged between 351 and 476 per cent for the country as a whole during 1986/87. The burden was relatively lower for outpatient care, which ranged between 45-63 per cent for the country as a whole during the same period. However, in both inpatient and outpatient care, the burden was found to be higher among rural than urban populations. This could be due to the difference in the cost of living between rural and urban areas than the cost of treatment itself because most of the rural patients have to avail themselves of hospital facilities located in urban centres. Further, poor households are spending a relatively higher proportion of their income on health care than the better-off section of society. According to the NCAER survey of 1993, the bottom 20 per cent households were spending 12.3 per cent of their income on health care as compared to only 3.1 per cent by the top quintile (Table 6.8). The burden of treatment is unequally distributed across different

TABLE 6.8: **Average Annual Health Expenditure by Households according to Income Quintile, 1993**

	Health Expenditure (Rs.)			Health Exp. as % of Income		
Income Quintile	All	Rural	Urban	All	Rural	Urban
1 (Bottom 20%)	772	782	699	12.3	12.6	10.4
2	696	664	826	5.6	5.4	6.6
3	1210	1286	1005	6.9	7.3	5.7
4	1084	1037	1176	4.4	4.3	4.7
5 (Top 20%)	1657	1506	1806	3.1	2.9	3.3
All	1052	973	1254	6.0	6.1	5.9

Source: NCAER Survey, 1993.

population groups reflecting the inefficiency in the public delivery system and indicating the potential for voluntary comprehensive health insurance schemes for the poor in society.

Equity in Benefits Received from Government Health Spending

The NCAER has recently completed a World Bank commissioned study assessing the extent to which health expenditure benefits the poor throughout India (Mahal and Gumber, 2000). The study looks at utilisation of health services (inpatient admissions, short hospitalisations, inpatient admissions for childbirth, outpatient visits, immunisation, ante- and post-natal visits) according to socio-economic attributes of the population in terms of scheduled and non-scheduled population, below and above poverty line and MPCE quintile groups. Data are broken down by state, urban/rural location, sex, type of facility (hospitals, PHCs and others) and by type of provider (public, private). It also assesses the extent to which the burden of user fees is shared between income groups. It further estimates total net subsidies by MPCE groups from public health expenditure. The key findings are:

- *The better off utilise health services more than the poor* : the top quintile are hospitalised over seven times more frequently than the lowest quintile and almost 10 times more often in rural areas. In terms of outpatient visits the top quintile made 65 per cent more outpatient visits than the bottom quintile in urban areas and 125 per cent more in rural areas. In terms of immunisation a child in the top quintile has on average 4.6 immunisation shots whilst a child from the lowest quintile has 3.8. The top quintile account for 27 per cent of all inpatient days associated with childbirth (despite the fact that they only account for 10.9 per cent of children aged under one).
- *The rich are the main users of public sector facilities* : the top quintile account for almost 40 per cent of inpatient days in public hospitals; the bottom quintile just over 10 per

cent. At PHCs and other facilities the majority of inpatient days are accounted for by middle income groups. For short stay hospitalisations the picture is less extreme. An exception is childbirth where the poorer groups make far greater use of public facilities accounting for almost five times more in patient days, than the top quintile.

- *The poor make relatively more use of the public sector but still make significant use of the private sector* : for the poorest quintile 61.9 per cent of inpatient days were spent in public facilities compared to 28.5 per cent for the top quintile. The private sector dominates the provision of outpatient services although the poorest quintile are slightly more likely to use the public sector with 20.8 per cent of treatments being made in the public sector compared to only 7.9 per cent for the private sector. As a result utilisation of public facilities is shared relatively evenly between income groups. Immunisation is mainly carried out in public facilities. In rural areas 96.6 per cent of shots for the lowest quintile are provided in the public sector; for the top quintile the figure is 85.7 per cent. In urban areas where the private sector is more developed the figures are 88.9 per cent and 31.6 per cent respectively. A percentage of 57.7 inpatient days related to childbirth for the lowest quintile are spent in the public sector compared to only 13.3 per cent in the top quintile. The lower quintile groups benefit predominantly from pre/post-natal visits and childbirth conducted by ANMs and LHVs. In urban areas, 78.2 per cent of such pre/post-natal visits are to those in the lowest quintile. For childbirth 40.7 per cent are to those in the lowest quintile. In rural areas ANMs and LHVs serve a broader clientele though the lower income groups predominate.
- *Formal user fees are primarily paid by the better off* : Nearly 89.2 per cent of hospital charges in rural areas are paid by those in the top income quintile. Also, 92.9 per cent of charges at PHC level and below are paid by those in the top two income quintiles.
- *Public sector subsidies benefit the better off more than*

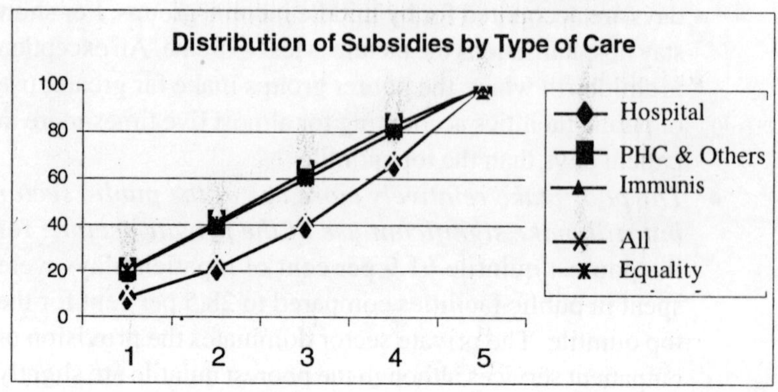
Distribution of Subsidies by Type of Care
100
80
60
40
20
0
1
2
3
4
5
Hospital
PHC & Others
Immunis
All
Equality

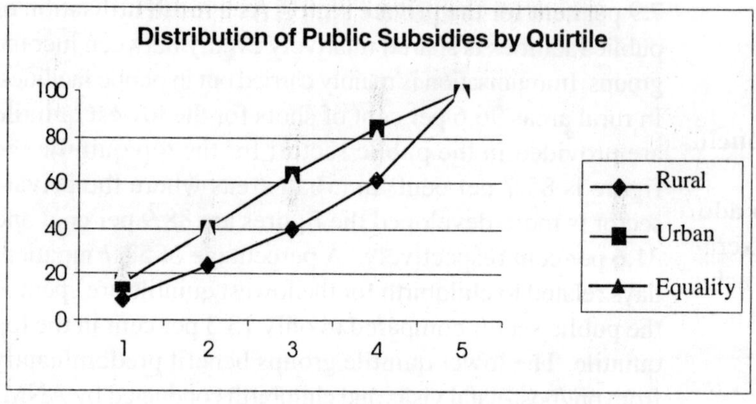
Distribution of Public Subsidies by Quirtile
100
80
60
40
20
0
1
2
3
4
5
Rural
Urban
Equality

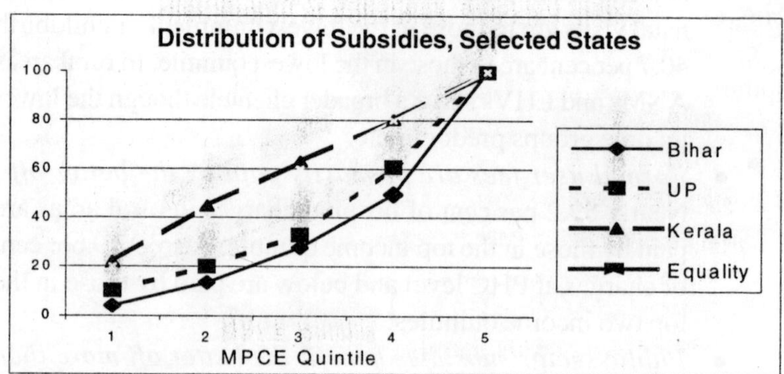
Distribution of Subsidies, Selected States
100
80
60
40
20
0
1
2
3
4
5
MPCE Quintile
Bihar
UP
Kerala
Equality

the poor : this reflects the trends outlined above. Whilst public sector subsidies for PHC and immunisations tend to benefit the poor, this is more than offset by the concentration of public subsidies for inpatient care on middle and higher income groups (Table 6.9). Estimates for distribution of public subsidies are also provided for major states. As hospital care accounts for a large part of the share in the total subsidies (86 per cent at all India level), it would be interesting to analyse inter-state variations in this aspect. The distribution of public subsidies in Bihar, Haryana, Himachal Pradesh, Madhya Pradesh, Northeastern states, Orissa, Rajasthan and Uttar Pradesh is less equitable than for India as a whole (Table 6.10). On the other hand, it is more equitable in Gujarat, Tamil Nadu, Kerala and to some extent Punjab, because the poor tend to have relatively more access at all levels of facilities in these states.

Conclusions and Policy Options

To address equity in distribution of public health subsidies, government must adopt better targeting mechanisms. These could be achieved through (i) focusing more on resources in areas where the poor already get significant benefits, (ii) improving the targeting of resources in areas where the poor do not currently benefit, (iii) shift resources from areas where the poor do not benefit to those where they do, and (iv) enabling measures to improve targeting of public resources.

Given the fact that the bulk of current subsidies goes to the hospital sector this is where initial emphasis might be placed on:

- Shifting of resources from hospitals to PHCs which could be achieved through holding overall allocation to hospitals constant in nominal (real) terms; greater self financing of hospital services (e.g., pay beds for the better off, in the longer term looking at insurance); shifting resources from tertiary to district hospitals; allocating resources according to workload and good performance of the facility.

TABLE 6.9: **Distribution of Net Public Subsidies by Level of Care by MPCE Quintile, Rural and Urban India, 1995-96**

	Type of Service				
MPCE Quintile	Short Hospitali-sations	All Hospitali sations	PHC & Others	Immunisations	All (2+3+4)
		Rural India			
1 (Bottom)	10.6	7.7	17.0	22.6	9.6
2	14.4	12.5	19.6	22.2	13.8
3	17.9	15.8	21.2	20.7	16.7
4	24.3	21.5	10.8	19.7	21.2
5 (Top)	32.8	42.5	22.4	14.8	38.6
		Urban India			
1 (Bottom)	18.0	15.6	18.8	26.7	16.1
2	23.7	23.6	26.5	25.9	23.7
3	23.2	23.7	16.8	21.2	23.4
4	20.9	21.4	17.5	17.0	21.2
5 (Top)	14.3	15.7	20.4	9.2	15.7
		All India			
1 (Bottom)	11.1	8.4	20.3	23.7	10.2
2	14.3	13.0	20.7	22.2	14.1
3	20.6	18.2	21.7	22.0	18.7
4	26.4	26.9	20.3	19.6	26.0
5 (Top)	27.6	33.5	17.0	12.5	31.0
Total subsidy distribution (%)	57.1	86.1	9.1	4.8	100.0

Source: Ajay Mahal and Anil Gumber (2000), *Who Benefits from Public Health Spending in India?* National Council of Applied Economic Research, New Delhi, October 2000.

- Increasing the share of hospital subsidies going to the poor through investigating the potential for better targeting; better monitoring of performance of autonomous hospitals in

TABLE 6.10: **Distribution of Net Public Sector Health Subsidies by Level of Care & MPCE Quintile Across States**

State	Type of Facility	MPCE Quintile					Total Subsidy	
		1	2	3	4	5	Rs. million	%
Andhra Pradesh	Short hospitalisations	18.1	17.0	16.6	30.5	17.8	1229	49.7
	All hospitalisations	14.8	14.4	15.0	25.5	30.4	2053	83.0
	PHC & others	20.5	21.6	33.5	15.2	9.2	263	10.6
	Immunisations	29.3	23.0	21.5	17.9	8.4	158	6.4
	Total	16.3	15.7	17.4	23.9	26.7	2474	100.0
Bihar	Short hospitalisations	3.1	12.9	19.1	27.4	37.5	586	52.9
	All hospitalisations	2.3	8.3	12.5	21.8	55.1	949	85.7
	PHC & others	7.2	8.5	31.6	25.6	27.2	68	6.1
	Immunisations	20.7	21.7	21.3	18.3	18.0	91	8.2
	Total	4.1	9.4	14.4	21.8	50.3	1108	100.0
Gujarat	Short hospitalisations	17.9	24.4	17.8	21.4	18.4	663	46.3
	All hospitalisations	12.4	16.9	38.6	14.8	17.3	1189	83.1
	PHC & others	26.9	15.6	27.1	21.4	9.0	149	10.4
	Immunisations	28.4	25.1	20.0	17.7	8.8	93	6.5
	Total	15.0	17.3	36.2	15.6	15.9	1431	100.0

(contd.)

TABLE 6.10 *(contd.)*

State	Type of Facility	MPCE Quintile					Total Subsidy	
		1	2	3	4	5	Rs. million	%
Haryana	Short hospitalisations	18.6	17.4	13.3	19.5	31.2	464	58.2
	All hospitalisations	12.7	11.9	12.7	27.0	35.7	677	85.1
	PHC & others	13.8	22.6	25.8	19.4	18.5	59	7.4
	Immunisations	21.4	25.7	23.3	19.8	9.7	60	7.5
	Total	13.5	13.7	14.4	25.9	32.5	796	100.0
Himachal Pradesh	Short hospitalisations	6.4	11.1	18.0	24.5	40.0	474	64.7
	All hospitalisations	6.4	11.0	12.6	23.9	46.1	675	92.1
	PHC & others	21.2	15.2	22.7	24.0	17.0	45	6.2
	Immunisations	18.9	22.7	20.5	24.8	13.1	12	1.7
	Total	7.5	11.4	13.4	23.9	43.8	732	100.0
Karnataka	Short hospitalisations	10.1	17.8	23.3	26.5	22.3	1148	54.1
	All hospitalisations	7.6	14.2	18.9	24.1	35.2	1803	85.0
	PHC & others	17.1	31.3	20.7	15.5	15.4	216	10.2
	Immunisations	22.5	23.6	26.3	17.9	9.8	101	4.8
	Total	9.3	16.4	19.5	22.9	32.0	2120	100.0

(contd.)

TABLE 6.10 *(contd.)*

State	Type of Facility	MPCE Quintile					Total Subsidy	
		1	2	3	4	5	Rs. million	%
Kerala	Short hospitalisations	28.1	20.9	24.3	15.6	11.1	2490	61.5
	All hospitalisations	21.7	23.3	17.8	17.3	19.9	3921	96.8
	PHC & others	28.3	11.7	30.4	14.8	14.7	93	2.3
	Immunisations	30.8	23.7	22.4	12.8	10.4	34	0.8
	Total	21.9	23.0	18.2	17.2	19.7	4049	100.0
Madhya Pradesh	Short hospitalisations	8.6	9.3	12.2	32.3	37.7	1601	60.3
	All hospitalisations	6.4	9.2	12.5	29.1	42.8	2179	82.1
	PHC & others	17.2	22.5	29.4	18.8	12.1	302	11.4
	Immunisations	24.1	21.1	20.9	19.1	14.8	172	6.5
	Total	8.8	11.5	15.0	27.3	37.4	2653	100.0
Maharashtra	Short hospitalisations	16.8	17.6	22.7	27.3	15.5	1728	54.3
	All hospitalisations	13.1	13.5	21.3	32.1	19.9	2624	82.4
	PHC & others	35.6	24.8	23.4	7.0	9.2	387	12.2
	Immunisations	30.4	23.2	23.9	14.0	8.6	172	5.4
	Total	16.8	15.4	21.7	28.1	18.0	3183	100.0

(contd.)

TABLE 6.10 *(contd.)*

State	Type of Facility	MPCE Quintile					Total Subsidy	
		1	2	3	4	5	Rs. million	%
North East	Short hospitalisations	9.5	11.3	19.4	22.5	37.3	1099	61.6
	All hospitalisations	9.0	10.9	17.7	21.0	41.2	1387	77.7
	PHC & others	19.9	23.5	20.2	21.9	14.5	346	19.4
	Immunisations	23.3	21.0	18.8	22.0	15.0	51	2.8
	Total	11.6	13.6	18.2	21.2	35.3	1784	100.0
Orissa	Short hospitalisations	7.8	16.2	20.4	17.3	38.3	950	49.8
	All hospitalisations	8.6	13.6	15.5	11.8	50.5	1605	84.1
	PHC & others	11.2	23.2	20.6	22.6	22.4	240	12.6
	Immunisations	24.4	27.9	18.6	15.7	13.3	64	3.3
	Total	9.4	15.3	16.3	13.3	45.7	1909	100.0
Punjab	Short hospitalisations	11.6	16.1	18.1	20.1	34.1	412	76.9
	All hospitalisations	11.5	15.1	18.5	29.7	25.2	447	83.5
	PHC & others	30.4	30.6	15.7	19.0	4.3	39	7.3
	Immunisations	31.2	24.5	20.4	14.9	8.9	49	9.2
	Total	14.7	17.1	18.5	27.6	22.2	535	100.0

(contd.)

TABLE 6.10 *(contd.)*

State	Type of Facility	MPCE Quintile					Total Subsidy	
		1	2	3	4	5	Rs. million	%
Rajasthan	Short hospitalisations	7.2	12.6	12.0	23.1	45.1	1085	66.1
	All hospitalisations	8.8	9.6	10.8	19.7	51.2	1425	86.8
	PHC & others	10.1	26.6	21.6	11.0	30.6	130	7.9
	Immunisations	23.0	21.4	21.3	20.9	13.3	86	5.3
	Total	9.6	11.5	12.2	19.1	47.6	1641	100.0
Tamil Nadu	Short hospitalisations	19.5	18.2	24.1	22.6	15.5	2203	62.7
	All hospitalisations	13.7	20.1	20.7	25.4	20.1	3177	90.5
	PHC & others	22.8	14.1	20.5	18.8	23.8	209	6.0
	Immunisations	30.8	25.5	18.6	17.2	7.9	125	3.6
	Total	14.8	19.9	20.7	24.7	19.9	3511	100.0
Uttar Pradesh	Short hospitalisations	12.4	11.9	17.2	20.0	38.5	1764	49.9
	All hospitalisations	8.1	8.1	12.3	30.3	41.2	2875	81.3
	PHC & others	17.4	13.1	11.6	16.5	41.4	364	10.3
	Immunisations	22.1	21.5	20.0	20.9	15.6	297	8.4
	Total	10.2	9.8	12.9	28.1	39.0	3537	100.0

(contd.)

TABLE 6.10 *(contd.)*

State	Type of Facility	MPCE Quintile					Total Subsidy	
		1	2	3	4	5	Rs. million	%
West Bengal	Short hospitalisations	12.6	13.0	20.0	26.8	27.5	2163	59.1
	All hospitalisations	9.2	18.0	19.3	22.9	30.7	3260	89.0
	PHC & others	25.5	25.5	16.0	18.2	14.9	283	7.7
	Immunisations	25.6	24.6	19.6	19.9	10.2	120	3.3
	Total	11.0	18.8	19.0	22.4	28.8	3662	100.0
All India	Short hospitalisations	11.1	14.3	20.6	26.4	27.6	20063	57.1
	All hospitalisations	8.4	13.0	18.2	26.9	33.5	30252	86.1
	PHC & others	20.3	20.7	21.7	20.3	17.0	3198	9.1
	Immunisations	23.7	22.2	22.0	19.6	12.5	1687	4.8
	Total	10.2	14.1	18.7	26.0	31.0	35136	100.0

Source: Same as for Table 6.9.

providing services for the poor; learning from experiences of a few states (such as Kerala and Tamil Nadu) which have been extremely successful in focusing public hospital subsidies on the poor and replicating these in other states.

- Strengthening network amongst public, private and NGO sectors in poor and under-served areas. Encouraging the private sector to establish a bigger presence in rural areas so that the better off rural section, which enjoys a major share of public subsidies, can seek care from non-public facilities. Regulate this private sector to ensure it at least delivers an acceptable quality of care at reasonable cost and provides at least some essential services.

The foregoing analysis and articulation has clearly demonstrated that the economic reforms initiated in the country since the 1990s have had little (if any) impact on the health sector. This is so whether we consider the trends in the allocations made for the health sector or in the health outcomes since the initiation of reforms in the country. The central budgetary allocation to the health sector was 1.2 per cent of the total allocation in 1991/92 and during 1993/94 to 1998/99 it was around 1.4 per cent and marginally stepped up to 1.7 per cent during 1999/2000 and 2000/01 and further to 1.8 per cent in 2001/02. Although, in nominal terms the allocation to health sector increased from Rs.1734 crore in 1991/92 to Rs. 6752 crore in 2001/02, in real terms the increase could be marginal.

One possible reason for this behaviour may be our belief that economic reforms would necessarily be accompanied by all round improved outcomes in the health sector on its own. However, since health is a state subject and almost all decisions are taken by the state governments in the areas of their domain, economic reforms which are initiated by the union government may not thus have much impact on the health sector (and that too indirectly) unless the state governments on their own undertake such reforms in their respective states in the health sector. Indeed the World Bank, under the State Health Systems Project operating in seven major states[3] in the country, has attempted to influence the health outcomes in these

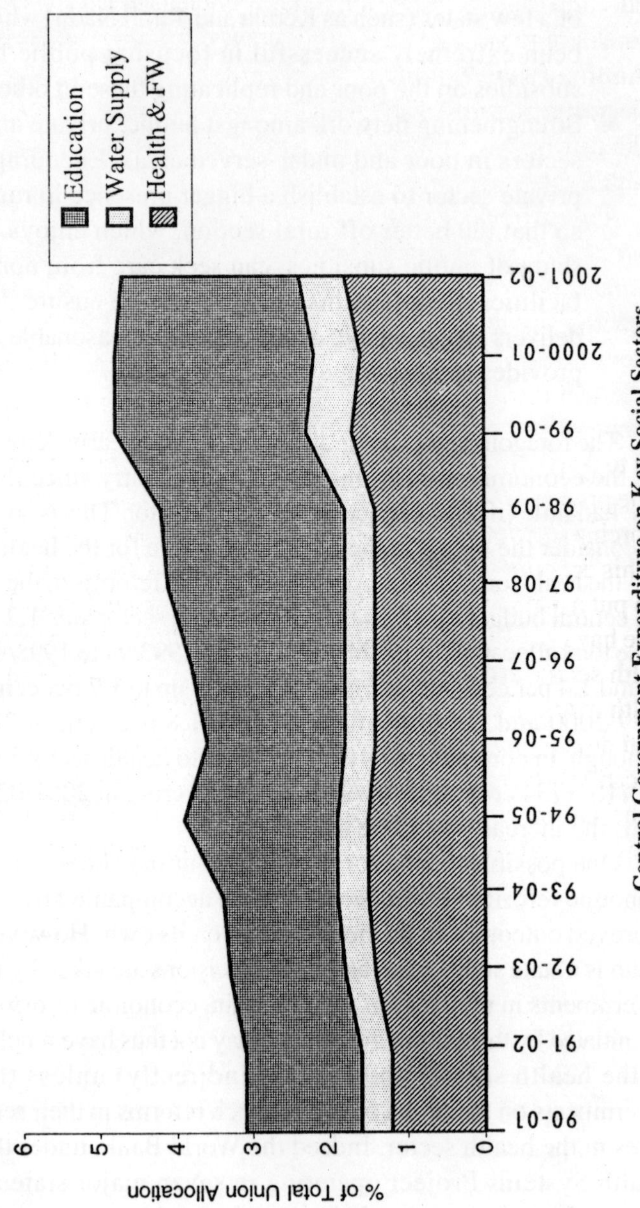

Central Government Expenditure on Key Social Sectors

states through specifically focusing on reforms at the secondary level health care facilities. However, certain deficiencies have been pointed out in this approach, and it is in this context we may cite the example of Andhra Pradesh where, apart from the State Health Systems Project, recently under the AP Economic Reform Project, primary health care has been emphasised and resourceful links with the State Health Systems are being attempted.

A word of caution in regard to the aspect of equity is in order. Most of the recent health projects have underlined the need to promote user charges/cost sharing mechanisms as a means to overcome the financial problems experienced by hospitals. Clearly the levy of user charges is likely to hurt the cause of equity, as a large section of hospital beneficiaries is the poor who are generally exempted from payment of user charges. Also, at the same time the well to do people are shifting away from the public health care system to the private. This situation has resulted in a dismal performance of enforcing user charges as is evident from the rather small collections on this account. Thus user charges apart from hurting equity have also put a question mark on the sustainability aspect as well. Hence if we have to ensure both equity and sustainability of projects in the health sector, we have to seek other options of raising funds (e.g., health insurance and providing additional resources). In addition a good deal of attention needs to be paid to the aspect of improving allocative efficiency within the health sector. This exercise should be in the nature of a stand alone exercise largely independent of economic reforms, but within its broader framework.

APPENDIX: **Health Spending for Major States in India, 1993**

State Ranked by Col. 6	Per Capita Annual Health Exp.			Share of House hold Health Exp. (2 as % of 3)	House hold Health Exp. as % of House hold Income	Total Health Exp. as % of NSDP/ NNP
	Govt.	Household	Total			
	1	2	3	4	5	6
Jammu & Kashmir*	238	325	563	57.7	NE	10.7
Kerala	111	482	593	81.3	11.9	9.5
Himachal Pradesh	209	370	579	63.9	6.7	8.9
Bihar	51	223	274	81.4	6.1	7.5
Orissa	74	276	350	78.9	8.2	7.4
Andhra Pradesh	66	421	487	86.4	7.8	7.4
Karnataka	93	360	453	79.5	8.8	6.5
Rajasthan	83	196	279	70.3	4.2	5.4
Uttar Pradesh	55	175	230	76.1	4.5	4.9
Gujarat	78	259	337	76.9	4.7	4.4
Madhya Pradesh	63	168	231	72.7	6.9	4.3
Tamil Nadu	100	202	302	66.9	6.5	4.2
West Bengal	73	154	227	67.8	3.4	3.8
Haryana	83	267	350	76.3	4.1	3.4
Punjab	110	282	392	71.9	6.2	3.2
Maharashtra	85	259	344	75.3	5.4	3.2
Assam	66.	96	162	59.3	2.4	2.8
All-India	84	250	334	74.9	6.0	5.5

Note: Estimates for Jammu & Kashmir are based on the previous NCAER survey of 1990.

NSDP – Net State Domestic Product, NNP – Net National Product

Source: Abusaleh Shariff et al. (1999:56) *conomic Reform and the Poor*, National Council of Applied Economic Research, New Delhi, mimeo.

NOTES

1. This paper is dedicated to the memory of my "guru" Professor Pravin Visaria who inspired, nurtured and guided me to work in the area of health economics.
2. Shariff and Gumber (1998) have attempted a comprehensive review of the impact of economic reforms on poverty. Beside exploring the linkages between GDP growth rate and incidence of poverty, the analyses also focus on poverty influencing parameters (availability of food grains, food prices and general inflation, central budgetary allocations for poverty alleviation programmes, etc.) and changes in the income distribution of households.
3. These states are Andhra Pradesh (SHS-I), Karnataka, Punjab and West Bengal (SHS-II), Maharashtra and Orissa (SHS-III), more recently Uttar Pradesh (SHS-IV) is included. Rajasthan is under consideration.

REFERENCES

Gumber, Anil (1997), "Burden of Disease and Cost of Ill Health in India: Setting Priorities for Health Interventions During the Ninth Plan". *Margin*. Vol. 29, No. 2, pp.133-172.

Gumber, Anil and Veena Kulkarni (2000), "Health Insurance for Informal Sector: Case Study of Gujarat". *Economic and Political Weekly*, Vol. XXXV, No. 40, September 30-October 6, pp. 3607-3613.

India, National Sample Survey (1980), "Notes on Morbidity: NSS 28th Round (October 1973-June 1974)", *Sarvekshana*, Vol. 4, Nos. 1 & 2, July-October, pp.17-21 and S137-180.

—— (1992), "Morbidity and Utilization of Medical Services: NSS 42nd Round (1986-87)", *Sarvekshana*, Vol. 15, No. 4, April-June, pp. 50-75.

Mahal, Ajay and Anil Gumber (2000), *Who Benefits from Public Health Spending in India?* National Council of Applied Economic Research, New Delhi, October 2000.

National Council of Applied Economic Research (1992), *Household Survey of Medical Care*, NCAER, New Delhi.

Shariff, Abusaleh (1995), "Health Transition in India", Working Paper No. 57, National Council of Applied Economic Research, New Delhi.

—— and Gumber, Anil (1998), *Economic Reform and the Poor*, National Council of Applied Economic Research, New Delhi (Mimeo).

——, Anil, Gumber, Ravi Duggal and Alam Mooner (1999), "Health Care Financing and Insurance: Perspective for the Ninth Plan, 1997-2002", *Margin*, Vol. 31(2), Jan-Mar, pp. 38-68.

Sundar, Ramamani (1992), "Household Survey of Medical Care", *Margin*, Vol. 24, No. 2, January-March, pp. 169-175.

Tulasidhar, V.B. (1993), "Expenditure Compression and Health Sector Outlays", *Economic and Political Weekly*, Vol. XXVIII, No. 45, pp. 2473-2477.

Visaria, Pravin and Anil Gumber (1994), *Utilization of and Expenditure on Health Care in India, 1986-87 (A Study of Five States)*, Gujarat Institute of Development Research, Ahmedabad.

——, Anil Gumber and Paul Jacob (1996), *Morbidity, Health Care Utilization and Expenditure Pattern in Andhra Pradesh, Kerala, Madhya Pradesh and Punjab, 1986-87*, Gujarat Institute of Development Research, Ahmedabad.

—— and Anil Gumber (1997), *Level and Pattern of Morbidity, Health Care Utilization and Expenditure in India, 1986-87*, Gujarat Institute of Development Research, Ahmedabad.

—— and Anil Gumber, *Utilization of and Expenditure on Health Care in India, 1986-87 (A Study of Five States)*. Ahmedabad: Gujarat Institute of Development Research, 1994.

World Bank (1993), *World Development Report 1993: Investing in Health*. New York: Oxford University Press.

—— (1995), *India: Policy and Finance Strategies for Strengthening Primary Health Care Services*. Population and Human Resources Operations Division, Report No. 13042-IN, Washington DC, 1995.

7

ECONOMIC REFORMS: Where are the Women ?

NIRMALA BANERJEE

It is now 10 years since the Indian government officially came to adopt a new economic policy with a structural adjustment programme. So, it is indeed time now for taking stock of what has been done and with what outcome. In this process, the experts usually focus on the state of the macro-economy and of its important sectors, and largely ignore the changes in the conditions of the people at large. Although there is always a mention of changes in the levels of poverty as well as overall employment and unemployment, little is said about the nature of the work that people have been doing to overcome poverty. Also, in the growing concern for efficiency and competitiveness of economic activities in the country, much of the blame for shortfalls in it is laid at the doors of workers for their low productivity. But even in the recent budget, which ventured into formulating labour-related policies, few concrete schemes have been included for improving productivity. In the general apathy about the situation of labour, it is only to be expected that there is little concern for the situation of women who after all form a small, unskilled minority in the workforce.

In this paper, I want to briefly look at the actual developments in India over the last decade or so in women's employment as compared to those for men. Available data for this period shows that, for neither men nor women are there indications of an unambiguous improvement in the labour status. For women workers, the trends appear to be rather mixed; for the majority who are rural, employment prospects have stagnated and the minor gains they had begun to make in the earlier decade have not really been consolidated. For urban women, it seems that some new possibilities may have opened up in this period. In this paper, I have focused mainly on women's work opportunities in manufacturing and services where some positive or negative changes have been appearing. My concern is to put these possibilities at the margin against the background of the overall situation of women who have been in the workforce. This is because it is important to identify the bottlenecks that hinder the majority from making the necessary adjustments for taking advantage of the positive changes and to cope with the negative ones. The overall conclusion that suggests itself is that, unless some special policies are pursued by the state, the positive changes are very likely to bypass the existing workers.

So, What has been Happening?

Before going further, it is essential that we familiarise ourselves with facts. If we look at available data for each quinquennium starting from 1983, which preceded the trends towards liberalisation, to 1999/2000 which is the latest year for which we have official information, the surprising part is the complete absence of any dramatic shifts; particularly in women's work, trends over this time have moved, but gently, in a kind of inexorable reiteration of past directions. As Table 7.1 shows, till the latest available year, women's workforce participation rates by any definition have been on the decline. For men too the trends are not dissimilar though perhaps of a somewhat lesser order. As we know, these rates can decline with more children staying longer in school, and that may well have been part of the explanation in this case. But we do know that, at least for urban women, the rates of workforce participation have been so low that given a chance, they could have increased fast even with the withdrawal of child labour. Therefore, it is obvious that, in India, unlike in several Asian countries outside this sub-continent, nothing has happened to draw a greater percentage of women into the labour force.

TABLE 7.1: **Workforce Participation Rate of Males/Females by Different Definitions**

		Usual Status				Current Weekly Status				Current Daily Status			
NSS Rounds		38	43	50	55	38	43	50	55	38	43	50	55
Area	Sex	1983	1987-88	1993-94	1999-2000	1983	1987-88	1993-94	1999-2000	1983	1987-88	1993-94	1999-2000
Rural													
	Male	51.7	539	553	531	51.1	504	530	510	48.2	501	504	478
	Female	34.0	323	328	299	22.7	220	267	253	19.8	207	220	204
Urban													
	Male	51.2	506	520	578	49.2	492	571	509	47.3	477	498	490
	Female	15.1	152	154	139	11.8	119	139	128	10.6	110	120	111

Sources: NSS Report No.455 : *Employment & Unemployment in India,* 1900-2000, Key Results (tables 4 & 5).

NSS Report No. 406: *Employment & Unemployment in India,* 1993-94, Key Results (tables 4.2.1 & 4.2.2).

Secondly, rural women remain concentrated in agriculture; from 1983 till date the share of agriculture in rural women's total employment is about 85 per cent. And since urban employment forms a very small share of women's total employment (both because a majority of women live in rural areas, and also because a much smaller percentage of urban women join the workforce in India), agriculture remains the occupation of more than three quarters of all the women who work.

Agriculture as an occupation for urban workers has in fact declined sharply; for both men and women this has meant a relatively faster growth of tertiary or service sector employment. Women's share in the total secondary sector has been gently declining as seen from Table 7.2.

TABLE 7.2: **Per 1000 Distribution of Usually Working by Broad Groups of Industry in Different NSS Rounds**

		Rural				Urban			
NSS Rounds		38	43	50	55	38	43	50	55
	Sex	1983	(1987-88)	(1993-94)	(1999-00)	1983	(1987-88)	(1993-94)	(1999-00)
Primary PS	Male	772	739	737	712	97	85	87	65
	Female	862	825	847	841	255	218	193	146
Secondary PS	Male	103	123	113	127	344	343	331	329
	Female	78	112	91	93	307	324	295	293
Tertiary PS	Male	123	138	149	161	551	572	581	606
	Female	52	63	63	66	430	458	510	561

Source: NSS Report No. 455, *Employment & Unemployment in India,* 1999-2000, Key Results (Table 2).

In the distribution of workers by their labour status between the categories of self-employment, regular service and casual labour, there have been some significant changes even in the short period of five years between 1993/94 and 1999/2000. Table 7.3 shows that from 1987/88 onwards, there was a mild but significant shift towards casual employment in the case of male workers: in rural areas this

TABLE 7.3: **Per 1000 Distribution of Usually Employed by Category of Employment in Different NSS Rounds**

		NSS Round	38	43	50	55
Principal Status	Area	Sex	(1983)	(1987-88)	(1993-94)	(1999-00)
Self-employed	Rural	Male	595	575	569	544
		Female	541	549	573	500
	Urban	Male	402	410	411	412
		Female	373	393	364	384
Regular employees	Rural	Male	106	104	85	90
		Female	37	49	34	39
	Urban	Male	445	444	427	419
		Female	318	342	355	385
Casual labourers	Rural	Male	299	321	346	366
		Female	422	402	453	461
	Urban	Male	153	146	162	169
		Female	309	265	281	231

Source: NSS Report No. 455: *Employment & Unemployment in India*, 1999-2000, Key Results, Table 10.

shift was at the cost of both self-employment and regular service. The same was true of rural women. In urban areas, for men there was a move from regular service to casual labour, with self-employment remaining at the same level. For urban women, there was a more significant shift in favour of regular employment at the cost of both self-employment and casual labour. Interestingly, these shifts have not been uniform across the board in all sectors. Table 7.4 shows that, for rural men and women, the shift from self-employment to casual labour is mainly in the primary sector. This is as to be expected with the growing trend towards landlessness. For urban men, the increase in casual labour is mainly in the secondary sector, and comes from a fall in the share of regular service jobs in that sector. For both rural and urban women, there was an increase in self-employment in the secondary sector. For urban women, there was also a marked increase in regular service jobs in the secondary sector. In the case of the tertiary sector in rural areas, there was an increase in the share of women in regular service, mainly at the cost of the self-employment category. In the case of urban women in the tertiary sector, this trend was reversed. It was self-employment that had made some gains.

TABLE 7.4: **Incidence of Different Status Employment in Sector-wise Employment of Rural and Urban Men and Women, 1993/94 and 1999/00**

	Rural				Urban			
	Male		Female		Male		Female	
	93/94	99/00	93/94	99/00	93/94	99/00	93/94	99/00
0 - Primary								
Self-employment	60.4	58.1	50.1	48.20	59.1	60.6	43.5	41.2
Regular services	1.8	1.9	-	1.02	4.5	3.0	-	5.9
Casual labour	37.8	40.0	48.7	50.26	36.7	36.4	56.5	58.8
1-5 - Secondary								
Self-employment	36.6	36.4	52.4	66.6	28.2	29.0	41.7	50.0
Regular services	18.3	18.2	9.5	9.5	47.1	42.0	19.5	23.5
Casual labour	45.0	45.5	38.0	23.9	24.7	28.4	38.9	26.5
6 - 9 - Tertiary								
Self-employment	54.9	52.4	56.2	50.3	45.9	45.6	30.7	33.3
Regular services	34.2	34.5	31.3	37.5	45.9	45.9	58.1	54.4
Casual labour	11.0	13.1	12.5	13.0	8.2	8.4	11.3	10.6

Sources: NSSO Report No. 406, for 50th Round 1993/94, Table 1A, p. 46 and Statement 3A, p. 76.

NSSO Report No. 455, for 55th Round 1999/2000, Table 1, p A-1 and Table 5, p. A- 25.

With respect to unemployment rates, which our system tries to measure but rather unsatisfactorily, there are signs that, in rural areas, current daily status unemployment is slightly on the rise, as one would expect with increasing casualisation of employment. In urban areas, unemployment rates by all definitions have declined between

1987/88 and the last year. These rates by any definition have always been the highest in the case of urban women, and in the latest round this relative position remains unchanged; but the decline in urban women's unemployment rates has certainly been the fastest (NSSO Report No. 455, Table 14, p. 28).

Manufacturing

In the early years of reforms, there was a general expectation that, in the process of liberalisation, India would also undergo what has been rather inelegantly called feminisation of the workforce, especially of the manufacturing workforce. The term was to signify that women would come to form the bulk of the labour in manufacturing; and/or, the terms and conditions offered to all workers in more and more manufacturing jobs would come to resemble those traditionally offered to women. The hypothesis was based on the experience of most faster developing countries of the last quarter century (Standing1989, 1999, Cagatay and Ozler 1995 among others). It was assumed that in all countries accepting the SAP, the two engines of growth would be foreign direct investment and rapid growth of foot-loose export-oriented industries. Also in the eighties, much of such investment was in industries and operations using labour intensive technologies. Since no country had any clear comparative advantage in terms of natural resources for attracting investment into those kinds of foot-loose industries, the choice of the locale had been mainly on grounds of the availability of cheap, docile and flexible labour in plentiful supply. In most countries women seemed to be the logical choice in the quest for such labour. Hence the generalisation, according to which it was expected that with the liberalisation of state policies vis-a-vis foreign direct investment and the low wage rates paid to women workers in general, India would become one such country with feminized manufacturing labour.

The Reality

The actual experience of Indian women regarding manufacturing employment in this first decade of reforms has been quite mixed and differs significantly from these expectations. Women's employment in manufacturing in the public sector increased fairly fast in the 1980s, but at the same time, it went down in absolute terms in the private sector. On the other hand, in the years between 1991 and 1994, their employment continued to grow in the public sector, and also picked up sharply in the private sector. This is in line with the hypothesis of feminization of manufacturing employment. On the other hand, unlike the argument made under that sarne thesis, there were no indications that increase in the numbers of women workers had a significantly negative effect on the terms offered to workers in general in the organised sector. At least till 1994, real wages and real costs of labour per man day were rising in the organised sector of all manufacturing industries (Anand and Sundaram, 1998, tables 7 and 8, p. 827).

TABLE 7.5: **Women Workers as Percentage of Total Manufacturing Employment**

Year	Rural	Urban	Total
1987-88	31.06	17.45	24.7
1993-94	30.81	17.62	24.5
1999-2000	30.95	17.74	24.7

Sources: NSSO Report on 43th Round 1987/88 Table No. 53.1 p. 79 and Statement 34, p. 101.
NSSO Report No. 406, for 50th Round 1993/94 Table 1A p. 46 and Statement 3A, p. 76.
NSSO Report No. 455 for 55th Round 1999/2000 Table 1, p. A.1 and Table 5, 5 A, p. 25.

But that is far from the complete story. Manufacturing employment in the organised sector in 1994 constituted about 20 per cent of the total manufacturing employment in the country. For women, the share of the organised sector in their total manufacturing employment at that time was no more than 13 per cent. Women formed around 11 per cent of all manufacturing workers in the organised sector. One cannot thus draw any conclusions about trends in their manufacturing employment without taking account of developments in the organised and unorganised sectors together.

According to NSSO data, total manufacturing employment in India went up very slowly, by less than five per cent between 1987/88 and 1993/94. In that period women's total manufacturing employment remained almost stagnant. Over the next five years, total manufacturing employment went up by about 16 per cent for both men and women (NSSO, Employment and Unemployment Surveys, various rounds). Because of these mixed trends, Table 5 shows that throughout this period there are no indications that women have increased their share in total manufacturing employment whether in the rural or in the urban sector. This was in spite of the fact noted above, namely, that their employment had lately gone up in the organised sector. Actually as Table 7.6 shows, the increase had tended to be in the organised sector alone. In the unorganised manufacturing sector, which accounted for nearly 80 per cent of all manufacturing employment, the numbers of workers were falling slowly between the late eighties and the mid-nineties.

The Reasons

Why has the experience of Indian women been so different from that of women in other countries? One reason of course is that the growth of the modern sector in India is nowhere as large compared to the total size of the Indian economy; nor have exports from India been anywhere as important a contributor to the national income as in the countries of south-east or east Asia that remain as the models of feminized workforce.

But far more important is the fact that in India the growth of the organised or modern manufacturing sector has been far too slow in comparison with the size of the workforce that was already engaged in manufacturing activities. The fortunes of this large majority of workers therefore remained tied with their traditional enterprises. Why these traditional enterprises were doing badly is also obvious from Table 7.6; invested capital per worker in the unorganised enterprises was a small fraction of that in the rest. In a recent enquiry by the NSSO (NSSO Report No. 456, Table 8, p. 75), it appeared that over 40 per cent of all such units in manufacturing suffered from a shortage of capital. Since over 85 per cent of them were own account enterprises (ibid, statement 2, p. 16), it is possible that the bulk of these at least in rural areas were traditional cottage or household enterprises using their family equipment, such as a loom or a potter's wheel and had not updated the machinery in several generations.

TABLE 7.6: **Manufacturing Industry in Mid-nineties**

Category		Agro-based	Non-agro based	All
Capital per Worker	Organised	55700	197940	155770
	Unorganised	5000	10 000	5700
Share in employment of	Urban	73%	62%	69 %
unorganised sector	Rural	93 %	87 %	92 %
Annual compound rate	Organised	2.26 %	3.01 %	2.09 %
of growth of employment 1986 - 87 -1990 / 91	Unorganised	-2.6 %	-1.5 %	-1.9 %
1991 - 1995 - 96	Organised	3.34%	4.24%	3.89%
1989 90 - 94 – 95	Unorganised	- 2.1%	- 0.9%	- 1.5%

Source: G. K. Chadha (1999), "Trade, Technology and Employment", *The Indian Journal of Labour Economics*, Vol. 42, No. 4, tables 3-4, pp. 896-903.

At the same time, globalisation has increased the competition faced by these units; this is as true of enterprises which have been producing non-tradeables as it is of those engaged in producing tradeables. Earlier many goods like flour, edible oil or dry snacks were being produced by traditional means for local markets. These are now increasingly being produced by modern large-scale enterprises for much wider markets and their sales everywhere are being promoted by attractive advertisements and packaging that appeal to consumers everywhere. With modern communications, rural markets are also well within their reach. As a result, these commodities can no longer be considered non-tradeable.

In the case of commodities that have traditionally been tradeable, small enterprises have again been badly hit mainly because of growing competition. This could be for the raw materials they use, as in the case of handlooms; since the early nineties when government policy of allowing exports of cotton and cotton yarn pushed up their prices by 500 per cent or so in two or three years, the industry has reportedly been undergoing a crisis. Or the competition can be in markets for their products: for example, reports are that the Indian household-based sericulture industry is reeling under the competition of silk cocoons and yarn from China that have flooded the Indian markets. All in all, for small enterprises producing both tradeable and non-tradeable manufactures, the years since the opening up of the Indian economy have largely been traumatic. The NSSO report for 1999/2000 found that among unorganised manufacturing enterprises, 76 to 80 per cent were either stagnating or contracting (ibid., Table 11, pp. 88-93).

The process is particularly likely to have adverse implications for women in manufacturing because most work in small enterprises is mainly engaged in processing of agro-based materials. These industries constitute the more traditional of India's industries. These include food processing as well as textiles and leather industries. As Table 7.6 has shown, these are also the industries which are particularly under-capitalised. Historically these units had survived for two reasons: as argued before, their products were earlier consumed locally where similar goods of large enterprises were not being marketed. The second factor that had helped these units to survive in the past was the support of some government policies. Many among the agro-based groups had been subsidised by the Khadi and Village Industries Corporation, either singly or as cooperatives. Many had been further protected from competition from large units through the policy of reservations. Now that all such support policies are being withdrawn, the future for the enterprises and their workers is supposedly quite bleak.

Possible Adjustments

So what happens to women who become unemployed when their family enterprises collapse? Two small studies, one in the Janakpuri slum of Delhi (conducted by Action Aid in 1994), and another in a few villages in the handloom weaving villages of the Hoogly district of West Bengal (conducted by Sachetana in 1997) indicated that when family based enterprises collapsed, most women who had earlier worked in those as part of the family labour then tried to find employment elsewhere. In Delhi this was a study of a community of Jolahas who had earlier made a living weaving cheap bedcovers on their traditional pitlooms. The industry became non-viable after the new textile policy was initiated. For the women it then became imperative to get some wage work. Being in Delhi, they had a choice of occupations, but because of their family backgrounds, many of those options, especially in trade or domestic service were taboo for them. Most therefore had accepted manufacturing work on piece-rates, either at home or in distant sweatshops. In West Bengal, women of weaver families who had been forced to seek some other work had faced similar taboos against agricultural work which would have been the only alternative for them; but at that time most had found work on piece-rates from the many powerloom factories coming up in the region, where they did their traditional work of preparing the yarn.

It is a moot point whether or not on balance, this shift had benefited the women. Working for a money wage meant that, perhaps for the first time, they had a regular cash income of their own and that income was a significant part of the family income. That had got some recognition for them as workers which the earlier unpaid work had seldom done. But the stress of work had often increased because they had to adjust between the priorities and demands of their employers as well as of their household authorities. It is possible that over time, those women would come to some better arrangements, but in those early days, they were obviously having a hard time coping.

Also, these kind of lateral shifts in their occupations may not always be feasible in the case of all women who are made redundant by the collapse of their traditional family enterprises. A major problem is of their location. For rural women workers who are situated in villages across the country, there may be no other local work available except in agriculture or trade and even that may require their moving out of the house or travelling some distance. Many communities of traditional artisans have strong taboos against such moves by their women. Mulberry silk in West Bengal is produced mostly by Muslim households whose women so far have not been allowed to take up work outside the home. Under such constraints, the women may find work, but under extremely exploitative terms. For example, in 1976/77, in a study of the ready-made garment industry in Kolkata, we had found that work on many of the manual tasks in the industry, such as sewing on buttons used to be put out to home-based workers in Kolkata. At that time we had thought that the piece rates they were being paid for that work were appallingly low. But in another survey conducted 20 years later, we found that the tasks were no longer being put out in Kolkata. Instead, They were increasingly being sent out of Kolkata to women in somewhat inaccessible villages; and the rates paid in the 1990s were the same as they had been in the city at the time of the earlier study 20 years earlier.

Women who are made redundant in their traditional occupations also have another problem; skill training in India is predominantly through family upbringing. For women this means training only for the work they were traditionally supposed to do in the family enterprise, be it cultivation or manufacturing. Therefore, the skills they possess are usually specific to the traditional household occupation. When they look for work outside the household, they can either offer to do the same work for others or they can aspire only for some unskilled work. Men who become similarly redundant also face that problem; but they face few taboos in their choices of alternative occupations and can move into some other work such as transport or construction that are expanding in rural areas. They also have the option of migrating seasonally or for long periods. and there is considerable evidence of their increasing migration even if only for seasonal work. Many studies have brought out the growth in even single female migration for work in recent years. Nevertheless they are relatively more handicapped on the one hand by their lack of education, to which I will come later and also by the lack of access to relevant information. More important, I have shown elsewhere how, the Indian tradition of women joining the labour force relatively later in their life cycles than in most countries, reduces their mobility and further restricts their choices of occupations. I have further argued elsewhere that, a major cause of the spread of dowry in all sections of Indian society is linked with this; the collapse and degradation of traditional household industries tend to reduce the relative value that families put on women's labour and of the skills they had used in family enterprises. Men, because of their access to alternative occupations, thus come to attain a comparatively higher status within their communities. The growing differential in the life-time contributions that will be made by men and women to family incomes has led to a revision in community-based marriage practices and a replacement of bride-price by dowry (Banerjee, forthcoming).

Of course, there is the example of Bangladesh women from similar backgrounds who had no previous tradition of wage work or single migration, but who suddenly began to come to the cities to work in garment factories. In India in the last century or more of industrialization, records show that, whenever there was a rise in the demand for labour, it was quickly met by additional workers offering their services so that, at no time did any industry find itself starving for labour, whether male or female. In the early part of this century, the jute industry could not attract sufficient numbers of local Bengali labour. But the gap was quickly filled by migrant workers coming from Uttar Pradesh, Bihar and Orissa. There were women coming singly to work from as far away as Andhra Pradesh. Given the proper incentive, traditional cultural barriers against women's work have always been circumvented. And in today's situation too, for any conceivable possibility of Indian industry demanding more female labour, it is unlikely that they will meet with any supply bottlenecks. In a very short while adequate numbers of duly qualified women will be coming forth to offer their labour. . The question is, will the women who are now being made redundant be able to make inroads into that market? Or will the jobs go to a different section of women who may have come from a group hitherto under-represented in the Indian manufacturing industry?

Services

Table 7.2 had shown that in the last quinquennium, there was a rise of about 10 per cent in the share of tertiary work in urban women's employment. And although the number of urban women workers is small compared to other groups of male and female workers, the development may be important as a signifier of the events to come. This section includes workers in both trade and various services, and as Table 4 has indicated, among them, there was a rise in the share of those working as self-employed. Among the regular service holders in this group, a section works in the organised sector and in the post-liberalisation period there has been some increase in that group in the private sector. . But the total number of organised sector women workers (urban and rural) in services and trade was no more than six lakh in 1994 as compared to the estimated number of 41 lakh (principal status only) for 1999/2000 of urban service workers. Also, it would not be unreasonable to assume that the additions to organised service sector workers have come mainly from among better educated women. I am more interested in examining the situation of the uneducated or poorly educated woman worker who is still the typical example of the Indian worker; therefore, the next few paragraphs are mainly about this latter group which is concentrated in the unorganised sector.

According to the recent survey of unorganised enterprises by the NSSO (Report No 456), employment of urban women in unorganised trade (category G) in urban India was about 14 lakh in 1999/2000. In that year, urban women's combined employment in services including education, health, community and personal services and entertainment etc., (categories G standing for trade and M, N, and O) was about 15 lakh. Interestingly, in trade, the share of urban workers among all women workers was less than half; but in the combined total of above-mentioned services, the share of the urban section was over 77 per cent. In other words, for those services, the market was concentrated in urban areas. This was so in spite of the fact that even there, more than two-thirds of the category worked as owner-workers or helpers in family enterprises.

The Potential

One advantage of the tertiary sector is that it does not face competition from products coming from outside the local area. Large capital may displace the small providers of those services, but the labour input remains local. So its growth creates net additions to local employment. Even if commuters join the work, the fact that they have to be personally near the consumers of work every day means that the hinterland sending such workers has to be relatively small. Also, while many services such as education and personal care are unlikely to be mechanised, others like health may substantially add to the equipment in use; but this too will usually mean a greater demand for workers to operate that equipment.

It can also be shown from available data on consumer expenditure that there is a very close correlation between levels of total consumption expenditure and of expenditure on these services The rank correlation in a cross-section of 28 major Indian states between their ranks as per the state-wise levels of per capita total consumption expenditure and of per capita combined expenditure on the services of education, health and miscellaneous consumer services (NSSO Report No. 454, tables 4R and 4U, pp. 51-56) for the year 1999/2000 worked out to be 0.83 for rural areas and 0.94 for urban areas. In other words, one can expect that as levels of per capita consumption expenditure rise, consumers can be expected to raise their expenditure on such services in tandem. So, while the distribution of the first round of gains from economic reforms may be extremely skewed, supply of services may be one of the few channels through which a part of those gains may trickle down to the less fortunate groups.

Moreover, service jobs admittedly are very much subject to gender stereo-typing, But in India, in many of the major consumer services, job segregation has gone in favour of women. Education of younger children is very much seen as a woman's job; so is nursing and many of the health-care tasks. Domestic service has now become mainly a woman's job. Women have faced few barriers to entry in most personal care services. Indeed given the fact that, traditionally, women's wage rates in such service occupations have been relatively low in the past has meant that employers often give them a preference. So, there is every possibility that it is the service trade that may get feminised in India and rates of pay in it may get relatively degraded because of that.

India enjoys a special advantage as a potential supplier of several of these services. It has generated a large number of highly qualified education and medical personnel. Already, several Indian cities including Kolkata, Mumbai, Chennai and Hyderabad attract a large number of consumers of those services from neighbouring countries and the Middle East. There are several centres for delivering technical education of high standards. Tourism has considerable still unexploited potential in the country. So apart from a growth in the demand from the local population, there are possibilities of external demand developing fast.

The Problems

Once again, the question is, what group of women are likely to get those additional jobs? Will they provide any openings for the women who are being displaced from their earlier occupations? Since there are no hard data available on these points, our thinking is mostly speculative but may not be unrealistic.

One characteristic of service enterprises is that since the products are for immediate consumption, there is need for a critical mass of demand from local consumers for the service for the occupation to yield a viable living for one worker. This means that even for something like tutoring young children, the prospects would be much better in urban than in rural surroundings. Even rural residents would seek the more expensive services by moving to cities. So probabilities are, the majority of additional jobs will come to be located in urban areas.

For rural women, it will be difficult to compete for these jobs mainly because of this. Many of them with responsibilities for younger children are unable to commute daily or migrate singly. In several small studies of domestic worker women who commute to the city every day for work, it was found that, most had young children and family responsibilities. Their coming to work depended on either having the help of an older relative, mother or mother-in-law or of a daughter or daughter-in-law. Migrating to urban areas was not possible because of difficulties in finding somewhere to live; also part of the family income was from rural activities. The process involved very long hours with bad transport facilities and quite often the sacrifice of a girl child's education. And in almost all cases, commuting was possible only for women on the periphery of the city. Women from distant rural areas could not do that.

Secondly, it is very probable that for the service jobs that are being newly generated, some educational qualifications may be necessary. A rural health worker has to keep many kinds of records; a doctor's receptionist often has to work on a computer. A paramedic has to read and familiarise herself with names of medicines and their dosages.

This is why existing workers may find it difficult to make a lateral shift into the new openings. Table 7.7 shows that, even in 1999/00, the extent of illiteracy was higher among workers than among the general population. But for urban male workers, the percentage of illiterates was falling more rapidly than even among the general population. Remarkably, this was true also for rural women but not for the urban females. But in urban areas, for both men and women the percentage with secondary and above education among workers in 1999/00 was significantly higher than in the general population. It does seem that for urban employment, education of

TABLE 7.7: **Level of Education among General Population and Workers (in 1000)**

		Males		Females	
5+ Years		Rural	Urban	Rural	Urban
Illiterates in population	1993-94	37.8	15.9	63.4	31.8
	1999-2000	33.8	14.4	56.7	28.4
	Percentage change	(-10.6)	(-9.4)	(-10.6)	(-10.7)
Illiterates among workers	1993-94	45.1	18.9	80.0	48.6
	1999-2000	40.3	16.4	74.9	44.0
	Percentage change	(-10.6)	(-13.2)	(-6.4)	(-10.4)
Secondary and above	In general population	13.3	34.9	5.6	24.9
	In workers	16.0	42.5	3.7	28.9

Sources: NSS Report 406 for 1993-94, Table 2.
NSS Report 455 for 1999-2000, Table 7.

some recognised level may become a key to the job market. Again, this is a bad news for women who are trying to change their occupations because the jobs are more likely to go to the vast numbers of hitherto unemployed educated.

The third problem is of women getting access to training for skills required in the new kinds of jobs. For rural people to become aware of the kinds of skills in demand, it is essential to build a machinery for dissemination of that information on a regular basis. Although radio and television have reached most parts of the country, no other agency except a state-sponsored one would be interested in undertaking this task. In itself it is likely to require considerable expertise on the part of the advisers. In the next analysis, even when people become aware of the need for such training, there are very few sources within their reach for obtaining that training. The training itself is expensive so families would be reluctant to give it to the girls; they would tend to reserve it for the sons.

Positive Interventions

On the whole, it appears that, even if the new directions given to the economy were to generate some employment, it is unlikely that these openings will accommodate the existing workers. For women who are at present in the workforce but may be facing a shrinkage of their traditional opportunities, the problem is likely to be even more serious because of their lack of mobility as well as of autonomy. In spite of these handicaps they have been trying to adjust to the changed circumstances; in these unequal struggles, they need some positive intervention in their favour from the state. There are three kinds of interventions needed, all of which are well within the realm of public policies even in the current changed perspective.

Firstly, the state has to take an active part in disseminating information about the developments that are taking place and are likely to affect different groups of workers. Too often workers, especially women workers are faced with a major change in the outlook for their occupations for which they have had no notice at their level.

Secondly, there was much talk earlier of a fund for reskilling workers. There have also been schemes for providing capital without collateral to small enterprises. So far one can give numerous examples when such official schemes for workers have deliberately by-passed women. In recent years, the state has been leaving this job mainly to NGOs and confined its role to providing some capital through micro-credit schemes. I have elsewhere dealt at some length with the lacunae in those schemes. Here suffice it to say that there is need for serious rethinking on those (Banerjee and Mukherjee, 1999).

Thirdly, in the long run, the state has to vigorously pursue its professed aim of making it compulsory for all children to get some years of education. This is a minimum requirement for preparing all persons to be receptive to ideas and information about new developments and possibilities.

Apart from the state, it is vitally important on the part of women's organisations and political parties to aggressively promote workers' organisations among women. Our dialogues especially with the commuter worker women have shown that, these are no passive victims. Over the years they have carved a definite niche for themselves in cities and also improved the terms of their employment to a significant extent. But their main demand is for some kind of organisation to represent them and fight for their rights. For example, they talked about the government scheme for night shelters which they could not pursue for want of such an organisation. We all have before us examples of organisations like SEWA, WWDF, or Annapoorna. But these models have not been copied elsewhere. Political parties and their trade union wings have been particularly remiss about this. In the situation that is developing on the labour front, many of the problems facing labour have to have political solutions. Who is to work for them if the political parties and their sponsored unions continue to concentrate only on the miniscule organised sector?

REFERENCES

Action India (1995), "The Charkawallis of Delhi" Paper submitted to UNU/INTECH under the project, Impact of Globalisation on Women, Maastricht.

Anand, T.C.A and K. Sundaram (1998), "Wage Policy in India: A Review", *The Indian Journal of Labour Economics, Conference Issue,* Vol.41, No. 4, Oct.-Dec.

Banerjee, N. (Forthcoming), "Between the Devil and the Deep Sea" in K.Kapadia (ed). *Volume on Violence on Women in India,* Kali for Women, New Delhi.

Banerjee, N. and M. Mukherjee (1999), "Micro Credit for Women's Employment", Occasional Paper No.1, Sachetana Information Centre, Kolkata.

Cagatay, N. and S. Ozler (1995), "Feminization of the Labour Force", *World Development,* Special Issue on Gender Adjustment and Macro Economics, Vol. 23, No. 11, Paragon, U. K.

Sachetana (1997), *Impact of SAP on Women: A Case Study of Hoogli District,* West Bengal, Report prepared for the Department of Women and Child, Ministry of Human Resources, Government of India, New Delhi.

Standing, G. (1989), "Global Feminization through Flexible Labour", *World Development: Special Issue,* Vol. 17, No. 7.

8

LABOUR IN A GLOBALISED ECONOMY: Social Security and Safety Nets in India

ALAKH N. SHARMA and PIUSH ANTONY

Introduction

The era of reforms, which began in the early 1990s, consisted of measures for attaining macro economic stabilisation and structural reforms to push the Indian economy to a higher growth path. This involved liberalisation and globalisation of the economy to correct the backlash of excessive control and inbuilt inefficiency by a market friendly policy framework where the role of the government is more of a strategic intervention. This meant considerable departure from one of the most regulated economies, with a model of accumulation based on the domestic market and import-substitution, to one oriented towards the international market. The impacts of such a transition in the short and medium term, it is argued, will be more pronounced in the labour market which will have a direct bearing on poverty. However, the nature of the actual impact of reforms on employment conditions and labour market is a contested terrain where opinions and predictions range from highly optimistic replication of East Asian experience to the disheartening plight of Latin American countries. As this paper is primarily concerned with the impact of globalisation on workers, an elaboration of both predictions seems appropriate.

Those who believe in the positive impact, adhere to a particular trajectory of events to result in enhanced growth of employment and economy. The structural adjustment would remove the 'rigidities', and factor price distortions in the economy, they argue, and that it would change the industry-mix and factor-mix in favour of labour (Singh, 1993; Deshpande, 1992) as well as increase the demand for labour due to the shift to labour intensive products and techniques. Consequently, the demand for unskilled labour would increase. According to the new policy, the extent of protection and its distorting effects would be reduced considerably except in the manufacture of luxury goods. Women workers would find easy entry into production process related jobs in manufacturing. This, in turn, would diversify their occupational structure, leading to reduction in sex-labelling of occupations. The quality of the labour force would increase as has happened in the East Asian countries. New industries would be located away from the centres as they are today. This will continue the process of regional dispersal further—even leading to greater equality in rural-urban wage differentials.

On the contrary, apprehensions about such an outcome are articulated by many, as in the Latin American countries where structural adjustment and search for flexibility in the labour market have both lowered the employment growth and brought about deterioration in conditions of employment. Unemployment will grow not only in response to the new entrants to the labour force in the face of a decline in employment opportunities, but also as an outcome of a liberal exit policy and privatisation (Mundle, 1992). The efforts towards labour flexibility and acute international competition and the consequent increasing emphasis on the reduction of costs, mainly labour costs, in order to retain both domestic and international markets will see the erosion of many institutions of labour welfare. It would lead to further segmentation of the labour market and expansion of low-income informal sectors in the economy. Increasing casualisation, use of contract labour, subcontracting, home-working and increased working hours will also form the inevitable outcomes of this shift. Feminisation of the labour force might increase, but would constitute a flexible and cheap labour force catering to the needs mostly of contract work and of the informal sector (Deshpande and Deshpande, 1992). Thus, reforms would further accelerate segmentation of the labour market by informalisation of the economy wherein labour standards are not kept at the minimum standards.

In this paper we make an attempt to understand the impacts of the reforms from the vantagepoint of workers. By following the conventional categorisation of workers into formal and informal sectors, we take a critical look at the changes in the labour market by analysing the trends in the employment scenario in the post-reform period from the macro level studies as well as from micro level evidences. In the context of the changes that are discernible from these studies, the paper reviews the existing social security and safety net measures available for the workers.

The paper has five sections. Following the introductory section, Section two discusses the changes in the growth of employment, employment status, and trends in unemployment and gathers micro level evidences of the impact of globalisation on the labour market. Section three discusses security mechanisms pertaining to workers in the formal sector. Section four is devoted to an understanding of the existing social security measures and safety nets for the informal sectors and their adequacy in the context of globalisation. The last section concludes the discussion by drawing upon the major arguments from the earlier sections towards policy implications.

Post-reform Period: An Analysis of Trends in the Growth in Employment

The growth of employment in India has been rather low with an average annual rate of around 2 per cent over the past four and half decades or so. However, different sub-periods recorded variations in the growth rate. In the 1950s, it grew at less than 1 per cent. It picked up in the 1960s and 70s to over 2 per cent, which decelerated to about 1.8 per cent during the 1980s. The early 1990s witnessed further deceleration but rose to over 2 per cent after 1992. Though in the initial two years of economic reforms the rate of growth of employment declined, it picked up when there was a revival in the economy in terms of growth of GDP. The UPS and UPSS employment growth during 1994-2000 for all the sectors together has been 2.42 and 2.21 respectively. The employment (UPS) growth during this period in rural areas has been 2.2 per cent whereas in urban areas it has been 3.1 per cent.

The sector-wise distribution of employment growth shows a lower figure for the long-term growth rate of employment in agriculture. It has been only 1.5 per cent per annum during the 21-year period of 1973-94, while the non-agricultural sector and sub-sectors showed growth rate of over 3 per cent. Most of the employment growth has come from construction (7.27 per cent), trade (7.05) and transport and storage (6.0 per cent). At the same time, the service sector showed a stagnated growth rate of 0.30 per cent.

There has been a long-term shift in the composition of the workforce from agriculture, but it is less pronounced than the shift that has happened in the structure of GDP. During the period of 1972/73 to 1993/94, the share of agriculture in employment declined from 74 per cent to only 65 per cent, but its share in GDP reduced from 41 per cent to 30 per cent. In rural areas the share of agriculture declined by 7 percentage points during 1973-94, while the secondary and tertiary sectors have shown considerable increase. The share of rural non-farm employment also rose from 14 per cent to about 22 per cent during the same period. The structure of rural non-farm employment also shifted in favour of the tertiary sector, with remarkable improvements in the share of trade and transport, along with an increase in the share of female employment in the rural areas.

While these trends in the growth of employment need to be understood in relation to the changes in the economy in terms of investment patterns and in the nature of the GDP growth, the consequent changes in the employment status of the workers are more relevant to our present analysis.

Changes in Employment Status

There has been a distinct long-term shift in the structure of employment by employment status in favour of casual wage employment. In the rural areas the shift in the structure has been away from self-employment and to some extent from regular wage/salaried employment towards casual wage employment. On the other hand, the shift in the structure of urban employment has been away from regular wage/salaried employment towards casual wage employment. The shift in the structure of male employment has mostly been away from self-employment and regular wage employment towards casual wage employment and in the case of females from self-employment to casual wage employment and regular wage employment.

The structural shifts are clearer if they are considered separately for rural and urban areas. In urban areas the shift in the structure of male employment has been away from regular wage employment towards casual wage employment. In rural areas the shift has been mostly away from regular wage employment towards casual wage employment. The overall structure of female employment has shifted away from self-employment largely towards casual wage employment but to a sizeable extent also towards regular wage employment. Most of the shift away from self-employment in urban areas has been towards regular wage employment while in rural areas it has been towards casual wage employment. The rise in the share of casual wage employment during 1994/2000 has been larger in the case of females and in urban areas. Among urban females during 1999/2000, the share of casual employment rose by 5 percentage points after showing a decreasing trend from 1983 to 1993/94. Since casual wage employment as the usual principal status employment is certainly inferior in quality to regular wage employment from the point of view of employment security, income security and certain other benefits, it can be said that there has been a long-term deterioration in the quality of employment.

The rate of growth of employment of the educated, which had risen from 5.60 per cent per annum during 1978-83 to 7.13 per cent per annum during 1983-88, rose further to 7.20 per cent during 1988-94. However, this growth rate declined to around 6 per cent during 1999/2000. Most of the growth in educated employment has come not from regular wage/salaried employment but from the larger growth in casual employment and to a lesser extent from self-employment. As a result, the composition of educated employment has changed over the years. During 1999/2000, the shift in the structure of employment has been from regular employment to self-employment and casual employment. The regular wage/salaried worker constituted 59 per cent of the total educated employed in 1978, which declined to about 43 per cent in 1999/2000, while self-employed and casual workers increased from 38.4 and 2.8 per cent to 47.8 and 9.2 per cent respectively. Judging from the structure of educated employment and shifts therein the growth of educated employment seems more a result of supply than induced by demand. The jump in the share of casual employment at the expense of regular wage employment is a cause for concern.

Trends in Unemployment

The overall unemployment rate is not high in India. The lower incidence of unemployment is mainly because of the prevalence of widespread poverty. The poor cannot afford to remain unemployed and they take up whatever unremunerative work is available. However, unemployment ratios among certain specific categories like the educated, the youth etc., are higher than those overall ratios. Among the youth (15 to 29 age group) the UPS unemployment ratios vary from 3.7 per cent among rural females to 16.6 per cent among urban females as per the latest NSSO survey of 1990/2000. For males it varied from 5.1 per cent in rural areas to 11.5 per cent in urban areas. The latest NSSO survey results also show no noticeable change in the unemployment ratios over the period across various categories. However, the decline in the unemployment rate, till 1993/94 which was noticed earlier, has been halted in 1990/2000. In fact, in some categories, i.e., in rural areas the CWS ratios have been higher in 1999/2000 by about one percentage point than attained in 1993/94, both for males and females.

The structure of chronic open unemployment has changed significantly in favour of the educated. The proportion of the educated among the UPS unemployed has risen steeply in the case of females—from 40 per cent in 1972/73 to 74 per cent in 1999/2000 in urban areas and from 11 per cent to 63 per cent in rural areas during the same period. It has also increased in the case of males, though not as sharply. Overall, around 63 per cent of the unemployed are educated.

Thus, the incidence of overall unemployment is not very high in

India. Even if we take into account the underemployment (visible or invisible) the combined rate does not go beyond 10 per cent. The fact that the percentage of people below poverty line is much higher than 35 per cent in 1993/94 and about 27 per cent in1999/2000 (which is not comparable with earlier surveys) shows that more than unemployment *per se*, the real problem is that of the working poor.

Changes in the Labour Market: Micro Level Evidences

The evidences at micro-level point towards an increasing labour market flexibility in the wake of economic reforms in India. A comprehensive survey of 233 firms located in Ghaziabad district and 16 fertiliser units across the country (Sharma and Sasikumar, 1996) reveals this phenomenon. Most of the surveyed firms (78 per cent) in Ghaziabad reported employment growth during 1991-95, albeit with some variations. All in all, total employment in the sample units grew by 24 per cent during 1991-95. On examining employment change by size of the units it was found that small and tiny firms experienced the highest employment growth (39 per cent), followed by medium-scale firms (31 per cent), while large firms showed a decline in their employment by about 2 per cent during 1991-95. The survey in Ghaziabad showed a clear relationship between change in employment and change in business in terms of turnover. Business and employment increased in tandem in 56 per cent of the surveyed firms. However, the survey of the fertiliser industry in this study reported that during 1991-95 the overall employment—permanent and non-permanent—declined. Unlike in the case of the Ghaziabad survey, the fertiliser industry did not demonstrate any clear relationship between direction of change in employment and change in business.

An important finding of the Ghaziabad survey was that in 76 per cent of the sample units, total employment grew by way of increase in the employment of the non-permanent type of workforce. In the fertiliser industry, although temporary employment declined, casual employment registered a rise. Interestingly, in the fertiliser industry non-permanent female employment increased more than permanent male employment. The rise in casual female employment was quite significant. In view of this, trend along with the increasing feminisation of the workforce, the rising tendency of casualisation turns out to be a remarkable feature of employment generation during 1991-95 in both the samples. It is interesting to find that within the non-permanent category of employment, there is a rise in contract employment.

The increase in female contract employment is more than that of male contract employment. The dominant reasons for contract labour employment are lower supervision costs, specialisation and coping with uncertain and fluctuating product demand apart from the co-operative attitudes of the contract workers. Growth/fall in turnover was found to be the most important reason of rise/fall in employment. However, company restructuring was somewhat important in accounting for the fall in employment of managerial and professional staff, whereas shortage of qualified workers was found to be an important cause of employment fall in the case of supervisors/foremen. An interesting finding in this connection is that, in the survey only a few firms considered rising wage/salary costs as a reason for the employment fall in non-manual occupational categories whereas no firms considered this as a reason at all for the fall in employment of manual occupational categories.

The enterprise survey in the fertiliser industry also pointed to uneven but significant changes in permanent employment across different occupational categories. Although permanent employment declined on the whole, the employment of managerial/administrative, professional and clerical personnel increased significantly and that of technical personnel increased marginally while employment in sales and service and manual employees declined significantly during 1991-95. Among the manual employees, the decline in the employment of higher categories such as supervisory and skilled operatives was modest whereas the decline in employment of lower categories was quite significant. In general, it seems that the sample units tend to dispense with manual employees and substitute white-collar workers in their place. However, the employment gain through white-collar recruitment was much less than the employment loss of manual workers.

The Ghaziabad survey also shows that during 1991-95, real

wages of clerical and supervisory staff and skilled, semi-skilled and unskilled operatives in all the main product groups except for semi-skilled operatives in electrical machinery and appliances declined. The matter of concern is that the decline in real wages was more for semi-skilled and unskilled workers, especially the latter. The employees survey of this study also generally corroborated this, especially in the case of blue-collar workers.

A recent study carried out by the Institute for Human Development for the Ministry of Statistics and Programme Implementation of more than 1300 manufacturing firms in nine industry groups spread over 10 Indian states shows that employment grew by 2.84 per cent per annum between 1991 and 1998 (Deshpande et al., 2001). Non-manual employment increased at 5 per cent per annum whereas manual employment increased at 2.29 per cent. It is found that employers brought about an increase in total employment by increasing the share of non-permanent employees and an increase in manual employment by increasing the share of women workers. Smaller firms grew faster than bigger firms. Firms, which increased sales, increased manual employment, as did those who employed contract workers. Employers who increased fixed capital for workers reduced manual employment. Employers increased employment but only of one or other category of non-regular flexiworkers.

The findings of this study show that proportionately bigger firms (covered by exit ban) have been able to reduce employment in comparison to smaller firms. The reasons being that bigger firms have a greater flexible composition of manual labour (higher proportion of non-permanent employment) and it facilitates changing of the employment level in a more effective manner. However, presence of union, being larger in bigger firms, hinders employment reduction. Within flexible categories of manual employment, the share of casual in total employment is more influenced by state- and industry-specific factors whereas the share of contract labour is largely determined by location of the firm in a specific state and employment size group. Among different flexible categories of manual employment, it is observed that firms with a lower level of feminisation are likely to record faster rise in contract labour. Again, union presence works against feminisation of the workforce but higher share of non-permanent employment favours it. Basic wages are largely determined by minimum wages and to a very small extent by collective bargaining. Consolidated wages seem to be the norm as reported by three-fourths of all reported forms. One qualification of this study is that more than two- thirds of all reported firms are in the 0-50 employment size-group in 1998.

There are several ways by which labour flexibility is being achieved, the most popular being the so-called Voluntary Retirement Scheme (VRS). The impact of this can be seen very clearly in the pharmaceutical industry in Mumbai. In the early 1980s, large pharmaceutical companies were the source of some of the best paid and most secure employment in Mumbai; by the late 1990s employment had been decimated and a large number of factories closed down (Hensman, 2001). This was mainly done through VRS, and in many cases, due to fear psychosis of imminent closure of the factories, union campaigns against these schemes have had limited success. But the net result has still been closure after closure. The factories of Ciba-Geigy, Geigy, Roche, Hoechst, Abott Laboratories, Parke-Davis, etc., have disappeared from the landscape of Mumbai, and along with them their workforce and unions. The public sector has not been affected to the same degree but is threatened by privatisation which would certainly be followed by large-scale job losses (Hensman, 2001).

A recent study on lockouts in India with specific reference to West Bengal (Datt, 2001) reveals that the share of person days lost owing to lockouts has increased after liberalisation. Relying on the data supplied by the Ministry of Labour the study shows that the share of person days lost in the public sector owing to lockouts has increased from 4.4 per cent in the pre-liberalisation period to 9 per cent in the post-liberalisation period. The contagion effect of the lockout phenomenon is observed in the private sector too. The relative social intensity of lockouts in the private sector over the public sector is also much higher in the post-liberalisation period. State-wise picture of lockouts is also disturbing in many states, pointing out that the share of person days lost because of strikes increased in the post-liberalisation period. The study attributes the dominance of lockouts to the change in the attitude of the state towards employers as against employees. In the case of West Bengal, the major cause of lockouts was an effort on the part of employers to downsize the firm by getting rid of redundant labour. The study also points out that lockouts were used as an instrument to casualise the workforce.

Another pertinent observation that many micro level studies put forward is that of feminisation of the labour force. A study by UNNATI (1996) reports an influx of women coming for work in urban areas of Ahmedabad after 1991. A majority of them entered the urban informal sector, which does not follow fair labour practices. Though the construction sector in the city shows some rise in employment, textile and pottery industries are facing stagnation or decline. The reasons for stagnation in both textile and pottery industries are mainly the closing down or lay off of factories and low capacity utilisation resulting in lower labour use. The study points out that it is the urban traditional manufacturing sector workers who are the immediate victims of globalisation related industrial policy changes.

Another comprehensive study of the impact of industrial restructuring on women workers in five industries—pharmaceuticals, plastics, soaps and detergents and gems and jewelry in Bombay and electronics in Delhi also highlight the growing casualisation of labour, particularly of women (Chhachi et al., 1996). The study also reports significant job losses in these industries.

All these developments in the labour market have their implications for industrial relations also. The trends in unionisation in India, which began in the late nineteen-seventies, are being further strengthened in this period. (Sen, 1993). These are: (a) there has been a decline in the absolute membership of unions as well as in density of unionisation as more and more temporary and contract or casual non-unionised workers enter industry; (b) secular stagnation or decline in permanent employment has affected the trade unions considerably, although the concentration of unions is in the organised sector of industry; (c) confusion has prevailed over the methods of trade union, particularly in terms of the union's inability to counter new offensives from management and government, and consequent changes in employment pattern; and (d) trade unions have been contained in the area of organising new sections of workers or in storming the citadels of management prerogatives either through or outside collective bargaining. Trade unions have in general been vocal in their opposition to the reforms as they are especially concerned about the possible drastic reduction in employment in the organised sector which is already thin and the reduction of the public sector which they themselves find difficult, in some ways, to defend (Venkatratnam, 1996). While the management have been pleading for relaxation of the rigidities of the labour laws, particularly employment, the trade unions have been opposing profound changes in the management strategies also. According to Rao (1995), private sector units including multinationals have shifted production from the organised to the unorganised sector for taking advantage of tax holding and other incentives. Ramaswamy (1996) points out that the organised sector has not grown because work is siphoned off to the unorganised sector to take advantage of cheap labour. Recruitment in the bargaining category has been literally banned. Further, in recent years, more particularly after the reforms, there is ascendancy in managerial rights and decline in trade union rights. New technologies, together with structural and other changes seem to have put unions in a much more vulnerable position today than at any time in the past.

As a whole the impact of recent economic changes and reforms on the labour market reveals a mixed picture. While the overall pace of employment generation has not declined, the quality of employment has generally deteriorated. This is because most of the employment is being created in the informal sector where there is practically no provision of insurance and social security. The labour market has witnessed significant change in its nature and character. The trend towards casualisation, subcontracting and flexibilisation has increased. Although the process of feminisation has also simultaneously occurred, it is mostly in the case of flexible categories of labour. Industrial restructuring has led to significant reduction in organised sector employment, in the bargaining category, and increase in non-bargainable category. All these developments have led to weakening of the power of trade unions.

Thus, one of the most conspicuous effects of globalisation is that the small proportion of the labour force that enjoyed job security is gradually shrinking and the proportion of those who are devoid of any security is multiplying. This trend is intensified by shifting certain categories of workers from the lower cadres to non-bargainable categories by simply altering their designations.

Social Security: Provisions for the Organised Sector Workers

The enactment of social security provisions for workers in the organized sector can be traced back to the colonial period. Since independence, these provisions were further strengthened and made more comprehensive through various legislative measures, such as, labour welfare legislation , minimum wage legislation, job security legislation and industrial relations legislation.

(i) *Labour welfare legislation:* These legislations aim to provide basic decent working conditions, adequate safeguards against disease/affliction and some support beyond the working life span. They include a large number of legislative measures in areas covering compensation to workers in case of disability or death; provision of provident fund/pension to employees; maternity benefit in case of women workers; health insurance and medical benefits; regulation of working conditions such as hours of work and minimum age of workers, etc.

(ii) *Minimum wage legislation:* In view of the extremely low levels of wages in many occupations, the Minimum Wage Act was enacted in 1948 and is applicable to a large number of occupations in addition to that for agricultural workers. Minimum wages fall within the jurisdiction of state governments and some of the progressive ones have extended its application beyond these scheduled types of employment enumerated in the Act. The stipulated level of minimum wage is fixed on the basis of subsistence level requirements and as such does not ensure anything beyond a bare minimum.

(iii) *Job security legislation:* The objective of these legislations is to provide not only avenues of employment but also some degree of stability to those already in employment. The 1976 legislation made it mandatory for enterprises employing 300 or more workers to seek government's permission before any enterprise could be closed. In addition, in the event of a closure being permitted, the enactment provides for compensation to retrenched workers at a specified rate. An amendment in 1987 further widened the scope of the Act by making it applicable to firms employing 100 or more workers.

(iv) *Industrial relations legislation:* These legislations pertain to various legislative and other measures governing trade union activity and the machinery for improving the state of industrial relations. They safeguard the rights of trade unions and provide a framework for maintaining industrial peace through detailed procedures of settlement of industrial disputes. All the above legislative measures apply to enterprises in the organised sector only except the minimum wage, which also covers the unorganised sector.

The legislative measures enacted in India have often been described as excessive and have been held responsible for slowing down the growth of employment by discouraging investment and growth. It has also been argued by many that as such protection is provided to only a small section of the workforce (about 8 per cent), the generation of employment will take place mostly in the unorganised sector with deplorable conditions of work, and as a result, the proportion of protected workers would decline. In the process, the very objective of providing social protection to a large majority of workers gets defeated.

In the wake of economic reforms, this debate has intensified and it has been argued that overprotection to a small section of workers is not only inimical to growth of employment, but also goes against social justice as the number of workers with deplorable conditions of work is increasing. Of late, restrictive provisions in this regard have come under attack, as they are supposed to negate an 'exit policy' considered necessary for industrial restructuring and attracting foreign investment. In the wake of liberalisation, this problem has been brought onto centerstage and there have been frequent demands by the industry and foreign investors to have some kind of 'exit policy'—the right of hiring and firing. In this respect the provisions of the Industrial Disputes Act which lay down conditions and procedures for retrenchment of workers have been widely criticised. It is contended that the provisions are so restrictive that reduction in workforce or closures is extremely difficult even if the employer agrees to pay the required compensation to retrenched workers, and to effect closures in the case of enterprises employing more than 100 workers is not generally granted permission by the government (mostly state governments).

The issue has generated considerable debate in the wake of declining manufacturing sector employment, particularly after the 1980s. Scholars like Fallon and Lucas (1991) and Ahluwalia (1992) attributed the decline in manufacturing employment to the faster growth of industrial wages relative to consumer prices for industrial workers, abetted by union militancy and job security provisions, resulting in a significant long-term reduction of employment. However, Papola (1994) argues that though the stringent job security regulation may be one of the reasons for the slower growth of employment, this may not be the sole or even major factor in restricting growth in employment in the organised manufacturing sector. An important reason for the decline in the growth of employment seems to be the structural and technological characteristics of industrial growth induced primarily by demand and efficiency considerations.

Nevertheless, this does not mean that there is no rigidity in the Indian labour market. Irrespective of its impact on employment, a degree of protection to labour may lead to inflexibility in labour adjustment required for restructuring of enterprises in the interest of competitive efficiency. Although, in spite of these obstacles many enterprises were able to adjust their workforce by rationalisation and technological changes, the process has been tardy. Several routes have been found illegal closure by the employers, as for example, not paying electricity bills, etc. All these have only added to the problem of labour—since they have neither been paid their wages nor their due compensation. This has also resulted in significant industrial sickness as well as prevalence of redundancies leading to their non-competitiveness. Although unions have generally resisted any legislative or executive move to make closure and retrenchment easier, in recent years, unions at enterprise level have generally been found to be accepting the inevitability of adjustments in workforce in the face of globalisation and industrial restructuring.

The government is contemplating bringing changes in the labour laws to make the labour force more flexible in the interest of competitive efficiency. In the wake of the second-generation reforms, changes in the labour laws are put on top of the agenda. Already in the budget of 2001/02, the government has put forth a proposal for amendment of the Industrial Disputes Act, by which firms employing up to 1000 workers will not be required to seek government permission for closures or retrench workers if required by technological change. The amount of separation benefits has been proposed to be enhanced. Further, the government has suggested amending the Contract Labour (Regulation and Abolition) Act, by which firms will be allowed to employ contract labour more liberally. These changes will satisfy industry to a great extent but in the light of experiences at micro level it will further exacerbate casualisation and contractualisation, leading to general worsening of labour standards in India. Trade unions are bound to resist these changes. The privatisation of BALCO and the stiff resistance by the trade unions show the shape of things to come. The most important challenge before the industrial relations system is how to combine competitive efficiency along with genuine interest of the workers. If the country has to retain its industrial democracy, a balance has to be struck.

Labour Redundancies and National Renewal Fund

The government has set up a mechanism in the form of an organisation called Board of Industrial and Financial Reconstruction

(BIFR) to examine and decide whether sick private and public sector enterprises could be revived with restructuring or have to close down. In the case of public sector enterprises, the pronounced policy of the government is to effect closures or retrenchments only as a last resort, after all avenues of reviving the unit and maintaining employment are exhausted. And where these measures are inevitable, a National Renewal Fund (NRF) has been constituted to enable enterprises to pay reasonable separation benefits, and assist the workers rendered redundant by their retraining and redeployment. The NRF has three parts: (a) an Employment Generation Fund (EGF) to provide resources for approved employment schemes, to regenerate employment opportunities for employees affected by industrial restructuring in the unorganised sector; (b) the National Renewal Fund (NRF) to deal with the immediate requirements of labour in sick units arising from revival or closure of such units; (c) an Insurance Fund for Employees (IFE) to deal with future changes in employment structure in the context of changes in technology and modernisation.

While the main objective of NRF was to help in retraining, counselling and redeployment of affected workers, and also employment generation, both in organised and unorganised sectors of the economy, a major part of the NRF expenditure was utilised for compensation payments under the Voluntary Retirement Scheme (VRS). It is worth noting that only a quarter of the VRS availees were retrained and merely 8 per cent could be redeployed (Government of India, 1999).

Displacement of a large number of the workforce through the mechanism of VRS, without equipping them with adequate skill and training to re-enter the job market, has resulted in a huge loss of productive humanpower. Though no major study has been undertaken to follow up the post-VRS vocation of labour, a few studies have pointed out that a majority of these redundant workers have joined the unorganised sector as the 'new poor' (Roy Choudhary, 1996). Displaced workers also face income loss—the average income of those re-employed dropped by about 44 per cent (Noronha, 1999). Therefore, it is urged that retraining for redeployment of displaced workers should be seen as a social safety net and be assessed in terms of its efficacy in reducing the period of unemployment, enhancing or maintaining the income level of displaced workers and equipping them for sustainable employment in industrial environments which may increasingly require different and higher levels of skills. Thus, it is necessary to provide retraining well before the workers are out of work. In effect, retraining should be considered to be an extension of placement efforts.

Unfortunately, the overall performance of retraining for redeployment under NRF has also been less than desirable. A small proportion of VRS availees (25 per cent) opted for training. This is a matter of concern because it shows that retraining is not perceived as a skill improvement strategy for redeployment. Counselling may also act as an important factor in popularising retraining, though in some cases it has been restricted to giving advice regarding optimum utilisation of VRS funds received. An important factor responsible for the limited interest in training can be the time that elapsed between displacement and availability of counselling. Counselling should, therefore, begin early—ideally; right from the time when those potentially affected by retrenchment have been identified.

The budgetary provisions for the NRF have been abolished since the budget for the year 2000/01. The Department of Public Enterprises, in a recent notification to all PSUs, has made it clear that only those companies which are financially sound and can sustain a scheme of VRS on their own surplus resources may devise and implement it. On the other hand, budgetary support will be provided to the marginally profit/loss making/sick PSUs for implementing the VRS only in case bank credit is not available. There is much enthusiasm in the government about revised voluntary scheme, which does not envisage as to how to retrain and absorb the affected workers in the wake of the ongoing economic reforms process.

All this makes it extremely desirable to strengthen the retraining activities as a measure of social safety net. At the outset, the focus of retraining should not be just some other skills for employment but enhancing core skills and intellectual skills of the workers which make them more flexible, adaptable and useful to the changing pattern of production. As more and more industrial firms undertake restructuring and start operating in leading edge technologies, the requirement of enhancing the core skills and higher order cognitive skills would become more important. This is a basic requirement not only for retraining but even more importantly, for the initial training system. Sustainability of employment will depend on this focus (Chandra, 1999). The labour reform process must lay stress on retraining and redeployment strategies rather simply, making VRS more attractive for a small section of the workforce.

Security Provisions for Workers in Unorganised Sector

The social security provisions for the unorganised sector workers are mainly in the form of minimum wage legislation, welfare funds, and anti-poverty employment generation programmes. This section discusses various security provisions made available to the workers under each of these provisions.

Minimum Wage Legislation

Under the Minimum Wage Act, 1948, both the central and state governments have set minimum wages for agriculture as well as for a range of occupations in unorganised industries, which are thought to be particularly vulnerable to exploitation. There are a fairly large number of occupations for which minimum wages are currently fixed. Though the different state governments have revised the minimum wages from time to time, the wages fixed are still very low. In most cases the government while fixing statutory minimum wages has apparently not taken into consideration the minimum requirements of a worker's family to rise above the poverty line (Bhagat, 1997). But even these bare subsistence level wages, in an overwhelmingly large number of occupations across various regions of the country, have not been enforced. Nor has adequate attention been paid to treat minimum wages as an important instrument of employment security and poverty alleviation. On the contrary, it has been argued that higher and stricter enforcement of minimum wages may lead to a rise in prices which may erode the real gains of higher wages; and further that it may reduce the demand for labour consequent to rise in real wages. Ghoshe (1997), while examining the issue in depth strongly refutes these arguments and finds that they are not really relevant in the context of India. In fact, the minimum wages, even at very low levels and poor reinforcements, have served some useful purposes. First, in many regions they have set the floor level wages. They have a role in pushing wages upward in slack seasons and in depressed areas including the wages of women. They have also contributed to the strengthening of the bargaining power of labour (Parthasarthy, 1997).

There have been strong and persistent demands from several quarters for wider coverage of minimum wage legislation, higher levels of revisions and stricter enforcement of minimum wages so that they serve the objective of poverty alleviation for the large number of casual workers in agriculture, unorganised industries and services in the country who belong to the poorest segment of the population—they are poor in an absolute sense and low wages is the principal cause of their poverty. Organisations like National Centre for Labour are campaigning for the enactment of a national level legislation on minimum wages, which takes into account the minimum wages equivalent to the norms for the poverty line. While it is true that there are problems in the enforcement of this legislation, this should not be cited as an excuse for the non-implementation of the Act. The revised rates and provisions of the Act could be widely publicised throughout the country through the media, and village panchayats may be activated towards their implementation. Their wide publicity can become a rallying point for organising the unorganised workers. Further, determined efforts should be made to use the existing labour inspection machinery of the government to enforce the provisions of the Minimum Wages Act. And, of course, the government must ensure that the officially announced minimum wages are paid in all government-sponsored activities such as special employment programmes, public works, etc. (Ghoshe, 1997).

Welfare Funds

To extend social assistance to workers in the unorganised sector, several legislations have been enacted by the Government of India to set up five welfare funds in the Ministry of Labour. This is to provide housing, medical care, and educational and recreational facilities to workers employed in the beedi industry, certain non-coal mines and cine workers. Efforts have also been made towards substantially expanding the application of the welfare fund approach to cover categories and sub-categories of workers in the unorganised sector.

The scheme of welfare funds is outside the framework of the specific employer-employee relationship in as much as the resources are raised by government on a non-contributory basis and delivery of services is effected without relating to individual worker's contribution. Apart from the welfare funds set up by the central government, various state governments have also formulated welfare programmes and are implementing these through funds created by them for certain categories of unorganised labour.

In India, the ideal example of social security benefits in the unorganised sector that is often quoted is the welfare fund for beedi workers under the Beedi and Cigar Workers Act. A tripartite body consisting of the representatives of government, employers and workers regulates this welfare fund. Identity cards are provided to the workers, who receive minimum wages. Education of their children is supported through scholarships and money is provided for the purchase of uniforms for their children. Charges of hospitalisation, insurance in case of sudden death, travel facilities for recreation of the worker are some of the benefits extended to the workers. However, provident fund/pension is not included in the benefits provided and this issue has been taken up for consideration by the government (Unni, undated). Apprehensions are often raised about the funding of these social security benefits. The Beedi Worker's Welfare Fund has been a success because it is funded through a cess of tax on the commodity. Similar options for the benefit for other workers have to be devised. Here again a mix of public and private sector responsibility may be most appropriate—the government, industry (employers) and workers, all contributing to a social security fund. The modus operandi for such a fund and its disbursement is of course crucial if the benefits are to accrue to the most insecure groups in the labour market (Unni, ibid.).

Although the welfare funds have played an important role in

minimising risks associated with the occupations of such workers, their coverage is very small in comparison to the vast number of workers in the unorganised sector, particularly those involved in home-based work. Obviously, similar funds for other trades and for contract workers should be devised. Moreover, these measures are far from adequate for providing some minimum income to such workers in the unorganised sector. As such, there is no alternative to implementing the appropriate support system in the form of training, credit, appropriate technology, etc., for the large number of home-based workers and micro enterprises both in rural and urban areas. There are many examples of proper support systems along with organisations of workers that have contributed to the growth of income of such workers/enterprises in several parts of the country. SEWA is one telling example of such an initiative but there are others as well.

Anti-poverty and Employment Programmes

Integrated Rural Development Programme (IRDP): The (IRDP) programme was formally started in the year 1980/81, though it was initiated in 1977-78 in a limited form. From April 1999, it has been restructured and merged with Swarn Jayanti Gram Swarojgar Yojana (SGSY). It provides support to the rural households below the poverty line, with a package of assistance consisting of a subsidy and a bank loan to enable them to acquire productive assets such as livestock, manufacturing and processing equipment and business space. Its also stipulates a minimum coverage of disadvantaged groups and women. In order to provide training support for self-employment under the programme and to provide special focus on women and children, two sub-programmes allied to IRDP, namely, Training of Rural Youth for Self Employment (TRYSEM) and Development of Women and Children in Rural Areas (DWCRA) were also put into operation.

The programme, as envisaged in its design, has succeeded to some extent in reaching the poor and amongst them the more disadvantaged groups like the scheduled castes (SC) and scheduled tribes (ST) but it suffers from certain serious limitations to be an effective instrument to raise the income levels of assisted households substantially and permanently to lift them above the poverty line. First, though the programme is termed as integrated, it, in fact, lacks any link with other development programmes of the area and thus tends to ignore input and market linkages and infrastructure requirements of assisted activities. Second, in relation to the requirements of meeting a quantitative target in terms of the number of families covered, the identification of activities and projects often tends to be arbitrary, and viability and sustainability aspects are often neglected. Third, the provision of outright cash subsidy often leads to misappropriation of benefits due to lack of a stake and interest from the beneficiaries. Fourth, there was an implicit assumption that the prospective beneficiaries possessed information and skills to enable them to choose viable options, had access to raw materials and were aware of markets. These are the disabilities from which the poor suffer which the IRDP did not take into account, particularly those relating to community decision-making. Fifth, bureaucratic red-tapism delays delivery at several levels.

Swarna Jayanti Gram Swarozgar Yojana : With the addition of several programmes, viz., TRYSEM, DWACRA, Supply of Improved Toolkits to Rural Artisan (SITRA) and Ganga Kalyan Yojana (GKY) in IRDP over the years, there has been a complete lack of sectoral integration in their implementation as each one started operating as an individual programme and focussed entirely on achieving its own goals. With a view to ensuring sectoral integration and making poverty alleviation programmes more meaningful, these are merged into a simple Programme—the Swarna Jayanti Gram Swarozgar Yojana (SGSY), with effect from April 1, 1999.

The SGSY aims at establishing a large number of micro enterprises in the rural areas with an emphasis on the 'cluster' approach. In each block four to five key activities are to be identified, based on their resource endowments, occupational skills and the availability of markets. The results of evaluation of the scheme are yet to be known. However, since SGSY is still a credit-cum-subsidy programme, it is feared that the scheme may face similar difficulties as in the case of IRDP unless the old loopholes and shortcomings are removed effectively.

Wage Employment Programmes

Short-term wage employment on public works has been an old and conventional device used by governments to provide relief to poor households from hardships caused by drought, flood and other natural calamities. The first major programme called 'Food for Work' was initiated in India during the 1970s. Subsequently, National Rural Employment Programme (NREP) and Rural Landless Employment Guarantee Programme (RLEGP) were started with the objectives of providing gainful employment to the unemployed and underemployed and building community assets and rural infrastructure.

Jawahar Rozgar Yojana and Employment Assurance Scheme : The experience of implementation of NREP and RLEGP showed that large investments made in generating employment did not yield commensurate returns in terms of creation of durable and useful assets. Even on the employment generation front, administrative procedures were not cost-effective and thus a sizeable part of the funds got utilised in overheads. With a view to removing some of these shortcomings a new programme, Jawahar Rozgar Yojana (JRY), was launched on April 1, 1989 by merging NREP and RLEGP. Some basic changes in the modus operandi of the implementation were also introduced. The basic objectives of the programme, however, remained the same, except that the creation of additional employment opportunities for the unemployed and underemployed was emphasised as a primary objective, and creation of sustained employment by strengthening rural economic infrastructure and also that of assets in favour of the rural poor and improvements in the quality of life in rural areas as a secondary objective. A major change introduced in JRY in 1993/94 in comparison with the earlier programmes, was that funds based on pre-determined criteria would be provided to every village panchayat, itself based on the overall guidelines provided by the central and state governments.

The Employment Assurance Scheme (EAS) was launched on October 2, 1993 in identified backward blocks situated in drought-prone areas, desert areas, tribal areas and hill areas. Initially it covered 1,772 blocks in the country. The scheme provides for assured employment of up to 100 days during the lean agricultural season to those seeking work, where the work would be of an unskilled manual type. The secondary objective is the creation of economic infrastructure and community assets for sustained employment and development. EAS has been restructured in 1999/2000. It is now an allocation-based scheme under which funds are shared by the centre and the state in the ratio of 75:25. The allocation of funds to the state is made on the basis of incidence of poverty and district-wise allocation within a state on the basis of the index of backwardness.

The conflict between employment generation and asset creation objectives, common to all wage employment programmes, has assumed greater significance in the case of JRY, particularly in view of its large outlays. It is, therefore, argued that while the provision of additional gainful employment to the rural poor is the primary objective of the programme and is being met to a significant extent, it is desirable to ensure that such large outlays help simultaneously create useful community and productive assets for sustaining development and employment generation in rural areas.

With an objective to develop village infrastructure, JRY has been strengthened and restructured as Jawahar Gram Samridhi Yojna (JGSY) with effect from April 1, 1999. The primary objective of JGSY is the creation of village infrastructure including durable assets at the village level and assets to enable the rural poor to increase opportunities of sustainable employment. Another objective is to generate supplementary employment for the unemployed rural poor. Though there is no sectoral earmarking of resources under JGSY, 22.5 per cent of allocation must be spent on schemes for SC/ST families living below the poverty line and 3 per cent for the creation of barrier-free infrastructure for the disabled. Nearly 30 per cent of employment opportunities are to be reserved for women. Under the programme, each village panchayat has to prepare an annual plan, which shall be approved by the Gram Sabha. Priority will be given to the completion of incomplete works. The village panchayats are empowered to execute work schemes up to Rs. 50,000 without seeking any technical approval.

As regards EAS, its success in providing employment has been rather limited. The scheme also suffered from several limitations, such as bogus reporting, providing employment without assets entailing the risk of again falling below the poverty line, etc. It has been suggested by many that in order to improve efficacy of the programme and ensure that the poor and unemployed get up to 100 days of employment in the lean agricultural season, the programme should be restricted to backward areas characterised by poor agriculture, chronic poverty and hunger.

Employment Guarantee Scheme (Maharashtra): Apart from the major rural employment and poverty alleviation programmes sponsored by the Government of India, described above, a unique initiative for guaranteeing gainful employment was taken up in the State of Maharashtra in the early seventies and has been in operation since then. Aimed at providing gainful and productive employment to the people in rural areas and small towns who are prepared to do manual work but cannot find it on their own, the Employment Guarantee Scheme (EGS) guarantees work to any person above the age of 18 years normally residing in the villages requiring work. The work can be provided anywhere within the district of the applicant's residence though it is normally provided within eight kms of the residence of the job-seeker. The guarantee is restricted to only unskilled manual work. Failure to provide work creates a liability on the state to pay an unemployment allowance. The scheme is self-targeting in nature and is totally financed by the state government through a special levy. Wages are paid on a piece-rate basis, but are so fixed for different items of work that an average person working diligently for seven hours a day will earn an amount equal to the minimum wages prescribed for agricultural labour in that area under the Minimum Wages Act.

The EGS, it is generally agreed has made a somewhat significant impact on the current employment and unemployment situation in rural Maharashtra. Various evaluation studies show that EGS by itself may not have enabled the participating households to cross the poverty line, but it has raised income levels of the participating households to a significant extent. Thus, the programme should be assessed on the basis of the criterion for reducing the severity of poverty rather than the head count incidence of poverty, and on that score, it has contributed significantly as is indicated by a substantial supplementation made by it to the incomes of the poor households (Datt and Ravallion, 1991; Mahendra Dev, 1992). In addition, it has brought several indirect benefits. These include: (a) the creation of rural assets; (b) an upward pressure on agricultural wages; (c) an insurance for the rural workers; (d) extension of the right to work for rural women, and (e) making employment an entitlement enabling collective political action by the poor, and facilitating political mobilisation (Mahendra Dev and Ranade, 1996). Thus, the EGS has benefited the poor in terms of employment and income, notwithstanding its defects like leakages to non-poor and prevalence of corruption among officials and contractors.

Urban Employment and Anti-poverty Programmes

Over the years, it has been realised that poverty in urban areas is as persistent as in rural areas though its magnitude is smaller. Anti-poverty and employment generation programmes in urban areas was initiated in 1986 with the introduction of the Self Employment Programme for Urban Poor (SEPUP). It provided assistance to urban households living below the poverty line for starting self-employment ventures on the basis of a bank loan up to Rs. 5,000 of which 25 per cent was to be a government subsidy. However, the programme was scaled down as the banks through which it was implemented showed scant interest in it.

Nehru Rozgar Yojana : A major initiative in promoting urban employment was taken in 1989 with the introduction of the Nehru

Rozgar Yojana (NRY). It aims at providing employment to the urban unemployed and underemployed poor, through wage work and self-employment ventures as well as upgradation of housing of the poor. The earlier scheme (SEPUP) was merged into NRY, with effect from 1992/93. The NRY consists of the following three schemes:

(i) The Scheme of Urban Micro Enterprises (SUME): Under this scheme, the unemployed and underemployed persons belonging to poor families are encouraged to set up small enterprises in service, petty business and manufacturing. Assistance is given on a bank loan-cum-subsidy basis. The scheme is applicable in all urban settlements.

(ii) Scheme of Urban Wage Employment (SUWE): Under this scheme, wage employment is sought to be provided to the unemployed and underemployed from poor families in public works in urban settlements with less than 1 lakh population. The works to be undertaken are to be decided by urban local bodies and could be in the nature of construction of public utilities.

(iii) The Scheme of Employment through Housing and Shelter Upgradation (SHASU): This scheme aims at improving the shelters of the urban poor through repair, construction and additions to their existing housing units. The assistance consists of government subsidy of 25 per cent of the cost subject to a ceiling of Rs. 1,000 and loan from the Housing and Urban Development Corporation (HUDCO), at a concessional rate of interest and with a repayment period of 10 years. The scheme is applicable to urban settlements with a population upto two million.

It may be noted that even if the envisaged targets were reached and the programmes were effectively implemented, the coverage of the programme would still be too meagre in relation to the magnitude of the problem in urban areas. It may be noted that all urban unemployment cannot be tackled through wage employment in public works. A large proportion of the urban unemployed who are educated, and openly unemployed, look for regular full-time work as a result of which the scope for wage employment programmes like the rural JRY are limited in urban areas. But self-employment offers substantial scope in urban settlements, particularly in the informal sector. The SUME scheme under NRY seems to be a very limited attempt in this regard in relation to the magnitude of unemployment.

Swarna Jayanti Shahri Rozgar Yojana : The Swarna Jayanti Shahri Rozgar Yojana (SJSRY) was launched in April, 1999 subsuming the earlier urban poverty alleviation programmes, namely, Nehru Rozgar Yojana (NRY), Urban Basic Services for the Poor (UBSP) and the Prime Minister's Integrated Urban Poverty Eradication Programme (PMIUPEP). The objective of the scheme is to provide gainful employment to the urban unemployed or underemployed poor through encouraging them to set up self-employment ventures or provision of wage employment. There are two schemes under SJSRY—the Urban Self-Employment Programme (USEP) and the Urban Wage Employment Programme (UWEP).

USEP has three distinct components: (i) assistance to individual urban poor for setting up of gainful self-employment ventures; (ii) assistance to groups of urban poor women for self-employment—the scheme is called Development of Women and Children in the Urban Areas (DWCUA); and (iii) training of beneficiaries, and other persons associated with the urban employment programme for upgradation and acquisition of vocational and entrepreneurial skills.

Prime Minister's Rozgar Yojana : The Prime Minister's Rozgar Yojana (PMRY) was launched in urban areas during 1993/94, and the most important national level scheme for promotion of self-employment launched earlier, the Self-Employment for the Educated Unemployed Youth (SEEUY), has been subsumed in it since then. PMRY is now extended to rural areas from 1994/95. The objective of the scheme is to provide self-employment opportunities in industry, business and services to one million educated unemployed youth. The scheme is applicable to youth in the age-group of 18 to 35 years, who have passed or failed in the matriculation examination or qualified from ITI or who have undergone a government-sponsored technical course for a minimum duration of six months, and have a family income not exceeding Rs. 24,000 per annum from all sources. The entrepreneur is required to contribute 5 per cent of the project cost as margin money and the balance of 95 per cent would be sanctioned as composite loan by banks without any collateral guarantee. The central government would provide subsidy at the rate of 15 per cent of the project cost subject to a ceiling of Rs. 7,500 per individual.

Though many more youth are seeking assistance under PMRY, almost half of the total applications are rejected by the taskforce committees of the district industry centres, mainly owing to inadequate technical skills. Also, there is a lack of public campaigns focussing on various aspects of PMRY such as eligibility, fund availability, skill requirement, market, etc.

Existing Programmes: Emerging Needs and Adequacy

The safety net envisaged for the poor to cope with the hardships of the new economic policy did not offer anything particularly new but is linked to the overall poverty alleviation strategy. The objective of minimising the hardships of the poor during the period of structural adjustment would best be met by ensuring that the overall strategy and programmes for poverty alleviation are suitably revamped and expanded. Given the vast magnitude of poverty, unemployment and underemployment, it would not be feasible to remove them through direct government expenditure. Such expenditure should be enhanced to the extent that resources permit and the coverage of existing programmes should be substantially expanded. But the extent to which poverty could generally be alleviated and the adverse effects of structural adjustment on the poor mitigated would primarily depend on the pace at which the generation of productive employment opportunities is accelerated. And that, in turn, would depend on how quickly the economy can attain a high and sustainable growth rate. Fortunately, India has been able to quickly absorb the shock of adjustment and the growth rate of the economy has been over 6 per cent during the last few years. However, there are certain developments in the labour market, like rise in casualisation and informalisation of the economy, which are disquieting. Although poverty levels have not risen in India during reforms, it continues to be high and hence there is need for the continuation of direct measures for poverty alleviation and employment generation.

The strategy adopted for tackling the issues of poverty and unemployment is a two-track one in which the benefits of normal growth process are supplemented by social safety nets. This seems inescapable at least as long as the present high levels of poverty persist. As Bhagwati (1988) points out, the optimal strategy for poverty alleviation is bound to be a mixed strategy involving some consideration of the direct and indirect approaches. A question that is sometimes raised in this context relates to the relative efficacy of the two tracks in this strategy. Special employment programmes like JRY claim investible resources, which could otherwise have contributed to the growth process. A study on costs and benefits of the rural works programme in India has indicated that the benefits accruing from such employment programmes contribute directly to the growth process, thereby reducing the force of the 'growth foregone' argument.

The importance of these programmes also lies in their contribution in holding the wage rate and in creating some infrastructure in the rural areas, thereby adding to the existing stock of infrastructure every year. In wage employment programmes, the emphasis has been more on employment creation than on the building up of infrastructure of a durable or productive type. Although in recent years there have been some changes in the approach to infrastructure building, emphasis on creation of durable infrastructure is still rather weak. The creation of infrastructure, particularly minor irrigation, watershed development and roads will enhance agricultural productivity and thereby increase employment in agriculture on a more sustainable basis. In the face of persistence of high levels of poverty along with increasing casualisation of labour market, this kind of safety-net mechanism seems to be desirable, but its linkage with the growth process is also essential.

However, an all-out effort is needed to streamline and strengthen the delivery mechanism of these anti-poverty and employment programmes so as to improve their better targeting and effectiveness. Often the absence of proper coordination among different programmes has been pointed out as an important reason behind the poor performance of these programmes. The government's recent efforts in merging several programmes may be an attempt to remove this lacuna to some extent.

Another important reason behind the unsatisfactory performance of these anti-poverty and special employment programmes has been the lack of people's participation. It has often been said that the approach in implementing these programmes seems to be more technocratic and top-down with poor delivery systems. However, an important landmark in the 1990s is the 73rd and 74th amendments to the Constitution bringing about significant decentralisation by providing for a system of local government based on mandatory elections. This provides an opportunity to strengthen the panchayats to effectively implement the various anti-poverty employment schemes. The panchayats must serve as the principal agencies of programme implementation. The experiences of implementing such schemes in West Bengal and Karnataka have shown that there is enormous potential in this regard. However, the success achieved through decentralisation will depend to a large extent on whether acute inequalities in endowments have been eliminated. In such a setting, the panchayats would be free from the domination of rich and powerful landlords and would be more responsive to the needs of the rural poor. Further, careful consideration should be given to concentrate these programmes in the more depressed regions and states where poverty is endemic rather than spread them thinly in all areas of the country. Some agriculturally developed states and districts have very little use of the rural works programmes. They have, though, a low incidence of poverty, and the openly educated unemployed, who are unlikely to opt for work in a wage employment programme, mainly account for relatively high unemployment rates in these areas.

Labour Market Characteristics and Social Security Needs

Based on the above discussion, certain characteristics of the Indian labour market are significant in the context of providing social and economic security to the workers. The first and foremost characteristic is that the employment-unemployment scenario is not a dichotomous one with organised employment on the one hand and open, long-term unemployment on the other. Most people are employed in India as per the time-disposition criterion. This brings out the next major characteristic of Indian labour market, that is the issue of the working poor. Though most people are employed, much of the employment is not adequately productive or remunerative. The obverse of this constitutes the third characteristic, that employment is largely concentrated in the unorganised sector. It accounts for about 92 per cent of the total workforce in the country. While workers in the organised sector (about 8 per cent) are covered by various social security provisions, the unorganised sector workers lack basic securities related to income or employment. Further, the preponderance of self-employed, constituting largely of home-based workers, with no clear-cut employer-employee relationship makes insecurity of income an inherent feature of the unorganised sector. Thus, the fourth characteristic is that most of the employment in India suffers from income insecurity. The fifth characteristic concerns the discriminations in the labour market. Of significance is the gender-based discrimination. Women have a lower probability of employment and earning the same remuneration for the same kind of work on par with men, even with equal educational and skill levels. The sixth pertains to the variations across the states. While there are relatively advanced states (in socio-economic terms) with high unemployment rates and states that are considered backward show low levels of unemployment. The pre-capitalist relations in the latter category of states can be explained in terms of their low levels of unemployment, but is accompanied by low levels of earning, high levels of underemployment and less productive self-employment which causes impediments to skill acquisition. In the case of the former category of states, more skilled labourers are present for the non-farm sector but deterred away due to the unacceptable wage rates.

Finally, a large section of people are yet to be integrated or are very loosely connected with the mainstream consisting mostly of independent producers/service providers, both in rural and urban areas, such as pavement-dwellers and rag-pickers in urban areas, landless and very small peasants in the rural areas, forest-dwellers, etc. These workers have limited market contacts and have high degree of uncertainty in their production conditions and hence their livelihood base.

It can be discerned from the above discussion that these characteristics are important to understand the social security needs of the workers belonging to various categories and sectors. Moreover, it necessitates strategies at different levels to address the vulnerabilities of various categories of labour. The following section is devoted to outlining the social security needs specific to each category.

Regular salaried/wage workers: These workers are largely in the organised sector, either in the public/government or private sectors. With regard to their social security needs two issues are of importance. One pertains to the recent changes in the sector resulting in the employment of a large number of contract and temporary workers, which is likely to increase significantly after the initiation of labour market reforms in the coming years. Although these workers are technically in the organised sector, they may be only marginally better off than such workers in the unorganised sector. The government enforcement machinery and trade unions have the responsibilities to safeguard the interests of such vulnerable workers. Although the employers need some kind of flexibility in adjusting the workforce in the face of global competition, it has to be by way of innovatively combining efficiency with the interest of the labour in the Indian industrial relations system. In a poor country like India, adequate separation benefits to workers should be assured. While selective relaxation may be brought in the case of job security regulations, there is a need to make minimum wages even more comprehensive for the organised sector workers. The second issue is related to National Renewal Fund. The NRF has not so far been able to address the problem of labour redundancy and retrenchment properly. It needs to incorporate retraining and redeployment along with counselling as integral to its agenda.

Irregular wage workers: This category of workers including that of casual and contract workers, are largely unprotected, and suffer from high level of uncertainty in their income and employment. Though most of them are covered by the minimum wage regulations and provisions like welfare funds are available for certain categories of workers, implementation is very poor. More importantly, there is no assurance of any specified minimum income. Therefore, for such workers employment security implies a mechanism of ensuring minimum income and employment through labour market and other interventions. The proposition of formulating national minimum wage in the country, has been withheld due to the disagreement raised from many quarters. Their main contention is that it would increase the rigidities in the labour market. But experiences show, at least at the state level, that effective implementation of minimum wages has many other positive impacts and it is an effective tool in reducing poverty. There should be a concerted policy advocacy to bring this issue to the center stage of debates and further for implementation.

Equally important is the programme for generating supplementary employment and incomes for these workers. The role of direct poverty alleviation and employment generation programmes need to be strengthened to generate supplementary employment and incomes. Beyond these employment and income security needs also, as many micro level experiences show, there is a large scale need of other social security measures such as health security among these workers.

Self- employed workers: Provisioning of social security for a large number of self employed people, especially for those engaged in household and micro-enterprise activities including home-based workers, street vendors etc., poses a greater challenge. Largely unreported and faced with the uncertainties of the market their security needs involve adequate access to inputs, services and marketing facilities. A large number of workers in this category also need security of work premises as well as legal recognition of their activity. For them, social and economic security essentially implies income security through various interventions—fiscal, labour market and, organisational.

Increasing the earnings of such workers is crucial for securing a minimum income level, as with regular wage employment shrinking the educated unemployed have to find job opportunities as self-employed and these are mostly in the informal sector or outside the organised sector. There is a need for creating a more supportive environment for self-employment, both in rural and urban areas. Earnings depend on productivity of the worker, for which technology, infrastructure, capital formation and skills are of importance. The level of skill acquired is related to a basic level of education and therefore, increase in literacy and school enrolment will have to aim for their long-term impact. Similarly, support to informal sectors in urban areas through access to credit and technology are crucial for raising the productivity of the urban self-employed and casual workers.

Women workers: As a category of workers, they demand special attention in terms of their social security needs. One of the important issues concerning women workers is that of gender discrimination in the labour market. There should be effective policy amendments and interventions to address this. There still exist substantial wage disparities between males and females. On a priority basis, there should be efforts towards this as an increase in women's income has more effect on the overall welfare of the household. Further, as the 'educated component' of female unemployment has exceeded that of male employment in urban areas, and unemployment rates for urban females, educated or otherwise, have not come down since 1993, the strategy for employment creation has to be around to improving the access of women to education and skills which are relevant and responsive to the needs of the economy. Women's specific security needs such as maternity benefits, childcare etc., in the unorganised sector are yet to gain attention in the discourse on social security. And, a lion's share of women workers are in the unorganized sector. Gender sensitive policies need to be implemented towards this, to increase the productivity of women as well as to increase their work participation in the economy.

Independent producers/service providers: Faced with acute

uncertainties with respect to their production, social security for them is essentially their livelihood security itself. Further, as they are yet to be integrated to the market, they are more vulnerable to uncertainties of nature such as drought, flood, crop loss, etc., as well as to the incursions of the market forces. Marginal farmers, forest-dwellers, pavement-dwellers in urban slums, etc., are some examples of such workers. These workers need livelihood security through insurance schemes and access to credit.

Though all the abovementioned dimensions and issues are important for formulating a comprehensive social and economic security in India, the most needed security across the category of workers is of income and employment. Sectors and occupations should be identified for employment potential and efforts should be made to strengthen them. It is the informal sector both in rural or urban areas but mostly in the latter where most of the employment is going to be created. This will be both in manufacturing and services, but the trend shows that the services sector has a much higher employment potential than manufacturing. A well-planned support system should be provided for the growth of this sector considering all key inputs such as marketing, credit, training, upgradation of technology, etc. For enhancing the capabilities of vulnerable workers in the informal sector, a proper blend of education and training is extremely desirable. Experiences across the world show that skill development and training are the most important factors in increasing the employability of the workforce in the wake of on-going globalisation. India is taking steps in this regard, but efforts have so far been limited to the organised sector only. Further, in any scheme of a comprehensive socio-economic security, policies with regard to primary health and elementary education are very important. These are crucial in the development of human resources and a workforce in the country. They can considerably lower the requirement of financial burden on socio-economic security in the future if proper policies are implemented at present.

More importantly, for any positive impact, long term and short term interventions need to be planned with adequate linkages amongst the interventions. Provisioning of quality health care and primary education along with vocational training and provisions for institutional mechanisms for skill up-gradation are to be prioritised as long-term and short-term initiatives. At the risk of repetition, it needs to be emphasised that effective implementation of minimum wages and its periodic upward revision are urgently required to ensure the basic security of income to the workers to sail through the troubled tides of globalisation.

This paper draws substantially from Sharma and Mamgain, (2001) .

REFERENCES

Ahluwalia, Ishar J. (1992), *Productivity and Growth in Indian Manufacturing*, Oxford University Press, Delhi.

Bhagat, Manju (1997), "Poverty and Minimum Wages", *The Indian Journal of Labour Economics,* Vol. 40, No.4.

Bhagwati, Jagdish (1988), "Poverty and Public Policy", *World Development,* Vol. 16, No. 5.

Chandra, Ashoka (1999), "The Role of Training in Productivity: The Objectives of NRF", in M.L. Nandrajog (ed.), *National Renewal Fund: A Look Ahead,* International Labour Organisation, New Delhi.

Chhachi, Amrita et al. (1997), "Mediating the Macro and the Micro: Industrial Restructuring and Women Workers Lives", Paper Presented at a Seminar organised by FREA (1997).

—— (1997), "The Electronic Industry", Paper presented at a seminar organised by FREA (1997).

Datt, Ruddar (2001), *Lockouts in India: A Case Study of West Bengal,* Institute for Human Development, New Delhi.

Deshpande, L.K., Alakh N. Sharma, A.K. Karan and S.Sarkar (2001), *Economic Liberalisation and Labour Market Flexibility in India,* Institute for Human Development, New Delhi.

—— (1992), "Economic Liberalisation and Labour", *The Indian Journal of Labour Economics,* Vol. 35 No. 4.

Deshpande, Sudha and L.K. Deshpande (1992), "New Economic Policy and Female Employment", *Economic and Political Weekly,* October 10.

Datt, Gaurav and Martin Ravallion (1991), *Impact on Time Allocation and Poverty of Public Works in Two Maharashtra Villages,* Welfare and Human Resources Division, World Bank, Washington, D.C.

Fallon, P.R. and R.E.B. Lucas (1991), "The Impact of Changes in Job Security Regulations in India and Zimbawe", *World Bank Economic Review,* Vol. 5, No. 3.

Ghoshe, A.K. (1997), "Should There be a National Minimum Wage in India?", *The Indian Journal of Labour Economics,* Vol. 40, No. 4.

Government of India (1999), *Annual Report 1998-99,* Ministry of Industry, New Delhi.

—— (1990), *Concurrent Evaluation of Integrated Rural Development Programme: The Main Findings,* Department of Rural Development, New Delhi.

Guhan, S. (1995), "Social Security Options for Developing Countries", in Figueirdo, Jose B. and M. Shaheed (eds.), *New Approaches to Poverty Analysis and Policy-II,* International Institute of Labour Studies, Geneva.

Hensman, Rohini (2001), "Employment as Social Security: Pros and Cons", in IDPAD Workshop on Collective Care Arrangements Among Workers and Non-workers in the Informal Sector, Centre for Economic and Social Studies, Hyderabad, March 1-2.

ILO (1996), *India: Economic Reforms and Labour Policies,* International Labour Organisation, New Delhi.

IAMR (2000), *Evaluation of Prime Minister Rozgar Yojana,* Institute of Applied Manpower Research, New Delhi.

Mundle, Sudipto (1992), "The Employment Effects of Stablisation and Related Changes in India, 1991-92 to 1993-94", in ILO-ARTEP, *Social Dimensions of Structural Adjustment in India,* ILO, New Delhi.

Mahendra Dev, S. (1992), "Poverty Alleviation Programme: A Case Study of Maharashtra with Emphasis on Employment Gurarantee Scheme", Discussion Paper No. 77, Indira Gandhi Institute of Development Research, Mumbai.

—— and Ajit Ranade (1996), *Background Paper for World Bank Country Memorandum for India,* World Bank, New Delhi.

Mathur, Ashok (1999), "Economic Reforms, Employment and Non-Employment: Theory, Evidences and Policy", *Conference Volume of the Indian Economic Association,* 80th IEA Conference, Chandigarh.

National Sample Survey Organisation (NSSO) (1996), *Key Results of the 50th Round Survey on Employment and Unemployment,* Revised Report No. 406, Department of Statistics, Government of India, New Delhi.

Noronha, Ernesio (1999), "Duration of Unemployment and Re-employment", *Management and Labour Studies,* Vol. 24, Nos. 2 and 3, April.

Papola, T.S. (1992), "The Question of Unemployment", in Bimal Jalan (ed.), *The Indian Economy,* Viking Delhi.

—— (1994), "Structural Adjustment, Labour Market Flexibility and Employment", *The Indian Journal of Labour Economics,* Vol. 37, No. 1, New Delhi.

Parikh, K. (ed.), 2000, *Indian Development Report,* Oxford University Press, New Delhi.

Parthasarthy, G. (1997), "Minimum Wages within Agriculture", *The Indian Journal of Labour Economic,* Vol. 40, No. 4.

Planning Commission (1956), *Second Five Year Plan,* New Delhi.

—— (1962), *Third Five Year Plan,* New Delhi.

—— (1992), *Eighth Five Year Plan,* New Delhi.

—— (1999), *Ninth Five Year Plan,* Vol. 1, New Delhi.

Rao, Praveen (1995), "Liberalisation, Structural Adjustment and the Working Class", in *Redeployment of Labour in South Asia,* AMDISA, Hyderabad.

Ramaswamy, E.A. (1996), "Organised Labour and Industrial Relations", in *Selected Readings for Discussion at the National Conference on the Future of Industrial Relations and Industrial Relations in Future,* New Delhi.

Ranade, Ajit (1998), "Maharashtra's Employment Gurantee Scheme: Regional Patterns, Scope for Reforms and Replication", *The Indian Journal of Labour Economics,* Vol. 41, No. 2.

Roy Choudhary S. (1996), "Industrial Restructuring, Unions and the State: Flexible Mill Workers in Ahmedabad", *Economic and Political Weekly,* Vol. 31, No. 8.

Singh, Manmohan (1993), "Economic Reforms and Challenges before the Labour Economics, *The Indian Journal of Labour Economics.* Vol. 35, No. 1.

Shrouti, Arvind and Nandkumar (1994), *New Economic Policy and Changing Management Strategies: Impact on Workers and Trade Unions,* Maniben Kara Institute, Mumbai.

Sharma, Alakh N. (2000), *Employment Generation Policy in India and Social Safety Needs,* Working Paper, Institute for Human Development, New Delhi.

—— and R.P. Mamgain (2001), "Employment Generation and the Question or employment Security", in S. Mahendra Dev, P. Antony, V. Gayathri and R.P. Mamgain (eds.), *Social and Economic Security in India,* Institute for Human Development, New Delhi.

—— and S.K. Sasikumar (1996), *Economic Liberalisation and Labour,* National Labour Institute, Noida.

Unni, Jeemol (undated), *Security in the Labour Market: Self-employed Workers and Employment in South Asia,* Gujarat Institute of Development Research, Ahmedabad, mimeo.

UNNATI (1996), *Participatory Study of the Poor Household Economy of Gujarat, Towards Understanding the Impact of Structural Adjustment Programme,* Organisation for Development Education, Ahmedabad.

Venkatratnam, C.S. (1996), "Economic Liberalisation and the Transformation of Industrial Relations Policies in India", *National Conference on Future of IR and IR in Future,* New Delhi.

III

ECONOMIC INTEGRATION AND EMPLOYMENT

9

WTO AND EMPLOYMENT FOR RURAL HOUSEHOLDS: Challenges from Within and Without

G.K. CHADHA

When an Economy Starts Globalising Itself ...

When an economy decides to open up its frontiers and become a part of the world economic system, varying degrees of structural changes set in, practically in each of its sectors. Depending on how much, and how quickly the opening-up process proceeds, as also the size of the economy and the level of sectoral diversification it has already achieved, some sectors register direct, and more radical changes in their investment, production, marketing and pricing regimes while others get indirectly affected, partly through demand-supply linkages with domestic producers now facing international competition and partly through newer and market-responsive roles that all actors in the game have to play.

It is inconceivable that in a globalising economy, economic life of certain sections can stay aloof. For example, even petty farm operators, producing exclusively for the domestic market, may get linked with the international movement of input prices, just as their brethren engaged in tradable commodity production may face more severe earning swings under the new and volatile price regimes. Similarly, even a small scale, family-based industrial enterprise in a village may face a decline in its economic fortune just because the demand for its product is declining now that cheaper substitutes are available through imports, or else, its production efficiency may improve now that raw material costs are lower under the open trade regime, or else, it is now ancillarised to an urban-based, modern industrial enterprise, and so on. Impact on people engaged in trade, banking and finance, the wide range of service activities, etc., can likewise be visualised, on short- as well as long-term basis. In sum, the whole economic system gets a shake-up. Many of the old economic paradigms have to go and new rules of the game come in. New efficiency norms get evolved, new production milieu takes roots, new marketing and pricing perceptions step in. Product/service quality and marketability are the new commercial concerns; price competitiveness becomes the watchword.

The switchover from an inward-looking, closed or import-substituting development strategy to an outward-looking, open or trade-linked strategy necessitates changes in policy perceptions, investment priorities and newer inter-sectoral linkages, all geared to gain competitiveness in the external trade sector. The role of the state needs to be re-defined now that financial, trade and investment flows transcend national frontiers; the facilitating role of the state has now a new and wider canvas to cover. Again, under the new dispensations, the public institutions, most ostensibly the banking and other corporate financial institutions, have newer and 'tougher' priorities to observe. The public and private sector partnership has now to proceed along different lines because, on one hand, a 'level playing field' has to be assured to the export-linked domestic producers, and, on the other, the state's interventionist stances have to be selective and market-responsive. The state policy and apparatus have now to encompass new political economies. On a broad plane, in a globalising economy, the organised system of production and servicing expands steadily, relative to its unorganised counterpart; this is unmistakably the case with the economic activities directly linked with the external sectors, and indirectly those which are getting more and more affected by foreign influences. Technology upgradation becomes the most inescapable and all-encompassing prerequisite for 'staying in the game'. While in some sectors or activities technology-on-ground has to be straightened out, in terms of the conventional parameters (viz., introduction of new products, new inputs, new methods of using inputs, new marketing methods and strategies, etc.,), in others it is the newer god of information technology that does the whole trick. And then, the people who can effectively grapple with the ticklish requirements of the new technologies, can no more be the lot of the uneducated, unskilled or untrained workers; the quality of manpower emerges as the most binding determinant of its effective participation in global trade, financial and investment exchanges. The quality of manpower, in turn, is a direct function of human resource development policies adopted over years.

Again, for big countries characterised by sharp rural-urban divides, in numerous fields of their economic existence, most noticeably in infrastructure, sectoral diversification of production and employment, technology-in-use, market linkages, etc., the rural-urban gaps get sharpened. Consequently, an urban-ward shift of production locales becomes an attractive proposition. Again, in big countries, especially those riddled with queer gender perceptions, social prejudices, religious dogmas (leaving aside caste rigidities), the male-female differentials, most notoriously in the less-enlightened rural areas, are likely to get exasperated. The rural females suffer the most.

In brief, the economies under globalising influences are bound to mark departures from their past. Usually, left to itself, the break is slow. But the preceding two decades are a witness to the quickening of the process because, in many cases, the new band of national policy makers have been extraordinarily eager to prove that the past regimes have failed to mitigate people's distress. Consequently, new bases for conducting their economic affairs, both external and internal, have been evolved and put into practice, in one developing economy after the other. Apart from its uneven regional and inter-personal impact on income, employment and welfare, globalisation has been responsible for exasperating the prevailing labour market segmentations now that the educated, trained or skilled job aspirants would ride over their uneducated or unskilled brethren. The past two decades or so have clearly demonstrated that the future belongs to the former while the latter suffer many reverses.

Opening-up of the Indian Economy

On January 1, 1995, just after the most comprehensive GATT trade round was concluded, the first and most powerful world trade regulating agency – WTO – came into existence. India joined it along with 131 other founding members. Under the circumstances that had been governing the Indian economy, both internally and externally, during the eighties, and the difficulties into which it had landed itself during the early nineties, it was both natural and inevitable for India to join the WTO. It is in the fitness of things to briefly sketch the background that made the opening-up of the Indian economy inevitable during the nineteen-eighties and early nineteen-nineties, and its entry into the WTO fold during the mid-nineteen-nineties.

Beginning of the Opening-up

The initial compulsions to open up a window or two to the world trade system were largely driven by international oil price crisis. However, the feeling that the Indian economy could no more continue with its import-substitution strategy, so assiduously cultivated during Nehru's economic regime and doggedly carried forward through the fifties, sixties and seventies, had started gaining a firm ground in policy and academic circles only when we stepped into the eighties. Hence, during the latter half of the eighties, the Indian economy started opening up its frontiers to the world outside. It was the first time ever that loud voices on improving 'productivity', 'efficiency' and 'competitiveness' were raised in official circles (Government of India, 1985). India could no more keep aloof from the rest of the world, particularly if technological advances occurring elsewhere were to be assimilated and adapted to India's own production requirements. Anticipating export growth potential of certain sectors/areas, a selective import liberalisation approach was put into operation to gain international competitiveness. Import of technology, modern capital equipment and its ancillaries, specified categories of industrial raw materials, etc., all on a highly selective basis, was the summary of the trade liberalisation philosophy of the eighties. Naturally, its impact, especially on domestic employment in general and rural employment in particular, was limited. Nonetheless, it set the trail ablaze. Since 1986 or 1987, every now and then, the economy witnessed one or the other liberalising element till we entered the nineties.

Augmented Opening-up Since 1991

In July 1991, a new economic era ensued. Wide ranging policy reforms, encompassing all major sectors of the economy (trade, industry, agriculture, foreign investment and foreign technology, financial sector, public sector, and so on) were put through, with a rare degree of political resoluteness. It is beyond the purview of this paper to spell out details of each set of reforms. Nonetheless, to comprehend the degree of trade liberalisation that India had already reached around the time that the Uruguay Round negotiations were wound up in 1994, and the likely impact that the WTO's emergence in 1995 would make on employment situation in India, it is in the fitness of things to concentrate on trade and draw a broad sketch of the trade policy reforms effected since 1991.

The new trade policy aimed at eliminating discretionary controls on international trade transactions, reducing the nominal as well as the effective protection available to domestic industry, and bringing domestic prices closer to world prices. Three dimensions of the new trade policy, namely, a rapid dismantling of quantitative restrictions on imports and exports, a substantial reduction on taxes and subsidies on trade and suitable adjustments in exchange rate, need to be underlined.

The process of a near total dismantling of quantitative restrictions on imports and exports signaled a dramatic departure from the past policy regimes. Only a few items (often referred to as the negative lists) remained under import/export restrictions. On the import side, the negative list was made up of three categories: the prohibited, the restricted and the canalised lists, each one of which contained a few items which could be imported under some conditions. In essence, the negative list included most consumer goods; for all items outside this list, there were no restrictions on imports.

In the sphere of exports also, the negative list consisted of the same three principal categories. Nonetheless, very few items remained on the prohibited and the canalised lists. The restricted items, which were still subjected to licensing limits on quantities, or minimum exports prices, comprised a wide range that included most agricultural commodities and several unprocessed or semi-processed materials.

Reduction in import and customs duties was the other landmark of the new trade policy. Since 1991/92, the customs duties on import of most capital goods, project imports for crucial sectors (e.g., coal mining, petroleum refining, power generation, etc.,) and a wide variety of raw materials and manufactured intermediates, were slashed, in varying proportions, almost on a year-to-year basis. Appropriate rationalisation in the structure of customs duties was also introduced from time to time, to facilitate freer flow of imports. The third component of the new trade policy was exchange rate adjustments which came between July 1991 and March 1994, in varying form and content.

From the brief description of trade policy reforms given above, it is abundantly clear that what was hesitatingly pursued earlier was now put through with a rare degree of political resoluteness. Practically, the whole of the old policy fabric came under change. Foreign investment was now invited (perhaps, competitively wooed by all regions of India!), in a wide range of areas; investment collaborations were negotiated by dozens; technology import was no more a forbidden word; the public sector had started 'shedding its unproductive weight' while the private sector, mature enough as it was believed to have grown by then, had started entering into those difficult and strategic areas that were once beyond their investment capability; external trade had opened up in a significant manner and the flow of exports and imports was freed of numerous procedures; a wide range of quantitative restrictions was done away with; international market calculations and 'getting the prices right,' both nationally and internationally, were now given out to be the infallible panacea for growth, employment and economic welfare. In brief, every sector of the Indian economy was attuning itself to the changing economic environment. The state itself was striving to define its role in the new economic order.

Full Opening-up under WTO Regime

It is against this background that India's going to the WTO in 1995, and accelerating further the process of trade liberalisation, would seem to be natural and inevitable. In the opinion of the then policy makers, duly supported by a strong academic and public lobby, WTO's membership was likely to bring higher growth, accelerated export expansion, and a better earning and living standard to the so-called 'average citizen of India'. Perhaps, the hope of benefiting from expanding export opportunities weighed heavily, compared with the apprehension of damage that an unbridled flow of imports under the neo-liberal free-trade discipline of the WTO might inflict on the domestic economy. In any case, during the past five to six years, India has gone quite afar with the implementation of most of the agreements signed with the WTO. The process is still on and yet disturbing signals have started surfacing on many fronts. An intense, all-round debate on the likely impact of the full implementation of the WTO agreements is already on; the adverse effect on employment, particularly rural employment, has already emerged as an acutely disturbing issue. It is essential, therefore, to make some conjectures about the kind of internal and external challenges that the Indian economy has to absorb if employment setbacks are to be averted. First, however, a word about WTO agreements, especially the ones which are likely to put their pressure on the employment side.

So far, India has done well in observing its commitments to WTO. For example, concrete action has been taken or initiated on all agreements applicable to India under GATT, GATS and TRIPs. Broadly, these relate to the removal of quantitative restrictions and tariff restructuring, simplification of customs procedures, evolving international standards in trade and industry (in compliance with the Agreement on Technical Barriers to Trade and that on Sanitary and Phyto-sanitary measures), Agriculture, Textiles, IPR, Trade Related Investment Measures, Anti-dumping Measures and Safeguards, Services Sector, and so on. The most contentious issue is the conversion of non-tariff barriers into equivalent tariff barriers and the reduction in the base tariff structure. Even under the pre-WTO GATT commitments, this process had been initiated in the right earnest. For example, the regime of industrial protection that prevailed prior to the signing of the WTO agreements, through a high tariff wall as well as a rigorous import licensing regime, was getting dismantled around the time that we stepped into the WTO regime. Till 1997, Quantitative Restrictions (QRs) on imports, notified to the WTO on Balance of Payment (BoP) grounds, were operative only for 2714 tariff lines; in March 2000, their number had come down to 1429, including 685 tariff lines under special import license. In compliance with the tariffication commitment, QRs on 714 (out of 1429) tariff lines stood withdrawn with effect from April 1, 2000, while those on the remaining lines were to be lifted by March 31, 2001. Moreover, all the items on which QRs were maintained on BoP grounds, except 36 canalised items, can now be freely imported. Furthermore, as many as 576 of the 812 items reserved for small scale industry, that were earlier protected through QRs, are already put under OGL. This aspect alone may create serious problems for India's small scale industrial sector which provides employment to a very large proportion of industrial workforce and which, under the existing economic dispensation, cannot compete with cheap imports; the adverse impact may get magnified once the effect of the end-of-transition-periods in WTO Agreements (e.g., TRIMs, TRIPs and tariff bindings) was felt in 2001 and beyond.

Compliance on the front of tariff reductions/adjustments has been even more disciplined. For example, India is committed to bind about 67 per cent of its tariff lines which include nearly the whole lot of agricultural lines and some 62 per cent of lines for imports of industrial goods. The remaining unbound lines include those on consumer goods and a few select industrial items. Further, the import schedule is divided into two sections, one for agricultural products and the other for some industrial items including textiles. For non-agricultural goods, India undertook, with a few exceptions, ceiling bindings of 40 per cent *ad valorem* on finished goods and 25 per cent on intermediate goods, machinery and equipment.

The tariff restructuring for agricultural commodities needs to be noted in particular. For 2000/01, the average basic duty rate for all agricultural tariff lines is 34.9 per cent against the negotiated bound tariff rate of 114.9 per cent. Against 686 agricultural commodities for which India stood committed for tariff reduction, the 2000/01 levels of her MFN tariff rates are lower than those of Uruguay Round final bound rates for as many as 676 commodities (Dhar and Chaturvedi, 1999); in fact, in respect of more than 85 per cent of the commodities (numbering 587 out of 686), the difference between the Uruguay Round bound rates and India's MFN tariff rate was 50 per cent and more. The 10 commodities for which India's actual rates were higher than the negotiated bound rates were largely hard drinks such as whiskies, rum, gin, vodka, other compound alcohols, and so on (Gulati and Narayan, 1999).

Let us, very briefly, look at the track record of the developing world compared with what the developed economies have been doing. While the developing world was cajoled to remove non-tariff barriers to smoothen out the international trade environment, the developed world has been consistently expanding the network of non-tariff measures and imposing various trade restrictive impediments including the latest outcry of environmental concerns, labour standards, child labour, and so on. For example, going by the 1998 UNCTAD estimates, as many as 22 non-tariff barriers were operative in Japan, as many as 16 in the EU, nine in Australia, four in the USA, and so on (Panchamukhi, 2000: 61). The story about tariff reduction is perhaps more depressing. A large and influential part of the developed world (notably Japan, USA and the EU) has not gone in for full tariffication of agricultural products; instead, they have gone in for the so-called tariff rate quota system for several commodities which, in essence, restricts their entry and denies legitimate gains to the developing economies. The US tariff schedule, for example, includes as many as 192 tariff lines to administer product-specific tariff quotas, used particularly for dairy products, sugar, peanuts, tobacco, cotton, etc. The implicit hurt to the developing world can thus be imagined, even without calculations. The most telling example comes from the dairy sector. In 1999, the peak tariff rate for milk powder, granules, etc., (fats <= 1.5 per cent) was 99 per cent in the EU, 336 per cent in Japan, 213 per cent in Canada, 211 per cent in Korea, against zero per cent in India. Again, for the same tariff line but with fats >=1.5 per cent, the peak tariff rate in 1998 was 58 per cent in US, 171 per cent in the EU, 557 per cent in Japan, 313 per cent in Canada, 211 per cent in Korea against zero per cent in India. Similar examples can be located for some other commodities.

In contrast, most of the developed economies have observed their commitment more in breach than in implementation. For example, during 1997-99, producer subsidy equivalent (PSE, a working alternative of AMS) was 60 per cent or more in EFTA (especially Norway, Switzerland and Iceland) and the East Asian (especially Japan and Korea) countries; such a high support to agriculture grossly violates the spirit of free trade and extended market access to developing countries. But then, the PSE ranges between 30 to 45 per cent in the case of the EU, Turkey and OECD countries; it ranges between 15 to 25 per cent in the case of Canada, Czechoslovakia, Mexico, US and Poland. Subsidies on the basis of per hectare cultivated or per unit output or per cultivating household throws bare the non-compliance of the developed world in an ever more blatant manner. In sum, therefore, the retention of domestic subsidies at a high rate by many developed countries continues to give us cause for concern. So far, free trade has not worked as fair trade. It is not difficult to visualise that under such a contrived flow of cheaper imports, domestic agriculture would suffer an output setback, and with that employment in agriculture is bound to suffer, most ostensibly in terms of the earning content of on-farm employment, if not in terms of number of persons working under the self-employing family farm systems. But then, non-farm employment cannot remain unaffected if purchasing power of the cultivating households gets jeopardized. Moreover, not only is domestic agriculture to be safeguarded against 'cheaper' imports, concerted efforts have also to be made to gain greater market access for its agricultural products. Still further, the freer inflow of all varieties of imports would directly generate labour-displacing effects in domestic industry, most certainly the small and tiny rural industry where a sizeable chunk of rural non-farm work-force is employed. For all these developments, many challenges lie ahead on the domestic and external fronts with their serious consequences for employment that must be thoroughly grasped.

Let us now look at the services sector and our commitments

under GATS. Recognising the importance of this sector for accelerating the process of growth and, more importantly, in facilitating the to and fro trade flows, the government has been making drastic changes in investment and ownership policies to improve services such as telecommunications, shipping, roads, ports and air transport. The foreign direct investment regime has been liberalised to attract foreign capital in this sector. Foreign equity upto 51 per cent is now automatically allowed in support services for land and water transport, business services including software, and health and medical services; for mining services, non-conventional energy generation and distribution, and storage and warehousing, the automatic approval goes upto 74 per cent; and in the case of electricity generation, transmission and distribution, the limit is 100 per cent. While the insurance sector has recently been opened to private investment, railway transport continues to remain among four industries reserved for the public sector.

India's schedule under GATS provides for specific commitments covering business services, communications, construction work for civil engineering, financial services, health-related and social services, and tourism services (WTO, 1998: 152). India has not so far made any commitments on services relating to distribution, education, environment, recreational, cultural and sporting, etc. Undoubtedly, a path of gradual liberalisation has been followed so as to have wider acceptability of the reform process, especially because of the fragile political climate that pervaded most part of the 1990s. Nonetheless, India actively participated in the Uruguay Round negotiations on services, and made commitments in 33 activities, against the average of 23 for the developing world as a whole. India also participated in the recently concluded financial services negotiations and improved its offer by enhancing the annual limit for foreign bank branches from eight to 12 and withdrawing India's MFN exemptions relating to banking services. Again, India is among 43 countries participating in the Information Technology Agreement covering computers, telecommunication equipment, semi-conductors, manufacturing equipment for semi-conductors, software and scientific instruments; she has offered zero tariff rate on 217 information technology related tariff lines (six-digit level) by 2005.

Guided by the current goings, it seems, a fairly substantial part of the services sector is one area where India has a real prospect of becoming a dominant world player. Thanks to its comparative advantage in the field of human resources and availability of supporting research institutions and universities, there is a tremendous unexplored market potential for a variety of services. India has already acquired a substantial market share in the global cross-country customized software development market. Its share in the global market increased from 12.0 per cent in 1991 to about 19.0 per cent in 1998 and is expected to reach 25.0 per cent in a year or so. India's cost competitiveness is very likely to stay on for another decade or so, and the Indian computer professionals and software experts are going to benefit under the GATS' 'movement of natural persons' clause. The extent to which USA's Silicon Valley is getting increasingly manned by Indian professionals, the speed at which collaborations are being forged between software companies in India and abroad, the calculated manner in which the Indian companies and professionals are being 'wooed' by the US, Germany, Japanese, UK and other European companies, all testify to India's solid expertise, on the one hand, and its comparative cost advantage, on the other. Thanks again to the recently amended EXIM policy, exports have already begun in the areas of accountancy and tax, architectural services, engineering, surveying and technical consultancy, repair and maintenance of equipment, health care and educational services, printing and publishing services, insurance services, oil and gas services, advertising and promotion, film production, recreational and entertainment, and so on (FISME, 1999: 32).

It should thus be fairly obvious that the Indian labour market would have to contend with two sets of challenges: one that would arise out of the freer movement of goods into and from the country, and the other connected with the augmented external demand for a variety of technical and professional workers. Different policy approaches would have to be devised and worked for.

Technology and Employment Prospects under New Trade Regime

How would people's working conditions and general standard of living look like after a decade or so, is the question that needs to be examined with some degree of empirical firmness. Central to these questions is the issue of employment. It is time to pose questions such as the direction in which the rural labour market is likely to move in the near future now that new trade and other policy regimes have taken roots in the Indian economy. But then, the impact of new trade policies on employment can be seen only through the technological changes that have started taking shape in diverse areas of production, both in rural and urban areas, with their accompanying impact on employment that needs both to be explored and projected. To be sure, technological changes could be employment-friendly just as they could be employment-reducing; much depends upon how the opportunities coming up under the open trade regimes are made use of by the domestic policy makers.

It would be naïve to suggest that changes in trade policy alone make impact on technology which, in turn, determines the pace and pattern of employment expansion. It is possible, and in many situations it is indeed the case, that under the ongoing politico-economic system, technological changes in a wide spectrum of production and service activities are propelled by domestic compulsions and supported by internal institutions, usually through public exchequer. For an economy that has started liberalising its external trade and other policies, especially big economies such as India which have had a long history of domestic policy regimes, it is difficult to isolate the technology-changing impact of the newly emerging open trade regime from such impacts occurring under the normal development process. Moreover, it is not the trade policy alone that has undergone a substantial reorientation; practically all other major policy spheres have also been modified in conformity with the rules of the global economic system. For example, foreign investment, not always a constituent of trade exchanges, is also welcome to India. If such investment comes into the specified sectors of the domestic economy, along with a committed package of capital goods, and production technology gets geared to international competitive standards, it is difficult to say that this has happened because of the open trade regime; foreign direct investment too makes its direct impact. But then, it is not really essential to work out precise magnitudes of individual impacts; it should be sufficient to acknowledge that opening the frontiers of the domestic economy to foreign trade, foreign finance, foreign investment and technical know-how (including collaborative and joint production ventures), etc., must make a decisive impact on technology-in-use, in specified sectors/activities, which in turn, would make its impact on employment, not only in the specified sectors but elsewhere also.

The above limitations of figuring out a one-to-one correspondence between a liberal trade regime and technological changes notwithstanding, it is important to emphasise that the open trade policy succeeds only if production and service activities satisfy international norms of efficiency, cost effectiveness, product quality, timely dispatches of consignments, and so on. These obligations apply as much to producers in one tradable sector as to the other. For example, both agricultural and manufactured exports would expand if only they conform to international quality standards, are price competitive and reach their destination according to agreed time schedules. Similarly, on the import side, to insulate domestic goods from the onslaught of their competitive counterparts coming from abroad, production efficiency and price competitiveness are inescapable prerequisites for the domestic producers. Progressive updating of technology is a must; otherwise, domestic producers might steadily get edged out. Perhaps the inroads that a wide assortment of foreign consumer goods has now been making for some years into the upcoming Indian market, both in rural and urban areas, prove the point. And then, the updating of technology is equally inescapable for the services sector. For example, domestic banks are already facing a tough competition vis-à-vis the foreign banks operating in India; unless they change their total modus operandi, introduce new schemes, offer new incentives, and so on, they might lose their clientele further. Likewise, there is a clear indication of increasing export competition in the areas of air transport, tourism (foreign tourists choosing or not choosing India as their destination) and other associated service sectors.

But then, whatever the shape in which the technological change manifests itself, a few other changes associated with new technology may also be underlined. For example, production and marketing management now needs new visions, initiatives and networking, both at home and abroad. Concerns for environment, labour standards and product acceptability, etc., acquire added significance. Human element becomes the kingpin, from the beginning to the end; the era of captive domestic market is over and with that, quality consciousness and price competitiveness become prime considerations, for staying on in the market. The new production regimes are greatly propelled by superior human capabilities. New skills are needed; new working attitudes are insisted on, and accordingly, new and demanding recruitment standards are prescribed. Even for self-employing ventures, uptodate knowledge of the trade and market networking are essential ingredients for success. Education, training and skills become the inescapable prerequisites for more efficient production and marketing.

When all this happens, the dualism in the labour market not only endures itself but gets further sharpened. A market for educated, trained and skilled job aspirants, typically characterised by new and upcoming production/marketing/management standards, significantly higher levels of productivity, wage rates and earnings, etc., steadily expands simultaneously with a steady (and perhaps surreptitious!) decline in the job market for their less educated, semi- or un-skilled and untrained brethren. Employment prospects thus brighten up for the more qualified while a squeezing scenario sets in for the untrained and the uneducated job seekers; differences in employment prospects get magnified between self-employment and wage-paid jobs, and still more significantly, between urban and rural areas. Rural job aspirants, especially females among them, suffer far more severe setbacks, primarily because of their own educational, training and skill deficiencies.

Indian Economy in Recent Years

Ever since the arrival of economic reforms in July 1991, practically every sector of the Indian economy has started undergoing one structural change or the other which, in turn, has begun to show its impact on growth, employment, distribution, and so on. All available evidence points towards disturbing signals on the employment front. However, before we look through the employment scenario, it may be useful to see through the overall growth record of the 1990s.

Growth Profile of the Nineties

During the 1990s, the Indian economy has thrown up a mix of pleasing and depressing signals. On the positive side, four features attract our pointed attention. First, a consistent restructuring of the economy has been going on, without a break or undulation; the secondary and tertiary sectors have steadily improved their share in the GDP while the primary sector has done the opposite. Second, the 1990s have clearly witnessed a much faster pace of globalisation, compared with the 1980s; exports and imports as a percentage of GDP have witnessed a steady expansion, especially during the most recent years. Third, the structure of India's trade has been steadily tilting in favour of manufactured goods; the tilt is clearly more pronounced during the 1990s compared with the 1980s, and during the latter half of the 1990s compared with the first half. Finally, the overall growth of the economy during the 1990s has been no less pleasing. For example, keeping aside a few exceptions, the year-to-year change in GDP has generally been markedly higher during the nineties than during the eighties; in particular, the performance in the recent years has been consistently superior (Chadha, 2001:38).

In total terms, the GDP growth profile does not support the pessimism voiced by some analysts. However, marked differences are discernible as regards the recent performance of the three sectors. Without doubt, the primary sector has shown a highly uneven growth pattern during the 1990s, much the same way it did during the 1980s. The secondary sector too threw signals of concern, especially because of the steep decline in its year-to-year growth during the second half of the 1990s. It is only the tertiary sector which has generally maintained its year-to-year growth momentum during the post-1995 years. And it is precisely because of the steadily increasing share of this sector in national income that the latter half of the 1990s witnessed a steady improvement in the annual percentage growth of total GDP, and this saved us from reclining into a mood of pessimism.

But then, we have adequate evidence that substantiates the pessimism theory. The marked decline in the annual percentage change in total exports, total imports, agricultural exports and manufacturing exports during the post-1995/96 period is adequate proof of the adverse circumstances. The position during 1999/2000 is reported to be no better. As a matter of fact, for the whole decade of the 1990s, the highly undulating profile of the annual percentage change in respect of each of these four trade variables, especially for agricultural products, clearly signifies our incapability of building a stable trade base, in spite of the 1991 economic reforms or the post-1995 adjustments under our WTO commitments. There are many other indicators (e.g., increasing weakness of the Indian rupee, stock market up- and down-swings, the increasing hiatus between the negotiated and actual arrival of foreign direct investment, on the external front, and, an unrelenting increase in the cost of living index for industrial or urban non-manual employees, a slackening pace of investment, most notoriously the public sector investment, etc., on the domestic front), which reflect increasing vulnerability of the Indian economy in general, and the trade sector in particular (ibid: 41).

Employment Scenario

The employment scenario during the nineties lends itself to highly differing interpretations. To some observers, the worst has already arrived while to others, the post-reform or post-WTO years are essentially a transitory phase that throws up its own gains and losses, spread over different sectors or groups of workers. Here is a telling description of the pessimism given out by the first group of observers:

> Foreign imports have killed off thousands of small and medium industries in India, as many as 400,000 according to an estimate.

> A number of industries have closed down in Mumbai, Thana-Belapur, Bhiwandi, Aurangabad, Kanpur, Aligarh, Indore and several other towns ...In Bhiwandi 60 per cent of powerlooms are silent. In Aligarh, small firms making locks and other hardware for generations, are downing shutters. In Mumbai, if you motor down Thane-Belapur complex every other factory is closed. Since everybody cannot be a software engineer and take off for Silicon Valley, thousands, if not lakhs of people, have lost their jobs (Dubashi, 2000: 10).

Pessimism of this order is not authenticated by national-level survey data which nevertheless points towards sectors doing better and those doing worse during the post-reform years, compared with the pre-reform phase. Let us look at the NSS survey and economic census data on employment more systematically and then draw meaningful conclusions about the on-going situation on employment.

Growth of Employment

The proponents of economic reforms would make us believe that employment was expected to pick up primarily because the output growth was likely to pick up after economic reforms took roots. Dwelling more on the labour-displacing effects of these reforms, the critics would, however, believe that employment would not grow in the same proportion in which output would grow, given the compulsion of installing a more capital-intensive technology in many branches of production. Since technological changes of the above type are likely to come about only in selected production sectors, and labour-intensive technologies are likely to dominate in many others, a mixed overall picture on employment growth was likely to emerge for some years after the arrival of the reforms. This is what seems to be happening currently in the Indian economy in general, and rural areas in particular.

Employment Growth Rates: NSS Data

The NSS data for the nineties clearly throw up a mixture of gains and losses for rural as well as urban employment. To say the least, the tall employment-friendly claims of the 1991/92 economic reforms or the prospective gains from the WTO agreement, are nowhere in sight, most certainly for the rural work force. Table 9.1 shows growth rates of employment for two sub-periods: 1987/88–1993/94 and 1993/94-1999/2000. For notional convenience, we take these as pre- and post-reform periods; we have no other time-demarcation choice since the recent NSS survey data on employment are available only for 1987/88, 1993/94 and 1999/2000. That the overall rate of growth of employment witnessed a varying degree of decline during the post-reform period compared with the pre-reform phase, for each group of workers, both rural and urban, would lend some support to the pessimism expressed in some quarters; for rural workers, the rate of growth of employment declined steeply from 2.12 per cent during the pre-reform phase to 0.66 per cent during the post-reform years, for urban workers, it fell sizeably, *albeit* less steeply, from 3.39 per cent to 2.27 per cent; for male workers (rural+urban), the decline was from 2.49 per cent to 1.38 per cent while for their female counterparts, it was far more precipitous, falling from 2.17 per cent to as low as 0.26 per cent. In terms of overall employment growth rates, the years since 1993/94 have, therefore, brought no cheers to any section of the working population. It is nonetheless important to note that the rate of growth of urban employment continued to be much higher than that in the rural areas, just as the rate of growth of employment for male workers continued to be higher than that for their female counterparts; as a matter of fact, for female workers, the relative situation has considerably worsened during the post-1993 years.

The disturbing signals are clearly discernible in many production and service sectors, both in rural and urban areas. For example, in the rural areas, agriculture could absorb no additional hands during the post-reform years while during the pre-reform phase, a fairly respectable growth rate of employment (2.16 per cent per annum) was in operation. The other major sectors witnessing substantial employment reverses in rural India were mining-quarrying, utilities, trade, finance-insurance-real estate, and community-social-personal services. Other sectors of the rural economy did witness a higher rate

TABLE 9.1: **Annual Compound Growth Rate of Employment for Usual (Principal+Subsidiary) Status Workers by Sex, Residence and Sector of Production: 1987-88 to 1999-00**

	Total (R+U)		Rural		Urban		Male		Female	
Sector of Production	87-88 to 93-94	93-94 to 99-00	87-88 to 93-94	93-94 to 99-00	87-88 to 93-94	93-94 to 99-00	87-88 to 93-94	93-94 to 99-00	87-88 to 93-94	93-94 to 99-00
1	2	3	4	5	6	7	8	9	10	11
Field crop production	2.43	0.12	2.45	0.23	1.82	-3.23	2.31	0.33	2.63	-0.22
Plantation	3.48	-4.27	2.75	-3.35	11.36	-14.07	3.71	-5.97	3.04	-1.19
Livestock	-1.37	-1.08	-1.47	-0.83	-0.34	-3.75	-3.46	-1.23	-0.32	-1.02
Agricultural services	10.29	12.90	10.10	13.42	12.41	6.73	6.99	13.93	16.47	11.37
Forestry & logging	-8.23	-0.81	-8.52	-1.12	-4.72	2.27	-2.08	-4.62	-15.25	4.87
Fishing	5.68	-4.53	6.47	-6.37	2.35	2.51	4.96	-3.82	10.98	-9.58
Total agriculture	2.15	0.05	2.16	0.18	1.98	-3.40	2.12	0.21	2.20	-0.21
Mining	2.36	-2.78	2.14	-2.28	2.77	-3.71	2.65	-2.33	1.23	-4.75
Manufacturing										
Food products	4.57	2.78	5.88	2.26	2.64	3.60	4.36	3.43	5.13	1.00

(contd.)

TABLE 9.1 *(contd.)*

1	2	3	4	5	6	7	8	9	10	11
Beverages, etc.	3.88	1.83	4.62	2.62	2.39	-0.01	1.84	-1.81	4.93	3.31
Cotton, wool, jute etc.	1.16	-4.24	0.27	-3.32	2.03	-5.13	0.43	-4.31	2.76	-4.08
Textile products	-7.06	6.69	-8.93	7.22	-5.16	6.21	-7.71	8.58	-5.99	3.39
Wood products	1.28	3.77	0.68	3.66	2.77	4.04	0.37	4.89	4.17	0.28
Paper products	0.24	3.78	2.19	0.94	-0.20	4.42	0.71	3.55	-2.60	5.26
Leather products	-0.37	6.54	-8.96	0.94	4.54	8.19	-1.48	6.86	12.55	4.05
Rubber products	21.68	1.97	23.50	3.38	20.82	1.23	17.67	0.29	42.24	5.99
Chemical products	-6.86	5.67	-9.90	0.94	-5.76	6.95	-2.08	6.50	-22.97	-2.75
Non-metallic mineral products	0.93	1.81	1.38	2.74	-0.28	-1.07	1.64	1.73	-0.98	2.04
Basic metal ind.	-3.96	2.95	-8.96	13.30	-2.48	-0.40	-3.98	3.02	-3.39	0.94
Metal products	2.32	5.54	2.19	8.13	2.39	4.04	2.30	4.47	3.36	31.56
Machine tool & elect. machinery	3.00	2.54	5.14	-1.89	2.09	4.34	1.89	3.30	17.71	-5.17
Transport equipment	-6.77	-2.73			-3.19	-2.73	-7.01	-2.19	3.36	
Other manfg .	6.33	0.86	5.91	-2.86	6.65	3.20	7.58	-0.32	1.09	6.13
Repair services	5.86	-1.11	9.06	-3.18	3.67	0.42	8.61	-1.97	-17.53	13.15
(a) Agro-based (20-21 to 29)	0.56	1.97	0.46	2.16	0.68	1.72	-0.25	2.44	2.08	1.11

(contd.)

TABLE 9.1 *(contd.)*

1	2	3	4	5	6	7	8	9	10	11
(b) Others (30-38,97)	3.14	1.56	3.81	1.03	2.67	1.95	3.93	1.07	-1.52	4.78
Total manufacturing	1.57	1.80	1.54	1.78	1.60	1.83	1.66	1.78	1.31	1.87
Utilities	3.10	-4.77	2.19	-5.65	3.76	-4.19	2.88	-4.73	10.59	-5.66
Construction	-0.12	6.36	-3.51	6.43	6.25	6.26	2.23	6.76	-9.68	3.59
Trade	3.59	3.99	3.22	1.81	3.87	5.54	3.71	4.03	2.81	3.73
Wholesale trade	11.86	-0.86	16.42	0.88	9.89	-1.84	11.14	-0.87	27.49	-0.65
Retail trade	2.71	4.66	2.30	1.60	3.06	6.96	2.80	4.86	2.16	3.44
Hotel+Restaurant	2.63	4.20	2.15	3.91	2.98	4.40	2.93	3.69	1.12	6.79
Transport, storage and communication	3.66	5.31	3.78	7.29	3.58	3.91	3.57	5.33	6.90	4.73
Finance, insurance & real estate	5.23	6.07	4.44	2.51	5.48	7.05	4.16	6.54	16.88	2.18
Community, social and personal services	4.74	0.21	4.36	0.32	5.06	0.13	4.26	-0.002	6.07	0.76

(contd.)

TABLE 9.1 *(contd.)*

1	2	3	4	5	6	7	8	9	10	11
Public admin, defence etc.	1.17	0.17	-0.33	1.35	2.01	-0.46	0.84	0.36	3.97	-1.32
Sanitary services	10.85	-10.10	21.02	-15.60	5.29	-6.35	15.76	-14.33	5.31	-4.97
Education, scientific etc.	5.21	3.82	4.71	3.01	5.75	4.65	5.06	2.81	5.49	5.63
Medical & health etc.	2.73	4.00	2.14	0.73	3.14	5.88	2.88	3.56	2.43	4.92
Community services	0.23	-2.42	2.16	-4.62	-2.21	0.42	0.60	-3.37	-1.66	2.11
Recreational & cultural services	9.49	-3.60	14.71	-10.07	6.49	0.11	9.43	-3.92	10.59	0.94
Personal services	9.34	-2.14	7.70	-0.63	11.15	-3.73	10.28	-2.07	8.11	-2.23
Non-agriculture	2.81	2.65	1.97	2.31	3.60	2.95	3.01	2.86	2.09	1.81
All sectors	2.39	1.02	2.12	0.66	3.39	2.27	2.49	1.38	2.17	0.26

Sources: *Sarvekshana*, September 1990: S218-S247; NSS Report No.409, March 1997:A163-A176; NSS Report No 458-II, May 2001: A182-A194.

of growth of employment during the post-1993 years. But then, while a marked improvement is clearly discernible in respect of construction and transport-communications, it was rather a meek increase in respect of manufacturing and the total of non-farm employment. Likewise, a highly disparate picture is discernible for the urban economy as well. Here, the cheering spots are fewer, however. Clearly, the improved situation is visible only in trade and finance-insurance-real estate; for manufacturing, construction and transport-communications, only a meek or negligible improvement has been the fate of urban workers. On the other hand, the sectors where the rate of growth of employment witnessed a varying degree of decline were agriculture, mining-quarrying, utilities, and community-social-personal services. In overall terms, the urban areas too show a mixture of higher and lower employment growth rates after the onset of economic reforms.

Again, it is interesting to see that the employment reverses during the post-1993 years are shared, in varying form and content, by male and female workers. Except for transport-communications where the rate of growth of employment improved from 3.57 per cent during 1987/88-1993/94 to 5.33 per cent during 1993/94-1999/2000 for male workers while it declined from 6.90 per cent to 4.73 per cent for female workers, and, likewise for finance-insurance-real estate where it increased from 4.16 per cent to 6.54 per cent for male workers against a steep decline from 16.88 per cent to 2.18 per cent for female workers, in all other sectors the increase or decline in employment growth rate was seen simultaneously for male and female workers. In particular, the precipitous decline in agriculture, mining-quarrying, utilities, and community-social-personal services, a meek decline in non-farm employment as a whole, a sizeable increase in construction, and a meek improvement in manufacturing, during the post- compared with the pre-1993 years, were the common fate of male and female workers. In particular, the precipitous decline in community-social-personal services in respect of female workers, poses serious doubts on the employment-augmenting capabilities of economic reforms in their present outfits, since this sector has particularly been a stronghold for them. In total terms, relative to male workers, for the females, the employment setbacks have been more severe while their gains have been of a much lower order.

The fact that the rural economy stands well enmeshed with the rest of the economy, or the rural job aspirants can no more operate outside the precincts of the national labour market is authenticated, *albeit* indirectly and meekly, by a pattern of employment growth commonly shared by rural and urban workers. It cannot be a coincidence that employment growth rates in transport-storage-communications, construction, and manufacturing sectors improved during the post-reform years, both for rural and urban workers; likewise, the decline or slow-down in the mining, utilities, finance-insurance-real estates, and community-social-personal services, were the common fate of both the groups. It is only for trade that, during the post-reform years, the urban workers surged much ahead of their rural counterparts when the retail trade activity gained additional momentum under the informal sector of the urban economy, in addition to a high pace of employment expansion in the hotel-restaurant segment.

Let us now peep inside the major sectors, first with the rural workforce. For them, employment changes in agriculture must be dissected first of all. Practically, each sub-sector in the primary sector suffered a varying degree of setback; the worst sufferers are field crop production, plantations, and fishing. The employment growth rate in livestock and forestry-logging did improve but it was not able to switch over from a negative to a positive rate. On the whole, a fairly depressing agricultural employment scenario seems to have set in during the post-reform years; for a host of reasons, most ostensibly the rising pace of mechanisation, cropping pattern adjustments not necessarily attuned to labour-absorbing crop enterprises, the general preference of the young entrants to the labour market in favour of non-farm jobs, etc., it continued with its inability to take on additional work seekers, either in field crop production or agriculture as a whole. In other words, agriculture seems to have lost its verve as an expanding source of employment for the rural work seekers. Unluckily, as we see later, non-farm employment expansion has hardly compensated them for the sluggish labour absorptive capacity of agriculture.

A mingle of improved and shrunken employment growth rates was the fate of the manufacturing sector. Employment growth rates for rural workers improved during the post-reform years in textile products, wood and wood products, leather and leather products, chemical products, non-metallic mineral products, basic metal industries, metal products and the total of agro-based industries, while the opposite was true for food products, beverages-tobacco, jute-mesta, cotton and wool products, paper and paper products, rubber and rubber products, machine tools and electrical machinery, other manufacturing, repair services and the total of non-agro based industries. Improved employment expansion was particularly striking for textile products, basic metal products, metal products, and agro-based industries as a whole, while the squeeze in the pace of employment growth was substantially high for rubber and rubber products, machine tools and electrical machinery, other manufacturing and repair services. The mixed picture observed for the total of rural workers is discernible, in varying degree and form, for the rural male and female workers. The combined effect of these developments is that, for the total of manufacturing, employment growth rate could not increase beyond 1.78 per cent per annum in the post-reform years, against 1.54 per cent during the pre-reform period. This, by any objective reckoning, cannot be termed as a marked departure from the pre-reform years.

Has the urban manufacturing sector fared better in the post-reform period? Summarily, no. It is extremely revealing to see that the pattern of post-reform improvement or decline in the rate of growth of employment is very largely similar between rural and urban areas. In total terms, it is more than evident that the adverse or beneficial effects of economic reforms since 1991/92 or of India's entry into WTO since 1995, encompassed both rural and urban manufacturing activities; it is wrong to believe that the initial brunt of employment setbacks was borne by rural workforce alone.

The employment setbacks and gains under community-social-personal services, are fairly widely spread across individual segments, and are shared, in varying degree, by rural and urban, and male and female workers. For example, for rural workers, there was a decline in the rate of growth of employment during the post- compared with the pre-reform years, in six out of the seven segments; only public administration and defence registered an increase from -0.33 per cent to 1.35 per cent. For urban workers, the setback occurred in five of the seven segments; only medical-health, and community services witnessed an improvement. The most devastating decline, witnessed both by rural and urban workers, was in sanitary services, recreational and cultural services, and personal services. Nearly the same story unfolds itself when we look at the post- and pre-reform employment growth rate for male and female workers.

Employment Growth Rates: Economic Census Data

The economic census data, available for 1980, 1990 and 1998, can also throw light on some aspects of rural employment. It must, however, be noted at the very outset that economic census data are not entirely comparable with NSS data. In the former, there is no information on employment in field crops and plantations; the pre- and post-reform temporal setting has to be different between the two sets of data. Perhaps, some minor conceptual differences also exist between the two. Undeterred by these constraints, we look into the economic census data largely to check the veracity of our earlier conclusion that employment growth rates in the post-reform years do not reflect a marked departure from those in the pre-reform period. Table 9.2 answers this limited inquiry rather well. Constrained by the time setting of the economic census data, the decade 1980–1990 is taken as the pre-reform period while the years 1990–1998 are taken to represent the post-reform period.

A varying degree of slow-down in rural employment growth rates, in the post-reform period as compared with its pre-reform counterpart, is discernible in each of the three segments set out in Table 9.2. The drop in each of the rural employment growth rates is, however, not very big. In some sense, it lends support to our assertion that the ground realities so far support neither the proponents nor the critics of the reforms. Interestingly, consistent with what was observed earlier through the NSS data, employment growth rates in urban areas too show a slow-down. To put the record straight, the slow-down is relatively more pronounced in certain

TABLE 9.2: **Employment Situation in India: 1980s and 1990s**

		Allied Activities to Agri-culture*	Non-Agri-cultural Activities	Total
1	2	3	4	5
Rural	1980	2433018	21793510	24226528
	%	10.04	89.96	100.00
	1990	4206566	27969200	32175766
	%	13.07	86.93	100.00
	1998	6081232	32051302	38132534
	%	15.95	84.05	100.00
Absolute change				
	1980/1990	1773548	6175690	7949238
	1990/1998	1874666	4082102	5956768
	1980/1998	3648214	10257792	13906006
Annual compound growth rate (%)				
	1980/1990	5.63	2.53	2.88
	1990/1998	4.71	1.72	2.15
	1980/1998	5.22	2.17	2.55
Urban	1980	394866	28557279	28952145
	%	1.36	98.64	100.00
	1990	525847	37684600	38210447
	%	1.38	98.62	100.00
	1998	609229	41889478	42498707
	%	1.43	98.57	100.00
Absolute change				
	1980/1990	130981	9127321	9258302
	1990/1998	83382	4204878	4288260
	1980/1998	214363	13332199	13546562
Annual compound growth rate (%)				
	1980/1990	2.91	2.81	2.81

(contd.)

TABLE 9.2 *(contd.)*

1	2	3	4	5
	1990/1998	1.86	1.33	1.34
	1980/1998	2.44	2.15	2.16
Total	1980	2827884	50350789	53178673
	%	5.32	94.68	100.00
	1990	4732413	65653800	70386213
	%	6.72	93.28	100.00
	1998	6690461	73940780	80631241
	%	8.30	91.70	100.00
Absolute change				
	1980/1990	1904529	15303011	17207540
	1990/1998	1958048	8286980	10245028
	1980/1998	3862577	23589991	27452568
Annual compound growth rate (%)				
	1980/1990	5.28	2.69	2.84
	1990/1998	4.42	1.50	1.71
	1980/1998	4.90	2.16	2.34

Notes: 1. Figures exclude Assam and Jammu & Kashmir;
2. * includes activities (other than crop production and plantations) such as live-stock, agricultural services, hunting, trapping, forestry and logging, fishing etc.

Source: Government of India, *Economic Census, 1980*, 1990 and 1998, CSO. (http://www.nic.in/stat/stat_act.htm).

segments of the urban compared with those in the rural economy. This is consistent with the hypothesis that the first round of employment-displacing effects of liberalisation, globalisation and privatisation has to be borne relatively more by the urban economy. As a matter of fact, only a detailed product sector classification can inform us about the relative gains or losses of rural areas when the economy is heading towards globalisation and privatisation.

A relatively bigger setback of the urban workforce can also be seen through its shrinking share of the incremental employment.

During 1990-1998, out of the total of 8.29 million additional work-places coming up in non-agricultural activities, the urban areas had a share of 50.7 per cent, while during the previous decade (1980-1990), out of the total of 15.30 million additional jobs, the urban areas had a hefty share of 60.0 per cent. Again, during the pre-reform decade (1980-1990), the absolute number of additional non-agricultural jobs coming up in urban areas was 9.13 million against 6.18 million in the rural areas; during the post-reform years (1990-98), the urban areas could muster only 4.20 million additional non-farm jobs against 4.08 million in the rural areas. Clearly, the urban performance is relatively less satisfying. The first round impact thesis thus gets a bit more of empirical firmness. It must, however, be stressed that employment gains and losses can never be a one-sided affair; for certain product lines, the rural areas do have the wherewithal to withstand competition, both from within the country and outside, while for others, their inferior technology or product quality or diseconomies of scale become their Achilles' heel. As we see later, this indeed has been the case in recent years.

Increasing Casualisation of Employment

Table 9.3 shows the changing mode of employment between 1972/73 and 1999/2000 in rural areas. It is at once clear that in rural India, the incidence of self-employment has been consistently on a relative decline, both for rural male and female workers; for rural males, it declined from around 66 per cent in 1972/73 to 55.0 per cent in 1999/2000 and for rural females, it dropped from 65 per cent to 57 per cent. Second, regular salaried jobs have unmistakably been on the decline, both for rural male and female workers, especially the former. Third, and quite strikingly, employment under casual labour basis has increased for both categories of workers. The increase has been fairly steep in the case of rural male workers, and a little less so in the case of rural females. The point of economic substance is that in rural India, the casual wage-employment is steadily rising at the cost of self-employment. For rural areas, the switch-over is a more worrisome matter since the declining incidence of self-employment

TABLE 9.3: **Composition of Usually Employed Male and Female Workers**

Year	Rural Male			Rural Female			Rural Persons		
	Self-employed	Regular Employee	Casual Labour	Self-employed	Regular Employee	Casual Labour	Self-employed	Regular Employee	Casual Labour
1972-73	65.9	12.1	22.0	64.5	4.1	31.4	65.3	9.3	25.4
	(39.2)	(50.7)	(10.1)	(48.4)	(27.9)	(23.7)	(41.2)	(46.3)	(12.5)
1977-78	62.8	10.6	26.6	62.1	2.8	35.1	62.6	7.7	29.7
	(40.4)	(46.4)	(13.2)	(49.5)	(24.9)	(25.6)	(42.4)	(41.8)	(15.8)
1983	60.5	10.3	29.2	61.9	2.8	35.3	61.0	7.5	31.5
	(40.9)	(43.7)	(15.4)	(45.8)	(25.8)	(28.6)	(41.8)	(40.0)	(18.2)
1987-88	58.6	10.0	31.4	60.8	3.7	35.5	59.4	7.7	32.9
	(41.7)	(43.7)	(14.6)	(47.1)	(27.5)	(25.4)	(42.8)	(40.3)	(16.0)
1993-94	57.9	8.3	33.8	58.5	2.8	38.7	58.0	6.4	35.6
	(41.7)	(42.1)	(16.2)	(45.4)	(28.6)	(26.0)	(42.3)	(39.4)	(18.3)
1999-2000	55.0	8.8	36.2	57.3	3.1	39.6	55.8	6.8	37.4

Note: Figures in parenthesis are for urban workers.
Sources: Government of India, (1990a): 92; Government of India (1996); Government of India (2001): 106-111.

may be throwing some people out of self-cultivation only to swell the ranks of the landless agricultural labourers. In fact, for rural India, independent information through population census does confirm the rising proportion of the landless agricultural labourers from about 17.0 per cent in 1961 to as high as 32.0 per cent in 1991 (Haan, 1980, Part II: 2; Census of India, Paper 3 of 1991: 193).

It is as well possible that many among the self-employed sub-marginal and marginal cultivators, whose proportion among the cultivating households has been continuously rising during the 1960s, 1970s and 1980s, temporarily give up agriculture and seek work as non-agricultural labourers, on casual basis. That the temporary 'switch-over' or seasonal supplementation is a real possibility, and, by implication, is behind the increasing casualisation of wage labour, has its support from the much higher increase in casually employed males compared with their female counterparts.

The quickened pace of casualisation, and a more visible decline in the proportion of self-employed workers, during the nineties, lends some credence to the theory of increasing segmentation in the Indian labour market, in general, and increasing marginalisation of rural job aspirants, in particular. Interestingly, as some recent studies show, in most recent years, casualisation has not been discernible for urban workers; in fact, it has declined for urban females during 1993/94-1999/2000 (Chadha, 2001:503). This is plainly so because of the marked improvement in the educational and training capabilities of urban female job-seekers, almost at tandem with urban males; the future cadres of the urban female job aspirants are likely to be equipped with educational, training and skill accomplishments not much different from their urban brethren, and would thus be able to compete effectively in the information-, technology-, and management-intensive urban labour market. Their rural sisters do not seem to have a chance on such job frontiers. In plain terms, for a preponderant majority of rural workers—coming as they do from the landless labour, marginal and small cultivating households—self-employment on own or leased-in land and casual wage employment on others' farms or in one or the other non-farm activity are the only two choices; regular salaried jobs do not accommodate more than a handful of them, nearly to the total exclusion of the female job aspirants. It bears some conjecture, therefore, that in terms of quality of employment, rural job seekers have undoubtedly a long gap to cover.

Challenges Ahead

The foregoing descriptions should not throw us to despair. Instead, we better take stock of our weaknesses, especially in trade-related employment policies and act fast, both at home and abroad. On the home front, suggestions given from time to time in the past, and now hastened under the WTO exigencies, have revolved around infrastructural improvements, removal of bureaucratic hassles, down-sizing of the public sector, encouraging technological up-gradation through economies of scale, imported technology and know-how, forging public-private sector partnership in strategic areas, strengthening of human capital base, public investment in social sectors, bridging rural-urban gaps in socio-economic development, strengthening of agriculture to reap the benefits of strong forward-backward linkages including employment multiplier effects, labour market reforms, promotion policies for small industry, fostering a market-friendly development of the banking and insurance sectors, and many more. On the external front, we have to prepare ourselves to fight against the existing asymmetries in the WTO agreements, most ostensibly for the crucial changes needed in the Agreement on Trade-Related Intellectual Property Rights, encompassing issues of patentable matter, bio-diversity preservation, production and promotion of community knowledge, etc., plead for a free movement of labour in the vein of the free flow of goods and services, sort out diverse non-trade issues, especially those related to environment and labour standards. For paucity of space, we cannot go into all these issues. Given our concern for the worsening employment situation for the rural households, we are strongly advised to concentrate on the most crucial issue of the poor quality of India's rural workforce, on the home front, and, on issues of free movement of labour and non-trade issues, on the external. The critical import of these specific issues for domestic employment in general, and of rural households in particular, hardly needs to be emphasised.

Poor Human Capital Base in Rural India

There is absolutely no doubt that the quality of the existing workforce in general, and of rural workforce in particular leaves much to be desired, especially when judged by international standards. The narrow band of technically qualified, highly skilled and professional hands, largely hailing from the upper-middle class urban households notwithstanding, the wide mass of Indian workers emerging from the lower and middle strata of the rural households, are hardly equipped to absorb the challenges being thrown by the open economic regime. Admittedly, a sizeable proportion of these rural workers would have to be written off in the context of both the urban market pressures and external trade and investment competitions. But then, are we preparing the future cadres of our workers, most expressly the rural job seekers, to acquire higher levels of educational, training and skill capabilities so as to absorb the onslaught of the economic reforms and of WTO? Can rural India pin its hope on its future labour force, if not on the present army of its workers? Perhaps, we have to peep into the human capital base of the existing workforce, as also the quality of the labour force that will emerge within the next five, 10 or 15 years.

Education and Skill Capabilities of the Existing Rural Workforce

In our view, a poor human capital base of India's rural economy in general, and of rural industrial workforce in particular, is indeed its Achilles' heel. Educated workforce in any economy is essentially a byproduct of its educational system. In India's federal democratic system, education and health are the development responsibilities of individual states. Although an overall policy umbrella is set out, from time to time, by the central government, yet priority thrusts on different levels and types of education, per capita expenditure on basic and higher levels of education or on primary and advanced levels of health services, etc., remain within the purview of the state governments. Numerous studies on social infrastructure in India show sharp inter-state variations in education and health services, on the one hand, and the increasing rural-urban gaps, on the other. For paucity of space, we cannot sketch out the state-level picture. Nonetheless, even the national-level position shows a fairly depressing scenario.

In quantitative terms, educational facilities in India have witnessed a tremendous expansion during the past decades, yet millions of children and adolescents, most markedly in the rural areas have had no education, or could not go too far. The situation regarding skill up-gradation is particularly weak. For example, only about 5.0 per cent of secondary school level students were found to opt for vocational stream against a target of 25.0 per cent set during the eighth plan (Government of India, 1999: 122). Training systems suffer from limited flexibility, poor curricula and weak links with industry. The most serious lacuna from the point of rural industry is that training in government training centers is mostly focused on the organised sector which has extremely limited relevance for the kind of household, tiny and cottage enterprises that dominate the rural industrial scene.

The weaknesses and lopsidedness of the Indian educational system never revealed themselves as blatantly as in recent years, when the Indian economy opened itself to the world outside. The Indian workforce clearly stands divided into three broad compartments in terms of its educational and training capabilities. The top segment comprises a very small number of highly educated and professionally trained persons, hailing nearly exclusively from the urban areas, who are progressively becoming a part of the international labour market or the highly lucrative segment of the domestic market; undoubtedly, they are the product of a few top-class educational institutions (e.g., Indian Institutes of Technology, some engineering colleges, management institutes, etc.) that exist side by side with the thousands of India's average or low-quality schools, colleges and other institutes. The bottom consists of those who still remain illiterate or could not go beyond, say, primary schooling, not to speak of their remaining devoid of technical training and professional skills. A fairly high proportion of India's working population falls in this category; by any reckoning, rural workers take a lion's share in this segment of workforce, and acquiesce to stay on in agriculture or in low-paid non-agricultural, including industrial, jobs.

Finally, the middle segment, again constituting a fairly sizeable proportion of India's working population, is 'educated' in a formal sense but the quality of their education and training leaves much to be desired. It is this segment of 'educated job aspirants' that has entailed the widening of the mis-match between what the economy or industry can offer and what they are looking for. Rural workers who have a fairly big share in this segment of workforce, are no exception.

We can substantiate our view on the poor quality of workforce in rural India through two sets of data. The latest nation-wide survey by the National Sample Survey Organisation (NSSO), for 1999/2000 in respect of the non-farm workforce in rural India as a whole is the first set. The second set comes through our own recent (April-June, 2000) survey. First, let us look at the rural industrial sector as mirrored through the rural non-farm sector as a whole. Table 9.4 reveals rural workers' educational weaknesses in many different ways.

It is clear that till as late as 1999/2000, nearly 40.0 per cent of the rural male, about three-fourth of rural female and more than a half of the total rural workers were totally illiterate. By any reckoning, it is a national shame, and in spite of the hype that India claims in the arena of information technology, it clearly shows the inherent weakness of a large part of the Indian economy. But then, the actual level of educational accomplishment among the non-illiterate rural workers is a matter of equal distress. For example, not more than 28.0 per cent of the rural male, 16.0 per cent of the rural female and less than a quarter of the total rural workers could go beyond primary level of schooling. The most disappointing feature of the rural workforce is an excessively low percentage of educated workers, i.e., those with a background of secondary and higher level of schooling; (in common parlance, secondary level of schooling provides the dividing line between 'educated' and 'uneducated' workforce). It is indeed disgusting to see that, even around the turn of the new century, only 16.0 per cent of the rural male, just about 4.0 per cent of the rural female, and 12.5 per cent of the total rural workers could be categorised as 'educated workers'.

For each level of educational accomplishment, the urban workers are way ahead of their rural counterparts. Two implications stand out for the future of the rural economy and rural labour market. First, with the present stock of its uneducated or semi-educated workforce, especially the womenfolk among them, the rural economy cannot stand up to the challenges already unleashed and those soon to follow through globalisation and free trade regime. Second, the rural-urban hiatus in each aspect of employment, most markedly the capability for job aspirants to get onto more remunerative jobs through formal market channels, is bound to increase manifold, unless some extraordinary interventions are initiated in favour of the rural boys and girls, currently in their early teens or adolescence.

Table 9.4 also shows separate proportions of agricultural and non-agricultural workers, at each level of education. The markedly inferior educational background of agricultural against non-agricultural workers is yet another cause of worry, not only for those who are staying on in on-farm employment but also for the future of agriculture itself; gone are the days when agricultural production and exports could be sustained through the army of semi- or un-educated farm workers. Agricultural technology, especially the complicated nuances of the emerging bio-genetic regimes, production efficiency and cost, marketing techniques including the premium attached to timely information flows inside and outside the national frontiers and external bindings such as TRIPs and TRIMs, etc., are all going to be in the forefront of a decision matrix. The human capital in agriculture is going to be of as much critical significance as in other sectors. Rural India is clearly throwing up highly disturbing signals in this regard too.

Finally, Table 9.4 shows that the prospects for rural workers to walk into non-farm jobs improve as we move from low to higher levels of education. For example, while as many as 46.0 per cent of the illiterate rural males stay back in agriculture, not more than a quarter of them are accepted by non-agricultural sectors. The corresponding proportions for the rural female workers are 78.3 and 56.7, respectively. The secondary and higher level of schooling shows it impact much more clearly, for a switch-over from agriculture to non-agriculture. For example, not more than 12.0 per cent of the

TABLE 9.4: **Educational Background of Workers in the Indian Economy by Level of Schooling and Place of Residence**

Level of School Education	Rural Male			Rural Female			Rural Persons			Urban Male			Urban Female			Urban Persons		
	Agr.	Non-Agr.	Total	Agr.	Non-Agr.	Total	Agr.	Non-Agr.	Total	Agr.	Non-Agr.	Total	Agr.	Non-Agr.	Total	Agr.	Non-Agr.	Total
Not literate	46.2	25.8	40.3	78.3	56.7	74.9	56.9	31.6	50.6	38.2	14.9	16.4	78.2	38.1	44.0	51.0	18.7	21.2
Schooling upto primary level	27.5	28.1	27.7	14.6	21.5	15.7	23.2	26.9	24.1	25.7	22.0	22.2	14.9	18.3	17.8	22.2	21.4	21.5
Middle level Schooling	14.4	19.7	15.9	4.9	9.2	5.6	11.2	17.7	12.8	15.8	18.9	18.7	4.7	10.0	9.2	12.3	17.5	17.1
Secondary schooling and above	11.9	26.4	16.1	2.2	12.6	3.8	8.7	23.8	12.5	20.3	44.2	42.7	2.2	33.6	29.0	14.5	42.4	40.2

Source : Government of India, *Employment & Unemployment in India: 1999-2000,* Key Results, NSS 55th Round (July 1999-June 2000), NSSO, Dec. 2000: A37-A42.

'educated rural males' and just about 2.0 per cent of their female counterparts, stay back in agriculture; it is equally clear that more than a quarter of the 'educated rural males' and about 13.0 per cent of their female counterparts do get absorbed in one or the other type of non-agricultural job.

The above picture cannot, however, obliterate the fact that the proportion of educated rural workers (say, with secondary and higher levels of education) who cannot get out of agriculture is still very high (Table 9.5); 53.0 per cent of rural males and 48.0 per cent of rural females, having secondary and higher levels of schooling, are still 'accommodated' in agriculture, presumably because adequate non-farm avenues of employment are not forthcoming.

TABLE 9.5: **Percentage of Usual Status Farm and Non-Farm Rural Workers by Level of Schooling and Sex : 1987-88 and 1999-2000**

Level of School Education		Rural Male		Rural-Female		Rural Persons	
		Agr.	Non-Agr.	Agr.	Non-Agr.	Agr.	Non-Agr.
Illiterate	99-00	81.67	18.33	87.96	3.04	84.43	15.57
	87-88	81.40	18.60	86.70	13.30	84.68	15.32
Primary level schooling	99-00	70.80	29.20	78.23	21.77	72.21	27.79
	87-88	70.70	29.30	78.80	21.20	73.45	26.55
Middle level schooling	99-00	64.40	35.60	73.81	26.19	65.59	34.41
	87-88	66.20	33.80	82.10	17.90	70.65	29.35
Secondary level schooling and above	99-00	53.00	47.00	48.23	51.77	52.41	47.59
	87-88	50.50	49.50	48.50	51.50	50.05	40.95
All levels	99-00	71.40	28.60	85.40	14.60	76.3	23.70

Sources: 1. Government of India, *Sarvekshana*, Special Number, September 1990: S94-S96.

2. Government of India, *Employment & Unemployment in India:* 1999-2000, Key Results, NSS 55th Round (July 1999–June 2000), NSSO, Dec. 2000: A37- A42.

The vulnerability of rural workers surfaces more blatantly in respect of technical/professional education, the expanding network of these educational facilities during the post-Independence decades notwithstanding. For example, studies based on the 1993/94 NSS data show that the rural females are completely devoid of degrees in engineering/technology, medicine and agriculture; their position is nearly the same as regards diploma in these branches of learning (Chadha, 1999: 162-3). They have some share, *albeit* very small, in diploma in crafts and other miscellaneous vocations, which can at best help them compete in a second grade rural job market, scarcely with a prospect for expansion. The contrast between rural and urban females is a painful reading of the prevailing situation. The urban females have been steadily improving their position, practically in all technical/professional degrees/diplomas while their rural counterparts, in all age-groups, have had no noticeable improvement to report. In brief, the expanding network of technical/professional educational facilities in India has very largely bypassed rural females born some 20 years back or earlier; those born in more recent years are striving to gain a foothold in technical/professional education, yet their actual achievement, as recorded by the 1993/94 NSS data, is too trivial to catch anybody's eye (Chadha, 1999: 159).

Education and Training of Workers in Rural Industry

Let us now look through the evidence that we gathered ourselves during April-June 2000 through a survey of an assorted mix of tiny and small enterprises in rural and urban areas of three Indian states (West Bengal, Haryana and Maharashtra). Table 9.6 reveals a highly disappointing educational and training background of workers engaged in such industries. Hardly 39 per cent of rural and 42 per cent of urban workers engaged in such enterprises report having acquired matriculation or higher level of schooling; the rural percentage varies from (a ridiculously low level of) 13.0 in West Bengal to 47.0 in Maharashtra. On-the-job training was reported by as many as 80 per cent of the rural and 88 per cent of the urban workers; the rural percentage varies from 59.0 in West Bengal to 90.0 in Haryana. Just about 8 per cent of them in rural and about 5.5

TABLE 9.6: **Educational and Training Background of Workers Engaged in Tiny and Small Enterprises in India: April-June 2000 Survey**

State/Area		General Education				Technical Education				Training			
		Illiterate	Upto Matric*	Matric & Above	Total	ITI & Polytechnic	Engg.	MBA & Other	Total	On-the-Job	Family	Govt. Agency	Total
1	2	3	4	5	6	7	8	9	10	11	12	13	14
West Bengal													
Rural	No.	63	158	32	253	1	0	0	1	149	102	2	253
	%	24.9	62.5	12.6	100.0	0.4	0.0	0.0	0.4	58.9	40.3	0.8	100.0
Urban	No.	2	270	139	411	7	14	6	27	368	37	6	411
	%	0.5	65.7	33.8	100.0	1.7	3.4	1.5	6.6	89.5	9.0	1.5	100.0
Total	No.	65	428	171	664	8	14	6	28	517	139	8	664
	%	9.8	64.5	25.8	100.0	1.2	2.1	0.9	4.2	77.9	20.9	1.2	100.0
Haryana													
Rural	No.	17	181	151	349	23	11	3	37	313	8	28	349
	%	4.9	51.9	43.3	100.0	6.6	3.2	0.9	10.6	89.7	2.3	8.0	100.0
Urban	No.	16	142	88	246	20	8	5	33	216	0	30	246
	%	6.5	57.7	35.8	100.0	8.1	3.3	2.0	13.4	87.8	0.0	12.2	100.0
Total	No.	33	323	239	595	43	19	8	70	529	8	58	595
	%	6.8	51.7	41.6	100.0	7.2	3.2	1.3	11.8	88.9	1.3	9.7	100.0

(contd.)

TABLE 9.6 *(contd.)*

1	2	3	4	5	6	7	8	9	10	11	12	13	14
Maharasthra													
Rural	No.	75	224	268	567	37	14	5	56	467	41	59	567
	%	13.2	39.5	47.3	100.0	6.5	2.5	0.9	9.9	82.4	7.2	10.4	100.0
Urban	No.	21	78	151	250	9	4	1	14	214	22	14	250
	%	8.4	31.2	60.4	100.0	3.6	1.6	0.4	5.6	85.6	8.8	5.6	100.0
Total	No.	96	302	419	817	46	18	6	70	681	63	73	817
	%	11.8	37.0	51.3	100.0	5.6	2.2	0.7	8.6	83.4	7.7	8.9	100.0
All Three States													
Rural	No.	155	563	451	1169	61	25	8	94	929	151	89	1169
	%	13.3	48.2	38.6	100.0	5.2	2.1	0.7	8.0	79.5	12.9	7.6	100.0
Urban	No.	39	490	378	907	36	26	12	74	798	59	50	907
	%	4.3	54.0	41.7	100.0	4.0	2.9	1.3	8.2	88.0	6.5	5.5	100.0
Total	No.	194	1053	829	2076	97	51	20	168	1727	210	139	2076
	%	9.3	50.7	39.9	100.0	4.7	2.5	1.0	8:1	83.2	10.1	6.7	100.0

Notes: 1. Small-scale industrial units are defined as those employing workers ranging between 2 to 15, irrespective of the technology in use, nature of product produced and the range of market linkages reported; 2. * those with 10 years of schooling are defined as matriculates.

Source: Kokko, Ariere, Chen Jiyuan and G.K. Chadha, "Institutional and Technological Base of Rural Industrialisation in India and China", On-going Research Project, CSRD/SSS, JNU, New Delhi.

per cent of them in urban areas, received training through government agencies. This source of training for the rural workers is conspicuous by its absence in West Bengal while in the other two states also, it is only a marginal phenomenon. This lends itself to two different interpretations. First, most of the people receiving training from government technical training institutes do not opt to work in tiny and household type rural enterprises either because they do not see any future for themselves or else the technical capabilities acquired by them generally are of no avail to the simpler production and management requirements of such industries. On the other hand, the employers in such industries can easily catch hold of untrained and raw hands, pay them fairly low wages, and cause them to learn the 'basics of the craft' during the notional period of probation. Moreover, recruiting trained hands entails the prospect of losing them before long possibly because such workers are demanded elsewhere also besides having to pay them higher wages. Productivity is bound to suffer.

Technical education reveals the most distressing part of the story. For example, only 8 per cent of workers engaged in such industries, both in the rural and urban areas, have had the benefit of technical education; a substantial proportion (65 per cent of rural and 48 per cent of urban workers) of them nonetheless stopped at the level of an industrial training institute (ITI) or a polytechnic; workers with management degrees (e.g., MBA) were nearly conspicuous by their absence, both among the rural and urban enterprises. Our survey data also show that substantial differences do exist between family workers employing themselves in such enterprises and those hired from outside on wage-paid basis. The contrast between family and hired workers is most appalling in respect of training. It is even more gruesome when we see their rural-urban divide.

It is thus absolutely evident that a preponderant majority of the existing workforce engaged in the tiny and small industrial enterprises is hardly qualified to grapple with the managerial and technological challenges of free international trade. In the coming years, the rigour of competition that the rural enterprises would face vis-à-vis their urban counterparts as also under the unbridled influx of imported goods cannot be adequately answered with the educational, training and skill background of the existing lot of workers. In total terms, the picture is fairly gloomy.

Preparing for the Future

Is rural India preparing itself for the impending job market challenges? Unluckily, the answer seems to be a big 'No'. One can venture to answer this question in more ways than one. Perhaps, a critical scrutiny of the current status of attendance in educational institutions may capture the size, nature and the rural-urban break-up of the army of job seekers that would transcend the Indian labour market five or 10 years hence. The limitation of time and space would not permit us to do more than this.

Rural Job Aspirants in the Near Future

Table 9.7 throws up many depressing features, for rural people compared with their urban brethren, and for females contrasted to males. First, in each age-group, the proportion of rural people not attending any educational institution is much higher than that of their urban counterparts. Even as late as in 1999/2000, nearly one-third of rural children (age group five to nine years) do not go to school while for the corresponding urban children, the absenteeism does not touch more than 18 per cent of them. Again, the fact that nearly 28.0 per cent of the rural children (age group 10-14 years) do not go to school is a highly disconcerting feature inasmuch as this is the age at which they should ordinarily be pursuing at least middle level of schooling. Finally, around two-third of the rural children in the age group 15-19 years do not attend any educational institution; some of them never ever went to school while others might have dropped out at one stage or the other. In total terms, for each specified age group of children, the rural people are way behind their urban counterparts in terms of their status of attendance in educational institutions.

Second, the rural children, compared with their urban counterparts, in each age group, are late in reaching a given level of

TABLE 9.7: **Distribution of Persons (Age 5 Years and Above) by Status of Current Attendance in Educational Institutions for Different Age Groups in Rural and Urban India: 1999-2000**

Age Group (Years)	Current Status on Attending Educational Institutions	Rural Areas			Urban Areas		
		Male	Female	Persons	Male	Female	Persons
5- 9	Not attending school	29.2	37.1	32.8	16.1	19.0	17.5
	Pre-primary schooling	18.8	16.8	17.8	25.7	25.5	25.6
	Primary schooling	50.3	44.9	47.7	54.9	52.6	53.9
	Middle & higher levels	1.7	1.4	1.6	2.9	29.3	2.9
10-14	Not attending school	21.6	35.2	27.7	12.9	18.5	15.5
	Pre-primary to primary	36.2	30.2	33.3	30.3	27.3	28.9
	Middle level schooling	35.1	29.0	32.3	45.4	42.6	44.2
	Secondary & higher levels	7.1	5.7	6.4	11.1	11.6	11.4
15-19	Not attending school	56.0	73.4	63.5	41.1	48.0	44.2
	Pre-middle to middle levels	11.5	7.1	9.4	8.4	7.2	7.8
	Secondary to higher Secondary level	29.3	17.3	23.6	39.8	34.0	37.2
	Technical degree and diploma	3.0	2.2	2.6	10.4	10.9	10.7
20-24	Not attending school	89.3	96.1	93.0	76.6	83.1	79.7
	Pre-secondary to higher secondary	4.2	1.4	2.8	5.1	2.9	4.2
	Technical degree	4.6	1.7	3.1	12.8	10.1	12.0

Source: Government of India, NSS Report No. 458-1, May 2001: A119-A124.

schooling. For example, in the age group five to nine years, 54.0 per cent of urban children reach primary level of schooling against 48.0 per cent among the rural children; in the age group 10-14 years, 44 per cent of urban against 32.0 per cent of rural children reach middle level of schooling; the differences manifest themselves most conspicuously in respect of technical degrees/diplomas, especially when the adolescence is crossed over.

Third, the worst placed are the rural females, in terms of attending school or acquiring varying level of education, in each age group. It is a clear proof of their social handicap that nearly 73.4 per cent of the rural females (against 46.3 per cent of their urban sisters) have given up education by the time they enter the age-group 15-19 years; the handicap encompasses nearly the whole lot of rural females as soon as they move beyond their teens. They are the worst placed in respect of technical degrees/diplomas. Just about 2.2 per cent of rural females (age group 15-19 years) are engaged in such professional studies against as many as 11.0 per cent of the corresponding urban females. In the next age group (20-24 years), their relative position is far worse, for the simple reason that most parents, especially those in rural areas, would like their daughters to be married off, latest in their early twenties. To complete the story, technical qualifications for the rural females, confined as they are to a microscopic minority among them, do not go beyond diploma in (village!) crafts. The rural lasses may better be trained in tailoring, weaving, embroidery, stenotyping, or still better, trained in cooking and 'better child rearing'!

It is thus abundantly clear that the rural-urban gaps in respect of education and skills are tending to become sharper. And then within the rural areas, the girls are losing their ground to boys. There is absolutely no doubt that in the matter of 'schooling', which already is and is likely to become a sharper surrogate of 'human capital formation' in the years ahead, the rural females are getting the least attention. In other words, they are getting least prepared for education- and skill-intensive jobs and consequently, in the intensely competitive future job markets, they are bound to get a severe battering. In contrast, their urban sisters seem to be assiduously improving their stock of 'human capital' and preparing themselves well to compete with urban males.

Finally, to comprehend the existing realities in a somewhat unconventional, and admittedly approximate, manner, we look at the educational attainment of the present-day children, adolescents and the adults/youth among rural/urban males/females (Table 9.8).

Before we discuss Table 9.8, a few clarifications may be in order. First, for every age group, we have indicated a notionally expected range of educational achievement; this roughly takes care of the age differences among children in the same class. Second, for every two adjoining age groups, we have deliberately kept some overlap in respect of the notionally expected levels of educational attainments, once again to accommodate the reality of some children joining late. Third, the notionally expected ranges have been kept the same for rural and urban children as also for males and females; this enables us to see the rural-urban and the male-female gaps in a more telling manner. Finally, people benefiting through the non-formal channels of education (e.g., adult literacy programme) are included among those at the pre-primary stage of schooling.

Table 9.8 gives us adequate material to reiterate some of our earlier conclusions. First, the proportion of children, adolescents and the youth who are below the (notionally) expected level of educational attainment is uniformly the lowest among the rural females, followed by rural males, urban females and urban males; to put the record straight, while a substantial gap exists between the males and females in rural India, the male-female gaps are indeed very small in urban India. The male-female gap in rural India (better interpreted as discrimination against females) sets in right when the child reaches the school-going age (five to nine years), and keeps on widening itself as we go upto older children, adolescents and adults, and so on. In comparison, the proportion of urban females below the (notionally) expected level of educational attainment, is only a shade higher than that of their urban counterparts, in each age group. Happily, the gap shows no tendency to increase as we move up on the age group ladder. In one word, by and large, the urban girls and women are doggedly striving to stay close to urban boys and men, for all levels of education.

Second, the obverse side brings more distressing comparisons. The proportion of children, adolescents and the youth falling within the (notionally) expected range of educational attainment is the lowest for the rural females, next higher for rural males, followed upwards for urban females and urban males, for each age group or

TABLE 9.8: Distribution of Persons by Level of Educational Attainment for Different Age Groups, Separately for Rural and Urban Males/Females: 1999-2000

Category of Persons	Age Group (Years)	Notional Expected Range of Educational Attainment Specific to the Age Group	% Distribution of Persons in Terms of Actual Educational Attainment: Below the Notionally Expected Range	Amidst the Notionally Expected Range	Above the Notionally Expected Range	% of Persons Falling in Each Age Group
1	2	3	4	5	6	7
Rural	5-9	Pre-primary to primary	29.0(29.0)	69.0	2.0	13.7
Male	10-14	Primary to middle	28.0(21.6)	65.0	7.0	12.8
	15-19	Middle to secondary	58.0(56.0)	39.0	3.0	9.9
	20-24	Secondary & above	90.0(89.3)	10.0	-	7.8
	25-29	Professional degree	98.8(98.0)	1.2	-	7.5
Rural	5-9	Pre-primary to primary	37.0(37.)	62.0	1.0	12.9
Female	10-14	Primary to middle	39.5(35.2)	54.5	6.0	11.7
	15-19	Middle to secondary	75.0(73.4)	23.0	2.0	8.8
	20-24	Secondary & above	96.0(96.0)	4.0	-	8.6
	25-29	Professional degree	99.8(99.4)	0.2	-	8.4

(contd.)

TABLE 9.8 (*contd.*)

1	2	3	4	5	6	7
Rural	5- 9	Pre-primary to primary	32.8(32.8)	65.6	1.6	13.3
Persons	10-14	Primary to middle	33.0(27.9)	60.5	6.5	12.3
	15-19	Middle to secondary	65.9(63.9)	31.5	2.6	9.4
	20-24	Secondary & above	93.5(93.0)	6.5	-	8.1
	25-29	Professional degree	99.0(98.7)	1.0	-	7.9
Urban	5- 9	Pre-primary to primary	16.0(16.0)	81.0	3.0	10.9
Male	10-14	Primary to middle	17.4(12.9)	71.5	11.1	11.6
	15-19	Middle to secondary	42.5(41.1)	47.0	10.5	11.0
	20-24	Secondary & above	77.0(76.6)	23.0	-	9.6
	25-29	Professional degree	96.0(95.6)	4.0	-	8.5
Urban	5- 9	Pre-primary to primary	19.0(19.0)	78.0	3.0	10.9
Female	10-14	Primary to middle	23.0(18.4)	65.5	11.5	11.4
	15-19	Middle to secondary	49.2(48.8)	39.	11.0	10.2
	20-24	Secondary & above	84.0(83.1)	16.0	-	9.4
	25-29	Professional degree	98.7(98.2)	1.3	-	9.0

(*contd.*)

TABLE 9.8 *(contd.)*

1	2	3	4	5	6	7
Urban	5- 9	Pre-primary to primary	17.5(17.5)	79.5	3.0	10.9
Persons	10-14	Primary to middle	19.9(15.5)	68.7	11.4	11.5
	15-19	Middle to secondary	46.1(44.2)	43.2	10.7	10.7
	20-24	Secondary & above	80.3(79.7)	19.7	-	9.5
	25-29	Professional degree	97.6(96.9)	2.4	-	8.8

Notes: 1: Pre-primary comprises literates through NFEC/AEC, TLC, etc., plus children at pre-primary stage.

2: Secondary and higher level include higher secondary, graduates and postgraduates in agriculture,engg./technology, medicine, etc.

3: Professional degree means graduates and postgraduates in agriculture, engineering/technology, medicine, etc., and

4: In Column 4, the figure in parenthesis is the percentage of persons in the specified age group currently not attending any educational institution.

Source: Government of India, NSS Report No.458-1, May 2001: A1-A6 and A119-A124.

each range of educational attainment. It is rather frightening to see that just about 4.0 per cent of rural females (against 16.0 per cent for their urban counterparts) in the age group 20-24 years are within the expected range of educational attainment (secondary level schooling and above); the corresponding proportions for the rural and urban males are 10.0 per cent and 23.0 per cent, respectively. The rural females' attainment of professional degrees makes a shameful reading. In brief, the relative 'neglect' of rural areas, and within those areas, of females compared with the males, is very apparent.

Finally, the 'neglect' becomes all the more apparent if we look at the proportion of persons currently not attending any educational institution, in each age group (figures in parentheses under col.4, Table 9.8). In spite of the 'national effort', spanning over the past five decades, towards providing *universal primary education*, in 1993/94, no less than 37.0 per cent of rural females and 29.0 per cent of rural males, in the age group, five to nine years, were not going to school; in comparison, the position was much better in the urban areas. Admittedly, these are the people who will swell the ranks of labour market after about 10 years. We are bound to witness rural females, and to a lesser extent rural males, waging a losing battle in the future non-farm employment market largely because they would have no 'educational attainment' to support their case. Again, no less than 35.2 per cent of rural females and 21.6 per cent of rural males in the next higher age group, 10-14 years were not attending any educational institution; the corresponding proportions for the urban children being 18.4 per cent for females and 12.9 per cent for males. These people would join the labour market after about five years, making matters worse not only for themselves but also for those of their senior but illiterate and unskilled fellow job-aspirants. Yet again, about 73.0 per cent of rural females, in the most determinative age group 15-19 years ,against 56.0 per cent among rural males, 48.8 per cent among urban females and 41.0 per cent among urban males, were not attending any educational institution. Some of them had either completed their education and were currently out of school, while others may have never had gone to a school. In any case, this is the age group which must have released, by now, job-aspirants with 'educational qualifications' that will not let them have an easy foothold in the rural and urban job markets

Needed a Conscious Bias

The foregoing analysis delineates the relatively stronger and weaker partners in the future labour market; unquestionably, the rural job seekers in general, and their female counterparts in particular, seem to be getting highly marginalised in the matter of education, training and skill formation. Compared with their urban brothers and sisters, their relative inferiority five or 10 years hence in competing for education- and skill-intensive jobs is transparent, besides the numerous other infirmities usually inflicted on rural areas that they will continue to suffer from. Their Achilles' heel is no more a secret.

This is not to deny that India has achieved great strides in education, skill improvement and human capital formation. Again, the progress registered so far could be anybody's pride, especially because the state's involvement in these areas has been high and increasing; for example, (a) expenditure on education in India has increased remarkably and (b) its relative share in total government expenditure on education has also increased from less than 40 per cent at the time of transfer of power from colonial rulers to independent government in India to more than 85 per cent in the recent years (Tilak, 1997:2241).

But then, an increasing share of public expenditure on education does not automatically guarantee 'adequacy of investment in human beings'. As a proportion of GDP, we are spending far less than what is needed to (1) provide universal elementary education, (2) sustain expanding requirements of secondary and higher levels of education, and (3) improve the overall quality of education. Among 166 countries surveyed in 1995, India ranked 98th as regards the proportion of GDP spent on education (ibid: 2239). No wonder, therefore, even around the mid-1990s, India accounts for the largest number of illiterates in the world; we are still far away from the goal of providing free universal elementary education; enrolment ratio in higher education is still a meagre 5-6 per cent of the eligible age group population, and so on.

Is it too late for us to learn from our own past lapses? Is it difficult to draw upon the experiences of our east Asian neighbours and redefine our social investment priorities? We have abundance of human resources but their development has yet to catch up; a conscious and vigorous pro-human resource development bias is yet to come. Let the jingle of a few thousand highly lucrative jobs not muffle the meek aspirations of many million job-seekers in India.

Outside Concerns and Issues: Free Movement of Labour

We choose to make a brief mention of the most crucial issue on the external front. This is to plead for a free movement of labour. At all future forums, India should work for freer movement of labour across countries, just as globalisation through free trade in goods and free movement of capital are now accepted as being beneficial to all, under the open and transparent multilateral trade regime . India has already created a unique niche for itself in the high-skill and professional labour markets of the US, Germany, France, the UK, Finland and other countries. The pull factor is getting equally dominant for middle-level and low-end workers, such as accountants, architects, educationists, nurses, merchant seamen, airline stewardesses, cooks, carpenters, construction workers, not only in the Gulf but elsewhere also. In simple terms, free international movement of workers should become a part of the WTO provision rather than through bilateral agreements which are not only restrictive but wage-discriminatory as well. It is high time, therefore, that comprehensive pro-active policies should be evolved for leveraging India's unique strengths in this new area. Among other safeguards, it should be ensured that manpower export grows transparently, along legal channels and that our citizens working abroad do get the best consular services that they are entitled to from our embassies.

REFERENCES

Birdsall, N. et al. (1997), "Inequality and Growth Reconsidered: Lessons from East Asia", in F. Ackerman et al., (eds) *Human Wellbeing and Economic Goals*, Island Press, Washington DC.

Chadha, G.K. (1999), " Economic Reforms and Emerging Demand Supply Hiatus in India's Rural Labour Market", *Indian Economic Journal*, Conference Volume.

—— (2000), "Non-Farm Employment for India's Rural Households: Looking Ahead Through Recent Setbacks", mimeo.

—— (2001), " Impact of Economic Reforms on Rural Employment: No Smooth Sailing Anticipated", *Indian Journal of Agricultural Economics*, Conference Number, July-September.

Dhar, B. and S. Chaturvedi (1999), *WTO Agreements and Agricultural Sector: Implications and Options for India,* Research and Information System for the Non-Aligned and Other Developing Countries, New Delhi, October.

Dubashi, Jay (2000), "Is the Finance Minister Painting an Overly Optimistic Picture of the Economy", *The Sunday Times*, New Delhi, October 22.

EPW Research Foundation (2000), "Current Statistics", *Economic and Political Weekly,* Vol. 35, No. 30, July 22-28.

FISME (1999), Federation of Indian Micro and Small and Medium Enterprises, *A Brief Guide to the WTO for Small Businesses*, New Delhi.

FICCI (2000), Seminar on "Impact and Implications of WTO on SSI Sector", Federation of Chambers of Commerce and Industry, New Delhi, March 1.

Government of India (1980, 1990 and 1998), *Economic Census*, CSO, New Delhi.

—— (1999-2000), *Economic Survey,* Ministry of Finance, New Delhi.

—— (1997), *Employment and Unemployment in India, 1993-94,* NSS 50th Round (July 1993-June 1994), NSSO, Report No. 409 , New Delhi, March.

—— (1985), *Seventh Five Year Plan 1985-1990*, Planning Commission, New Delhi, October.

—— (1991), *Census of India*, "Provisional Population Totals, Workers and their Distribution", Paper 3, Census Commission.

Gulati, A. and S. Narayan (1999), " Indian Agriculture in the Global Economy: What Should India Negotiate in Seattle and Why?", *Focus WTO*, Indian Institute of Foreign Trade, New Delhi, September.

Haan, H.H. de (1980), "Rural Industrialisation in India", Discussion Paper No. 54, Erasmus University, Rotterdam, September.

Kokko, Ariere et al. (2000), "Institutional and Technological Base of Rural Industrialisation in India and China: An On-going Research Project", CSRD-SSS, Jawaharlal Nehru University, New Delhi.

Kwa, A. (1998), "In Focus: WTO and Developing Countries", *Foreign Policy in Focus: WTO and Developing Countries*, Vol. 3., No. 37, November.

Panchamukhi, V.R. (2000), "Trade, Technology and Employment: Profile of Systematic Dilemmas and Paradoxes", *The Indian Journal of Labour Economics*, Vol. 34, No. 1., pp. 59-94, Jan-March.

Reddy, C.R. (2000), "WTO Stirs Again", *The Hindu*, May 11.

RBI (1999), *Handbook of Statistics on Indian Economy.*

Sundaram, K. (2001), "Employment and Poverty in India in the Nineteen Nineties: Further Results from NSS 55th Round *Employment-Unemployment Survey, 1999-2000*", Paper Presented at the International

Seminar on "Understanding Socio-Economic Changes through National Sample Surveys", organised by NSSO at New Delhi, May 12-13.

Tilak, J.B.G. (1997), "Five Decades of World Trade Organisation of Under-investment in Education", *Economic and Political Weekly*, September 6.

WTO (1999), *Statement on India's Position in WTO*, by Murasoli Maran, India's Commerce Minister, WTO's Ministerial Conference, Seattle, Nov. 30-Dec. 3.

WTO (1998), *Trade Policy Review – India*, World Trade Organisation.

10

WTO, GLOBALISATION AND INDUSTRIAL SECTOR: The Case of Market Access

RAJESH MEHTA

The different rounds of General Agreement on Tariff and Trade (GATT)/ World Trade Organisation (WTO) system have led to increase in market access of industrial goods. This is being carried out by the trade liberalisation process, including removal of quantitative restrictions (QRs) and providing tariff (custom) cuts on a large number of commodities by different countries across the world. At present, almost all the commodities of developed countries are bound and the level of average tariff rate is very low (around 5 per cent). In the Uruguay Round (UR), developing countries like India had taken part in negotiations on trade liberalisation in a comprehensive way. These countries are now committed to reduce the tariff rates for a large number of commodities/lines. As a result, a number of tariff bindings for industrial products of developing countries have increased from 13 per cent to 61 per cent. In the pre-Uruguay Round, India had bound tariff rates for around 6 per cent of its tariff lines. It had agreed to increase the number of lines with bound rates to 67 per cent in the UR.

India was opposed to the inclusion of "market access of industrial sector" in any forthcoming (if any) new round of WTO negotiations.[1] India had probably taken this stand because the average level of developed countries' tariff rate is low.[2] It was presumed by India that the inclusion of industrial tariffs in the new round (of WTO) would not increase market access for India, because the further reduction in tariff rates of developed countries can not be substantial. On the other hand, India may have to give market access to its trading partners by significantly cutting down further its tariff rates and spread of tariff bindings.

Although the Seattle meeting of the WTO collapsed and consequently the agenda for a new round could not be adopted, still significant progress was made on a number of issues. At present, there seems to be some change in India's stand on the inclusion of industrial products in the forthcoming multilateral negotiations.[3] A number of issues arise in this context. Should the negotiations be comprehensive? Which issues such as tariff bindings, tariff reduction, peak tariffs, tariff escalation and elimination of non-tariff barriers (NTBs) should be covered in the new round of negotiations? What modalities should be used for the conduct of the negotiations such as request/offer, formulae, sector-specific? The objective of this paper is limited. It analyses some issues concerned with India's trade liberalisation—in the context of strategies and options for a new round of multilateral trade negotiations—such as tariff peaks, tariff escalation and NTBs. It also summarises a review of India's commitments made in the Uruguay Round, the present state of its trade policy and the process of trade liberalisation initiated by it since the early 1990s. The paper reiterates the challenges arising out of globalisation and tries to suggest possible policy options and strategies available to India, if a new round of multilateral negotiations is started in future.

The paper is divided in five sections. Section one gives the present position of India's trade policy and process of trade liberalisation set in since the early 1990s. The next section gives a review of the commitments made in the Uruguay Round by the member-countries, particularly India. Section three deals with major issues of market access in forthcoming negotiations of the WTO, such as tariff peaks, tariff escalation, non-tariff barriers and problems of customs duties which are defined in the form of specific rates. Section four summarises the possible policy options and strategies available to India, in the context of the forthcoming negotiation of a multilateral trading system. The paper concludes with a summary.

Trade Liberalisation of Indian Industries

The main objective of this section is to observe the changes in the estimates of India's level of protection with respect to the tariff structure and quantitative restrictions (QRs) in the 1990s. For the purpose of quantifying the changes in the protection owing to import customs duty, emphasis has been given to the 'nominal rate of protection' measure. Estimates have been carried out by using Most Favoured Nation (MFN) tariff rates as are announced by the Government of India from time to time. The average values of MFN tariff rates have been worked out for the total economy. These values have been calculated by using the weights, based on the value of imports at six-digit HS. The weights have been calculated at six-digit HS, because the MFN import duty rates are available at HS six-digit level.

The Government of India levies different types of customs duties on goods imported into India, mainly: the Basic Customs Duty (BCD) and Additional Customs Duty (ACD). The basic duty rates are also known as the scheduled rates of basic customs duty. Earlier an auxiliary customs duty was announced every year along with the Union Budget. But in the year 1993/94 the auxiliary duty was merged with the basic customs duty, Presently there are two categories of scheduled rates: the standard rate (called MFN rate in literature) and the preferential rate. The preferential rate is applicable to preferential areas which are announced through separate notifications and are generally governed by specific (e.g., regional, bilateral, etc.,) agreements. The standard rates of basic customs duty are generally *ad valorem*. The Government of India has not announced *ad valorem* tariff rates for select products, but a specific amount (in Rs.) of customs duty per unit of quantity imported (in addition to the absence of *ad valorem* tariff rates). The standard rates are also called Most Favoured Nation (or MFN) rates.

In order to raise revenue, in the Budget of 1996/97, a Special Customs Duty (SCD) rate of 2 per cent was announced (in addition to other duties), for all products whose basic duty rate was not zero. This rate of special import duty was also increased to 5 per cent in 1997/98 to meet the revenue deficit. The special import duty was valid till March 1999. In the Budget of 1998/99, a Special Additional Duty of Customs (SADC) of 4 per cent (in addition to earlier announced categories of import duties) was announced with the objective of offsetting the sales tax on domestic goods. However, the effect of this SADC will be actually more than 4 per cent, because the SADC is calculated at aggregate value of imports, the basic duty, the special duty and the additional duty. In the Budget 1999/2000, a surcharge of 10 per cent on BCD was also announced.

The Union Budget for 2001/02 has done away with the surcharge of 10 per cent on basic customs duty. This will lead to simplification as well as a slight decline in the peak rate of customs duties. However, the basic customs duties have been changed only for a few commodities. Most of these changes are for agricultural commodities. This is being done with the objective of providing protection to Indian agriculture, keeping in view the removal of QRs on many consumer goods, including agricultural products from April 1, 2001. Customs duties on some raw material and intermediate goods have been reduced to make corrections for the anomaly in the tariff rates for final products. The Budget once again reconfirms the trade liberalisation policy regime by indicating clearly that the levels of India's tariff rates will be brought down to those of East Asian economies. It has also been announced that the number of customs duty rates will be brought to the minimum, and the peak duty rate too will come down to 20 per cent.

The standard rates of duty specified in the customs schedules, however, do not determine the actual duty rates applicable on different goods. The actual applicable customs duty rates, called the effective duty rates, are determined by the BCD, ACD, SCD or surcharge, SADC and various exemption notifications issued by the government. The additional duty of customs (ADC) equals the excise duty on the similar articles produced in India. The additional duty is calculated as the percentage of the aggregate of the c.i.f. value of imports and the basic duties (if applicable). Again, the additional duty is subject to various exemptions, notified from time to time. In this section (unless mentioned otherwise) we have not incorporated the additional customs duty while calculating the average rates because their protective effects are offset by the excise duty on domestic goods.

TABLE 10.1: **Import-weighted Average MFN Tariff Rates of Indian Economy, 1993-94 to 2001-02**

Year	Average MFN Tariff Rate[1]		Collection Rates[3]	Peak Tariff[4]
	Simple Avg.	Import-weighted[2]	Gross	
1993-94	83.00	82.76	31	85
1994-95	61.58	56.65	30.17	65
1995-96	48.83	44.75	29.45	50
1996-97	39.26	32.7	31.32	42
1997-98	35.12	30.91	29.29	45
1998-99	35.25	30.3	22.8	45
1999-00	35.54	29.81	23.67	44
2000-01	34.62	31.15	21.29[5]	38.5
2001-02	32.27	28.92	-	35

Notes: In some select products, the import custom duties are defined in the form of specific duties, we have tried to convert these specific duties into *ad valorem* equivalence using appropriate method.

1. Based on Basic Custom Duty (BCD) + Special Customs Duty (SCD) or Surcharge of products defined at six-digit HS level. It does not take into consideration specific exemptions of select products. The rate of SCD was 2 per cent for the year 1996-97, and (2+3=)5 per cent for the years 1997-98 and 1998-99. The surcharge of 10 per cent was imposed during 1999-00 and 2000-01.
2. Import Weights are based on the value of imports (in Rs.) during the same year, at six-digit ITC-HS classification. For 1997-98 to 2001-02, Import weights are based on the values of the imports for the year 1996-97.
3. Based on the Value of Custom Revenue (based on all types of duties on import) Collected/Value of total imports, from different volumes of G.O.I., Budget Documents, and DGCIS.
4. Excluding some products, whose custom duty is in the range of "Mega-tariff".
5. Based on Revised Estimate in Budget document, and assuming increase in total imports of 14.2 per cent during 2000-01.

Sources: Adopted from B.N. Goldar and R. Mehta (2001), "The Budget and Custom Duties", *Economic and Political Weekly*, pp. 989-991.

1. G.O.I., D.G.C.I.&S, *Monthly Statistics of Foreign Trade of India, Vol. II (Imports)*, various issues.
2. G.O.I., *Custom Tariff of India*, various issues.
3. G.O.I., *Budget Documents*, various issues.

In Table 10.1 we summarise some select indicators of India's tariff liberalisation for 1993/94 to 2001/02: import weighted average MFN tariff rate, simple average, MFN tariff rate, collection and peak rate. In calculating the import-weighted average MFN tariff rates, the weights are based on the value of imports for respective years and in calculating the average MFN tariff rates for 1997/98 onwards, the weights are based on the value of imports for 1996/97.

One can notice from this table that the average rate of MFN customs tariff has been declining since the adoption of the reform process in early 1990s. The average MFN customs duty rate has declined consistently and significantly from the level of more than 80 per cent in early 1990s to 30 per cent in the mid-1990s (Table 10.3). However, there has been no significant change in India's average custom tariff rates from 1997/98 onward, including the average rate for 2001/02, based on the proposals made in the present Budget. The decline in import-weighted average customs rates was almost negligible during 1998/99 and 1999/2000. In fact, the average tariff rate has increased slightly during 2000/01. The tariff changes proposed in the Budget of 2001/02 will lead to a marginal decline in import-weighted average customs tariff rate from 31.1 per cent in 2000/01 to 28.9 per cent in the coming financial year. It is likely that the average tariff rate will be more than 28.9 per cent because the tariff rates of some commodities (particularly agricultural products) may be enhanced in the coming financial year.

There has also been a decline in the peak tariff[4] of Indian customs duty rates in the early and mid-1990s. It declined significantly from more than 100 per cent during early 1990s to around 42 per cent in 1996/97. However, there has been no significant change in the peak tariff rates during the last four years as well as in the proposals made in the present Budget of 2001/02. Going by these trends, it seems that India will have to accelerate its process of tariff liberalisation so that it reaches the peak tariff of 20 per cent in the next three years, as announced in the Budget of 2001/02. To bring the level of India's customs tariff to that of East Asian countries, and keeping in view the long run objectives, a medium-term strategy needs to be worked out. East Asian economies have been reducing their tariff rates significantly. The average rate of Common External

Preferential Tariff (CEPT) of select countries of East Asia[5] was 3.64 per cent in 2000. It is expected that the tariff rates of these countries will come down further in the next three years. The CEPT average tariff of ASEAN-6 is expected to be around 2.4 per cent in 2003.

The customs tariffs will become the crucial trade policy instrument after the removal of The Indian Quantitative Restrictions (QR) regime. The present Budget proposal also acknowledges this fact. The following paragraphs summarise the present state of India's position on QRs for imports.

In the pre-reform period, India's trade policy was complex and cumbersome. There were different types of import licenses, alternate ways of importing, different categories of importers, etc. Imports of almost all commodities and goods, except especially permitted (sometime called commodities under Open General License), were restricted and they could be imported against a license. The items that can be imported under the open general licenses are sometimes called 'Free'. In the pre-reform period, the total number of goods and commodities falling under the open general license category was less than 10 per cent of importable commodities.

In the post-reform period, the coverage of open general license has been enhanced. Table 10.2 gives the number of items/lines which have been categorised under open general license or 'Free' from 1995/96 to 2001/02. One can notice from this table that India has been consistently removing its quantative restrictions (QRs) for the last couple of years. Although the dismantling of the QRs was started by India on a unilateral basis during the mid 1990s, most of the QR removals during 1997-2001 were due to dispute settlement proceedings of the WTO. In this context, it should be remembered that the reduction in tariff rates was started in the early 1990s on a unilateral basis, there has been no significant decline in India's applied rates after their level was brought close to the bound levels for industrial products. The following section gives a brief outline of India's tariff commitments in the GATT/WTO.

GATT/WTO Commitments in Industrial Sector

In the different rounds of the GATT/WTO, including the UR, a

TABLE 10.2: **India's Imports Subject to QRs, 1995-2001**

Year	Number of Lines which are Free (as % of total number of lines*)
April 1995	56.00
April 1997	65.80
April 1998	70.20
April 2000	86.41
April 2001	94.37

Note : * At 8 or 10-digit HS level.

Sources: 1. R. Mehta (1997), 'Trade Policy Reforms, 1991-92 to 1995-96: Their Impact on External Trade', *Economic and Political Weekly*, April 1997, pp. 779-784.

2. —— (1999), *Tariff and Non-Tariff Barriers of Indian Economy: A Profile*, RIS.

3. —— (2000), "Removal of QRs and Impact on India's Import", *Economic and Political Weekly*, Vol. XXXV, No. 19, May 2000.

4. B.N. Goldar and R. Mehta (2001), "The Budget and Customs Duties", *Economic and Political Weekly*, Vol. XXXVI, No. 12, March 2001.

number of steps were taken to enhance market access in a large number of industrial products. This is being carried out by providing tariff liberalisation for a large number of commodities/items. In this context, it needs to be remembered that member countries have to remove all types of prohibitions and quantitative restrictions, as per commitments made in different rounds. The multilateral trading arrangements not only provide a platform for increase in market access, but also give security through different provisions such as tariff binding, comprehensive rules and provisions for dispute settlement mechanism, etc. In the Uruguay Round the spread and frequency of tariff bindings and tariff cuts were large, as compared to the commitments made in the earlier rounds.

Owing to the tariff commitments in the UR, the average tariff rate of industrial products imported by developed countries from all sources will reduce by 40 per cent, i.e., from the average level of 6.3 per cent in pre-UR period, to 3.8 per cent in the post-UR period. The reduction in the average tariff rate of developed countries, imports from developing countries and least developed countries (LDCs) was relatively on the lower side—the respective declines being 37 per cent and 25 per cent (Table 10.3). This was mostly due to lower rates of tariff cuts in some sectors like textile and clothing (22 per cent), and fish and fish products (26 per cent). Developed countries import a significant proportion of these sectors from developing countries.

TABLE 10.3: **Tariff Reductions on Industrial Products by Developed Countries from Different Groups of Countries**

(percentages)

Import from:	Trade-weighted Tariff Average		Percentage Reduction
	Pre-UR	Post-UR	
All countries	6.3	3.8	40
Developing economies (other than least developed economies)	6.8	4.3	37
Least developed economies	6.8	5.1	25

Source: WTO, Uruguay Round, "Market-Access for Industrial Products", www.wto.org.

The UR commitment will lead to significant increase in duty-free imports on a significant number of lines by developed countries from all sources. Once the UR is fully implemented, the number of tariff lines subject to zero duty for developed countries will increase from 21 per cent in the pre-UR period to 32 per cent in the post-UR period. The frequency distribution of national lines by different ranges of tariff rates in the pre-UR and post-UR periods is given in Figure 10.1.

In the UR commitments, different procedures were adopted for changes in tariff rates. Most of the countries opted for a mixture of tariff reductions and ceiling bindings, while some countries such as India, Korea and Singapore have offered tariff reductions and no ceiling bindings. India agreed to reduce its average tariff rate from 71.4 per cent to 32.4 per cent, Korea from 18 per cent to 8 per cent, Brazil from 40 per cent to 27 per cent. The trade-weighted average

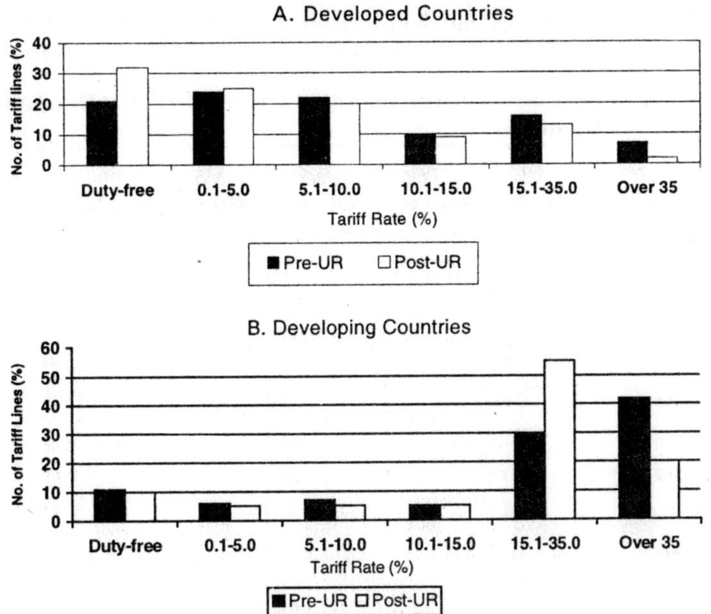

Fig. 10.1: **Frequency Distribution of Tariff Lines (Pre- and Post -UR)**

tariff rates of some selected countries in the pre-UR and the post-UR (due to tariff bindings in the UR) are given in Table 10.4. The table also gives the average of applied tariff rates for 1998. One can notice from this table that the average rate of applied tariff is significantly lower than the corresponding average bound rate for a large number of developing countries. This is mostly due to the unilateral liberalisation process adopted by these developing countries.

The UR has led to increase in security of market access by increase in frequency of tariff bindings. The developed countries have increased the number of bound tariff lines from 78 per cent in the pre-UR period to 99 per cent in the post-UR period. The developing countries have also significantly increased the number of committed lines from the level of 21 per cent to 73 per cent. As a result, the number of tariff bindings for industrial products of developing countries has increased from 13 per cent to 61 per cent. In the pre-UR period, India had bound tariff rates for around six per cent of its tariff lines. India has agreed to increase the bound rates for 67 per cent of tariff lines in the UR. As a result of this binding, 62 per cent lines of India's industrial sector have become bound.

TABLE 10.4: **Tariff Reduction on Industrial Products by Select Developing Countries**

	Trade-weighted Tariff Averages**		
Country	Pre-Uruguay*	Post-Uruguay*	Applied, 1998
Argentina	38.2	30.9	15.6
Brazil	40.6	27.0	16.3
Chile	34.9	24.9	11.0
Colombia	44.3	35.1	11.6
India	71.4	32.4	30.3
Indonesia	20.4	36.9	11.6[1]
Korea Rep.	18.0	8.3	7.5[1]
Malaysia	10.2	9.1	8.6[2]
Philippines	23.9	22.2	9.3
Sri Lanka	28.6	28.1	17.9[2]
Thailand	37.3	28.0	18.0[3]
Venezuela	50.0	30.9	11.8

Notes : * Pre- and Post-Uruguay Round tariff averages are computed as the trade weighted average of tariff rates on bound lines and applied tariff rates on unbound rates. Due to the significance of ceiling bindings in post Uruguay Round tariff averages, no reductions are reported. It excludes petroleum sector.

** HS Chapters: 25-97

1. for the year 1997
2. for the year 1995

Sources : 1. WTO

2. UNCTAD, *Trade Analysis and Information System*, Winter 1998-99.
3. R. Mehta, *Tariff and Non-Tariff Barriers of Indian Economy: A Profile*, RIS, 1999.

In the UR, India agreed to reduce tariff rates for 2701 commodity groups at six-digit HS-level[6] for industrial sector. The tariff commitments for all commodities were made in terms of *ad valorem* rates except for two commodities of the agriculture sector whose bound rates are committed in the form of a specific amount (Rs./kg.). The detailed list of the bound rates of committed lines is given in the WTO *India Schedule-II, 1994*[7]. A large number of industrial commodities, whose tariff bindings have been committed in the UR, belong to the sectors like machinery, chemicals, iron and steel, etc. A comparison of the levels of MFN applied tariff rates in 2000/01 and corresponding UR final bound rates (to be committed by March 2000) shows that India has not only maintained the levels of UR final bound rates, but has also reduced the levels of applied rates for a large number of products that are committed in the UR[8]. Although the level of applied tariffs is lower than (or equal to) the corresponding bound rates, the difference seems to be negligible. One can notice from Table 10.4 that India is committed to reduce tariff rates to 32.4 per cent (average) for industrial products, and India's applied MFN rates have been hovering around 32.7 per cent in 1996/97 to 28.9 in 2001/02.

In the GATT, it had been decided to have all types of QRs removed. India had also agreed to phase out its QRs on all commodities, except for around 600 commodities/lines for reasons related to security, etc., under Articles XX and XXI of the UR agreement. However, India maintained QRs on imports of some more items under provisions of Article XVIII:B of the Uruguay Round Agreement. This article recognises that member countries, whose economies can only support a lower standard of living and are in the earlier stages of development, may apply quantitative restrictions for their balance of payments (BoP) position. The article relating to BoP mentions that a member country has to announce publicly a time-schedule for elimination of QRs. Keeping this factor in view, the US filed a dispute against India. A panel was constituted in November 1997 to examine the US allegation that the continued maintenance of QRs on India's imports was inconsistent with India's obligations under the WTO agreement. In a report of the Appellate body of WTO[9] it is recommended that Indian quantitative restrictions are inconsistent with articles of the GATT. Keeping this factor in view, India and the US signed a mutual agreement[10] on December 28, 1999, which ended the dispute between the two countries on the earlier phase out of QRs. In this agreement, India had agreed to lift the QRs for all the items (i.e., 1429 lines at six-digit HS level), by March 31, 2001. Out of these 1429 items, the QR of 714 items were removed on April 1, 2000, while the QRs of the remaining items have been removed on April 1, 2001.

A recent study[11] has attempted to estimate the likely increase in India's import demand, owing to removal of QRs under the Indo-US agreement. It is expected that India's import demand will increase by 8.7 per cent, if no appropriate steps (like increase in tariff rate, imposition of NTBs) are taken. The study also shows that India's imports are likely to shoot up in commodity groups like vehicles other than railway, chemical fertilisers, plastic and plastic products, cereal products, electric plant and machinery, natural and cultured pearls; other vegetable textile fibres; coffee, tea and spices, paper and paperboard, man-made filaments and rubber and rubber products.

The items whose QR will be removed for BoP reasons can be categorised into two groups: (i) Those whose tariff rates have been bound in the GATT, and (ii) Those whose tariff rates are unbound. It has been noticed that a large number of these items are not bound in the multilateral negotiations. Further, the present levels of tariff rates of the items, whose QRs will be removed, are lower than the corresponding Uruguay Round bound rates for a significant number of committed items. In future multilateral negotiations for market access (including tariff rates) of the industrial sector, India should take into consideration the above discussed factors and various other characteristics of the industry. It should also identify the list of sensitive products and keep appropriate cushions to protect the domestic industry.

Trade Liberalisation in Forthcoming Negotiations: Issues for India

Specific Tariffs vis-à-vis ad valorem Tariff Rates

A large number of India's major trading partners are used to the practice of imposing specific duties rather than *ad valorem* rates. In most cases, specific custom duties[12] consist of one single specific tariff. However, many are mixed and complex, consisting of several specific and *ad valorem* tariffs associated with a condition of relationships between them. There are many variants of specific duties in the schedules of different countries. Different forms of specific duties are: (i) addition or subtraction of specific and/or *ad valorem* tariffs; (ii) choice between specific and/or *ad valorem* tariffs; (iii) choice between specific and/or *ad valorem* tariffs subject to upper and/or lower limits; (iv) unspecified variable tariffs; (v) two or more tariffs specified but without indication of what condition to apply, and (vi) tariff element applicable to input content. Some of these variants are very complex. For example, Japan defines the specific rate for 'groundnut not roasted' (HS 120910010) as "70 yens per kilogram + 7 yen for every 1 per cent exceeding 10 per cent by weight of lactose content". It is very difficult to calculate the effective rate of duties of such cases[13].

Specific duties are generally imposed to avoid customs valuation of imported quantity. It has been noticed that developed countries have imposed specific duties on a large number of commodities as compared to the number by developing countries. Although most of the countries believe that specific duties should be replaced by *ad valorem* rates, no decision was made in the UR. In fact, a significant number of UR bound rates have also been committed in the form of specific duties. There was no mention about this in the draft declaration of the Seattle meeting. It has been noticed that these specific duties conceal the fact that countries are indirectly imposing high tariffs without explicitly mentioning them in different forums.

The total number of commodities for which customs duties are given in the form of specific duties, is very large for countries like the EU (1780 lines), the US (1455 lines), as shown in Table 10.5. The Table clearly shows that 12 per cent of the EU's national lines (or commodities) were subject to specific duties in 1998. Similarly, 14 per cent of the national lines of the US were subject to specific duties in the same year. In India, the total number of lines with specific duties is very small. In the Indian Union Budget of 1999-2000, only 11 lines (out of the total 5113 lines) were subject to specific duties.

Specific duties are not suitable for analytical and comparative purposes, and require more common *ad valorem* tariffs. Hence, these specific duties are converted to *ad valorem* equivalence[14].

TABLE 10.5: **Number of Tariff Lines Subject to Specific Customs Duty by Select Countries, 1998**

Country	Number of Tariff Lines		Subject to Specific Tariff		% of Lines Subject to Specific Tariff	
	Total	HS 25-97	Total	HS 25-97	Total	HS 25-97 (%)
Australia	5817	5083	49	18	0.84	0.35
Brazil	9272	8354	0	0	0.00	0.00
Canada	8022	6639	229	8	2.85	0.12
EU	14251	10208	1780	77	12.49	0.75
India	5114	4410	11	9	0.22	0.20
Japan	9102	7158	469	92	5.15	1.28
Korea	10851	9207	20	20	0.18	0.21
Malaysia	8593	7341	55	41	0.64	0.55
New Zealand	7244	6207	257	246	3.55	3.96
US	10191	8340	1455	697	14.28	8.35

Sources: 1. UNCTAD, ibid., Winter 1998-99.
2. G. O. I., *Customs Tariff,* 1999-2000.

A study by UNCTAD has computed *ad valorem* equivalence of specific tariffs for 18000 commodities (of different countries) for the year 1996. It shows that the *ad valorem* equivalence of a large number of products, whose customs duties are defined in the form of specific tariffs in national custom tariff schedules, is very high. It also shows that a large number of these products belong to the agriculture sector. However, the study also identifies significant numbers of industrial commodities (of HS 25-97) whose *ad valorem* equivalence is more than 25 per cent. In the Japanese schedule, there were 76 national lines (of HS 25-97) whose *ad valorem* equivalent is more than 25 per cent but their customs duty is defined in terms of specific tariffs. The corresponding numbers for Australia, Malaysia, New Zealand, the EU and the US are 14, 47, 162, 14 and 136, respectively.

The customs tariff database of the US for August 1999[15] also proves the above-mentioned observation. In this database, the US defines specific duties for around 600 industrial commodities (national lines) and provides the corresponding *ad valorem* equivalent rates of most of the specific duties. It has been noticed that a large number of these items, whose customs duty is defined in the form of specific rate, have relatively higher tariff rates (as compared to other commodities), and belong to sectors like textile and textile products, footwear, etc. For example, *ad valorem* equivalent of customs duties of 'footwear with outer soles of rubber/plastic and upper of textile' is 58.8 per cent. Based on this detailed tariff information, we calculated simple average tariff rates of industrial products (HS 25-97) for two different categories of national lines: (i) those whose tariff is defined in the form of *ad valorem* rates, and (ii) those whose tariff has been defined in the form of specific duties. The estimated average (simple) rate of commodities, whose customs duty is defined in the form of *ad valorem* rates, comes to 3.9 per cent while the average *ad valorem* tariff equivalence of commodities whose customs duty is defined in the form of specific duties, comes to 11.4 per cent. This shows that the average tariff rate of commodities with specific duties is almost three times higher than the average tariff rate of the commodities whose customs duties are defined in the form of *ad valorem* rates.

Tariff Peaks

The recent statistics of customs duties show that the average tariff rates of different countries have declined. However, it has been noticed that the problem of high tariffs is still prevalent in certain sectors. These high tariffs are generally noticed in developed countries. The unusually high tariffs in the frequency distributions of tariff rates are called 'peak tariffs' in literature. Even if all the tariff commitments of the UR are implemented, peak tariffs seem to be a major hurdle in the market access of certain sectors. In this section, we analyse tariff peaks of certain developed countries, and identify different sectors where the tariff peaks are prevalent for a significant number of commodities. It is generally said that the reduction in peak tariff rates is one of the important issues for enhancing market access. In this context, it should be noticed that the tariff commitments in UR may lead to: (i) increase in the number of national lines with zero duty, and (ii) decrease in the number of lines with tariff rates exceeding an upper limit (see figure 10.1).

In most of the literature[16] a cut-off point has generally carried out the identification of commodities with peak tariffs. The level of the cut-off point is generally taken as 12 per cent (and sometimes 10 per cent or 15 per cent). All those commodities whose tariff rate is more than 12 per cent *ad valorem* rate, are called commodities with peak tariffs. In this existing literature the selection of a cut-off point is arbitrary and has no relation with average tariff. Although this method is simple, it has a number of disadvantages such as (i) no distinction is made between different levels of peak tariffs, and (ii) no distinction is made between different groups of countries (developed, developing, and least developed countries).

In a recent study, Mehta and Mohanty (1999) have suggested a method which is based on the upper limit of confidence interval of statistical distribution of tariff rates. In this method, the levels of peak tariffs are identified on the basis of a statistical formula[17]. This method is not simple and levels of cut-off points for identification of commodities with peak tariff vary from country to country. But it does have a number of advantages. It takes into consideration (i) average rates of tariffs, (ii) a proper measure of dispersion, (iii) tariff rates of all the national lines of a country (or commodity group), and (iv) difference between the average tariff rates and the level of tariff rates of each line.

In this context, it should be remembered that tariff negotiations in the multilateral rounds take into consideration the level of average tariff rates, present level of applied rates and depth of tariff cuts. But little emphasis is placed on tariff peaks.

In the existing literature, a number of attempts have been made to identify the commodities with peak tariffs. A study by the UNCTAD[18] has identified the commodities from different sectors (of eight countries) which are subject to peak tariffs. The identification has been carried out by taking into consideration the MFN tariffs/GSP[19] tariffs (whichever are applicable). Based on the findings of eight countries, the study concludes that, "both frequency and levels of tariff peak rates remain a matter of concern. Over 10 per cent of the tariff universe of the Quad countries, corresponding to an aggregate of 4,000-tariff lines, will continue to exceed 12 per cent *ad valorem*. All four countries maintain high variance in tariff rates. One-fifth of the peak tariffs of the US, one quarter of those of EU and Japan, and about one-tenth of those of Canada exceed 30 per cent. In the four selected developing countries, tariff peaks are more frequent but reach less extreme rates than in the major developed countries". This study also identifies a number of sectors with peak tariffs. Tariff peaks are largely prevalent in textile, clothing, footwear, leather and leather goods, automobile, other transport equipment and electronics. Summary results of the frequency of peak tariffs on exports from developing countries for the industrial sector (HS 25-97) are given in the Annexure.

Mehta and Mohanty[20] have shown that the problem of peak tariffs is still prevailing in major trading partners of India, i.e., the US, the EU, Japan, etc. It is observed that a large number of developed countries have imposed peak tariffs in sectors like textile and textile products, articles of plastics/rubber, chemical and chemical product, plant & machinery and transport equipment. In Japan, tariff peaks have been observed in leather and leather products and footwear products.

Table 10.6 gives a summary result of the Mehta and the Mohanty study on the basis of two methods: (i) cut-off point and (ii) statistical formulae. Based on the statistical formulae, the country-wise analysis shows that the US has imposed peak tariffs for around 11 per cent of national lines, Australia on five per cent of national lines and so on. The number of national lines which have peak tariffs in the Japanese market, is small (106 out of 7158), but the level of tariff peaks is very high. Comparing the two alternate methods for identification of peak tariffs, the study suggests that India and the other developing countries should opt for statistical formulae in the forthcoming negotiations.

Tariff Escalation

Tariff escalation occurs when tariff levels increase with the level of processing, providing high level of effective protection to the

TABLE 10.6: **Number of Lines[1] Subject to Peak Tariff[2], 1998**

Country	TR 12%	With Statistical Formula[3] TR M + SD
Australia	881	253
EU	861	1456
Japan	751	106
US	986	884
India[4]	4064	2
Korea[5]	21	15
Malaysia[6]	74	10

Notes :
1. Of HS 25-97
2. National Lines, it also includes some national lines with specific duties. The specific duties have been converted to *ad valorem* equivalent.
3. TR = Applied Tariff Rate, M = Average Tariff Rate, and SD = Standard Deviation of Tariff Rates
4. For the year 1999
5. For the year 1996
6. For the year 1997

Source: R. Mehta and S. K. Mohanty, *WTO and Industrial Tariff: An Empirical Analysis for India*, RIS, 1999.

importing countries' processing sectors. Tariff escalation has been a major concern for developing countries, which fear that it may inhibit their efforts towards industrialisation.

Tariff structures of different countries have traditionally displayed significant escalation favouring domestic processors for a large number of commodities. It was expected that tariff commitments in the UR would provide for gradual reduction of escalation by applying relatively higher cuts to finished goods. However, rapidly rising tariffs have been noticed from low rates for raw material to higher rates for intermediate goods and sometime peak tariffs for finished products. A number of studies[21] have confirmed that tariff escalation has continued after the UR for a large number of sectors, particularly, metals, textile and textile products, leather and rubber products and to some extent wood and wood products. This analysis is based on the estimation of two alternative measures commonly known as (i) effective rate of protection (ERP),

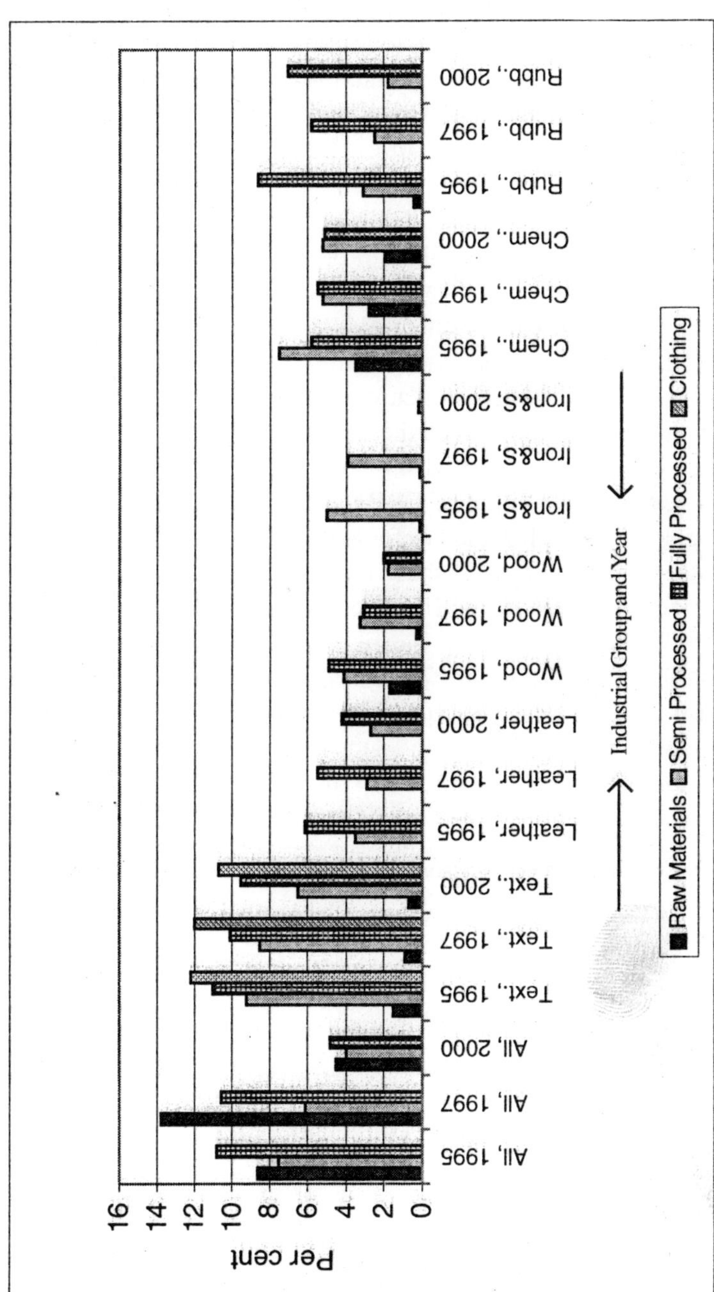

Fig. 10.2: **EU: Tariff Escalation, 1995, 1997 and 2000**

and (ii) levels of average tariff rates at different stages of processing, i.e., raw material, semi-processed items and finished goods. The results, based on estimated average tariff rates at different stages of processing, confirm the persistent high tariff escalation for a large number of countries/commodities. In Japan, tariff escalation is evident in a number of sectors, most notably between semi-processed and fully processed items, particularly in sectors such as, textile, petroleum refinery, rubber products, metals and footwear[22]. In the case of the EU, significant tariff escalations have been noticed in sectors such as textile, leather products, wood products, industrial chemicals and rubber products. The implementation of UR may lead to disappearance of tariff escalations in iron and steel of the EU[23]. However, it will continue in textile, leather and rubber products, etc., during the post-UR period, as shown in Figure 10.2.

The estimated value of ERP confirms the abovementioned finding. In the US, ERP doubles for leather and leather products, and rises steeply for textile products to the level of 35 per cent. The ERP rises more steeply in Japan: from 66 per cent for leather to 260 per cent for leather shoes. A significant increase has also been noticed for a large number of sectors in Malaysia and Korea. These results confirm that tariff escalation is still a major constraint for major export industries of developing countries.

Table 10.7 gives an estimate of the ERPs[24] of 55 sectors of the Indian economy for 1998/99. Our results show that there has not been

TABLE 10.7: **Estimate of Effective Rates of Protection for Indian Industries, 1998-99**

I/O Sector No.	Description	1998-99	
		NRP*	ERP**
1	2	3	4
1.	Paddy	0.00	-6.31
2.	Wheat	0.00	-5.70
3.	Other cereals	5.0	1.57
4.	Pulses	5.0	1.69
5.	Sugarcane	40.0	42.13

(contd.)

TABLE 10.7 *(contd.)*

1	2	3	4
6.	Jute	30.0	31.04
7.	Cotton	40.0	43.54
8.	Tea and coffee	10.0	8.83
9.	Rubber	20.05	18.70
10.	Other crops	29.31	30.55
11.	Animal husbandry	16.50	12.14
12.	Forestry and logging	3.86	3.14
13.	Fishing	31.24	31.40
14.	Coal and lignite	10.0	4.53
15.	Crude pet. & natural gas	19.45	18.84
16.	Iron ore	5.02	2.49
17.	Other metallic minerals	6.90	5.65
18.	Non-metallic minor minerals	37.54	28.82
19.	Sugar	5.0	1.31
20.	Khandsari	10.0	13.87
21.	Edible oils	30.04	35.15
22.	Other food & beverage industries	56.23	102.61
23.	Cotton textiles	38.96	40.62
24.	Woolen textiles	31.83	33.70
25.	Silk textiles	30.00	36.63
26.	Art. silk and synthetic fibre	33.85	33.37
27.	Jute hemp mesta textiles	39.95	45.91
28.	Readymade garments	40.0	43.68
29.	Other textiles	36.38	37.26
30.	Wood and wood products	30.79	40.37
31.	Paper and paper products	17.56	15.63
32.	Leather & leather prods.	27.08	28.53
33.	Rubber products	39.21	49.68
34.	Plastic products	30.19	30.18
35.	Petroleum products	25.19	29.77
36.	Fertilizers	24.91	22.53
37.	Pesticides	30.00	32.40

(contd.)

TABLE 10.7 *(contd.)*

1	2	3	4
38.	Synthetic fibre & resin	31.56	34.73
39.	Paints, drugs, cosmetics	31.90	35.91
40.	Other chemicals	27.57	29.25
41.	Cement	40.00	45.36
42.	Other non-metallic mineral products	34.14	36.69
43.	Iron and steel	29.26	32.27
44.	Non ferrous metals	32.35	35.78
45.	Tractors & oth. agri. mach.	20.00	16.51
46.	Other non-electrical machinery	20.70	15.29
47.	Electrical machinery	25.25	24.46
48.	Comm. & electronic equip.	21.88	19.32
49.	Rail equipment	39.84	45.60
50.	Motor vehicles	40.00	43.44
51.	Motorcycle, scooter & bicycles	40.00	45.80
52.	Other transport equipment	35.52	39.73
53.	Other manufacturing	18.61	10.74

Notes : * NRP for a sector is calculated on the basis of Import-Weighted MFN tariff rates. The weights are computed using the value of imports during the year 1996-97. The tariff rates are MFN tariff rates at six-digit HS level, without taking into consideration the exemption notifications. The correspondence, between an I-O sector classification and trade classification, has been carried out using trade statistics at eight-digit HS-ITC classification.

** Based on the co-efficient of Input-Output Table for the year 1998-99, for 65 sectors. Sectors numbered 54-65 are mostly service sectors.

Sources : 1. G.O.I., *Input-Output Transaction Table 1998-99*, Planning Commission.

2. G.O.I., *Custom Tariff of India*, 1998-99.
3. G.O.I., D.G.C.I.&I.S., *Monthly Statistics of Foreign Trade of India*, March 1997.
4. G.O.I., *Input-Output Transanction Table 1989-90*, C.S.O., November 1997.

any significant increase in estimated values of ERPs for almost all sectors of industrial products, except for "other food and beverages industries". There has been some minor increase in the ERP of some products like wood and wood products, rubber products, rail equipments, etc.

In short, the tariff commitments in the UR may not lead to decline in the tariff escalation for a large number of sectors in which India has huge export potential.

Non-Tariff Barriers

In the GATT, the developed countries have been forceful advocates of open and liberal trade and their message to developing countries has been to follow a similar process. In a truly amazing act of self-denial, they have an impressive array of new measures of protection and government interventions. These have been imposed through different instruments, including non-tariff barriers (NTBs).

The agreements of the UR have changed the intensity of different types of NTBs. Some measures of NTBs have lost their importance. The agreements on agriculture and safeguards have virtually made it impossible to impose any type of QRs. On the other hand, a significant increase has been noticed in some other measures of NTBs. Most of these measures have been designed and imposed to protect domestic production. These measures are sometime called "contingent protection measures" in the literature.

The strengthening of a dispute settlement mechanism is considered as one of the major achievements of the UR. Since the formation of the WTO, a number of disputes referred to the dispute settlement body has increased significantly as compared to the number of cases referred during the pre-UR period[25]. These disputes refer to anti-dumping duties, countervailing duties, sanitary and phytosanitary measures, technical barriers to trade, government procurements, transparency, TRIMs, national treatment, etc. These measures have affected the market access for a large number of industrial sectors, particularly textile, electrical and mechanical equipment, and agriculture products. Developing countries like India have huge trade potential in these sectors.

This section provides a brief outline of the present position of the NTBs in select trading partners of India. The UNCTAD has identified around 36 categories of NTBs, which Japan is imposing on its imported goods. Out of these 36 categories, 16 had been imposed on industrial imports of Japan (Table 10.8). At least one or other type of these NTBs has been imposed on 2742 commodities (or lines) of Japan's industrial sector. A significant number of Japan's imported items were subject to multiple types of NTBs and most of these items belong to commodity groups like mineral fuel (HS chapter 27), organic chemical (chapter 29), pharmaceutical product (chapter 30), furskin and artificial fur (chapter 43) and wood and wood products (chapter 44). Apart from these tariff barriers, the import of a large number of commodities require licenses, must meet particular specifications, and be imported through specific agencies, etc. Some examples of these specific restrictions for Japanese imports are given in part II of Table 10.8.

UNCTAD[26] categorises the identified NTBs in two groups: (i) hard-core and (ii) soft. It presents a measure of hard-core[27] NTBs for different countries. The results based on the UNCTAD information show that 8.7 per cent of EU's national lines have been subject to one or another type of NTB, during 1998. Similarly, the corresponding estimated values for Japan has been 5.9 per cent, for Australia 6.4 per cent, and for Brazil 36.6 per cent. The proportion of India's items subject to hard-core NTBs (restricted/canalised) comes to 10.7 per cent in 2000/01. It also includes those items whose QRs will be phased out under Indo-US Agreement on QR removal.

Non-tariff barriers continue to affect the growth of world trade and the UR could not tackle these issues successfully. On the one hand, the importing countries generally term them as NTBs, and on the other, the imposing countries insist that 'these instruments are policy objectives'.

The incidence of hard-core NTBs for different commodity groups varies significantly from one country to another. The hard-core NTBs have been frequently noticed in sectors like pharmaceutical products, essential oils, soap and organic surfaces, chemical products, leather and leather products, wood and wood products, textiles (particularly in the markets of Canada, Japan and

TABLE 10.8: **Types of NTBs Imposed by Japan on Industrial Sector**

I.	Broad Categories of NTBs Imposed
1.	Tariff quota
2.	Variable charges
3.	Anti-dumping duties
4.	Automatic license
5.	Non-automatic license
6.	Authorisation for wildlife protection
7.	Authorization ensure national security
8.	Authorization for political reasons
9.	Global quota
10.	Quota for sensitive products
11.	State monopoly of imports
12.	Sole importing agency
13.	Product characteristics requirements to protect human health
14.	Product characteristics requirements to protect environment
15.	Product characteristics to protect wildlife
II.	**Some Select Examples of NTBs**
(i)	Tariff quotas on certain food products, alcohol, leather and footwear products.
(ii)	Prior to importation motor vehicles generally need to meet a type-approval test.
(iii)	Only some select branded vehicles approved for cars imports: (a) BMW (46 types), (b) Volks wagen/Audi (84 types), (c) Mercedes Benz (62 types), (d) Opel (20 types), (e) GH (12 types), and (f) Chrysler (6 types). Examination period two months.
(iv)	Auto components regarded as essential to vehicle safety, called "critical parts", must be replaced either by a certified garage approved as capable of repairing all critical parts, or the replacement needs to be checked by the Ministry of Transport (MOT).
(v)	According to the provisions of Law, importing pharmaceuticals requires a license from the Ministry of Health and Family Welfare (MHFW).
(vi)	For granting a license to import of cosmetics, the MHFW uses a positive list, such that only ingredients with prior approval can be used. Each product to be imported must have a separate license, and in principle meet labelling requirements.
(vii)	Iron and steel production can apply for government assistance, such as low interest loans, loan guarantees and tax breaks.

the European Union), iron and steel, plant and machinery and miscellaneous manufactured products (in European Union and Australia), in a large number of major trading partners of India.

Tariff Liberalisation in the Forthcoming Round: Strategies and Options for India

In the Seattle meeting, India along with other member countries of the WTO, had agreed to a draft text (though not adopted) which reiterates further liberalisation of the industrial sector. It also includes many issues relating to market access for the industrial sector. A detailed analysis of these issues is essential to understand the nature of benefits and costs, including employment, accruing to India. In the forthcoming negotiations (if started), India should not concentrate on reduction in average tariffs but its concern should be the reduction in peak tariffs, and tariff escalation. In the negotiations, India should put emphasis on higher reduction of the tariff rates of finished products as compared to the tariff rates of unfinished or semi-processed products. Further, the conduct of negotiations, for possibility of deeper reduction, should be based on a formulae. Even if average tariffs are negotiated, they should be based on simple averages (and not import-weighted averages) of all commodities including those items whose customs duties are defined in the forms of specific rates. In fact, developing countries should demand that all the countries define their customs duties (even commitment rates) in the form of *ad valorem* rates.

Since the formation of the WTO, the number of disputes relating to NTBs has increased significantly as compared to the number referred to during the pre-UR period. These measures continue to affect the growth of world trade. India should demand a coherent approach for dealing with such issues and participate actively in setting up new (and clear) rules and provisions. Further, the forthcoming negotiations should not be based on a sector-by-sector approach. In fact, they should be more comprehensive, where reduction/commitments for agriculture, industry and textile should not be dealt with separately.

Concluding Observations

In the last round of GATT/WTO, India committed herself to reduce the average MFN customs duty rate from the level of 71.4 per cent in the pre-Uruguay period, to 32.4 per cent in the post-Uruguay era. It also agreed to increase the bound rates from six per cent of its tariff lines to 67 per cent.

The levels of India's MFN customs tariff rate and peak tariff rates have consistently and significantly declined in the early and mid-1990s. The average MFN customs duty rate declined from the level of more than 80 per cent in the early 1990s to around 30 per cent in 1997. Similarly, the peak tariff of Indian customs duty declined from more than 100 per cent during the early 1990s to around 42 per cent in 1996/97. However, India's average as well as peak customs tariff rates have not significantly changed from 1997/98 to 2001/02.

There has also been a significant decline in the incidence of quantitative restrictions. The imports of almost all commodities were subject to one or another type of quantitative restriction during the early 1990s. The removal of the QRs began during the mid-1990s, and imports of all commodities will be permissible without any licence from April 1, 2001, as per the decision of the WTO appellate body.

In short, one can say that India's trade liberalisation process has led to a significant decline in tariff/peak rates during the early and mid-1990s. However, India's average applied rates have been hovering around their committed levels for the last five to six years.

A number of the policy statements/commitments have been reiterated in the continuation of India's trade liberalisation process. Even the Budget proposals of 2001/02 reconfirm that the level of Indian tariff rates will be brought down to those of the East Asian economies. It seems that the process of reduction in the Indian customs duties will be restarted after the complete removal of the QRs. Since India will be reducing its customs duties on a unilateral basis, it has to work out the strategy for the forthcoming multilateral trade negotiations. Further, since the developed countries (particularly India's major trading partners) will not be able to substantially reduce their average (levels being already very low) tariff rates, India has to identify other issues in the requests/offers method of WTO negotiations.

In the next round of the WTO negotiation process India should concentrate on reduction in peak tariffs and tariff escalations. It should emphasise higher reduction in the tariff rates of finished products as compared to the tariff rates of unfinished or semi-processed products. It should also demand that all the countries should define their customs duties (even commitment rates) in the form of *ad valorem* rates, because it has been noticed that *ad valorem* equivalence of specific duties is relatively very high and in most cases falls in the range of peak tariffs.

It is well known that the successful completion of multilateral negotiations takes a couple of years. It is very difficult to believe that the new round will be completed before 2005. What in such case should be India's strategy for trade liberalisation during this period? India should not wait for the completion of the next round. During this period, India should (i) continue its unilateral liberalisation process, (ii) strengthen its bilateral/regional arrangements through preferential tariffs, and (iii) take steps towards removal of anti-export bias.

NOTES AND REFERENCES

1. This was India's position, in December 1999, before the ministerial meeting of WTO in Seattle. The main objective of this meeting was to decide the agenda of the next round of multilateral trade negotiations.
2. It is possible that this stand may have been taken due to 'strategic' reasons.
3. There was almost consensus in Seattle meeting among the members of WTO on draft declaration of the working group: *Market access negotiations on non-agriculture products.* India had also no objection to this draft.
4. Not for some commodities like beverages, and select agriculture commodities which have mega tariff.
5. Brunei, Indonesia, Malaysia, the Philippines, Singapore and Thailand.
6. Out of 2701 commodity groups, 59 lines were defined for sub-groups of HS six-digit level, while the commitment for one commodity group was offered for a subgroup of HS four-digit level.
7. India had to maintain its applied rate at or below the bound rates by March 2000, except for the commodities of textile sector. The commitments for the textile sector has to be carried out by March 2005. See also Academy of Business Studies (ABS), *Easy Reference Customs Tariff, 1999-2000,* March 1999.

8. For India's (i) UR bound rates and (ii) present levels of MFN Tariff rates (2000-1), see Mehta, 1999, *Tariff and Non-tariff Barriers of Indian Economy: A Profile*, RIS, 1999, and ABS, ibid.
9. WTO, *India-Quantitative Restrictions on Imports of Agricultural, Textile and Industrial Products: Report of the Appellate Body,* WT/DS90/AB/R, and August 23, 1999.
10. See, WTO, *India-Quantitative Restrictions on Imports of Agricultural, Textile and Industrial Products: Agreement under Article 21.3 (b) of the DSU*, WT/DS90/15, Jan. 17, 2000.
11. See, Mehta, R., "Removal of QRs and its Impact on India's Imports", *EPW*, May 2000; See also Mehta; R, *QR Removal and India's Import: The Case of India's Unilateral Offer for SAARC Countries*, RIS, 2000.
12. Amount of value per unit of imported commodity.
13. See Mehta, R. and S.K.Mohanty, *WTO and Industrial Tariff: An Empirical Analysis for India*, RIS, 1999.
14. See, for example, UNCTAD, *Trade Analysis and Information System*, Winter 1998-99, for different formulas for conversion of specific duties to *ad valorem* equivalence.
15. USITC, *Interactive Tariff Database*, August 1999.
16. See, UNCTAD, *The Post-UR Tariff Environment for Developing Countries: Tariff Peaks and Tariff Escalation,* TD/B/COM/1/14/Rev/1, 14, September 1999-2000 and UN, *Market Access since UR, Implications, Opportunities and Challenges,* Report prepared by UNCTAD and WTO, May 1998.
17. The statistical formula is defined as

Peak Tariff ≥ Mean + è.Standard Deviation,

$\geq M + \theta.\ SD,$

where

$$M = \frac{\text{Sum of Tariff Rates } (TR_i) \text{ of all Lines of a country}}{\text{Total No. of Lines (N)}}$$

$$= \frac{\sum_{i=1}^{N} TR_i}{N},$$

$$V = \frac{\sum_{i=1}^{N} (TR_i - M)^2}{N},$$

and the standard deviation (SD) is defined as

$$SD = \sqrt{\text{Variance}}$$

θ = a constant which can take values 1, 2 or 3

18. UNCTAD, *The post-Uruguay Round Tariff Environment for developing country exports* (TD/B/COM. 1/14), Geneva, 1999/2000.
19. Generalised System of Preference.
20. Mehta, R. and S.K. Mohanty, 1999, ibid.
21. UN, ibid.
22. WTO, *Trade Policy Review: Japan 1998*, Geneva, June 1998.
23. WTO, *Trade Policy Review: EU 1998,* Geneva, March 1998.
24. The Effective Rate of Protection (ERP) for commodity j is defined as

$$ERP_j = \frac{t_j - \sum_{i=1}^{n} a_{ij} TR_i}{1 - \sum_{i=1}^{n} a_{ij}}$$

where a_{ij} = input-output coefficient, TR_i = import tariff rate of ith good. The values of a_{ij} are taken from the input-output tables for the year 1998-99 prepared by Planning Commission, while the values of tariff rate(TR_i) are based on 'scheduled tariff rates' as announced by government. See also Mehta, R., "Trade Policy Reform 1991-92 to 1995-96: Their Impact on External Trade," *EPW,* 1997, for estimation procedure of ERPs of different Industries.
25. See for example, UNCTAD/WTO, ibid., 1998.
26. UNCTAD, ibid., Winter 1998-99.
27. The hard-core NTBs, defined by UNCTAD, include the three major categories: (i) *Quantity control measures* (referred to as QRs): such as non-automatic licensing, quotas, prohibitions, export restraint arrangements but excluding tariff-quotas and enterprise-specific restrictions., (ii) *Financial measures*: they include advance payment requirement, multiple exchange rates and restrictive official foreign exchange allocation, but exclude regulations concerning terms of payment and transfer delays/queuing, and (iii) *Price control measures:* which effect the cost of imports in a variable amount on the basis of difference between domestic prices and its corresponding foreign prices. They include administrative price fixing, voluntary export price restraint, variable charges, anti-dumping measures, and countervailing measures.

ANNEXURE

Tariff Peak Products; Post-UR Tariffs Faced by Exports from Developing Countries (Industrial Products)

(Percentage)

Products Description	EU	Japan[a]	US	Canada	China	Malaysia
Bovine skin leather, tanned	5	30	0	0	9	0
Sheep and lambskin leather, prepared	2	30	2	0	14	0
Suitcases, briefcases of leather	1	10	8	7	25	25
Suitcases of plastics or textiles	4	8	20	7	35	25
Small pocket leather goods	1	10	20	5	25	25
Leather gloves	7	10	14	10	25	25
Woven fabrics of>80 per cent combed wool	12	8	25	14	30	0
Cotton, raw	0	0	79[1]	0	3	0
Carpets, knotted, of wool or fine animal hair	6	8	0	10	32	30
Babies' garments, knitt.or crocheted, of syn. Fibr	11	22	16	18	33	20
Women's blouses, knitt. or crocheted, of man-made fibres	11	11	32	18	35	20
T-shirts, knitted or crocheted, of cotton	11	11	17	18	30	20
T-shirts, knitt.or crocheted, of syn. fibres	11	11	32	18	35	20
Pullovers, knitted or crocheted, of man-made fibre	11	11	32	18	32	20

(contd.)

ANNEXURE *(contd.)*

Men's coats, woven, of wool or fine animal hair	11	9	17	18	35	20
Men's trousers, woven, of wool or fine animal hair	11	9	17	18	35	20
Men's trousers, woven, of cotton	11	9	17	17	31	20
Men's trousers, woven synthetic fibres	11	9	28	18	35	20
Women's dresses, woven of wool or fine animal hair	11	9	14	18	35	20
Women's trousers, woven, of synthetic fibres	11	9	29	18	35	20
Men's shirts, woven, of cotton	11	7	20	17	31	20
Men's shirts, woven, of man-made fibres	11	7	28	18	35	20
Women's blouses, woven of man-made fibres	11	9	27	18	35	20
Babies' garments, woven of synthetic fibres	9	9	29	18	33	20
Ties, bow ties and cravats, woven, of man-made fibres	11	0	14	18	33	25
Bed linen, printed, of man-made fibres	11	5	15	18	33	30
Waterproof footwear	13	27	38	20	25	30
Footwear with outer soles and uppers of rubber/plastic	13	7	56	18	25	30
Footwear with leather uppers	6	140	10	18	25	30
Sports footwear (with textile uppers)	13	8	58	16	25	25
Parts of footwear, uppers and parts thereof	3	25	42	8	25	25

(contd.)

ANNEXURE *(contd.)*

Ceramic tableware, kitchenware, and so on (excluding china)	9	0	28	0	30	30
Drinking glasses of glass	8	0	29	0	30	25
Glassware for kitchen, toilets etc.	8	0	38	0	30	25
Television picture tubes, colour	10	0	15	5	18	0
Cars, capacity<2500 cubic centimetres	7	0	3	6	80	140
Diesel trucks	15	0	25	6	40	30
Bicycles	11	0	11	9	25	25
Watch movements	2	0	33	5	20	0

Notes: [a] GSP rates exist at half the MFN rate for most of these products, but are limited by tariff quotas.
[1] Progressive additional safeguard duties are levied if import prices are below the level indicated in the tariff.

Source: UNCTAD/WTO, *The Post-Uruguay Round Tariff Environment for Developing Country Exports: Tariff Peaks and Tariff Escalation* (TD/B/COM.1/14/Rev.1), September 14, 1999.

11

GLOBALISATION, LABOUR MARKET AND LABOUR STANDARD

BIPLAB DASGUPTA

Introduction

In this year's budget the Finance Minister has conceded to a long standing demand of the global agencies, that the labour laws protecting the workers from sudden closure and lay offs by the management, should be scrapped. Prior to this amendment, this decision in the case of enterprises employing more than 100 men, could only be taken in consultation with the authorities. By proposing to amend the required number of employees from 100 to 1000, the Finance Minister is in effect taking away protection from lay off and closure.

In future, there may be other bills coming that would further dilute the provisions of labour welfare legislation on minimum wages and compensation for workplace damage, and providing crèches, toilets etc., in order to transform labour market conditions in India to the requirements of the large multinational companies. To the wealthy MNCs, with their empire spread over a large part of the globe, the rights to 'hire and fire' are inalienable ones, and are indispensable preconditions for their entry to a particular market in a big way.

'The overriding tendency (of the World Bank)', as one ILO document suggested in 1994, 'has been to criticize existing labour laws and regulations, whenever they may raise the cost of labour and otherwise impede the freer operation of market forces.' The ostensible objective was to remove rigidities and distortions in the labour market (Plant, 1994: 57). Labour market regulations are cited specifically as constraints to successful reform. A World Bank document on Africa (1989) says : 'Experience suggests that, except on grounds of health or worker safety governments should resist interfering in labour markets. If left alone, they work well. The political imperative is to interfere, but the economic logic is not to. ...Minimum wage legislation, regulations restricting the ability of employers to hire and fire, and related interventions tend to raise costs, reduce competitiveness, and restrain the growth of employment. During the next generation, the rapidly expanding labour force will tend to drive wages down. In these cases, any attempt to obstruct this process administratively will fail in the long run, at the cost of lower growth in production and employment in the short run' (Plant, 1994: 63-64).

This change is going to be in line with the labour market reform under structural adjustment, which also proposes reform in trade, industry, finance and fiscal sectors. The World Bank (1992) talks generally about poverty reduction, safety nets and the need to go for labour-intensive community work, but is critical of minimum wages, labour market and job security legislations (Plant, 1994: 58). All the three major international agencies, collectively known as the 'trinity' seek these reforms including labour market reform.

Two Contrasting Views on the Labour Market

It is not usually recognised that these three major international agencies—World Bank, IMF and WTO—though sharing the same market-oriented economic philosophy, speak with diverse and contradictory voices when it comes to labour market reform. While the World Bank and the IMF desire non-intervention of the state, and prefer the determination of wages and other labour conditions through the interaction of the forces of demand and supply in the market, in contrast, the World Trade Organisation (WTO) seeks a certain amount of state intervention to achieve what they describe as 'labour standard'. The present author is unsympathetic to both these views, for reasons given below and elsewhere, but feels that those who support labour market reform owe a duty to specify which type of labour market reform they are advocating, and why. They can not support both these types of mutually exclusive labour market reform at the same time.

Why Structural Adjustment is Anti-labour

We begin with a bland statement that these so-called labour market reforms are anti-labour and anti-poor country. These reforms are parts of the Fund-Bank structural adjustment programme that seeks total, unobstructed mobility of capital and commodities across national frontiers, but would not allow corresponding privileges to another equally important factor of production, labour, to move without restrictions from labour-surplus areas such as India, to labour-deficit ones, such as Australia. The globalisation programme that they advocate is, for this reason alone, partial, discriminatory and biased.

This paper has been organised in the following way : The paper begins with an analysis of the work of Olson, whose New Political Economy(NPE) provided the theoretical underpinning of the structural adjustment programme (Section one). For those who would like to understand structural adjustment, to boost or to demolish it, or to arrive at his own judgement about it, Olson is compulsory reading. Olson is even more relevant on the issue of trade unions and wages, which occupy an important segment of Olson's analysis. He is a keen protagonist of the flexible labour market, that allows the wages to move easily up and down and provides jobs to those seeking jobs, even at wages lower than those ordained by the trade unions, to clear the market.

In Section two, we show, how this advocacy of a flexible labour market leads to a concept of an authoritarian state, with the idea that authoritarian governments are generally more effective in keeping wages down and making business lucrative. In other words, as NPE goes, for the successful implementation of a market-based liberal economy, one requires its political obverse, an illiberal authoritarian state like Singapore or Indonesia. In this section we tried to show that, on the contrary, most economically successful governments are democracies and are not in the habit of repressing labour.

Fourth section deals with the admitted world-wide failure to introduce labour market reform and to make them effective. It also discusses many of the negative consequences of structural adjustment for the toiling masses, such as poverty, regional and personal disparity, unemployment and so on, as the economy collapses under the weight of structural adjustment and bread riots spread. And, ultimately the structural adjustment package itself is scrapped either by the exasperated donor or by the disgruntled donee who can not continue with it any further. Such things, well documented, have happened many times over the past two decades, particularly in Sub-Saharan Africa.

In Section five we discuss labour standard as proposed by the World Trade Organisation (WTO). Though all the three members of the global trinity share a common economic philosophy, their attitude towards labour market reform is far from similar. While, through the labour market reform the World Bank wishes to keep the wages low and to make dynamic MNC investment attractive, WTO's concern is to protect high, wage, decaying western industries, such as the garment industry, from low wage third world competitors.

In the last section, we discuss why WTO's attempt to impose a uniform labour standard world-wide failed, and also the implications of such failure for developed-poor country trade relationships. We particularly discuss the author's experience at the Seattle Ministerial Conference of WTO, where he participated as a member of the core official Indian delegation and where the rich countries lobbied hard and twisted the arms of the vulnerable third world countries to reach a consensus favouring a labour standard.

NPE and Olson

The philosophical basis of structural adjustment lies in the writings of Olson and other exponents of the so-called new political economy (NPE). Since we have discussed the new political economy elaborately elsewhere, here we do no more than draw the attention of the reader to this particular aspect of Olson's writings (Dasgupta, 1998: Chapter One; Olson, 1982).

Rationality and Self Interest

At the base of NPE is the concept of 'rationality', which is taken as synonymous with self interest. A person or a self interested group seeks a higher share of the national cake through his actions. It is, however, debatable whether self interest is the main motivating force behind human action. The history of mankind is replete with examples where people have risen above their own narrow interests to sacrifice a great deal, including their lives, for a cause. NPE does not explain philanthropy, martyrdom, nationalism, ethnicity, giving and taking of life in ugly communal outbursts, or fights between two groups of (non-gambling) football fans. People can and do go beyond their immediate self interest quite regularly. Further, joining of a group (e.g., 'save the baby seal' campaign) is not merely prompted by the desire to get a share of the national cake. Emotions, sentiments, concerns for others and enjoyment in being a part of a larger group are matters that go beyond personal book-keeping and cost-benefit analysis. One can even go to the extent of saying that if rationality is defined only in terms of self interest, the most rational behaviour would be an irrational one.

From Individual Self Interest to Group Interest

Taking the Olsonian definition of rationality as self interest for the purpose of our understanding NPE, the transition from individual self interest to 'group interest', a major concern of Olson and NPE in general, takes place when these two are not in conflict. Generally speaking, a rational self interested individual in the Olsonian sense has no incentive to contribute to the provision of a public good if he can do without, more so where there is no close and direct connection between his contribution and the social good that results (Hindess, 1988: 14). He would not join a union or pay taxes and would rather enjoy a 'free ride' of higher wages from collective action or contribution by others, unless not being a member of the union or tax-payer would confer some disadvantages (e.g., social exclusion or imprisonment) that are, in his reckoning, more costly than the amount he will have to pay as union subscription or taxes (Olson, 1982: 21).

According to Olson, the only exceptions are 'encompassing organisations', when unions represent almost all earners in a society, and where pursuing national wellbeing would also further their own interests (Olson, 1982: 63). But in the case of 'encompassing organisations' the success of the organisation will depend largely on its ability to frame rules that benefit the vast majority of its members or avoid conflicts among members, but, in most cases, at the cost of efficiency, such as, the seniority rule in promotions prevailing in many workplaces (Olson, 1982:58).

We know that, to be effective, a cartel has to fix both the price and the quantity of the product it is offering. But in this situation the encompassing organisations, who function like a cartel, tend to fix only the price, namely, the wage in case of a union, leaving the quantity, that is the number employed, to be determined by the market (Olson, 1982:48-59). This, in the case of the labour market, would imply the presence of unemployed on the one hand and the prevalence of high wages for the employed on the other. Wage will not be adjusted downward to allow the market to be cleared and to make unemployment disappear.

Distributional Coalitions

Further, according to Olson, such interest groups as labour unions, are likely to form 'distributional coalitions' with other interest groups, and seek various types of state intervention in the economy, for example, controls against imports and other competitors and licenses and permits for themselves, at the cost of the welfare loss for the nation as a whole. Lobbying, taken as a positive feature of the pluralist-competitive society so far by the neo-classicists, is considered by Olson and NPE to be harmful.

A major question raised by NPE is whether such pursuit of self interest by individuals and interest groups operating in an economy, with conflicting aims and with unequal access to decision-makers, brings about a desirable 'optimum allocation of resources' for the country as a whole. Until NPE, an assumption underlying neo-classical micro-economics was that the sum of individual welfare and utility maximisation adds up to social welfare. Olson, however, disagreed. Indeed, as his analysis attempted to show, this would lead to an irrational economic outcome. The special interest groups would only cater to the interests of their members, and, thus, will reduce efficiency and the aggregate income of the society as a whole in which they would operate (Olson, 1982:47).

Distributional coalitions, whose objective was to maximise the share of its members in the national cake, would be quite inefficient in their manner of functioning. Because of the diversity of interests they represent to achieve a common aim, coalitions would tend to have a crowded agenda and, thus, would be rigid and slow in decision-making. Once a bargain has been struck, it would be difficult to change the terms within a short period, even if that becomes necessary because of altered market or technology conditions (Olson, 1982: 59). Further, distributional coalitions, once big enough to succeed, would tend to limit diversity of interests and values of their membership, and to make themselves more and more exclusive (Olson, 1982:69). In other words, the politically rational goals of private interests would 'lead to ends that are economically irrational' (Grindle and Thomas, 1991:25). They will induce the government to make rules and pass legislation that would benefit them exclusively. The coalitions will strive to capture the largest possible share of national income, at the cost of the vast majority, who are poor and unorganised (Olson, 1982:69-73).

Olson raised the question: why was there more unemployment among the groups with lower skill and productivity—as for example, teenagers, or disadvantaged racial minorities—while it was the least among the highly skilled workers. He then proceeded to answer that question himself. When wages are set above market clearing levels, the argument goes, it is inevitable that the employer will choose and attract the more skilled, and, inevitably, the less skilled and young would go without jobs (Olson, 1982:195-205). Though he also blamed the monopsonistic policy followed by enterprises for this, he made the trade unions more of a culprit by saying that they block 'mutually advantageous transactions between individual employers and workers to keep wages below competitive levels.' The fact that the unions would not allow the unemployed to work at low wages by displacing those who are already working at higher wages is considered to be wrong. The unions are made responsible for the stickiness of wages, and for not letting the market be cleared. Olson's anti-Labour views even take him to support inflation, which apart from being inequitable erodes real wages (Olson, 1982:206).

Distributional Coalition of the Potential Beneficiaries of Reform

While critical of all types of 'distributional coalition', Olson, in his efforts to make the organised trade unions his main target, entangled himself in another serious double-talk. Not all interest-groups or coalitions are decried by NPE. On the contrary, its proponents argue for mobilising support for structural reform by bringing together the potential and actual beneficiaries of such market-based reform, away from the interventionist state. To quote one influential World Bank publication: 'Adjustment programs should thus be designed and presented with an awareness of the importance for political sustainability of building a coalition of groups benefiting from and expanding as a result of the reform process' (Webb and Shariff, 1992: 84). One World Bank official was glad to note that the military regime in an African country, was receiving the support of the beneficiaries of reform (Foroutan, 1993:27). In other words, coalitions of a different kind, of the potential beneficiaries of reform, are welcome, while those sponsored by the trade unions are not.

The trade unions are blamed for producing irrational economic outcomes, because they seek to maximise their own share of the national cake by forming a coalition of similar interest groups, and yet NPE urges the possible beneficiaries from structural adjustment to form a coalition in its support in order to make it politically sustainable. The theory does not reveal why such a coalition of possible beneficiaries of reform would be any different from other types of distributional coalitions seeking to maximise their share of the national cake, and in that case how can they avoid inefficiencies and irrationalities associated with distributional coalition in general, as discussed by Olson himself. Given this ambiguity, one might argue, despite the elaborate arguments of Olson and other proponents of NPE, that there is nothing basically wrong with coalitions as such, the more critical question being: on whose side are you?

NPE and the Authoritarian State Repressing Labour and Wages

Violent Nature of the State

The NPE protagonists entangle themselves in another serious argument on the nature of the state and its relationship with the unions. Like Marxists, NPE proponents take the view that the essence of the state lies in its right to legally use violence in favour of interest groups (read classes- BD) in control of the state machinery (Lal and Myint, 1996: 11, 263). But unlike the Marxists, they take the view that only an authoritarian regime can control those trade unions of organised workers which seek wages that are higher than the average earnings of the multitude of unorganised workers more effectively (Hoggard, 1995: 209).

Liberal Economics Requires Authoritarian Politics

In other words, liberal neo-classical economics requires, for its success, its political obverse—an illiberal, authoritarian political structure: a ruling party (or leader) which can rise above interest—groups such as trade unions, make decisions and impose it on the rest of the society, and sustain unpopular but desirable policies over what is likely to be a number of difficult years. The economic success in several of the Southeast and East Asian countries in recent years has been attributed to the success of their authoritarian governments in keeping wages in check (Agarwal et al., 1996).

The main justification put forward for such an attitude towards labour is that high wages, prompted by trade union activities, operate as a disincentive to private investment. While according to this view, there is nothing wrong in the management making huge profits and accumulating wealth, trade unions are not permitted to procure for their members wages that are far in excess of the average wage. This, again, looks at the issue from one side: that is the requirement to induce the rich to make efforts to become richer by producing more, but ignoring a task that is no less important, of providing incentives for the vast majority of workers who would actually turn the wheel. In fact, the literature on structural adjustment and new political economy is replete with policy prescriptions that would keep wages within limits, even by way of repression of organised labour, while allowing the industrialists and traders to maximise profit.

A simple linear relationship between economic success and the political form of the government is hard to establish (Hoggard, 1995:200). In fact, taking all the countries of the world into account, generally speaking, the better off countries tend to be more democratic than the poorer ones. On the contrary, autocratic governments—whether ruled by Mobutu, Trujillo, Batista, Duvalier, Idi Amin, Rhee, and Ayub Khan, just to name a few with long records of governance, all generously supported, financially and militarily, by the Western governments, World Bank and IMF—do not seem to have done much for the economic progress of their people. The fact that many economically successful East or Southeast Asian countries are mainly governed by autocratic regimes, is a mere coincidence and this correlation between the two can not be generalised (Healey et al., 1992: 1-2;).

Further, as Taylor argues, if the authoritarian generals, because of their total control over the country, are so efficient in keeping the government out of the market, what prevents them from taking over the market too? 'The record of the Third World authoritarian states in avoiding corruption and distortions is not encouraging in this regard', he concludes (Taylor, 1995:42). Generals ousting corrupt politicians in a coup, and making trains run in time and the clerks attending the office punctually, usually end up being worse than those they replace, as the experience of many countries—from Pakistan and Bangladesh in Asia to Central American Republics through Africa south of Sahara confirm.

Anti-labour Policies of the East Asian States

However, whether autocratic or not, the governments of East Asia were notorious for their repressive labour policies, for controlling the organised labour movement, for suppressing dissent and unrest, and for ruthlessly restraining wages. Struggles of the working people for higher wages and/or an equitable share of the national income were brought down with a heavy hand. To quote the World Bank study on the *East Asian Miracle,* in almost all the East and Southeast Asian countries (except Hong Kong) the 'governments restructured the labor sector to suppress radical activity in an effort to ensure political stability .... Labour movements in Indonesia and Thailand, while not subject to systematic restructuring, were nonetheless routinely suppressed at the first sign of radicalism' (World Bank, 1993: 164-165).

Where permitted, the labour unions were mostly controlled by the ruling party or the management, and had no independent voice. Labour legislation was non-existent, or weak or diluted in order to encourage private, including foreign, investment. Formation of industry-wide unions was prohibited, enterprise unions were encouraged, while the government gave bureaucracy and business a long hand in dispute settlement. The management had the unrestricted right of hiring and firing. In Japan too, the management was far from friendly to the trade unions, particularly the left wing variety, but their harshness was partly mitigated by the norm of life-time employment for a bulk of employees within a paternalistic social-administrative corporate framework (Bagchi, 1987). To what extent such a policy eventually contributed to social welfare and high growth, and, even to democratic trade unions, in the long run, is a moot question.

One major objective behind this ruthless suppression was to keep wages low. However, after this policy of wage repression had succeeded in promoting a certain amount of increase in production and achieving a higher level of GNP, the government took a more relaxed attitude towards wages, helped by the switch-over to more capital intensive and less labour intensive industrial strategies. It was realised that, for further growth, repressive policies would not do, and would in fact be counter-productive (Hoggard, 1994: 96). However, even when allowed to grow, wages lagged behind labour productivity increases and the share of labour in national income was deliberately kept low. to make room for profit, accumulation and investment (Agarwal et al., 1996).

There is no doubt that low, repressive wages played a certain role in East Asian development. But so did a vigorous public sector and an interventionist state, 'directed' investment and saving, 'created' comparative advantage in high-quality industrial goods, and so on, that were at variance with the theology preached by the World Bank. A multi-dimensional phenomenon like the high growth rate in East Asia, sustained over more than three decades, can not be explained in terms of a single factor alone. The fact is that the strategy of low, repressive wages was abandoned and the anti-trade union policy was modified, as soon as a certain amount of progress was achieved in East Asia (Dasgupta, 1998: 282-284, 307-311, 313).

The NPE view on trade unions does not take into account the historical process by which the trade unions emerged in the modern industrial world, to fulfil a certain need, as the guilds of artisans and craftsmen emerged in the middle ages, to protect their collective interest. In the beginning, the employers were too powerful in relation to the individual workers who were in their employ, exploited them at will, hiring and firing them when these suited their interests.. The trade unions grew as a collective body of workers to protect them from exploitation. They are as much a part of the industrial reality now so that they can not be wished away, not even where they are very weak, as in India.

Labour Market Reform: Global Experience in Practice

In most countries, because of strong local opposition, the governments have not been able to make much headway in this area.

As one World Bank document puts it, 'the Bank has acquiesced in the desire of the governments to avoid the politically sensitive issue of labour retrenchment.' (Corbo and Fischer, 1992;11; Webb, and Shariff, 1992: 78). Only in a country like Ghana, where ghost workers constitute a significant proportion of the public pay roll, a substantial public saving has been achieved by removing many (not all) of those from the list (Toye, 1991: 175).

Frozen Organised Employment

In general, structural adjustment leads to a freeze in public employment. Organised private sector employment also grows seldom because of the low level of private investment and high capital intensity of what takes place. Most of the unemployed fall back on the low productivity 'informal sector' which acts as a 'natural safety net'. The organised sector also takes full advantage of the surplus labour situation by opting for contract labour and casualisation, and for putting out systems that avoid establishment costs and make it easier for them to offload surplus workers as demand falls. This high social cost of structural adjustment programmes has been a recurrent theme in studies by UNICEF and ILO among others. In sub-Saharan Africa structural adjustment has destabilised many poor households, which have been hurt by inflation and food scarcity (ILO, 1995: 4-9; Cornea et al., 1987).

Mobility of Capital Across Frontiers, but Labour Mobility Highly Restricted

As we have noted at the very beginning, the trinity's concern for free trade and global mobility of capital, inputs and products does not entail free flow of labour power across national frontiers. If anything, over the past three decades, immigration laws in the rich countries have become more rigid, and their implementation more severe against labour exports from the poor countries. Unlike capital and products that are supposed to move from anywhere to anywhere in response to demand, movement of people from labour-surplus to labour-deficit areas is actively discouraged. The question is, why the philosophy of free trade in the case of rich country capital, is not applicable in the case of third world labour.

No 'national treatment' for Labour and No 'local content requirement' for Capital

During the pre-reform days, particularly in East Asia, foreign firms competing with domestic ones, had to meet a long list of 'local content, requirements', that greatly blunted their competitive edge. They had to hire a certain percentage of local engineers and other skilled manpower, use local raw material, had to reinvest a part of their profit in the host country market, had to export a certain proportion of the production to foreign markets, and so on. Now, under the new WTO dispensation, capital is to be given 'national treatment' and freed from 'local content requirements' and any kind of discrimination in favour of local enterprises. Given this, why should not labour, irrespective of its source, enjoy a similar 'national treatment' and protection from discrimination. It can not be that 'local content requirement' is bad for capital and good for labour, while 'national treatment' is good for capital but bad for labour. Obviously, the global trinity's love for free trade is confined to the factor the rich countries have in plenty, that is capital, and does not extend to labour, that the poor countries have in plenty.

Japanese Case of Lifelong Employment

Some liberal thinkers wish to take the issue of local market to its logical conclusion. They prescribe the complete overhauling of the labour market, with 'labour power' rather than 'labourer' as the unit. They argue for the replacement of regular labourers working for a scheduled number of hours in a day and for a scheduled number of days in a week, and for all practical purposes for their entire working life, by 'flexi-time workers', many of whom like married women would drop in and out of the labour market in accordance with their family needs, whose contribution would be measured by 'hours' and who would not be required to stick to a given time format. This, they claim, would improve efficiency as it would no longer be necessary for an enterprise to carry permanent workers on the pay roll even when the demand for its product declines.

Those opposed to such radical change in the pattern of labour use point to the Japanese and IBM examples, where a person is recruited for life. Seniority, rather than merit, determines promotion in Japanese enterprises. The Japanese and IBM models, based on a stable and regular workforce, have cemented the bond between the worker and the management, while no such loyalty is expected from the flexi-time workers, they argue (Vittorio and Fischer, 1992:20). Things are of course changing in IBM and Japan. They are no longer what they used to be in the past. Still, the morale of the story remains: one has to make allowance for the national and corporate heritage and the diversity of culture.

MNC Salaries: A Distorting Factor

One major impact of globalisation on labour use and labour market, that has serious implications for a country like ours, is rarely, if ever, discussed. This relates to the distorting impact of the MNC salaries on the wage structure for the country as a whole. With the entry of the multinationals, the pay structure for the higher level of management has been catapulted to a very high level. Though not at par with salaries for the same jobs in the rich countries, these are now high enough to gravitate the ablest of the skilled work force towards them in the poor countries. This is forcing the non-MNC companies, in their turn, to raise the salaries of their own management staff to MNC levels, realising that not to do so, in this age of globalisation, would mean losing them to MNCs. Two major consequences have followed. First, the economy is being divided clearly into those enterprises which can offer MNC level salaries to their professionals and managers, and those who can not.

Second, the disparity between the highest and the lowest paid within the same enterprise is widening alarmingly. The company's balance sheet, while capable of offering astronomical salaries to a few, would not allow a similar hike in the salaries and wages of all other employees. While the ratio between the highest and the lowest paid is around 30:1 in the rich countries, 10: 1 in East Asia, it is around

100:1 in many of the Indian enterprises. Such gross inequality is not sustainable, and is bound to lead to widespread industrial unrest. The Indian companies are, thus, facing a serious dilemma as it is not easy to reduce this disparity – either by raising the wages of the lower order given their vast number, or by restraining wage increases at higher level in the face of global competition.

Anti-poor

Most studies show that structural adjustment, with its attendant policy of sacking workers and reducing wages, gives rise to poverty, unemployment, lowering of wages and a lower level of access to health and education, as government social spending and subsidies are reduced and wages are held back in the face of inflation. (Mzulu, 1993:32). One Bank study admits that 'Little is known about how poor people at large are affected when countrywide subsidies have to be cut back to reduce the government deficit.' But then adds hastily: 'But experience with adjustment programs has already shown clearly that failure to adjust is likely to hurt the poor' (Development Committee, 1990: 31). Another World Bank study, evaluating the performance of the adjustment programmes in the 1980s, admits that calorie intake had stagnated or declined during the 1980s, and the poor had been hurt by pruning of government activities or privatisation of health and other services; in the latter case the richer are targeted by those providing services (World Bank, 1992:4-6; Zuckerman, 1991: 254). The World Bank document edited by Corbo et al. takes a contrary position, that it would have been worse for the poor without SAP. 'Adjustment to adverse external shocks or the effects of previous policy mismanagement inevitably carries some short-run social costs... The report did not find evidence that adjustment lending was associated with an increase in the overall misery of the poor. To the contrary, orderly adjustment supported by Bank lending seems to have been less costly for most of the poor and for the general populace than disorderly adjustment without Bank support was' (Corbo, and Fischer, 1992; 14).

For a long time, social issues were ignored by the World Bank, but from the early 1990s, thanks to a campaign launched by the

UNICEF, a 'social dimension' is now added to structural adjustment loans (SALs), as for example, with a safety net and renewal programmes that cushion the impact of retrenchment in non-viable industries by offering some funding and training for self- employment and other jobs (Development Committee, 1993: v). However, the amount available for these activities have usually proved to be inadequate. On this issue there appears to be a serious contradiction between the Bretton Woods twins and ILO (Development Committee, 1993: 123).

Public Distribution System

On the issue of the public distribution system, the overwhelming opinion inside the Fund-Bank establishment is in favour of trimming it to its minimum size and targeting it in favour of the rural poorest. The opinion on the other side is that, in a situation where the administration is not equipped to identify recipients and perform such targeting, such a policy does hurt the most vulnerable section in a poor country. Further, the higher administrative cost associated with targeting may significantly exceed the benefit it derives from reaching the poorest. (For arguments in favour of targeting, see Knudsen, and Nash, 1991: 143; and against targeting, see Islam, 1991: 157; Development Committee, 1993: 75).

It has been found that the breakdown of the adjustment programme and a policy reversal is more likely in cases where the social cost is high, in terms of its impact on vulnerable sections, e.g., in Zambia in 1987 and in Madagascar in 1991, leading to suspension of adjustment programmes (Foroutan, 1993: 31). A food riot here and a strike there, or, in case of democracies, a few election debacles, are likely to unnerve the government in power and to lead to a rolling back of the economy from structural adjustment.

Labour Standard

While the issues relating to the right to 'hire and fire' and diluting existing labour legislations have been raised by the World Bank and

IMF as a part of their structural adjustment or stabilisation programmes, those relating to 'labour standard' have been, in the main, sponsored by the third of the trinity, the WTO, founded in 1995. The former advocate the unrestricted spread of dynamic, competitive, MNCs, all over the world, but the latter cater to the survival needs of the old, decaying, non-competitive industries of the west, otherwise unable, on their own, to face the competition of the Third World products. In the former case, the two major international agencies wish the government to stay out of the market and advocate the survival of the fittest, while in the second case, WTO seeks state intervention in the form of legislations and implementation of laws relating to child labour, old labour, bonded labour, trade unions, and so on. Most US statesmen, including the president of the country, sometimes advocate one position and sometimes the other, without explicitly recognising the contradiction between the two.

The idea of a labour standard has been prompted less by the concern for the plight of the exploited poor country workers, than by the fear of competition from cheaper third world imports. It may be noted that the first official Commission to enquire into the conditions of workers in the Indian jute industry, in 1895, was inspired by their global rivals, the jute textile industry of Britain whose centre was located in Dundee, Scotland (Buchanan, 1966: 42). In both cases, the management was in the hands of the British, more specifically the Scottish, but they were sworn enemies. The Indian counterparts were seen by their Scottish rivals as intruders in a field that they looked upon as their exclusive preserve. The interest they took in the labour conditions in the Indian jute industry was prompted less by their concern for the low wage and poor working conditions of the proletariat that was in the making in India at that time, but by the fear that the Dundee industry was being swamped by products from this cheap source and its own survival was threatened.

Wages Equalised, GDP Not

The issue of 'labour standard' that the rich countries pushed for acceptance at the WTO ministerial conference at Seattle in 1999

December, was prompted by the same capitalist desire to keep away competition from cheap sources. At Seattle, the rich countries proposed a set of global rules that would standardise labour market behaviour and establish some parity in terms of wages paid and conditions under which the workers operate. The argument being given to justify such standardisation was that cheap wages were conferring on the poor countries a differential advantage in global trade, and that such differential was unfair and was threatening many of the rich country industries.

Such a partisan view ignored what was obvious. The wage level of a country can not be out of tune with the overall state of its economy and its per capita GNP. There can be no mechanical parity between wages, say, in Japan and India when Japan's per capita income is one hundred times more than India's. To demand that wages paid in India should be made comparable with those in rich countries, would amount to driving Indian exports out of the world market.

Low Wages: A Trade Advantage

It can also be argued that a poor country like India, with little capital, technology and management resources, enjoys advantage over the rich countries only in terms of the prevailing low wages. To force them to adopt western wage levels would ruin their industries and would take away whatever little chance they still have in making some of their products competitive in the world market. It might also be asked why the rich countries should grudge this very small advantage the poor countries have over them, when they dominate the world trade so comprehensively and ruthlessly. The share of the poor countries in the global trade is pitifully small and is getting smaller over time. The terms of trade are consistently against the poor country exports as they keep on producing and exporting more to earn less, activities ancillary to trade such as shipping and insurance are also under their near absolute control, while the multinational companies (MNCs) decide, in the case of most poor countries, what to produce and what to sell.

Appalling Labour Conditions in India

Our criticism of the attempted imposition of 'labour standard' by the rich countries does not take away the fact that the conditions in which Indian labourers work are appalling. Many of the issues the Dundee competitors raised in the 1890s regarding the conditions of labour in the jute industry were undeniable, nor was there anything wrong in the support, monetary and otherwise, their trade unions gave to their Indian counterparts. In India, the management had always been reluctant to share its profit with those who toil on the floor, while the continued employment of child labour is an unpardonable sin. The International Labour Office, rightly, takes the view that the provision of social insurance and social protection are basic human rights. . But our present analysis serves the purpose of providing a proper global perspective.

Trinity's Attempt to Standardise Global Rules and to Hijack UN Agenda

This controversy over labour standard is yet another example of two current global tendencies, both emanating from the rich countries and both of which are in the judgement of the author, harmful to poor country interests. First, the tendency to universalise and standardise everything in terms of a set of global rules, that are framed mainly by the rich countries with the interests of their own MNCs in focus. Whether it is patent, investment, competition policy, labour or environment, an obsessive and vulgar desire to bind the world with a uniform set of rules is evident. Such attempt at standardisation ignores the wide divergence that exists between countries in terms of level of development, resource endowment, human resources, historical background and so on. Such standardisation is also opposed to the spirit of the 1993 Convention on bio-diversity, that followed the Rio Earth Summit and emphasised diversity (and not conformity) as something essential for the sustenance of life on this planet (*The World Commission on Environment and Development*, 1987: 13, 65, 151). It is needless to add, that such standardisation is also at the cost of national sovereignty. If forced and child labour exists it is for the government concerned to adopt remedial legislative measures; why should an external agency frame rules on those? When talking about labour standard, ILO has been always keen on social insurance and social protection, as essential ingredients of this concept: items conspicuous in their absence from the WTO agenda (*Development Committee*, 1993: 123).

Trinity's Subordination of UN Agencies

The second is to subordinate the United Nations and its affiliated bodies to those promoted by the G7 countries and the powerful global trinity—World Bank, IMF and WTO—three organisations that are effectively owned and/or controlled by the former and share a common market-oriented economic philosophy. WTO now deals with matters such as investment, patents, agriculture, environment and labour, that should have been left with specialised UN institutions that were created in response to those specific needs, as for example, United Nations Industrial Development Organisation (UNIDO), World Intellectual Property Organisation, Food and Agriculture Organisation, United Nations Environment Programme and the International Labour Office, respectively. Almost all these UN-affiliated organisations had, for a long time, opposed various aspects of globalisation sponsored by the trinity. Over the past few years, by way of intense G7 pressure, almost all of them have been brought in line with the economic philosophy of the trinity.

While in the original format of 1944, the World Bank and the IMF were supposed to report their activities to the Economic and Social Council of the United Nations, this was never done. The agenda of various UN bodies has been hijacked by the institutions patronised by the G7 countries, so much so that today people hardly know of the Economic and Social Council, but, whether they love it or hate it, the trinity influences their lives. The G7 preference for the trinity over the United Nations and their active, financial and political patronage of the former over the latter is understandable, because by their voting power and otherwise, they control the trinity more easily.

In this particular case, by no stretch of imagination can labour standard be taken as a trade matter to be discussed and resolved by WTO, particularly when ILO has been constituted precisely with the objective of dealing with issues such as the labour standard.

The Fiasco at Seattle

The Ministerial Conference of the World Trade Organisation, held at Seattle, Washington, from November 30 to December 3, 1999, was convened with a crowded and diverse agenda, labour standard being only one of the many items discussed. From the point of view of the rich countries, the objective was, first, to consolidate the gains they made at Marakesh in 1994, and second, to spread the idea of standardisation to new areas, such as labour, environment, e-commerce and government procurement, to name a few. From the point of view of the poor countries, the objective was the other way round: that is, first, not to allow standardisation to proceed further, and second, to rectify as far as possible, the damage done to the poor countries at Marakesh. Seattle presented to poor countries like India an opportunity as well as a danger. An opportunity because, we hoped, if the poor countries of the world managed to form an effective trade alliance, did their homework well and bargained hard, they might succeed in rectifying, at least to some extent, the injustice that had been done to them during the 1994 Marakesh agreement on TRIPs (Trade related aspects of Intellectual Property Rights). On the other hand, our fear was, should they fail to present a united front, there was a real and ominous possibility that whatever little remained of their economic sovereignty in the TRIPs agreement would also be taken away by the rich countries. In the language of economics it was a zero sum game: the poor countries could not play for a draw, it was a win situation.

However, as it turned out, while the rich, northern countries, as always, were ready with their drafts prepared in consultation with several hundreds of experts in various fields, over several years, virtually nothing remotely comparable had been done by the poor countries by way of preparation for a meeting that was to decide, effectively, whether they would ever be able to move out of the poverty trap, and to meet the very modest objective of advancing a few inches towards becoming a middle-level income country such as South Korea or Taiwan, in a few generations time.

The Indian government, facing an election in October, a month away from Seattle, was fully preoccupied with the question of its own political survival, and had no time to ponder over the broader issues of globalisaton and trade. It never called a meeting of the undissolved Upper House or of various parties to form a national consensus, that could form the basis of our position on various issues, whatever the outcome in the election, or publish any white paper setting out the government's position on those.

For India time was running out fast for yet another reason. Injustices done in 1994 at Marakesh could not be rectified by India alone, and would have to be done by way of forming trade alliances with other less developed countries. Given its appallingly low share of the world trade—0.6 per cent, compared with 2.67 per cent at the time of Independence—India alone was not going to count for much. The rich countries, no matter how rich they are, also take care to form alliances to augment their bargaining strength, namely, the Common Market in Europe or NAFTA covering the USA, Canada and Mexico, or the Japanese connection with South-East Asia, apart from organisations and institutions such as OECD and G7, the World Bank, the International Monetary Fund and the World Trade Organisation that maintain year-round vigil to protect rich countries' interests.

Among the poor countries too one finds many similar regional trade alliances, such as the ten-member ASEAN (Association of South East Asian Nations) in South-East Asia, Andean Pact, CACM (Central American Common Market), Caricom (Caribbean Community), and Mercosur (Mercado Caomu del Sur) in Latin America, and PTA (Preferential Trade Area for Eastern and Southern Africa), and UDEAC (Union Douaniere et Economique de l'Afrique Centrale) in Africa. A major incentive for the formation of such alliances was that these were permitted, under GATT rules, to extend additional concessions to intra-regional members of those bodies that were denied to other GATT members.

Where is the trade alliance that India belongs to? The most natural of such alliance could have been called the South Asian Common Market, comprising India and her immediate neighbours, countries that were once parts of the British Empire and share a common historical experience and common cultural roots. These countries also share many common economic interests, for example, the world prices of jute and tea, opposition to patenting of basmati by a Texan company, and the distribution of trade gains that would follow from the dismantling of the textile quotas with the ending of the infamous multi-fibre agreement in 2005, to name a few. Such a trade alliance, joining hands with other trade alliances in Asia, Africa and Latin America, could have effectively changed the world trade scenario and vastly improved the bargaining position of the poor countries. Virtually nothing had been done in this direction.

India could also learn from experiences in the past trade negotiations: that, unless united as a rock, the third world countries, given their very low trade shares, count very little in those negotiations. The three key players in the 1994 Marakesh negotiation were the United States, Europe and Japan who exchanged drafts among themselves and finalised everything and did not bother to seek the opinion of the poor countries. Apart from these three, a fourth player that was sometimes consulted was the Cairns group of 14 members, representing rich and middle income countries specialising in agricultural exports and having close links with the G7, namely, Australia, New Zealand, Argentina, Brazil, Canada, Chile, Colombia, Fiji, Hungary, Indonesia, Malaysia, The Philippines and Thailand. This collection of countries, accounting for one-tenth of world GDP and manufacturing output and 30 per cent share in world agricultural exports, made a much bigger impact than the much larger group of less developed counties. If the main players ever wanted to consult the less developed countries, they talked to the South Koreans or the Taiwanese. The poor countries operated on the periphery, remained as shadows, seldom consulted until the rich ones had completed negotiations amongst themselves. As one commentator pointed out: 'Whatever the skills of negotiators from the South, for the most part they are like extras on the GATT stage: the show can't go on without them, but nobody is remotely interested in what they have to say' (Watkins, 1992:37).

One major reason for the poor performance of the less developed countries in the Marakesh negotiations, apart from their weak economic power and lack of unity, was the absence of specialised staff and advice. In the 1990 Brussels meeting during the Uruguay round negotiations, Ms. Carla Hills, US Trade Representative, brought 400 advisers, a number that exceeded the combined strength of all the sub-Saharan Africa and Latin American trade missions put together. The formidable intellectual strength of those 400 was augmented by another 200 or so, lent to Hills by corporate giants such as American Express, Citibank and IBM and, on Intellectual Property Rights, by a coalition of agro-chemical conglomerates led by Pfizer, Monsanto, Cargill and Du Pont (Watkins, 1992: 37-38).

The experts had the ability to examine an issue from all possible angles, and then to project in their drafts selfish US interests as being in the interest of entire mankind. Though 70 countries out of the 108 countries in the GATT negotiations were the less developed ones, they had no voice and expressed their views, on the few occasions that they did, 'within a framework scripted by the major industrialised states' (Hopkins, 1993:143-149). It is hardly possible for India to bring together such an array of skill or to match the US in the number of experts, but the least one would expect of a government is not to surrender without a fight and to devote as much time and energy as possible to proper homework.

The Indian delegation reached Seattle without adequate and comprehensive homework and without any significant skilled assistance. The delegation did not even have a lawyer to examine various drafts. The present author was one of the three MPs (the other two being Sri Kamalnath of Congress and Sri Yerran Naidu of TDP), who formed the core of the official delegation along with the Minister of Commerce, Sri Murasoli Maran. However, as the Seattle drama unfolded, and Labour Standard became the main item that the rich countries wanted to push, the political consensus that eluded us in Delhi for so long, arrived at Seattle.

Some US Congressmen and members of the European

Parliament asked us during the bilateral talks how we could avoid supporting the labour standard, which involved, among other things, banning of child labour and forced labour, recognising trade unions and the right of collective bargaining etc., and our answers were three-fold. First, there was an agency of the United Nations, called International Labour Office (ILO), whose job it was to deal with labour issues in consultation with governments, workers and management. Why should the World Trade Organisation arrogate to itself the specialised task of another international agency, going far beyond its mandate to deal with trade issues? Second, there is something called 'economic sovereignty' that is enjoyed by every independent nation; why should WTO attempt to bind the world with a standardised set of rules, irrespective of wide differences among countries in history, levels of development, factor endowment, comparative advantage and culture? Why should not matters like this. be left with the countries concerned, their governments and the labour movement, not dictated from above by a super world state? Third, we reminded then of our fear that, while proposing a labour standard, the welfare of the poor country workers was far from their minds. Labour standard was to be used as a 'non-tariff barrier' to keep the Third World exports away. We reminded them that the rich countries in general, and US in particular, had a poor record in terms of signing ILO labour conventions; US has signed only 12 out of the 100-odd conventions. We told then that we believed that their expression of sympathy for Indian workers was hypocritical.

What happened at Seattle? Let us begin at the very end. On December 3, 1999, the fourth day of the much-hyped WTO Ministerial Conference at Seattle, the last plenary session began around 10 at night. But it ended quite soon, in less than half an hour, without a joint declaration, without any resolution having been approved, without any decision on the next round of talks, and without even thanking the chair and the participants. Every one on the dais seemed to be in a hurry to draw the curtain. Cerelene Bershefsky, the 49-year old Chair, the host, the US trade representative, admitted in a dull tone, that the conference had to end inconclusively as there was no consensus. She was followed by chairs of the five working groups, each of whom made some brief remarks taking two-three minutes each. The last to speak was Mike Moore, the Director General of WTO who hails from New Zealand, whose job it would be to pick up the pieces and to hold wide-ranging consultations to decide on the future course of action. Humour, wit and pleasantries that normally characterise the final session in such international conferences were conspicuous by their absence. The only touch of humour or poetry in an otherwise grim presentation was Cerlene Bershefsky's reference to 'we, the sleepless at Seattle'. As soon as Mike Moore finished his speech, those on the dais, all of them, got up and ran, as if they were catching the last bus. There was not even a round of applause to mark the ending. It took some while for us to realise that the conference had actually ended.

The meeting ended as badly as it began, as the inauguration ceremony had to be scrapped because of demonstrations. Though their demands varied and were often in conflict with one another, the NGO protesters operating outside were united in their antagonism towards WTO. The most militant amongst them strongly opposed the corporate domination of the world, their ruthless exploitation of the poor countries, and the evils of modern capitalism. While the members of this group were described as 'criminals' and 'trouble-makers', and were at the receiving end of tear gas shells, rubber bullets and truncheons, the demands of about 30000 workers, for labour standard, organised by AFL-CIO, the official union, who marched through downtown Seattle, were publicly supported by none less than President Clinton himself.

Before I reached the WTO conference on November 26, I could not foresee that the Seattle talks would collapse, and so completely. One of our expectations remained unfulfilled, the other more than fulfilled. Our expectation, that, at least a part of the damage done by the Marakesh agreement of 1994, would be rectified, by forming trade alliances with other poor countries did not materialise because on this issue the government lacked political will. But, further attacks to restrict the access of Third World exports to the rich country markets, in the name of labour and environment standards, and further invasion of our markets in the name of standardised global rules on e-commerce, rules on government procurement and so on, were successfully resisted.

India's leading role, buttressed by the efforts of Egypt, Indonesia and some others, helped the smaller countries, some heavily indebted and therefore vulnerable to blackmail, polarise around us. However, some prophets of doom, a section of the Indian business interests associated with the delegation, kept on cautioning us that we would be isolated and punished for our misdemeanour by the mighty USA unless we compromised.

The fact that no agreement emerged was not a bad thing in itself. 'No agreement' was better than a 'bad agreement' imposed on us by the rich countries. The biggest achievement of Seattle was that, for the first time since many years, the hegemony of the United States was challenged and its bullying effectively countered in an international forum. Seattle confirmed, that the world on the eve of a new millennium, in 1999, was not the same as it was in 1994, when the rich countries could make the poor countries dance to their tune on anything they wished.

Seattle failed largely because of the strong resistance given by the poor countries to rich country machinations. Some amongst them could see through President Clinton's crude manipulation of protesting US workers, whose jobs were threatened by Third World exports, to make out a case in favour of a protectionist universal labour standard, despite his erstwhile loud public rhetoric of liberalisation. His threat of trade sanctions against countries violating such core labour standards helped to unite the poor countries: India with Pakistan, the 'less developed' with the 'least developed' led by Bangladesh, and the net food importers with the net food exporters. Third world unity was as solid as a rock. The last straw on their back was the humiliation more than 100 of those countries—mostly smaller, poorer and blacker than others—suffered, when they were excluded from the privileged 'green-room consultations', where only 23 countries were accommodated in the final phase of the negotiations, and others were forced to loiter in the corridors.

That was one of the immediate causes for the resentment. The great majority were resentful because the promised gains from trade expansion, under the 1994 Marakesh agreement and WTO monitoring since 1995, did not materialise in their case. Their boiling anger against the unequal nature of world trade, their small share in it, and MNC domination were forcefully articulated in the plenary. Further, the rich country double-speak on trade liberalisation—when they themselves had been continuing to practice protectionism under various guises, and to give astronomical subsidies to their own agricultural and industrial producers, while asking the poor countries to do otherwise—stood fully exposed.

There were also differences between Europe and the USA on a number of points that could not be reconciled such as on agricultural subsidy, on the naming of the coming round of trade negotiations ('Seattle round', as the US wanted, or the 'millennium round', as the Europeans wanted) or on the strategy (Should this be confined to a few items, as the US wanted, or should this be a comprehensive package so that at the end of the negotiations everybody could write back home saying that it had gained at least something, as the Europeans wanted).

Where do we go from here? Having taken a principled stand, and having acquired some prestige in the process, should we not build on the advantage gained to press for the renegotiations of the Marakesh agreement itself? And should we also not try to unify the poor countries and take their leadership on issues like labour standard or labour market reform, rather than chasing the rich nations in order to obtain an elusive permanent seat in the Security Council.

REFERENCES

Agarwal, Pradeep, Subir V. Gokarn, Veena Mishra, Kirit S. Parikh and Kunal Sen (eds.) (1996), *Policies for Industrial Competitiveness : What India Can Learn From the East Asian Experience*, Indira Gandhi Institute of Development Research, Project Report to International Development Research Centre, Ottawa, Canada, Bombay, (mimeo).

Bagchi, Amiya Kumar (1987), *Public Intervention and Industrial Restructuring in China, India, and Republic of Korea*, International Labour Organisation, Asian Employment Programme (ARTEP), New Delhi.

Buchanan, Daniel Houston (1966), *The Development of Capitalistic Enterprise in India*, Frank Cass & Co, London, First Edition 1934.

Corbo, Vittorio and Stanley Fischer (1992), "Adjustment Programmes and Bank Support: Rationale and Main Results", in Vittorio Corbo, Stanley Fischer & Steven B. Webb (eds.), *Adjustment Lending Revisited - Policies to Restore Growth, A World Bank Symposium,* World Bank, Washington DC.

Cornea, Andrea, Richard Jolly and Frances Stewert (1987), *Adjustment With a Human Face*, Oxford University Press, Oxford.

Dasgupta, Biplab (1998), *Structural Adjustment, Global Trade and the New Political Economy of Development,* Sage (Delhi) and Zed Books (London).

Development Committee (1989 and 1990), Development Committee, Number Twenty Three, Problems and Issues of Structural Adjustment, April and September.

Foroutan, Faezeh (1993), "Trade Reform in Ten Sub-Saharan African Countries: Achievements and Failures", Policy Research Working paper 1222, World Bank, Policy Research Department, Trade Policy Division.

Grindle, Merilee S. and John W. Thomas (1991), *Public Choices and Policy Change - The Political Economy of Reform in Developing Countries*, John Hopkins University Press, Baltimore and London.

Healey, John, Richard Ketley and Mark Robinson (1992), *Political Regimes and Economic Policy Patterns in Developing Countries*, 1978-88, ODI No 67, London.

Hindess, B. (1988), *Choice, Rationality and Social Theory*, Unwin-Hyman, London.

Hoggard, Stephen (1994), "Politics and Institutions in the World Bank's East Asia," in Fishlow, Albert, Catherine Gwin, Stephen Haggard, Dani Rodrik & Robert Wade (eds.), *Miracle or Design: Lessons from the East Asian Experience*, Overseas Development Council, Policy Essays No 11, Washington DC.

—— (1995), *Democracy and Economic Growth*, in Schydlowsky, Daniel, (ed), *Structural Adjustment - Retrospect and Prospect*, Praeger, Westport, Connecticut, London, Chapter 11.

Hopkins, Raymond F. (1993), "Developing Countries in the Uruguay Round : Bargaining Under Uncertainty and Inequality", in Avery, William P (ed.), *World Agriculture and the GATT*, Lynne Rienner Publishers, Boulder & London.

ILO (1993), "Structural Change and Adjustment in Zimbabwe", Interdepartmental Project on Structural Adjustment, Occasional Paper 16.

—— (1995), Sectoral Activities Programme, Joint Meeting on the Impact of Structural Adjustment in the Public Services (*Efficiency, Quality Improvement and Working Conditions*), Geneva 24-30 May

Islam, Nurul (1991), "Comments", in Thomas, Vinod, Ajay Chibber, Mansoor Dailami, Jaime De Melo (eds.) *Restructuring Economies in Distress Policy Reform and the World Bank*, World Bank, Oxford University Press, Oxford.

Knudsen, Odin, and John Nash (1991), *Agricultural Policy*, in Thomas, Vinod, Ajay Chibber, Mansoor Dailami, Jaime De Melo (eds.) *Restructuring Economies in Distress Policy Reform and the World Bank*, World Bank,

Oxford University Press.

Lal, Deepak and H. Myint (1996), *The Political Economy of Poverty, Equity and Growth- A Comparative Study*, Clarendon Press, Oxford.

Mzulu, Joseph (1993), "Real Exchange Rate Depreciation and Structural Adjustment : The Case of the Manufacturing Sector in Zimbabwe (1980-1991)", IDS, Ph. D. thesis.

Olson, Mancur (1982), *The Rise and Decline of Nations: Economic Growth, Stagflation and Social Rigidities,* Yale University Press, New Haven and London.

Plant, Roger (1994), *Labour Standards & Structural Adjustment*, ILO, Geneva.

Taylor, Lance (1995), "Policy Reform in the 1980s", in Daniel M. Schydlowsky (ed.), *Structural Adjustment - Retrospect and Prospect*, Praeger, Westport, Connecticut, London.

Toye, John (1991), Ghana, in Paul Mosley, James Harrigan and John Toye, eds.), *Aid and Power - the World Bank and Policy-based Lending*, Volume 2, Routledge, London.

—— (1996), "Structural Adjustment, Labour Markets and Employment Policy, in Charles Avery (ed.), *Constraints on the Success of Structural Adjustment Programmes in Africa*, Macmillan, London.

Watkins, Kevin (1992), *Fixing the Rules: North - South Issues in International Trade and GATT Uruguay Round*, Catholic Institute for International Relations, London

Webb, Steven B and Karim Shariff (1992), "Designing and Implementing Adjustment Programs", in Vittorio Corbo, Stanley Fischer and Steven B. Webb (eds.), *Adjustment Lending Revisited - Policies to Restore Growth, A World Bank Symposium,* World Bank, Washington DC .

World Bank (1992), Policy Planning and Research Department, *Adjustment Lending: An Evaluation of Ten Years of Experience*, Washington.

—— (1992), Poverty Reduction: Handbook and Operation Directive.

—— (1993), *The East Asian Miracle - Economic Growth and Public Policy*, Oxford University Press, Oxford.

—— (1989), Sub-Saharan Africa: From Crisis to Sustainable Growth.

WCED (The World Commission on Environment and Development) (1987), *Our Common Future*, Oxford University Press, Oxford (The Brundtland Report).

Zuckerman, Elaine (1991), "The Social Cost of Adjustment", in Vinod Thomas, Ajay Chibber, Mansoor Dailami, Jaime De Melo (eds.), 1991, *Restructuring Economies in Distress Policy Reform and the World Bank*, World Bank, Oxford University Press.

IV

STATE EXPERIENCES

12

ECONOMIC REFORMS, PACE OF DEVELOPMENT AND EMPLOYMENT SITUATION IN PUNJAB

SUCHA SINGH GILL

Introduction

Punjab had been one of the most vibrant regions of India before the introduction of the economic reforms of 1991, popularly known as the New Economic Policy. Though it had shown signs of fatigue in the disturbed decade of the 1980s yet the past momentum had kept its dynamism at the level of the all India average. When the economy needed corrections in the distortions of the pattern of development, a paradigm shift had already taken place replacing state intervention by market mechanism. In the effort to manage the fiscal crisis, the capability of the administration to intervene got seriously undermined. When the economy of the region is at the crossroads, the government has no resources to introduce any correction/ restructuring. In this paper, an attempt is made to study the economy of Punjab in the post-reform period. The main objective of the paper is to understand the process of employment generation and throw some light on the emerging unemployment situation in the state. The paper is organised in four sections. Section I compares the growth performance of the state in the post-reform period with the pre-reform period. Section II shows the broad trends of employment/ unemployment in the state. Section III analyses the declining employment potentials in agriculture. The last section shows the pattern of employment in the organised sector, job preferences of the job-seekers and makes a brief comment on the policy options.

Unlike other advanced regions in India, the Punjab economy has become crisis ridden in the post-reform period. This is reflected through a relative slow down in economic growth, which began in the 1980s. With the petering out of the green revolution, the Punjab economy began to lose its dynamism. During the 1960s and 1970s, the rate of growth of the state's gross domestic product was substantially higher than the all India average but during the decade of the 1980s, Punjab's annual rate of growth was lower than the all India average during four out of the ten years. The situation took a serious turn in the 1990s when Punjab's rate of growth consistently (except in 1996/97) remained lower than the all-India average. Between 1992/93 and 1997/98 (the Eighth Five Year Plan Period), the average annual growth rate of Punjab was 5.1 per cent compared to the all India average 6.8 per cent. Punjab's position has been reversed vis-à-vis the Indian economy in the 1990s compared to the 1970s. The average annual rate of growth of the Punjab economy during 1974/78 (the Fifth Five Year Plan) was 6.7 per cent compared to 5.1 per cent for India as a whole. The slow down in Punjab's economic growth rate in relation to the Indian economy is manifested in all the three sectors namely, primary, secondary and tertiary in the 1990s as compared to the 1970s.

The deceleration in the growth process is more pronounced in the primary sector which is identified in the state with agricultural and allied activities only. During the disturbed decade of the 1980s, this sector experienced a negative growth rate only in one year (1983/84) whereas it has shown a negative growth rate in three years (1991/92, 1995/96, 1997/98) during the 1990s. As compared to an average annual growth rate of more than 5 per cent in the 1980s, the primary sector's annual growth rate has been 2.41 per cent in the 1990s. Negative growth rates are caused by occasional crop failure in a situation of exhausted potentials of future increase in per acre yield of principal crops. With the present level of technology, the state has already realised the potential yield for wheat and paddy to the extent of 77 per cent and 75.45 per cent respectively (PAU, 1998). These two crops account for nearly 70 per cent of the area under cultivation and further marginal increase in per acre yield although possible would be with a very high marginal cost. The state is not moving towards crop diversification, as there are high risks due to instability in yield, return and prices of competing crops. Diversification is almost impossible in the absence of minimum support prices, assured market clearance, storage and other support systems for the new crops. When there is a dire need of a state support mechanism for the introduction of diversification of the economy in general and that of agriculture in particular, the policy environment has changed against state intervention and in favour of market forces. In fact, the orientation of the government in the state underwent a major change. In the 1980s, the whole focus of the government policy shifted from development expenditure towards non-development expenditure owing to disturbed conditions. Development expenditure which used to be 71.92 per cent of the total government expenditure of the Punjab government in 1980/81 declined to 64.92 per cent in 1990/91. When the situation normalised in the early 1990s the same trend continued owing to fiscal crisis in the state and also due to the policy shift introduced in India in 1991 with reflection on the policy of the Punjab government. Development expenditure further declined from 64.92 per cent of the total expenditure of the state in 1990/91 to 46.49 per cent in 1998/99 (Table 12.1). The relative fall in public investment has contributed to the slowdown of the development process in the state. This decline is more pronounced in capital expenditure (at constant prices 1980/81) in agriculture during the 1980s and 1990s compared to that of the 1970s (Chand, 2000). The slowdown in economic growth and decline in public expenditure in agriculture has serious negative implications for employment generation in the state.

Trends of Employment and Unemployment

Recently, the Planning Commission has estimated that Punjab would experience an increase in unemployment, although the rate of growth of labour force would be low compared to the all-India average. In this category, the state is bracketed with Kerala and Tamil Nadu. Punjab is expected to have a low growth rate of employment, that

TABLE 12.1: **Expenditure of the Punjab Government**

(Rs. crores)

Year	Development Expenditure	Non-Development Expenditure	Grant-in-aid	.Total
1	2	3	4	5
1978-79	283.61	101.60	1.08	386.57
	(73.36)	(26.37)	(0.27)	(100.00)
1979-80	296.44	113.91	1.51	411.86
	(71.98)	(27.66)	(0.36)	(100.00)
1980-81	395.25	153.20	1.08	549.33
	(71.92)	(27.88)	(0.20)	(100.00)
1981-82	432.02	186.26	1.10	619.98
	(69.78)	(30.04)	(0.18)	(100.00)
1982-83	466.41	214.14	3.01	683.56
	(68.23)	(33.63)	(0.41)	(100.00)
1983-84	583.05	235.14	1.67	819.86
	(71.12)	(28.68)	(0.20)	(100.00)
1984-85	615.17	319.45	6.72	941.34
	(65.35)	(33.94)	(1.50)	(100.00)
1985-86	773.19	372.24	17.47	1162.90
	(66.49)	(32.01)	(1.50)	(100.00)
1986-87	773.45	418.33	10.31	1202.09
	(64.34)	(34.80)	(0.86)	(100.00)
1987-88	1190.57	432.27	10.70	1633.54
	(72.88)	(26.46)	(0.66)	(100.00)
1988-89	1302.21	546.19	19.08	1867.48
	(69.73)	(29.25)	(1.02)	(100.00)
1989-90	1313.31	685.31	22.44	2121.02
	64.98	(33.91)	(1.11)	(100.00)
1990-91	1635.98	855.54	28.28	2519.91
	(64.92)	(33.96)	(1.12)	(100.00)
1991-92	3183.44	981.94	31.33	4196.71
	(75.85)	(23.40)	(0.75)	(100.00)

(contd.)

TABLE 12.1 *(contd.)*

1	2	3	4	5
1992-93	1936.72	1452.66	33.14	3422.52
	(56.59)	(42.44)	(0.97)	(100.00)
1993-94	2131.77	1875.35	57.12	4138.98
	(51.49)	(46.38)	(1.41)	(100.00)
1994-95	2192.70	3802.33	47.73	4336.91
	(36.29)	(62.92)	(0.79)	(100.00)
1995-96	2552.93	3017.67	64.39	5634.99
	(45.31)	(53.55)	(1.14)	(100.00)
1996-97	3947.16	2911.90	66.61	6925.67
	(56.99)	(42.05)	(0.96)	(100.00)
1997-98(R)	4463.32	3661.46	70.87	8195.65
	(54.46)	(44.68)	(0.86)	(100.00)
1998-99(B)	4441.70	5042.47	71.16	9555.33
	(46.49)	(52.77)	(0.74)	(100.00)

Notes: Figures in brackets are percentages. R-Revised, B-Budget.

Source: Economic Advisor to Government of Punjab, *Statistical Abstract of Punjab* (various years).

is, 0.73 per cent per annum during the Ninth Plan period, that is, 1997-2002 (Table 12.2). The labour force is projected to grow at the rate of 2.27 per cent per annum during the corresponding period. Punjab's projected growth rate of employment is the lowest among the major states. Consequently, the average level of unemployment during the Ninth Plan is estimated at 10,65,000 persons (Planning Commission, 1999). The estimates of the Planning Commission indicate that among the major states, the employment situation is likely to deteriorate most seriously in Punjab. It is placed at the worst position even among the low performing states like Bihar and Uttar Pradesh. The estimates of the Planning Commission are based on the National Sample Survey Usual Status concept of measurement of unemployment. This has been considered as a better measure compared to the Current Weekly Status and Current Daily Status concept in a situation where economic compulsion forces the unemployed to undertake subsidiary work for survival owing to lack of a public social security system. Further, these estimates have been based on information pertaining to 1987/88 and 1993/94 NSS data.

TABLE 12.2: **Employment Growth and Growth of Labour in Major States***

State	Employment Growth Rate 1997-2002	Labour Force 1997-2002	Growth Rate 2002-2007
All-India	2.44	2.51	2.47
Andhra Pradesh	3.11	2.39	2.34
Assam	3.73	2.73	2.79
Bihar	1.29	2.58	2.85
Gujarat	2.53	2.37	2.18
Haryana	3.49	2.99	2.84
Karnataka	2.81	2.47	2.26
Kerala	1.26	2.30	1.90
Madhya Pradesh	2.61	2.39	2.48
Maharashtra	2.54	2.26	2.20
Orissa	2.35	2.10	2.13
Punjab	0.73	2.27	2.08
Rajasthan	2.71	2.84	2.91
Tamil Nadu	2.00	1.98	1.70
Utter Pradesh	2.07	2.57	2.68
West Bengal	2.75	2.52	2.45

Note : * Employment and labour force estimates are on usual status basis.

Source: Planning Commission, *Ninth Five Year Plan*, Vol. I., Government of India, New Delhi, 1999, p. 200.

The data collected by the Economic and Statistical Organisation of Punjab indicate that the unemployment situation in the state is more serious than projected by the Planning Commission. These data were collected as part of the Fourth Economic Census conducted in Punjab on the direction of the Central Statistical Organisation,

Government of India during April-June 1998. The additional information on unemployed persons in the age group of 18-35 years was collected along with this census. This was carried out by deploying school teachers and staff of other departments under the supervision of Tehsildars, BDPOs and EOs of municipalities. The data thus collected bring out that there were 14,71,527 unemployed persons in the state. Out of this number 10,40,269 (70.69 per cent) belong to rural areas and 4,31,258 (29.31 per cent) belong to urban areas. Of the total estimated unemployed persons 8,97,860 (61.02 per cent) are educated with qualifications of matriculation and above and 5,73,667 persons (38.98 per cent) are uneducated, both literate (below matric) and illiterate. There are visible differences in the nature of unemployment between rural and urban areas. In rural areas the educated and uneducated unemployed are evenly distributed with respective share of 56.17 per cent and 43.87 per cent. But in urban areas of the state 72.81 per cent are educated and 27.19 per cent are uneducated (Table 12.3). This indicates that educational needs are better served in urban areas while rural areas are lagging behind, resulting in a large proportion of the workforce with little education. The unemployed workforce which is labelled as uneducated cannot be absorbed in the secondary and tertiary sectors without their being provided with further schooling

TABLE 12.3: **Unemployment in Punjab, 1998**

Area	Educated	Uneducated	Total
Rural	583851	456418	1040269
	(56.13)	(43.87)	(100.00)
Urban	314009	117249	431258
	(72.81)	(27.19)	(100.00)
Total	897860	573667	1471527
	(61.02)	(38.98)	(100.00)

Note: Figures in the brackets are in percentage.

Source: Economic Advisor, "Report on Unemployed Persons (Age Group 18-35 years) Desirous of Seeking Self Employed in Punjab", unpublished, Government of Punjab, Chandigarh, 1998.

and raising their skill levels. In the absence of the necessary training programmes aimed at imparting skills, the uneducated rural unemployed are destined to stay in the rural areas and remain underemployed visibly engaged in agriculture.

Information about the educational qualifications of unemployed persons shows that a vast majority of them are matriculate freshers and undergraduates. The second largest number consists of craftsmen, that is, trained ITIs and work experienced followed by trained teachers. The least unemployment is found among doctors, engineers and agricultural specialists (Table 12.4). Evidently, the overwhelmingly large number and proportion of unemployed among the educated belong to those with general education (Chand, 1993).

A survey of unemployment and underemployment carried out during 1979-81 brings out that among the unemployed in rural Punjab, nearly 80 per cent were those with qualifications of matriculation and above. But among the underemployed, a majority of them were either illiterate or just literate. Persons with qualifications of matriculation and above constituted 17.25 per cent of the total underemployed. Thus, unemployment is mainly the problem of the educated while underemployment is that of uneducated persons in Punjab (Krishan, 1986, pp.135-146 and 193-196).

The 50th round of NSS (1993-94) has brought out that the major portion of unemployment comes to the share of the youth. In Punjab, rural males and females are placed in the category of medium unemployment with respective rates being 2.9 per cent and 3.4 per cent by Usual Principal occupation plus subsidiary occupation, while urban male and urban female youth are experiencing high rate of unemployment with respective rates being 6.8 per cent and 17.3 per cent (Parthasarathy and Nirmala, 2000).

Declining Labour Absorption and Underemployment in Agriculture

The labour absorption capacity of agriculture is on the decline in the state. The per acre requirement of labour for all the major crops except cotton declined between 1970/71 and 1983/84. The annual

TABLE 12.4: **Number of Unemployed according to Qualification in Punjab**

Year	Matriculate Freshers	Undergraduate Freshers	Graduate Freshers	Postgraduate Freshers	Graduate Engineers	Diploma Engineers	Craftsman Trained ITI and Work Experienced	Doctors		Agriculture Specialists	Teachers			Total Including (others)
								Allopathic	Others		M.Ed. and B.Ed.	Language	PTI CPED DP.BP &MP	
1980	72215	27660	28221	6454	246	2430	25849	44	262	331	18480	1488	9948	214738
1990	158989	42893	35934	10581	437	5189	34104	27	275	643	23425	956	4925	409211
1996	165091	36089	29984	8305	1052	7213	33516	60	481	340	28051	481	2625	387192
1997	180419	46100	31285	7682	1000	7124	35006	75	409	604	37038	541	3029	405426
1998	185055	52251	30239	7832	931	7205	38997	106	394	653	35798	498	2162	410161

Source : Economic Advisor, *Statistical Abstract of Punjab 1999*, Government of Punjab, Chandigarh, 2000, p. 459.

rate of decline was highest for paddy (2.36 per cent) followed by wheat (2.22 per cent), rapeseed and mustard (1.69 per cent), maize (1.61 per cent), bajra (1.34 per cent), sugarcane (0.98 per cent) and jowar (0.25 per cent). Only in the case of cotton, an increase at the rate of 0.19 per cent per year was noticed. But the overall requirement of labour increased at the rate of 1.08 per cent per annum. The same pattern has been observed in the case of Haryana (Bhalla, 1987). As shown in Table 12.5, per acre labour absorption had been declining but the overall labour absorption in agriculture has been increasing during the 1970s. The increase in total labour absorption was due to the increase in gross cropped area and shift in cropping pattern from low labour absorption crops towards high labour absorption crops. The major contribution in the process had been the introduction of paddy in the kharif crops.

TABLE 12.5: **Crop-wise Trend in Growth Rates of Labour Absorption Per Hectare 1970-71 to 1983-84 in Punjab and Haryana**

Crops	Punjab	Haryana
Paddy	-2.36	-1.99 ***
Jowar	-0.25 ***	-0.50 **
Bajra	-1.34	-0.86
Maize	-1.61 ***	1.58 ***
Wheat	-2.22 ***	-1.88
Rapeseed and Mustard	1.69 ***	-2.35
Cotton	0.19	0.12
Sugarcane	-0.98 ***	1.23 ***
Total	1.079 *	0.230

Notes : * significant at 95 per cent. ** significant at 98 per cent. *** significant at 99 per cent.

Source: Shiela Bhalla, "Trends in Employment in Indian Agriculture, Land and Asset Distribution", *IJAE*, Vol. 42, No. 4, Oct-Dec. 1987, pp. 545, 548-549.

The gross cropped area expanded from 56,78,000 hectares in 1970/71 to 67,63,000 hectares in 1980/81. The gross cropped area increased by 19.11 per cent between 1970/71 and 1980/81. The net sown area increased by only 3.40 per cent during this period. The major factor which contributed to the increase in gross cropped area was the increase in the area sown more than once. Along with the expansion in the double cropped area, the shift in cropping pattern in favour of paddy cultivation increased the labour requirement more than the decline caused by the declining per acre requirements.

The trend of overall increase in labour absorption in the 1970s has been reversed in 1980s and 1990s. The total labour absorption in agriculture of the state stood at 480.38 million man-days during the triennium ending 1983/84. This declined to 445.56 million man days during the triennium ending 1992/93 and further to 431.67 million man days during the triennium ending 1996/97. The overall decline in employment in 1992/93 over 1983/84 is estimated at 7.25 per cent and in 1996/97 over 1983/84 is estimated at 10.14 per cent (Table 12.6). The major factor in the decline of absolute employment of labour in agriculture is the sharp decline in mandays requirements per hectare in paddy cultivation. Per hectare labour requirements in this crop stood at 104.34 man days during the triennium ending 1983/84. This declined to 70.60 man days during the triennium ending 1992/93 and 63.37 man days per hectare during the triennium ending 1996/97. The per hectare decline in employment in paddy cultivation in 1996/97 over 1983/84 is estimated at 39.27 per cent. This is accompanied by continuing decline in per hectare labour absorption in the wheat crop. The per hectare labour requirement in wheat stood at 49.44 man days during the triennium ending 1983/84 but declined to 43.89 man days during the triennium ending 1992/93 and 42.79 man days during the triennium ending 1996/97. The labour requirements per hectare in wheat cultivation declined between 1996/97 and 1983/84 by 13.45 per cent. Per hectare labour requirement increased mildly in case of cotton and rapeseed and mustard between 1983/84 and 1992/93 but declined between 1992/93 and 1996/97. The labour absorption per hectare stood at 94.42 man days during 1983/84 in cotton, increased to 98.59 man days during 1992/93 but declined to 95.08 man days in 1996/97. The cotton crop showed a positive employment absorption during 1996/97 over 1983/84 by 0.70 per cent. The rapeseed and mustard crops showed a similar trend in per

TABLE 12.6: **Estimated Total Employment in Principal Crops ('000 mandays) in Punjab**

Year (Triennium ending)	Paddy	Wheat	Cotton	Rapeseed and Mustard	Others	All Crops
1983-84	141519.47	149786.39	61184.16	3943.11	123946.73	480379.86
1992-93	144871.20	143271.44	69735.66	3527.01	84152.21	445557.52
1996-97	139836.04	139281.45	65351.34	3557.21	83644.51	431670.55

Notes: 1. Employment is calculated by multiplying area under different crops by per hectare employment in respective crops (that is, paddy, wheat, cotton, rapeseed and mustard). In case of other crops weighted average (of four crops) per hectare employment is multiplied by the total area under other crops.

2. Total employment in 1992-93 over 1983-84 declined by 7.25 per cent; the employment declined by 10.14 per cent in 1996-97 over 1983-84.

Source : Calculated from Directorate of Economics and Statistics, *Cost of Cultivation of Principal Crops in India*, Ministry of Agriculture, Government of India, New Delhi, 1991, 1996 and 2000.

hectare labour absorption. Per hectare labour requirement stood at 41.22 mandays during the triennium ending 1989/90, increased to 44.46 man-ays during the triennium ending 1992/93 but declined to 37.98 mandays during the triennium ending 1996/97. This indicated a decline in employment in 1996/97 over 1989/90 by 7.86 per cent. The average per hectare labour absorption in these four crops declined by 20.31 per cent between the triennium ending 1983/84 and 1996/97 (Table 12.7).

TABLE 12.7: **Per Hectare Employment of Labour in Major Crops of Punjab (Man days)**

Year (Triennium ending)	Paddy	Wheat	Cotton	Repeseed and Mustard	Weighted Averaged of the Four Crops
1983-84	104.34	49.44	94.42	41.22*	69.96
1992-93	70.60	43.89	98.59	44.46	59.22
1996-97	63.37	42.79	95.08	37.98	55.75
	(-63.37)	(-13.43)	(0.70)	(-7.86)	(-20.31)

Notes: 1. * Figure relates to year triennium ending 1989-90.
2. Figures in parenthesis indicate percentage change in 1996-97 over 1983-84.

Source: Same as for Table 12.6.

The factors which operated in favour of increasing total labour absorption in agriculture during the 1970s in spite of the falling per hectare labour requirements are not present in the 1980s and 1990s. In the 1970s, the increase in cropping intensity and change in cropping pattern in favour of more labour intensive crops more than compensated for the negative factor (per hectare decline in labour requirement), leading to net increase in the total labour absorption in agriculture. In the 1980s and 1990s the cropping intensity has grown at a slower rate approaching towards saturation level (184.5 in 1996/97). Secondly, the cropping pattern has also stabilised. The wheat-paddy rotation has come to occupy the leading position and share around 70 per cent of the total cropped area with cotton finishing as a distant third crop with its share of nearly 9 per cent of the area. All other crops account for around 20 per cent of the total cropped area (Table 12.8). The increase in the area owing to increase in cropping intensity has been absorbed by paddy. In addition, whatever area has been released by displacing other crops has also been absorbed by wheat and paddy. The largest share in increased cropping area (75 per cent) has been captured by paddy and the rest (25 per cent) has gone to wheat. The decline in total absorption of labour in agriculture of Punjab is explained by the decline in per hectare labour requirement in both the crops. In the case of wheat the per hectare labour requirement was very low (42.79 man days in 1996/97); as for paddy, it is fast approaching a low level (it was 63.37 man days in 1996/97).

TABLE 12.8: **Area under Major Crops in Punjab**

('000 hectares)

Year Triennium Ending	Paddy	Wheat	Cotton	Rapeseed and Mustard	Others	Total Cropped Area
1983-84	1356.33	3029.96	687.00	95.66	1771.68	6940.33
	(19.54)	(43.65)	(9.90)	(1.38)	(25.33)	(100.00)
1992-93	2052.00	3264.33	707.33	79.33	1421.01	7524.00
	(27.27)	(43.39)	(9.40)	(1.05)	(18.89)	(100.00)
1996-97	2206.66	3255.00	687.33	93.66	1500.35	7743.00
	(28.50)	(42.04)	(8.88)	(1.21)	(19.38)	(100.00)

Notes: 1. Figures in parenthesis are percentage of the total cropped area.

2. Increase in total cropped area in 1996-97 over 1983-84 is 11.57.

3. Net sown area has declined marginally from 4208,000 hectares in triennium ending 1983-84 to 4196,330 hectares in triennium ending 1996-97.

The high level of mechanisation in sowing, irrigation and harvesting of both these crops has continuously replaced human labour by machine. This is confirmed from the estimated increase in the number of agricultural machinery and implements in Punjab between 1977 and 1996 (Table 12.9). In 1977 agricultural machinery was dominated by bullock operated ploughs (iron and wooden), tubewells, carts and bullock operated cane crushers. In 1996, implements such as ploughs (iron and wooden), carts, bullock operated cane crushers nearly disappeared from the scene nor was their number reported in various statistical publications. In 1990s the scene has been dominated by power operated machinery and implements. They include tubewells, tractors and trailers, threshers, tractor drawn disc harrows, tillers, combines, spray pumps and so on. The implements in use in the agriculture of the state, at present, show

TABLE 12.9: **Agricultural Machinery and Implements in Punjab ('000 number)**

	Implements and Machinery	1977	1996
1.	Tractors/Trailers	64.3	330
2.	Tiller/Cultivators	-	228
3.	Disc harrows (T. drawn)	-	248
4.	Seed cum-fertiliser drill	-	135
5.	Spray pumps	-	510
6.	Tractor drawn combines	-	4.6
7.	Self propelled combines	-	2.3
8.	Threshers	-	305
9.	Cane crushers (bullock cooperated)	75	-
10.	Cane crushers (power operated)	17	35
11.	Tubewells	468	875
12.	Wooden ploughs	602	-
13.	Iron ploughs	907	-
14.	Carts	332	-

Source: Economic Advisor, *Statistical Abstract of Punjab, 1983*, Government of Punjab, Chandigarh, 1984. Statistician, Department of Agriculture, *Agricultural Statistics of Punjab*, Government of Punjab, Chandigarh, 2000.

high level of mechanisation, which has displaced (completely) animal power and human labour to a considerable extent. In fact, the double crop system and commercial (investment intensive) nature of agriculture require quick sowing and harvesting and induce greater use of power operated machines. This is beneficial for intensive use of land (fixed factor) and to overcome the risk of unfavourable weather conditions damaging the matured crops.

The shrinking absolute labour absorption in agriculture has created a very serious problem of underemployment in agriculture. Using the definition of 273 standard man days of employment with 42 hours per week as full employment of a person (Krishan, 1986), the level of underemployment can be worked out. The total work-force available in Punjab agriculture consisted of 19,17,210 cultivators, 14,52,828 agricultural labourers plus 3,63,207 migrant labourers (available even during the lean period). Thus, the total workforce available for work turns out to be 37,33,245 but a full year's work is available for 24,48,118 persons. This means 12,85,127 persons, or one-third of the total can be withdrawn from agricultural (and livestock) activities. Out of this, full work is available for 9,09,673 cultivators and 15,38,445 agricultural labourers. Thus, 10,07,537 cultivators and 2,77,590 agricultural labourers are surplus, causing underemployment for the rest of the workforce (Table 12.10). The problem of underemployment is very serious among cultivators compared to agricultural labour. The majority of small and marginal cultivators suffer from this problem more acutely. This is partially on account of the small size of holdings which generate work for fewer man days and partially on account of hiring in of agricultural labourers for certain activities which cultivators themselves do not undertake owing to various social and economic factors. At the same time, the fast shrinking time gap between harvesting of one crop and sowing of another crop (because of increasing cropping intensity), forces the small (and marginal) cultivators to hire in some agricultural labour.

Employment Pattern of Organised Sector, Job Preference and Policy Options

The discussion on the trend and level of unemployment and under-

TABLE 12.10: **Underemployment/Unemployment in the Workforce in Agriculture and Livestock of Punjab, 1991**

Category of Persons	Number of Persons Working	Full Work Available for the Number of Persons	No. of Surplus Persons
Cultivators	1917210	909673	1007537
Agricultural labourers	1816035*	1538445	277590
Total	3733245	2448118	1285127

Notes: 1. * indicates that this figure includes 3,63,207 estimated migrant labourers who stay in rural Punjab even during the lean period. This is based on estimates of M.S. Sidhu, P.S. Rangi and Karam Singh, "A Study on Migrant Agricultural Labour in Punjab", Panjab Agricultural University, Ludhiana, 1997.

2. Total employment in agriculture is estimated on the basis of per acre labour requirement multiplied by total area under different crops (Table 12.4 in this paper). Nearly 50 per cent labour requirement of livestock is added on the basis of the share of third sector in the total SDP in ratio to the share of agriculture in SDP.

3. The distribution of labour requirement between hired and family labour is estimated on the basis of share of respective labour in cost of cultivation of different crops. The family labour attributed solely to cultivators and hired labour to agricultural labour.

employment brings out several dimensions of the problem. There is a serious problem of underemployment among the farmers (for more than half of the time there is no work for them) and agricultural labourers. At the same time, open unemployment is on the rise, either among the uneducated or the educated in the rural areas. Among the educated unemployed, the largest proportion consists of matriculates, fresh undergraduates and fresh graduates with general education. Most of the unemployed are in the younger age group from 15-29 years and can be grouped as unemployed youth. The employment generation strategy and policy has to be multipronged depending on the capabilities and aspirations of the unemployed and the resource endowment of the state.

A long-term strategy demands that in the foreseeable future

(say 10-15 years) nearly half the farmers/cultivators and 20 per cent of the agricultural labourers and the entire growth of their numbers in these years must be shifted outside agriculture both within and outside the rural areas. This requires fast expansion in non-farm employment to absorb a major share of the present and potential work force engaged in agriculture and allied activities. But in the near future this must be accompanied by swift increase in the employment within the agriculture and allied activities through crop diversification. To achieve this, decentralised development (block planning) has to be accompanied by major investment in marketing, storage, processing and minimum support price programme of the new/ proposed crops. This process can take care of employment for the uneducated also.

Tackling the problem of open unemployment is a difficult and more complex process. First, there is a mismatch between the aspirations of the unemployed and the policy environment in the state. Rural job seekers aspire to get the secure government and semi-government jobs (Krishan, 1986; Rao and Singh, 1989). The government is not willing to act as a major employer. This mismatch has to be corrected both by changing the attitude of the job seekers as well as that of the government. In fact, the government has to take the initiative and come forward with policies and programmes which encourage creation of job opportunities for the job seekers. The government cannot downsize at a lower level without downsizing at the top. This attitude makes a mockery of the argument of downsizing and keeps alive hopes of filling vacancies at the lower level. At the same time job seekers' preference for government jobs cannot be changed if employment and its quality in the private sector is not improved by observing labour standards. The present trends of employment generation (Table 12.11) indicate that employment in the organised private sector moves along with employment in the public sector. If this is so the government may have to continue as a major employer for some more time. This would require a still greater role for the government in employment generation, particularly in infrastructure building and in the social sectors like education, health and so on. This would create the necessary inducement/incentives

TABLE 12.11: **Employment in Organised Sector in Punjab (in numbers)**

	Sector	1990	1991	1992	1993	1994	1995	1996	1997	1998	1999
1.	Public Sector										
	(a) Central govt.	68819	72308	79904	81394	82787	83693	83662	80823	80483	79880
		(8.88)	(9.14)	(9.75)	(9.75)	(9.96)	(9.95)	(9.82)	(9.55)	(9.43)	(9.43)
	(b) State govt.	289787	293577	301770	302945	299930	296476	298202	298597	310654	307146
		(36.85)	(37.10)	(36.84)	(36.65)	(35.98)	(35.23)	(34.93)	(35.29)	(36.39)	(36.26)
	(c) Quasi govt.	173104	171618	175447	175040	177842	182526	188203	180329	177175	180329
		(22.01)	(21.69)	(21.42)	(21.18)	(21.34)	(21.69)	(22.04)	(21.32)	(20.75)	(21.29)
	(d) Local govt.	33487	32556	33554	34232	33605	32764	32942	32834	34241	33602
		(4.26)	(4.11)	(4.10)	(4.15)	(4.03)	(3.90)	(3.86)	(3.88)	(4.01)	(3.97)
	Total (1)	566197	570059	590675	593611	594364	595459	603209	592583	602553	599088
		(72.00)	(74.02)	(72.11)	(71.83)	(71.31)	(70.77)	(70.65)	(70.04)	(70.57)	(70.72)
2.	Private sector	220237	221230	228485	232813	239158	246000	250551	253424	251223	248023
		(28.00)	(27.96)	(27.89)	(28.17)	(28.69)	(29.23)	(29.35)	(29.96)	(29.43)	(29.28)
	Grand total (1+2)	786434	791289	819160	826424	833522	841459	853760	846007	853776	847111
		(100.00)	(100.00)	(100.00)	(100.00)	(100.00)	(100.00)	(100.00)	(100.00)	(100.00)	(100.00)
	Increase of grand total over the previous year	-	4855	27871	7264	7098	7937	12301	-7753	7769	-6665

Source: Economic Advisor, *Statistical Abstracts of Punjab 1995 and 1999*, Government of Punjab, Chandigarh.
Growth of Employment between 1990 and 1999 = 7.72 % per year = 0.86 %

for the private sector to expand directly productive activities (DPA). In the long run there has to be synchronisation between agricultural (and allied) production, manufacturing and human resource development. This synchronisation cannot be smooth via market forces, it has to be co-ordinated by planning at the state and decentralised level.

Fast agricultural growth assisted industrial development in Punjab during the pre-Green Revolution as well as in the post-Green Revolution period. This occurred through the provision of surplus production of foodgrains, agricultural inputs for industry at competitive prices as well as through a sustained growth of demand both for industry's capital and consumer goods. In other words agricultural development promoted industrial growth through backward and forward linkage effects (Macrae, 1971). In value terms production of agricultural implements recorded an annual growth rate of 10.2 per cent, hand tools at 15.4 per cent, domestic production of fertilisers at 18.7 per cent, cotton ginning at 9.42 per cent, sugar at 8.82 per cent, cotton textiles at 16.2 per cent between 1970/71 and 1982/83. The higher growth rate in agro-based industries also gave a substantial annual growth rate of employment at 4.5 per cent in agricultural implements, 13.7 per cent in hand tools, 3.66 per cent in cotton ginning and cotton textiles at 19.11 per cent during 1970/71 and 1982/83 (Bhalla, 1990).

The process of fast agricultural development resulting in industrial development put the Punjab economy on a fast development path. This was also accompanied by fast expansion in employment outstripping the internal growth of labour supply. This process worked very well till the end of the 1970s decade showing scarcity of labour force. It is during this period that a large influx of migratory labour started in the state in agriculture as well as in the manufacturing sector. The industrial sector being largely small and unregistered appeared unattractive to the local labour. This was due to the fact that labour legislation could not be implemented in the small unregistered industrial units. At the same time difficulty in organising trade unions to ensure minimum wages and procure better conditions of work kept the jobs in industry really low paid, making them absolutely non-acceptable to the local labour. But these low-paid jobs remained very attractive to the labour from the backward states such as Uttar Pradesh, Bihar and Madhya Pradesh (Sidhu, Rangi and Singh, 1997). Thus, a process which was emerging to absorb the workforce from the rural areas and ultimately to start transformation of the economy by shifting the workforce from agriculture to industry was thwarted at the early stage (in the late seventies). The entrepreneurs in the private sector initially but later in the co-operative and public enterprises began to prefer migrant labour being cheaper as well as docile in claiming/asserting their rights of fair wages and reasonable conditions of work.

Punjab being part of the all India economy could not retain within its boundaries the multiplier effects of investment/development efforts. Thus the fruits of agricultural prosperity and supported industrial development of Punjab were shared with the rest of India which was growing at a relatively slow pace (Bhalla, 1990). The employment policy of Punjab has had to grapple with the question of retaining employment effects of economic expansion without effecting the efficiency/cost of production and avoid being chauvinist in approach.

Self-employment generation is a very popular measure suggested by policy makers and is high on the government agenda in India (Ninth Plan, p.212). To make this viable, the imparting of self-employment skills among the unemployed is of paramount importance. This requires identification of self-employment opportunities (tradewise), organisation of effective training programmes, followed by requisite financial support/credit availability and strictly followed by marketing arrangements for the produce of the self-employed. The majority of the unemployed particularly from the rural areas have no skills at present for self-employment. The earlier experience of TRYSEM in Punjab has not been very encouraging (Singh, 1996, pp.122-32). The present system of promotion of self-employment programmes is handicapped by the bureaucratic system of identification, selection and implementation. This needs to be changed and replaced by the involvement of professionals from academic institutions in implementation and evaluation of such programmes. At the same time, the planning machinery needs to be activated to play its relevant role. The task is colossal and needs co-ordinated effort from multi-directions.

In this context it is relevant to discuss the capability of the provincial government. During the last two decades (1980s and 1990s) the Punjab government's own capability has suffered a setback. The disturbed decade of the 1980s changed the orientation of the administration from development to law and order. This led to considerable neglect of development issues and resource mobilisation did not get any attention. A state government which could spare a major part of its revenue for development began to face a resource crunch for shouldering its routine functions of maintenance of law and order and to administer justice. Owing to the distortions in the orientation of the administration and considerably diminished capability because of a serious resource crunch, the state government no longer remains a model for intervention in economic affairs. The performance of the government has been considerably impaired for the role expected from it (Gill, 2000). But as yet there is no substitute for the state government. Given the higher base of development and considerable level of the potential resources, the resource crunch can be overcome through better tax compliance, widening of the tax base and giving up of the policy of populism. At the same time developmental orientation of the government administration can be built by sensitisation of the political leadership and bureaucracy.

The process of introduction of the second generation of economic reforms involving withdrawal of the Union Government from procurement of foodgrains and public distribution system, reduction of subsidy on power, irrigation and fertiliser and privatisation of public enterprises and forcing the state government to withdraw from economic intervention would make the employment situation worse in Punjab. The economy needs critical support in vital areas such as agriculture and industry which are facing a very serious threat from global players in the wake of the opening up of the economy under the WTO regime.

REFERENCES

Bhalla, G.S. (1990), "Agricultural Growth and Industrial Development : A Case Study of Punjab", CSRD, JNU, New Delhi, mimeo.

Bhalla, Shiela (1987), "Trends in Employment in Indian Agriculture, Land and Asset Distribution", *Indian Journal of Agricultural Economics*, Vol.42, No.4, October-December.

Chand, Himal (1993), "Educated Unemployed in Punjab", *Man and Development*, Vol.15, No.2.

Chand Romesh (2000), *Emerging Trends and Regional Variations in Agriculture Investment and Their Implications for Growth and Equity,* NCAP, New Delhi.

Directorate of Economics and Statistics, *Cost of Cultivation of Principal Crops in India, 1991, 1996 and 2000,* Ministry of Agriculture, Government of India, New Delhi.

Economic Advisor (1998), Report on Unemployed Persons (Age-Group 18-35 years) Desirous of Self-Employment, Government of Punjab, mimeo.

—— *Statistical Abstract of Punjab*, various issues, Government of Punjab, Chandigarh.

Gill, Sucha Singh (2000), "Punjab : Fiscal Crisis and Non Governance", *Economic and Political Weekly*, Vol. XXXV, Nos. 20-21, May 27-June.

Krishan, Gopal (1986), *Spatial Dimensions of Unemployment and Underemployment*, Concept Publishing House, New Delhi.

Macrae, John (1971), "The Relationship between Agricultural and Industrial Growth, With Special Reference to the Development of the Punjab Economy from 1950-1965", *Journal of Development Studies*, Vol. 7, No. 4.

Planning Commission (1999), *Ninth Five Year Plan, Vol. I*, Government of India, New Delhi.

Partharsathy, G. and K.A. Nirmala (2000), "Employment and Unemployment of Youth", *Indian Journal of Labour Economics*, Vol.43, No.4., October-December.

Punjab Agricultural University (1998), *Proceedings of Brain Storming Meeting on Farmers and Farming in Punjab*, Ludhiana.

Rao, K. Venugopal and Harvinder Singh (1989), "Nature and Extent of Educated Unemployment in Punjab: With Special Reference to Border Districts", in Promod Kumar et al. (eds.) *Research Project on Border Area of Punjab, Jammu and Kashmir and Rajasthan: A Search for Development Strategy (A Report on Punjab)*, Vol.II, CRRID, Chandigarh, mimeo.

Sidhu, M.S., P.S. Rangi and Karam Singh (1997), *A Study on Migrant Agricultural Labour in Punjab,* Panjab Agricultural University, Ludhiana.

Singh, Baldev (1996), *Self Employment Through Entrepreneurship Development*, M.D. Publications, New Delhi.

Statistician (2000), *Agricultural Statistics of Punjab*, Department of Agriculture, Government of Punjab, Chandigarh.

13

ECONOMIC REFORMS AND EMPLOYMENT: KARNATAKA

R.S. DESHPANDE

Introduction

The Karnataka economy has a typical characteristic of intermittent phases of growth and stagnation. This is a matter of concern, as it creates a direct impact on the overall growth performance of the state economy and complicates the analyses of the reform process. Thereby it becomes difficult to relate the policy responses to an intervention. During the last decade, efforts at policy as well as at implementation levels are being made to overcome the constraints and encourage growth boosters across sectors. The constraints mainly relate to utilisation of resources, generation of employment, existing infrastructure facilities, forward and backward linkages, and allied supportive activities. Besides these, the liberalisation process introduced through economic reforms has led to the emergence of the new sectors, such as, information technology, international trade, horticulture, floriculture, fisheries, agro-processing etc. These sectors require better quality of supportive infrastructure for sustained development and only then, can they contribute significantly to the output and employment growth of the state.

Karnataka has a large share of its area under severe climatic constraints with a highly diversified agricultural sector. The state has a traditional culture and hence could not make strong forays in industrial development except in the regions surrounding the cities of south Karnataka and specifically in the IT sector. Typically, the state has a large population of poor, located in rural areas, specifically among agricultural labourers, scheduled castes, and scheduled tribes. Finding work therefore remains an extremely important pursuit in rural livelihood. Despite these constraints, the economy is quite resurgent, having an intense potential for growth. The fact that the state has the largest share of drought-prone areas of the country and higher than the country's share of poor did not deter the state from achieving better rates of reduction in the poverty ratio (Rao, 1992). The high density of low value and high-risk crops typifies the state agriculture. On the contrary and at the same time, the state has entered in a big way in the high-tech agriculture and industrial growth only next to a chosen few states in the country.

Karnataka's recent emergence as an important partner in boosting the export growth of the country has also been underlined. As history tells us, Karnataka has always been the first to take initiative on many occasions—be it pragmatic land reforms, democratic decentralisation, well-designed anti-poverty programmes, understanding human development (through HDI) at a desegregated level, fresh initiatives in rainfed agriculture or rigorous participation in international trade. In most of the cross-section comparisons across states, Karnataka occupies the unenviable position at an average or at the median level. From one point of view, this can be interpreted as an average response to the developmental initiatives and not sliding down in a comparative position despite the acute constraints faced. From another point of view, this can indicate inability to climb up in the developmental hierarchy despite remaining at an average (threshold level) level for a long time. Probably, the developmental efforts are so critically managed that the state continues in a position without sliding down in the hierarchy and at the same time unable to climb up in comparison with other states of the country. This directs us to an obvious policy conclusion that it is high time to focus on a fresh look at the developmental efforts with strong initiatives to cross the barrier of being at an average level for a long time. In the liberalised economic scenario, such impetus should come from the private investment as well as efforts towards participating in the market with vigorous market drives. That will require growth in the most crucial sectors (after locating such sectors) that hold ahead a promise and finding out new investment avenues in similar areas. The efforts, therefore, must be directed towards optimising the value added and at the same time not losing the human face of development.

Growth in State Income (SDP) and Sectoral Contributions

The state has experienced a significant change in its Gross State Domestic Product (GSDP) during the last decade. Growth has taken place especially during the second half of the decade, and specifically after 1993/94. As the trends in net state domestic product (NSDP) suggest, the economy has experienced continuous and reasonably good growth during 1993-2000 (Table 13.1). The trends in net state domestic product at constant prices indicate a growth rate of about 5 per cent per annum which is less than the 5.9 per cent per annum growth rate assumed at the country level. This low growth rate is mainly due to the shortfall in the production of major agricultural crops and the deceleration in the agriculture sector. The sectoral origin of the net state domestic product of Karnataka specifically for three major sectors, namely, agriculture and allied activities, manufacturing, industrial sector and services sector are presented in Table 13.2. Estimates of net state domestic product for the period 1993/94 to 1998/99 are presented in the table by industry of origin at constant prices (1993/94).

Agriculture and allied activities as well as the service sector has grown at 14.2 per cent and 11.8 per cent, respectively. The industrial sector has grown at a lower rate of growth, i.e., around 6 per cent. The mining sector has also shown a significant decline in its contribution towards NSDP. Similarly, forestry as well as fisheries have shown declining trends in growth. This does not bear a telling effect on the employment scenario (see Appendix Table 13.1).

Fiscal Situation in the State

The strength of the economy is reflected both through the rates of

TABLE 13.1: **Net State Domestic Product (NSDP) at Factor Cost**

Year	1991-92	1992-93	1993-94	1994-95	1995-96	1996-97	1997-98 (*)	1998 1999 (**)	1999 00 ($)
NSDP (Rs. in '000 crores)	10.27	10.49	38.64	41.78	44.5	49.36	51.48	57.01	59.61
Per capita income in Rs.	2262	2272	8190	8694	9089	9919	10200	11153	11504

Notes: 1. At 1993-94 Prices; 2. * Partially Revised Estimates; 3. ** Quick Estimates; 4. $ Anticipated Estimates.
Source: Economic Survey, 1999-00, Government of Karnataka, Bangalore.

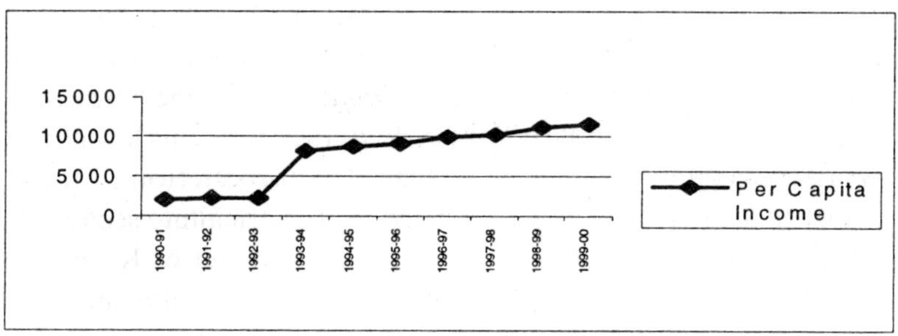

FIG. 13.1: **Per Capita Income 1990-2000**

TABLE 13.2: **Sectoral Contribution to State Domestic Product at Constant Prices**

No.	Sector	1993-91	1994-95	1995-96	1996-97	1997-98 (*)	1998-99 (**)
1.	Agri. and allied sectors(%)	39.1	36.9	33.7	31.3	28.6	29.5
2.	Industry (%)	23.6	25.2	26.8	28.3	29.4	28.1
3.	Services (%)	37.3	37.9	39.5	40.4	42.0	42.4
4.	Total NSDP (Rs. crores)	38641	41787	44504	49358	51478	57013

Notes: 1. * Partially Revised; 2. ** Quick Estimates.
Source: Economic Survey, 1999-00, Government of Karnataka, Bangalore.

growth and the fiscal situation that dictates them. Together these two factors indicate the potential for the overall employment situation in the economy. Therefore, while analysing the employment situation it is necessary to consider the fiscal situation to comment on the second phase of reforms. The White Paper on the state finances (GoK, 2000c) has recorded significant deterioration in the fiscal position of Karnataka over the last decade, particularly since 1995/96. The fiscal position was transformed from a revenue surplus of Rs. 159 crores in 1995/96 to a revenue deficit of Rs. 1163 crores in 1999/2000. Similarly, during this period, the fiscal deficit increased from Rs. 513 crores to Rs. 2781 crores. This has created an unstable fiscal situation characterised by a vicious cycle of interest payments feeding into deficits and debt servicing. The continuation of the prevailing trend will surely place Karnataka in a crisis within the next few years. An important cause of the deteriorating fiscal situation in the state is the declining share of revenue (including water fees, mandi cess and others) to gross state domestic product (GSDP). While the tax revenue has been stagnant, the ratio of non-tax revenue to GSDP has actually shown a decline from 2.2 per cent in 1990/91 to 1.3 per cent in 1998/99. This happened mainly owing to low and declining cost recoveries from non-merit public services and poor performance of the public enterprises (GoK, 2000c). Implicit subsidies owing to uneconomic pricing of irrigation, water supply, higher and technical education and urban health services amount to about 1.2 per cent of GSDP. An equally worrisome issue of the state finances of Karnataka is the dismal financial performance of public enterprises. Another major cause is lower user charges and slow growth in revenue receipts from agriculture and allied sectors in Karnataka over the last fifteen years i.e., from 1985/86 to 1999/2000 (BE). The declining productivity of public expenditures added to the problem.

As can be seen from Table 13.3 the annual expenditure through the state plan has gone up from Rs. 1774 to Rs. 5888 crore marking an increase of more than three times. This also reflects substantial change in the per capita outlay from the state plan. Therefore, such investment should have generated employment commensurating with this rate. But this will happen only when the per capita annual plan

TABLE 13.3: **Expenditure on Annual Plans, Centrally Sponsored and Central Plan Schemes**

(Rs. crore)

Year	State Plan	Centrally Sponsored & Central Plan Schemes (GOI) Share	Irrigation Projects Pending Approval	Western Ghats Development	Total	
					Outlay	Per Capita Outlay (Rs.)
1980-81	359.43	53.79	25.13	1.94	470.28	126.00
1990-91	1301.93	264.35	89.09	9.47	1664.84	372.47
1991-92	1774.53	277.96	131.13	9.53	2193.15	483.01
1992-93	2032.95	390.48	192.68	7.91	2624.02	564.31
1993-94	2798.40	457.15	209.62	9.65	3437.82	771.94
1994-95	2974.09	495.11	218.10	9.50	3696.80	751.38
1995-96	3390.84	397.09	238.86	10.49	4037.28	842.86
1996-97	3972.57	491.02	288.73	10.28	4762.60	979.96
1997-98	4424.48	503.93	296.23	9.00	5233.64	1063.75
1998-99 (RE)	5131.54	1110.78	267.00	15.00	6524.32	1310.10
1999-00 (BE)	5888.00	1198.63	280.00	15.00	7381.63	1461.71

Note: R.E.-Revised Estimates, B.E.-Budget Estimates Irrigation projects pending approval and Western Ghats development for 1980-81 and 1990-91 to 1998-99 and outlays for 1999-2000.

Sources: 1. Details of Provisions for Plan Schemes, Finance Department, Government of Karnataka.

2. *Economic Survey, 1999-00.*

outlays get converted into investment and thereby transformed into capital formation across sectors. Given the precarious fiscal situation it would have been difficult to sustain the rates of capital formation in the economy. Despite the constraints on growth and allocation across sectors, the capital formation trends in the state are not relatively bad. At 1991, the total gross capital formation in the state stood at about Rs. 430 crore which increased almost four times by 1998/99 (Table 13.4).

TABLE 13.4: **Capital Formation through State Resources in Karnataka 1980-81 and 1990-91 to 1999-2000**

(Rs. crore)

Year	Value of Assets Created			Changes in Stock	Gross Capital Formation
	By Departmental Commercial Undertakings	By Govt. Administration	Total		
1980-81	112.20	101.45	213.65	6.29	219.92
1990-91	279.41	135.78	415.19	14.58	429.77
1991-92	398.91	158.92	557.83	16.38	574.21
1992-93	547.35	187.42	734.77	15.73	750.50
1993-94	738.00	249.00	987.00	10.00	997.00
1994-95	768.60	275.69	1044.29	14.43	1058.72
1995-96	760.28	307.43	1067.71	73.06	1140.77
1996-97	817.75	408.02	1225.77	34.00	1259.77
1997-98	685.75	470.83	1156.58	-6.48	1150.10
1998-99 (R.E)	746.42	766.09	1512.51	NA	1512.51
1999-2000 (BE)	770.09	834.87	1604.96	NA	1604.96

N*ote:* R.E. -Revised Estimates, B.E.-Budget Estimates

Source: "Reports on An Economic-cum-Purpose Classification of the Karnataka Government Budget: 1999-2000", and earlier issues, Directorate of Economics & Statiistics.

This has given rise to sufficient investment in order to generate employment in organised as well as unorganised sectors. The per capita expenditure on annual plans and the central and state sponsored schemes has also increased during the period 1991-2000. It was about Rs. 483 during 1991/92 and has increased to Rs. 1462 within a span of nine years. Overall, this has given a hope that we should be able to manage the employment growth rates during this phase. The revenue receipts have shown declining trends in the aggregate fiscal scenario and it is well known that revenue receipts are significantly susceptible to fluctuations in the agriculture sector. Therefore, it is necessary to look into the trends in revenue generation from the agricultural sector. Moreover, the agricultural sector receives a good amount of subsidies and protection from the state exchequer. These have a direct bearing on employment generation in the unorganised sector as well as in the agriculture dependent organised sector. The stagnation during the last five years is quite evident from Table 13.5 as well as Figure 13.2.

(Rs. lakh)

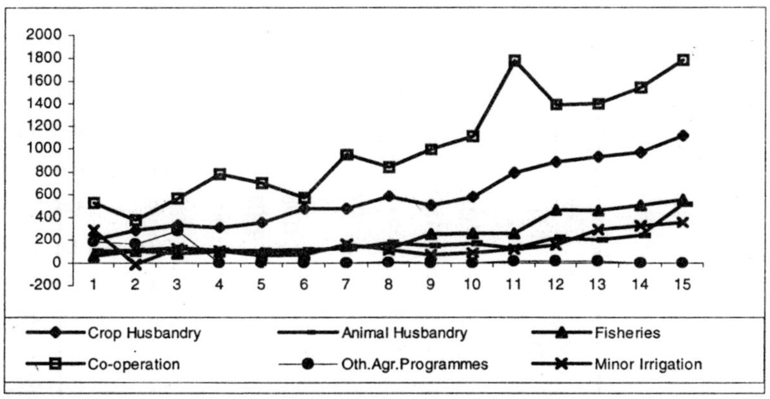

FIG. 13.2: **Revenue from Agriculture and Allied Sectors (1985-86 to 1999-2000)**

Source: Finances of State Governments, RBI, various issues.

Employment Situation in Karnataka

The employment situation in Karnataka during the last decade has not been very encouraging. Aggregate employment can be grouped into organised and unorganised sectors. Employment in the unorganised sector comes mainly from the agricultural and unorganised service sectors whereas, in the organised sector it is

TABLE 13.5: **Revenue Receipts from Agriculture and Allied Sectors of Karnataka, (1985-2000)**

(Rs. Lakh)

Year	Crop Husbandry	Animal Husbandry	Fisheries	Forestry & Wild Life	Cooperation	Other Agricultural Programmes	Major & Medium Irrigation	Minor Irrigation	Total
1985-86	203	98	58	5645	527	185	479	289	7484
1986-87	287	107	98	5314	377	163	809	-15	7140
1987-88	331	134	84	5251	570	281	1335	128	8114
1988-89	313	106	92	4639	778	0	1431	103	7462
1989-90	359	106	88	5157	702	0	1614	64	8090
1990-91	481	111	80	5818	572	0	1689	69	8820
1991-92	476	128	144	6169	949	0	3015	165	11046
1992-93	585	175	123	6909	842	2	1645	111	10392
1993-94	501	151	255	9198	995	0	1355	70	12525
1994-95	578	169	262	9508	1113	0	1319	90	13039
1995-96	791	132	262	10609	1775	10	1693	122	15394
1996-97	889	222	462	11335	1390	12	1710	156	16176
1997-98	931	205	457	11381	1401	13	1636	294	16318
1998-99	969	240	503	11157	1541	0	1635	324	16369
1999-00	1115	519	553	12500	1785	0	2520	356	19348

Note: 1998-99- RE - Revised Estimates, 1999-00-BE - Budget Estimates.
Source : *Finance of State Governments*, RBI, various issues.

generated in industries and government sponsored schemes. Organised sector employment constitutes about 10 per cent of the total employment and this has grown by about less than one per cent per annum during the last decade (Economic Survey of Karnataka, 2000). There are no clear estimates about unorganised sector employment but there is enough evidence to believe that this has grown at about 1.5 per cent per annum which can be arrived at from the analysis of the growth of the sector. This is certainly a matter of concern. In the organised sector, employment in the social sector contributes about 40 per cent of the employment and this has grown much faster as compared to the other sectors.

Any analysis of employment has to deal with the statistics from the employment exchange registers as well as the industrial employment in the state. It is noted that the registrants in the employment exchange have grown much faster than the jobs found for them. Across the industry groups, social and personal services have provided the largest number of jobs. Employment in the private sector has shown signs of deceleration specifically during the nineteen-nineties (Table 13.6). It is intriguing to note that only 11 per cent of the jobs have gone to women workers. The ratio is much lower in the public sector as against the private sector. Karnataka has an Employment Assurance Scheme (EAS) which provides about 11 crore man-days per year. This is usually utilised towards the creation of productive assets in the rural areas such as roads, watershed management, minor irrigation, and other such works. In addition to these, there are a few other programmes which also generate employment to the tune of about seven crore man days per year.

While the organised sector employment has decelerated in terms of its growth, job seekers as per the live registers of the employment exchanges have increased by about 3 per cent during the nineties (Fig. 13.3). Among different categories of registrations, the Industrial Training Institute certificate holders and the personnel below matriculate level have increased by more than 7 per cent (Table 13.7). Among the employment exchange registrants, matriculates and below constitute about 85 per cent. These are non-skilled workers and therefore they need vocational training.

TABLE 13.6: **Employment in Public and Private Sectors in Karnataka for the Years 1990-91 to 1999-2000**

(In lakhs)

Years	Public	Private	Total
1990-91	10.17	4.30	14.47
1991-92	10.28	4.52	14.80
1992-93	10.26	4.75	15.01
1993-94	10.33	4.97	15.30
1994-95	10.52	5.28	15.80
1995-96	10.59	7.00	17.59
1996-97	10.84	7.32	18.16
1997-98	10.86	7.57	18.43
1998-99	10.92	7.57	18.49
1999-2000 as on 30/9/1999	11.1	7.50	18.60

Source: Collected from *Economic Survey*, Karnataka, various issues.

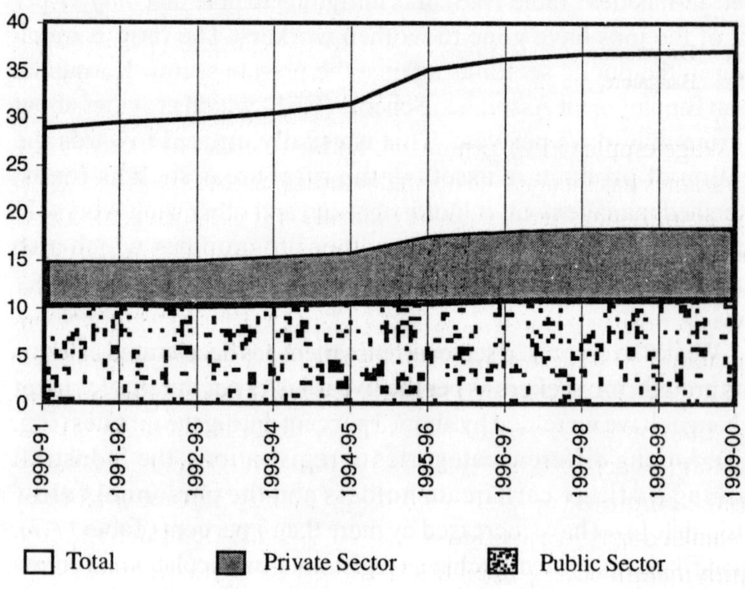

FIG. 13.3: **Employment Trends in Organised Sector in Karnataka**

TABLE 13.7: **Registrants on the Live Registers of Employment Exchanges in Karnataka 1980-81 and 1990-91 to 1999-2000**

(in thousands)

Year	Post-graduates	Graduates	Diploma Holders	ITI Certificate Holders	Matriculates	Non-Matriculates	Total
80-81	5.51	69.10	5.52	8.40	290.78	228.48	607.40
90-91	10.35	112.71	24.31	38.53	773.49	368.37	1327.70
91-92	11.96	119.61	28.38	41.95	867.77	374.00	1443.60
92-93	13.02	129.38	31.20	45.94	941.61	350.33	1511.40
93-94	14.11	156.07	33.13	45.92	1007.87	323.56	1580.60
94-95	14.85	160.85	34.50	49.08	1055.15	336.69	1651.10
95-96	14.82	163.59	32.57	51.58	1126.76	349.69	1739.00
96-97	14.24	166.04	36.89	58.32	1164.15	340.58	1780.20
97-98	13.81	171.70	37.59	61.17	1187.67	335.01	1806.95
98-99	14.49	159.34	38.16	65.02	1235.65	305.39	1818.05
99-00	14.77	158.93	38.03	69.99	1256.07	332.42	1870.21

Source: Directorate of Employment and Training, Government of Karnataka, Bangalore.

Wage employment generation under government-sponsored programmes has increased marginally during the period. Among the wage employment programmes, the state has nine categories and their achievement was about 872 lakh man days of employment created during 1999-2000. This is slightly lower than what was achieved during the earlier years. Even otherwise, employment generation in the organised sector has not been of a very high order. The incremental employment during 1991 to 2000 has been in the range of about some one lakh man days per year. Given the supply of labour this achievement is miniscule. We have presented in Table 13.6 the employment generated in public and private sectors in Karnataka during this period. It can be seen that the public sector employment has stagnated but there are quite positive signs of increase in employment in the private sector.

Performance of Agricultural Sector

We are reviewing the performance of the agricultural sector in order to assess the probable changes in the employment scenario. This is an indirect method of arriving at the changes in employment in the agricultural sector. The agricultural sector has the largest employment potential in the state. The Agricultural Policy Resolution adopted by the Government of Karnataka in 1995 (GoK, 1995) has, by and large, covered six issues, namely: (i) land and land use policy to improve growth prospects; (ii) policies to improve yield and achieve self-sufficiency in food-grain production; (iii) policy towards increasing the availability and improving the efficient use of scientific inputs and other supporting services like credit; (iv) policy to reduce regional imbalances in agricultural development within the state by identifying the needs and growth potentials of different sub-regions based on agro-climatic conditions; (v) policy to sustain the growth in output and yields through creating proper marketing and pricing structure; and (vi) potential for employment growth in other sub-sectors.

The Agricultural Policy Resolution of Karnataka State emphasises that agricultural production policies need to aim at achieving higher growth rates in production and employment which would help in meeting the requirements of the state. The objective of the policy documents was to spell out a clear direction for a strategy to create a prosperous rural society in Karnataka. It aimed at spurring growth in the agriculture and allied sectors by taking advantage of opportunities opened up by trade at national and global levels in an overall environment of economic liberalisation. The policy document assumed that growth in agriculture would provide a momentum to growth in other sectors through its backward and forward linkages. The kind of the growth that has been envisaged would generate more employment and cut down poverty in rural areas in due course.

The Karnataka policy favours the government stand on granting industrial status to agriculture while the national agriculture policy (GoI, 2000) is vague on this issue. While maintaining that giving agriculture the status of an industry is the ultimate goal, it envisages this objective to be achieved gradually. In the transitional period, the strategy should be to provide agriculture with appropriate modifications, incentives and safeguards of the type available to industry, ensuring elimination of discrimination against agriculture in the matter of credit, costing, returns to investment, infrastructure, markets, exports and research and technology. It also wants foreign capital flow in agriculture and allied fields.

Declining investment and capital formation in agriculture are key factors causing deceleration in employment trends and not realising the sector's real potential. This is also an important reason for the unabated poverty in rural areas. The Karnataka policy suggests a solution for finding the wherewithal for additional private and public investments. While it proposes that private sector investment be financed through institutional credit and farmer's own funds, it feels that public sector investment should be arranged through normal government allocations.

Review of Agricultural Performance

Agriculture and allied activities accounted for 37 per cent of the state income of Karnataka and 69 per cent of the population of the state is engaged in this sector. Within the sector, crop husbandry accounted for 34 per cent of the output, 32 per cent of the state income and 25 per cent of the employment generated by the sector (GoK, 1998). The dominant role of this sector in the state economy as core contributor to growth of employment and income is quite clear even ignoring the estimates relating to its forward linkages. The growth rate in agriculture, which was quite commendable till the end of 1970s decelerated during 1980s. The production of foodgrains stagnated and productivity was low, both under rainfed as well as under irrigated agriculture, during the eighties (GoK, 1993). This was attended to immediately by taking quick policy steps. In the eighth plan period, the emphasis was on integrated watershed development, strengthening the infrastructure base and ensuring adequate supply of inputs. During the late eighties and early nineties, with the help of state level policy interventions, the state achieved a recovery from the large looming stagnation. A number of centrally sponsored thrust programmes were implemented like the Intensive Rice Development Programme, the Pulses Development Programme and the Oilseeds Production Programme, focused on stepping up production and productivity on watershed basis. All these have helped to enhance the availability of employment in the sector.

Since, 1997/98, the emphasis of the state's policy has been directed towards hi-tech agriculture. These included incentives for registered seed growers, the popularization of plant protection measures and strengthening of agricultural laboratories. To train women and youth, an extension project has been taken up with external assistance. In the last decade, area under horticulture increased by over three lakh ha., indicating an average annual growth rate of about three per cent per annum. The emphasis was on rainfed horticulture. Karnataka Horticultural Producer's Co-operative Marketing Federation is functioning effectively. These programmes are likely to have mixed impact in terms of employment creation. On one hand, these activities will require additional manpower, but on the other, the demand will be more for skilled personnel. Specific skills will be required. It is proposed to strengthen the existing research stations, equip them with new technology, and provide training facilities.

The development of the agricultural sector in the state thus began with the seemingly formidable constraints in the form of large rainfed areas, meagre irrigation, low value, low yield dominant cropping pattern and large share of dependent population with low employment elasticity. The struggle of the sector to achieve respectable growth pattern is well documented (GoK, 1993) but what has been achieved in the face of constraints sets a role model. Rainfed agriculture also participated and contributed equally in the growth in the sector (Rao, 1992). This is the main component of the role model of achievement despite hard constraints. Now, the state is poised to enter sectors like food processing and horticultural exports. Therefore, the investment needs, employment creation and capital formation in the sector assume significance during this phase.

In the following paragraphs, we trace the development of the agricultural economy of the state during the last four decades.

Crop Diversification

Diversification of cropping pattern provides greater change in the quantum as well as composition of employment. The area under total cereals in the state stood at 45 per cent, down by 11 per cent (in 1990/00) from 56 per cent (in 1955-58). The decline is mainly owing to reduction in area under jowar and bajra. The area under paddy increased by 3 per cent (from 8.7 to 11.6 per cent) between 1955-58 and 1990-93 and stabilised around that level after that. The area under maize increased from about 0.1 per cent in 1955-58 to 2.5 per cent of the gross cropped area in 1990-93 and further to 4.31 per cent. Though there is a decline in the proportion of area under cereals, paddy, jowar, bajra, maize and wheat, continue to be the dominant cereal and millet crops in the state. The decline in the area under cereals indicates lower requirement of manpower in this production activity.

The cereals in general dominate the cropping pattern of the state. Rice is the major cereal crop in the coastal and Malnad districts whereas, jowar and ragi are the important staple foodgrains in northern and southern districts of Karnataka, respectively. Area under pulses (Table 13.8) remained more or less unchanged (around 14 per cent) during the last four decades. However, the introduction of a technology mission for oilseeds and favourable price regime helped in expansion of area under oilseeds. The area under oilseeds in the state, which was around 12 per cent till the late 1970s, increased to 24.4 per cent after the 1980s but slid down to 19.6 per cent, subsequently. The gains in the oilseeds area during the eighties were at the cost of cotton. The area under groundnut and sunflower in the state shared about 4.6 and one per cent of the total area under the respective crops in the country. Cotton is an important cash crop of the state. The area under cotton has declined from 10 per cent to 5 per cent and much of the decline came after 1980/81. The area under other cash crops such as sugarcane, coconut, arecanut etc.,

TABLE 13.8: **Changes in Cropping Pattern**

(Area as per cent to GCA)

Crops	1955-58	1979-82	1990-93	1997-00
Rice	8.68	10.41	10.86	11.60
Wheat	2.91	3.17	1.80	2.16
Jowar	25.45	19.04	17.76	15.61
Bajra	5.11	5.67	2.98	3.04
Ragi	8.64	10.15	8.71	7.95
Maize	0.10	1.40	2.50	4.31
Total cereals	56.46	53.28	44.97	45.31
Gram	1.55	1.32	1.90	--
Tur	2.80	3.31	3.60	3.74
Total pulses	12.64	14.19	13.59	14.62
Groundnut	8.80	7.74	10.53	9.95
Sesamum	--	1.02	1.09	--
Safflower	--	1.48	1.35	--
Sunflower	--	1.00	10.22	--
Total oil seeds	12.08	12.56	24.39	19.56
Cotton	10.21	9.31	4.88	4.83
Sugarcane	0.52	1.50	2.32	2.71
Chillies	1.03	1.40	1.36	--
Tobacco	0.39	0.44	0.47	0.64
Coconut	0.86	1.59	2.02	-
Arecanut	0.29	0.50	0.55	-
Banana	--	0.35	0.27	-
Citrus	--	0.28	0.19	-
Mango	--	0.42	0.45	-
Coffee	0.61	1.03	1.19	-
Mulberry	--	1.07	1.29	-
Others	16.27	13.47	9.51	-
Gross cropped area	100.00	100.00	100.00	100.0
(Total GCA in lakh ha.)	(104.3)	(110.3)	(121.9)	(120.02)

Note : '-' indicates data not available presently.

Source: Directorate of Economics and Statistics, Government of Karnataka, Bangalore.

has increased over the years. The area under cotton declined in the traditional cotton growing districts of northern Karnataka though it increased in Malnad district during the 80s.

At the macro level, cash crops shared a relatively larger irrigated area when compared with the foodgrain crops across the farm sizes and social groups. The proportion of cereal area under irrigation was relatively higher on small farms when compared to large farms and the opposite was true in the case of oilseeds. The changes in the cropping pattern in Karnataka and in India are in terms of proportion of gross cropped area under different crops presented for four points in time in Table 13.8. The crops included here cover more than 85 per cent of the gross cropped area in the state and are triennium averages. One can visualise three broad trends in the area allocation across crops. Firstly, it is found that the area under cereals and millets is decreasing over the years and this area is largely transferred to commercial crops. Secondly, a large share of resources (in terms of irrigation and inputs) is allocated to irrigated high value crops and thus the yield rates of irrigated crops are comparable to the national averages. Lastly, northern Karnataka and rainfed portions of southern Maidan have a largely diversified crop pattern whereas coastal Karnataka and irrigated regions seem to prefer mono cropping.

Production trends of important crops are analysed here with the help of compound rates of growth for production and productivity for the period 1955/56 to 1993/94 and separately for 1990 to 2000. It was observed that the production of cereals in the state has grown at 2.13 per cent per annum during the period 1955/56 and 1993-94. The entire growth was contributed by yield as area under cereals in the state decelerated during this period. The expansion in area under cereals during 1955/56 through 1967/68 resulted in significant growth in cereal production in the state. The cereal production in the state had increased marginally (by 0.0116 per cent per annum) between 1980/81 and 1990/91 and this miniscule growth was due to lower levels of production during the late 1980s. Concerned with this the state government appointed an Expert Committee (under the Chairmanship of Sri Satish Chandran) to probe into the factors responsible for stagnation in agricultural production. However, there was a recovery during 1992/93 and the analysis of production data for 1980/81 through 1993/94 indicated a growth rate of around 1.78 per cent. It is essential to underscore that the growth in production during this period came mainly through yield improvements. But the deceleration is again visible during the nineties.

Pulse production in the state accelerated by 1.79 per cent per annum during the last 40 years and by 2.71 per cent during the seventies. Oilseed production in the state was almost stagnant during the mid-fifties through the seventies. However, it grew at a rate of 7.33 per cent per annum between 1980/81 and 1993/94. The performance indicators of the crop economy at state level merge the differences across regions. These regional differences are of greater significance to policy formulation than the state aggregate performance.

In the cropping pattern of the state, cereals and oilseeds are the two major crop groups followed by pulses. The principal cereal crop in terms of area is jowar with 18.97 lakh hectares followed by paddy with 13.53 lakh hectares (1997/98). In the total oilseeds area of 23.72 lakh hectares, groundnut and sunflower account for 83 per cent of the area. Pulses account for 16.82 lakh hectares of area and it is distributed over a variety of pulses. In the year 1999/2000, the anticipated production of cereals has been 79.47 lakh tonnes, 6.58 lakh tonnes of pulses, 11.66 lakh tonnes of oilseeds, 293.33 lakh tonnes of sugarcane, and 8.38 lakh bales of cotton. There has been no increase in the production levels of these crops in the year 1999/2000 compared to the production levels of 1995/96. However, 1998/99 appears to have been a good agricultural crop year for the state (Table 13.9).

TABLE 13.9 (i): **Compound Growth Rates in Crop Economy: 1955-56—93-94**

(Per cent per annum)

Crops	Area	Production	Productivity
1	2	3	4
Rice	0.60	2.21	1.60
Wheat	-0.63	2.73	3.38
Jowar	-0.84	1.26	2.12

(contd.)

TABLE 13.9 (i) *(contd.)*

1	2	3	4
Ragi	0.44	2.17	1.72
Maize	10.76	15.52	-
Total cereals	-	2.13	2.43
Gram	1.02	1.80	0.77
Tur	1.42	1.94	0.52
Total pulses	0.83	1.79	0.95
Groundnut	0.65	1.55	0.90
Total oil seeds	2.18	2.74	0.54
Cotton	-1.60	2.39	4.06
Sugarcane	4.40	4.87	0.45

TABLE 13.9 (ii): **Growth Rates in Crop Economy: 1990-2000**

(Per cent per annum)

Crops	Yield	Production	Area
Rice	-0.45	2.09	2.55
Ragi	-1.14	-4.32	-3.22
Jowar	-3.3	-4.54	-1.28
Bajra	-7.89	-9.18	-1.4
Maize	-0.83	6.86	7.75
Wheat	0.77	4.78	3.98
Minor millets	1.35	-5.43	-6.68
Total cereals	-0.17	-0.03	0.14
Tur	-2.72	-1.26	1.5
Total pulses	-4.84	-1.11	3.92
Total foodgrains	-1.12	-0.12	1.02
Groundnut	-8.54	-10.4	-2.03
Total oilseeds	-5.98	-9.56	-3.81
Sugarcane	2.21	1.49	-0.7
Cotton	-0.42	-3.42	-3.01
Tobacco	-0.93	4.75	5.74

Source: Based on the data collected from Directorate of Economics and Statistics.

Emerging Employment Generating Sectors in State Agriculture

Horticulture

Karnataka occupies a very important position in the horticultural map of India. The shift from subsistence farming to more remunerative horticultural crops has been a marked phenomenon in the recent past. In the recent years, the area under horticultural crops is growing much faster because of liberalisation and NEP induced market changes, availability of infrastructure, and the incentive structure. The area under horticultural crops in the state has increased to 1.4 million hectares (from 0.8 million ha.) registering a growth rate of 4 per cent per annum over the period of 1980/81 to 1995/96. This is higher than the all India growth rate as well as that of China and Brazil. The production levels have gone up to 11 million tonnes in 1995/96 from 5.6 million tones in 1978/79. Karnataka had accounted for 10 per cent of the area and production in this during this period (Table 13.10).

TABLE 13.10 (i): **Area under Important Horticulture Crops in Karnataka**
(Area: Hectares in Lakhs Production: Tonnes in Lakhs)

	Area		Percentage to Total		Production		Percentage to Total	
Items	1978-79	1995-96	1978-79	1995-96	1978-79	1995-96	1978-79	1995-96
1. Fruits	1.41	2.66	17.05	19.10	23.41	45.14	42.00	41.39
2. Vegetables	1.26	2.29	15.24	16.44	20.10	46.72	36.06	42.84
3. Garden/ Spices crops	5.56	8.81	67.23	63.24	12.02	16.17	21.56	14.83
4. Commercial/ Flowers	0.04	0.17	0.48	1.22	0.21	1.02	0.38	0.94
5. Total	8.27	13.93	100.0	100.0	55.74	109.05	100.0	100.0

Source: Statistical Data on Horticultural Crops in Karnataka State, 1993-94 and 1995-96, Government of Karnataka.

In terms of value, the horticultural production in Karnataka in 1995/96 was worth Rs.5819 crore, accounting for 44 per cent of the state's value of production from agricultural sector. This is increasing every year although the share of agricultural sector in the state total domestic product is declining. The value of exports of horticultural crops in the state increased from Rs. 3719.42 lakh in 1994/95 to Rs. 5190.45 lakh in 1996/97. This has accounted for 1.42 per cent of the total horticultural exports of the country (GoI, 1997). During the last five years the area under most of these crops increased at a faster pace compared to the other crops. The area under spices increased from 3.91 lakh hectares in 1995/96 to 6.15 lakh hectares in 1999/2000.

TABLE 13.10 (ii): **Area under Horticulture 1995-2000**

(Lakh hectares)

Crops	1995-96	1996-97	1997-98	1998-99(P)	1999-00(A)
Flowers	2.76	2.86	3.14.	3.25	3.36
Coconut	4.25	4.31	4.94	5.14	5.35
Spices	3.91	3.96	5.61	5.87	6.15
Vegetables	2.43	2.45	2.59	2.65	2.71
Cashew	0.67	0.68	0.67	0.68	0.69
Flowers	0.19	0.20	0.20	0.20	0.20

Note: P-Provisional, A-Anticipated
Source: Directorate of Horticulture.

Floriculture

Floriculture is emerging as an important commercial crop both in Karnataka and also at the country level owing to its multiple use and export potential. The major traditional flowers used are marigold, jasmine, rose, aster crescendo, while the cutflowers with stems include rose, gladiolus, tube rose and carnation. Floriculture in Karnataka has achieved an impressive growth. Karnataka occupies second position both in terms of area and production, next to Tamil Nadu. In Karnataka, the area under floriculture has grown from 4,000 hectares with 21,000 tonnes of production in 1978/79 to 17,419 hectares (46 per cent share in the country area) with 102,205 tonnes of production by 1995/96. Export of floriculture produce has impressively increased to 607 tonnes (value Rs. 425 lakh) in 1996/97 from just eight tonnes (Rs. 15 lakh) in 1994/95. The current export level of the state forms 7 per cent of the total earnings of the country's floriculture (GoI, 1996/97). The Government of Karnataka has taken some important steps to create a proper incentive structure for floriculturists. These measures have now started yielding positive results. The new policy has resulted in approval of 134 floriculture export units till December 31, 1995 with a total outlay of Rs. 1091 million in the country. Already, 32 units of floriculture have started functioning in different parts of the country. These trends indicate that Karnataka may emerge as the hub of floricultural activities in India. This activity promises great scope for employment especially women workers.

Agro-processing and Rural Industries

Agro-processing activity in the state, particularly in respect of food processing is quite subdued. Realising the importance and the scope of food processing within the state, the government brought out an exclusive industrial promotion policy for agro-food processing from April 1999 by offering concessions and incentives for promoting food processing within the state. The Karnataka Agro Industries Corporation Ltd. has a fruit-processing unit. The unit processes fruits into jams, juice and tomatoes into squashes, crushes, sauce etc., and sells the products through a network of sales points spread over the state. Under the aegis of the Department of Industries and Commerce various corporations are functioning for development of village and small industries. These corporations are playing a vital role in providing training to the artisans to improve their skills. In addition there are 1519 industrial cooperatives in the state in the small, village and cottage industries sector in the areas of coir, leather, handloom and allied artisan oriented activities.

Emerging Challenges

Enabling Environment

The state of Karnataka faces threefold challenges for employment generation and tackling the new phase of reforms in the current environment (see Box). The agro-climatic situation of the state divides it into a large number of agro-climactic zones. The crop patterns as well as employment generation differ across these zones and thus policy mixes have to be conducive keeping in view the requirements. Hitherto, even directing public investment towards agricultural development across regions for the purpose of employment generation has not yielded desired results and has failed to merge the differences in developmental initiatives across these regions. In the absence of data on regionwise investment, we cannot conclude about the extent of the failure. But sensing the acuteness of the problem, the state of Karnataka has taken the initiative in constituting a committee to investigate into regional imbalances across the state and searching for employment avenues is one of the important aspects.

The fiscal situation and the policy philosophy adopted may not allow creation of new jobs under the public sector; thus, the onus of creating employment falls more on the private sector. The most important challenge that the state faces presently is facilitating private investment in the backward areas of the state. While initiating such schemes, it is essential to understand the resource endowments, employment multipliers, and competitive advantages of these regions to participate in the mainstream growth pattern. Hitherto, agriculture was considered as the only alternative to bring these regions into mainstream growth. Therefore, the growth culture needs to be created even in the allied agricultural sectors. Horticulture development, especially dry land horticultural crops, has proved to be a promising alternative both in terms of income generation and employment creation. In the recent past, it has been observed that horticultural crops have been picking up in terms of area as well as productivity in the northern dry regions despite the climatic constraints. The state government is taking sufficient initiatives to boost horticultural development in these regions.

The second major impediment that poses a challenge for the state government is the availability of funds to initiate agricultural and rural development schemes in the fragile regions. Therefore, private initiatives are required either in terms of corporate farming of bulk purchase and marketing facilities. The requirement of investment in the backward regions can also be met by siphoning the excess savings from well-endowed regions to the deserving backward areas. This can be achieved by floating low interest investment bonds to be purchased by private contributors from the developed regions of the state. Development boards specially set up to guide the process of development of these regions can take the initiative in this respect.

Sl. No	Major Challenges	Responses for Enabling the Acceptance
1.	Threatened stagnation in agri-growth, Employment and possibility of decelerating growth	Locating growth in the emerging growth inducing crops/ sectors
2.	Low value added in agricultural sector and tardy employment generation in the organised sector	Removal of marketing bottlenecks and enabling remunerative price situation
3.	Fast approaching optima on technological front	Investment boosting in R & D sector
4.	Large proportions of rainfed/ dryland area	Technological options and diversification of economic base
5.	Marginalisation of agricultural base	Group initiatives and arresting the process through institutional options
6.	Inadequate growth in public and private investment, deceleration of SDP growth	Attracting private investments in the sunrise sectors; locating sub-sectors with new growth options
7.	Regional disparities	Prudent regional allocation of growth inducers
8.	Inadequate safety nets	Revamping and redesigning the safety net programmes; effective delivery
9.	Conflicting growth vs. environmental options	Resolving the issues amicably; reducing the intensity of negative externalities

The third and an important problem faced by the state is in terms of participation in the process of liberalisation by enabling a proper conduit towards the most deserving regions and groups of farmers. The state has been performing well as far as its participation in international trade is concerned. In the past four years, the state has shown good progress in the exports of agricultural products. If this tempo has to be continued and enhanced in future, it is necessary to support the agricultural and horticultural sectors in terms of crucial information as well as creating an enabling environment for participation. These are likely to boost employment trends.

Next Phase of Reforms

Gradual and graded reduction of the state role in directing the path of growth without compromising equity

The gradual and graded reduction of the role of state in directing the path of development, rural development, and natural resource management is an essential prerequisite of the current phase of the reforms. This however, has to be accomplished without influencing the welfare of the weaker sections, which was tied hitherto strongly with state policies. Such optima can be achieved only by simultaneously creating employment along with growth push. The process must gradually reduce the dependence of the population on the state schemes, thereby reducing public expenditure on these sectors and initiating the process of participation on the part of the people. Thus, generation of jobs is expected more from the organised sector. This is a major challenge as employment seekers are more densely located in the unskilled sector.

Dealing with a process of deceleration on six fronts, namely: technology, efficiency, markets, carrying capacity, lagged regions and weaker sections

Deceleration in agricultural productivity has been noted in the state. This is also coupled with not so encouraging employment trends. This has two important connotations. Either production efficiency is going down or those technological options are reaching their plateau. In this context, it is essential to act on the four fronts indicated above. Presently, an immediate task is to look for enhancement of the existing technology and at the same time improve the efficiency in the use of current technology. Efficiency in the production process in the agricultural sector is marred mainly due to the high dependence of the sector on the state. Thus, market reforms should address not only the issue of improving the marketing conditions in terms of infrastructure but also in terms of price spread and market margins so as to help weaker sections in properly marketing their products. The carrying capacity of the agricultural sector comes under discussion mainly when we think of the failure of the Lewis process. In the current two decades the carrying capacity of the agricultural sector will increase at a rate of about 2 per cent per annum and will put pressure on the resources. Therefore, it is necessary to plan a proper employment strategy adjusting the constraints.

Management of agricultural sector, natural resources and rural development with full participation of the stakeholders for growth and employment

The development paradigms hitherto have emphasised planning from the top. It is from the second plan onwards that Indian planners have been insisting on 'bottom up' planning, but nothing significant was done in this regard till the end of the seventh plan. Even the not-so-recent amendments to the Constitution (73rd and 74th) have not been put into full action despite the lapse of seven years. The non-governmental organisational network has been making dents sporadically into this sector and only in selected regions. These have not caught the attention of the policy makers in a significant way. Even here the replication has been questioned and there are umpteen numbers of examples where replication has failed. Therefore, the management of growth and employment has to be through a people oriented plan frame.

Integrating the Reforms

Reforms have been taking place in the Indian economy and subsequently in the state economy in various sectors including services, legal framework, governments, and industrial sectors. These have direct and indirect bearing across sectors and on employment trends. One of the lacunae of our developmental process has been the lack of horizontal and vertical integration in the implementation of policy and visualising the results. This has to be understood well and attended to while integrating the reform process across the sectors. There is an urgent need to initiate the integration so that stakeholders across sectors are not taken unawares.

APPENDIX

TABLE 13.1: **Employment in Organised Sector in Karnataka**

(In lakhs)

Sl. No	Industry	1991-92	1995-96	1998-99
1.	Plantation and forestry	0.56	0.57	0.56
	a) Public sector	0.40	0.41	0.39
	b) Private sector	0.16	0.16	0.17
2.	Mining and quarrying	0.28	0.27	0.21
	a) Public sector	0.24	0.20	0.16
	b) Private sector	0.04	0.07	0.05
3.	Manufacturing	4.07	6.08	6.29
	a) Public sector	1.27	1.06	0.96
	b) Private sector	2.80	5.02	5.33
4.	Construction	0.64	0.59	0.53
	a) Public sector	0.58	0.56	0.50
	b) Private sector	0.06	0.03	0.03
5.	Electricity gas and water	0.50	0.47	0.46
	a) Public sector	0.49	0.46	0.45
	b) Private sector	0.01	0.01	0.01
6.	Trade and commerce	0.32	0.36	0.37
	a) Public sector	0.08	0.10	0.10
	b) Private sector	0.24	0.26	0.27
7.	Tpt Storage and communication	1.48	1.60	1.62
	a) Public sector	1.43	1.53	1.54
	b) Private sector	0.05	0.07	0.08
8.	Finance, insurance and real estate	1.08	1.19	1.34
	a) Public sector	0.91	0.94	0.97
	b) Private sector	0.17	0.25	0.37
9.	Social and personal	5.87	6.46	7.11
	a) Public sector	4.88	5.33	5.85
	b) Private sector	0.99	1.13	1.26
10.	TOTAL	14.80	17.59	18.49
	a) Public sector	10.28	10.59	10.92
	b) Private sector	4.52	7.00	7.57

Source: Government of Karnataka (2000). *Manpower Profile: Karnataka*, Manpower and Employment Division, GoK, Bangalore.

TABLE 13.2: **Districtwise Employment in Organised Sector (As on 30-06-99)**

(In thousand man days)

Sl. No.	District	Employment		
		Public	Private	Total
1	Bangalore	295.3	268.0	563.3
2	Bagalkote	23.4	5.6	29.0
3	Belgaum	54.6	36.5	91.1
4	Bellary	34.8	15.7	50.5
5	Bidar	22.6	7.4	30.0
6	Bijapur	27.8	5.6	33.4
7	Chamrajnagar	14.6	2.1	16.7
8	Chickmagalur	24.2	12.2	36.4
9	Chitradurga	21.9	4.0	25.9
10	Davangere	27.8	10.4	38.2
11	DakshinaKannada	40.9	208.5	249.4
12	Dharwad	57.3	23.0	80.3
13	Gadag	13.6	5.6	19.4
14	Gulbarga	50.5	12.2	62.7
15	Hassan	35.3	7.8	43.1
16	Haveri	12.9	6.7	19.6
17	Kodagu	12.7	9.6	22.3
18	Kolar	50.0	6.5	56.5
19	Koppala	14.3	3.0	17.3
20	Mandya	34.3	4.1	38.4
21	Mysore	69.2	29.7	98.9
22	Raichur	27.8	3.3	30.9
23	Shimoga	39.9	7.6	47.5
24	Tumkur	40.0	10.4	50.4
25	Udupi	17.1	33.1	50.2
26	Uttara Kannada	36.2	11.9	48.1
	Grand Total	1099.0	750.5	1849.5

Source: Directorate of Employment and Training, Government of Karnataka (2000), Bangalore.

TABLE 13.3: **Karnataka: Some of the Important Infrastructure Development Indicators for the Year 1999-91 to 1998-99**

Year	Villages Electrified (Numbers)	IP Sets Electrified (Numbers)	Total Rcad Length (km.)	Total Railway (km.)	Post Offices (Numbers)	Total Hospitals (Numbers)	Total PHCs PHUs Dispensary (Numbers)
1990-91	26733	733100	130924	3060	9665	293	2032
1991-92	26733	805400	133987	3063	9704	293	2093
1992-93	26733	856700	134592	3069	9762	293	2127
1993-94	26733	904900	134832	3079	9781	293	2178
1994-95	28483	973288	134832	3079	9784	306	2726
1995-96	28483	1001209	135104	3079	9787	312	2777
1996-97	28483	1049465	137520	3192	9827	313	3398
1997-98	28483	1082150	139520	3192	9838	320	3513
1998-99	28483	1141824	142901	3270	9852	390	3516

Source: Collected from various issues of *Karnataka at a Glance*.

REFERENCES

Agro-Climatic Regional Planning Unit (1989), "Agro-Climatic Zones: Profiles and Issues". Working Paper No.2. ARPU, Ahmedabad.

Deshpande, R S. and V.M. Rao (2000), "Prospects for Coarse Cereals in Drought-prone Regions: An Exploratory Study in Karnataka", Research Report, ISEC, Bangalore.

Government of India (1997), "Approach Paper to the Ninth Five-Year Plan (1997-2002)", Draft paper circulated during the Meeting of the National Development Council held on 16 January 1997, at New Delhi, Planning Commission, New Delhi.

—— (2001), *Economic Survey 2000-2001*, New Delhi.

—— (2000), *National Agricultural Policy, 2000*, Ministry of Agriculture, July.

Government of Karnataka (1993), *Report of Expert Committee on Stagnation of Agricultural Productivity in Karnataka during 1980s* (Chairman: Satish Chandran), Bangalore.

—— (1995), *Agricultural Policy: 1995*, Department of Agriculture and Horticulture, Bangalore.

—— (1998), *Annual Plan 1997-98,* Vol. I. Planning, Institutional Finance and Statistics and Science and Technology Department, Bangalore.

—— (2000a), *Economic Survey (1999-2000),* Planning, Institutional Finance and Statistics and Science and Technology Department, Bangalore.

—— (2000b), *Karnataka Agriculture: a Profile*, Department of Agriculture, Bangalore.

—— (2000c), *White Paper on Financial Status of Karnataka*, Finance Department, Bangalore, March 31, 2000.

—— (2000d), *Manpower Profile: Karnataka-Year2000-2001,* Planning, Institutional Finance and Statistics and Science and Technology Department, Government of Karnataka, Bangalore.

Lanjouw, Peter (2000), "Poverty in Karnataka: Profiles and Emerging Issues", (Draft Paper) Development Economics Research Group, The World Bank, Washington.

Rao, V.M. (1992), "Change Processes in Dryland Communities", Presidential Address, Indian Society of Agricultural Economics, 51st Conference, *Indian Journal of Agricultural Economics*, Vol.47 No.1. Jan-March.

14

READY FOR SECOND GENERATION REFORMS? An Evaluation of Progress Made by Maharashtra*

AJIT KARNIK

Introduction

There has been much talk about the introduction of Second Generation Reforms (SGR) at the level of central and state governments in India. In fact, a few governments (central government included) have gone ahead and proclaimed that they have already initiated SGR. Of course, it is not made clear whether these SGR are being initiated after having already achieved all that was expected of the First Generation Reforms (FGR). Generally, it is not even spelt out exactly what constitutes the SGR that are being ushered in. Further, at the level of state governments it is not clear what the exact ingredients of FGR were. This difficulty, however, does not encumber evaluation of FGR at the central government level, since these mainly pertained to the highest level of government in the economy.

* I would like to thank Professor Atul Sarma who was kind enough to offer detailed comments on the paper. Thanks are also due to the participants at the National Seminar on "Economic Reforms and Employment in the Indian Economy", Organised by the Institute of Applied Manpower Research, New Delhi, March 22-24, 2001. Needless to add, I alone remain responsible for any deficiencies that remain in the paper.

FGR, by and large, dealt with items in the Washington Consensus (Holden and Rajapatirana 1997, World Bank, 2000) which included (among others):

- Fiscal discipline
- Redirection of public expenditure toward education, health, and infrastructure investment
- Tax reform—broadening the tax base and cutting marginal tax rates
- Interest rates that are market determined and positive (but moderate) in real terms
- Competitive exchange rates
- Trade liberalization—replacement of quantitative restrictions with low and uniform tariffs

A glance at the list of FGR given above shows that many of these have little relevance for state governments in India with the exception of government finances. This is an essential component of FGR since for the economy as a whole, it is stability in the fiscal balances of all levels of government that is crucial. This necessarily implies that as far as FGR are concerned, the very least that state governments should aim for is to set their fiscal balances in order.

I will be focusing on government finances in Maharashtra as a means of evaluating whether there has been any success as far as FGR are concerned. In section one, I look at the profile of various measures of fiscal balance for Maharashtra. I will simultaneously be comparing Maharashtra with all other states in India clubbed together. In section two, I look at the growth of the fiscal balance measures. This is studied in a pooled cross-section time series context so as to estimate differential rates of growth for Maharashtra as compared to other states. Section three looks at the impact of fiscal imbalances on real growth in Maharashtra. Finally, in section four, I look at some aspects of SGR, including transparency in government operations, issues in local finance and institutional factors such as law and order, political stability, etc. Section five concludes the discussion.

A Profile of Various Fiscal Balance Measures

A variety of measures are available for judging fiscal balances at any level of government. The level of government, whether central, state or local, determines which are the most appropriate measures. We propose to employ a variety of measures of fiscal balance as discussed in this section for the state of Maharashtra (MAH) and the Rest of India (REST). It may be pointed out that REST includes all states (numbering 25) as listed in the RBI publications on State Finances. It is possible that the inclusion of all the states of the Indian Federation may bias results owing to the inclusion of numerous small states. In the exercises of this paper we have not made any corrections on this score, but plan to do so while extending this work.

Throughout the analysis in this paper a distinction will be made between MAH and REST. The analysis is intended to offer a basis of comparison between Maharashtra and other states and help us to judge whether the state is better or worse than all other states put together. Note that a positive verdict on this score need not be a matter of comfort: the depressing conclusion to be drawn could well be that Maharashtra is doing badly but the other states are doing worse. It has not been possible for us to study the finances of all the (major) states of India and compare Maharashtra with the best of these. This would be an important exercise and help compare the performance of Maharashtra with these other states. However, such a study will have to wait for another time.

The measures of fiscal balance that will be used in this paper are the following:

(a) *Revenue Deficit*: This is measured as:

$$RD = RE - RR \tag{1}$$

Where,
RE = Revenue Expenditures
RR = Revenue Receipts
RD = Revenue Deficit

(b) *Capital Deficit*: This is measured as:

$$CD = CE - CR \quad (2)$$

Where,
CE = Capital Expenditures
CR = Capital Receipts
CD = Capital Deficit

(c) *Gross Fiscal Gap*: This is measured as follows:

$$GFG = (RE+CE) - RR \quad (3)$$

Where,
GFG = Gross Fiscal Gap

Note that the measure used here is different from that used by, say, Pattanaik et al. (1994, 1999). Specifically, we do not exclude from consideration discharge of internal debt and repayment of loans to the centre. Both of these involve a commitment of resources for the states and to the extent that these are factored out of CE, the requirement of resources is reduced. We have not done that. In order to avoid confusion and in view of differences with the approach of Pattanaik et al. we do not call our measure Gross Fiscal Deficit, even though it closely resembles it.

(d) *Basic Resources Gap (1):* This is measured as follows:

$$BRG1 = (RE + CE) - (OTAR + ONTR) \quad (4)$$

Where,
OTAR = Own tax revenues
ONTR = Own non-tax revenues

(e) *Basic Resource Gap (2)*: This is measured as follows:

$$BRG2 = (RE + CE) - [(OTAR + ONTR) + (ID - ML) + (PFS + RFD + OCR)] \quad (5)$$

Where,
ID = Internal Debt
ML = Market Loans
PFS = Provident Funds

RFD = Reserve Funds and Deposits
OCR = Other Capital Receipts

(f) *Basic Resource Gap (3):* This is measured as follows:

$$BRG3 = (RE + CE) - [(OTAR + ONTR + SCT + SGFC) + (ID - ML) + (PFS + RFD + OCR)] \quad (6)$$

Where,
SCT = State's share in Central Taxes
SGFC = Statutory Grants from the Centre

In the tables that follow we give the profiles of the various fiscal measures discussed above for both Maharashtra and Rest of the States in India. The time series listed below cover the period from 1990/91 to 1999/2000.

TABLE 14.1: **Standard Fiscal Balance Measures**

(Rs. lakh)

	Revenue Deficit		Capital Deficit		Gross Fiscal Gap	
Year	MAH	REST	MAH	REST	MAH	REST
1990-91	5465	525432	-33060	-520385	207324	2254803
1991-92	27613	537462	-125728	-495369	227897	2511478
1992-93	72849	438557	-1427	-692918	319535	2504817
1993-94	12190	369057	-6285	-328789	299633	2608850
1994-95	-27729	643346	-32895	-1029498	493685	3433323
1995-96	61220	802434	7856	-680981	513430	3609807
1996-97	94654	1014358	-44927	-661971	518370	4157215
1997-98	257994	1375300	-282376	-1561208	735857	5047543
1998-99	392594	3971584	-468049	-3544155	858010	8133302
1999-2000	948396	4731764	-625210	-4133679	1599966	9482457

Notes: 1. MAH - Maharashtra; REST - All states excluding MAH
2. A minus sign indicates a surplus.
3. Calculations for 1999/2000 are based on revised estimates of the relevant data; all others are based on accounts data.

Source: Computed from Reserve Bank of India Bulletin: Finances of the State Government, various issues.

The numbers in Table 14.1 are worrying but unsurprising. It is common knowledge that both the centre and states have been running up deficits on the revenue account and financing these by borrowings. In the process the capital account of the budget has been running surpluses, in order to keep the overall fiscal gap manageable.

TABLE 14.2: **Additional Fiscal Balance Measures**

(Rs. lakh)

	BRG1		BRG2		BRG3	
Year	MAH	REST	MAH	REST	MAH	REST
1990-91	385837	4764766	276535	3866489	106271	1452539
1991-92	430957	5515772	277583	4338512	85740	1438827
1992-93	551968	6106281	434356	4630773	211813	1144347
1993-94	590391	6675174	457901	5532092	179863	1582106
1994-95	766886	7649034	507186	5519185	247466	1363512
1995-96	829508	8722362	585403	7285091	301625	2743980
1996-97	889462	9750577	634666	8308528	282654	3118890
1997-98	1031499	11215273	653134	8936969	363545	3140721
1998-99	1254213	14065567	807644	9847105	419601	4112390
1999-2000	2037755	16998548	1329036	11990099	915359	4778597

Notes: 1. MAH - Maharashtra; REST - All states excluding MAH.

2. Calculations for 1999/2000 are based on revised estimates of the relevant data; all others are based on accounts data.

Source : Same as for Table 14.1.

The measures listed in Table 14.2 have been proposed by Pattanaik et al. (1994). Each of the BRG measures reveals the extent of fiscal dependency of the state on the Central Government, RBI and other agencies. The presence of a BRG automatically implies that it has to be financed from resources beyond the control of the state. The following means of financing the BRG may be noted:

$$BRG1 = SCT + GFC + CR + WMA \quad (7)$$

$$BRG2 = SCT + GFC + ML + LAC + WMA \quad (8)$$

$$BRG3 = NSGFC + ML + LAC + WMA \quad (9)$$

Where,
GFC = Grants from the Centre
WMA = Ways and Means Advances
LAC = Loans and Advances from the Centre
NSGFC = Non-statutory Grants from the Centre.

BRG1 gives the highest level of financing requirements given that only own resources of the state are taken into account on the revenue side of the gap. However, the state may still have some control over at least some of the financing items of BRG1 listed above. At the other extreme is BRG3, which quantifies the extent of dependency on completely exogenous factors over which the state does not have any control at all.

A measure of fiscal stress on a state can be computed as the ratio of BRG3 to BRG1.

$$\text{Fiscal Stress Ratio (FSR)} = \text{BRG3/BRG1} \qquad (10)$$

Further, considering the total resource requirement of the state as given by its total expenditures (TE = RE + CE), we can compute the fiscal dependency ratio (FDR) as follows:

$$\text{FDR1} = \text{BRG1/TE} \qquad (11)$$
$$\text{FDR2} = \text{BRG2/TE} \qquad (12)$$
$$\text{FDR3} = \text{BRG3/TE} \qquad (13)$$

Table 14.3 gives a profile of the ratios listed in equations (10)-(13).

The FSR for Maharashtra is substantially higher than it was at the beginning of the economic reforms process in 1991/92. An increase in the ratio indicates that the dependence on resources over which the state has little control has been growing over the years. On the other hand for the REST, the FSR has shown a decline over the same period. This leads to the conclusion that the REST is doing better than MAH in terms of managing fiscal stress. The next section will look at trends in the growth of this as well as the other ratios more closely.

TABLE 14.3: **Various Ratios Based on BRG**

(Percentage)

	FSR		FDR1		FDR2		FDR3	
Year	MAH	REST	MAH	REST	MAH	REST	MAH	REST
1990-91	27.54	30.49	35.82	59.33	25.67	48.14	9.87	18.09
1991-92	19.90	26.09	35.76	57.53	23.03	45.25	7.11	15.01
1992-93	38.37	18.74	39.39	57.98	31.00	43.97	15.11	10.87
1993-94	30.47	23.70	36.94	56.25	28.65	46.62	11.25	13.33
1994-95	32.27	17.83	38.29	54.05	25.33	39.00	12.36	9.63
1995-96	36.36	31.46	37.28	54.96	26.31	45.90	13.55	17.29
1996-97	31.78	31.99	36.77	56.19	26.24	47.88	11.69	17.97
1997-98	35.24	28.00	37.27	55.95	23.60	44.58	13.14	15.67
1998-99	33.46	29.24	41.37	59.59	26.64	41.72	13.84	17.42
1999-2000	44.92	28.11	50.43	59.60	32.89	42.04	22.65	16.75

Notes: 1. MAH - Maharashtra; REST - All states excluding MAH.

2. Calculations for 1999/2000 are based on revised estimates of the relevant data; all others are based on accounts data.

Source : Computed from Table 14.2.

As far as the FDRs are concerned, the ratio using the broadest measure of BRG, namely FDR1, shows an unmistakable increase for MAH while that for the REST, considering only the end points of the time period, shows stability. Again, FDR2 for MAH has worsened over the years but that for the REST shows a distinct improvement. The same story is repeated for FDR3 as well—MAH shows a deterioration while REST shows some improvement.

Growth of Fiscal Balance Measures

In this section we propose to investigate whether after the initiation of reforms there has been a worsening of the various fiscal balance measures, as well as the fiscal stress and fiscal dependency ratios in Maharshtra. We will also have a subsidiary objective of comparing Maharashtra's performance with that of the other states of India. For this purpose we propose to estimate pooled cross-section time series trend growth models using the *least squares dummy variables* technique. This will enable us to examine whether the growth of a fiscal measure or fiscal ratio in Maharashtra is lower than in the rest of the states.

We estimate the following pooled model for the purpose:

$$Y_{it} = a + b*TIME + c*(TIME*DUMM) \qquad (13)$$

Where,

Y_{it} = fiscal measure of interest for the ith cross-section unit in the tth time period; i= MAH, REST and t= 1...10 for each cross-section unit

TIME = trend variable taking values 1....10

DUMM = 1 if i = MAH

0 otherwise

Estimation of (13) will enable us to obtain the differential trend growth for MAH. For instance, when DUMM=1, the sum of the coefficients, (b+c) will yield the trend growth for MAH. The sign of the coefficient 'c' and its significance will indicate whether the trend growth for MAH is greater or lower than the trend growth for the REST. Table 14.4 reports results of estimating (13) for various fiscal balance measures.

In Table 14.4 the row (b+c) gives the differential trend growth for MAH. The major conclusions that emerge are :

1. Revenue Deficits (RD): The differential trend growth for MAH at $0.1068*10^6$ is lower than the REST. Of course, RD for MAH continues to increase at a rapid rate, but at least it out-performs the REST.
2. Capital Deficits (CD): The differential trend growth for MAH at $-0.0516*10^6$ is higher than the REST. MAH too has been using surpluses on the capital account to finance RD, but it has been doing so at a lower rate.
3. Gross Fiscal Gap (GFG): The differential trend growth for MAH at $0.0579*10^6$ is lower than the REST. Of course, GFG for MAH continues to increase at a rapid rate, but the performance is better than that of the REST.

4. Basic Resource Gap 1 (BRG1): The differential trend growth for MAH at $-0.0104*10^7$ is lower than that of the REST. Thus, while BRG1 is increasing for REST, it is declining for MAH.
5. Basic Resource Gap 2 (BRG2): The differential trend growth for MAH at $-0.0112*10^7$ is lower than that of the REST. As in the case of BRG1, while BRG2 is increasing for REST, it is declining for MAH.
6. Basic Resource Gap 3 (BRG3): The differential trend growth for MAH at $0.0320*10^6$ is lower than that of the REST. Thus even though BRG3 is increasing for MAH, it is at a lower rate than that of the REST.

TABLE 14.4: **Results of Estimating Equation 13**

	RD	CD	GFG	BRG1	BRG2	BRG3
Coefficient						
A	–0.4378	0.1669	0.3113	0.1424	0.1267	0.1663
	(–1.63)	(0.74)	(0.94)	(2.96)	(2.91)	(0.80)
B	0.3228	–0.2628	0.7215	0.1484	0.1038	0.4180
	(6.23)	(–6.03)	(10.80)	(13.41)	(12.55)	(11.16)
C	–0.2160	0.2112	–0.6636	–0.1588	–0.1150	–0.3860
(–5.10)	(5.96)	(–11.46)	(–15.18)	(–14.61)	(–11.96)	
(b+c)	0.1068	–0.0516	0.0579	–0.0104	–0.0112	0.0320
Adj. R^2	0.8613	0.8706	0.9602	0.9934	0.9830	0.9419
DW	2.12	2.32	2.17	2.04	1.65	2.02

Notes: 1. Coefficients of RD, CD, GFG and BRG3 have been given in truncated form. True values require exponentiation of 10^6. Thus, the coefficient –0.4378 should be read as $-0.4378*10^6$.

2. Coefficients of BRG1 and BRG2 have been given in truncated form. True values require exponentiation of 10^7. Thus the coefficient 0.1424 should be read as $0.1424*10^7$.

We also estimated pooled cross section time series growth models for fiscal stress and fiscal dependency ratios. The equation that we estimate is a slight variation on (13).

$$Y_{it} = \alpha + \beta*TIME + \chi*(TIME*DUMM) + \delta*DUMM \quad (14)$$

Where,

Y_{it} = fiscal stress or dependency ratio of interest for the ith cross-section unit in the tth time period; i= MAH, REST and t= 1...10 for each cross-section unit.

The only change in (14) as compared to (13) is the presence of DUMM as a variable by itself. It would not have served any purpose to include DUMM in (13) since it would have merely conveyed the fact that a measure of fiscal balance in *absolute terms* is lower for MAH than for all other states put together. This, in any case, is to be expected. In the case of (14), however, the variable of interest is a *ratio* and it is not automatic that a ratio for a state should be lower than the ratio for a collection of states. Table 14.4 reports results of estimating (14).

TABLE 14.5: **Results of Estimating Equation 14**

	FSR	FDR1	FDR2	FDR3
Coefficient				
α	0.2322	0.5876	0.4672	0.1329
	(4.78)	(30.81)	(32.07)	(6.34)
β	0.0061	–0.0026	–0.0037	0.0034
	(0.74)	(–0.81)	(–1.54)	(0.99)
χ	–0.0125	0.0207	0.0051	0.0059
	(–1.44)	(4.91)	(1.59)	(1.25)
δ	0.1898	–0.3261	–0.2052	–0.0528
	(2.83)	(–12.56)	(–10.32)	(–1.79)
$(\beta+\chi)$	–0.0064	0.0181	0.0014	0.0093
Adj. R^2	0.2639	0.8706	0.9177	0.3137
DW	1.77	1.53	2.09	2.13

As in Table 14.4, the row $(\beta+\chi)$ in Table 14.5 gives the differential trend growth of the relevant fiscal ratio for MAH. The sign of the coefficient ä indicates whether the ratio is higher or lower for MAH as compared to REST. The major conclusions from the results of Table 14.5 are the following:

1. Fiscal Stress Ratio (FSR): This ratio is higher for MAH (the coefficient of DUMM is positive and significant) as compared to the REST even though the differential trend growth is lower for MAH. This indicates that even though the finances of MAH experience a higher level of stress, the situation is not worsening.
2. Fiscal Dependency Ratio 1 (FDR1): The ratio is lower for MAH (the coefficient of DUMM is negative and significant) but the differential growth is higher for MAH. For all states trend growth is falling while it is positive for MAH.
3. Fiscal Dependency Ratio 2 (FDR2): The ratio is lower for MAH (the coefficient of DUMM is negative and significant) but the differential growth rate is higher for MAH. The trend growth is negative for all states but positive for MAH.
4. Fiscal Dependency Ratio 3 (FDR3): Once again this ratio is lower for MAH but the trend growth is higher for MAH as compared to the REST.

Impact of Fiscal Imbalances on Growth in Maharashtra

In an earlier paper we (Karnik and Lalwani, 1997) had tried to examine expenditure levels of various state governments as a measure of the size of the government. We had then tried to establish links between interest group activity, government size and growth. However, it had not been possible to obtain any clear cut links between expenditures and rates of growth across Indian states. That was possibly due to the fact that the paper studied a heterogeneous group of states with sharply divergent growth and expenditure patterns.

In this section we try to examine whether it is possible to establish any links between various measures of fiscal balance and the rate of growth in Maharashtra. Each of the fiscal balance measures was employed in this exercise as a ratio to Maharshtra's

SDP at current prices. This was then sought to be linked to the rate of growth of Maharashtra's real SDP. Before we ran the regressions we tested each of the variables for presence of unit roots. Our data spanned the period 1980/81 to 1996/97. The results are given in Table 14.6.

TABLE 14.6: **Unit Root Testing Using Phillips-Perron Test**

	Series in Level	Series in First Differences
RDR = RD/SDPC	Non-stationary: Unit Root present	Stationary
CDR = CD/SDPC	Non-stationary: Unit Root present	Stationary
GFGR = GFG/SDPC	Non-stationary: Unit Root present	Stationary
BRG1R = BRG1/SDPC	Non-stationary: Unit Root present	Stationary
BRG2R = BRG2/SDPC	Non-stationary: Unit Root present	Stationary
BRG3R = BRG3/SDPC	Non-stationary: Unit Root present	Stationary
SDPR (growth rate)	Stationary	–

Note: SDPC - SDP of Maharashtra at current prices.
SDPR - SDP of Maharashtra at 1980-81 prices.

Given the results of unit root testing in Table 14.6, we ran regressions of various lags of the first-differenced fiscal balance ratios on growth rates of SDPR. Ideally, we would have preferred to employ lag selection criteria such as Akaike Information Criteria or Final Prediction Error to select appropriate lags for the independent variable. However, the paucity of our data set precluded that. Hence the maximum lags that we have experimented with are three time periods. Even though we ran regressions for each of the six fiscal balance ratios, the results for CDR, BRG1R, BRG2R and BRG3R were uniformly poor. We do not report these results. Equations (15) and (16) report results for RDR and GFGR.

$$\underset{(19.93)}{GRTH = 8.2262} - \underset{(-5.71)}{6.6137}*DRDR + \underset{(4.05)}{3.5584}*DRDR(t-1) - \underset{(-7.94)}{9.2293}DRDR(t-2) \qquad (15)$$

Sum of lag coefficients = –12.2850
(–6.50)
Adjusted R^2 = 0.7284
Unit root testing on residuals – stationary

$$GRTH = \underset{(6.90)}{7.3115} - \underset{(-2.89)}{3.9407}*DGFGR(t\text{-}2) - \underset{(-1.86)}{2.8689}*DGFGR(t\text{-}3) \qquad (16)$$

Sum of lag coefficients = –6.8095
(–3.23)
Adjusted R^2 = 0.4376
Unit root testing on residuals – stationary

Where,
GRTH = Growth rate of real SDP
DRDR = First differenced ratio of revenue deficits to SDP
DGFGR = First differenced ratio of gross fiscal gap to SDP
The figures in parenthesis are t-statistics

The crucial result of equations (15) and (16) is given by the 'sum of lag c6efficients'.

In the cases of both RD and GFG, these are significantly negative, pointing to the adverse effect of revenue deficit and gross fiscal gap on real growth in Maharashtra.

Second Generation of Reforms

There has been strong criticism that many countries that followed the tenets of FGR found that economic development had eluded them (Stiglitz, 1998). This led to calls for ushering in SGR whose objective would be to make the gains of FGR more broad-based and sustainable. There is however no unanimity on the exact content of SGR. The term has been used in diverse ways by academics and policy makers. Stiglitz (1998), for instance, focuses on equity as an essential element in designing SGR. Jacobs (1999) notes that the central problem to be addressed by SGR is variable institutional adaptation. Transparency in government operations is included in this as are issues of decentralisation and fiscal federalism. Holden and Rajapatirana (1997) mention maintenance of law and order, protection of property rights, provision of basic education and health as important elements of SGR. In the Indian context, the term has been used merely to indicate progression to the next stage of the reforms process, without necessarily ensuring that the earlier stage has been completed. Thus, Maharashtra claims to have launched SGR, while crucial elements of FGR have remained incomplete, as we saw in previous sections.

In this section I look at some of the elements that make up SGR and examine whether Maharashtra has taken any preliminary steps in this direction. I will specifically look at the following:

1. Issues of transparency
2. Issues in local public finance
3. Institutional factors

Transparency: Fiscal Marksmanship

There has been considerable debate regarding transparency in government operations, especially its public finances. The Government of Maharashtra too had appointed a committee to give recommendations regarding transparency in government operations. The report of this committee is, however, not yet publicly available.

Fiscal transparency has been defined as openness towards the public about government structure and functions, fiscal policy intentions, public sector accounts and projections (Kopits and Craig, 1998). Such transparency strengthens accountability and increases the political risks associated with maintaining unsustainable policies (IMF, 1999). One of the important dimensions of fiscal transparency is what RBI (2000) calls Fiscal Marksmanship. This is a desideratum of the minimum standard of fiscal transparency and requires the revised and budget estimates for the two years preceding the budget to be included in budget documents. This allows an assessment to be made of recent performance compared to the budget and draws attention to the realism of the budget being presented (IMF, 1999).

It has often been noticed in budgets presented by both the central and state governments in India that the revised estimates diverge considerably from original budget estimates. This divergence may be due to events beyond the control of the government, but enough suspicion is often created regarding other factors at work. In a couple of earlier articles I had tried to find political economy explanations for such divergences in central government budgets (Karnik 1997, 1998).

In this section we attempt to quantify the extent of divergence between budget estimates and accounts data for MAH and REST over the period 1991/92 to 1999/2000. We measure fiscal marksmanship as the gap between budget estimates and accounts data as follows:

$$GAP(\%) = (AD-BE)/BE(\%) \qquad (16)$$

Where,
BE = Budget estimates of the relevant variable
AD = Accounts data of the relevant variable

We present graphical pictures of GAP for (a) Revenue Receipts (Fig. 14.1) (b) Own Receipts (Tax + Non-tax) (Fig. 14.2) (c) Revenue Expenditures (Fig. 14.3) (d) Capital Receipts (Fig. 14.4) (e) Capital Disbursement (Fig. 14.5) and (f) Capital Outlay (Fig. 14.6). The figures make it amply clear that Maharahtra's fiscal marksmanship is way off target. Fig. 14.1 for Revenue Receipts shows some kind of a cyclical pattern, which needs investigation. Specifically, it may be interesting to see if the pattern can be connected to an electoral cycle.

While the graphs do convey an interesting picture, it would be useful to compute a summary measure to quantify the quality of fiscal marksmanship in MAH and compare this with the REST. We compute the Root Mean Square Percent Error (RMSPE) for divergence between budget estimates and accounts data. Since our interest is in divergence from budget estimates, we take the ratio of divergence to budget estimates and not actual data as is usually done in computing RMSPE. Table 14.6 presents these results.

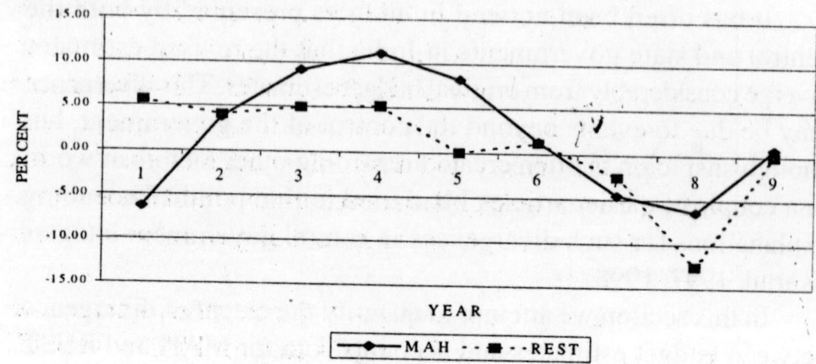

Fig. 14.1 : Revenue Receipts

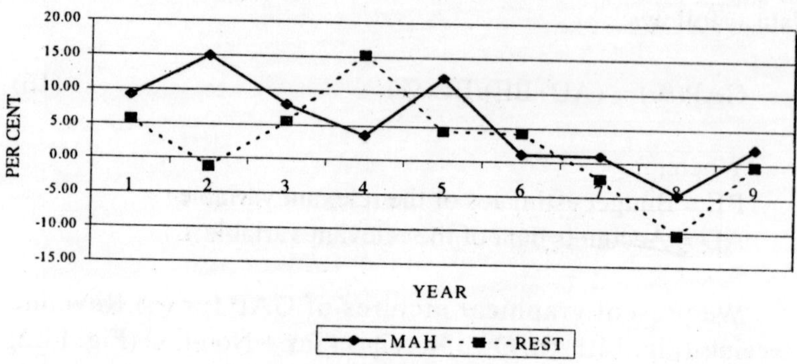

Fig. 14.2 : Own Receipts

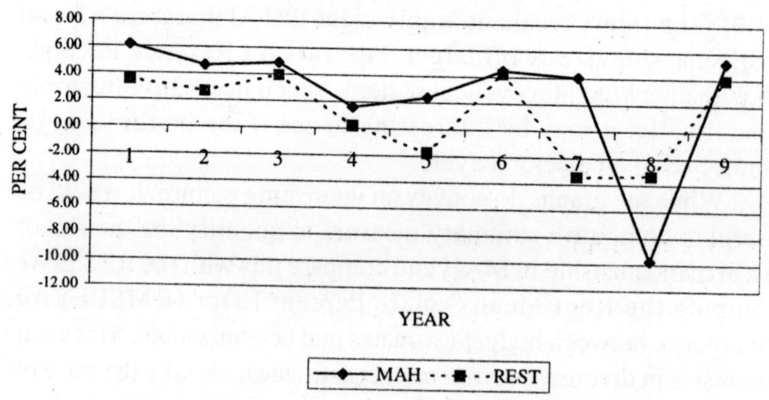

Fig. 14.3 : Revenue Expenditures

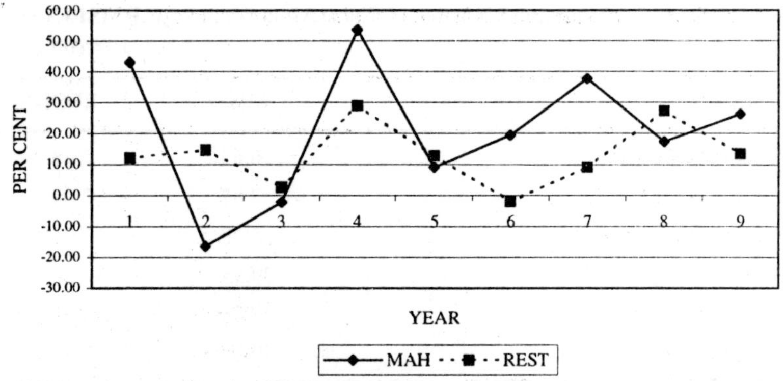

Fig. 14.4 : Capital Receipts

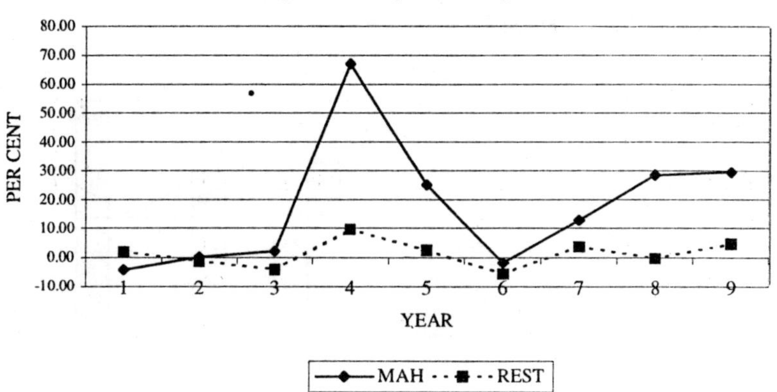

Fig. 14.5 : Capital Disbursement

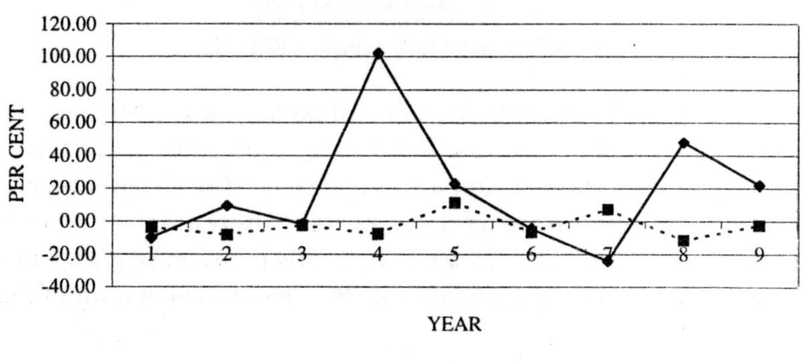

Fig. 14.3 : Capital Outlay

TABLE 14.7: **Summary Measure of Fiscal Marksmanship: RMSPEs**

(*Percentage*)

Category	MAH	REST
Revenue Receipts	6.63	5.43
Own Receipts	7.87	7.04
Revenue Expenditures	5.28	3.25
Capital Receipts	29.55	16.26
Capital Disbursements	27.88	4.65
Capital Outlay	40.08	7.52

Note: RMSPE have been computed for the period 1991-92 to 1999-2000.

Source : Same as for Table 14.1.

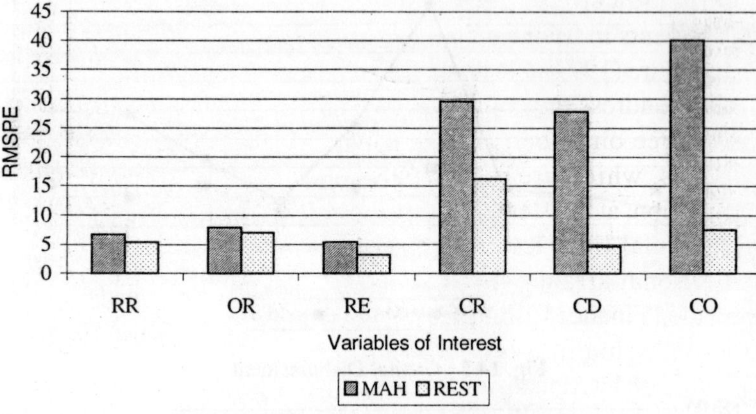

Fig. 14.7 : Fiscal Marksmanship: RMSPEs

Not only is the quality of Maharashtra's fiscal marksmanship poor, its performance relative to other states, .especially in the capital account of the budget is appalling. Clearly, if transparency in government operations is an important ingredient of SGR, Maharashtra has a long way to go. Very little faith can be placed in the budget estimates that are given in the budget documents of this state.

Issues in Local Public Finance

An important aspect of SGR must be decentralisation. This involves not only decentralisation from the central government to the states, but also further downwards to lower levels of government, such as urban or rural local bodies. Decentralisation must occur not only with respect to functions that must be performed by local bodies but also in terms of finances available. Constitutional provisions (Eleventh Schedule of Article 243(G) of the Indian Constitution gives a long list of functions to be performed by the Panchayat Raj institutions) now place a large number of functions at the doorstep of local governments. Only a few of these functions have public goods characteristics and most defy economic logic (See Karnik, 1999 for a critique). There has not been, however, assignment of appropriate revenue sources to these governments for the discharge of these functions. Hence, the fiscal health of most local bodies in the states is very fragile.

An indication of the fragility of the fiscal health of local governments in Maharashtra is available from the Government of Maharashtra (1997). Finance commissions were set up by numerous states to address the complaint of the 1983 Planning Commission Task Force on Urban Development: "Unlike the federal-state relations, which are regulated by an explicit provision in the constitution, at the state-municipal level, these relations are wholly on informal lines and in the absence of any well-established institutional arrangements for periodical review through state appointed Finance Commissions, the entire area of state-municipal relations remains vague". While the setting up of a Finance Commission by Maharashtra is certainly a welcome step, much needs to be done to tone up the health of local bodies. Even though I do not go deep into the details of the Report of the Finance Commission here (see Karnik, 1999 for details) I would like to present some computations to indicate the fragility of local public finances in the state of Maharshtra.

Ideally, it should be possible to relate fiscal balance measures to levels of income of the concerned locality/jurisdiction. However, ncome figures are generally not available for each locality. Consequently, we have used the State Domestic Product (Factor Cost) figures of Maharashtra to compute various fiscal ratios at the level of municipalities in Maharashtra. These ratios make it quite apparent that the fiscal situation of Urban Local Bodies is deteriorating. The surplus on the revenue account is seen to be declining. As this balance falls that much less is available for capital expenditure, which forces the local body to look for grants from the state government as well as loans from state government and financial institutions. This is reflected in the deteriorating overall fiscal balance of municipal corporations (Table 14.8).

TABLE 14.8: **Fiscal Balances: Municipal Corporations in Maharashtra**

(Rs. crore)

	Mumbai		All Municipal Corporations	
	1990-91	1994-95	1990-91	1994-95
Revenue account	-113	-157	-213	-353
Balance	(-0.194)	(-0.14)	(-0.36)	(-0.32)
Capital account	121	259	2.9	426
Balance	(0.21)	(0.23)	(0.36)	(0.38)
Budget	8	101	-22	74
Balance	(0.01)	(0.09)	(-0.04)	(0.06)
Overall fiscal	60	188	83	215
Balance	(0.10)	(0.17)	(0.14)	(0.19)

Notes: 1. Figures in brackets are ratios to Maharashtra's State Domestic Product (%)
2. Revenue Account Balance - Revenue Expenditure - Revenue Income
3. Capital Account Balance - Capital Expenditure - Capital Income
4. Budget Balance - Total (Revenue + Capital) Expenditure - Total (Revenue + Capital) Income
5. Overall Balance - Total (Revenue + Capital) Expenditure - Revenue Income
6. Plus sign indicates a deficit and minus sign indicates a surplus.

Source: *Fiscal Balances: Municipal Corporations in Maharashtra*, Government of Maharashtra, 1997.

Institutional Factors

In this section we examine the institutional environment prevailing in Maharashtra. As stated earlier, Holden and Rajapatirana (1997) mention maintenance of law and order and protection of property rights as important components of SGR. Institutions and institutional environment, however, have a much wider connotation than maintenance of law and order and security of property rights.

Institutions define and limit the set of choices of individuals and in the process reduce uncertainty by providing a structure to everyday life (North, 1990). The institutional constraints that delimit the set of choices of individuals are similar to rules of the game. Of all the rules that constitute the institutional structure, those pertaining to the legal environment have received the most attention.

However, apart from the legal environment as it exists in the statutes, enforceability of law and order is equally important. Inadequately enforced laws impinge on the security of property rights, which may be more harmful to the incentive to invest than is non-arbitrary taxation (Clague et al., 1997). Impartial and predictable enforcement of law and order make property rights secure and reduce the extent of uncertainty that is inherent in any investment decision.

As North (1994) has pointed out, it is apparent that, apart from security of property rights (including contractual rights), the quality of the polity is equally important. The efficiency with which governments manage provision of public goods and the creation and implementation of government policies are important determinants of the speed with which countries/regions grow (Knack and Keefer, 1995). In short, the quality of the political system is an important determinant of the level of investment in a region and the consequent growth. Of all the various qualities of a political system, the following merit attention:

1. *Political Stability:* This is an important consideration in both democratic and non-democratic environments. In both environments instability would clearly have a detrimental impact on investment.
2. *Policy Implementation:* The smooth flow of investment requires that policies announced are implemented in a consistent, transparent, rule-based manner. This eliminates

the need for lobbying and other influence peddling measures to get favourable policies implemented.

3. *Administration:* The quality of administration is reflected in the efficiency with which public goods are provided, the efficiency with which applications for investment are cleared, etc. Efficient administration will serve to reduce the transaction costs of investment decision making.

In this paper we do not examine in detail the links between institutional factors and investment flowing into Indian states (see Karnik et al., 2001 for an empirical investigation along these lines). What we wish to do here is compare Mahrashtra's institutional setting with that of some other states. The data that we employ has been gleaned from an opinion poll of about 100 companies, both Indian and transnational, conducted by The Gallup Organisation. The poll asked respondents to rank Indian states on the basis of their perceptions regarding institutional / political conditions prevailing in these states. Three such opinion polls have been conducted, for 1995, 1997 and 1999, and these have been reported in various issues of *Business Today*. The data set that we employ is similar to that employed by Knack and Keefer (1995) in their cross-country study on institutions and economic performance. Table 14.8 gives the ranking for select variables for Maharashtra and four other states which are its close competitors.

The results of Table 14.9 show clearly that Maharashtra has been losing its pre-eminent position among the states of India. There has been deterioration in each and every measure between 1997 and 1999. The quality of local administration has gone down by two ranks, as have policy implementation and political stability. As far as flexibility of state government policies and law and order are concerned, Maharashtra's rank has slipped by one. The state to have made the greatest strides over the years has been Andhra Pradesh. While it is true that Maharshtra retains its overall top ranking in the opinion poll, the slippages on institutional and political fronts do not augur well for the initiation of SGR.

TABLE 14.9: **Changes in Perception Ranks for Select Institutional and Political Variables**

	Maharashtra			Gujarat			Andhra Pradesh			Karnataka			Tamil Nadu		
	1995	1997	1999	1995	1997	1999	1995	1997	1999	1995	1997	1999	1995	1997	1999
Flexibility of state govt. policies	2	2	3	1	1	2	8	5	1	3	4	5	4	3	4
Policy implementation	2	1	3	1	2	2	20	4	1	3	5	5	4	3	4
Quality of local admin.	1	1	3	2	2	2	15	5	1	5	4	5	9	3	4
Law and order	1	1	2	2	2	1	11	6	3	3	3	4	4	4	5
Political stability	2	2	4	1	1	2	23	4	1	22	5	5	3	7	3

Source: "The Best States to Invest In: A Business Today – Gallup Organisation Research Projects", *Business Today*, December 1997 – January 2000 and December 1999 – January 2000.

Conclusions

The objective of this paper was to examine the progress of economic reforms in the state of Maharashtra. Specifically, we were concerned with the achievements of FGR and the portents for SGR. On both counts the performance of the state has been disappointing. The most relevant component of FGR for state government is fiscal discipline. However, our analysis covering the last ten years, that is, since the beginning of economic reforms, suggests very poor performance of all states in India. Especially worrying has been the performance of Maharashtra which has a reputation for being one of the more progressive states in the federation. Our econometric exercises demonstrated the adverse impact of fiscal imbalances on the real rate of growth of Maharashtra.

Our analysis of SGR focused on issues of transparency, local public finance and political and institutional aspects. On each of these issues the report card for Maharashtra shows very poor achievement so far. Clearly, the portents for the introduction of SGR in the state are not very encouraging.

Extension of the work done in this paper will compare Maharashtra, not with all the states in the Indian Federation as has been done here, but only with the 15 largest ones. This, it is expected, will remove any bias that may have crept in owing to the inclusion of smaller states in the analysis. It is also proposed to compare Maharashtra with a few specific states, such as Gujarat, Karnataka, Tamil Nadu and Andhra Pradesh, which are its closest competitors.

REFERENCES

Clague C., P. Keefer, S. Knack and M. Olson (1997), "Institutions and Economic Performance: Property Rights and Contract Enforcement" in C. Clague (ed.) *Institutions and Economic Development: Growth and Governance in Less Developed and Post-Socialist Countries*, The Johns Hopkins University Press, Baltimore.

Government of Maharashtra (1997), *Report of the First Maharashtra Finance Commission*, Government of Maharashtra, Mumbai.

Holden P. and S. Rajapatirana (1997), "Emerging Issues in Latin America: A Second Generation Agenda", http://www.eri-la.org/Papers/2ndgen.htm; also available in *Nordic Journal of Latin American and Caribbean Studies*, Vol. XXVIII, 1-2, 1998.

International Monetary Fund (IMF) (1999), *Manual on Fiscal Transparency*, http://www.imf.org/external/np/fad/trans/manual/index.htm

Jacobs S.H. (1999), "The Second Generation of Regulatory Reforms", IMF Conference on Second Generation Reforms, November 8-9, 1999.

Karnik A. (1997), "An Analysis of Union Budget 1997-98 From the Perspective of Devising an Appropriate Role of the State". *Economic and Political Weekly*, May 31.

—— (1998), "Budget 1998-99: Focusing on Wrong Issues", *Economic and Political Weekly*, July 18-24/25-31.

—— (1999), "Comments On The Report Of The First Maharashtra Finance Commission", Seminar On Municipal Finance Issues of Transparency, Accountability and Civil Society Participation for Poverty Alleviation. 29th-October 30, 1999, All India Institute of Local Self Government, Mumbai.

—— and M. Lalwani (1997), "Interest Groups, Government Size and Growth". In D.M. Nachane and M.J.M. Rao (eds) *Macroeconomic Challenges and Development Issues: Essays in Honour of Professor C.N. Vakil*, Himalaya Publishing House, Mumbai.

——, A. Samant and N. Asher (2001), "Institutional and Political Determinants of Investment in Indian States" in B.L. Mungekar, D.M. Nachane and M.J.M. Rao (eds.) *Indian Economy in the New Millennium*, Himalaya Publishing House, Mumbai.

Kopits G. and J. Craig (1998), "Transparency in Government Operations", IMF Occasional Paper No. 158, IMF, Washington D.C.

Knack, S. and P. Keefer (1995), "Institutions and Economic Performance: Cross Country Test Using Alternative Institutional Measures", Centre for Institutional Reform and the Informal Sector, Reprint No. 65, University of Maryland at College Park.

North D.C. (1990), *Institutions, Institutional Change and Economic Performance*, Cambridge University Press, Cambridge.

North, D.C. (1994), "Economic Performance Through Time", *American Economic Review*, Vol. 84, pp. 359-68.

Pattanaik R.K., R.D. Bangar, S.M. Pillai and Rekha Sharma (1994), "Resource Gap of the State Government: Measurement and Analysis", RBI Occasional Papers, Vol. 15, No.4.

——, S.M. Pillai and S. Das (1999), "Budget Deficit in India: A Primer in Measurement", RBI Staff Studies, Department of Economic Analysis and Policy.

Reserve Bank of India (2000), *State Finances: A Study of Budgets of 1999-2000*, RBI, Mumbai.

Stiglitz J. (1998), "Distribution, Efficiency and Voice: Designing the Second Generation of Reforms", Conference on Asset Distribution, Poverty and Economic Growth, Brasilia, Brazil.

World Bank (2000), *World Development Report*, World Bank Washington D.C.

APPENDIX

List of Abbreviations

AD	Accounts Data
BE	Budget Estimates
BRG	Basic Resource Gap
BRG(i)R	BRG(i) /SDPC; i takes values 1, 2, 3.
CD	Capital Deficit
CDR	CD/SDPC
CE	Capital Expenditures
CR	Capital Receipts
FDR	Fiscal Dependency Ratio
FGR	First Generation Reforms
FSR	Fiscal Stress Ratio
GFC	Grants from the Centre
GFG	Gross Fiscal Gap
GFGR	GFG/SDPC
ID	Internal Debt
LAC	Loans and Advances from the Centre
ML	Market Loans
NSGFC	Non-statutory Grants from the Centre.
OCR	Other Capital Receipts
ONTR	Own non-tax revenues
OTAR	Own tax revenues
PFS	Provident Funds
RD	Revenue Deficit
RDR	RD/SDPC
RE	Revenue Expenditures
RFD	Reserve Funds and Deposits
RR	Revenue Receipts
SCT	State's share in Central Taxes
SDPC	SDP of Maharashtra at current prices
SDPR	SDP of Maharashtra at 1980-81 prices
SGFC	Statutory Grants from the Centre
TE	Total Expenditures
SGR	Second Generation Reforms
WMA	Ways and Means Advances

15

REVIEW OF SECOND GENERATION ECONOMIC REFORMS: ASSAM

H.S. DAS

Assam – Background

Assam is situated in the North-East of the country. With 2.41 per cent (78,438 sq. kms) of the country's area, it is home to 2.66 per cent (26.6 million-2001 Census) of the country's population.

The present position of the economy of Assam gives a rather disquieting picture. In the beginning of the planning process, Assam was ranked as one of the prosperous states of the country. The per capita income of Assam was about 4 per cent above the national average in 1950/51. Thereafter, the growth rates of the state economy, and consequently of per capita income, started declining. The per capita income of Assam came down to the all-India average level by 1954/55. After that the per capita income of Assam has not only been lower than the all-India average, but the gap has been widening (Table 15.1).

The recent GDP growth rate of Assam has been much lower than that of the country as a whole. Table 15.2 will illustrate the point :

Assam today is ranked the third poorest among the large and medium states in terms of per capita income.

Another disturbing scenario is the change in the sectoral

TABLE 15.1: **Status of Economy (Per Capita Income)**

(at constant 1980-81 prices)

Year	India	Assam	Difference
1950-51	1127	1173	46+
1960-61	1350	1140	210-
1970-71	1520	1221	299-
1980-81	1630	1284	346-
1990-91	2267	1544	698-
1995-96	2664	1606	1002-
1996-97	2814	1628	1133-
1997-98	2955	1677	1278-
1998-99	3132	1707	1425-

Source: Directorate of Economics and Statistics, Government of Assam.

TABLE 15.2: **GDP Growth Rate Per Annum**

(Per cent)

Period	India	Assam
Seventh Plan period	6.0	3.7
Eighth Plan period	6.8	3.7
1997-98	5.0	3.0
1998-99	6.0	(-) 2.2
1999-2000	6.4	8.2

Source: Same as for Table 15.1.

composition of the state GDP. In 1970/71, the shares of the primary, secondary and tertiary sectors were 54.7 per cent, 14.0 per cent and 31.3 per cent respectively. In 1998/99 this changed to 43.77 per cent, 13.73 per cent and 42.50 per cent respectively. The declining percentage contribution of the secondary sector to the state SDP is a matter of serious concern. On the other hand, rapid growth in the share of the tertiary sector at the cost of both the primary and secondary sectors in a rural, agrarian and underdeveloped state like Assam is rather alarming. According to available statistics public services appear to be the main contributor to the increasing share of the tertiary sector. Had the share of agriculture declined because of increasing shares of the secondary and tertiary sectors due to their faster growth rates, then there would not have been any cause of concern. Rather, it could have been viewed as a positive development. But in case of Assam this does not appear to be the case. The percentages of population depending on the primary sector and living in rural areas still remain very high at about 70 per cent and 89 per cent respectively. So, the decreasing share of the primary sector in the state GDP implies impoverishment of the rural masses. This is borne out by the fact that the proportion of people living below the poverty line in the rural areas of Assam is a very disturbing 45.01 per cent. This also explains the phenomenon of unsustainable rural unemployment, particularly among the educated unemployed youths in the rural areas and resultant unrest and discontentment among them. The negative impact of this situation in the social, political and economic life of the state are there for all to see.

Other areas of serious concern are (a) High growth rate of population, (b) poor infrastructure, (c) low agricultural productivity, (d) deteriorating power situation, (e) recurring flood, erosion of soil and environmental degradation, (f) inadequate health care facility, particularly in the rural areas, (g) low rate of capital formation and industrial stagnation and (h) brain-drain from the state.

First Generation Reforms and Assam

The fiscal and balance of payment crisis of the late nineteen-eighties and early nineteen-nineties accentuated by the Gulf War of 1990/91, are primarily responsible for the beginning of the era of economic reforms in the country. The first generation reforms were externally induced and, of necessity, crisis-driven. Fiscal stabilisation, especially fiscal-deficit control, liberalisation of foreign trade, industrial policy and foreign exchange regulations, and a modest beginning of the process of partial disinvestment in and privatisation of PSUs were the highlights of the first generation reforms. These reforms, also called the New Economic Policy, were mostly at the central government and national level. Except for a few southern states, the other states were not seen to be playing much of a proactive role in adapting to the changing economic environment. Assam, unfortunately, appears to be one of those states. As brought out clearly by tables 15.1 and 15.2, the state economy was more or less stagnant during the period of the first generation reforms. The benefit of the reforms at the national level hardly touched this peripheral state. Nor could any significant reforms be initiated by the state government. It was completely engrossed in fighting, with its back to the wall, the problems of insurgency and terrorism, ethnic uprisings and violent clashes, and natural calamities, mainly floods. At the same time, the State Government's financial position went from bad to worse. For all practical purposes, it was incapacitated to initiate any significant reforms or development initiative on its own. Meanwhile, as in the rest of the country, the old order was crumbling. But in Assam the new order was yet to be born.

Second Generation Reforms and Assam

The National Scene

The first generation reforms helped the nation tide over the crisis. The dreadful prognosis of disintegration of the national economy apprehended in some quarters did not come true. But the reforms generated an intense national debate. The mid-nineties witnessed serious political instability. But the heartening feature of all this is that the debate on reforms has now stabilised into a national consensus on reforms—cutting across party lines. The reforms are now coming from within, consciously.

The debate now is on the details—how much and when. It is in this environment of national consensus that the second generation reforms are unfolding. They are both vertical and horizontal. Vertical in taking the reforms of the first generation farther and deeper. Horizontal in extending the reforms process to include hitherto untouched areas of the national economy. The recently introduced Union Budget 2001/02 is the best testimony of this. Fiscal deficit is targeted to be lowered further to 4.7 per cent in 2001/02 from 5.1 per cent in 2000/01. The Fiscal Responsibility Bill, already introduced in Parliament, seeks to reduce it further to 2 per cent and completely eliminate the revenue deficit in the next five years. Reduction of civilian staff strength of the Union Government by 2 per cent per annum over the next five years, reduction of administered interest rates, including those on small savings by 1.5 per cent from March 1, 2001, reduction in personal and corporate income taxes, incentives for agricultural growth, infrastructure development, power sector reforms, opening up and reforms of the financial sector including insurance, further liberalisation of the provisions regulating foreign investments both ways, proposed reforms in the labour market, acceleration of the process of disinvestment in and privatisation of PSUs, continued restructuring of the industrial sector in tune with the fast unfolding WTO regime and focus on health, education and social security are the other highlights of the budget. Annual GDP growth rate is projected at 6.5 per cent during 2001/02 against 6.0 per cent in 2000/01. Hiccups and transition troubles in some sectors of the economy notwithstanding, the average growth rate of the GDP has been 6.4 per cent since 1992/93. The percentage of population below the poverty line has fallen from 36 per cent in 1993/94 to 26 per cent now.

The reform process is essentially one of freeing the economy from the suffocation of excessive government control and allowing the market forces to play the dominant role. It means freeing the latent human energy and enterprise from unnecessary regulation and control. The process of reforms is essentially one of removing the inefficiencies from the system.

Regional Disparity

But India is a vast country. Different states and regions of the country are at different stages of development. The reform process has ushered in a new economic environment. No doubt, it has opened up new opportunities. At the same time it has also brought to centre-stage new problems. One such problem is regional disparity. The already developed regions are at a more advantageous position as compared to less developed regions like Assam and the North-East. The trend so far indicates further widening of the already existing regional disparity. During the reform period, the northern and eastern regions of the country seem to have fallen behind the southern states. The North-South divide within the country may become a matter of serious concern if not mended in time. The position of Assam (and the North-East) is even worse.

Table 15.3 illustrates how the industrial sector in Assam has been completely bypassed by the reforms process.

TABLE 15.3: **Percentage Share of Assam in the Industrial Sector vis-à-vis All India (From August, 1991 to March, 2000)**

Category	Assam	India	Assam's Percentage Share
IEMs	96	39,268	0.24
LOIs	11	3.419	0.32
100 per cent EOU's	2	3,615	0.35
FDIs	nil	8,310	0.00

Notes : IEM-Industrial Entrepreneurs Memorandum, LOI-Letter of Intent, EOU-Export Oriented Unit, FDI-Foreign Direct Investment.

Source: Assam Industrial Development Corporation.

Another indicator of Assam's failure to benefit from the reforms process is the bank credit-deposit ratio. It has been falling steadily during the period of reforms and now stands at 34.1 per cent only, against the national average of 57.6 per cent as on June 30, 2000. If we exclude the advances to the tea and oil industries then the figure falls to shockingly low levels.

Initiatives by the State Government: White Paper on State Finances

Of late, however, an introspective debate has started in the state on the government's initiatives. In May 1999 the state government brought out a white paper on the state of its finances. This revealed with clear focus some very disturbing trends, some of which are:

(a) A sharp increase in revenue expenditure and a corresponding fall in capital (includes development) expenditure in relative terms (Table 15.4).

TABLE 15.4: **Trends in Revenue and Capital Expenditure**

(Rs. in crore)

Year	Revenue Expdr.	Capital Expdr.	Total	Share in Total Expdr. Revenue Expdr.	Share in Total Expdr. Capital Expdr.
1984-85	837.08	245	1082.08	77.36	22.64
1985-86	958.07	271.77	1229.84	77.9	22.1
1986-87	1160.39	347.12	1507.51	76.97	22.95
1987-88	1316.34	347.95	1664.29	79.09	20.91
1988-89	1436.49	247.86	1684.35	85.28	14.72
1989-90	1668.78	396.94	2065.72	80.78	19.22
1990-91	1915.3	429.66	2344.96	81.68	18.32
1991-92	2148.1	530.11	2678.21	80.21	19.79
1992-93	2450.93	376.87	2827.8	86.67	13.33
1993-94	2901.18	404.25	3305.43	87.77	12.42
1994-95	3270.7	408.31	3679.01	88.9	11.1
1995-96	3575.76	460.67	4036.43	88.59	11.41
1996-97	3571.31	366.46	3937.77	90.69	9.31
1997-98	3959.37	438.33	4397.7	90.03	9.97
1998-99 (R.E)	6095.87	720.63	6816.5	89.43	10.57
1999-2000 (B.E)	6686.5	887.66	7574.16	88.28	11.72

Source: State (Assam) Finances, Factual Position (May 1999), Finance Department, Government of Assam.

(b) An alarming increase in the state's fiscal deficit (Table 15.5).

TABLE 15.5: **Assam's Fiscal Deficit**

(Rs. in crore)

1984-85	1989-90	1994-95	1998-99	1999-2000
(-) 361.23	(-) 521.95	(-) 465.82	(-) 1312.45	(-) 1595.85

Source: Same as for Table 15.4.

(c) An alarming increase in the outstanding debt burden of the state (Table 15.6). Twenty-three per cent of the total expenditure from the state's consolidated fund goes in debt servicing.

TABLE 15.6: **Outstanding Debt Position (Year-ending)**

(Rs. in crore)

1984-85	1989-90	1994-95	1997-98	1999-2000	2000-01
1736.13	3704.74	4613.15	6083.87	8388.07	9967.20

Source: Same as for Table 15.4.

(d) An abnormal (average 4.22 per cent per annum) increase in the number of state government employees during the period 1981/82 (2,27,734) to 1998/99 (4,59,701). In addition to the 4,59,701 regular employees (for a population of 2.6 crore) as on April 1, 1999, there were 47,000 additional employees of the work charged, muster roll and casual categories. In the 2001/02 budget, expenditure on salaries, wages and pensions account for 72 per cent of the total revenue receipts and 58 per cent of the total revenue expenditure.

Progress so far: Fiscal Reforms in the State

(a) Publication of the White Paper on the state finances was followed by a great deal of introspection and debate. This resulted in the signing of an MoU with the Government of India in November 1999 and adoption of a fiscal reforms programme by the state government.

(b) As a sequel to this, creation of additional posts has been banned; 5000 vacant posts have already been identified for abolition. The exercise of identifying another 10,000 posts is on. Filling up of any vacant post anywhere in the government needs prior approval of an Empowered Committee headed by the Chief Secretary. Provincialisation, that is, taking over of private educational institutions by the government, has been stopped. Tax collection drives have been stepped up. Against a total state tax collection of Rs. 1224.75 crore in 1999/01, the revised estimate for 2000/01 is Rs.1424.54 crore—an increase of over 16 per cent. The state government has implemented Uniform Floor Rates of tax from January 1, 2000. This move has reduced the rate-war with the neighbouring states and is expected to rake in additional revenue of Rs.45 crore. Similarly, The Assam Taxation (Settlement of Disputes) Act, 2000 has been implemented from May 17, 2000. The objective is to expedite settlement of cases pending before various courts and tribunals and thus mobilise withheld tax revenues. Another important development is the receipt of Presidential assent for introduction of the Entry Tax Bill. Assam acts as the transport corridor for the other six North-Eastern states. Some unscrupulous traders and transporters avoid payment of tax to the Assam Government by showing one of the neighbouring states as the destination of the taxable goods by manipulation although they actually unload the goods in Assam. This piece of legislation is expected to plug this loophole. To arrest the growth of increasing debt-servicing liability, a ceiling has been imposed on government guarantees against institutional loans availed of by State PSUs, local bodies and cooperative institutions. Past experience shows that debt servicing liabilities on account of most such loans fall ultimately on the state government as the guarantor.

PSU Restructuring

(a) Another area where the state government has initiated affirmative action is in the realm of privatisation of state level PSUs. There are 49 PSUs under the state government. Together they employ 57400 employees. Cumulative investments made in all the PSUs put together amount to Rs.4400 crore (1999/00) of which Rs.2990 crore are direct government investments by way of equity, loans and grants. The balance is mainly institutional borrowings with government guarantee. The accumulated loss over the years in the PSUs has eroded their equity bases completely and their collective current negative net worth is Rs.1400 crore. Of the total investments in the PSUs, the Assam State Electricity Board (ASEB) accounts for 75 per cent, followed by the Assam State Transport Corporation(ASTC) with 10 per cent, the remaining 15 per cent being in the other 47 PSUs. In return, ASEB and ASTC contributed around 70 per cent and 10 per cent respectively of the total accumulated loss. Around half of the PSUs have already become non-functional. Additional government investment in PSUs has virtually stopped. Imposition of ceiling on issue of government guarantee has limited their scope to avail institutional finances as well.

(b) Against the above background, the state government has taken concrete steps for revival of seven PSUs through varying degrees of privatisation by way of (i) long-term lease to private sector participants; (ii) private sector management; and (iii) custom-milling. VRS is being resorted to in four other PSUs including ASTC, to make them viable entities. A few other PSUs like the Assam Tea Corporation have been subjected to critical scrutiny about their viability and about the future course of action — which include the

options of disinvestment and privatisation. As for those PSUs which have lost their relevance under the changed circumstances and have outlived their utility, there is no alternative but to close them down. Creation of a state-level BIFR is under consideration. As for the two major PSUs—ASEB and ASTC—revival and restructuring proposals have been worked out. For tariff rationalisation of the ASEB, it has been decided to set up a single member Assam Electricity Regulatory Commission. An MoU to be signed with the Union Government for Power sector reform in the state is in the final stage of preparation. But with utilisation of only about 25 per cent of the installed capacity of power generation, almost 50 per cent being the T & D loss, huge outstanding dues to outside power suppliers and large accumulated loss, the ASEB is in dire straits. Some degree of privatisation in generation and distribution is possibly unavoidable.

State Government's Limitations

(a) As can be seen from the above, the initiative taken by the state government so far is limited to correction of its own fiscal imbalance and reform/restructuring of its PSUs. But the manoeuverability of the state government in its fiscal reform is somewhat limited. On the expenditure side, the upward revision of pay scales of the state government employees in line with the Fifth Pay Commission hike by the Centre and implementation of UGC Pay scales for College/University teachers have put unsustainable strain on the state finances. This is in spite of the fact that the pay hike given to the state employees in Assam is well below what their counterparts in the central government got under the Fifth Pay Commission. These are decisions taken at the centre but they have expensive ramifications for the states.

(b) On the revenue side, only 30 per cent of the state's total receipts (tax and non-tax) are raised by the state itself. The balance 70 per cent are transferred from the centre by way

of state's share of central taxes, grants-in-aids and other central assistance. Viewed from this angle, success in mobilising additional tax revenue by the centre means a larger share for the state in absolute terms. Similarly, improvement in the financial health of the centre and increase in the size of the national cake means larger devolution to the state by way of grant-in-aid and other central assistance. Under the present constitutional arrangement, therefore, success of the fiscal reform measures at the centre is, in a way, more important and meaningful to the state than the success of its own fiscal reforms. This is not to say that the state should do nothing. It must do everything possible to increase revenue and curb the growth of non-plan revenue expenditure. It is encouraging to note that the buoyancy co-efficient in collection of state taxes, which declined till the mid-1990s has, once again started moving upward. But then, agricultural income tax, land revenue, taxes on vehicles, state sales tax and excise duty being the only major sources of tax revenue, and NSDP growth rate being sluggish in Assam for quite some time as already illustrated, there are inherent limitations in the state's capability to raise additional resources and thereby correct its fiscal imbalances. Similarly, with 47 per cent of the total expenditure accounted for by payment of salaries, wages and pensions (58 per cent of the revenue expenditure), 23 per cent by debt servicing and 9 per cent by essential administrative expenditure including that for fighting the counter-insurgency operations, the room for expenditure curtailment by the state is indeed limited.

(c) The award of the Eleventh Finance Commission has dealt another blow to the State of Assam. Assam has been awarded only Rs.110.68 core as non-plan revenue grant for the entire award period of 2000-05, as against Rs.712.03 crore awarded by the 10th Finance Commission. The entire deficit grant will be sanctioned to the state during the first year of the award period, i.e., 2000/01, which would imply that the EFC award assumes that the state government's

revenue account would be generating surpluses for the remaining four years of the award period. This is quite contrary to the actual position as detailed in the previous paragraphs.

A comparison with other Special Category States and some non-Special Category States reveals how little Assam has been awarded by way of deficit grants.

TABLE 15.7: **Non-plan Revenue Deficit Grants**

(Rs. in crore)

State	TFC	EFC
Assam	712.03	10.68
Himachal Pradesh	772.18	4549.26
J & K	1184.13	11211.19
Meghalaya	316.42	1572.38
Nagaland	529.78	3536.24
Orissa	371.74	673.60
Punjab	Nil	284.21
West Bengal	Nil	3246.09

Source: Assam Government Finance Department and Reports of the 10th and 11th Finance Commissions.

The EFC has awarded a sum of Rs.12,362.05 crore as share of central taxes to Assam over the period 2000-05 as compared to Rs.7,064.14 crore awarded by TFC. Even in this case, the interest share of Assam has declined to 3.285 per cent of the net proceeds of all shareable union taxes and duties from 3.42 per cent awarded by TFC. Thus, contrary to expectations, the award of the EFC will not in any way help alleviate the state's precarious financial position.

What is Possible within the Limitations

There is, however, some room for improving the administrative efficiency in the collection of taxes and quality of expenditure. India's

ranking on the Corruption Perception Index (CPI) for the year 2000 has improved from 72nd position last year to 69th. However, India still remains one of the (22nd) most corrupt countries in the world. Perhaps no state of the country can be said to be free from this debilitating affliction. Corruption is eating into the vitals of our society and the state apparatus and it has badly tarnished the national image. It not only erodes the moral authority and credibility of the government in the public eye, but also impairs its capability. Enlightened opinion today says that corruption is not a necessary evil or unavoidable side-effect of economic growth. It is morally reprehensible and bad in economics. It retards economic growth, generates social inequality and abets criminal proclivities. But unfortunately, this important issue has not found its due place and prominence in an otherwise lively and healthy national debate on the reform process.It is perhaps high time that reduction of corruption is put firmly on the agenda for second generation reforms. In Assam also reduction of corruption will improve the quality of governance and help correct the fiscal imbalance of the state by improved revenue collection and quality of expenditure. The bouyancy coefficient of tax collection can surely be improved by improvement in tax collection administration even at the current level of GDP/ NSDP growth rates.

Decentralisation

(a) Decentralisation of power from the centre to the states and from the state to the urban and rural local bodies also needs to be included in the agenda for the second generation reforms. Each layer of government should concentrate on its area of core concern. Just as the central and state governments are gradually withdrawing from their PSUs, so also the Central Government may gradually withdraw from the sphere of a large number of centrally sponsored schemes(CSSs), which, in any case, are implemented mostly by the state governments. The CSSs are mostly in education, health and family welfare, social welfare, agriculture, industry, forestry, public health, irrigation and rural

development including rural roads and infrastructure sectors. These are subjects in the state or concurrent list of the Constitution. Uniform national programmes under these sectors ill-fit the heterogeneous regions of a vast country like India, particularly regions like Assam and the North-east. The large central ministries in these sectors may be downsized and they may be given limited coordination roles. Conceptualisation of programmes and their implementation may be left to the states and necessary funds may be transferred to them through the mechanism of Finance Commissions or as central assistance under the State Plans.

(b) Similarly, the state governments may delegate many of their present functions to the local bodies with corresponding devolution of funds as provided under the 73rd and 74th amendments of the Constitution. Assam's record in this regard is below expectation. For one reason or the other, Panchayat elections in the state have not been held since February 1997. The last elections were held in 1992. The position with regard to the urban local bodies is however, satisfactory.

Centrally Sponsored Schemes and the State's Annual Plan

(a) As regards some important centrally sponsored schemes like rural development programmes, the funding pattern between the centre and the state is 75 per cent and 25 per cent respectively. But due to acute resource crunch of the state, Assam has not been able to avail itself of the central allocation in full because it cannot provide its 25 per cent share. As a result, much needed poverty alleviation and rural infrastructure programmes remain under-implemented although the incidence of rural poverty in the state is an alarming 45 per cent. Perhaps, in the larger interest of the rural poor, the centre may enable the state to avail itself of the central allocation in full by substantially reducing the percentage of the state share.

(b) Another unintended consequence of the existing

arrangement of State Plan financing is that the negative BCR (Balance from Current Revenue) is met from the Plan resources. For instance, in 2000/01 the aggregate resources for the state's annual Plan is Rs.2893.85 crore. But after offsetting the negative BCR of Rs.916.76 crore and Rs.290.53 crore toward negative contributions of ASEB and ASTC, the core plan outlay is only Rs.1520.00 crore, which is lower than even the quantum of central assistance (Rs.1686.56 crore) which Assam receives as 90 per cent grant and 10 per cent loan, being a special category state since 1990/91. Even from the outlay of Rs.1520.00 core, more than 50 per cent goes on payment of plan salary and wages. What remains is grossly inadequate for development works in the infrastructure and social sectors. Drastic cuts in non-plan expenditure together with generation of additional resources for development cannot possibly be deferred any longer.

Central Government Initiatives

(a) Taking cognizance of the abysmally low level of infrastructure and the basic minimum needs of Assam and the other six N.E. states, the Government of India set up a high level Commission under the chairmanship of Shri S.P. Shukla. The Commission submitted its report in March, 1997. The Commission recommended a number of projects to remove the infrastructure backlog of the N.E. region requiring an investment of Rs.93,619 crore, including Rs.18,807 crore for Assam. Similarly, Rs.9395 crore was recommended for meeting the basic minimum needs, including Rs.3952 crore for Assam. But unfortunately the Commission's recommendations have remained largely unimplemented for want of finances of such high magnitude. However, one welcome development is that, following the Shukla Commission recommendation, some concerned Union Ministries are now required to earmark 10 per cent of their plan budget allocations for the North-east.

Moreover, a Non-Lapsable Central Pool of Resources has been operationalised since 1998/99 for the North-east. Ministries who do not spend their stipulated 10 per cent for the North-east would transfer the unspent balance to this pool. Various developmental projects for the North-East are taken up with funding from this pool. The total annual accrual to the pool has averaged around Rs.400 crore.

(b) As is clear from the above discussion, both the state and central governments are now fully seized of the problem of underdevelopment of Assam and the North-east, particularly under the emerging liberalised economic environment in the country. Serious and sincere efforts are being made to give a kind of new deal to the North-east after years of neglect. But yet things do not somehow seem to look up. It does not move as if a deadweight is holding it back. What could it be?

Non-Economic Factors

History and Geography

The entire North-east is land-locked—the nearest port Kolkata being about 1000 kms. away. Ninety-eight per cent of the region's boundary is international border—with Bhutan, China, Myanmar and Bangladesh. The 23 kms. strip of land in North Bengal that separates Nepal from Bangladesh is its only link with the Indian mainland. The terrain is difficult. Except for the Assam plains, it is mostly hilly and forest land—interspersed with many turbulent rivers. Rainfall is heavy. In such a terrain maintenance of the surface transport network is a very difficult and expensive proposition. The partition of the country in 1947 blocked the road and rail transit routes from the region through erstwhile East Pakistan. With this began the saga of transport bottlenecks, a sense of geographical isolation and the process of economic deceleration.

Next came the great earthquake of 1950 and resultant topographical changes of unprecedented magnitude including change in courses of major rivers and consequent flood havocs.

The 1962 China war left a great psychological scar in the minds of the people of the region. This war changed the North-east perspective of the policy planners from development to one of defence.

The Indo-Pak wars of 1965 and 1971 also left their adverse effects on the economy of the region. The Brahmaputra and Barak river routes through erstwhile East-Pakistan were also lost after 1965.

Next came the reorganization of Assam in 1971 and the creation of a number of new states. The six-year long Assam agitation beginning in 1979/80 also meant major disruption of normal economic activities.

Insurgency and Militancy

Before the state could get down to economic reconstruction, there arose the problem of insurgency and militancy from the mid-1980s. The Armed Forces Special Powers Act and the Disturbed Areas Act have been in operation in Assam for many years now. The problem of insurgency in the region dates back to the 1950s with the Naga problem. This was followed by Mizo insurgencies in the sixties and later in Manipur.Today, barring Arunachal Pradesh and Mizoram, all the other five N.E States are facing problems of insurgency and militancy. In Assam alone there are 16 such groups operating. Apart from ULFA and Bodo militant groups, there are various ethnic tribal militant groups such as the Bengali Tiger Force (BTF), as well as Islamic fundamentalist terrorist groups like Harkat-ul Mujahideen, Muslim United Liberation Force of Assam(MULFA) and Muslim Liberation Tigers of Assam (MULTA) etc. Some of these groups receive training and other logistic support and strategic guidance from abroad, including from Pakistan's ISI. The problem is no longer a mere law and order problem affecting only the State of Assam. It has assumed new dimensions which have the potential to jeopardise the security and integrity of the nation. Frequent killings, kidnapping and extortions have badly vitiated the economic environment in Assam and the North-east. Table 15.8 illustrates one dimension of the problem—the number of militancy related deaths in the state in the past five years.

TABLE 15.8 : **Number of Militancy Related Deaths in Assam**

Year	Civilians Killed	Security Personnel Killed	Total
1996	261	80	341
1997	237	89	326
1998	387	77	464
1999	179	87	266
2000	412	80	492
Total	1476	413	1889

Source : Home and Political Department, Government of Assam.

The state government has taken a number of initiatives within the country and abroad to invite investment. The Government of India had also launched an attractive package of incentives in July 1999, including Central Excise Duty exemption for 10 years, to promote industrialisation of the North-east. Yet the results are not so encouraging as illustrated in Table 15.3. Security concerns, coupled with poor infrastructure perhaps explain the shyness of the investors despite the attractive incentives.

The tourism potential of Assam and the North-east is immense. But due to poor infrastructure and a perceived sense of insecurity, tourists normally tend to avoid visiting this region. The Assam Government has, of late, been participating in some tourism meets and fairs abroad. But it has now transpired that some foreign embassies in New Delhi have been advising their citizens to avoid the North-east for security reasons, although not a single foreign tourist has been killed or kidnapped in Assam during the last 20 years of militancy. Some image-correction by the state is necessary. Restricted Areas Permit for Assam and some other parts of North-east were abolished way back in 1995. But tour operators complain that some Indian missions abroad still exclude Assam and parts of North-east from the Indian visa.

Migration Problem and Ethnic Conflicts

The treaty of Yandaboo in 1826 brought Assam under British Rule.

With this came a large number of personnel from Bengal to man the new administration. The discovery of oil, tea and coal and exploitation of the virgin forests also attracted many traders and fortune seekers. Assam went through a rapid economic transformation in the 19th century. In the second half of the 19th century and early part of the 20th century large scale migrant labour came from the tribal belts of eastern and central India for the tea plantations in Assam. Since the beginning of the 20th century Assam has been the destination of large scale migration from erstwhile East Bengal. The availability of large tracts of virgin cultivable land was the attraction. The 1947 Partition and the 1971 Bangladesh War also caused large-scale influx of refugees to Assam from the then East Pakistan. Some migration originated from Nepal too. Tables 15.9 and 15.10 illustrate the extent of migration.

TABLE 15.9: **Assam 1901-1991 : Per cent Increase of Population**

Year	Growth Rate Assam	Growth Rate All-India	Variation
1901-11	16.99	5.73	11.26
1911-21	20.48	-0.31	20.78
1921-31	19.91	11	8.91
1931-41	20.4	14.22	6.17
1941-51	19.93	13.31	6.62
1951-61	34.98	21.51	13.34
1961-71	34.95	24.8	10.15
1971-91*	52.44	48.24	4.2
1991-01	18.85	21.34	(-)2.49

Note: * No census was held in Assam in 1981. Hence the growth rate is for the twenty-year period 1971-91.

Sources: 1. 1901-71, *Census of India, 1971*, p. 59; 1971-91, calculated based on *Census of India, 1991a.*

2. Sanjib Baruah (1999), *India Against Itself,* Oxford University Press, p. 51.

As is seen from Table 15.9, during the last hundred years, the growth rate of population in Assam has been substantially higher than

TABLE 15.10: **Assam 1911-1921 : Population Growth by Migration and Natural Growth**

Area	Total Increase, 1911-21	Gain/Loss by Migration	Increase by Natural Growth	Per cent Total by Migration	Increase by Natural Growth
Assam	+929,725	+411,941	+517,784	+44.3	+55.7
Brahmaputra Valley	+784,650	+416,350	+332,300	+55.6	+44.4
Surama Valley	+ 97,771	-14,216	+111,987	-14.5	+114.5
Hills	+ 83,304	+ 13,613	+ 69,691	+16.3	+83.7

Source: 1. *Census of India 1921*, p.8.
2. Sanjib Baruah, ibid.

the all-India growth rate. The 2001 Census is a pleasant surprise. Assam's population growth rate for the decade 1991-01 has declined to 18.85 per cent. This is lower than the all-India figure of 21.34 per cent. Although the 2001 Census data are yet to be critically analysed, it is generally believed that after the anti-foreigner agitation of 1979-85, the number of fresh migrants and settlers to the state has come down. Perhaps this is one of the contributory factors responsible for the noticeable fall in Assam's population growth rate in the last decade. But the problem of population pressure and ethnic tension had already assumed alarming proportions.

Pressure on land has increased tremendously as a result of migration as also due to natural growth. The average density of population in Assam is 340 per sq. km as against the all-India average of 324 per sq. km (2001). Hitherto protected tribal belts and blocks are being encroached upon by the new migrants. Precious forest lands are being depleted. Assam has witnessed a number of communal clashes involving the new migrants and the indigenous people, particularly indigenous tribals, in the last couple of decades. The roots of these violent conflicts lie in conflict over land. It will perhaps not be an exaggeration to say that such violent conflicts over land and subsequent displacement of people resemble, in some cases, the ethnic cleansings in Bosnia, Serbia, Cosovo and the neighbouring areas. Such a situation is certainly not congenial for economic growth and development.

Fall in Standards of General Law Enforcement

Along with the rest of the country Assam has also experienced a fall in the standards of general law enforcement. What is also disturbingly discernible is the growing tendency among the people to disrespect and disobey the law of the land. The prevailing feeling among the people is that even legitimate wants can be fulfilled only by circumventing the lawful route and by exploiting the legal loopholes. The low rate of conviction, large number of pending court cases and inordinate delay in disposal of court cases give the message that the chances of criminals and law-breakers getting away scot free are much more than the chances that they will be brought to book and punished. Such a situation is also not congenial for rapid economic growth and reforms.

Flood Problem

Assam is very prone to floods and natural calamities. Whatever little infrastructure is created is damaged again by the annual floods. As for example, in 1998 alone there was a loss of Rs.1000 crore to the public utilities and various other infrastructures. Till now, these damaged assets have not been fully repaired. The loss of property and infrastructure in 2000 was estimated at Rs.700 crore. The fury of the floods and the extent of damages to life and property have increased many fold after the great earthquake of 1950. The cost of providing gratuitous relief to the affected people also runs into hundreds of crore every year. The Calamity Relief Fund corpus of about Rs.80 crore a year is grossly inadequate.

Unemployment

The inadequate economic development and backwardness of Assam has a natural fall-out in terms of its capability to provide adequate employment opportunities to its unemployed youths. This has not only led to a lot of dissatisfaction among them but has also contributed to the problem of insurgency and millitancy as witnessed at present in Assam. As per available data on the live register of the employment exchanges, the number of job-seekers at the end of the year, 1999 stood at 16.35 lakh compared to 16.19 lakh registered at the end of 1998. Out of the total job-seekers as at the end of 1999, the number of educated job-seekers was 12.39 lakh constituting about 75.78 per cent of the total. While the state government is not in a position to provide large-scale employment because of its financial problems, business and industry have also not come up to provide an alternative.

The Prevalent Mindset: Dominated by Politics, Not Economics

The scenario described above explains the prevalent mood in the state. It is one of despondency and cynicism. The public debate on issues centres round the government. While government is the object of criticism for almost everything that is wrong, it is also looked up to and depended upon for almost everything that is needed. Unlike the southern states, very little is actually happening outside the governmental sphere in Assam. Public debate and thinking in the state is dominated more by political and cultural issues rather than by economic issues. In recent years many well-researched, well-written books have come out on the politics of the state, but none such on the economy of the state. This situation has to change to clear the way for reforms and economic regeneration.

Future Vision

According to the State Directorate of Economics & Statistics, the estimated population in Assam as on October 2000, stood at 26.4 million. This is projected to reach 36 million by 2000, putting even more pressure on land and infrastructure. The state will not only have to cope with this additional population pressure but also raise the standard of living and improve the quality of life of this significantly larger population at an accelerated rate to catch up with the projected national levels by that time. According to the estimates of the State Directorate of Economics & Statistics, the per capita income of the state is projected to reach Rs.11,496 by the end of 2019/20 from Rs. 5919 during 1997/98 at constant (1993/94) prices if the current growth rates of population and NSDP continue. As against this, the projected per capita income for the country in 2019/20 is Rs.27,799 as compared to Rs.9660 in 1997/98 at constant (1993/94) prices, if we go by the current rates of growth of national population and GDP. This, in other words, means that the per capita income of Assam by 2019/20 will be only 41.35 per cent of the national average as against 61.27 per cent in 1998/99. This situation is obviously not acceptable and the trend must be reversed. Assam must aim to catch up at least with the national average in terms of per capita income by the year 2019/20. Even this reasonable target will necessitate an annual NSDP growth rate of 8.6 per cent. This is a tall order by any standard but not an impossible one if we take into account the resource base and other plus points of the state.

Advantages Assam has: Resources

a) The state is very rich in natural resources. Table 15.11 shows the major mineral resources of the state.

TABLE 15.11: **Assam's Mineral Resources**

(Estimated reserves)

Resource	Availability
Crude oil	140.00 M.T.
Natural gas	156 BMSCM
Coal	320 M.T.
Limestone	800 M.T.
Granite stone	More than 1 billion cu.mts.

Source : Assam Industrial Development Corporation.

Its forest resources, tea plantations, fertility of the soil, bio-diversity, water resources and a traditional handloom and handicraft industry are other areas of strength.

b) Apart from natural resources and water resources, Assam's other strong point is its human resource. According to the 54th round of the National Sample Survey, the literacy rate of Assam increased to almost 80 per cent (December, 1999) against the all India average of less than 60 per cent. Assam's rich secular, composite cultural heritage, absence of social evils such as, dowry, casteism and communal harmony are also some of its strong points. Other areas of potential strength are Tourism and Information Technology. While traditional industries may be handicapped because of geographical isolation, industries based on information technology defy such natural obstacles.

c) All these years we have been complaining about geographical isolation and transport bottlenecks. Now, however, in the context of the globalisation process, Assam and the North East appear to be rather strategically located between the East/South East Asian economies on one side and the Indian mainland economy on the other. With improved infrastructure Assam's perceived locational disadvantage can be turned into a strategic commercial advantage in the changing global context. In any case, our country is committed to the new WTO arrangements. They are going to affect Assam also. We must strategise our future planning for our economic development with an eye on the process of globalisation.

Conclusion

As has been discussed in the previous pages, the economic situation in Assam today is one of stagnation. It has barely been touched by the economic reforms. The economic progress of the state has been badly affected by a number of serious problems—both economic and non-economic. If Assam does not resolve those problems quickly enough, the state may go down like one of the many sub-Saharan African countries which are very rich in resources but torn by civil strifes, natural calamities and diseases. They are today among the poorest countries of the world in terms of income and infrastructure.

Fortunately, some positive developments are taking place slowly. The people of the state are getting weary after years of militancy and violence. Realisation seems to have dawned on the youth that they have to look beyond government jobs for a productive and meaningful life. A beginning has been made in opening border trade with the neighbouring countries. Above all, a parametric change seems to be happening on the agriculture front. Absence of proper irrigation facilities kept agricultural productivity at a very low level. According to one estimate, from 1978 to 1998, the gross cropped area in Assam increased by almost 300 per cent. But agricultural production increased by only 220 per cent during the same period, which means a fall in productivity by 17 per cent and that agricultural growth in the state was horizontal and not vertical.

With financial assistance from the Central Non-Lapsable Pool and loans from the World Bank and NABARD, the state government launched a scheme of installation of Shallow Tube Wells with a view to exploiting the vast ground water resources of the State for irrigation purposes during the dry months. More than one lakh STWs have been installed during the last one year. Suddenly the farmers, who were till now practising single cropping, have switched over to double cropping. With this the consumption of fertilisers and use of HYV seeds have also gone up. What is happening is almost a mini green revolution. What is more important is the new-found self-confidence after years of despondency among the farmers. Agriculture holds one of the major keys to economic regeneration of Assam. Although it is too early to affirm that a green revolution has already happened, it is important to note that a break through of sorts has been made. It must be sustained in the coming years.

If it can happen in agriculture, then it can happen in the other sectors also. Assam has got immense natural resources and potential to turn around and enter into an era of rapid economic growth and join the process of economic restructuring and reforms. The opening up of trade with the neighbouring countries of Bangladesh, Myanmar, China and Bhutan as well as re-opening of the much shorter rail, road and waterways transit routes through Bangladesh can really open up the entire North-eastern region which has a strong resource base. The initiative must come from the people themselves. The people of the State must change their mindset, give up the irredentist issues and focus on economic regeneration. If this happens, Assam can become a really rich and prosperous state.

ABOUT THE CONTRIBUTORS

Antony, Piush is currently a Visiting Fellow at the Institute for Human Development, New Delhi. She holds an M.Phil. degree in Applied Economics from the Centre for Development Studies, Thiruvananthapuram. She has earlier worked as Research Associate at the Gender Studies Unit of the National Institute of Advanced Studies, Bangalore. Her areas of interest include decentralisation, women and development, food economy, child labour, informal sector workers and migration. She has co-edited a book on social and economic security in India.

Banerjee, Nirmala was trained as an economist in Bombay University and at the London School of Economics and Political Science. She recently retired as a Professor of Economics from the Centre for Studies in Social Sciences, Calcutta where she had worked for more than a quarter of a century. Her fields of interest are the informal economy and labour reforms. She has worked extensively in the area of women's work on the basis of secondary data as well as her own fieldwork.

Chadha, G.K. is the Vice-Chancellor of the Jawaharlal Nehru University, New Delhi. Prior to joining the Vice-Chancellorship, he was Chairman of the Commission for Agricultural Costs and Prices, Government of India, New Delhi. Professor Chadha has had a long and meritorious teaching and research career in Economics, mostly at the Jawaharlal Nehru University, New Delhi. He has been Visiting Fellow/Professor at various institutions abroad, and Chairman/Member of many Expert Committees/Teams at the national and international levels. He has to his credit 12 books and many research papers in national and international research journals, on development issues relating to India and other developing countries of Asia. Professor Chadha has also been consultant to several international organisations.

Dasgupta, Biplab, now working as the Honorary Chair of Planning and Development Unit, Jadavpur University, has retired from Calcutta University in the year 1998. He is also a member of the Upper House (Rajya Sabha) of the Indian Parliament. A Ph.D. in Economics from the London School of Economics and an M.Sc. in Computer Science from London University's Institute of Computer Science, Professor Dasgupta has been Professor/Visiting Fellow in many reputed institutes and universities in India and abroad. He has undertaken assignments for various U.N. agencies. Professor Dasgupta has contributed numerous articles in professional journals and has a few books to his credit.

Das, H.S. is a member of the Indian Administrative Service (1982: Assam). A Master's Degree holder in Economics, during the last 20 years he has served in posts as diverse as Director of Border Areas, Director of Industries, Deputy Commissioner, Secretary Finance, Commissioner and Secretary, P&D, Cultural Affairs, Hill Areas, Home and Political Departments in Government of Assam. Currently he is Commissioner and Secretary, Home and Political, Border Areas and Passport Departments.

Deshpande, Lalit, Ph. D., taught at the Department of Economics, University of Mumbai and retired as Professor and Head of the Department. Author and editor of a few books, research monographs and papers published in India and abroad, Professor Deshpande has been an external collaborator and consultant to the ILO and its regional offices and the World Bank Mission in India. He has been Visiting Fellow at various institutes/universities abroad. He has been on official committees of the Government of Maharashtra and the Government of India. Currently, Professor Deshpande is an Honorary Visiting Professor at the Institute for Human Development, New Delhi.

Deshpande, R.S., a Ph.D. in Agricultural Economics from Marathawada University, Aurangabad, is currently Professor and Head of Agricultural Development and Rural Transformation Unit at the Institute of Social & Economic Change (ISEC), Bangalore. He has also worked at the Gokhale Institute of Politics and Economics (GIPE), Pune. He has worked in various capacities on policy bodies both at the centre and state levels. He is the author of two books and published several research papers in national and international journals. Professor Deshpande has worked on World Bank and Ford Foundation assignments and has been Visiting Fellows at Universities abroad.

Deshpande, Sudha, Ph.D. taught at the Department of Economics, University of Mumbai and retired as a Reader in Demography. She has written both singly and jointly with her husband, Prof. Lalit Deshpande, working papers and reports for the ILO and its regional offices, the World Bank and Department of Women and Children, Ministry of Human Resource Development, Government of India. She has worked extensively in areas of employment and unemployment, management of cities and city slums. She has held prestigious visiting positions in universities abroad. Dr. Deshpande has contributed research papers in various professional journals. Currently, she is an Honorary Senior Visiting Fellow at the Institute for Human Development, New Delhi.

Gill, Sucha Singh is Professor of Economics at the Punjabi University, Patiala. He has also been Professor and Head of Punjab School of Economics at Guru Nanak Dev University, Amritsar. He served on two study panels of National Commission on Rural Labour (1989-90), and is also a non-official member of Punjab State Planning Board. Professor Gill has to his credit books on wide-ranging themes. He has also contributed articles and research papers to leading journals.

Gumber, Anil, is a Ph.D. from Gujarat University, Ahmedabad and has been a Post-Doctoral Takemi Research Fellow in International

Health from Harvard School of Public Health, Boston (USA). Currently, he is Senior Research Fellow at the Centre for Health Services Studies, Warwick Business School, and Coventry (UK). Dr. Gumber previously worked at the National Council of Applied Economic Research, New Delhi. His research work has focused on issues relating to human development including health, nutrition and poverty. He has two books to his credit of which one is co-authored by him.

Karnik, Ajit is the RBI Ambedkar Professor of Political Economy at the Department of Economics, University of Mumbai. He has been Visiting Scholar at various universities abroad. His areas of specialisation are political economy, public economics and applied econometrics. Professor Karnik has written extensively in national and international journals as well as published four books. He is consultant to UNDP, Government of Maharashtra, and several private sector organisations.

Mahendra, S. Dev, is presently Director, Centre for Economic and Social Studies, Hyderabad. He has made significant contributions in the field of development economics, and written extensively on agricultural development, poverty and public policy, food security, employment guarantee schemes, social security and farm and non-farm employment. He was awared the Ph.D. degree from the Delhi School of Economics and did his Post-Doctoral research at the Economic Growth Centre, Yale University. Dr. Mahendra Dev has been teaching at the Indira Gandhi Institute of Development Research, Mumbai for the last nine years. He has been a consultant to many international organisations like the UNDP, World Bank, International Food Policy Research Institute, ESCAP and has also worked as a member in various committees set up by the Government of India.

Mathur, Ashok is Professor of Economics at the Centre for the Study of Regional Development, Jawaharlal Nehru University, New Delhi. He obtained his doctorate from the London School of

Economics. Prior to joining the Jawaharlal Nehru University in 1972, he had been on the Faculties of Economics at the Kurukshetra University, Haryana and the Enfield College of Technology, U.K. Professor Mathur has served in many important positions in his career and is currently Editor of ICSSR's Journal of Abstracts and Reviews in Economics. His publications and research are in the spheres of: regional economic development and disparities; economic growth in India; labour economics; economics of education and manpower planning.

Mehta, Rajesh is a Senior Fellow at the Research and Information System for Non-Aligned and Other Developing Countries (RIS), New Delhi. He obtained his Ph.D. degree in economics from the Delhi School of Economics, University of Delhi. He has been consultant to various national and international organisations. Earlier, he was Adjunct Professor in the Indian Council for Research on International Economic Relations. He has also served on the faculty of University of Western Ontario. Professor Mehta has written widely in the areas of regional integration, trade policies of South Asian countries, WTO-related issues, etc. He has authored and co-authored seven books/monographs and has contributed regularly to national and international journals.

Mitra, Arup, Ph.D., is currently based at the Institute of Economic Growth, Delhi. His research interest lies on areas relating to urban development, employment, migration, rural non-farm sector, total factor productivity growth, infrastructure and gender—areas in which he has several publications.

Panchamukhi, P.R. has formerly been the Director, Indian Institute of Education (IIE), Pune; Professor and Head, General Economics, University of Bombay; Chief, Financial Resources Division; and Advisor in the Planning Commission, Government of India. Professor Panchamukhi's areas of specialisation include public finance, economics of education and health. He has to his credit more than 10 books and numerous articles. His major contribution in institution building is seen in the developing of Research Units in Economics of Education at the Bombay University, IIE, Pune and CMDR, Dharwad. Professor Panchamukhi has been a consultant with several international organisations.

Sharma, Alakh N. is the Director of the Institute for Human Development, New Delhi. He has served in several important positions at national-level institutions. He was a faculty member of the A.N. Sinha Institute of Social Studies, Patna for several years. Professor Sharma has made significant contributions in areas such as poverty, labour market, migration and development economics. He has been closely associated with the Indian Society of Labour Economics and has been the Editor of the Indian Journal of Labour Economics for the last ten years.

LIST OF PARTICIPANTS AT THE SEMINAR

1. Dr. S.P. Gupta
   Member, Planning Commission
   Government of India, New Delhi

2. Dr. Montek Singh Ahluwalia
   Member, Planning Commission
   Government of India, New Delhi

3. Professor G.S. Bhalla
   Emeritus Professor
   Jawaharlal Nehru University, New Delhi

4. Professor Ashok Mathur
   Jawaharlal Nehru University, New Delhi

5. Professor K.L. Krishna
   Indian Council for Research on International
   Economic Relations (ICRIER), New Delhi

6. Professor Suresh Tendulkar
   Delhi School of Economics, Delhi

7. Professor Biplab Dasgupta
   Member of Parliament (Rajya Sabha)
   New Delhi

8 Professor B.B. Bhattacharya
   Institute of Economic Growth
   University of Delhi, Delhi

9. Professor Lalit Deshpande
Formerly Deptt. of Economics
University of Mumbai,
Mumbai

10. Professor Ruddar Dutt
Institute for Human Development, New Delhi

11. Professor C.P. Thakur
Formerly Faculty of Management Studies
University of Delhi, Delhi

12. Professor G.K. Chadha
Jawaharlal Nehru University, New Delhi

13. Professor Amitabh Kundu
Jawaharlal Nehru University, New Delhi

14. Professor Nirmala Banerjee
Centre for Social Sciences, Calcutta

15. Dr. Pranob Sen
Adviser (PPD)
Planning Commission,
Government of India, New Delhi

16. Professor Ravi Srivastava
Jawaharlal Nehru University, New Delhi

17. Shri Shailendra Sharma
Adviser (LEM)
Planning Commission, Government of India
New Delhi

18. Dr. Prem Vashishtha
Director
Agricultural Economic Research Centre
University of Delhi, Delhi

19. Professor Ajit Karnik
    Deptt. of Economics
    University of Mumbai, Mumbai

20. Professor Sucha Singh Gill
    Deptt. of Economics
    Punjabi University, Patiala

21. Dr. Alakh N. Sharma
    Director
    Institute for Human Development,
    New Delhi

22. Dr. B. Bhattacharya
    Dean
    Indian Institute of Foreign Trade (IIFT)
    New Delhi

23. Dr.A.C. Kulshrestha
    Deputy Director General
    Cental Statistical Organisation, New Delhi

24. Dr. J.B.G. Tilak
    Senior Fellow
    National Institute of Educational Planning & Administration
    (NIEPA), New Delhi

25. Professor Atul Sharma
    Indian Statistical Institute, New Delhi

26. Professor P.K. Chaubey
    Indian Institute of public Administration, New Delhi

27. Dr.R.S. Deshpande
    Institute of Social & Economic Change, Bangalore

28. Dr.(Mrs.) Sudha Deshpande
    Formerly Deptt. of Economics
    Universityof Mumbai,
    Mumbai

29. Professor Binod Khadria
    Zakir Hussain Centre for Educational Studies
    Jawaharlal Nehru University, New Delhi

30. Ms. Mervi Karikorpi
    European Commission, New Delhi

31. Shri A.K. Angurana
    Deputy Director General, CAPRAT
    India Habitat Centre,
    New Delhi

32. Dr. Abusaleh Shariff
    Chief Economist
    National Council of Applied Economic Research (NCAER)
    New Delhi

33. Dr. Sonal Desai
    Senior Consultant
    National Council of Applied Economic Research (NCAER)
    New Delhi

34. Shri K.Narayanan Unni
    Deputy Registrar General and Census
    Commissioner of India, New Delhi

35. Shri H.S. Das
    Commissioner and Secretary
    Government of Assam, Guwahati

36. Shri K.S. Jangpangi
    Inspector General of Police
    Directorate of Border Security Force, New Delhi

37. Dr. B. Nagarjuna
    Deptt. of Economics
    Central University Hyderabad
    Hyderabad

38. Dr. J.P. Singh
    Professor
    Agricultural Economic Research Centre,
    University of Delhi, Delhi

39. Dr.(Mrs.) Nira Ramachandran
    C-1822, Palam Vihar, Gurgaon

40. Shri U.S. Pant
    Chief Controller of Accounts
    Ministry of Steel & Mines, New Delhi

41. Shri M.N. Siva Subramaniam
    Director
    Planning Commission, New Delhi

42. Padmaja Mehta
    Director (LEM)
    Planning Commission, New Delhi

43. Dr. Nisha Srivastava
    Department of Economics
    Allahabad University, Allahabad

44. Dr. (Mrs.) Kumud Sharma
    Senior Fellow
    Centre for Women's Development Studies (CWDS)
    New Delhi

45. Dr. Anil Gumber
    National Council of Applied Economic Research
    New Delhi

46. Shri A.S. Ahluwalia
    Director, Ministry of Labour, Chandigarh

47. Shri S.R.S. Gill
    Director, Ministry of Labour, Chandigarh

48. Dr. Pandurang Rajaram Kinare,
    Rajlaxmi, Near Parvartha Niketan
    Thane(W), Mumbai

49. Dr. Arup Mitra
    Institute of Economic Growth
    University of Delhi, Delhi

50. Dr. Rajesh Mehta
    Senior Fellow
    Research and Information System for Non-Aligned
    and Other Developing Countries (RIS), New Delhi

51. Dr. Naushad Ali Azad
    Deptt. of Economics
    Jamia Milia Islamia University, New Delhi

52. Shri S. Nigam
    Economic Adviser
    Ministry of Industry, New Delhi

53. Shri Deepak Rastogi
    Joint Director
    Central Statistical Organisation
    New Delhi

54. Ms. Preeti
    Deputy Director
    National Commission on Labour, New Delhi

55. Dr.C.Bal Krishna
    Bharat Vikas Vikalpa
    C-40 Sector 27, NOIDA

56. Shri Nilambuj Sharan
    LEM Division
    Planning Commission, New Delhi

57. Shri Raj Kumar
    LEM Division
    Planning Commission, New Delhi

58. Shri Pratap Jena
    National Institute of Public Finance and Policy
    New Delhi

59. Ms. Roli Asthana
    Research Scholar
    C-1/5, Lodi Gardens, New Delhi

60. Dr. Piush Antony
    Institute for Human Development, New Delhi

61. Dr. Narayan Prasad
    Deptt. of Economics
    Indira Gandhi National Open University, New Delhi

IAMR Faculty

Dr. H. Ramachandran, Director
Dr. A.K. Yadav, Chief
Dr. M.R. Prasad, Chief
Dr. (Mrs.) Mridula Sharma, Chief
Dr. Saseendran Pallikadavath, Chief
Dr. Lalita Manocha, Chief
Shri S.B.Lal Saxena, Jt. Chief
Smt. Santosh Aggarwalla, Jt. Chief
Shri K.C. Veoli, Jt.Chief
Smt. Harsh Sharma, Jt.Chief
Shri Bal Krishan, Jt. Chief
Dr. Nandita Khadria, Editor
Smt. Madhu Srivastava, Senior Research Officer
Shri A.K. Verma, Senior Research Officer
Shri I.C. Awasthi, Senior Research Officer
Shri B.S. Prakash, Senior Research Officer
Dr. K. Sambandan, Research Associate

Consultant

Dr. A.B. Bose, Senior Consultant
Dr. K.K. Tripathy, Consultant

INDEX